THE BASEBALL BOOK 1991

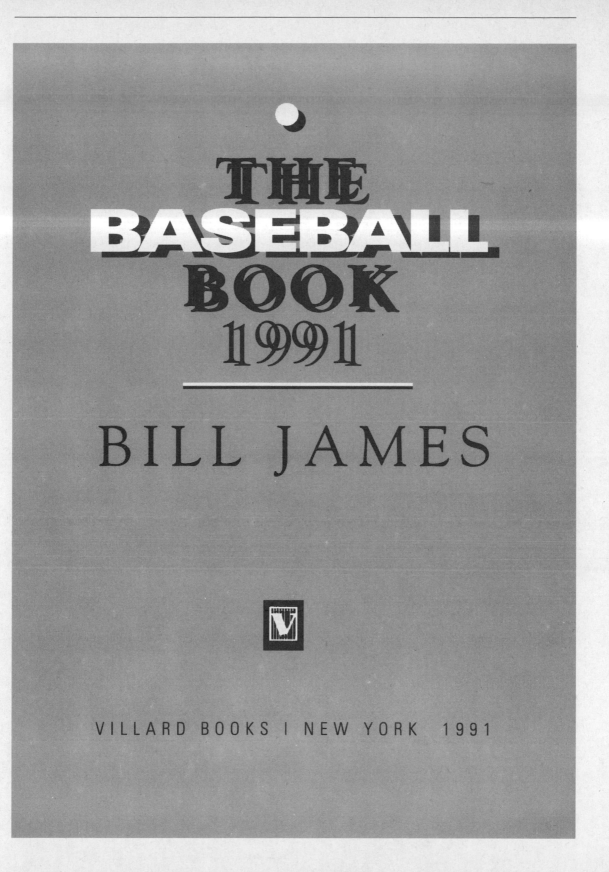

THE BASEBALL BOOK 1991

BILL JAMES

VILLARD BOOKS | NEW YORK 1991

All rights reserved under International and Pan-American Copyright Conventions.
Published in the United States by Villard Books, a division of Random House, Inc.,
New York, and simultaneously in Canada by Random House of Canada Limited, Toronto.

Villard Books is a registered trademark of Random House, Inc.

ISSN 1055-1433

Designed by Robert Bull Design

9 8 7 6 5 4 3 2

First Edition

ACKNOWLEDGMENTS

Producing a book is something that one surely could do all by one's self, if only one were perfect in every way. I'm not, unfortunately, so I need the help of at least twenty or thirty people to make it through an average day. These include:

Susan McCarthy, who is my wife. Susie also did the cover art, did the drawings of Luke Appling, Richie Ashburn and Luis Aparicio which appear in the Biographic Encyclopedia, and took over all the responsibilities of the house while I was confined to a word processor.

Rob Neyer, who works with me each day. The way it works is, if I don't know anything I ask Rob, and he has to find out.

Mike Kopf and **Jack Etkin,** who also wrote pieces for the book.

Liz Darhansoff, who has been my agent for many years.

Peter Gethers, who has been my editor for many years.

Bob Bull, who designed the book.

John Dewan of STATS, Inc., who provided the Stats.

Dick Cramer of STATS, Inc., who wrote the program which generated the stats.

Tom Heitz and **Bill Deane** of the Hall of Fame library, without whom it would be difficult to do research.

Rachel and **Isaac,** who are my children.

Corinne Lewkowicz, who does the publicity for the book.

Many people also contributed to this book in one form or another, and I hope you will appreciate that I am sincere when I express the usual paranoia about forgetting someone. I steal ideas from and exchange information with everybody I talk to or exchange letters with; God knows who all that might include. My thanks to Eddie Epstein, Jim Carothers, Peter Sprengelmeyer, James J. Skipper, Miles McMillin, Hal Bodley, Joe Garagiola, Dan Quisenberry, Mark Hulsey, Lisa Marshall, Don Zminda. My thanks to all the people who corrected errors in last year's book; these are listed in the article about Errata and Addendum. Thanks to you all.

CONTENTS

INTRODUCTION

This is a book of basic questions and basic information.

Section I is basic questions, and the outlines of answers.

Section II is basic data.

Section III is fun stuff.

I've been writing books with player comments for more than ten years, and I've tried it all different ways—but I've never tried anything remotely like this before. When I started writing player comments in the late seventies, my assumption was that I was writing to an audience which already knew a great deal about each player, but wanted to know more. My goal was to find *something* about the player—any little thing—that *the reader did not already know.*

It is difficult to remember now how desperately little statistical information was available then, and how easy it was to push back the boundaries. Since the average fan had no way of knowing whether Larry Bowa had hit .205 or .378 against left-handed pitching or whether Bob Horner had hit four home runs in his home park or 26, I thought it was useful to round up the data and point out what was interesting within it.

As time passed more and more statistical information became available, and so it became harder and harder to find something to say about the player that my reader would not already know. If one year it was enough to point out that the player hit better at home than on the road, the next year it would be required to compare what he hit in grass parks to what he hit on turf, and then the next year we might look up what he hit in day games and what at night, and then the next year what he hit leading off the inning. As each new breakdown became available each existing one became less significant and less interesting. The search for *new* and *interesting* information about each and every player became more frantic, until eventually I was no longer pursuing the boundaries of the data, but being pursued by the data which was exploding behind me.

What puzzled and irritated me throughout the eighties was that the information explosion seemed wholly irrelevant to the discussion. Although vastly more information became available to the average fan, his comprehension of what it meant and how it fit in with what he knew or believed about the game advanced not at all. TV screens spewed out meaningful and meaningless information in interchangeable bytes, relevant information mixed with irrelevant, polluted information mixed with clean. To introduce new information into this environment became a fool's errand, for no matter how clearly the news was sent out it would soon be garbled, and if it was relevant it would soon be misplaced, and if it was sent out clean it would soon get dirty.

In 1987 I decided that I was contributing to the problem, and that therefore I should stop and go in some other direction. I stopped doing the *Baseball Abstract,* abandoning the thing a writer loves most: a reserved spot on The List. I decided to start doing a different kind of baseball book, which is *The Baseball Book.*

The concept of *The Baseball Book,* when it was made real (the first edition was 1990) turned out to have some obvious flaws. Material which was intended to be of lasting interest, such as *The Biographic Encyclopedia of Baseball,* was mixed together with material which was clearly intended to be of transient interest, and thus stuff which obviously should have been in a hardcover book was mixed with stuff which more or less had to be in a paperback. Material which needed to be spun out quickly was mixed with material which needed to be handled carefully. Material which appealed to people with an interest in baseball history was in the same covers with material of interest to rotisserie players, which was intentional, but when it came out proved not to have been such a good idea. The *Biographic Encyclopedia of Baseball* required that we keep the *form* of a comprehensive resource, although the material was meant not as a reference, but meant to be read.

I wouldn't tell you that I have solved all of these problems in the last year. What I'm going to do, eventually, is split *The Baseball Book* into two books, a paperback and a hardcover.

What I've tried to do in the first section of this book this year is talk about, write about, as many of the things which are on the minds of the average baseball fan as I can. For each player, I tried to find the basic questions about each major league player. The basic questions about Darryl Strawberry: How's he going to do in Los Angeles? How will he hit in Dodger Stadium? How much will his loss hurt the Mets? How much will he help LA? What are his career totals going to be? Is he going to hit 500 home runs in his career? 600? How many?

The basic question about Marquis Grissom: Is he going to be a star? The basic question about Joe Girardi: Is he better than Berryhill? The basic question about Ron Gant: Is he for real? The basic questions about Dennis Eckersley: Is he the most effective reliever ever? Should he have won the Cy Young Award? Is he going to be a Hall of Famer?

There are certain questions which recur constantly throughout the section, the most common of which is "Who is he?" I would assume that if you look up Tom Gilles, what you probably want to know is "Who is Tom Gilles?" At whatever level the player rests, there is an implied question mark. Can he play? Does he help the team? Can he be a star? How long will he last? Why didn't he play well last year? Can he come back? Why did he play *so* well last year? Will he go in the Hall of Fame? Can he get 3000 hits? Has he slipped a notch? Where does he rank? Can he win 300 games? Can he hit 756 home runs?

These questions recur because these are the basic questions we ask ourselves when we think about major league players. There are also individual questions, which pertain to maybe half of the players. I mention the Griffeys, and you naturally think about father/son combinations. I mention Ripken, you're naturally going to wonder about the streak.

I stopped writing the *Abstract* because I was concerned about information pollution. The *Abstract* was committed to the search for *new* information, perhaps without appropriate respect to whether that information was relevant or important, and certainly without any regard for whether the average man could understand it or could not. This section opens up a new chapter in my career, beginning the process of searching among the thousands of pieces of information which have become available for those which relate to the fundamental discussion about the player. Yes, we can find out now what a player hit with two out and a runner on third base, but what does that matter? We are overwhelmed by details. What we need now—what I think the public needs now—is someone to help them search among the thousands of pieces of evidence about each player for the data and the underlying principles which help to answer the basic questions. That is what I have tried to do here.

In many ways this is a more difficult thing to do, to look at the *whole* picture of the man, rather than merely trying to make that picture a tiny bit clearer in some detail. To try to answer the basic questions about every player requires an arrogance, or a self-confidence at least, that I did not have five years ago. There are a thousand players here, which gives me a thousand chances to be dead wrong. But that represents what I think we need to do in the 1990s. We need to take the information explosion of the 1980s, and harness it to the issues that we are interested in.

THE BASEBALL BOOK 1991

BASIC QUESTIONS

•A•

Don AASE, Los Angeles
Can he still pitch?

There isn't any reason to think he can. I had his career over in last year's book, but the Dodgers decided to extend it a year. He pitched poorly for the third straight season, and one would have to assume his career was over.

Jim ABBOTT, Angels

It was widely reported a year ago that Jim Abbott's 12 wins in his first professional season set a record for the most major league wins by a pitcher in his first pro season. We have discovered that this is not correct.

A pitcher named Ernie Wingard, who won 13 games for the St. Louis Browns in 1924, had never pitched professionally before that season. A note on page 100 of the 1925 *Reach Guide* says that Ernie Wingard "never had a great deal of training in the art of heaving before becoming a big leaguer. He made the major leagues, it must be remembered, in one long jump from the semi-pros." We called the National Association, which maintains records of minor league contracts, and confirmed that they had no record of Wingard pitching in the minor leagues prior to his thirteen-win season in 1924.

Kyle ABBOTT, California
Who is he?

Left-handed starting pitcher, similar to Jim Abbott in size. Throws very hard, regarded as the best pitching prospect in the California system but didn't pitch well at Midland (Texas League) last year.

Shawn ABNER, Padres
Is he ever going to be a regular?

Probably not, no. He played so much better last year than he had before that there was some renewed optimism about him, but if you look at what he did in 1990 compared not to his own past but to what is expected of an outfielder, it's apparent that he has little chance of playing regularly. The basic elements of offense are hitting for average, power, speed and strike zone judgment. He hit .245, homered once in 184 at bats, was two for five as a base stealer and struck out three times as often as he walked. He was nowhere near the standards of an average outfielder in any area.

Jim ACKER, Toronto
What happened to him last year?

Acker, who pitched extremely well in 1989, started out well last year (1.77 ERA through the end of May) but was hit hard the last four months (5.14 ERA). I can't give you an answer as to why, which from his standpoint may be the worst answer of all. He had no injury, or at least had no periods of inactivity such as one would associate with an injury. The frequency with which he got ahead of hitters was the same in 1990 as in 1989. Left-handers have always hit him, and hit him about the same last year as in 1989 (.286 in '89, .289 last year). But right-handers, who he limited to a .190 batting average in 1989, jumped to .276 against him last year, meaning that he wasn't getting anybody out.

Steve ADKINS, Yankees
Can he pitch major league baseball?

I am optimistic about Adkins' *long-term* future, less optimistic about his immediate future but certainly not down on him. Adkins, a six-foot-six inch left-hander, has been in the Yankee system since 1986, posting consistently good won-lost records (aggregate 54-26) and earned run averages. Last year at Columbus he was 15-7 with a 2.90 ERA, but walked 98 men in 177 innings. Called to the majors, he walked 29 men in 24 innings, and posted a losing record for the first time in his career.

Obviously, Adkins can't win with that kind of control, and you probably know that most young pitchers who have ability but can't find the strike zone never do. They don't overcome the control problem, as a rule, until they lose the good stuff. I give Adkins a good shot at being in the blessed minority. First, he's always been a winner. In the minor leagues he was able to succeed pitching outside the strike zone probably 60% of the time. To succeed in the majors he'll have to hit the strike zone a little more often—but not a lot. There are still a lot of major league hitters who will swing at a bad pitch if you give them the chance, and *every* hitter will chase a bad pitch once in awhile.

Second, Adkins (due to some minor injuries) has not pitched a lot of innings—less than 150 a year as a rule. That's a big plus to me, because it probably means his arm is in better shape now, at age 26, than it would have been if he had been healthier.

I make Adkins a good prospect—not an "A" prospect, like Offerman or Gonzalez, but a good Grade B prospect.

Troy AFENIR, Oakland
Who is he?

27-year-old catching prospect, has been around. In 34 major league at bats he has struck out 18 times, has yet to draw a walk. He can't hit enough to play, but if he's a good guy his glove rep might get him a spot as somebody's number three catcher. Or maybe they'll expand the rosters to 45; that would help.

Juan AGOSTO, St. Louis
Will he bounce back?

Agosto, who had pitched well for two and a half years as the left-handed spot reliever for the Astros, posted a 1.34 ERA through May last year, but then was pasted the rest of the year, posting ERAs of 4.70 in June, 7.52 in July, 5.59 in August, 5.40 in September and 5.40 in October. Basically the same story as Jim

Acker. Despite not pitching well he pitched in 82 games, the most of any major league pitcher.

In view of the fact that there is no generalized degeneration of his pitching record, I would say that there may be a chance of a comeback. His hits/innings ratio, home runs allowed and strikeout/walk data were not substantially different last season than in his better years.

Will he help the Cardinals?

He'll be trying to replace Ken Dayley. He won't be any *better* than Dayley.

Rick AGUILERA, Twins

In the September 25, 1990 edition of *USA Today* it said that "Minnesota's young starting rotation needs a pitcher who piles up a lot of innings, and if Rich Garces . . . is good enough to close, the Twins will consider moving Rick Aguilera back to the rotation. GM Andy MacPhail says he will talk about it with Aguilera first."

GM Andy MacPhail should have his head examined to see if there are any moving parts. Aguilera is a fine pitcher, but how in the world would anyone conclude that he was a pitcher who was capable of piling up a lot of innings? He has been put in the starting rotation in the major leagues time and time again, and every time he has immediately hurt his elbow. The most innings he has ever been able to pitch in a major league season is 145. He has struggled for years to find a role he can fill in the major leagues, and last year he did it, moving into the closer role and saving 32 games in 39 chances . . . so now you're going to move him back to the starting rotation? So you can see if a 19-year-old kid out of A ball is good enough to be the closer? What the hell is wrong with you people?

(**Late Note:** The acquisition of Steve Bedrosian presumably means that Aguilera will be in the rotation.)

Darrel AKERFELDS, Philadelphia
Does he have the ability to be a relief ace?

Probably not. His strikeout/walk ratios are very poor—less than even. It is hard to name a relief ace who had those kind of ratios. I suspect his current job is as much as he can do.

Scott ALDRED, Detroit
Who is he?

Aldred is a left-handed pitcher, regarded a year ago as the top pitching prospect in the Tiger system. He went 6-15 with a 4.90 ERA for Toledo but the Tigers called him up in September anyway. He pitched well in three starts for the Tigers, and Sparky Anderson said that "After he plays winter ball and then goes through a full spring training, we should have ourselves a pitcher."

There is a temptation, of course, to use this situation as an illustration of the shortage of pitchers around nowadays, how little talent is in the minor leagues. Can you imagine a pitcher in the fifties getting called up after going 6-15 with a 4.90 ERA?

Yes, I can—because in fact it happened, many times. In 1956 a pitcher named Truman Clevenger went 2-11 with a 5.94 ERA for Louisville. The Washington Senators called him up. In 1954 Jim Brosnan went 4-17 with an ERA of 4.70 for Des Moines. The Cubs called him up. In 1957 a pitcher named Fred Kipp went 8-17, leading the International League in losses, with a 4.09 ERA and a bad strikeout/walk ratio. The Brooklyn Dodgers called him up late in the year, and he pitched 40 games for the Dodgers in 1958. That was when the farm systems were at their peak.

There have always been guys like that. In 1937 a wild left-hander named Ken Chase went 3-10 for Chattanooga in the Southern League, walking 108 men in 153 innings and posting a 4.65 ERA. The Senators gave him a look late in the year

anyway. He got shelled so they sent him back to Chattanooga for 1938, where he started the season with a 5-12 record, at which point they called him back up. He stayed in the league for several years, and even won fifteen games in 1940. He hung around for several years after that because for some reason he could always beat the Cleveland Indians.

It *is* true that most of the time when you see something like this happen, you're talking about a bad team, desperate for pitching. There are even some cases where it has worked, and the guy has turned out to be more effective in the majors than he was in the minors, like Bob Purkey and Mickey Lolich, who worked his way through the minors with a nifty 27-44 record.

Mike ALDRETE, Montreal
Would you want him on your team?

Aldrete isn't of any use to a rotisserie team or a fantasy league team, because his chance of being a regular has evaporated and he doesn't contribute anything in the large areas of play which are the basis of most of those games. On a real team, he is a useful fifth outfielder and early-in-the-inning pinch hitter. Even last year, hitting .242, he was useful because he had almost as many walks (37) as hits (39), and consequently a good on-base percentage.

Jay ALDRICH, Baltimore
Is he going to be in the majors?

Almost certainly not. He's 30 years old this April, was given an emergency trial by Baltimore and bombed. He'll be fighting to keep his career alive.

Gerald ALEXANDER, Texas
Who is he?

Alexander is a right-handed starting pitcher for the Rangers who has definite star potential. Alexander was a twenty-first round draft pick out of Tulane (1989) who impressed the Rangers a year ago with microscopic ERAs in rookie ball. He started 1990 at Charlotte (A ball) where he was 6-1 with an 0.63 ERA. Promoted to AAA Oklahoma City, he went 13-2 there, a total of 19-3 on the season.

While recognizing that he could take the league by storm, I wouldn't place him too high on my list of potential American League Rookies of the Year. The positives are 1) he pitched brilliantly last year, 2) he has decent control, and 3) his strikeout/walk ratio is good. The negatives are 1) Texas may be due for an off season, 2) Tom House has a dreadful record of developing pitching prospects into pitchers, 3) he has been brought along awfully fast, 4) while his strikeout/walk ratio is *good*, it isn't *great*, and 5) if he's that damned good, why was he a twenty-first round draft pick a year ago? I'd like him better if the record of having succeeded was sustained over a longer period of time, in other words. A good prospect, but not high on my draft list.

Manny ALEXANDER, Baltimore
Who is he?
Very young shortstop, listed a year ago as a top prospect in the Oriole system. He hit .178 in the Midwest League in '90, which probably didn't move him up the list any.

Beau ALLRED, Cleveland
Will he be in the majors this season?
If Maldonado departs as a free agent, Allred has a good chance of being on the major league roster. He'll fight for a job with Turner Ward.

I was high on Allred a year ago, when he hit over three hundred in AA, but he didn't help himself last year, when he played at Colorado Springs, a hitter's haven, and didn't do anything much.

Allred's problem is that he's a "medium" guy, the kind of guy who could hold up a bank and get by with it because the only thing anybody would remember about him was that he seemed kind of average. He's not large or small six foot, 193 pounds. He runs well enough, but he's not *fast*. He has some line-drive power, but he doesn't have *power*. His strikeout/walk ratio is pretty good, but it's not good enough to attract any attention.

Allred is 25 years old now, getting long in years for a prospect. The odds are that he will never play regularly in the major leagues, but I think he might turn out to be a decent player if he does.

Roberto ALOMAR, Toronto
How good is he going to be?
A year ago I wrote that "There are three truly great second basemen in history . . . and then some guys who are almost in the same class. I think by the time he is through, Roberto Alomar is going to be talked about along with those guys."

Alomar last year had basically the same season that he had in 1989, so there is little to add to or subtract from what I wrote last year. Of course, I would have liked to see him take another step forward, but he is only 23 years old, so there's no immediate pressure for dramatic improvement.

Who won the trade?
I'll discuss that in the Joe Carter comment.

Sandy ALOMAR JR., Cleveland
Is he going to be a big star?
I think he'll be a minor star, maybe comparable to Tony Pena, but I doubt that he'll be a big star. First, although he played well last year, he didn't play *that* well. He hit .290 but with limited secondary offensive skills, so that on the whole he was just a little bit better *as a hitter* than the average American League catcher, and probably also somewhat better defensively. Compare Alomar to Mickey Tettleton of Baltimore, who was considered to be having a poor season.

Their at bat totals were almost the same (445, 444). Alomar hit .290, Tettleton .223, which is a difference of thirty hits, thirty singles. Tettleton drew 106 walks, Alomar only 25—so who was better? Which is worth more: thirty singles or 81 walks? Tettleton also hit more home runs than Alomar (15-9), and the other differences between them were minor.

If what Alomar did last year was a typical season, he'll be a star. I'm inclined to think that the season was near the top of his ability. I doubt that he is truly a .290 hitter; I think it is more likely he's a .265 hitter having a good season. That's still pretty good—but I doubt that he's any better hitter than Steinbach, Mike Heath, Mike Macfarlane, Pat Borders, B. J. Surhoff or most of the other catchers around the league.

Who won the trade?
Cleveland, for several reasons:

- The Indians traded for one player (Alomar) with others thrown in who might develop. One of those extras, Carlos Baerga, now has a chance to be a pretty good player.
- San Diego made the trade to try to put them over the top, to make 1990 their season. It didn't happen for them.
- The critical downphase of the Padres' season occurred when their star catcher was hurt. Because of the trade, Alomar was not available to control the damage.
- Even though he was third in the league in RBI, it would be hard to argue that Carter played particularly well for San Diego.

Note: Alomar's .376 average against left-handed pitching was the best in the American League.

Moises ALOU, Montreal
Is he ready to come to the majors and contribute?
Alou is a major league player, but in my opinion not a championship quality

player at this time. Moises, who is Felipe's son, seems to have more in common with Jesus Alou than the other two brothers. He's a big guy (6-3, 185—about the same size as Jay) but like Jay has never hit for power. I think he'd hit around .270 if the Expos stuck him in the lineup, has a good arm and may develop power later on.

Wilson ALVAREZ, Chicago White Sox
What happened to him last year?

Alvarez, listed by one publication as the best prospect in minor league baseball in 1989, was completely ineffective at AAA Vancouver (7-7, 6.00 ERA), and dropped down to Birmingham, where he pitched fairly well. He's 21, so he has plenty of time to come back.

Richie AMARAL, Seattle
Who is he?

He's kind of a strange story. Amaral's major league equivalencies show him to be one of the better-hitting second basemen in baseball. As a major league regular he would hit .265–.290 with a good number of doubles, seventy to a hundred walks and twenty-five to fifty stolen bases. The White Sox, who need help at second base, drafted Amaral from the Cub system two years ago, but never gave him a look although he hit extremely well at AA in 1989 and AAA last year. They let him leave the organization as a six-year free agent.

Amaral is 29 years old. His defensive stats at shortstop were terrible, and obviously he has never impressed anyone as a defensive wonder—yet the Cubs and then the White Sox have persisted in playing him at shortstop, or playing him half the time at shortstop and half at second base, where his defensive stats are actually pretty good. Why? It's a puzzle. If you've got a minor league shortstop who can hit, why don't you give him 150 games at second base to let him develop? Why do you draft him and then ignore

him even when he plays well? What am I missing here?

Amaral signed with Seattle, which may mean he is going to try to play short. If he does, he's probably doomed to failure. His fielding percentage at short was .923 in '88, .900 in '89.

Larry ANDERSEN, San Diego
Will he be able to pitch in San Diego the way he did in Houston?

It would not be fair to Andersen to suggest that his ERA in Houston was created by pitching in the dome. His ERA in 1989 was 1.22 in Houston, but still 2.00 on the road, which isn't too bad. When he moved to Boston in 1990 he was better than ever. He throws strikes, and gets ahead of the hitters an extraordinary percentage of the time (61% last year.) I'm sure he won't be *as* effective in San Diego as he was in Houston, but there is no reason to think that he won't remain an extremely effective pitcher.

Allan ANDERSON, Twins
What happened to him last year?

Pitchers who strike out less than four men a game are virtually never successful over a period of years. The Twins scored a lot of runs for Anderson in '89 but very few last year (Tim Leary was the only American League starter with less support), which caused his won-lost record to dramatically over-state his loss of effectiveness between '89 and '90.

Brady ANDERSON, Orioles
Does he still have a chance to be a star?

Anderson now has 825 major league at bats, with a batting average of .216. I've always liked Anderson, and on some level I still do, but you can't be stubborn in evaluating talent. A player who hits .216 through that many at bats is *not* going to be a star, and faces an uphill battle to play regularly.

There are still things to like about Anderson. I refuse to believe that he's a .216

hitter; I still think he could hit .250 as a regular. His defense is good, and his secondary offensive skills are *very* good. If he could get the corner turned, he's a player who could walk 80 times and steal 50 bases, and a guy like that can help you. But he's going to run out of chances pretty quick.

Dave ANDERSON, Giants
Is he the best utility infielder in the majors?

People take batting averages in small trials too seriously. Anderson hit .350 last year in a hundred at bats, which caused some people to cite him as the best backup infielder in the majors. He's a decent enough player, but he's a lifetime .239 hitter. His .350 batting average last year produced six RBI—six—and his peripheral stats were mostly poor.

Kent ANDERSON, California
Is he going to be a regular?

No. Anderson hit .308 last year, which is like Dave Anderson's .350 average—in 143 at bats, it means almost nothing. Schofield is a good player, basically the same age as Anderson, and I doubt that Anderson will be able to take his job.

He may have a better shot at second base.

Scott ANDERSON, Montreal
Who is he?

Six-foot-six inch, 29-year-old right-hander, had a shot with Texas several years ago.

Anderson is no prospect, but he's the kind of no prospect who can fool you, like Mike Bielecki or Dave Johnson. He was drafted by the Rangers in 1984, and pitched quite well as a starter for two years in their system (1984–1985). In 1986 the Rangers moved him to AAA and converted him to relief, after which his career began to go in the toilet. He floundered as a reliever from 1986 through 1988, switched back to a starting role with Indianapolis in 1989 and has pitched fairly well as a starter for a year and a half. His K/W ratios and ERAs have been pretty good. He's the kind of pitcher that Buck Rodgers has worked miracles with before, and I wouldn't bet against it happening again.

Willie ANSLEY, Houston
Who is he?

Outfield prospect, a big guy who can run (Oklahoma offered him a scholarship as a running back.) He didn't play real well at AA last year, and I don't think he'll surface before 1993.

Eric ANTHONY, Astros
Is he going to be a star?

A year ago Anthony was a highly touted prospect whose arm and awesome power were supposed to make him a star. He struggled, and of course a lot of people have given up on him.

I didn't see Anthony as a coming star a year ago, so naturally I don't now. He is going to strike out so much that he can't hit for average, and he does not have great speed. What does that leave?

But his .192 batting average last year now has people unrealistically pessimistic about him, just as a year ago people were unrealistically optimistic because of his power. He's not a .190 hitter. He'll hit .230, .250 maybe, with enough home runs and defense to keep him in the league. He's a Cory Snyder, Rob Deer type.

Kevin APPIER, Royals
How good is he?

Appier pitched awfully well last year, going 12-8 with a 2.76 ERA; among his wins were a one-hitter against the Tigers (Game Score: 87) and a three-hit shutout of Boston in which he struck out ten (Game Score: 90).

As is well known, the Royals' organization in the John Schuerholz years produced more quality pitchers than any other major league team, and there is a strong possibility that Appier will be another one. He was better than the league

average in almost every area of performance—strikeouts, walks, hits allowed, home runs allowed, won/lost record—and fourth in the league in ERA. That's unusual even for a *successful* young pitcher, who normally will be a combination of strong positives and lingering negatives.

Appier doesn't need to *improve* to be one of the better pitchers in the league; he just needs to stay where he is while pitching 225 innings a year. It isn't absolutely clear that he'll be able to do that. He's never pitched anywhere near that many innings, and with his youth (he's 23) and slight frame, it's uncertain how he'll react to the challenge.

He does *not* have a pretty motion; there's a lot of energy consumed in his delivery in ways that don't seem related to what he is doing. He flops around, is what I'm saying; his arms and legs fly this way and that. The impression is that it is very difficult for him to be throwing this hard—as contrasted with, say, Roger Clemens or Roger Salkeld, who seems to throw a 94-MPH heater with no wasted effort. On the other hand, there is nothing about his delivery that seems *destructive*; it just seems inefficient. I'm not sure that Appier will be able to pitch 225 innings a year without an injury—but if he can he'll be one of the league's best pitchers.

Note: Base stealers were 13 for 14 against Appier last year, the highest *percentage* against any major league pitcher. One can't help but note, however, that while the *percentage* is high the *total* isn't—in fact, it's a little below average. My reading of this peculiarity is that Appier did a decent job of keeping the runners close, but Macfarlane didn't throw them out anyway.

Luis AQUINO, Royals
Why have the Royals been so reluctant to start him?

I commented a year ago that if you compared Jeff Montgomery and Mark

Davis at some length, you would wonder why the Royals put out $13 million to replace Montgomery with Davis. What may be harder to understand, in its own way, is why they would spend good money to bring in Storm Davis, rather than giving a look to Aquino as a starter. In 1988, when Davis posted a pretty good ERA for Oakland (3.70), Aquino posted a 2.79 ERA for the Royals, granting that was only 29 innings. In 1989, when Davis was posting a 4.36 ERA for Oakland, Aquino was posting a 3.50 ERA for the Royals—in almost the same number of innings. So why put out a lot of money to get Davis, rather than take a look at Aquino?

Wait a minute—I have the answer. "We're not interested in ERA," explained Royals pitching coach Frank Funk. "We're after *wins.*" I think that gives you a hint at the Royals' problem last year.

Aquino pitched well again last season—much better than Davis—until his season ended on July 20. As it happened, I was at that game, and had a great seat right behind the third base dugout. Aquino was dead in the sixth inning; we were screaming for Wathan to come out and get him. I can't remember when I have seen a starting pitcher so obviously tired sent back to the mound, not once but three times, until the game was over. Funk felt it was important for him to finish the game, to build his confidence, you know. That's what he explained to the reporters the next day.

First, Aquino had been pitching great for several weeks. He was making his third start of the season, and his third *effective* start; his ERA in the three starts (all in July) was 2.05. So what was wrong with his confidence?

Second, what exactly is the value of being confident that you can finish a game, in today's baseball? Does Bob Welch have this confidence? Seems to me he's doing alright, and he's finished three games in two years. Storm Davis has completed two games in four years.

Third, what kind of sense does it make to build up a pitcher's "confidence" by forcing him to pitch when he is tired?

He didn't pitch again for more than two months. It was announced that he had hurt himself while warming up for his next start. With the exception of two innings in October, he was done for the year.

Johnny ARD, San Francisco
How's he doing?

Ard, a right-handed pitcher, was the Twins #1 draft pick in 1988, and was one of the top prospects in the organization. He's a sinker/slider pitcher, throws hard. He went 12-9 at Orlando (AA) last year, and will probably move to AAA in 1990, but his strikeout/walk data was poor (101 to 85) and *Baseball America* did not list him among the top prospects in the Southern League. He was traded to San Francisco for Bedrosian.

Jack ARMSTRONG, Reds
Will he ever pitch a whole season the way he did the first half last year?

Armstrong started the All-Star game for the National League last year, faded to nothing in the second half of the season and was criticized for working too hard between starts, bringing to mind the question Ron Swoboda once posed ("Why am I wasting so much dedication on such a mediocre career?") My comment about Armstrong a year ago was that he could be real good, but then so could half the guys in the league. That's still pretty much how I feel about him, granting that the comment works at a different level now, after he has won twelve games in a season, than it did a year ago. In the long run it is always preferable to bet on people who work too hard rather than people who work too seldom.

Brad ARNSBERG, Texas
Has he gone as far as he can go?

Arnsberg, once a bright prospect in the Yankees' system, posted a 6-1 record, 2.15 ERA in 53 games last year, prompting people to wonder whether he had the ability to move into a key role. The answer is probably *not*, although you never know for sure. He didn't pitch anywhere near as well as the 2.15 ERA would suggest.

Paul ASSENMACHER, Cubs
Could he do the job of a relief closer, or is he locked into the role of a left-handed spot reliever?

Assenmacher is a Rodney Dangerfield of relief, a Zane Smith of the bullpen. If there is a reason why he couldn't be an effective closer, I don't know what it is. He's a big ugly guy, skinny and kind of sloppy looking, but he's pitched extremely well for several years. His entire career has been spent pitching for bad teams in the two worst pitcher's parks in baseball, County Stadium in Atlanta and Wrigley Field. Despite this massive handicap, his records are pretty good. His ERA last year was 2.80, and he struck out nearly a batter an inning. His career strikeout/walk ratio, not counting intentional walks, is about three and a half to one. I think the big ugly son of a gun can pitch.

The Cubs, despite the collapse of their bullpen, were reluctant to let Assenmacher close, and have now added Dave Smith to obviate the possibility.

Don AUGUST, Brewers
Will he ever get back to where he was two years ago?

I doubt that he will. Pitchers who don't strike people out have good years, but they are almost never effective over a period of years. This is just one more case in point.

Joe AUSANIO, Pittsburgh
Who is he?

Right-handed relief pitcher, an 11th-round pick in 1988 who has pitched sensationally in the Pirate system for three years. Obviously the Pirates aren't impressed, as he is being promoted very slowly and isn't usually listed among the top prospects in the organization. He throws a fastball and a forkball and has a terrific strikeout/walk ratio. I'd compare him to Drabek, in that his arm isn't awesome but his mental makeup appears to be outstanding. I think he's going to be a good pitcher.

Steve AVERY, Atlanta
How large a shadow does his terrible performance cast over what appeared to be a brilliant future? Can a young pitcher recover from a start like this to go on to an outstanding career?

Avery, tagged a year ago (by me, among others) as one of the top pitching prospects in the game, came to the majors in June and was terrible, going 3-11 with a 5.64 ERA. It would be nice to blame his park, The Launching Pad, for some of this, but his record in road games was 0-7 with a 7.71 ERA. He had only a few good starts, and right-handed hitters hit .309 against him.

Most pitchers who are destined to be great, truly great, do not struggle *in this way* on coming to the major leagues. Many young pitchers fight their control for several years before finding themselves, like Koufax, Bob Gibson and Nolan Ryan. But *if* a young pitcher can throw strikes, and *if* he is destined to be a good one, normally he will be effective from the start of his career, as for example Tom Seaver was, or Warren Spahn, or Juan Marichal, or Jim Palmer or Catfish Hunter or Roger Clemens.

Of course there are young pitchers who have had seasons like this and went on to be outstanding; I'm just saying that you have to adjust your estimate of the probabilities. I still like Avery quite a bit. His strikeout/walk data was good, and the strikeout/walk ratio is a better indicator of future success than any other element of a pitcher's record. The Braves have a bad defense, and it is tough to pitch well with a bad defense around you.

I don't know exactly what to make of this, but when opposing hitters hit the first pitch against Avery, they hit .460 (29 for 63). When they hit the second pitch, whether it was 1-0 or 0-1, they hit .368 (25/68). Avery was *much* more effective when he got deeper in the count. I don't know what that means—maybe he was taking *too much* off the fastball early in the count, trying to get ahead of the hitters. I suspect that it indicates some problem in adjusting his thinking from how one gets minor league hitters out to how one gets major league hitters out, and I suspect that once he gets past that point, he's going to be an effective pitcher.

Oscar AZOCAR, San Diego
Is he going to be a star?

No. Azocar brings the Padres good defense, excellent speed and the ability to hit .255–.280. It is questionable whether that will be enough to keep him in the lineup, but it definitely is not enough to make him a star.

Azocar, who I think is the first player to have two cars in his name, grounded into only one double play last year in 65 games. In the minor leagues, however, he has grounded into many more double plays than you would expect from a left-handed hitter with speed.

•B•

Wally BACKMAN, Philadelphia
With the apparent development of Jeff King, is he going to continue to have a job?

Backman hit .292 with an excellent .374 on-base percentage, so you'd think he would be valuable to *somebody*. The Pirates in 1989 were uncertain who their leadoff hitter was, and Backman helped to clear that up, since he's obviously a leadoff hitter. He also hit .358 last year with men in scoring position.

Carlos BAERGA, Cleveland
Is he going to be a star?

Baerga has several of the things you look for in trying to spot a young star. He hit well enough in the majors last year (.260) at a very young age (21). He has a combination of skills to build on—some speed, but also some pop in his bat and a good throwing arm.

I like Baerga about as well as, but no better than, the other guy in this trade, Sandy Alomar. I'd say his chance of developing into a star player is maybe 15 to 20%.

Kevin BAEZ, New York Mets
Who is he?

Shortstop prospect, spent the year at AA. No hitter, no speed. On the last day of the season Jay Horwitz put a line in the press notes claiming that he was the nephew of Joan Baez, but he's not that, either.

Jeff BAGWELL, Houston
Who is he?

Terrific young hitter; the Red Sox traded him to Houston for Larry Andersen. You never know *exactly* how good a young player will be, but with some luck (for Bagwell) Lou Gorman will hear about the Bagwell trade until the day he dies. It could be one of those deals, like

Lou Brock for Ernie Broglio, Nolan Ryan for Jim Fregosi and Frank Robinson for Milt Pappas, that haunts the man who made it.

Bagwell is a third baseman and singles hitter, like Wade Boggs. If he had come up in Fenway, in my opinion, he would have won some batting titles. Playing in Houston, of course, he probably won't, but still might. He'll probably take the third base job away from Caminiti within a year and a half, though.

Scott BAILES, California
Will he be on a major league roster?

No.

Mark BAILEY, San Francisco
Mark Bailey? Is this the guy that used to be with Houston?

Yes. He's 29 now, runs like Ernie Lombardi. I don't expect him to be on a roster.

Harold BAINES, Oakland
Will he hit in Oakland the way he did in Chicago and Texas?

Baines has never played in a good park to hit in. In view of his age (32) and extreme lack of speed (he hasn't stolen a base in four years) he is probably of less real than perceived value.

Doug BAIR, Pittsburgh
Is his career over?

Unless they revive the Senior's League, yes.

Doug BAKER, Minnesota
Can he help a major league team?

Baker, an infielder with a good defensive reputation, hit .295 in 1989 (78 at bats) but spent almost all of 1990 in the minors, anyway. I don't understand why. He's not very good, but I don't understand why he couldn't play for somebody like Seattle or Boston, a team which needs another shortstop.

Steve BALBONI, Yanks
Will he make a team this year?

Let's look at the factors which would influence that:

1. The Yankees have three first basemen, with Mattingly and Maas, and Balboni is third among the three.
2. He hit .192.
3. The Yankees aren't going to contend anyway, so what do they want with a 34-year-old first baseman?
4. He does have a guaranteed contract for $900,000 plus a $200,000 buyout on an option. So it would cost the Yankees a million-one to release him.
5. His home run rate is still terrific.
6. He's not *really* a .192 hitter.
7. He's a good guy to have around the clubhouse.

Hm. Balancing it all out, I'd say it's 50-50 whether he's going to get another year in the Show, maybe a little less than 50-50. Even if the Yankees don't sign him, somebody else might, somebody who plays in a better home run park.

Balboni now has had a slugging percentage in the .400s—between .406 and .498—for seven straight seasons. His career slugging percentage is .450.

Jeff BALDWIN, Houston
Who is he?

Left-handed hitting outfielder, called up from AA after hitting .316. He's a line drive hitter, no speed or power, so he'll be trying to latch on to Danny Heep's old job, more or less. Trying to fill the shoes of Harry Spilman. I think he can probably do the job, but he may need another decade or two in AAA before he gets a good shot.

Jeff BALLARD, Baltimore
Can he bounce back?

Ballard is like Allan Anderson of Minnesota, another pitcher who had a couple of good years without any strikeouts. In fact, Don Zminda pointed out last year in *The Scouting Report* that Ballard was the first pitcher since 1941 to win as many as 18 games with as few as 62 strikeouts. Pitchers like that are almost never successful over a period of years.

I expect Ballard to have other good years. I expect him to win 14, 16 games again. But I *don't* expect that he will ever be a pitcher that you can count on from year to year.

Jay BALLER, Kansas City
Is he through?

Through? I thought the sumbitch was *dead*.

Scott BANKHEAD, Seattle
Can he come back?

There are some pitchers—John Tudor is maybe the best example right now—who are physically unable to pitch a large percentage of the time, but who are nonetheless effective when they are able to pitch. This seems wrong, intuitively; it seems that a pitcher should not jump from "unable to pitch at all" to "pitching very well" without an intervening gray area—and in fact that is how it usually happens. Normally, a pitcher who can't stay healthy won't be effective when he is able to take the mound, but there are a few exceptions like Tudor and Spud Chandler. Rick Aguilera.

I suspect—from his standpoint I would hope—that Bankhead may be one of those. Bankhead's injuries (knee, back and elbow problems) are of a type that simply aren't going to go away. He isn't ever going to be able to pitch 225 innings a year consistently. But, despite a superficially unimpressive career record, he *is* a good pitcher, and he may be able to help the Mariners (or somebody) if they can spot him.

Willie BANKS, Minnesota
Who is he?

A right-handed pitcher with a 90+ fastball, Banks was the Twins' first-round draft pick in 1987. He struggled at first, got untracked in 1989 and is expected in the majors perhaps this year, perhaps next. Young and talented, but he walked 98 men in 162 innings at Orlando in '90. A year ago he was regarded as the #1 prospect in the Twins' system, but has been passed by four or five other pitchers.

Jesse BARFIELD, Yankees
Is he a championship quality player?

He is, yes. Barfield has taken some criticism since he came to New York for not hitting 40 home runs every year, but then, what can you expect of a city that refuses to respect Rickey Henderson and Darryl Strawberry?

Barfield isn't Henderson or Strawberry, but he's a consistent 20, 25 homer man with a reasonable batting average. He runs alright, rarely grounds into double plays and has the best arm of any major league outfielder. On a losing team people will focus on his weaknesses, but he's a good player.

John BARFIELD, Texas
Who is he?

26-year-old left-hander, doesn't throw hard enough to break wind. It will come as a great surprise to me if he can pitch effectively.

Brian BARNES, Montreal
Who is he?

Young left-hander, on the small side (5 foot 9) but has a good fastball, an excellent curve and changes speeds well. He struck out 213 men in the Southern League last year.

It seems likely that Barnes will get some major league innings this year. His control isn't great, and one would like to see him spend a year in long relief before he moves into a starting job. I suspect that Barnes may emerge as a devastating relief pitcher within a couple of years, and might also succeed in a starting role. The Expos have many candidates for the starting job vacated by Kevin Gross.

Marty BARRETT, Boston
Will he play regularly again?

He'll probably get another shot. He's not that old—two years younger than Tom Herr, a similar player—and not that bad, still moves around fairly well. He may not be able to help a championship team anymore, but he could plug a gap for somebody.

Barrett was angry when he was benched last spring and, since the effect of his benching was to get Luis Rivera in the lineup, took the liberty of comparing his own offensive statistics to those of Rivera. Barrett is certainly a better hitter than Rivera, but we all know what is wrong with this analysis. Leaving Barrett in the lineup forces Jody Reed to play shortstop, which stretches his skills; moving Reed to second improves the Red Sox defensively at two positions. This is not to say that I agree with Morgan's choice. Luis Rivera can't hit and isn't anything special at shortstop, either. But Naehring and Reed will be the Red Sox best-hitting double play combination since Petrocelli and Andrews.

Kevin BASS, San Francisco
Will he bounce back?

Sure. He's just 31; he can still play even if he's lost some speed after the knee injury. He may not be stealing 30 bases in a year, but even if he doesn't he'll hit better than the people the Giants had playing right field before he came.

Billy BATES, Cincinnati
Who is he?

Little second baseman, was in the Milwaukee system until late last summer. You probably saw him in post-season play, as a pinch runner, and that appears to be his role if he is on a major league roster. He stole 51 bases for Denver in 1987, and is 8 for 9 as a thief in the major leagues. Probably will never hit enough to play regularly.

Bill BATHE, Giants
Is his job safe?

Despite the development of Steve Decker, the odds are that he will be on the roster. The Giants have five catchers in the picture as of December 1—Decker, who should be the regular, Kennedy and Carter, who platooned last year, and Bathe and Bailey, who would both like to be the number three catcher. Well, six if you count Manwaring. Common sense tells you that the Giants aren't going to keep around two former stars (Kennedy and Carter) to back up the rookie, and Bathe played well in scarce appearances last year.

Jose BAUTISTA, Baltimore
Will he get another shot at a starting job?

Bautista, who started 25 times for the Orioles when they were terrible in 1988, is probably about ready for another shot at a major league job. He's a big guy with a major league average fastball and very good control (he walked only 15 men in 108 innings at Rochester last year.) I'd give him maybe a 30, 40% chance of being an effective pitcher sometime, and that's very high for a guy who isn't on anybody's list of hot prospects.

Kevin BEARSE, Montreal Expos
Who is he?

Bearse is a left-handed pitcher, who is very fortunate to be with the Montreal Expos. His handling by the Cleveland Indians is a textbook illustration of how an organization with its head up its ass destroys young players.

Bearse was a 22nd-round draft pick in 1987, meaning that he doesn't have outstanding stuff. He proved to be a heady pitcher who could change speeds and locations well enough to tie the hitters in the low minors in knots. In Rookie Ball in 1987 he was 7-1 with a 1.71 ERA, 81 strikeouts and only 15 walks in 63 innings. In A ball in 1988 he was equally sensational as a relief ace, posting a 1.31 ERA with 127 Ks in 103 innings, excellent control.

In 1989 the Indians decided to convert him to a starter. At AA he was less dominating—only 67 strikeouts in 101 innings—but still had superb control (16 walks) and enough savvy to post a won-lost mark of 9-3 with a 2.05 ERA. Promoted to AAA in mid-season, he was 5-2 with a 3.94 ERA, which is superb for Colorado Springs, which normally has a team ERA around 5.00. In January of 1990 *Baseball America* listed him as the number three prospect in the Indians' organization.

So, with the benefit of three weeks of spring training and without an inning of major league experience, Bearse opened the 1990 season in the Indians' starting rotation. This is dumb to begin with—not that it can't work, but it's a bad gamble. The best place for a rookie pitcher is long relief, where the pressure is the least. This is true for *any* pitcher, but it is doubly true for a pitcher like Bearse, a pitcher that I think of as being in the Bud Black mold. While *sometimes* they are effective from the beginning of their careers—Randy Tomlin, Tom Browning—*most* of the time they take a little longer to find themselves as major league pitchers. The things that they did to get people out in the minor leagues don't work so well in the major leagues, so they need to re-think their approach to the game, find out what they can and can't do, and build up from there.

Well, this being the Indians, Bearse got three starts. He was hammered all three times, so they sent him back to Colorado Springs. At Colorado Springs he was 11-9 with an ERA of 5.00. Now wait a minute—that's not all that bad. Bearse had a winning record, a good strikeout/walk ratio and a normal ERA in that park. It wasn't a *good* year, certainly not by his own standards, but you can't expect a guy to be great every year. Heck, look at John Burkett just one year ago, when he was 10-11 with a 5.05 ERA at Phoenix.

The Indians put him on waivers; he was claimed by the Montreal Expos. "The way he pitched up here, and the reports we got on him down there . . . let's just say he was expendable," said John McNamara.

Steve BEDROSIAN, Minnesota
Can he hold the relief closer job?

He's not a relief closer at this point in his career. Bedrosian probably had as much to do with the Giants not winning last year as any individual. The Twins picked him up, no doubt hoping to repeat the Jeff Reardon saga. Reardon, who seemed to be slipping in the National League, pitched fairly well as a closer for the Twins in '87, when they won the World Championship.

Often a pitcher does gain a new life when he switches leagues, as Charlie Leibrandt and Oil Can Boyd did last year. But I think there is little likelihood that Bedrosian will be as effective as a stopper as Aguilera was, and a great likelihood that Aguilera as a starter will hurt his arm.

Kevin BELCHER, Rangers
Who is he?

A right-handed hitting outfielder, some speed and an above-average arm, line drive hitter who has had sporadic minor league success. Grade B prospect; center fielder now but could emerge as a Joe Rudi type player.

My MLEs show Belcher as a .270-range hitter with a slugging percentage around .400. According to *Baseball America* he has impressed his coaches as a very businesslike young man who works hard.

Tim BELCHER, Dodgers
Can he come back?

I never like to bet on a sore-armed pitcher, but the injury which stopped him in mid-season, 1990, does not appear to be serious. A small piece of carti-

lage was taken from his shoulder in arthroscopic surgery. Sixty-five, 70% chance of a comeback.

Stan BELINDA, Pittsburgh
What's his star potential?

It's very good. He wasn't great last year, but he certainly wasn't *bad*, either. He was good most of the year, but hammered for a stretch in June which ruined his ERA. His ERA was 5.50 in June, 2.68 for the rest of the year.

Leyland hasn't used a relief ace, but among the members of his bullpen committee—Belinda, Landrum, Patterson, Kipper and Power—Belinda has by far the best chance of emerging as a star.

Incidentally, although Belinda is a *right*-handed pitcher, he held *left*-handed batters to a .176 batting average last year. I don't know what that means . . . 91 at bats.

Derek BELL, Toronto
Who is he?

Outfielder, listed a year ago by *Baseball America* as the number two prospect in the system.

Bell is strong, runs and throws well, but I'm not impressed. He's one of those guys who is supposed to learn to hit someday. Sure.

George BELL, Chicago Cubs
How much has he lost, as a hitter?

Bell was having a great year last year through early July. As of July 1 he had 17 homers, 56 RBI and a slugging percentage around .500. Then he stopped hitting almost completely, and wound up the year with his poorest totals. In the first week of September Bell, who is almost never out of the lineup, missed eight games with a fluid buildup behind his right eye, but didn't hit any better in September than he had the previous two months.

Anytime you have an off year at the age of thirty people are going to attribute it to the birthday, but a player doesn't

suddenly lose the ability to hit a fastball in mid-season. In my opinion, it had to be the eye problem that was preventing him from hitting. Bell has an attitude rep so he doesn't always get credit for traits that would be regarded as leadership for another player, but he likes to be in the lineup every day, and he probably played last year when he shouldn't have. If his eye clears up, I think his bat will return in 1991.

How will he hit in Wrigley Field?

Andre Dawson came to Wrigley Field at the age of 32; Bell is going there at age 31. They're very similar hitters, although Bell may be a tiny bit better. I think that what Andre Dawson has done as a hitter in Wrigley Field is a very good estimate of what Bell is likely to do.

Jay BELL, Pittsburgh
Is this his permanent level of ability? Is he going to get better? Is he going to drop off? Why does he bunt so damn much?

A couple of things that I was wrong about, to begin with. I saw Bell play several games when he was with the Indians, and I agreed with them that he wasn't going to make it as a major league shortstop. I thought that he would eventually hit well enough for a shortstop, but I thought that he simply didn't have a shortstop's arm. Every throw to first base seemed to be either in the dirt or over the first baseman's head, not far enough off to be an error, but just not really where it was supposed to be.

Apparently, the arm is better than I thought it was; once he relaxed and began to play everyday, his throws got better. I don't know that he's going to win any Gold Gloves, but he's OK out there.

Also, when I saw the amazing bunt totals—he had 39 sacrifice hits last year, the most in the National League in the better part of a century—I assumed that he must be bunting for base hits, and then taking the sacrifice when the bunt wasn't quite good enough. Hitters like to do that sometimes because it protects their batting average, and I also think it's a good strategy—but apparently that's not what he's doing. He's really bunting to sacrifice. Leyland, who is a good manager in important respects but a God-Awful percentage manager, apparently likes for him to bunt even in the early innings.

Bell has had two seasons of almost identical production—.258 in 1989, .254 last year—so you have to assume that that's his real level of ability.

Tito BELL, Baltimore
Can he play?
Definitely. George Bell's younger brother, he's a major league shortstop all the way. The Orioles need to figure some way to get value for him.

Mike BELL, Atlanta
Who is he?
Left-handed, line-drive hitting first baseman for the Braves. He was signed as an undrafted free agent in 1986 and worked his way through the Braves' system. He is still young (turns 23 in April) and has a reasonable combination of skills—runs well, good defensive first baseman, some command of the strike zone. Basically, he's a young Dave Bergman.

The signing of Sid Bream probably means that he'll start the year at Richmond, which is probably the best thing for him. He hasn't played AAA yet. Also, even leaving Bream out of it, I like Cabrera better than Bell. That's not to put Bell down, because I think he's probably going to hang around the majors for several years, but I think Cabrera could be a star. I don't think Bell will.

Joey BELLE, Cleveland
Will he be in the majors this season?
In a better organization, you could say confidently that he won't. Belle was

called up in mid-season, 1989, after hitting twenty home runs in AA ball. He was unimpressive in the majors in 1989 (a .225 average in 62 games), and was mysteriously absent the first part of the 1990 season, the mystery being resolved when the Indians announced that he had started the season in an alcohol and drug rehabilitation center. Playing 24 games for Colorado Springs late in the year, he hit extremely well; in nine games with Cleveland, he didn't.

Belle *is* a major league hitter, and I'm not saying he won't hit if he has a major league job. I think he probably *would* hit fairly well. I'm saying it seems to me to be obviously better sense to give him a year at AAA. If I was running the Indians, I would want to do two things:

1. keep the pressure off of him, and
2. make him *earn* a major league job.

Rafael BELLIARD, Atlanta
Can he help a team?
As a regular, which he was much of 1988, he's way over his head. As a bench player, he's alright. He fights the Mendoza line and has no power, but he's a good defensive player at three positions, an 80% base stealer and he'll take the walk if the pitcher gives it to him.

Fred BENAVIDES, Cincinnati
Who is he?
Shortstop prospect, no hitter. *Baseball America* listed him as the number five prospect in the Cincinnati organization a year ago, but I can't understand why. Chief Bender, a Cincinnati exec, said that "he reminds you of a young Kurt Stillwell," but

a. he's only two years younger than the *real* Kurt Stillwell, and
b. who the hell is Kurt Stillwell? If you really like him, shouldn't he remind you of a young Ozzie Smith or a young Alan Trammell or somebody?

I don't think Benavides will ever be a player.

Bill BENE, Los Angeles
Who is he?
Arguably the worst number one draft pick of all time. Bene, a right-handed pitcher, has never been an effective pitcher anywhere, even as an amateur. In 1988 he had a 5.80 ERA at Cal State, walking 51 men in 50 innings, and almost nobody except the Dodgers had him pegged as anything better than a sixth-round draft pick. He can throw hard, for about two minutes at a time, and for some incomprehensible reason the Dodgers in '88 puffed out their chest in their arrogant, lovable way and pronounced him a first-round draft pick.

His records since then are amazing—not amazing like Nolan Ryan, and not even amazing like Steve Dalkowski. It's just amazing that anybody could be this bad. In 1989 he pitched 14 times, mostly as a starter, and lasted a total of 27 innings. He walked 56 men, finished 0-4 and posted a 10.33 ERA.

Last year he won a game, which was such an event that *Baseball America* did a story about it. He finished 1-10 with a 6.99 ERA. We're not talking AAA here; that's at Vero Beach. His strikeout/walk ratio was 34-96. That's 34 strikeouts, 96 walks. In his pro career he has walked 12.5 men per nine innings.

Andy BENES, Padres
Why did he struggle last year? Is he going to be a big star or not?
Benes has been fighting tendinitis in the shoulder for a year and a half. Even with it, he wasn't that bad last year—3.60 ERA, 140 strikeouts in 192 innings.

I still think Benes is going to be a star. The basic problem last year was that he hit the wall about the fifth inning. The first 60 pitches that he threw in a game last year, the batting average against him was .231. After 60 pitches it went up to .258. From the seventh inning on, it was

.313. Probably this reflects the tendinitis, but Benes is also a great big guy, and there may be an assumption that size and strength automatically mean endurance. It may be that, like Goose Gossage and Eckersley and others, he is best suited to come into the game and throw hard for two innings.

Mike BENJAMIN, San Francisco
Is he going to be a regular?

Probably not. Uribe may have a couple of years left, and Andrew Santana is the Giants' shortstop of the future. I also don't think Benjamin would hit enough to hold a regular job.

Todd BENZINGER, Reds
Will he regain his status as a regular?

I don't know why he would. I didn't think Benzinger should be a regular anyway, because I don't think you can carry a first baseman who hits .250 with not much power and a bad strikeout/walk ratio. With the development of Morris and the continued degeneration of Benzinger's offense, I don't know why he would get another shot at a regular job. His slugging percentages since he came to the major leagues: .444, .425, .381 and .340. And .444 ain't too good.

Juan BERENGUER, Twins
Is he being used appropriately?

Probably. When he started six times for the Twins in 1987 he pitched well, and he was a fairly effective starter for Detroit in 1983 and 1984. I'm not sure, given the Twins' need for a starting pitcher, that I wouldn't have given him a longer look in that role. Still, I can understand Kelly's thinking:

- Berenguer is 36 years old and overweight. You can bring him in to throw as hard as he can for as long as he can.
- He has been effective in the role assigned him. His won-lost record for the last four years is 33-13, which is

weighted because he usually comes in with the team behind, but still a good record. His ERAs are also good for the Minnesota park, consistently in the mid-threes.
- He's one of the most consistent pitchers in the majors in that role, so why take him out of it and gamble on having a mediocre starting pitcher at best, or an injured pitcher at worst? He's not a great pitcher but he's good where he is, so take the money and run.

Dave BERGMAN, Detroit
How much longer is he going to last?

Bergman will be 38 in June, and it is unusual for a player who was never a regular to last that long. Of course, I think Bergman *could have been* a regular for many years had he caught a break early on, so maybe that's not a relevant factor.

I think Bergman is a terrific role player, maybe the best I've ever seen to do the job that he does. The positives are:

- Good defense at first base.
- Good left-handed pinch hitter.
- Excellent strikeout/walk ratio.

He still runs well enough. Apart from his age, I don't see any reason he wouldn't stay around for two or three more years.

Geronimo BERROA, Atlanta
Is he ever going to make it?

Berroa played with the Braves in 1989 and played well enough (.265), but was returned to the minor leagues anyway. Time is running out on him as a prospect (he's 26).

I don't see Berroa as a coming star, but I don't see him as any worse than a dozen guys who have major league jobs, either. He's a Candy Maldonado type—good arm, line drive hitter with some power,

poor K/W, not going to hit .300. If I was running a team I'd rather pick up Berroa than Maldonado, because the odds on his having a good year are about the same, and he'd do it a lot cheaper. But I wouldn't be anxious to have either one of them.

Sean BERRY, Kansas City
Who is he?

Berry is a 25-year-old third baseman, hit .292 at Memphis last year with 14 homers and 77 RBI. He has a history of stealing bases (37 in 1989) but, in view of his build (5-11, 200 pounds) probably won't be a base stealer for more than a year or two, if that.

Berry is a decent prospect, maybe a B+ prospect. The Royals are trying to decide whether they like him better, or Terry Shumpert, with Kevin Seitzer swinging between them. If Seitzer can play second base, Berry will play third. If Shumpert takes second base, Seitzer stays on third.

Damon BERRYHILL, Cubs
Can he come back?

It's going to be an amazing story if he does, because I think the odds are stacked against him:

1. The injury that he suffered, a tear to the rotator cuff, is about as serious an injury as a catcher can have.
2. Berryhill wasn't a great player, anyway. He was a .250 hitter with no speed, not much power and a poor K/W ratio in Wrigley Field. You take 90% of that, and you've got a AA player.
3. He has serious competition for the job. Joe Girardi, who caught for the Cubs last year, is about as good as Berryhill was before the injury.
4. Name a young catcher who missed almost an entire season with an injury, and went on to have a good career. OK, Carlton Fisk, name another one. Most catchers who start to get hurt,

like Ray Fosse, just degenerate from that point.

Dante BICHETTE, California
How good is he?

Not very good. He has a great throwing arm and good overall defensive skills, but I don't think he'll ever hit enough to help a team win a pennant. He hit .253 last year with 15 home runs, and I doubt that he is capable of doing significantly better than that. I wouldn't mind having him on my team as a platoon player and defensive sub in the outfield, but I don't see him as a regular.

Mike BIELECKI, Chicago
What happened? Can he bounce back?

Bielecki was pitching well early last year, with a 3.76 ERA through May 22. On that date, Dazzling Don Zimmer let him pitch ten innings in a game, and he was pretty worthless for six weeks after that, posting an 8.02 ERA in his next nine starts.

Is he capable of having another big season like 1989? Yes, I definitely think he is. Bielecki posted a 2.32 ERA over his last six appearances (31 innings.) But there are three things to keep in mind:

1. It's tough for a pitcher to have a good career in Wrigley Field. Only three or four pitchers since World War II have been consistently successful here.
2. The Cubs aren't a great organization. Frey is a fool and Zimmer's been doing this to starting pitchers for twenty years, so what kind of support is he going to be getting from the organization? Not much.
3. Bielecki has a history of bouncing from very good to very bad. On balance, he's a .500 pitcher so far (38-37).

I suspect he's going to have some more good years, and I suspect he's going to have some more bad ones.

Craig BIGGIO, Houston
Where does he rank among National League catchers? Does he still have star potential?

Biggio doesn't throw well enough to be a star catcher, and the Astros, recognizing this on some level, have been experimenting with him in the outfield. Apparently, he doesn't look too bad in center field.

If I were the Astros, I would give up on him immediately as a catcher, and give him a full season in left field. If he continues to catch he's going to destroy his speed, which is one of his major assets as a player—in fact, I suspect that already he doesn't run as well as he did two years ago.

In the right role, whatever that turns out to be, Biggio is going to be a valuable player to somebody some time. He is going to be in a World Series sooner or later. Every year that passes without his developing into a star, the more unlikely it becomes that he will emerge as a star.

Dann BILARDELLO, Pittsburgh
Will he be on a roster?

Probably not. He's probably not all that bad a player if he could latch on to a job as a third catcher, but he's past thirty, and his performance last year (an .054 average in 19 games) has a good chance of bringing his career to a screeching halt.

Tim BIRTSAS, Cincinnati
Is he an effective middle reliever?

He's OK in that role, and might be up to a larger one. Early in his career Birtsas couldn't recognize home plate, walking 91 men in 141 innings in 1985. People still think of him as wild, but he really isn't anymore; the last two years he has walked just 37 men (unintentionally) in 121 innings. I wouldn't be shocked to see him succeed in a starting role if he gets another chance.

Joe BITKER, Texas
Who is he?

Right-handed pitcher, has been kicking around a long time in the Padre system and then the A's. He re-emerged as a prospect by saving 26 games for Tacoma last year, made the PCL All-Star team and then was included by the A's in the Harold Baines trade.

Obviously, Bitker is a Grade C prospect in view of his age (27) and trade history. On the other hand, he's a guy that you might want to focus on in a rotisserie league, in that here is a player that you might be able to pick up for ten cents and he could turn into a steal. There is no particular reason to think that he can't pitch major league baseball. At Tacoma last year he struck out 52 and walked only 20 in 56 innings, and his ERAs the last four years are unimpressive (3.58, 3.97, 3.53, 3.20) until you remember that this is the Pacific Coast League, where the league ERA is in the mid-fours. His minor league record doesn't look a lot different than Orel Hershisher's.

Bud BLACK, San Francisco
Who would you rather have: Bud Black or Tom Browning?

Black and Browning were both free agents over the winter. Black signed with the Giants for a reported $2.5 million a year, and Browning re-signed with the Reds a day or two later for about 25% more than that. The two pitchers are similar enough that it is likely that the Black deal set the framework for Browning's. My guess is that Browning wanted to re-sign with Cincinnati, and waited until a similar pitcher—Black—had signed as a free agent, thereby establishing his market value.

Anyway, who made a better deal—the Giants, or the Reds? I say the Giants did. I certainly respect Browning, and you'd be a damn fool not to respect a pitcher who leads the league in starts every year and wins 60% of his decisions. Browning has started 108 times in the last three years, which is certainly one of the top figures in baseball. Browning is three years younger than Black, and Browning has a better career record, 93-61 as opposed to 83-82.

On the other hand, while salaries are based on what you have done in the past, we still live in the future:

- Browning's strikeout ratios have declined so much, from 5.3 strikeouts/nine innings as a rookie to 3.9 last year, that it becomes questionable whether he can continue to win. Very few pitchers can pitch successfully over a period of years while striking out less than four men a game. Black, though not a strikeout pitcher, still strikes out 4.6 per game.
- Browning's won-lost record over the last two years is 30-21, but that's with Cincinnati, while Black's is 25-22, not that much worse, while pitching with Cleveland.
- Browning's ERA last year was .01 *over* the National League average; in 1989 it was .10 under the league average. Black was under the American League average by .52 in '89 and .34 in '90.

As I say, they're comparable pitchers and it's right that Browning gets more money, because you're paid by what you've done in the past, and Browning has done more over a period of years. But my guess is that time will prove that the Giants made a better deal.

Willie BLAIR, Cleveland
What's his future? Can he be a major league starting pitcher?

Blair, a long reliever with Toronto in '90, was traded to Cleveland after the season, and may start the season in the rotation.

I am thoroughly puzzled by the Blue Jays' handling of Blair. The Blue Jays *need* a starting pitcher, and they're not long in candidates. Why did they trade away Blair, who was one of their better options?

The Blue Jays, normally a deliberate organization to the point of being obstinate, were flighty in their handling of Blair. After drafting him in the eleventh round in 1986 they sent him to the minors as a reliever, in which role he pitched from 1986 through 1988. In 1989 he made 17 starts for Syracuse and was unimpressive, but came to the majors last year anyway, starting six times and relieving most of the year.

Blair appears to be a Grade B prospect—a player who should be a regular and could be a star, but also carries some question marks. For one thing, he has never been particularly impressive anywhere since St. Catharines in 1986, posting an aggregate won-lost record of 17-27 over a period of four years. At the same time, he hasn't really been hammered anywhere, either; he just pitches well enough to earn a look at the next level.

Kevin BLANKENSHIP, Chicago Cubs
Does he have a major league future?

Probably not, but you never know with a pitcher. Blankenship was an undrafted free agent signed by the Atlanta system in 1984, kicked around the Braves' system for several years until he took the Southern League by storm in 1988, and then went 13-7 in the American Association in '89. He's a year older than Dwight Gooden or Bret Saberhagen.

Lance BLANKENSHIP, A's
Can he play regularly?

I doubt that he can. I think in a good year, were he a regular, he could hit .240 with 70 walks and 30 stolen bases—but suppose you put him in the lineup and he didn't have a good year? He's a good defensive player and a good enough sub, but I'd be skeptical of him as a regular.

Jeff BLAUSER, Braves
Does he still have star potential? Why wasn't he playing regularly last year?

I still believe, as I did a year ago, that Blauser is going to be a star. He was on the disabled list early last year with a torn thigh muscle, one of many injuries which cost Russ Nixon any chance to keep his job. Blauser's a *good* hitter, one of the best hitting shortstops in the National League, and a better defensive player than Andres Thomas. He didn't have a great year last year, but he still hit .269, and how many NL shortstops did better than that? One—Barry Larkin. This guy is one of the ten best shortstops in baseball right now, and young enough to get better.

Mike BLOWERS, Yankees
Will he get another chance? Was 1990 his only shot at a major league job?

Blowers has never been considered a hot prospect, so he doesn't figure to get more than one more shot at best. His performance last year, when he hit .188 and fielded .899, is surely less than he is capable of doing (I wonder if he's the first player ever to hit below the Mendoza line *and* field below the Butch Hobson mark?) If he gets another chance I expect him to play better, but he's got no star potential.

Bert BLYLEVEN, California
Does he have a comeback left?

Sure. After you've had six comebacks, what's a seventh? His strikeout/walk ratio is still three to one, and how many guys strike out three times as many as they walk but can't win. He'll come back.

Mike BODDICKER, Kansas City
Why is he pitching so much better now than he did a couple of years ago? Will he help Kansas City? How much will his departure hurt Boston?

What baseball people say is that pitching for Baltimore when they had a bad defensive team undermined Boddicker's confidence, so that he started trying to be too fine. As a result he was getting pitches out over the plate a little too often, and giving up home runs. It is also said that he was more comfortable being the number two pitcher on the staff, behind Clemens, than being looked upon as the ace.

His signing by Kansas City strengthens them in their strongest area, starting pitching; he competes for time with Saberhagen, Gubicza, Appier, Gordon and Storm Davis. His addition doesn't substantially alter the outlook for the team. If the Royals don't find a second baseman and can't sort out the outfielders, they're not going to win no matter what Boddicker does. If they do those things and Oakland isn't invincible, they could win anyway. The addition of Boddicker just makes them maybe 3% more likely to win.

The effect on Boston will depend on how well Darwin and Matt Young pitch. Obviously you would rather start the year with Boddicker in your rotation than Matt Young.

Joe BOEVER, Philadelphia
What's his role? Should we give up on the idea that he's a closer, and move him into the set-up role?

Boever is now thirty years old, and his control still has not come around. Despite that, I think the Phillies could do worse than making Boever their closer. Compare him to Roger McDowell, who's the same age, and you find they pitched about the same number of games and innings, but Boever gave up fewer hits and runs, and struck out almost twice as many batters. Maybe that's unfair to Roger, who

a. is a ground ball pitcher, and
b. didn't have his best season,

but I would still rather have McDowell coming in in the seventh and Boever in the ninth, rather than the other way around.

Wade BOGGS, Boston
Is the change in the level of his performance permanent? Is he going to hit .360 again, or is he through as a 200-hit a year man?

Boggs is 32 years old, and very few players—less than ten percent, certainly—have their best major league seasons at that age. His major injury last year (a chipped bone in the middle toe of his right foot) will clear up over the winter, but even before that, Boggs wasn't on target to hit .360. I think Boggs will win at least one more batting title, with perhaps a .340 season, but I think his chance to hit .400 is probably gone.

In the August 20, 1990, edition of *The Sporting News*, Wade Boggs put forth one of those incredibly silly quotes that sportswriters for some reason insist on taking seriously. "Boggs said he was more comfortable batting third, instead of first, in the Red Sox' order," reported *TSN*. " 'I don't have speed, I'm not a leadoff hitter,' he said."

I don't know if you ever noticed this, but Wade Boggs *also* doesn't have any power. Yes, it is true that leadoff men usually have speed and Boggs doesn't have any, but isn't it also true that players who hit third usually have some power? Boggs has hit 14 home runs in the last three years. That's a prototypical number three hitter? He didn't have any speed when he scored 128 runs in 1988. He didn't have any speed when he scored a hundred or more runs every year from 1983 to 1989. When did he ever *drive in* 100 runs?

A few years ago the introductory article to *The Baseball Abstract* was a long discussion, entitled *Rain Delay*, about who was the best player in baseball. I tried to pick through the minefield of the discussion as carefully as I could and reach a logical conclusion, and the conclusion I reached was that Wade Boggs was the best player in baseball.

A conclusion, I now realize, which was obviously wrong. In retrospect, I made one critical error: I assumed that Boggs' 1987 power surge represented a real change in his abilities, rather than a one-year fluke. The article was in the 1988 book. 1987, you remember, was a "lively ball" season in which a lot of people hit home runs. Boggs, however, had announced in spring training, before any of us knew what kind of a year it was going to be, that he was going to try to hit more home runs, so I interpreted this as a real change: he had decided to try to hit more home runs, and had proven to be capable of so doing.

If Boggs could hit twenty-plus home runs a year, then perhaps he would be the best player in baseball. He doesn't; he hits five a year. My runs created formula estimates that Boggs has created more runs per out over the course of his career than any other active player, and I believe in the runs created formula, but it ain't *always* right. The fact that he is clearly *not* the best player in baseball was driven home to me last summer when I was working with a game-simulation routine. Both Boggs and Rickey Henderson have been basically leadoff men throughout their careers. I programmed the simulation to reproduce their *career* performance, the good years and the bad, through 1989. Then I put identical teams behind them in spots two through nine, and let those teams run for several thousand games.

The team with Rickey Henderson leading off scored more runs in the simulation than the same team with Wade Boggs leading off—in fact, they scored *a lot* more runs, almost twenty more runs a year. That's *before* 1990; if I repeated the experiment now, the Henderson team would be even further ahead.

I tried moving both Henderson and Boggs to the third spot, shifting another player to leadoff. Again, the Henderson team performed substantially better than the same team with Wade Boggs in the same offensive spot.

Wade Boggs' career statistics have

been compiled playing in Fenway Park, one of the best hitter's parks in baseball—and, in fact, Boggs has hit far better in his career at home than he has in other parks. Rickey Henderson's stats have been compiled in *poor* hitter's parks, and in fact Henderson in his career has hit much better on the road than he has at home. I did nothing, in the simulation, to adjust for this—and yet Henderson's stats still represent distinctly greater value than Boggs'.

So if Wade Boggs is not the best *lead-off man* in baseball, not the best playing the role that he plays, it is obvious that he cannot be the best player in baseball. What, you think he gets there on defense?

In my defense, I could point out that Rickey Henderson in 1987 had played only 95 games, and was taking a lot of criticism for his glovework and attitude. It's a poor alibi: the fact is that I should have been smart enough not to reach the conclusion that I reached, that Boggs was the best. Henderson is the greatest lead-off man in baseball history, and I was the first person to say that. I shouldn't have wavered on it just because Henderson was hurt part of one year, and I should have realized that if Boggs wasn't the best leadoff man in baseball, he couldn't be the best player. I think it's a good article, but I made a dumb choice, and that's all.

Note: The major league leaders in runs created per 162 games played: Boggs (118), Henderson (114), Brett (111), Mattingly, Raines, Will Clark, McGriff, Eric Davis, Kal Daniels and Eddie Murray. Strawberry is eleventh, so the Dodgers have the 9-10-11 men in the middle of their order if Daniels can play.

Brian BOHANON, Texas
Who is he?

Twenty-two-year-old left-hander, a first-round draft pick in 1987. Because of injuries Bohanon has pitched so little that it's hard to evaluate him. His minor league won-lost record, from 1987 to 1990, is 6-8. Six wins. In view of his major league performance last summer (6.62 ERA) it seems obvious that he needs to spend a couple of years in Oklahoma.

Tom BOLTON, Boston
Is he for real? Is he really this good?

Bolton posted a 3.38 ERA last year. I don't expect him to do that every year, nor to win two-thirds of his decisions every year. But the real question about him seems to be why he didn't receive a better chance earlier in his career. His ERA at Pawtucket was 2.72 in 1986, 2.79 in 1988 and 2.89 in 1989. The Red Sox would call him up, let him sit around and then send him back down. I don't see any reason to think that he can't pitch effectively in the major leagues.

Incidentally, Bolton pitched great in Fenway Park—6-1 record, 1.99 ERA—and was almost as effective against right-handed hitters as he was against left-handers.

Barry BONDS, Pittsburgh
Did he deserve the MVP Award?

I think that Bonds did deserve the MVP Award, for which he was almost a unanimous selection.

I think this was one of the first times that the new information which has become available in the last ten years has played a key role in the general discussion about who should be the MVP. Bonds hit .377 with men in scoring position, including a .440 mark the first half of the season, when the Pirates built their lead.

Bonds won the MVP Award although another outfielder on the same team (Bonilla, of course) drove in more runs (120-112) and scored more runs (112-104). Bonilla also played right field, which is normally considered the more demanding defensive position, while Bonds played left. Without looking, I would be willing to bet that that's never happened before, that a player won the MVP Award although a teammate drove in and scored more runs, except for the cases where the Award went to a shortstop or a catcher.

Of course, although Bonilla drove in and scored more runs, Bonds hit for a better average, hit more home runs and had a much higher slugging percentage. Bonds has an additional skill, stealing bases, which Bonilla does not have, and despite playing left field Bonds is obviously the better outfielder of the two. Those things made him the natural MVP, but *if it had not been known* that Bonds was hitting so sensationally with men in scoring position, a Bonilla faction in the voting would have developed. Some people would have said that Bonds has the individual stats, but Bonilla is the guy the Pirates count on to produce when it counts. The fact that Bonds had hit .377 with men in scoring position took an argument away from Bonilla, and made Bonds, who would probably have won anyway, an almost-unanimous selection.

There has been, in recent years, an ungodly proliferation of freak-show "combinations" of home runs and stolen bases. Bonds last year became the second player to hit thirty homers and steal fifty bases in the same year; in recent years we have seen the first player with 40/40 (Canseco), the third player with 300/300 in his career (Andre Dawson), the first player with 20/80 or 25/70 or whatever. It's guaranteed that if Bonds hits 35 homers this year and steals 49 bases within ten minutes someone will produce a list of players who have hit 35 homers and stolen 45 bases. Everything's a "club" now—a 20/20 club, a 30/30 club, a 30/50 club, etc. Everybody's got his own list—a Sandberg list, a Dawson list, a Canseco list, a Henderson list, a Howard Johnson list, an Eric Davis list—and everybody is at or near the top of his own list. Somebody discovered that Bonds was the first player in baseball history to hit .300, score 100 runs, drive in 100, swipe 50 bases and hit 30 homers.

The problem, of course, is that since each of these lists has a separate definition there are competing claims for the selection as the greatest power/speed combination. My solution to this mess, which I proposed more than ten years ago, is "Power/Speed Number." Power/Speed Number has no analytical meaning; it simply generates a single, coherent list out of a zoo of options. I used to call it the "Bobby Bonds number," after Barry's father, who was the dominant player of this type in his generation.

Anyway, in 1990 the two MVPs, Bonds and Henderson, were also the league leaders in power/speed number, which had never happened before. Bonds led the majors at 40.4, followed by Henderson at 39.1, Ron Gant at 32.4 and Ryne Sandberg at 30.8. Bonds was the sixth player in major league history with a power/speed number over forty, the others being Eric Davis, 1987 (42.5), Rickey Henderson, 1986 (42.4), Jose Canseco, 1988 (41.0), Bobby Bonds, 1973 (40.9) and Eric Davis in 1986 (40.4). Eric Davis probably would have set the all-time record in 1985 or 1986 except that Pete Rose kept sending him back to the minors.

Bobby BONILLA, Pittsburgh
Can he sustain this kind of performance over a period of years? Is he heading into the prime of a Hall of Fame career? Did he really deserve the MVP Award?

1. No, he did *not* deserve the MVP Award. I picked him last year as the best candidate for NL MVP, so of course I'd be thrilled to argue that he really was, but he wasn't. Bonilla hit .282 with men in scoring position—almost the same as his overall batting average. Whereas Bonds hit .344 with men on base, Bonilla hit just .258, and whereas Bonds hit 14 of

his 33 homers with runners on base, Bonilla hit 12 of his 32. Bonilla's higher RBI total is simply a function of the fact that, hitting fourth while Bonds hit fifth, he batted many more times with men on base (302-221) and many more times with men in scoring position (188-138). Also, the defensive stats support the subjective conclusion that Bonds is a vastly better outfielder than Bonilla. He had a much better range factor (2.45 to 2.06; that's based on plays made per nine innings), a much better fielding percentage (.983 to .961) and more assists (14 to 8).

2. Can he sustain this over a period of years . . . Bonilla's 1990 season was probably a career year, and it is unlikely that he will match it again, or at least regularly. But while Bonilla probably *won't* drive in a consistent 120 runs a year—how many players ever have?—I think he *can* drive in a consistent 100 runs a year with 25 to 30 homers. He's very durable, and hasn't had a slugging percentage lower than .476 since his rookie season in 1986. You put a guy slugging .500 in the middle of *any* lineup for 160 games a year, and you're going to get a hundred RBI.

3. Will that make him a Hall of Famer . . . I wouldn't scoff at the idea, but I doubt that it will. Bonilla's a 230-pounder, so I suspect that in just two or three years he'll be too slow to play the outfield. (He may be moved to first in '91.) He's not a multi-dimensional star; he's not a glove man anywhere or a baserunner. His strikeout/walk ratio isn't a positive, and he's not a .300 hitter. He's an RBI man. He's Rocky Colavito or Del Ennis or George Foster. Those guys are good ballplayers and they help teams win pennants, but they don't *ordinarily* go in the Hall of Fame.

Note: Bonilla had fifteen sacrifice flies last year, the most in the major

leagues. The record is 19, by Gil Hodges.

Greg BOOKER, San Francisco
Does he deserve a major league job?
He's a joke. He's been in the major leagues for eight years, and he's got five wins and one save. His strikeout/walk ratio is even, one to one. If *everything* went right for him, he'd be Dennis Lamp for a year or two.

Rod BOOKER, Cards
Is he a valuable player?
He's an average sixth infielder. He hits OK for an extra infielder, runs pretty well, does the job in the field. He's OK.

Bob BOONE, Kansas City
Will he play regularly again?
Despite his age (he's 43) Boone lost his job not by playing poorly, but because of an injury. He didn't hit terrible last year, although he didn't hit great, and he's still an above-average defensive catcher.

Contrary to what you often read, there really is *not* a shortage of catchers at the moment. If you look around the American League in particular but both leagues, you'll find that almost everybody has a decent catcher, and several teams have two or three. There is a shortage of *star* catchers, and there are teams which have problems, but there are teams which have problems at any position. The teams which have real catching problems, like Atlanta and Texas, have young players that they *should* be looking toward to fill the vacancy. Boone will be looking for a team which is ready to compete, but needs to fill a hole at catcher, and I don't know who that would be. Maybe the Mets.

Dan BOONE, Baltimore
Is he going to be on a roster?
I suspect that he *may* be on a roster for several years. Despite his age (37) and

size (140 pounds), Boone pitched great at Rochester, including a no-hitter, and pitched well in a brief shot with Baltimore. Boone throws a knuckleball, but unlike most knuckleball pitchers *doesn't* walk many people. I suspect that if he gets the chance, he could pitch effectively for several years.

Pat BORDERS, Toronto
Where does he rank among American League catchers?

Superficially, Borders appears to be one of the better catchers in the American League, hitting .286 last year with a slugging percentage just short of .500. He hits right-handed pitchers about as well as left-handers, and he throws well.

But if you look a little more carefully, you realize that there are some problems:

1. His power stats may have been inflated a little bit by playing in Toronto. Ten of his 15 home runs were hit in the Skydome.
2. He never walks, so despite a good batting average he's not on base very much.
3. He's slow as hell. He grounded into 17 double plays in 346 at bats, one of the worst rates in baseball, stole no bases and scored only 36 runs. Dave Valle having an off year still scored more runs with less playing time.
4. He hit just .225 with men in scoring position, so he didn't drive in a lot of runs, either.
5. He's got the arm but he ain't Tony Pena, either. He's not, at this point, a candidate for a Gold Glove award.

You have to respect a guy who can hit, because no matter what people say that's the one most important skill in the game. But taking his game as a whole, Borders is in the middle of the pack among American League catchers. Maybe he'll move up in '91.

Mike BORDICK, Oakland
Who is he?

Spare infielder, made the A's roster for the World Series when Walt Weiss was hurt. He's got no future—no power, not much speed, hits like Gallego.

Chris BOSIO, Brewers
Can he come back?

I always liked Bosio, and for years was urging my readers to draft him, or whatever, arguing that a guy who strikes out three times as many as he walks is going to start winning sooner or later. He started winning in 1989, but then was troubled early last year by a knee problem—it turned out to be a bone spur on his right knee—and didn't pitch well. He was effective very early in the games, holding hitters to a .220 batting average for the first thirty pitches, but then the roof caved in, and he was lucky to make it through five innings. He hit the disabled list April 29, had surgery on his left knee on August 7 and missed the rest of the year.

The party line is that he is expected to make a full recovery. I still like him, but my patience is running a little thin. He's 28, and he has a lifetime won-lost mark of 37-46. If he's going to make any money in this game, he'd better start pretty soon.

Shawn BOSKIE, Chicago Cubs
Can he be a rotation anchor, or was he just starting in desperation? Who is he? What's his future?

A right-handed starting pitcher, Boskie pitched consistently well in the minor leagues—never spectacularly well, but well enough to win more than he lost. Called to the Cubs last summer, he started 15 times with a good 3.69 ERA. Boskie's not at either end of any spectrums. His control has been a problem, but never a nightmarish problem, and now it seems pretty good. He throws hard but not *real* hard, not Dwight Gooden hard. He's a good prospect, but not a great prospect.

Wrigley Field is a big negative for a pitcher, of course. It's not just that Wrigley causes fly balls to become home runs, which is bad enough, but that also tends to create the perception that a pitcher is failing, which sets up a cycle of frustration. Very few young pitchers over the years have been able to overcome this and get established as successful starting pitchers. I also feel that a park like this gives a special advantage to a pitcher with great control, like Ferguson Jenkins. If I were running the Cubs I would look first for veteran starting pitchers in their thirties, and try to keep young pitchers in a support role for two or three seasons.

So, while actually I like Boskie's stuff and his delivery, I'd be reluctant to bank on him to succeed in these circumstances. If he stays healthy long enough, he'll eventually be a good pitcher.

Thad BOSLEY, Rangers
Will he be around? Is he through?
Released. Gone.

Daryl BOSTON, New York Mets
Is he really this good?

Probably not. Boston was 27 years old last year, which is the most common age for a player to have a season which is over his head. He's always had athletic ability, and many of us have always been puzzled by why he didn't play better. When a player combines a good season with obvious physical talent, like Boston, there is a tendency to write off the five previous years as a fluke. On the other hand, you could say the same thing about Mike Davis or Larry Sheets or a dozen other guys, and what normally happens to them is that they'll eventually give you one good year and then start to drift slowly back where they came from.

Denis BOUCHER, Toronto
Who is he?

Left-handed pitcher, jumped from A ball to AAA last year. A native Canadian, Boucher is compared to Jimmie Key, a control-type left-hander who spots the ball well.

Oil Can BOYD, Montreal
Is he back for good, or was this just a blip on the radar screen?

Boyd, who is very thin, pitched 272 innings in 1985, and began fighting a variety of emotional problems and blood clots in 1986. If he pitches 272 innings again, it's a good bet that he'll have arm problems again. He's past thirty now, and one would hope that the emotional stuff is behind him. My guess is that if he doesn't pitch more than 220 innings a year, he can pitch consistently well for the next five years.

Phil BRADLEY, Chicago White Sox
He's a free agent. Do you want him?

I was a supporter of Bradley's for years, but at this point I have to say no, I don't want him. He's the kind of *player* that I like—some speed, but also some power, good K/W, good percentage player, pretty decent outfielder. But the attitude rep has followed him from Seattle to Philadelphia to Baltimore, and it can't all be everybody else's fault. The production numbers have been slipping—he hit just .256 with 4 homers last year, although I know he's a better hitter than that. He's 32, and almost all players are beyond their prime by that age. He could come back, but if he's a free agent and I'm a general manager, I don't make him an offer.

Note: Bradley was hit by pitches 11 times last year, the most of any major league player. I mentioned this to a friend of mine who has had to deal with Bradley in the past, and he said "Yeah, and I bet ten of 'em were former teammates."

Scott BRADLEY, Seattle
Can he help a team win? Should the Mariners be looking for somebody better?

I expect his career to pick back up in 1991. He's a *very good* number two catcher, one of the best in baseball. He didn't play well in 1990, and the Mariners are talking about what they need to do to revive his career—maybe get him some playing time at other positions.

Glenn BRAGGS, Milwaukee
Is his improved performance for real?

It's Daryl Boston, chapter two; if you want to know what I think of Braggs, just read Daryl's comment and change the name. I was very surprised that he played as well as he did for Cincinnati. On the other hand, he was 27, and a lot of guys play over their head when they're 27. Now he's 28, and we'll see.

Jeff BRANTLEY, San Francisco
Can he do this every year?

Brantley had a 1.56 ERA last year, but his peripheral numbers weren't that good. His K/W ratio and hits per inning were near average. He doesn't have a great fastball, and has no real history of consistent success.

Mike Scott had no history of consistent success before Craig taught *him* the split-fingered fastball, either. I wouldn't move Brantley to the set-up role and make Righetti the closer. I would split the glamour job between Brantley and Righetti. But if Brantley can move into the class of the really good relief pitchers, Franco and Eckersley and Thigpen and Myers, etc., I'm going to be very surprised.

Sid BREAM, Atlanta
Will he help the Braves? Does his defense justify his offense?

My friend Pete DeCoursey makes a strong argument that I have shortshrifted Bream in the past, that in fact his defense *is* good enough to carry his bat. It's a technological argument, having something to do with vectors and range indexes, and to be frank I don't really understand what he's talking about, but in principle I can see that he might have a point. The fact that people often choose to put a slugger with no defense at first base doesn't mean that a good defensive player there can't shut off as many hits as he would at another spot.

Obviously, if Bream hits the way he did in 1990—.270 with power—he's a good player, no argument. If Bream goes back to hitting .250 without much power, the argument comes back. I like to make decisions, when I can, on real, tangible evidence, rather than speculation and theory—but the fact that the defensive contribution of a first baseman is difficult to put into numbers does not mean that it doesn't exist. It's just a question of putting it into some sort of coherent statement so that we can evaluate the trade-offs.

Will he help the Braves?

It's probably the dumbest free-agent signing of the winter. First, he's not a very good player. Second, he's thirty years old and signing with a team which still loses around a hundred a year, so it's very unlikely that he could last long enough to help them win. That means that *if* Bream plays well and stays in the lineup for two or three years, the Braves will have to replace him just at the time when they will be getting serious about moving into contention. Worst of all, the signing of Bream means that Francisco Cabrera, who is a far better hitter than Bream, will start the year on the bench.

John Schuerholz isn't a *bad* general manager, on balance. He does some clever things, and he does some fundamental things well. But for some reason, the man can't resist a mediocre thirty-year-old ballplayer. When he took over in Kansas City the Royals had no one like that. Everyone on the team was either a good ballplayer, a proven role player or a young player with potential. Within three years, Schuerholz had filled up the roster with mediocre 32-year-old players exactly like Sid Bream—Leon Roberts, Joe Simpson, Jerry Martin, Steve Renko, Eric Rasmussen, Don Hood. There's a lot of young talent in Atlanta, but that habit sure as hell isn't going to make the road to the top any shorter.

George BRETT, Kansas City
Is he a Hall of Famer?

Sure. Brett's batting title in 1990 does nothing at all to improve his chances of going in the Hall of Fame, because he was over-qualified anyway. The only way he could avoid the Hall of Fame is Pete Rose's way.

Is he going to get 3000 hits?

Yes. His chance of getting 3000 hits in his career is now estimated at 95%.

Note: Brett has now created more runs in his career (1,556) than any other active player.

Greg BRILEY, Seattle
Can he play everyday? Does he still have star potential?

Jim Lefebvre was a part of the Tony LaRussa crowd in Oakland, and because LaRussa speaks so well of him there has been a tendency among sportswriters to transfer the respect which LaRussa has earned to Lefebvre, and to speak of him as a bright young manager. But for a bright young manager, he sure pulls some rocks.

For one, I don't see how any manager can justify giving 478 at bats to Jeffrey Leonard and 355 at bats to Henry Cotto while trying to make a platoon player out of Greg Briley. Let's look at Greg Briley two years ago, 1989:

- 24 years old, left-handed hitting outfielder,
- hit .266,

- 13 home runs in part-time play, .442 slugging percentage,
- some speed, 11 stolen bases,
- decent strikeout/walk ratio, not good or extremely bad,
- hit .321 in limited at bats against left-handed pitching.

What any sensible manager would do, given that combination, is try to find out whether he can play every day and be a minor star. Given just very slight improvement with experience, Briley projects as a .280 hitter with 20 homers and 20 stolen bases.

Instead, to create playing time for a couple of guys who are absolutely useless, Lefebvre *reduced* Briley's playing time, and all but eliminated his playing time against left-handed pitchers.

Briley had an off year—but not all that bad, either. His batting average and power were off from 1989, but he stole 16 bases in 20 attempts. He substantially improved his strikeout/walk ratio, making it quite a bit better than the league average. He grounded into only six double plays.

A year ago I thought Briley had a chance to be an excellent player. Obviously, I have to be less optimistic now: good players get *better*, not worse, in their second seasons. But I still think it is stupid not to give this guy 600 at bats and see what he can do with them.

Greg BROCK, Milwaukee
Will he be better off somewhere else?

He's 33 years old, turns 34 in June. He's had nine years to prove himself, in two parks. It's silly to be talking about his getting better somewhere else. Maybe he'll be ten percent better, but he's never going to play a key role on a good team.

Rico BROGNA, Detroit
Who is he?

Left-handed hitting first baseman, regarded as the best prospect in the Detroit

system. Excellent defensive player, showed power for the first time last year at London in the Eastern League. May push Fielder to DH in 1992.

Tom BROOKENS, Cleveland
Is he going to hang around another year?

Sure. He had a good year in '90; he'll last until he has a bad one . . . McNamara used him more than he should be used against right-handed pitching (he has a big platoon differential), but he had a better-than-normal year against right-handers, so the effects of this weren't apparent.

Hubie BROOKS, New York Mets
What's his role with the Mets?

The Mets lost Darryl Strawberry and acquired two outfielders to replace him, Brooks and Vince Coleman. Since Coleman and McReynolds figure to play every day, if Brooks played fulltime that would move Boston to the bench, which doesn't seem likely. A platoon combination of Brooks and Boston seems like a natural. Brooks hit better the wrong way last year (against right-handers), but that's a one-year aberration.

Keith BROWN, Cincinnati
Who is he?

Good-sized right-hander, old for a prospect (27) and apparently doesn't have much of a fastball. He's earned a major league look by posting microscopic ERAs at all minor league levels, 2.45 last year at Nashville (AAA). Superb control but a long-odds prospect with an organization which has pitching; may get a chance somewhere else as a six-year free agent in 1992.

Kevin BROWN, Rangers
Is he going to win 12 every year? Is he going to get better? Is he going to get worse?

I'm less optimistic about him now than I was a year ago, and I'd be somewhat reluctant to have him on my team in 1991.

1. The Rangers have an absolutely awful record with young pitching prospects. They have had a dozen or more young starting pitchers in the Tom House era—Jose Guzman, Edwin Correa, Paul Kilgus, Jeff Russell. None of these people except possibly Bobby Witt is a good pitcher now.

2. A young pitcher's strikeout rate usually goes *up* for two or three years after he enters the league. Brown's strikeout rate went *down*.

3. The Rangers team indicators of 1990 are strongly downward. If the team has an off season, no individual starting pitcher on the team will be a good gamble.

Brown could still be an outstanding starting pitcher; I just don't want to be betting on him in 1991. He is a ground-ball pitcher, which gives him a chance to be successful without striking people out. Last year Brown led the American League in:

1. Groundball/Flyball ratio (3.44 to 1),
2. Double plays behind him per nine innings (1.20), and
3. Fewest pitches per batter (3.40).

Kevin D. BROWN, Milwaukee
Should he have a major league job?

Yes. This Kevin Brown is one out of the Mets' system. He's 25 years old, a left-hander with some history of arm problems, but he has nothing left to prove in the minor leagues after going 11-8 in 1989 and 10-6 last year. He doesn't have much of a fastball (83 to 86 MPH), but he changes speeds well. I like him, and I wouldn't be shocked to see him win the American League's Rookie of the Year Award.

Marty BROWN, Cincinnati
Who is he?

Overage infield prospect, 28 years old. He hit well in the low minors, but unim-

pressively in AAA ball. Defense marginal at third base. No future.

Jerry BROWNE, Cleveland
Where does he rank among American League second basemen?

Browne's weakness is that he doesn't turn the double play very well. His strengths are summed up in the fact that he scored 92 runs last year while everybody was talking about what a disappointing season he was having.

In my opinion only one American League second baseman, Julio Franco, rates distinctly ahead of Browne. Three other second basemen rank about even with him, those being Harold Reynolds, Steve Sax and Jody Reed. All four of those guys have important strengths and nagging but significant weaknesses. I think, myself, that I like Browne a little better than Sax, Reed or Reynolds, but they're all very close.

Tom BROWNING, Cincinnati
What's he worth? If he's a free agent, how much do you want him?

He's been an outstanding pitcher, but I'm leery of him. I always think of Tom Browning as the modern Johnny Podres. Browning was 30 last year, and Podres had his last good year at age 30. See also comments on Bud Black and Ron Robinson. I'd stay away from him.

Mike BRUMLEY, Detroit
Can he help a team? Is he an acceptable utility infielder?

I would regard him as an average or above-average utility infielder. He's a switch hitter, regarded as a decent short-stop, runs well and isn't any worse hitter than Wayne Tolleson or a dozen other guys. He deserves a job.

Tom BRUNANSKY, Boston
What kind of an effort should the Red Sox make to keep him? Can he help a team as a free agent?

Brunansky by reputation is a very good outfielder, a very smart outfielder

who knows what he can do and what he can't, although I am told he didn't play as well in the field with the Sox as he had in St. Louis. He has been, in the past, a potent power hitter. Still, if I were running the Red Sox, I would let Brunansky go, move Quintana to the outfield and let Mo Vaughn play first base.

Brunansky last year hit home runs in bunches at two times when he was under a magnifying glass. He had always hit well in Fenway Park when he was with the Twins, so the feeling when he came over was that he might have a monster season. In his second game in Fenway with the Sox he hit two homers and drove in seven runs, and then three days later had a homer, double and single in one game. In his first sixteen games with the Sox he hit .317 with four homers, 13 RBI and a .571 slugging percentage. "I want to see him in Fenway for two weeks in warm weather," said Red Sox hitting coach Richie Hebner. "He'll do some damage."

"He's a dead pull hitter and he'll attack that wall," said Tony Pena, Brunansky's teammate in St. Louis and Boston.

"This is probably the best hitting park in the major leagues for me," said Brunansky, who has been his own teammate for several years. The feeling was that he should hit about 40 home runs for the Red Sox—15 on the road, as he consistently has over the years, and 25 in Fenway.

When the pennant was on the line he got hot again, hitting three home runs in a game and five in the series against Toronto in the last week of the season.

What a lot of people around the country didn't realize was how truly awful his performance was in those intervening 100-plus games. Brunansky hit six times as many home runs at home as on the road—13 at home, 2 on the road. For the season (including games in St. Louis, he hit .333 with 13 homers, 52 RBI in his home park—but .180 with three homers and 21 RBI on the road.

One-season splits involve large flukes, and not *too* much should be made of the fact that Brunansky was so helpless away from Fenway Park. Maybe Fenway Park put him in the habit of trying to pull everything; maybe it was something that just happened.

It is not based on this that I would be reluctant to re-sign him; that's just another factor in a complex of concerns. Brunansky is 30 years old, and I've thought for years that, being a player with "old player's skills," he would not age well. He hasn't. If you look at what he's done in the last two years, one year in a good park for him and one year in a bad one, it just isn't very impressive. Over the last two years he's averaged .247 with 18 homers, 79 RBI, 5 stolen bases in 15 attempts, 66 runs scored as a full-time player.

Maybe he'll do better than that in his early thirties—but then, maybe he won't. As a free agent, you're taking a gamble at $3 million a year.

Mo Vaughn is a *good* young hitter, probably a better hitter than Brunansky. Carlos Quintana looks pretty awful at first base, but they say he isn't a bad outfielder. Quintana and Vaughn will be playing the next three years at an average of about $400,000 a season. Even if Vaughn fails, there's Phil Plantier, who *I think* is going to be a terrific power hitter, so even without Brunansky the Red Sox options are backed up. I just couldn't justify paying Brunansky $3 million a year to take the chance that he will finally have that 100 RBI season we have been waiting for.

Bill BUCKNER, Boston

I was in Fenway Park on opening day when Bill Buckner returned to the Red Sox. He was given a standing ovation, a hearty welcome back. As a Royals fan, I was cheering louder than anybody to see him back in a Red Sox uniform.

Think about this . . . the Red Sox last year took a gamble that all of us—you, me, everybody you talk to about these things—knew was certain to fail. We all knew that Bill Buckner could not possibly help the Red Sox win in 1990, and we were right.

And yet *they did win*. What does that tell you about baseball, that an organization which does something which makes no sense at all can still win?

Steve BUECHELE, Rangers
Will he keep his job?

Buechele had an awful year, but then so did the two guys who were candidates to take his job, Scott Coolbaugh and Dean Palmer (Coolbaugh was traded to San Diego). If it was up to me I'd dump him and get on with the future, but my guess is that Valentine will stick with him.

Jay BUHNER, Seattle
Will he ever make it as a regular? What's the holdup here?

Buhner keeps getting hurt, usually in June. In 1989 he started the season in the minors, and then sprained the ligaments in his wrist while robbing Jim Eisenreich of a triple (June 27), and missed a month or more. Last year he was on the DL with a sprained ankle until June 1, and then Brad Arnsberg broke his right forearm with a pitch on June 16, so he was out until late August.

When in the lineup, he has played fairly well, with a career average of just .249 but excellent power. In 650 major at bats—ten percent more than one full season—he has 42 doubles, 29 home runs, 105 RBI. If he can stay healthy a full year he'll hit over 20 home runs and over 30 doubles, but challenge Rob Deer and Bo Jackson for the league lead in strikeouts. Not much speed but good defense, good arm. The .276 batting average that he compiled last year may be near the top of his range.

Eric BULLOCK, Montreal
Is he going to be on a roster?

I doubt it. He's had looks with four teams and hasn't impressed anybody yet. At 31, he may be out of chances.

Dave BURBA, Seattle
Who is he?

Right-handed pitching prospect for Seattle, nothing impressive about him. Grade C prospect.

Tim BURKE, Montreal
Is he up to the role of a closer? Should the Expos be looking for somebody else?

Buck Rodgers likes to split his relief work among two or three pitchers, and I think that's the right role for Burke. He's effective as a late-inning reliever, but he's not *dominant*. A born-again Christian and a team player, he doesn't have an ego problem with sharing the spotlight, and in fact it has been suggested that he might be uncomfortable if he were asked to be Bobby Thigpen.

Burke has a larger-than-normal platoon differential, which might also make it difficult to use him as an unsupported relief ace. Last year left-handed hitters hit .285 against him, while right-handers hit .210. This makes him vulnerable to maneuvering by opposition managers.

John BURKETT, San Francisco
Can he do this every year? Is he going to be a consistent winner? Does he have star potential?

Burkett was one of the biggest surprises of last year, a guy who didn't even make the book, but pitched 200 innings, won 14 games and could have been, in some years, the Rookie of the Year.

The easiest question is as to his star potential, which is limited almost to the point of being non-existent. I *doubt* that he can be a consistent winner in the sense of being more than a couple of games a year over .500; he might go 15-12, 14-13 a lot. But as to whether he can pitch well enough to make a lot of money, I don't see why he can't. His mechanics seem to be good, his arm hasn't been abused and he has a record of being healthy, so I don't see why he can't pitch 200 innings a year and be as good as the next pitcher.

★ ★ ★
Ellis BURKS, Boston
★ ★ ★

Burks is probably the number one candidate for the American League MVP Award this season. He'll be 27 years old late in the season and in his fifth major league campaign, so he's about to the stage where most players have their best seasons. He's a very good player in a typical season, hits around .300 with power, speed and defense. He plays for a contending team in a hitter's park. That's as good an outline of an MVP candidate as you can find before the season starts . . . did you know that Ellis Burks had homered on Mother's Day for five straight seasons (two in the minor leagues) before being held to a triple last year?

Todd BURNS, Oakland
Will he move into a bigger role? Could he be a closer or a starting pitcher for another team?

In 278 major league innings Burns has a 17-10 record and a 2.79 ERA, so there is a tendency to think that he might be able to play a larger role on another staff. It is also possible that the Oakland park and defense make him look better than he is, and that exposed to a heavier workload he would just get hurt.

Burns doesn't throw hard, but he changes speeds exceptionally well. I don't see him as having much star potential, but I respect him as a pitcher who works very well with what he has. If the situation arises where the A's need to put him in the rotation, I wouldn't bet against his having a good season.

Randy BUSH, Minnesota
Will he get his regular job back?

Probably not. Like Todd Benzinger, Bush didn't really play well enough to justify a regular job when he had one, although he is a better hitter than Benzinger. At age 32 he seems more likely to stay at the 200 at bat level than to move back up.

Brett BUTLER, Los Angeles

What an amazing year he had. Butler, who has always been one of my favorite players, had probably his best major league season last year. Butler finished:

- Third in the National League in runs scored,
- Among the top ten in batting average,
- Third in walks,
- Fourth in the league in stolen bases,
- Third in triples,
- Fifth in on-base percentage,
- Tied for the league lead in hits,
- Third in the league in fewest double plays grounded into

(per at bat). Although he hits more ground balls than any National League player except Willie McGee, he grounded into only three double plays.

And yet, we heard almost nothing about him all season. You look at all the other guys who were among the league leaders in runs scored, and they're the players that we talked about all summer—Ryne Sandberg, Bobby Bonilla, Ron Gant and Len Dykstra. Those guys were the subject, among them, of five jillion feature stories. Butler scored just as many runs, and nobody said a thing.

A leadoff man's job is measured in about six categories: batting average, runs scored, hits, walks, on base percentage, stolen bases. Whatever combination of them you like, those are the elements. Butler was among the league leaders, high among the leaders, in every category that defines his job. How many players in baseball do *their job* that well, year in and year out?

A couple of stat notes: Butler made pitchers throw 2,902 pitches last year, the most of any major league player except Wade Boggs. He has now scored 90 or more runs in each of the last seven years, making him the only major league player who can make that statement. His stolen base percentage, which had seemed to be slipping in recent years, was the best of his career in 1990, although it still was not exceptional.

An interesting question is whether Butler has any chance to make the Hall of Fame. He has done more than a dozen things in his career which would be characteristic of a Hall of Famer, including scoring a hundred runs (five times), hitting .300 (twice), leading the league in triples (twice), runs scored (once) and hits (once), playing center field for a championship team (once) and stealing 50 bases in a season (twice). Those are all the sorts of things that Hall of Famers do. He *should* have a couple of other credentials. He should have won about four Gold Gloves, and he should have played in several All-Star games, but hasn't. With his exceptional 1990 season, he is now unquestionably one of the ten greatest leadoff men of all time.

Despite these credentials, Butler has little chance of making the Hall of Fame. Butler has done many things which would be *characteristic* of a Hall of Famer, but none of those which *define* a Hall of Famer. As such, he would have to show truly remarkable durability, continuing to play the way he is now for at least five more years, before the pile of credentials would begin to demand consideration.

There is some precedent for players of his type showing unusual durability. Sam Rice, a similar type of player, continued to hit over .300 annually into his forties. The late Doc Cramer, also somewhat similar but not quite as good, played regularly until the age of 39, collecting 2,705 hits despite a late start. Eddie Collins, a similar player but better, hit .349 and led the American League in stolen bases at the age of 37, and continued to hit a consistent .340 after that even though he was never healthy.

But that's not something you can expect Butler to do. Butler will need *at least* 2,300 hits to have any chance to make the Hall of Fame, and he's still five years away from that figure. At his age (he turns 34 in June), even three more years is asking a lot.

Will he help the Dodgers? Can he hit in Dodger Stadium?

Butler is the best bunter in baseball, so the long grass in the infield here should be perfect for him. I doubt that he'll hit any *better* in Dodger Stadium than he has in the past, but I don't expect him to lose much.

•C•

Francisco CABRERA, Atlanta

I love this guy, as a hitter. I thought a year ago, based on what he had done in the minors, that he could hit close to .300 and slug nearly .500 in the major leagues. His actual performance as a rookie (he hit .277 and slugged .482) didn't do anything to discourage me. The Braves have several candidates to play first base and I like some of the other guys, too. Sid Bream may improve the infield defense, which God knows the Braves need, but Cabrera's the best. He's got to play.

Greg CADARET, Yankees
Is he a starter or a reliever? Does he have any potential to be really effective either way?

Cadaret is *clearly* a reliever, not a starter, and the fact that the Yankees have not been able to recognize this just shows how messed up the organization has been.

There are two things which mark a man as being more effective in relief than as a starter. A pitcher with one really good pitch is more effective in relief than as a starter, because as a starter the hitters will have too many chances to see the out pitch.

A pitcher who wears out quickly is more effective in relief than starting.

Cadaret hits on both counts. He is a pitcher with one pitch, a marginal fastball. He has a curve and a forkball to show the hitters some variety, but his pitch is the fastball. To be effective at all, he has to throw it as hard as he can.

His record shows this as clearly as possible. Originally a starter in the minor leagues, he was completely ineffective from 1984 on. In 1985, as a starter, he was 6-16 with an ERA of 6.01 in two places. In 1986 at Huntsville, as a starter, he posted an ERA of 5.41. In 1987, with

the same team, he was switched to relief—and his ERA dropped to 2.90.

The next year, with Oakland, he pitched 58 times in relief with a 2.89 ERA. Traded to the Yankees as part of the Rickey Ripoff, he was switched to the starting rotation, and his career began to hit the skids again.

In 1990 he had an ERA of 6.11 as a starter, and 3.57 in relief.

Ivan CALDERON, Montreal
Will he help the Expos?

The Expos did have two legitimate leadoff men (Raines and DeShields) and were short of middle-of-the-order guys, so in that respect the trade makes sense. Calderon may hit better in Montreal than he did in Comiskey, which wasn't a great place to hit.

I wouldn't have made the trade, because I think Raines can be one of the best players in baseball, and I don't think Calderon could.

What's with the base stealing? Is he really fast?

Calderon isn't really fast, despite the 32 stolen bases, but then, neither is Canseco. Calderon was seven for eight as a base stealer in '89, lost some weight during the winter and decided to be aggressive on the bases. He was 32 for 48, which doesn't help the team or hurt it, but Torborg decided to go along with him. He also grounded into 26 double plays, leading the major leagues, and is the only major league player who has grounded into twenty or more the last two seasons. He's a good line-drive hitter and an above-average regular, but he's not fast.

Ernie CAMACHO, San Francisco
Isn't he out of chances yet?

Camacho has pitched 13 to 15 major league games, and 14 to 18 innings, for *four* straight seasons, with an aggregate ERA of 6.11. I wouldn't think he would get a chance to make it five, but you never know.

Ken CAMINITI, Houston
Did he just have an off year, or is he really not very good?

He's not very good. Last year he was awful—.242 with four homers in 541 at bats—but even in his one good year, 1988, he wasn't good enough to be very interesting. He may have his best major league season this year, with Bagwell pushing him, but I still don't see him as a championship quality player.

Jim CAMPBELL, Kansas City
Who is he?

Left-handed finesse pitcher, was being used as a reliever by the Royals until last year. He's pitched well most of his professional career, but he isn't regarded as having a major league fastball, so he has to be dominant at each level before he moves up.

Don't draft him for 1991; the odds against his having a big rookie year are huge. In the long run, I wouldn't bet against him, once he survives a few trials and figures out how to survive in the major leagues. But it will be a few years.

Sil CAMPUSANO, Philadelphia
Is he ever going to get out of the prospect class? Isn't he about 40 by now?

Actually, he's only 24; it just seems like he's old because we started hearing about him when he was 19. He doesn't seem to be any better player now than he was then. He has all the tools, as they say, but he doesn't know the strike zone, and the strike zone is the heart of the game. Lee Thomas has said that if he lost Dykstra for some reason, he'd be happy to open the season with Campusano in center. Maybe. He could probably hit .240 with 18 homers, but who wants that?

George CANALE, Milwaukee
Who is he?

Left-handed first base non-prospect; the Brewers seem to like him, but God knows why. Bruce Manno, the Brewers farm director, says that "He's got a bright future with us." Sure. There's always a demand for .230-hitting first basemen with power like Sammy Sosa.

Casey CANDAELE, Houston
What's the right role for him? Is he an infielder, an outfielder, what? Where'd he disappear to?

Candaele is basically Wally Backman, chapter two.

- Both men are small. Backman is listed at 5-9, 168, and doesn't seem that tall. Candaele is listed at 5-7, 165.
- Both are switch hitters.
- Both run fairly well, although Backman ran better when he was Candaele's age.
- Both men are originally second basemen.

Backman had his first shot as a regular in 1982, and hit well enough (.272), but was sent back to the minors because it was felt that he didn't play the bag well enough to be a regular second baseman, or hit well enough to be a regular anywhere else.

Candaele had his first shot as a regular in 1987, and hit well enough (.272), but was sent back to the minors because it was felt that he didn't play the bag well enough to be a regular second baseman, or hit well enough to be a regular second baseman, or hit well enough to be a regular anywhere else.

I doubt that Candaele can hold a regular job in the major leagues, and I think the Astros would be smarter to give the second base job to Dave Rohde. Like Backman, Candaele probably doesn't turn the double play well enough to be a regular second baseman. He doesn't have the overall offensive punch to be a regular left fielder, probably, or the arm to be a center fielder. To this point in his career he hasn't gotten on base enough or run the bases well enough to be an effective leadoff man (his career on-base percentage is .317, and he is 18 for 39 as a base stealer.)

What saved Backman's career was that Dave Johnson came along, sorted through the things that Backman could do and couldn't do, and devised a way to make use of the positives and minimize the negatives. One key to this was the realization that although Backman was listed as a switch hitter, he really couldn't hit at all right-handed; his career batting average against left-handers is around .150.

Interestingly enough, Candaele *may* have the same problem, although on the other side. In 1987, when Candaele batted 449 times, he hit .310 against left-handers, just .259 against right-handers. Last year, the same thing only more so: he hit .341 against left-handers, but .235 against right handers. Both seasons he also had a much better strikeout/walk ratio against left-handers.

So the proper job description for Candaele may begin by emphasizing that he should play mostly against left-handed pitching. If you start with that, I think you've got the basis of a major league career here. I know that as a table-game manager, I love to have a player on my roster who can play the infield *and* the outfield; it's like having an extra roster spot. If you look at Candaele as an infielder/outfielder who can hit .300 against left-handers, pinch run for the slowest guys on the team and not cause any problems in the clubhouse, I think you can see him as a twelve-year veteran.

John CANDELERIA, Montreal
What does he have left? Anything?

He's one of those guys like John Tudor (see Bankhead) that as long as he can get his arm above his shoulder he'll be able to get people out. Even last year, bad as he looked, he struck out 63 men in 80 innings, had a strikeout/walk ratio better than 4-1 (not counting intentional walks.)

With his age and injury history you're

never going to be able to count on him to pitch five innings a week, and he's a pain in the butt to have around if he's not pitching. So it's a close call, whether you want to save him a roster spot.

Tom CANDIOTTI, Cleveland

I can't think of what question you would ask about Candiotti; there don't seem to be any question marks left. He must have been the most consistent starting pitcher in baseball the last three years, going 14-8, 13-10 and 15-11 with ERAs in the mid-threes. He walks 53 to 55 men a year, and strikes out 124 to 137. His 1986 season was about the same (16-12, 3.57) before an off season in 1987. He's not a star, or going to be a star. Obviously he's a quality pitcher. There's no way of knowing how long he will last, and there's no reason to believe he'll collapse in the next two or three years.

Although Candiotti's won-lost records and ERAs are more similar to Charlie Hough's, the most-similar pitcher in the last twenty years was Joe Niekro. Niekro, like Candiotti, was a knuckleball pitcher who had a little Peggy Lee fastball that he would use to avoid getting behind the hitters. Hough throws the knuckleball all the time, regardless of the count; Candiotti spots the fastball and a twelve-mile-an-hour curve so that he doesn't walk as many men. Candiotti probably could pitch more innings than he has without hurting himself, and certainly could win twenty games if things broke right for him.

John CANGELOSI, Pittsburgh
Is he worth the roster spot?

Sure. He's a good baserunner, never grounds into double plays and has an excellent career on-base percentage (.364). I think he's one of the best fifth outfielders in baseball.

I don't know if you noticed this, but the Pirates in the last few months have seemed determined to decimate their outfield/bench:

- Moises Alou, one of two top outfield prospects in the Pirate system, was traded to Montreal for Zane Smith in the last weeks of the season.
- Wes Chamberlain, the other top outfield prospect, was lost to Philadelphia in a roster accident.
- R. J. Reynolds, one of the game's better fourth outfielders, hit .288 last year and said that he wanted to return to the Pirates, but went to Japan when the Pirates didn't make a decent offer.
- The Pirates are talking about moving Bobby Bonilla, their star right fielder, to first base.
- This talk became more serious when the Pirates lost Sid Bream to free agency. Although Bream is not an outfielder, he did compete for playing time with the same players.
- At the end of all this, the Pirates announced that they would not offer Cangelosi a contract, to make room on their forty-man roster.

I'm puzzled, not that one normally expects Larry Doughty to do things that make sense. Of course the Pirates have a great starting outfield, with Bonds, Van Slyke and Bonilla, but what if somebody gets hurt? It is unlikely that all of the Pirate stars (the outfielders and Drabek) will have great years together again. If they don't, the Pirates will need every hit they can get from the sword carriers. If Leyland has to re-build the bench during the first half of the season, it's a good bet the Pirates will be out of contention before the job is finished.

Jose CANSECO, A's

In the vast history of the minor leagues, there are three players I know of who hit forty home runs and stole forty bases in the same season. Note carefully: it may be that there are more than three, but I have only been able to find three. I waste a lot of time going through old Guides looking at minor league players, and I've only seen three players who did this.

The first of the three, and the most interesting, was a player named Wright who hit 52 homers and stole 42 bases for the Fort Wayne team in the Central League in 1930. Even allowing that this was 1930, the best hitter's season of the century, and that the Central League was not exactly Olympian competition, Wright had an eye-popping season, winning the triple crown with 52 homers, 169 RBI and a .419 batting average. He was a first baseman, and I believe his name was John Wright but apart from that I'm not even sure who he was. He never played in the major leagues, and is not listed in the SABR publications on minor league stars.

The second minor league player to hit 40 homers and steal 40 bases in a season was Frank Demaree, with Los Angeles of the Pacific Coast League in 1934. The Pacific Coast League in those days played a long schedule, and Demaree had the advantage of playing 186 games, which is not to detract from his accomplishment; if you scaled him down to 162 games you'd still have 39 homers and 36 stolen bases. Demaree hit .383 with 45 homers, 173 RBI and 41 steals, also 51 doubles and 190 runs scored. The Pacific Coast was an outstanding league, featuring players like Joe and Vince DiMaggio, Smead Jolley, Frenchy Bordagaray and Babe Dahlgren. Demaree, though forgotten today, was a legitimately outstanding player, good enough to start the All-Star game for the National League in 1936 and 1937.

The third player to hit 40 homers and steal 40 bases in the minors was a catcher, Dick Wilson, who hit .347 with 42 homers, 188 RBI and 41 stolen bases for Mexicali in the Sunset League in 1948. He was also the manager of the team. Wilson never played in the major leagues, but had an outstanding seventeen-year minor league career, the records of which are given in the second volume of *Minor League Baseball Stars.* Playing mostly in California, Wilson hit

.322 with 285 home runs in his long minor league career.

Note: Canseco last year hit .409 when not striking out. He was one of two major leaguers over .400, the other being Cecil Fielder, at .407.

Ozzie CANSECO, Oakland
Can he play? Is he ten percent as good as his brother?

If you have any faith in genetics, you have to think that he may eventually come around as a hitter. To be frank, he doesn't show the signs of it. He's been playing the outfield in AA ball for four years now, and he really isn't much better than he was in 1987. He'll never be more than a marginal regular, but he might be able to hit .240 with 25 homers sometime.

Mike CAPEL, Milwaukee
Who is he?

Right-handed pitcher, hasn't been able to stay healthy in the minors or get people out in the majors.

Mike Capel is from the Houston area, and graduated from high school the same year as Roger Clemens. The two of them went to the University of Texas together. Capel, at the time, was the star recruit, considered the best pitcher to come out of the Houston area in that class. He ain't going to be Roger Clemens, now, but he could probably pitch major league ball if he got the chance. Frank Wills' job, something like that.

Ramon CARABALLO, Atlanta
Who is he?

Delino DeShields-type player, shortstop/second base prospect who can run, takes a walk and can drive the ball. He hasn't advanced far enough that I can evaluate him, but I like what I hear.

Don CARMAN, Philadelphia
What's his problem? Why doesn't he win?

I wish I knew. I watch him pitch, he always looks good to me. He's regarded as intelligent and works very hard. I always think he'll win next year, but he never does.

Carman held left-handers to a batting average of .175 last year, but even this was not an unmixed blessing, since *most* of the hits that he gave up to left-handers were for extra bases, and almost half of them (seven of 18) were homers. The data in 1989 was similar but less extreme—six of 24 hits given up to left-handers in '89 were home runs. I guess that's the key to the riddle—if you can figure out why Carman gives up so many home runs to left-handed batters, you can probably turn his career around.

Gregorio CARMONA, St. Louis
Who is he?

22-year-old, 150-pound shortstop, regarded as Ozzie Smith's successor at short, and perhaps the best prospect in the Cardinal organization. Good defensive player, slap hitter with surprising plate discipline. Not expected in the majors for a year or two, but could be up earlier if Ozzie struggles with the bat.

Cris CARPENTER, Cards
Is he ever going to stick?

Definitely. Herzog didn't handle him very well, shifting him arbitrarily between starting and relief roles, but he has no history of failing. He's pitched very well in the minors—not very *much*, but well. He hasn't pitched badly in the majors. He has *extremely* good control, and decent enough stuff. He is said to be extremely intelligent and have a good knowledge of how to pitch. If he stays healthy, and his health record is good, he'll be a major league pitcher.

Chuck CARR, New York
Who is he?

Switch-hitting outfielder in the Mets' system, called up for a few games in September. He could have a future as a pinch runner, but it's not likely.

Mark CARREON, Mets
Could he play regularly? Is he in for increased playing time in the wake of Darryl Strawberry's departure? If he has to bat 400 times, how will he do?

Carreon is in for increased playing time not because Strawberry has gone, but because Mark Carreon has played damn well for two straight years, not that anybody has noticed. He has 342 major league at bats—six-tenths of a season—in which he has hit .281 with 17 home runs, a .488 slugging percentage.

Two years ago I wouldn't have believed that he could play regularly, and I remain skeptical. Two things:

- Most of his at bats have been *with* the platoon advantage. As a right-handed hitter, if he becomes a regular most of his at bats will be *without* the platoon edge.
- 342 at bats is not enough to truly evaluate a hitter.

I doubt that Carreon is a legitimate .280 hitter, and I doubt that he could sustain his power production as an everyday player. But you don't want to make the game more complicated than it is. When a player plays well, you increase his playing time to see what he can do. Carreon has played well.

Gary CARTER, San Francisco
Who needs him? Where's he going to land?

Carter played better last year than he had in several years. How much he could help a team in '91 would seem to depend on how realistic he is about his role on the team. If a team is looking for a right-handed hitting backup catcher and pinch hitter, Carter is a reasonable gamble. If he's looking for 450 at bats, then he's probably trying to pick up more than he could carry.

Joe CARTER, Toronto

Who got the better end of the trade? How good is Carter, really? Will he be the best left fielder in the American League?

Carter isn't a great player. The most important of the basic offensive statistics is on-base percentage, and Carter's on-base percentage is extremely low. The press and public wherever Carter has played have come to the conclusion that, while he will always drive in runs, he's a player of limited dimensions. He would rank fourth or fifth among American League left fielders, behind Rickey Henderson, Mike Greenwell and Tim Raines, about even with Bo Jackson. In fact, he and Bo are almost the same player, in broad outlines. Minor differences—Bo has a better arm, Carter is more durable.

The Alomar/Carter/McGriff/Fernandez trade, on paper, is as close to even as you could get—in fact, I think if you computer-designed a trade, asking which teams could trade two stars each way without anybody gaining or losing much, you'd have a hard time coming up with a better balance.

That being the case, the team which wins will be the team which

a. does a better job of re-configuring their talent to fit their needs, and

b. has more successfully dispelled the bad karma from the clubhouse.

Toronto is the team which is more likely to *win* in '91, and thus the team which is more likely to get credit for having made a good trade. I would have several concerns with the trade, from Toronto's standpoint. The Blue Jays, who had left and right fielders hanging from the rafters anyway, added another one in Carter, so it's hard to say that they improved the configuration of their tal-

ent. As for the clubhouse, if Joe Carter turns out to be a great team leader this will come as a great surprise in Cleveland and San Diego:

> As one A.L. executive said, "Toronto got rid of some problem players, but picked up Joe Carter and Devon White, who are two of the most selfish players in the game."
> —Moss Klein
> TSN, December 24

Criticism like that may push White and Carter to prove that they *are* team players, and may make the team. On a larger question, I wonder if Toronto isn't trying to fix tangible problems by changing the intangibles. The Blue Jays have a good team, but last year they played Mookie Wilson in center field, for no apparent reason, and used two starting pitchers with a combined record of 22-26 with a 4.51 ERA. If they don't fix *those* problems, then what was the point of the trade?

Steve CARTER, Pittsburgh

Who is he?

Two-hundred pound center field prospect for the Pirates. A poor percentage player, but I believe he could hit .290 in the major leagues. Line drive hitter; speed may be strained for center field but good for left or right. The Pirates don't have a job for him right now.

Chuck CARY, Yankees

Is it time to give up on him, or should the Yankees give him another season?

In a better world, one would think that an organization would make a careful decision about who they want to be their starting pitchers. Some organizations do—the Dodgers, the Royals, the Blue Jays, the A's.

If the Yankees had made a careful, thoughtful decision that Chuck Cary

could be a major league starting pitcher before they gave him 27 starts, then one would unquestionably have to say that they should stick with that decision. Cary's performance, despite a 6-12 won-lost record, wasn't all that terrible, and his strikeout and walk data was actually very good (134-55 in 157 innings). If this is a man that you believe in, then it would be foolish to give up on him after he has pitched at that level.

In the real world, of course, we know that the Yankees don't plan anything out that carefully; they just have pitchers around, and they give this one a start and then that one, and if anybody looks good they'll go a little longer with him. If there has never been an organizational decision that Cary should be a starting pitcher, then it is an open question as to whether he can start, and the evidence that he can is unimpressive.

But even so, given the Yankees' range of options, I would argue that Cary should get another year to try to get something done. If the Yankees dump Cary, which they very well may, then who will inherit the starts? Andy Hawkins? Cadaret? Dave LaPoint?

The Yankees *do* need to start giving a major league look to some of their minor league starting pitchers—but Cary isn't the man they ought to dump to accomplish that. In 256 innings in the last two years, he has struck out 213 men. That suggests that he has major league stuff, and his control record is decent. If I was the Yankees I would lock Leary, Cary and Witt in the starting rotation, with Eiland opening the season as the fourth starter. Then if Pascual Perez is ready to pitch a game or Hawkins is throwing well or Leiter or Adkins or whoever deserves another shot, give it to them in the fifth spot, or the fourth spot if Eiland doesn't work out, or the third spot when somebody gets hurt. But if the Yankees have any chance to get back on their feet, they need to stop diddling around with twenty-five starting pitchers.

Larry CASIAN, Minnesota
Who is he?

Left-handed starting pitcher, pitched well in three late-season starts with the Twins. He's a Grade C prospect, pitches well for a couple of starts at a time but no consistency. Doubt that he can be a rotation starter.

Carmen CASTILLO, Minnesota
What happened to him last year? Can he bounce back?

I would think it must be very hard to maintain consistent production figures in 200 at bats a year. Castillo as a fifth outfielder had had seven consecutive decent seasons—with a career high of 220 at bats. That's got to be tough to do, doesn't it? Even if you took George Brett or Don Mattingly and gave him 200 at bats a year, I'd think it would be tough for him to pile up good numbers every season.

Castillo is 32 years old. I don't think his failure to hit a home run in 137 at bats last year constitutes any *real* evidence that he can't produce anymore.

Tony CASTILLO, Atlanta
Can he pitch? Would he be the relief ace Atlanta has been desperately seeking?

I like him; I think he could surprise people. Castillo is small (5-10, 177 pounds) and not young (28 years old). He pitched brilliantly as a starter in the Carolina League in 1985, but then spent the entire 1986 season on the disabled list. But he has no real history of failing; he has always pitched well when he has been healthy.

I suspect that he might be best suited to the role of starting pitcher, give him six innings a start. Although his strikeout/walk ratio is exceptional, he has always given up a lot of hits, a high batting average. Apparently he would rather put one over the heart of the plate than walk a man. A starting pitcher can survive that; you give up seven hits in six innings but don't walk anybody, and you can still win. A relief pitcher can't. If you come in with a man on second, you have to risk the walk rather than give up a line drive. Castillo should start, and he should be protected, given a 100-pitch limit.

Andujar CEDENO, Houston
How good is he?

Not very good at this time. He's a shortstop prospect with the combined name of two of the Astros' most famous head cases, and at this time I doubt that he could break the Mendoza line. He's 21, so it's certainly possible that he'll eventually be a major league hitter, but if they bring him up now he's probably going to hit .180, have a strikeout/walk ratio of 10-1 and steal eight bases in 20 attempts.

Rick CERONE, Yankees
Even hitting .302, I'm not convinced that Rick Cerone helps anybody win. He hit .302 last year with a secondary average of .122—no walks, no power, no speed. He drove in eleven runs and scored twelve—and people talked about what a good year he was having with the bat.

John CERUTTI, Toronto
Do the Blue Jays need to replace him? Is he good enough for a number five starter?

He is *not* good enough for a number five starter, he is not improving, and the Blue Jays definitely need to replace him. He's been at .500 for two straight years, but whereas in 1989 he pitched better than that, last year he pitched worse. His strikeout/walk ratio has degenerated over the last five years from fairly good to unacceptable. In 1986 it was 89-47 (1.89 to 1); since then it's been 1.56 to 1 in 1987, 1.55 to 1 in 1988, 1.30 to 1 in 1989 and 1.00 to 1 last year. If this is one of those mathematical puzzles that starts out "what is the next number in this sequence," the answer is "the Blue Jays don't want to know."

Wes CHAMBERLAIN, Philadelphia
Is he going to be a star?

I was very high on him a year ago. He had a poor year at Buffalo, went to Philadelphia in a famous late-season screw up, and played well for the Phillies in 18 games.

Chamberlain is a big guy who can hit and run. Despite his awful season in 1990, his MLEs from 1989 show him as a *good* major league hitter. I think he might need another year of AAA, but if he is in the major leagues, I would make him about the number four candidate for the NL Rookie of the Year award, behind Decker, Lankford and Offerman at least. Eventually, I like his chances.

★★★
Norm CHARLTON, Cincinnati
★★★
How great is the star potential? Could he be one of the best pitchers in the league?

There are several things I look for in trying to spot a young pitcher who is going to be a star. The number one thing is that he has to be a power pitcher, since virtually all outstanding pitchers begin their careers as power pitchers. Beyond that, I like to see:

- A history of success,
- A good health record,
- A record of not having been worked too hard before the age of 25,
- A pitcher with a good organization,
- Pitching mechanics which aren't going to destroy his arm, and
- some evidence of intelligence.

Charlton seems to have positives in every area—not great big positives, but more positive than negative. He is something of a power pitcher, striking out 7.4 men per game. He has pitched fairly well, both in the majors and the minors. He has been healthy most of his career, although he did have one major injury, and his arm has not been abused. The

Reds, World Champions, have to qualify as a good organization. His mechanics are OK; he lands on his right foot a little bit early, I think, which causes his arm to hit his chest sooner than I think would be optimal. He has a degree from Rice University, which constitutes some evidence of intelligence.

So everything is in his favor. There are lots of guys who go 15-2 with a 1.71 ERA somewhere, but you run down this list and you find four negatives. Charlton has, that I can see, no reason why he wouldn't become a quality pitcher.

Scott CHIAMPARINO, Texas
Who is he?

He was considered one of the best pitching prospects in the A's organization, came over to Texas in the Baines trade and posted a 2.63 ERA in six starts. He could be Rookie of the Year, but I don't see anything to fall in love with about him. You run down the Charlton list (above), and there are two negatives and no major positives. The negatives are:

- Most young pitchers who are going to be stars strike out more men than he does. In the low minors he had good strikeout rates, but according to the September 25, 1990 *Baseball America* he "has discovered a new concept in pitching. Strike out fewer, win more." He's still a power pitcher, but it's a marginal classification.
- The Rangers have a poor record with young pitchers.

I haven't seen him pitch, so I can't comment on his mechanics. I think he's a good gamble for 1991, as rookies go, but not a pitcher who is going to be a star.

Steve CHITREN, Oakland
Will he make the A's? Will he pitch? Will he be Rookie of the Year?

Apparently the only thing that will keep him from being Rookie of the Year

is that, with Eckersley around, he won't be used in the glamour role. I expect Chitren to pitch about 65 times in a setup role, with an ERA below 3.00. If he's lucky, below 2.00.

Jim CLANCY, Houston

Needing a good year after a weak 1989, he went 2-8 with a 6.51 ERA. He's a survivor, but who can survive that?

Bryan CLARK, Seattle
Bryan Clark? The guy who came up ten years ago and never did anything? Is he still around?

Same guy. This is a *true* journeyman pitcher. Since starting with Bradenton in 1974 (4-6), he has pitched for Charleston (4-7) and Niagara Falls (3-10) in 1975, for Charleston in 1976 (1-13), for Salem in 1977 (5-13), for Charleston in 1978 (1-6) as well as Bellingham (no record), for Alexandria in 1979 (14-5), Spokane in 1980 (2-5) and then Lynn (9-5), for Seattle from 1981 through 1983 (1-1, 5-2, 7-10), for Salt Lake City in 1982, Syracuse in 1984, Toronto in 1984, Maine in 1985, Cleveland in 1985, Buffalo in 1986, Chicago (White Sox) in 1986 and 1987, Hawaii in 1987, Tacoma in 1988 and 1989, Calgary in 1990 and then back to Seattle.

He earned his way back by pitching outstanding baseball for two years in the Pacific Coast League (in '89 he was 15-7 with a 3.14 ERA.) His strikeout to walk ratios are poor even when he is pitching well, so that may not be a reliable indicator in his case. He pitched well enough with Seattle late in the year that he may be back in the majors this year.

Dave CLARK, Chicago Cubs
Could he play regularly?

I've always liked him, and I don't think that what he did last year (.275 with a .409 slugging percentage, seven for eight as a base stealer) is above his true ability in any way. He's 28, and not many guys get a chance to play regularly at that

age. The signing of George Bell closes off the position he would have to play. He's an expansion player, basically.

Jack CLARK,
Boston Red Sox
Will he help the Red Sox?

Jack Clark drives in and scores far more runs per at bat than Will Clark—always has, and still does. (Will C. last year drove in 91 runs and scored 95. Projected to the same number of at bats, Jack C. would have had 106 runs scored and 111 RBI.) Even in Will's best year, 1989, Jack was still more productive per at bat.

Although he didn't bat quite enough to qualify as the official leader, Clark's .441 on-base percentage last year was the best of any major league player (400 or more plate appearances.)

On the other hand, his career is in danger of being swallowed up by increasingly frequent injuries and constantly diminishing mobility. Sure, he puts a lot of runs on the scoreboard, but then, so did Ken Phelps. Three years ago Jack Clark was a star; now, he's a right-handed hitting Ken Phelps. His career will come to an end as soon as he goes into a major slump.

Note: Clark led the majors in secondary average last year, at .590. The top ten were Clark, Rickey Henderson (.583), Barry Bonds (.543), Randy Milligan, Cecil Fielder, Mark McGwire, Jose Canseco, Dave Justice, Fred McGriff and Eric Davis.

Jerald CLARK,
San Diego
Is he going to be a regular? A star?

He is probably not going to be a regular, much less a star. He hit .267 last year and I was surprised that he did that well, but that's 101 at bats. Walter Johnson hit .433 one year in that many at bats. He might hold a regular job for two or three years, but that's as far as he'll go at the outside.

Terry CLARK, California
Who is ho?

Minor league veteran, led the Appalachian League in saves in 1979. He tends to surface with organizations that are desperate for starting pitching, although in all likelihood he is no worse a pitcher than a dozen guys who have major league jobs.

Will CLARK, Giants
What happened to him last year? Is he still the best first baseman in baseball?

That's a definition of a superstar: a guy who hits .295 and drives in 95 runs in an off year. His season was within the normal range of random fluctuation, a little below his norms but not in a way that means anything. He revealed late in the season that he had been troubled by a nerve problem creating pain in his left foot.

Clark and Ruben Sierra have paralleled each other throughout their careers:

Year		G	HR	RBI	Avg.
1986	Clark	111	11	41	.287
1986	Sierra	113	16	55	.264
1987	Clark	150	35	91	.308
1987	Sierra	158	30	109	.263
1988	Clark	162	29	109	.282
1988	Sierra	156	23	91	.254
1989	Clark	159	23	111	.333
1989	Sierra	162	29	119	.306
1990	Clark	154	19	95	.295
1990	Sierra	159	16	96	.280

If you want to know who *eventually* will have better numbers, my money is on Sierra, but that's another story. The point is that this is just normal season-to-season fluctuation, which *both* Clark and the most-comparable player experienced. Sierra, incidentally, also had an ankle problem.

A couple of stat notes about Clark: in his first two seasons he was 9-for-33 as a base stealer, a horrible 27%. In the last three seasons he has jumped to the other end of the spectrum, stealing nine bases in ten attempts (1988), eight in eleven attempts (1989) and eight in ten tries (1990) . . . Clark has never grounded into even ten double plays in a season.

Stan CLARKE, St. Louis
Does he have a future?

Yeah, he's going to be traded to Houston for Terry Clark. Only his wife and children will know the difference.

Martin CLARY, Atlanta
Does he deserve another chance?

There is *nothing* in his record in 1990 (1-10, 5.67 ERA) or in his major league record as a whole which indicates to me that he can pitch.

Mark CLEAR, California
Does he have the worst control record ever?

Clear in his major league career has pitched 804 innings and walked 554 men, or 6.2 walks per game. I don't have a data base that I can search to find the worst ever, but I would guess there have been some worse. Probably the most comparable pitcher in history was Ryne Duren, who walked 6.0 per game, and had about the same ERA as Clear (3.83 for Duren, 3.85 for Clear.)

Roger CLEMENS, Bosox
Is he the best pitcher in baseball, or Stewart? Did he deserve the MVP Award?

My argument a year ago was that Clemens was clearly the best starting pitcher in the American League, and Dave Stewart would rank about fourth, behind Clemens, Viola and Saberhagen. The argument went:

- Although Stewart won twenty games in *each* of the three seasons 1987–1989, Clemens' record *over the three seasons as a whole* was much better.

- Clemens had pitched more innings over the three years than Stewart, during which he had given up fewer hits, fewer runs, fewer earned runs and fewer walks. Clemens had more strikeouts.

- Clemens had compiled distinctly superior statistics while pitching in a hitter's park. Stewart works in a pitcher's park. In the same park, Clemens' ERA would probably be a run a year better than Stewart's.

- Although Stewart's won-lost record was better than Clemens', it was only fractionally better. Clemens' won-lost *in the context of his team* was not only better than Stewart's, but *much* better.

So, with another year behind them, how does this argument change?

With Saberhagen injured and Viola in the National League, Stewart clearly moves up to the spot as the number two starting pitcher in the American League.

The distance between Clemens and Stewart, as individuals, is greater now than it was a year ago.

If we compared them both over a *five*-year period, there would of course be no contest, since this would include Clemens' 1986 season, when he was 24-4 and Stewart was 9-5. Going back more than five years would imbalance it even more, since Stewart had terrible records in 1984 and 1985. We will make a four-year comparison to give Stewart a break.

Over the four years as a whole,

- Stewart has pitched 35 more innings, 1062-1027, a difference of three percent.
- Clemens has given up fewer hits (and fewer hits per nine innings.)
- Clemens has given up fewer walks, and fewer per game.
- Clemens has more strikeouts, and more per game.
- Clemens has given up fewer runs, and fewer per game.
- Clemens has given up fewer earned

runs. Clemens' ERA over the four years is 2.77; Stewart's is 3.20.

- Clemens has thrown more complete games (47-41).
- Clemens has thrown three times as many shutouts (22-7).

Clemens has compiled these individual stat advantages despite playing in a park which is *much* tougher for a pitcher. There were reports last summer that, with the addition of the second-story press box in Fenway, Fenway could no longer be considered a hitter's park. When the final numbers were in, however, this proved not to be true, although it may be less of a hitter's park than it was a few years ago. The batting average of the Red Sox and their opponents in Fenway Park last year was .277; on the road it was .256. The Red Sox scored and allowed nine percent more runs per game in Fenway than on the road. The Coliseum, on the other hand, is a tremendous park for a pitcher. The A's scored and allowed 173 fewer runs at home than on the road in 1990 (565-738).

- Clemens' winning percentage over the four years is now *better* than Stewart's, even though Stewart has pitched for vastly better teams than Clemens. Clemens over the four years is 76-38, a .667 percentage. Stewart is 84-45, a .651 percentage.

The Red Sox have been less than a .500 team over the four years when Clemens was not pitching (.491)—and, in fact, they were less than a .500 team last year with other pitchers, although they won the division. They were fourteen games over .500; Clemens was fifteen games over.

The A's have been a .584 baseball team over the four years when Stewart wasn't pitching. Clemens' percentage is 176 points better than the rest of his team; Stewart's is 67 points better.

The fact that Stewart beats Clemens regularly when the two of them are matched against one another is an interesting phenomenon, and may be historically unique. I remember that Marichal used to beat Drysdale two or three times a year—I don't have the stats—but Drysdale lost twelve or fifteen games a season. The matchups with Stewart constitute a significant portion of Clemens' career losses, about one-sixth of them. I wonder if that's ever happened before, even when there were only eight teams and they played each other more often, that one-sixth of a great pitcher's career losses came against one other pitcher?

But that's not fundamentally how you evaluate a pitcher. If Stewart beats Clemens but loses to Minnesota and Baltimore, that's an intriguing puzzle, but it's no more than that. You evaluate a pitcher by

1. his earned run average, in the context of his park, his defense and the way he is used,
2. his won-lost record, over a suitable length of time and in the context of his team and offensive support, and
3. the individual components of his game.

Stewart is a great pitcher—but Clemens is unmistakably better. No thinking person can doubt that, if the two pitchers were on the same team, Clemens would emerge as that team's number one starter.

Did Clemens deserve the MVP Award? Not in my book. Clemens' absence from the team from September 4 to September 29 was used by both supporters and detractors in the Cy Young and MVP discussion. His detractors said that his absence from the team during most of the stretch run was reason enough not to vote for him. His supporters said that the fact that the Red Sox blew a six-and-a-half game lead while Clemens was out showed just how valuable Clemens was to the Red Sox.

My take on this issue is that Clemens' absence certainly *reveals* his value, in the same way that if the New York City police department were to be out of action for a few weeks it would certainly reveal how much New York City needs a police department. It *reveals* value, but it does not *constitute* value. I had no doubt anyway that Roger Clemens was extremely valuable to the Red Sox, who would be lucky to win the International League without him. The argument that a player on a ninety-win team is more valuable than a player on a great team because the ninety-win team couldn't win without him is, to me, an obviously specious argument, since it attributes to the player himself the value which is inherent in the position he occupies.

The absence from his team for three weeks in September of a close race has to weigh heavily against any award candidate. The fact that Clemens is a tough mugg and would have been out there pitching if there was any way he could, again, has nothing to do with the issue. I'd like to go out there and pitch myself, if I could, but this doesn't make me valuable to anybody. If Clemens had been able to pitch through September, I would have argued that he should win the Cy Young Award, despite Welch's 27 wins, and might have argued that he should have won the MVP Award. But I can't overlook the fact that, in a period when his team needed him most, he wasn't there.

Pat CLEMENTS, San Diego
Is there a job for him somewhere?
You'd think so; he's a left-hander and he's not terrible. He's also known as Jerry Don Gleaton, and has been known to check into motels under the name of Paul Mirabella.

Pete COACHMAN, California
Who is he?
29-year-old third base candidate, hit .311 in a late look with the Angels, who need a third baseman, and so may get a longer look this year. When he was

younger Coachman was a base stealer, stole 69 bases for Quad Cities in 1985. He still runs well enough to steal 20-30 bases in the majors, and his strikeout/walk ratios are good, but he has no power and I wouldn't expect him to hit above .260.

Dave COCHRANE, Seattle
Can he play?

He's Pete Coachman with a little power instead of a little speed. He's 28, a switch-hitting third baseman. He's not going to take the job away from Edgar Martinez, and wouldn't hold a regular job if he stumbled into one.

Chris CODIROLI, Kansas City
What was he doing in the major leagues?

Desperation.

Kevin COFFMAN, Chicago Cubs
Can he pitch?

No. He has no future as a major league pitcher.

Alex COLE, Cleveland
Is he going to be a star? Is he going to steal a hundred bases this year?

Ten years ago there were new young base stealers coming along every few weeks—Henderson and Raines, Willie and Mookie Wilson, Omar Moreno, Julio Cruz, Ron LeFlore and Rudy Law. If you think about it you'll realize that Cole is the first young player to come along in several years—the first since Vince Coleman—to make his mark primarily by stealing bases. I suppose you could argue for Harold Reynolds.

The most-comparable major league player to Alex Cole at the moment is Brian McRae. But the player that Cole most reminds me of, as a hitter, is not any of those other outfielders, but Maury Wills. Like Cole, Wills was stuck in the minors a long time, and his career

seemed to be going nowhere. What happened to set Wills free was that he started to switch hit, and when he did something clicked in his mind. He was challenged by the game, and he responded to the challenge. He became more aggressive on the bases, began to study the game and look for ways to make his mark on it.

I saw Cole a few years ago at Louisville, and I watched him carefully because at the time he was a prospect. At the time he was swinging hard, trying to drive the ball and yielding a combination of strikeouts and fly balls. But in the majors last year he seemed to be using a big bat and just slapping at the ball, flipping it over the infielders like Carew did and Willie Wilson did when he was young. Like Maury Wills did.

Officially, I'm a skeptic about Cole. You can ordinarily see almost exactly what kind of a hitter a guy is by his minor league statistics, and those statistics don't suggest that Cole is a .300 hitter. They suggest that he's a .250 hitter. A lot of times when a career minor leaguer gets a late shot he'll play over his head for half a season or so, and it's very possible that cole is one of those players.

But watching him last year, it seemed to me that something had clicked in his head, and his approach to the game was different than it was a couple of years ago.

Alex Cole has *no* chance of being Rickey Henderson or Tim Raines. He's starting too late, and his defense in center field is still not very good. But I think as long as he can remember what got him to the major leagues, stay aggressive and continue to punch at the ball, he could have a good career.

Vince COLEMAN, New York Mets
How will he hit in Shea Stadium?

Dave Nightingale in *The Sporting News* said that "The shift from artificial turf to grass will help him beat out hits." That was news to me; I thought I was the only

one who didn't believe that artificial turf created higher batting averages.

I checked Coleman's batting averages on grass and artificial turf since he came into the league in 1985. I might as well run the data:

	AB	H	2B	3B	HR	Avg.
In StL	1794	500	59	36	12	.279
Road Turf	818	201	29	12	1	.246
Road Grass	923	236	18	8	2	.256

His "home" performance, of course, has all been on artificial turf. Coleman has hit 28 points higher in St. Louis than on the road (.279–.251) which is three times the normal home field increase. He has, however, hit somewhat better on grass fields than in the other turf parks.

In my opinion, Coleman will probably prove a disappointment to the Mets. Because Shea Stadium has poor visibility, Coleman's strikeout to walk ratio will deteriorate in the move to New York. As a consequence of that his batting average, over a period of years, will drop by ten to fifteen points. Because one can run faster on turf than grass, his stolen base percentage may also decline slightly. The one thing most certain about the move to grass is that he will hit fewer doubles and triples. You can see this in the data, but I think you would know that anyway.

Coleman is 29 years old. Although he will not decline markedly because of age for the next three or four years, most players have had their best seasons before the age of 29.

Coleman, who stole 100 bases in each of his first three seasons, has *not* stolen a hundred in any of the last three.

Coleman is a lifetime .265 hitter, with a lifetime strikeout/walk ratio exactly two to one. If you take just a little bit away from that, you have a .255 hitter with a strikeout/walk ratio of 2.5 to 1, stealing 65 bases a year. Can a guy like that even play for a contending team? Probably not.

Darnell COLES, Detroit
What's the right role for him? Why is he so inconsistent? Should he be a regular? Should he be in the majors at all?

Coles, since we are dragging up players from the sixties (Wills), is the new Bill Robinson.

- Robinson was a right-handed hitter with some power but a relatively poor ability to make contact. Coles is the same.
- Robinson was originally a third baseman, switched to the outfield because of defensive problems. Coles is the same.
- Robinson was originally a hot prospect, but his career almost burned out after several seasons of hitting in the .220s. Coles is in the same position.

Robinson made a late-in-life comeback, having his best seasons in his mid thirties, which would be enough in my book to give Coles another look.

Coles clearly does not deserve consideration as a regular player at this point. He's got more than 2,000 major league at bats, and while he's played well at times the overall picture isn't very pretty—a .243 average with medium-range power. I don't understand why Lefebvre wanted to make him a regular at the expense of Brantley and then Briley. But I think he *is* a good enough player that he should be on a roster as long as his attitude is good, which everybody tells me that it is. My position would be to try to get him as many at bats as you can with the platoon advantage, use him as an extra third baseman, sixth outfielder and DH, and try to keep the pressure off of him. Maybe he'll move his production up a notch as Robinson did, probably he won't, but he'd be a useful 23rd or 24th man on the roster.

Dave COLLINS, St. Louis
Why did Herzog want him on a roster?

People like him and despite his age he still runs well. It was a silly decision, but then Herzog's human; he makes mistakes just like the rest of us.

Collins is now a coach.

Pat COMBS, Philadelphia
Can he still be a star? How much does a somewhat disappointing rookie season cause us to re-evaluate his future?

Combs' position is somewhat similar to that of Andy Benes. Regarded as a coming star a year ago, he pitched OK but not in a way that would suggest he was a star.

Having watched them for a year, it seems clear that Benes has a better chance to be a star than does Combs. But Combs major league record to this point—14-10 with a bad team, 3.73 ERA—certainly suggests that he is going to be around for a number of years, and still has some chance to be a star.

Keith COMSTOCK, Seattle
Why is he so much more effective than he was before he went to Japan? Where's his career going?

If you don't have a 95 MPH fastball, pitching's a mental game. A lot of guys don't figure it out until they're past 30. Lefebvre has also done a good job of limiting his role to what he can do best—face two or three hitters, including at least one left-hander.

Comstock, a left-handed pitcher, held *right-*handed batters to a .180 batting average last year. He also faded badly late in the 1990 season.

David CONE, New York
Where does he rank? Is he among the top ten starting pitchers in baseball? The top twenty?

He is, at all odds, the best number three starting pitcher in baseball. He's

better than that, and the elevator is still going up. Cone's strikeout/walk ratios, since 1987: 1.55 to 1 (which is OK) in 1987, 2.66 to 1 in 1988, 2.57 to 1 in 1989, 3.58 to 1 in 1990.

I think there is still a reasonable chance that Cone's arm troubles from the mid-eighties will come back, and obstruct his development. If that *doesn't* happen, I think he's going to bump past Viola and Gooden, and become the Mets' best starting pitcher, and one of the best in the National League. He's a smart pitcher, and he likes to experiment on the mound—change the angle a little bit, try this and that. That's my impression of him, anyway. When you're young and trying to establish yourself that can be a hindrance, in that you lose consistency within the game. But as you mature, it becomes an asset, in that it gives you more options. This is true of pitching as it is of many other things.

Cone, I think, has just reached the point where his tendency to experiment has become an asset. He was terrible for the first two months last year (6.27 ERA through June 4), but superb the rest of the year (13-6, 2.35 ERA.) He also gets stronger as a *game* goes on. Last year the batting average against him was .278 in his first thirty pitches, but .207 after that.

Three years is a reasonably good test of a pitcher. Cone over the last three years has a won-lost record of 48-21. Dwight Gooden is 46-20. Only two NL pitchers, Doug Drabek and Greg Maddux, have more wins than Cone over the three seasons, and both of those also have more losses. Cone is 27 games over .500 over the three years, the best of any National League pitcher.

He's capable of having a Cy Young season.

Jeff CONINE, Kansas City
Who is he?

Young first baseman, had a sensational first half with the bat at Memphis in 1990, slumped somewhat in the second half to wind up at .320 with 37 doubles, 15 homers, 94 walks. Playing winter ball in Venezuela he broke his wrist; no idea yet whether there will be long-term effects.

Conine was a pitcher in college. He had only one collegiate at bat, which caused him to be overlooked in the draft, so the Royals got him in the 58th round. He is a wonderful defensive player, extremely quick and agile (he was at one time one of the best racquetball players in the world).

The Royals' organization is long in first basemen/designated hitters, with George Brett still playing well, Kirk Gibson joining the team as a free agent, Luis de los Santos trapped in AAA and Bob Hamelin regarded as one of the best power-hitting prospects in the minors. Conine at the moment is the best of the young ones. If he develops as expected he'll be comparable to Mark Grace.

Dennis COOK, Los Angeles
What happened to him last year? Why did Philadelphia give up on him so quickly as a starting pitcher?

Left-handed hitters hit .296 against him, which makes it pretty hard to use him as a starting pitcher. I never did see him as a star, but he started out superbly last year (3-0 with a 0.77 ERA in April), stretched it to 5-0, then lost a couple of games. At the same time that the Phillies had to replace Ken Howell because of an injury, they decided to replace Cook just more or less for the hell of it. Last year he was 6-3 with a 4.03 ERA in 16 starts.

What's his job with the Dodgers?

The Dodgers have so many pitchers that the options are bewildering. If both Hershiser and Belcher prove to be healthy, Cook will be in the bullpen. If neither one can pitch, he'll be in the rotation.

Scott COOLBAUGH, San Diego
Is he going to be a regular?

Sure. He struggled last year in 67 games, but he's 24 years old, plays OK

defense at third base and has looked like a decent hitter in the past. The odds are he'll find himself.

Scott COOPER, Boston
Who is he?

Red Sox third base prospect, doesn't look as good as Bagwell but seems to be a major league player.

Cooper isn't going to move Wade Boggs, and isn't a Grade A prospect. He's not a .300 hitter or a speed demon or a power hitter or a great defensive player. His balance of skills would seem to me to be enough to provide a role for him in the major leagues in two or three years.

Joey CORA, San Diego
Why hasn't he been in the major leagues?

A. Irrational prejudice against small ball-players, or
B. No clearly defined offensive or defensive role.

I think he is obviously one of the better utility infielders around, and I'm not at all sure that he couldn't be a good everyday second baseman. With the trade of Alomar he may wind up as the Padre second baseman, but probably won't.

Sherman CORBETT, California
Can he pitch?

He's another guy who will battle for a job as a left-handed spot reliever. There's nothing impressive about him.

Wilfredo CORDERO, Montreal
Who is he?

Young shortstop, regarded as possibly the top prospect in the Expos' system. Only 19 years old, Cordero is said to be a major league defensive shortstop already, but is at least a couple of years away as a hitter.

John COSTELLO, San Diego
What's happened to him?

Costello supposedly is a very interesting person, has a degree in police science and is articulate and personable. He has a marginal major league fastball, is 30 years old and has no record of sustained success, so they're not real patient with him. He was hammered early in the year, was traded for Rex Hudler—a great trade for the Cardinals, as it worked out—didn't pitch well for Montreal, was sent down and posted a 7.04 ERA in AAA.

The Padres for some unexplained reason decided they had to have him, and rather than wait for Montreal to release him they traded Brian Harrison, who had a 1.19 ERA and 18 saves in A ball, to acquire him. Maybe they know something we don't.

Henry COTTO, Seattle
Is he helping the Mariners?

No. He's a good outfielder and a good baserunner, but he's never going to hit enough to help anybody win. He just hits enough, particularly early in the season, to hold his job. You can't even platoon him, because he hits left-handers and right-handers just the same. Cotto did have the best stolen base percentage in the American League (21 for 24).

Steve CRAWFORD, Kansas City
Why is he pitching better now than he did with Boston?

He's changing speeds more effectively.

Tim CREWS, Los Angeles
Could he be a closer?

He probably could, yes, but he isn't likely to get the chance. He'd have to be one of the top-ranked setup men in the league.

Chuck CRIM, Milwaukee
What happened to him last year? Why was he off his game?

With Plesac being less effective the Brewers had to try him in the closer role, and his stuff probably isn't at that level. He has good control and he's a competitor. I saw him knock George Brett on his butt last year, and how many Chuck Crims will do that, but he doesn't have much of a breaking pitch, and he's had trouble getting the first batter out.

His 1990 season, although he was clearly somewhat off, is within a normal range. He pitched 67 games, saved 11 and had a 3.47 ERA. That's OK.

Steve CUMMINGS, Toronto
Who is he?

Right-handed pitching prospect, may compete for John Cerutti's starting job. He's a sinker/slider pitcher, has pitched consistently well in the minor leagues. Grade B prospect; I suspect he will require a couple of years to settle into a major league job, if he ever does.

Earl CUNNINGHAM, Chicago Cubs
Who is he?

Power-hitting outfielder, regarded as perhaps the best prospect in the Cubs' system. He weighs 225 pounds in shape and has trouble staying in shape—a scout said he reported to camp last year looking like Eric Gregg—but is thought to be a potentially dominating hitter.

Milt CUYLER, Detroit
Can he play? Is he the American League Rookie of the Year?

Cuyler is a center fielder with great speed, often compared to Gary Pettis. Sparky said of him that "when you can run like that you get to play in the major leagues automatically. It's in the rules."

Cuyler's young enough to improve a great deal, but if he doesn't want to break the rules, he's going to have to. He's not terrible, and on the theory that anybody who can play can have a good year, he could win the Rookie of the Year Award. I think he's a .250 hitter, but let's say he hits .270 and steals 60 bases, which is possible, then he wins the Rookie of the Year. He's not one of my top candidates.

•D•

Kal DANIELS, Los Angeles

What a hitter he is. His injuries have taken away one of his skills prematurely (his speed), and his August injury may leave him unable to throw well enough to play the outfield. He plays in a park which costs him a few home runs and ten or fifteen points off his batting average. Even so, he's awesome—a career on base percentage over .400, a slugging percentage over .500. The Dodgers improved last year by 174 runs, from 554 runs scored to 728, which somebody told me was one of the largest improvements ever in that half of the game. Kal Daniels being healthy was the one biggest reason for that. This is a guy who can definitely win an MVP Award in the right year if he can get 80% healthy.

Ron DARLING, Mets
What should the Mets have done with him?

They should have traded him for a catcher, or if one wasn't available they should have traded him for a middle infielder. I know the arguments against it—you can never have too much pitching, you can't count on all your starting pitchers to stay healthy, you can't pay too high a price in talent to fill a hole, etc. The dominant considerations as I see them are:

• In a pennant race you can't afford to waste resources,
• A team gets a limited number of chances to win the pennant. Teams don't stay together forever, so when you have a chance to win it behooves you to make the effort.
• The Mets talent was abundant but horribly configured. The Mets had two third basemen, six starting pitchers and several first basemen, but no catcher, shortstop or second baseman to speak of.

That's a situation which calls out for something to be done. The obvious thing to do was to trade the surplus starting pitcher—Darling—for the best player available to cover one of the holes.

Can he come back and be a rotation starter?

Absolutely. I was never crazy about him, but I like him as well now as I did two years ago, maybe a little better. He had elbow surgery over the winter, but it wasn't anything that's going to keep him from being effective. He's just getting started; he'll be around a long time yet.

Danny DARWIN, Boston
Will he help the Red Sox? Why is he pitching so much better now than he did a few years ago?

Darwin had a wonderful year in relief in 1989, and then stepped into the starting rotation last year to go 8-0 with a 1.59 ERA in his first ten starts. Obviously Darwin's ERA in Fenway will probably be *at least* a run higher than it was in the Astrodome.

Despite the impressive performance as a starting pitcher, I think it's primarily a case of a pitcher being most effective when he was told to throw as hard as he can for as long as he can.

Darwin as I see him is the most-similar major league pitcher to Dennis Eckersley. The two men are about the same size and the same age. Both throw hard; both throw a slider and a fastball that sinks. Both will drop down sidearm and make the fastball ride in on a right-handed hitter. Both have good control. Eckersley washed out as a starter, and became a super-star as a reliever.

Darwin has always been a decent pitcher, maybe a better-than-decent pitcher. He is one of three major league pitchers who pitched through the 1980s with an ERA below 4.00 each year, the other two being Nolan Ryan and Bob Welch (minimum: 70 innings each season and 1200 innings total.) His strikeout to walk ratios have always been good, as was also true of Eckersley. He's always been healthy.

I think it was a mistake to make Darwin a starting pitcher. His first major league season (1980) he was a reliever, and he was excellent (13-4, 2.62 ERA.) Dandy Don Zimmer converted him to a starter in 1981 and he was just fair (9-9, 3.81 ERA); still, he remained a starter for most of his career.

Although Darwin's record in his years as a starter wasn't great, it was better than most people think. He never posted a high ERA, even once, and had generally good peripheral stats. His won-lost records were poor, but look at the teams that he was pitching for—Texas from 1980 through 1984 (they were never in contention in a weak division), Milwaukee in 1985–1986 (they lost 90 in '85 and were under .500 in '86), and Houston in 1987–88 (a .500 team.) Moved to relief in 1989, he has pitched brilliantly for two seasons.

Called on to relieve 31 times last year, Darwin got the first batter out 28 times, by far the best percentage in the major leagues. The leaders: Darwin, 90%, Duane Ward, 84%, Dan Schatzeder, 83% and Bob Kipper, 82.5%.

Darwin started seventeen times last year, and may be in the Red Sox rotation this year. I still think it's a mistake. I'm not saying that he will fail as a starter; he's never been a bad starter, and I can see him going 17-10, maybe. I just don't think it's a good gamble. If it was my team, I'd try him first as the relief ace. I think Darwin could be one of the best in the game in that role; I don't think Jeff Reardon is.

Doug DASCENZO, Chicago
Can he be a regular?
He's not terrible, but he should never be a regular. What he did last year is his true ability: he's a .250 hitter, no walks or power. He gives you speed and defense,

but that's not enough by itself. Walton is a better player.

Jack DAUGHERTY, Texas
Was he over his head last year? Having hit .302 and .300 the last two years, should he be considered a legitimate .300 hitter? Could he hit .300 as a regular?
I don't believe in him. When he hit .300 a year ago I didn't believe that was a real level of ability. He hit .300 again last year in 310 at bats. I still don't really believe that he's a .300 hitter, but I don't want to be stubborn, either, so let's say he's a .300 hitter. If he's a .300 hitter, is he a good ballplayer?

No, he isn't. If he's a .300 hitter he deserves a major league job, but not as an everyday player. His secondary average last year was .206, meaning that although he hit .300 he didn't do the other things that put runs on the scoreboard. Rob Deer, hitting .209, drove in and scored more runs (and more per at bat.)

His defense is marginal—he's a first baseman/left fielder/designated hitter.

He's 30 years old, so he's not likely to get any better.

Darren DAULTON, Philadelphia
Can he do this every year? Is he as good as he seemed to be last year?
Of course not. He's hit between .194 and .225 five times and over .225 once. I don't know about you, but in my book that makes him a lot more likely to hit .225 than .268.

Daulton is the opposite of Jack Daugherty; if he hits .225, he can still play. His secondary average last year was .320, and it's always been good. He does play a key defensive position, and he's an above-average defensive player at that position.

So he doesn't have to hit .270 to be a regular—but it would help if he'd hit .230. He's still got to prove that he can do that.

Mark DAVIDSON, Houston
Is he worth the roster spot?
No. The only thing he brings to the table is defense in the outfield. He doesn't hit for average or power or steal bases. A bench player has got to contribute in more than one area, or the manager has limited ability to maneuver.

Alvin DAVIS, Seattle
Should he be traded? What for?
As I write this, the Mariners are discussing trades involving Davis. The Mariners have three first basemen, in Davis, Tino Martinez and Pete O'Brien, all of whom are left-handed hitters. Reports are that they see trading Davis as their best option.

Were I running the Mariners, I would see trading Davis as the third option:

1. I don't think Tino Martinez is all that good. I think he's Sid Bream, rather than Don Mattingly.
2. Alvin Davis is the *best* of the three players. If you've got duplication at a position, you ordinarily try to keep the best of the available players.
3. Davis is the best player the Mariners have ever had. I would always prefer, when possible, to keep a player like that for his entire career, or as much of it as possible. Organizations benefit from stability. It is easier to sell to the public a product that they recognize.

Davis is a career .289 hitter who has power and walks a lot. This combination makes him, by the formulas that we use to measure these things, one of the best hitters in baseball—in fact, there have been years when he created more runs per out than any other major league player.

There is another side to the story:

1. There is some question whether Davis is actually as good a hitter as the formulas estimate. Although he "creates" a huge number of runs, he doesn't drive in or score a huge num-

ber of runs. He is very slow, one of the slowest runners in baseball, and with a man in scoring position they just walk him.

2. Stability means more if you have a tradition of winning than it does in Seattle. If the team has been winning, you want to keep the players who know what the price of winning is. If the team hasn't been winning, maybe it's time for a change.

3. Pete O'Brien is coming off his poorest major league season. If he was traded now, if he could be traded, his value would be down.

4. Davis is 30 years old. Branch Rickey always liked to trade a star player at age 30, before his value dropped. The Mariners may be faced with the options of trading him before his value drops, or waiting until after it drops. In view of his lack of speed, his value could drop quickly.

Davis is an average defensive first baseman, or maybe not quite. If I thought Martinez was as good as the Mariners think he is, I might trade Davis, too. As it is, I think the balance of advantages would dictate keeping Davis if possible.

Chili DAVIS, California
How good is he?

Middle of the pack. His speed has disappeared with a series of knee problems, making him, at 31, almost too slow to play the outfield. In the last two seasons he has stolen four bases and grounded into 35 double plays.

He's a wonderfully consistent hitter, hitting around .270 every year with some power. He gets on base. He can score eighty runs a year and drive in ninety, and that's not bad. He's not a star.

Eric DAVIS, Cincinnati
Is he a superstar?

When Davis hit the media in 1987 he was often compared to Willie Mays. Willie Mays arranged a meeting with him.

"Don't let them do that to you," Willie reportedly told him. "When time passes and you don't put up the numbers I did, they'll turn on you."

Willie's comments have proven prophetic. Eric Davis was a fine player last year, driving in 86 runs despite missing a month with aching wheels. He hit 24 homers, stole 21 bases. It wasn't good enough. He got booed.

Eric Davis uses a little whip-handled bat—don't ask me why—and strikes out in 26% of his at bats. Because of this, it really *should* have been apparent that he would never be a .300 hitter. If this wasn't apparent several years ago, it certainly is now.

He's not durable. He misses thirty games a year, regular as clockwork; his career high in at bats is 474.

I don't have a definition of a superstar, but to me, that's enough to keep Davis out of the club. He's got two major weaknesses.

Now, it's time to stop talking about that. It's time to stop holding it against Eric that he isn't Willie Mays. He's a remarkable offensive player, and a fine defensive player. He's a star, one of the twenty or thirty best players in the game. Let's try to respect him for what he is, rather than punishing him for what he isn't.

Notes: Davis has the highest career secondary average of any active player (.487). The eleven men over .400 are Eric, Rickey Henderson (.486), Ken Phelps (.457), Darryl Strawberry, Fred McGriff, Kal Daniels, Barry Bonds, Mark McGwire, Gary Redus, Jack Clark, and Tim Raines.

Eric's career stolen base percentage, 86.9%, is also the best of any active player, and is considered by the National League to be a career record, although if it was up to me I wouldn't consider a man eligible for a career percentage record until he had retired. The top five among active players: Davis, Raines, Willie Wilson, Vince Coleman and Barry Larkin.

Glenn DAVIS, Houston
Would he hit 40 homers a year in another park?

It's not likely. Over the years he has lost about four home runs a year to the Astrodome. He could certainly hit 40 homers a year in Wrigley Field or County Stadium in Atlanta, and he could hit 40 homers in a *good* year in most of the other parks.

Will he come back?

Sure. He had a torn muscle in the rib cage, and after that some strained muscles in the back. Nothing permanent.

John DAVIS, Chicago
Who is he?

He's a six-foot-seven right-hander, getting too old to be a prospect. He posted a 2.27 ERA in 27 games with Kansas City in '87, then was included in the Floyd Bannister trade. If his name was Carlos Chessman or something you'd remember him. He hasn't been able to find the strike zone for three years, and there's no reason to believe he will in 1991.

Mark DAVIS, Kansas City
Can he come back?

The Royals have hired Pat Dobson, his pitching coach in San Diego, to help ensure that the answer is "Yes."

Davis still throws as hard as ever, but I'm not certain that he'll be back in the saddle in 1991; I think it's a fifty-fifty proposition. Davis' control record in 1990 was not only the worst of his career, but *by far* the worst. When he was young he walked about four men per game. In 1988–89 he cut it to about three per game. Last year he walked almost seven men per nine innings.

I don't think there's a lot of precedent in baseball for a pitcher suddenly losing the strike zone to that extent. I haven't seen it happen that many times. But I think there is even *less* precedent for a pitcher like Davis suddenly losing the strike zone, and then suddenly finding it again. I think it is very possible that Davis will battle his control for the rest of his career.

Storm DAVIS, Kansas City
Why did he pitch so poorly for Kansas City?

Because he's not a very good pitcher. He was exactly the same pitcher last year that he was in 1989, when he won nineteen games for Oakland. The real question is, why on earth did the Royals not realize what they were getting?

Andre DAWSON, Cubs

Andre won his MVP Award in the wrong season. In 1987, when he won the MVP Award, I attacked the voting, arguing that while Andre had done one thing exceptionally well (he had hit 49 home runs), he wasn't outstanding anywhere else. The argument for him was home runs, defense and clubhouse leadership, and you don't give MVP Awards for leadership to a player from a last-place team.

But Dawson *did* do last year all of the things that he *didn't* do the year that they gave him the MVP Award. Whereas he hit only .287 that year—about average for an NL outfielder—last year he hit .310, ranking him third among the NL's 36 regular outfielders. Whereas he had a terrible strikeout/walk ratio in 1987 (103-32), last year he had fewer strikeouts and more walks (65-42). In his MVP year he didn't hit many doubles or triples or steal many bases, but last year he hit more doubles (28-24), more triples (5-2) and stole more bases (16-11) with a better stolen base percentage.

So I think he was a better player last year than he was the year he won the MVP award. That year I wrote, and I still believe, that he couldn't possibly have been one of the twenty best all-around players in the league. I don't think he was the MVP last year—but he was one of

the ten or fifteen best players in the league, as in fact he has been most of his career.

Note: With 346 career homers and 300 stolen bases, Andre ranks as the sixth-greatest power/speed combination in baseball history, with a power speed number of 321.4. I am amazed to discover that I apparently have not printed an updated list of the career leaders in power/speed number since 1983, and of course the list has changed a lot since then. Here is the current list:

		HR	SB	PSN
1.	Mays	660	338	447.1
2.	Bonds Sr.	338	461	386.0
3.	J Morgan	268	689	385.9
4.	Aaron	755	240	364.2
5.	Reggie	563	228	324.6
6.	DAWSON	346	300	321.4
7.	Baylor	338	285	309.2
8.	F Robinson	583	204	302.2
9.	Cedeno	199	550	292.3
10.	R Henderson	166	936	282.0

Among active players the highest career power/speed numbers are held by Dawson, Rickey, Dave Winfield (269.2), Robin Yount, Dale Murphy, George Brett, Darryl Strawberry, Ryne Sandberg, Claudell Washington and Kirk Gibson. The last time I wrote about this I wrote that it was very unlikely that any active player would supplant Willie Mays as the number one power/speed combination of all time, but it now appears that Rickey Henderson may. Henderson will need to hit about 270 home runs to rank as the top power/speed combo, which he may do in another four or five years.

Ken DAYLEY, Toronto
Dayley is a free agent, reportedly looking for a job as a bullpen closer. Can he carry the load? Would you sign him to be a stopper?

I would not sign him to be a stopper, and I would be reluctant to sign him at all. Dayley has had good ERAs for six

years in a row in St. Louis, but he was protected by three things:

1. Busch Stadium,
2. The magnificent Cardinal defense, and
3. Whitey Herzog, who does an exceptional job of spotting relief pitchers, not letting anybody get beat up.

Take those advantages away from him, and I'm not sure how effective he would be.

Late note: Dayley signed with Toronto, where he obviously will not be the closer. I don't expect him to have any real impact on the race.

★ ★ ★
Steve DECKER, San Francisco
★ ★ ★
Can he play?

You bet. Decker played last year at Shreveport, not an easy park to hit in, and hit .293 with 15 home runs. Reports on his defense are good. The October 10, 1990, edition of *Baseball America* listed him as the ninth-best prospect in the Texas League, with this entry:

The 6-foot-3, 215-pound Decker was impressive for the strength of his total game. He hit well and caught well this season, and at 24 figures to supplant San Francisco's aged catching platoon before long.
"He's a catcher from the old school—big, solid kid who throws well and can swing the bat," [Clint] Hurdle said.
"He's a solid, all-around catcher, and good offensive player," [Steve] Lubratich said.

Question: If he's a good defensive catcher and swings the bat well, why did *Baseball America* list him as the ninth-best prospect in the Texas League?

Answer: For precisely the same reason that they listed Ruben Sierra as the ninth-best prospect in the league five years ago, behind Kevin Elster and Mark McLemore.

I ain't whuppin' on them; it's a great publication. Anyway, we project him to hit .289 in the major leagues, with 16 homers and 75 RBI. Maybe he won't do that in 1991; maybe he won't do it until 1992—but he's going to do it. He's a hard worker and a take-charge personality. Get him on your team.

Rob DEER, Detroit
Will he help the Tigers?

He probably will help the Tigers, but he may prove an unpopular signing anyway because

a. all the strikeouts are frustrating, and
b. the Tigers are probably destined to have an off season, for which he may be blamed.

Deer should help the Tigers because their outfield last year was just awful—Gary Ward, Chet Lemon, Larry Sheets. A bunch of old guys hitting .258 with no power. Deer is a .225 hitter who strikes out as much as any player in baseball history, but he'll put a few runs on the scoreboard with his power and walks. He's better than Gary Ward.

The Tigers are trying to boost their team up to the point at which they can attract the really good free agents. They've made good offers to the top level free agents, but not many people want to go to Detroit, to begin with, and almost nobody wants to play for a bad team. They've brought in Moseby and Deer to try to get the team up to a more competitive level, but unless they get lucky—another Cecil Fielder—it will never work. Moseby is 31, Deer 30. By the time they collect enough of these guys to have a decent team, Moseby and Deer will be no better than Ward and Lemon were last year.

There are a couple of park factors working in Deer's favor this year. One is that he is leaving a home park, Milwaukee County Stadium, where he didn't hit particularly well. The other is that he can annihilate a left-hander. Be-cause of the dimensions of Tiger Stadium, the Tigers usually see a lot of left-handed pitching. On the other hand, with Cecil Fielder, Rob Deer and Alan Trammell in the middle of the lineup, I don't think the Tigers are going to be seeing any huge number of left-handers in 1991.

Notes: On lists of *types* of hitters, established by ratios between categories, Deer is often first or last in the major leagues. His career ratio of strikeouts to hits (1.59 to 1) is by far the worst in the major leagues. Next worst is Bo Jackson (1.39 to 1), then Pete Incaviglia, Mickey Tettleton and Steve Balboni. Deer would still be the worst if he lost a hundred strikeouts. On the other hand, his batting average last year accounted for only 33% of his offensive contribution, the lowest percentage in the major leagues. (He was followed on that list, the *good* side of the list, by Mark McGwire, Jack Clark, Mickey Tettleton and Cecil Fielder.) If Ken Phelps doesn't make a roster he will also be the career leader in that category, at 36%.

Deer went through the 1990 season without grounding into a single double play. This is a strange event. First, it's very rare. The records are indexed in a funny way and I'm not sure of this, but I think he may be the first right-handed hitter ever to do this, the only other players to get through a season without grounding into any being Dick McAuliffe in 1968 (a left-handed hitter) and Augie Galan in 1935 (a switch hitter.) I'm not certain—there may be others.

Galan and McAuliffe batted more times than Deer, but Galan and McAuliffe were leadoff hitters. Deer batted fifth and sixth and batted 237 times with men on base, so in a way his accomplishment is more remarkable.

More than that, however, Rob Deer is *not* an antelope. Not many of us, if asked to name the players who should ground into double plays least often, would name Rob Deer. We would name Rickey Hen-derson, Willie Wilson, Tim Raines, Devon White—left-handed hitters and switch hitters who can run. In his career, Deer has grounded into only twenty double plays, which just misses—literally by one at—being the best career record of any active player. The player who has grounded into double plays least often is Vince Coleman, with a career ratio of one DP for each 126.25 at bats, followed by Deer (126.2), Brett Butler (125), Lenny Dykstra (110) and Dave Martinez (104). The top seven men on the list are six leadoff men and Rob Deer.

Jim Rice used to ground into 25 double plays a year. The press would say that he grounded into so many because he hit the ball hard—but Rob Deer also hits the ball hard.

The occurrence isn't as strange as it might at first appear. Let's work through the data:

1. Deer batted 237 times in 1990 with men on base.
2. In probably 40 to 45% of those cases there was a runner in scoring position, but no runner on first base. That would cut the opportunities down to about 142.
3. In some of those cases, Deer was walked. Deer walks in one out of eight plate appearances, but that figure would be lower when there was a runner on first, so Deer probably walked about ten times when there was a runner on first. That leaves 132.
4. Deer hit .229 with men on base last year, so let's assume that figure applies here. That would mean that he had about 30 hits in those situations, which would mean that made about 102 outs with a man on first base.
5. Many of those, however, were strikeouts, which is a large part of the explanation for why Deer doesn't ground into double plays. Deer's strikeouts account for 46% of his outs, so there are a large number of outs which can't possibly be ground ball double plays.

If that 46% applies here, that would mean 47 strikeouts, and leave him with 55 ground-ball and fly-ball outs.

6. When Deer does hit the ball he usually hits it in the air. According to STATS Inc, Deer in 1989 hit the ball on the ground only 35% of the time, virtually tying Mark McGwire for the lowest such percentage in the major leagues. (This isn't quite the same as the Elias groundout/flyout ratio. STATS also includes the *hits* in their breakdowns.) If that 35% applies here, then Deer would have hit about 19 ground ball outs with men on base.

7. In almost half of those occasions there would have been two men out, which eliminates the double play possibility. Let's say nine of those ground ball outs were the third out. That leaves us with a field of ten ground ball outs.

That means that Deer probably hit about ten ground ball outs last year in double play situations, none of which happened to result in a GIDP. By random chance the number could be much lower than ten—maybe five or less. So when you understand it it's really not *that* remarkable that he didn't hit any ground balls right at anybody which could be turned into two. If you worked through the data for another player, who a) was in the lineup everyday, b) hit third or fourth instead of sixth, c) doesn't strike out much, and d) hits as many ground balls as fly balls, you might find that such a player would hit fifty ground ball outs a year in double play situations, rather than ten.

Deer's a right-handed hitter, which is a bias against him (in the double play category) but not that big a bias. Right-handed hitters, as a group, grounded into one double play every 43 at bats last year (not counting pitchers), while left-handed hitters grounded into one every 49 at bats.

The lowest percentages of ground balls: McGwire (35%), Deer (35%), Howard Johnson (38%), Kevin McReynolds (42%) and Tom Brunansky (42%).

Jose DE JESUS, Philadelphia
What's his star potential? Why did the Royals trade him for Steve Jeltz?

Irrational fear. DeJesus had a minor injury, and the Royals were afraid of going into the season with no backup infielder. The Royals a year ago thought they could win, and, perceiving themselves as having a winning hand, were afraid of losing because Frank White was old and they had no one behind him. In retrospect, it would have been wiser to head into the season with Frank White unsupported, and then try to make some arrangements on the fly if White couldn't cut it.

DeJesus has awesome stuff, but will probably battle his control for several years, and will probably have arm trouble before he finds his control. I'll be surprised if he becomes a star, and if he does it will be a couple of years yet.

Jose DE LEON, Cardinals
Will he come back?

He was on my fantasy league team last summer, and single-handedly kept me in the second division. I was sure he'd get it turned around in a couple of starts.

Looking at it analytically, DeLeon appears to be almost certain to have a better year. He's on the "Searcy list" of pitchers who are likely to have better years in 1991 than they did in 1990. DeLeon is high on the list, with a ratio of 23 strikeouts for each win (164 strikeouts, seven wins), which means that there is roughly a 95% chance that he will have a better record this year than last year.

Also, DeLeon had the worst offensive support of any major league pitcher in 1990 (2.96 runs per nine innings.) That honor will probably pass to someone else in 1991.

On the other hand, he was 7-19, so "a better record" might be 3-7 or something. No, DeLeon has pitched well over a period of years (11-12, 13-10, 16-12), and his 164 strikeouts in 183 innings are pretty good evidence that he has something left in the arm. I regard it as statistically very likely that DeLeon will be back at the level of his previous seasons in 1990.

My heart isn't in it.

Notes: The bottom five in the NL in offensive support were DeLeon, Joe Magrane, Mike Scott, Zane Smith and Mark Portugal . . . another note about DeLeon is that he threw to first base only thirteen times all year, the fewest of any major league pitcher with 162 innings. Bruce Ruffin, who never throws to first, didn't quite pitch enough innings to qualify.

Rich DeLUCIA, Seattle
DeLucia posted a 2.00 ERA late in the season. Is he really that good?

It's very unlikely that he is. DeLucia was drafted in 1986 but missed so much time following surgery on his right elbow in 1987 that he hasn't pitched enough innings to be evaluated reliably.

DeLucia has very good control, maybe exceptional control. He started 1990 at A ball, jumped to AA, AAA and the majors, and was sharp at all levels. He has no history of having failed, albeit a limited history of having succeeded. He could be good.

Rick DEMPSEY, Free Agent
Can he still play?

After two straight years under .200 he's dropped from a number two catcher to a number three catcher, if he can land a job at all. He's a free agent. His secondary average is around .300—exceptional for a catcher, and better than it was when he was a regular. At 41 he can still get out of a crouch and chase a fly ball, although he is awfully slow on the bases. I can see signing him as a #3 catcher.

Jim DESHAIES, Houston
What happened to him last year? Can he come back?

Deshaies pitches a little like Mike Boddicker—changes speeds to make a mediocre fastball look faster. Sid Fernandez type, pitches up in the strike zone.

He seemed to lose confidence in his ability to hit spots last year, and was getting behind hitters more than he had in the past. It was also suggested that the word had gotten around that if you could lay off the high fastball on the first pitch, you'd be ahead in the count and eventually get something better to swing at.

Deshaies needs to make an adjustment of some kind, obviously. Maybe he already has; he was pitching great at the end of the 1990 season (1.93 ERA in his last six starts, pitching at least six innings in every game). As long as his arm is OK, my guess is that he'll come back.

Note: Information compiled by STATS a year ago showed that Deshaies in 1989 threw to first more times than any other major league pitcher (355). This was published in a book entitled *The Stats Baseball Scoreboard*, which was just a wonderful book, full of all kinds of arcane little information like that.

The media picked up on the bit about Deshaies' pickoff throws, however, and used it as an example of the excesses of modern statisticians, but why? There is certainly a lot of useless statistical information floating around these days, which comes in two basic categories:

1. Lists of what people did in categories broken down so small that the data wouldn't become statistically significant in a hundred years, and
2. Formula-generated ratings the exact meaning of which is unclear.

This doesn't fit in either category. The fact that Deshaies throws to first more often than anybody else is just simple, basic information which didn't happen to exist before now. Everybody knows

what the statement means. There is no doubt that the data is statistically significant. It's worth knowing.

Anyway, Deshaies defended his title in 1990, making 2.4 throws to first base per baserunner, by far the most in the National League. Actually, Charlie Hough edged by him in total throws to first, but Hough had more baserunners to deal with.

Delino DE SHIELDS, Montreal
How good is he? Is he going to be a star?

He's awfully good. I think he took a step forward last year, and may need a consolidation year. But he's young, he can hit, he can run, he gets on base, he can play second base. He's got a chance to be a big star.

Who would you rather have: DeShields or Jeffries?

I'd rather have Jeffries, but it's close. DeShields is a better second baseman.

Mike DEVEREAUX, Orioles
Should he be a regular?

No. He's apparently reached his limits. He is probably due for his best major league season in 1991, but I wouldn't be looking at him as a franchise player. He makes a lot of mistakes.

Mark DEWEY, San Francisco
Who is he?

Right-handed reliever, knows how to pitch and has major league stuff as well. He'll be on my list of players who could win the National League Rookie of the Year Award, and would have been much higher on that list if the Giants hadn't signed Righetti.

Carlos DIAZ, Toronto
Who is he?

Good field, no hit catcher. He'll be around the fringes of the major leagues for the next five years or so, never a regular.

Edgar DIAZ, Milwaukee
Is there a job for him? Is he going to move up? Why has a shortstop who can hit .270 been in the minors all these years?

Diaz, who had a brief trial in 1986, finally made the majors last year and hit .271.

In 1986 he hit .315 at Vancouver (AAA), and seemed about ready to step into a major league job. (Vancouver is in the Pacific Coast League, but *not* a great hitter's park.) He dislocated his left shoulder in spring training, 1987, was disabled, sent out on a rehabilitational assignment and dislocated the shoulder again. He played badly in 1988 and 1989, and was apparently close to quitting the game. In the winter of 1989–90 he seemed to come to terms with the fact that he wasn't going to be a superstar, and got back on his feet.

Diaz would appear to be comparable to Felix Fermin, who is a regular. He is not thought to be as good a shortstop as Spiers, but he can play the position. If he continues to hit .270, somebody will look at him as a regular. I don't have a good line as to whether he will be able to do that. Certainly he played vastly better last year than he had in the previous couple of years, but was he over his head? It's more likely that he was *not* playing the way he was capable of the previous two years.

Mario DIAZ, New York
Could he be a major league backup infielder? Should the Mets make a place for him?

Diaz has followed two straight seasons over .300 (.304, .306) with two seasons in the .130s (.135, .136), which is certainly unique.

I'm inclined to think, on the basis of what little I know, that Diaz deserves a major league job. I'd rather start the season with Diaz as my shortstop than Howard Johnson, but he is 29 years old, has been in organized baseball more than a decade, and his chance of getting a regular job is roughly the same as your chance of getting a date with Kelly McGillis.

Rob DIBBLE, Cincinnati
Where does he rank among the game's top relievers? Should he be the Reds' closer?

Peter Gammons said over the winter that "one look at Rob Dibble's lifetime stats . . . and you'd rather have him right now than any reliever with the exception of Dennis Eckersley." I'm inclined to agree. Dibble has a career ERA of 1.90, one of the best ratios of strikeouts to innings in baseball history, if not the best, and good control. I'm not sure what else you would need to see, particularly if you watched the playoffs and World Series.

Myers is awfully good, too, but doesn't it seem to you that there are several advantages to sharing the "closer" job when you can?

1. Saves make stars. Saves are money. A pitcher with a 2.50 ERA and seven saves a season will earn $800,000 a year; a pitcher with the same ERA and thirty saves a year will earn $3 million a year. Whenever you take two people of roughly equal ability and make one of them a star and the other not a star, you've got a problem in the clubhouse. Maybe, if the guys are mature and/or get along well, it's not a big problem, but it's there. Dibble talks about leaving.
2. It keeps the pressure down. If you've got two closers you're in less danger of over-working one of them and blowing out his career.
3. You're less vulnerable in case there is an injury.
4. You're less vulnerable in case one pitcher has a slump, and not only for the obvious reason. If you have one ace reliever and he blows a couple of

games, everybody in the clubhouse is going to be looking over his shoulder until the situation is resolved. Having an ineffective closer is devastating to a team, because everybody knows it can blow you out of the pennant race as fast as anything. If you have one closer and he starts blowing leads and you have to switch him to another job, it's a big deal. It's in the newspapers. It's something to talk about in the clubhouse—did the manager wait too long to make the switch? Did he act too quickly?

But if you have *two* closers and one of them slumps, no big deal; you just start using the other one. You give the guy who is in a slump an opportunity to regain his confidence gracefully, with no need for controversy or discussion. In all likelihood, you give him a better chance to get headed in the right direction quickly.

5. If you have a lefty closer and a right-handed closer you can spot them and get the platoon advantage.

So anytime a team has two relievers of roughly the same ability, I'd rather split the saves between them, like Jim Leyland does. I'd split the saves between Brantley and Righetti. I think the team's stronger that way.

Lance DICKSON, Chicago
Is he going to be a star? Was he a good pick?

Dickson is a left-handed starting pitcher, medium size, pretty good fastball and terrific overhand curve. He struck out 141 men in 119 innings for the University of Arizona last summer, and became the Cubs' number one draft pick in June, 1990. He was sent to Geneva in the New York-Penn League, which brings up a question: why in the hell would you send a number one draft pick out of the University of Arizona to the NY-P League?

The correct answer, if you're curious,

is "because Jim Frey is a doofus." No, that's unfair, because even though Jim Frey certainly *is* a doofus, a lot of organizations do that. The White Sox did the same thing with Alex Fernandez, the Orioles with McDonald. It doesn't make any sense to me . . . what, you're trying to find out if he can pitch A ball? If you weren't pretty damn sure he could get out hitters in the NY-P League, you shouldn't have drafted him in the first round.

Anyway, Dickson gave up one run in three starts in Geneva (0.53 ERA, 15.4 strikeouts per nine innings), so they pulled him out and moved him . . . to another A league. They sent him to Peoria in the Midwest League, where he had a 1.51 ERA in five starts, and struck out 13.6 men per nine innings.

Well, that did it; the Cubs were convinced by now that he could pitch A ball. They sent him to Charlotte. AA.

The only thing this teaches him is packing and un-packing; send him to AAA and let him get on with his career. He'll figure out how to pack a suitcase sooner or later. In three starts at Charlotte he posted a 0.38 ERA, struck out 28 men and walked 3.

The Cubs brought him to the majors, but his arm was tired after striking out 250-some men for Arizona, Geneva, Peoria and Charlotte, and his vaunted overhand curve missed the plane.

How good is this kid? He's probably awfully good. I thought about marking him with stars, but didn't because:

1. He's a rookie, and rookie pitchers aren't often impact players,
2. He's got to pitch in Wrigley Field, and
3. I'm concerned about a twenty-year-old pitcher being worked as hard as Dickson was last year.

Still, if you've got a chance to get him in an APBA League or something, you'd better get him. He's got a chance to be Ron Guidry.

Frank DI PINO, St. Louis
Can he bounce back?

Of course he *can*, but I don't like the odds. He's been in the majors for ten years, and has had two good seasons, one pretty good. He's a left-handed spot reliever, and left-handers hit .293 against him last year.

Gary DiSARCINA, California
Can he play?

He's not even close. He hit .140 in eighteen games, and that's not far from his true level of ability. He might be a .220 hitter, but he's got a long way to go before he can hold a job.

John DOPSON, Boston
Will he come back?

Don't be drafting him, even if he pitches well in spring training. A guy who loses a whole season to an elbow problem is ordinarily going to take two or three years to get back up to speed. If he isn't a great pitcher to begin with, where does that leave you?

Bill DORAN, Reds
What's happened to him in recent years? Why did he slump off in the middle of his career, and why did he play so well last year?

Doran is a fine player, despite some ugly batting averages in recent years. It's very tough to hit in the Astrodome. Doran's not young—he's 33 in May—and when the Astros drifted out of contention he apparently got into a frustration cycle, based in his inability to achieve at the level of his expectations. My comment about him last year was "he'll bounce back, of course." No big deal; it wouldn't have mattered if he had hit .271 in 1989, rather than .219.

Is his injury in September going to slow him down in '91?

He had surgery to remove a herniated disc in his back. The doctors say he'll be ready for spring training, but I wouldn't want to bet the farm on it.

His age is probably as much a concern as his back, but remember, he's had the park working against his stats all of his career. Put him in another park, and he may yet have the best seasons of his life.

Brian DORSETT, Yankees
Is he ever going to get a chance? Would he succeed if he did?

Dorsett turns 30 in April and was released by the Yankees in December, so the odds are that he will never get a chance. He's not a bad hitter for a catcher—a better hitter than Geren, certainly. You'd think a third catcher who could pinch hit and put the ball in the seats once in awhile would be a useful player, a modern Aaron Robinson or Gene Oliver, but he was hurt by

1. the 24-man rule. He was a 25th-man type of player, and the 24-man roster gave an edge to a player who could play multiple positions, and
2. playing for the Yankees, who prefer high-salaried veterans to young players with something to prove.

I think he could have had a decent career, but I don't imagine we're going to find out now.

Richard DOTSON, Kansas City
Why did the Royals sign him?

It was a bizarre decision. The Royals offered two reasons for signing him:

1. "He's only 31 years old," and
2. "He's always pitched well in this park."

Weighing against these mighty considerations were the facts that

1. he was coming off of five consecutive bad seasons, and
2. any idiot could see that he couldn't pitch anymore.

Not to be too general or nothin', but *any* scout who filed a report on Richard Dotson which said *anything* other than "this sucker can't pitch" should be fired immediately. His best pitch was a change of pace, but *he had no fastball*.

The Royals traded Jose DeJesus to Philadelphia for Steve Jeltz, and to replace him took a chance on Richard Dotson. This, to me, is crystal clear evidence that the Royal front office had lost their direction, and changes had to be made. Good organizations still make many mistakes, because most decisions have both positives and negatives, and in the process of weighing them out the scales will inevitably tip the wrong way sometimes. But this decision had *no* valid positives to recommend it; it had *no* chance of working. The Royals made a decision, *as an organization*, which no one at the table should have advocated as an individual. If the Royals were still a good organization it could never have happened.

Brian DOWNING, California (released)
Why did the Angels release him? Can he still play?

Maybe I'm missing something, but the Angels' release of Downing seems to me to be a simple case of age discrimination. Downing last year, not having a particularly good year by his own standards, still drove in more runs per at bat than any other Angel except Dave Winfield, and scored about as many as he drove in. He hit for a decent average (.273) with power, and had a secondary average of .345.

Why do you release a player like that? I always thought the idea was that you got rid of the guys who *couldn't* play, not the ones who could. Dante Bichette and Lee Stevens will never be the hitters that Brian Downing is right now.

Kelly DOWNS, Giants
Can he come back from the injuries and pitch effectively?

I haven't seen him pitch since the injury. Many times a pitcher will adjust his pitching motion after a major injury to avoid a recurrence. Normally when this happens the post-injury pitcher won't have the same velocity, but may be just as effective because he has a better idea of what he's doing.

I think it's likely that Downs' chance of being an outstanding pitcher is gone forever. There is a good chance he can get back to being a 13-9 pitcher.

Doug DRABEK, Pittsburgh
Is he really that good?

I worked Drabek's arbitration case a year ago; real nice fella. Very bright.

When you do an arbitration case you break down the player's season inning by inning. Drabek's luck in 1989 was phenomenally bad. He had been stuck with a 14-12 won-lost record when he should have been about 18-10. Last year he pitched exactly as well as he had the year before—basically the same innings and ERA—but his luck evened out, and he wound up with a record somewhat better than he probably deserved, which was, again, about 18-10. He's an awfully good pitcher, but he's not likely to go 22-6 again anytime soon.

Did he deserve the Cy Young Award?

Sure. He pitched as well as Welch did, or better, and his competition was nowhere near as tough. Who else you going to give it to? Martinez was awesome, but Martinez had a higher ERA in Dodger Stadium—a pitcher's park—than Drabek did in Three Rivers, a hitter's park.

Jim Leyland could have started Drabek in the first game of the NL Playoffs, but did not do so, giving as his reason that Drabek is so methodical in preparing for a start that he did not want to interrupt his cycle by asking him to pitch on short rest. Did Leyland do the right thing, or should Drabek have started the first game of the series?

Well, you have to hand it to Leyland for doing what *he* thought was right and

the hell with all us second-guessers, but the decision itself doesn't make any sense to me. The Pirates won the division by four games, and it was pretty apparent that they were going to win certainly before Saturday, September 29, when Walk shut out St. Louis to put the Pirates four ahead with four to play. You're telling me that there's no way you can pull Drabek after five innings and bring him back a day early?

Gene Mauch was criticized after 1964, excessively criticized, for jumping his rotation to bring back Jim Bunning early, but this seems to me to be the polar extreme, and equally absurd: a superstitious refusal to nudge the starting rotation just a little bit to let your best pitcher open the playoffs. I can't see what you gain that could possibly be equal to the loss.

Tom DREES, Chicago
Who is he?

He's the guy who pitched three no-hitters for the White Sox' AAA team in 1989, including two in a row. Despite the no-hitters he wasn't considered a hot prospect then, and isn't now; it was apparently just a fluke thing. His hits/innings ratio isn't even all that great.

Drees is a six-foot-six left-hander, has pitched well in the minors for several years (last year he was 8-5, 3.98 ERA in the Pacific Coast League.) He doesn't have a great fastball or a trick pitch or anything, and doesn't strike out a lot of people. I still think if he's healthy (I'm not sure that he is) he ought to get a chance. I believe in a simple program: if you succeed at one level, you deserve a shot at the next level. I think whenever you get away from that, and start trying to figure the angles on who's going to adapt as he moves up, you're in real danger of outsmarting yourself, exactly as the Royals and Blue Jays did with Cecil Fielder. Drees has nothing left to prove at Vancouver, so why not find out if he can get people out in the majors?

Kirk DRESSENDORFER, Oakland
Who is he?

He's the latest stud from the University of Texas pitching farm, which has produced Clemens and Swindell, among others. He's small for a power pitcher (5-11, 180) and doesn't impress the radar guns, but had a fine college career and has started well in pro ball. The A's used one of their #1 draft picks on him. He could be in the majors this year. Great K/W ratios.

Cameron DREW, Houston
How's he coming along? Is he still a prospect?

Drew has had two operations to repair an elongated tendon in his left knee, apparently an old basketball injury. He is not able to run without pain, and hasn't played in two years. He played a few games in the Instructional League, and will report to spring training to try to make a comeback.

Tim DRUMMOND, Minnesota
Can he pitch? Will he be around? Will he move up?

You may remember Drummond as the guy who let fly a fastball at Mel Hall's head last May 23. Hall hit a home run in the second inning, and did a slow dance around the bases; Drummond knocked him down and precipitated a classic baseball "brawl"—lots of mad looks, no punches. Drummond likes to pitch inside, and at the time he appeared to be in a fair way toward acquiring a reputation as a head hunter, but there were no more incidents.

Drummond is about a Grade D prospect. He was a twelfth-round draft pick in 1983, got the hell beat out of him for a couple of years in the Sally League as a starting pitcher and converted to relief. He began picking his way through the minors like a broken-field runner, was shifted to the Mets system in the Mackey Sasser/Randy Milligan trade and then to the Twins in the Viola deal. He's 26; his park and his team will work against him. The odds are that he will never be a successful major league pitcher.

Brian DuBOIS, Detroit
Will he be back in the majors this year? Does he have a future?

He does have a future, yes; he's a strong Grade C prospect or a weak Grade B prospect. He's a left-hander with reasonably good stuff and reasonably good control. DuBois has pitched very well in the minors for the last three years, and has a 3.82 ERA through 16 major league starts, despite an ugly won-lost record. He should pitch 180 innings in the majors this year, and he should be alright.

Rob DUCEY, Toronto
Will he ever break through? Isn't he older than Claudell Washington?

No, but he is older than Sil Campusano. He turns 26 in May; we've been hearing about him since he was 21.

The Blue Jays won't return any of their starting outfielders. They traded Junior Felix, let George Bell walk away and won't play Mookie Wilson. Even so, Ducey has competition. The Blue Jays now have two regular outfielders (Joe Carter and Devon White) and several candidates for the third job (Glenallen Hill, Derek Bell and Mark Whiten as well as Ducey. That's assuming Olerud plays first.)

Three years ago I thought Ducey could be a star. His chance of being a star has probably evaporated, but he should be in the majors in 1991.

Mariano DUNCAN, Cincinnati
What was behind the big improvement last year?

Duncan's exceptional 1990 season can be attributed to three things—

1. Fired up by the trade from LA, he worked hard during the winter and arrived at the shortened spring training ready to go.
2. He was 27 years old, the age at which players often have their best seasons, and
3. He quit switch hitting.

I've been writing for years that Duncan was screwing up his career by switch hitting. He has always been a terrific hitter against left-handed pitching. In 1985 (his rookie year) he hit .286 and slugged .419 against left-handed pitching, but hit .224 with no power against right-handers. In 1986 he hit .260 against left-handers, .205 against right-handers. In 1987 he hit .275 against left-handers, .182 against right-handers. In 1988 he was in the minors, but in 1989 he hit .283, slugging .465 against left-handers, but .226 against right-handers.

Presumably, the reason that one switch hits is to eliminate the platoon differential, right? But if you're switch hitting and your platoon differential is three times as large as normal, then why do it?

Duncan still didn't hit right-handers well last year (.226), but led the majors in batting against left-handers, .410. He did show greatly improved power against right-handers, and if he'll stay with it the platoon differential will smooth out over the years.

Can he hit .300 again next year? Probably not, but he should remain a good player. He's always had the ability; he just couldn't get things going in the right direction. He had some health problems last year, was in an accident in a taxi and was suspended for a game for spreading rumors about an umpire or something. Duncan had never played second base for a full season before last year, and he still has a good deal to learn about the position. His ratio of double plays to errors was the lowest in the major leagues (the three lowest were Duncan, Jefferies and Samuel.) Another problem for Duncan is that it doesn't appear that Lou Piniella has much confidence in him. Piniella left Duncan hitting eighth all year even though Duncan hit .306. Often he hit seventh or eighth even against left-handers. The Reds replaced him with Bill Doran in the stretch run and then re-signed Doran. Duncan may be forced back into a utility role this year.

Mike DUNNE, San Diego
Are we ever going to hear from him again? What happened to him after his good year?

He'll never get it back. He was working at his limits in 1987–1988, and you can't do that over a period of years.

Shawon DUNSTON, Chicago Cubs
Where does he rank? Is he one of the best shortstops in baseball? What's the proper offensive role for him?

1. Dunston's power totals have *not* been inflated by playing in Wrigley, that one can tell. He has only one more home run at home than on the road (31-30).
2. Barry Larkin is obviously the best shortstop in the NL, and despite his off season I would stick with Ozzie Smith as the second best. Ozzie's on-base percentage last year was still almost fifty points higher than Dunston's.

   Beyond that, the best shortstops in the NL are Dunston and Spike Owen, and Dunston has to rate the edge. Three other NL shortstops are OK (Thon, Uribe and Bell), and five National League teams have shortstop problems or unproven shortstops (the Mets, Braves, Astros, Padres and Dodgers. Actually, Blauser's a good player but we don't know for sure that the Braves won't decide to see if they can get another bad year out of Andres Thomas.)
3. The problem with Dunston is that he really has no offensive role. With his very low on-base percentages he can't lead off, despite his speed and base

stealing skills, which are very good. With his strikeouts you don't want him hitting second, and while he is a good hitter for a shortstop, he doesn't hit enough to hit 3-4-5 ahead of Dawson, Sandberg, Grace, Bell, et al. He's just a very good hitter for a guy somewhere at the bottom of the order.

4. Dunston had the worst strikeout/walk ratio in the majors last year, among players with 400 or more plate appearances. The bottom five: Dunston, Cory Snyder, Sammy Sosa, Roberto Kelly and Jim Presley.

Jim DWYER, Minnesota
Why did he last so long? How can a guy who is never a regular last until he is 40 years old? Is there any precedent for this?

There are other examples of bit players lasting until they were 40, but they're rare—Johnny Cooney, Dave Philley. Dwyer was a good player who could have been a regular in his best years, but things just never broke right for him. He got his degree before he came into baseball, then spent several years bouncing up and down in the Cardinals' system when he probably should have been playing. He hit .387 in 87 games at Tulsa (American Association) in 1973, .336 there in '74 and .404 in 33 games in '75, indicating he was distinctly too good for the American Association.

But he couldn't get hot in the major leagues, and the Cardinals wouldn't let him play through his struggles. The Cardinals at that time were a confused organization, and did exactly the same thing at the same time to another young outfielder, Jose Cruz, who later proved that he could play. Dwyer couldn't break through it until he was almost thirty, and then never could land a regular job.

Lenny DYKSTRA, Philadelphia
Is he for real, or was this a fluke?
He was 27 last year . . . We shouldn't expect him to retreat to .237, because that was just a one-year abberation, but I don't expect him to stay at .325, either. I expect him to hit somewhere between .270 and .310, with a good strikeout/walk ratio and good stolen base percentage.

Dykstra last year hit .427 with men in scoring position, the best such average in the majors by 45 points (Dave Magadan was at .382.) He also hit .361 in the late innings of close games, sixth-best in the league. (He was 47/110 with men in scoring position, 30/83 in the late innings of close games.) Dykstra also had the second-best strikeout/walk ratio in the majors, behind Tony Gwynn.

•E•

Gary EAVE, San Francisco
Can he pitch? Why would Atlanta give up on a pitcher who had a 1.31 ERA in three starts?

Since when did the Atlanta Braves ever know what they were doing? Eave did nothing much from 1985 until 1989, when he went 13-3 at Richmond, was called up by Atlanta, started three times and went 2-0 with a 1.31 ERA.

The Braves, obviously impressed, shipped him to Seattle in the Jim Presley trade. The Mariners gave him a few games, but he was wild and they sent him down in May. He wound up the year in the Giants' system, pitching badly and walking seven men a game. I don't know what happened to him; he has major league stuff but at 26 he'd better find home plate pretty quick if he's going to have a career.

Dennis ECKERSLEY, Oakland
Is he the most effective reliever ever? Should he have won the Cy Young Award? Does he have a chance to go into the Hall of Fame? Can he pitch at this level again next season?

1. I think he is the most effective reliever ever. Rollie Fingers won the MVP Award in '81 because he gave up only nine runs all year—1.04 ERA, 61/8 strikeout/walk ratio—but even that pales beside what Eckersley has done the last three and a half years.
2. I would probably have listed him first on my Cy Young ballot. His chances were dead when Thigpen pulled away from him in the save column and Bob Welch was credited with 27 wins.

How many games would Welch have won if Eckersley had been ordinary? Over 20, surely, but probably not enough to win the Cy Young Award. I don't think that value inheres in the position one occupies, but in one's own performance. Eckersley didn't have as many save opportunities as Thigpen because he had a brief injury and the A's didn't play as many close games, but I still think he was the best pitcher.

3. Eckersley will be an interesting Hall of Fame debate because he has split his career between starting and relief roles. He was a good starter but didn't do a lot that would be characteristic of a Hall of Famer. He has awesome stats as a reliever, but no one really knows how those stats will look twenty years from now, when fifty-save seasons may be commonplace. His career totals are not impressive because of the divided role.

I think for Eckersley to get in the Hall of Fame, it is important for him to win a Cy Young Award or an MVP Award. Right now, I don't think he'd go in the Hall of Fame. If he has three more seasons like the last three and wins a major award, I think he definitely will go in. Anywhere between those two markers—between *three* more great seasons and no more great seasons—and he'll be in a gray area.

4. Can he pitch at this level again . . . if you mean will he have an 0.61 ERA again, the answer is of course not, don't be silly. If you mean will he continue to pitch at the level of the last three and half years, which is impressive enough, the answer is that he probably will.

Tom EDENS, Milwaukee
What does Milwaukee have here, anything? A starter? A reliever? Would they know a pitcher if they saw one?

They don't have anything; he's just a roster filler. And no, they wouldn't know a pitcher if they saw one.

Wayne EDWARDS, Chicago White Sox
Who is he? Can he move up?

A left-handed starter in the minor leagues, Edwards was the surprise of the camp for the White Sox, skipped AAA and made the majors as a reliever. He'll never be a star, a starter or a closer, but he'll probably be around for years and years and post generally good ERAs. Big, gangly guy.

Mark EICHHORN, Atlanta
Is his comeback for real? Why is he so inconsistent? Will he ever be consistent?

When he was effective with Toronto his workload was immense—69 games, 157 innings in 1986, 89 games, 128 innings in 1987. I associate his poor performances in 1988–89 with his excessive workload in those two seasons. Relief pitchers used to pitch that much, but then, relief pitchers used to bounce up and down like the price of oil, too. I think as long as they keep him within reasonable limits, he'll be consistently effective.

Dave EILAND, New York Yankees
Is he ready to help the Yankees? Can he pitch? Can he be a rotation starter?

Eiland has earned a chance to start in the major leagues. He proved last year that he's way too good for Columbus (16-5, 2.87 ERA), and really, he should have been in the majors last year, since

a. the Yankee starting rotation was dog meat, and
b. Eiland was 9-4 at Columbus in '89.

Let's use the "reasonable man" standard here, like they do in court. If your major league pitchers are getting hammered, and you have a young pitcher who is winning seventy percent of his decisions at AAA, what does a reasonable man do?

No, I don't think he'll be great. He's a control pitcher, and I usually figure that

a. a control pitcher takes a little longer to find himself in the major leagues, and
b. a control pitcher needs a good defense behind him more than a power pitcher does.

I figure that it will probably take a couple of years for Eiland to be consistently effective in the major leagues. But let's get on with it, OK?

Jim EISENREICH, Kansas City Royals
Why was he off his game last year? Why did his stolen base percentage go to hell in a handbasket? How good is he?

He wasn't nearly as good last year as he was the year before, despite comparable stats. His stolen base percentage dropped from 77% (27/35) to 46% (12/26) primarily because he was running into pitchouts a lot. I don't know if he was tipping something or if it was just bad luck, but I think he ran into a pitchout about seven times, which ruined his percentage.

He's a good player, rarely makes mistakes in the outfield. The media always says that he is the Royals' best defensive outfielder, and I guess he is, but he doesn't have a right fielder's arm.

Kevin ELSTER, Mets
Should he be a regular? Should the Mets find somebody else to play shortstop?

Let's start with this fact: he's got a .219 lifetime batting average.

Q. *Is that all he's going to hit?*
A. He could hit better for a season, but that's based on twelve hundred at bats, which is a fair trial.
Q. *Is it a* productive .219.
A. No. He has neither power nor speed.
Q. *Is he Ozzie Smith on defense?*

A. No.

Q. *Then why would he be a regular? Because you like him? Because you thought he was going to be better than this? Why?*

Elster had arthroscopic surgery on his shoulder in August, so he may not be ready to play in April, anyway. But even if he is, the Mets have got to stop kidding themselves about him.

Narciso ELVIRA, Milwaukee
Who is he? Can he pitch? Is that a name, or what?

He's a very young left-hander who has been blowing people away in the low minors, but has yet to put in a full season at AA. He should start the season in AAA, and it's simply too early to tell whether he is going to be good, great or nothing.

Luis ENCARNACION, Kansas City
Who is he?

He's the Rodney Dangerfield of the Royals' organization. Encarnacion is a small right-handed pitcher, marginal fastball, but he has pitched well in AA and AAA since 1986. You'd think sooner or later he'd get The Call.

Jim EPPARD, Angels
Can he play? Is there a place for him in the major leagues?

There isn't a great demand for first basemen who hit singles. Eppard's lifetime major league average is .281, which probably is about his ability. There is probably a job for him somewhere as a pinch hitter/DH.

Scott ERICKSON, Minnesota
Is he really that good? Should we expect him to be one of the top starting pitchers in the league this year?

First the basics; Erickson is a 23-year-old starting pitcher, a fourth-round draft pick in 1989 who stomped through the minors in 27 easy starts. Coming to the majors in mid-season, he was brilliant—an 8-4 record, 2.87 ERA.

That provides a basis for optimism among Twins fans, who naturally project for him a great career. Now the bad news:

1. He's park negative, meaning that he is pitching in a hitter's park.
2. He is team negative, meaning that he is pitching for a team that isn't likely to win anything.
3. He's on the "Robinson list", the list of pitchers who were probably over their heads last year, based on a ratio of 6.6 strikeouts per win.

Last year he had 53 strikeouts and 51 walks. How many successful starting pitchers can you name who have that ratio, over a period of years.

We don't want to be *overly* negative. His strikeout rate will probably go up this year (it normally does for a second-year pitcher) and his control record will probably improve. If he's less effective in '91 than he was in '90, what does that mean? That he's 15-12 with a 3.44 ERA? That's still pretty good. But do I project him as a top pitcher, the answer is no.

Nick ESASKY, Atlanta
Can he come back?

In December, when I'm writing this, there is no change in his condition. He is still, as of now, suffering from vertigo. If he does not recover by mid-season it will be unlikely that he will be able to hit when he does regain his health.

Alvaro ESPINOZA, Yankees
Should he be playing regularly?

We all like to say that at shortstop the number one thing is defense, but Espinoza tests the limits of the theory. He's a good shortstop but with the bat he's a joke. He played 150 games last year, scored 31 runs and drove in 20. He created fewer runs per out used than any other major league player batting 400 or more times.

My theory is that everything counts. If he's forty runs worse at bat than another shortstop, those forty runs cost you just as much as if you lost them at first base or left field or on the mound. And that's *too much* offense to give up to get a glove in the lineup. It's OK to have one-way players in the lineup if you're trying to play .500 ball, if you're just trying to stay in the league. But if you're trying to win the pennant, you can't do it with one-dimensional players.

Notes: Espinoza was also the only major league player with a secondary average below .100. The bottom ten were Espinoza (.091), Felix Fermin (.118), Alfredo Griffin (.119), Joe Girardi (.134), Jose Uribe (.137), Ozzie Guillen (.138), Johnny Ray (.146), Rafael Ramirez (.146), Charlie Hayes (.146) and Don Mattingly (.152).

Cecil ESPY, Rangers
Is he going to be around?

Probably not. All he gives a team is outfield defense, and that's not enough. He's not a good enough base runner to be a full-time pinch runner, even if he could find a manager who liked to keep a pinch runner around.

Dwight EVANS, Baltimore
Did the Red Sox act prematurely in releasing him? Is he finished?

The Boston Red Sox in 1990 said goodbye to two players who stood near the top of the lists of active totals, the one in an improbable triumph of determination over logic, and the other one of the game's unappreciated stars.

Bill Buckner, the major league career leader in games played, opened the season as Boston's platoon first baseman, but quickly lost his footing and was released at the end of April. Dwight Evans, the leader in runs scored and home runs, was troubled by an unruly back, and was notified at season's end that the Sox would not exercise his option.

The two players in many ways are diametric opposites:

Evans is right-handed, Buckner left-handed.

Evans leads active players in career strikeouts; Buckner struck out less often than any other active player.

Evans leads active players in career walks by a margin of more than two hundred; Buckner rarely walked.

Buckner was a high-average, line drive hitter; Evans was a fly ball hitter who didn't hit for a high average.

Evans played a position in the middle of the defensive spectrum, right field, and played it exceptionally well; Buckner played the defensive position where they put you when you can't run or throw, and was a below-average defensive player at that position.

Buckner, though thought of as a slow runner, stole 183 bases in his career, with a good stolen base percentage. Evans, though he ran better, stole less than half as many bases with a poor stolen base percentage.

In the last weeks of the 1985 season I heard an announcer say that "Bill Buckner virtually defines a tough out." Yes, and defines it frequently; Buckner made 505 outs that year, more than any other major league player. It always seemed so strange to me that a man who made so many outs would be thought of as a tough out, simply because he hit .299 and rarely struck out.

Evans, on the other hand, was a textbook illustration of an under-rated player: a good defensive player with a low batting average but a high secondary average. Because people look first at a player's batting average, a player who doesn't hit for a high average will never be a big star. But *if* he plays defense *and* does the other things that put runs on the scoreboard, he can contribute more to his team than the people who are stars.

In their careers they played in almost the same number of games (within one percent) and had almost the same number of plate appearances (within two percent). It makes for an easy offensive comparison: who drove in and scored more runs?

Evans, by far. Although Buckner hit for a higher average, Evans scored several hundred more runs, 33% more, and drove in more than a hundred runs more than did Buckner. Buckner made 841 more outs than Evans.

Buckner's career, I think, outlasted his abilities by about five years. Even by 1986, when he still drove in 102 runs, he was a pretty bad player.

And Evans career was hustled toward a premature end by a Sox front office which never regarded Evans as a star, and saw no point in seeing if he could surprise us once more. Evans scored more runs per game played last year than Greenwell, Jody Reed, Quintana, Brunansky, Pena or Rivera—six of the Sox' regulars. He drove in more runs per game than Boggs, Greenwell, Reed, Quintana, Pena or Rivera. He was way ahead of Mike Marshall in both areas—yet they didn't want him back. Think about it: they brought back Bill Buckner after he hit .216 for Kansas City and scored seven runs in an entire season. They didn't bring back Evans after he hit .249 and scored 66 runs. Why?

Will Evans help Baltimore?

Correctly used, as a right-handed platoon left fielder and DH, he should be a valuable player. If he gets out of his role he'll struggle.

Note: Evans has created more runs in his career than any active player except Brett and Winfield.

•F•

Paul FARIES, San Diego
Who is he?

Faries is a second baseman, obviously ready to play in the majors at the age of 26 and after hitting .312 at Las Vegas (AAA) with 48 stolen bases, 109 runs scored. My estimate is that as a major league player he would hit around .260, no power but some walks and some stolen bases.

Even with the Alomar trade, it will be hard for the Padres to get Faries in the majors. He is still behind Bip Roberts, if Roberts is at second, and Joey Cora. He can play, though.

Howard FARMER, Montreal
What happened to him? Is he going to make the Expos this year?

He just wasn't ready. Farmer started 1990 in the majors with almost no AAA experience. He should do better in his second try, but the Expos are hip-deep in starting pitchers.

Steve FARR, New York Yankees
How good is he? Will he help the Yankees?

Probably not. Farr lives on the edge. If everything is right for him, he generates outs; if something's not right, he has to be protected.

The Yankees have never shown themselves to be the kind of organization that could use a pitcher carefully—not in the last twenty-five years, anyway. Farr is 34. He could help the Yankees, but he's also got a good chance to be the next Ed Whitson/Doyle Alexander/Pascual Perez.

Will his departure hurt the Royals?

It is said in football that if the secondary is leading your team in tackles you've got a problem. Steve Farr, who was basically a garbageman, was the Royals' pitcher of the year in 1990, which is a fine tribute to him but, in the same way, surely not a good sign for the pitching staff.

Farr has developed into a deceptively good pitcher, and it is somewhat difficult to understand why the Royals considered his salary with the Yankees—reportedly $2.1 million a year—beyond their salary structure. Farr has pitched very well in five of the last six seasons. In 1988 he had 20 saves and a 2.50 ERA. In 1990 he was 13-7 with a 1.98 ERA in 127 innings, and held opponents to a .157 batting average with men in scoring position. In 1989 he had a 4.12 ERA, but that's misleading because he tried to pitch through some shoulder trouble; with the exception of one six-week period, he pitched probably the best ball of his career in 1989. I don't really understand why, if Mark Davis is worth $3.25 M and Mike Boddicker is worth $2.9 M, Farr isn't worth $2.1.

Maybe this is stating the obvious, but if the Royals' pitching is solid in '91, Farr will never be missed. For six years, Steve Farr has been the man who picked up the pieces of the puzzle that dropped under the table.

John FARRELL, Cleveland
What's his status? Will he be back?

He is expected to miss most of the 1991 season following elbow surgery.

Monty FARRISS, Texas
Who is he?

The Rangers first-round draft pick in 1988, a shortstop who is considering a switch to second or third. Actually, he probably should have moved a year ago, but he wanted to play short and the Rangers are so desperate for a shortstop that they were agreeable.

He can hit, I'll tell you that. He'll hit like Sabo or Toby Harrah, maybe better. Once he finds his position and spots an opening he'll be in the majors to stay.

Mike FELDER, Brewers
Can he play? Should he be a regular?

He's not a regular, no, because he's not enough of a hitter. Even if he were to hit .274, which he did last year, he'd be marginal. He's one of the better fourth outfielders in the American League because of his speed, defense and ability to make contact.

Junior FELIX, California
Who won the trade?

When Mike Kopf told me that the Blue Jays had traded Junior Felix for Devon White, I thought he was joking. Come on, I told him, the Blue Jays aren't that stupid.

As I see them, Junior Felix and Devon White are not players of comparable value—not remotely comparable value. Felix should be a star and could be a super-star. White is one of those guys with a world of ability who is a continual disappointment.

Felix was a good player last year at the age of 22. White was a marginal player at the age of 27. How do you make that trade?

I have a computer program which projects career stats on the basis of what the player has done in the past. The program estimates that Junior Felix will play more than 2,000 games in the rest of his career with more than 2,000 hits, a .266 batting average, more than 1200 runs scored, more than 1000 RBI, 237 home runs, 298 stolen bases and 355 doubles.

It estimates that Devon White will play 1,020 games in the rest of his career—less than half as many—with a .237 batting average, 85 homers, 177 stolen bases, and less than forty percent as many runs scored and RBI.

Wait a minute—it gets worse. There were two minor players involved in the trade—Luis Sojo and Willie Fraser. Sojo, the man given up by the Blue Jays, is obviously worth far more than Fraser—in fact, I would be willing to bet that Sojo

will do more for the Angels in '91 than Devon White did in '90.

More puzzling yet, the Blue Jays have always been an outstanding organization which did a good job of evaluating talent. The Angels have always been a bunch of clowns who have won a few times by spending a lot of money and hiring Gene Mauch.

How does this happen? How does a good organization make such an amazing decision?

Let's try to reconstruct the Blue Jays' logic:

1. Devon White has struggled with the bat, but he is still a fine defensive center fielder, maybe the best in baseball.
2. White will probably have a much better year in 1991 than he has had the last few years.
3. Yes, there is a talent sacrifice, but we (the Blue Jays) have lots of talent. We had lots of talent last year and the year before, but we didn't win.
4. We have to stop concentrating on getting as much talent as possible, and start worrying about improving the clubhouse chemistry, and pounding the talent into the shape of a ballclub.
5. Felix is a better hitter than White, but we'll score enough runs anyway. We have plenty of good hitters.
6. Felix has the raw ability to play center field—the speed and the arm—but we can't afford to be training him in midseason. If we put Felix in center field, his mistakes of inexperience could cost us several games early in the year, and that could cost us the pennant race. Where we are right now, we can't afford that. We've got to turn this talent into a pennant-winning team.
7. Felix may play for the next twelve years, but we have other outfielders. We have Olerud and Whiten and Glenallen Hill and Rob Ducey. We've always been able to come up with young outfielders.
8. Yes, Sojo is a valuable player, but we

have had multiple second basemen for several years, and it's just led to confusion and uncertainty. First we had Garcia and Sharperson, then we had Sharperson and Liriano, then we had Liriano and Manny Lee, then we had Manny Lee and Sojo. Maybe it's time we stopped worrying about having multiple middle infielders, and started concentrating on finding the best ones we have.

Individually, I agree with all of these points except number Five. I don't believe in saying that "we have enough hitting" because what you're saying is that the difference between what Felix hits and what White hits doesn't count. It damn well *does* count, even if you have other hitters, but that's a minor thing. Seven of the eight logical points which support the trade are correct as I see them. Devon White certainly could win the Blue Jays the pennant in '91.

But do these eight points add up to the conclusion that the trade has to be made? Not in my book they don't Why? Because the talent gap is just too wide. Felix is *too much* more valuable than White.

For years, the Blue Jays have been criticized for not making trades to round out the ballclub.

They make a few more trades like this, and Toronto will be begging them to stop.

Felix FERMIN, Cleveland
Should he be a regular? Can he help a team win a championship?

Despite a batting average around .250, Fermin is one of the least-productive regulars in the majors at bat, because he makes no other offensive contribution. Considering his defense and the fact that a lot of shortstops don't hit much, he's not the worst shortstop around. He probably ranks about 18th among the 26 regular shortstops—probably not good enough to play regularly for

a championship team, but probably not bad enough to replace. Mark Lewis will take the Cleveland shortstop job before long.

Alex FERNANDEZ, Chicago White Sox
How do you assess his star potential? Was he rushed too fast?

Fernandez was pretty good in the American League last year (5-5, 3.80 ERA) and it was generally agreed that he was tired after starting his season in February. The only question mark I see about him is whether the White Sox will work him too hard before his arm is mature, and destroy him in the long run. If they can avoid doing that, he should have a hell of a career.

Sid FERNANDEZ, New York Mets
Will he come back? Why didn't he win last year?

You always have to wonder about Fernandez' weight, and there is a natural tendency to associate his off season with that. I doubt that there is any real connection. He struck out 181 men in 179 innings last year, and had a 3.46 ERA. The reason he was 9-14 was simply that the Mets didn't score many runs for him.

Two things to remember if he is traded:

1. Shea Stadium is a strikeout park; he won't strike out as many somewhere else, and
2. The pitcher's record embodies the performance of his team. If the team doesn't play well, it's the pitcher's record that suffers—not only wins and losses, but hits, runs and everything else.

If he is still with the Mets in April, I'd put him on my draft list. He's still as good a pitcher as he was two years ago.

Sid may also be *helped* by the switch of McReynolds to center, if that occurs. Fernandez works almost entirely *up* in the

strike zone, and consequently gets fewer ground balls and more pop outs and fly outs than any other major league pitcher. (There were only four double plays turned behind him all last year, the fewest of any major league pitcher with 162 innings. His groundball-to-flyball ratio was also the lowest.) As a side-arming left-hander he faces almost entirely right-handed hitters, which means a lot of fly balls to left field. He can use Vince Coleman out there.

Notes: Fernandez held hitters to a .200 batting average last year, the lowest in the league. Although a left-handed pitcher he held right-handers to a .194 mark, also the best in the league . . . Fernandez is among five Mets who are under orders from Bud Harrelson to lose weight over the winter.

Tony FERNANDEZ, San Diego
Was he the best shortstop in the American League?

Trammell was the best last year, but Fernandez is the guy that I would most want to open the season with. The American League shortstops are a desultory lot—Ripken, Trammell, Guillen and Fernandez are really the only good ones. Trammell is 33, Ripken hasn't been Ripken since 1986, and Guillen is a good player but Fernandez is better.

Will he help San Diego?

Maybe. Garry Templeton was angry when the Fernandez trade was announced, saying that he had been stabbed in the back by the Padre management. I'd never before really heard of the idea that a player is entitled to keep his position, regardless of how he plays.

The Padres should have given Templeton the knife about five years ago, but is there not a certain irony in replacing Templeton with Fernandez? Look at them:

• Both players are switch hitters.
• Both are shortstops.

- Fernandez has tremendous range. So did Templeton when he was young.
- Fernandez at 24 set the major league record for hits by a shortstop, 213. Templeton at 23 became the first major league player to get 100 hits in a season left-handed and 100 right-handed. If you compare those two seasons you'll see they are strikingly similar.
- After a brilliant start Templeton stopped hitting, dropping gradually to the .250 range or below. Fernandez in the last two seasons has hit .257 and .276.
- Whitey Herzog said of Templeton that "when it's hot he doesn't want to play because it's too hot. When it's cold he doesn't want to play because it's too cold." Tony Fernandez doesn't have the same reputation, but at a game in Kansas City (August 11, 1989), Bret Saberhagen was at the top of his form, tying the Blue Jay hitters in knots. Fernandez went oh-for-three (I think it was three strikeouts) and then refused to come out and face Saberhagen the fourth time, saying that the way he was going he couldn't do the team any good anyway.
- To get Templeton the Padres traded a Hall of Famer, Ozzie Smith. To get Fernandez they may have traded another one, Roberto Alomar.

Mike FETTERS, Angels
Who or what is Mike Fetters?

Right-handed pitching prospect, Grade C prospect. He was a number 1 draft pick in '86, led the PCL in strikeouts in '89. Never outstanding in the minor leagues, but methodically pretty good with a good health record.

Cecil FIELDER, Detroit
Is he really this good? If he is, why didn't anybody realize it before? Should he have won the MVP Award?

As to whether we should expect him to hit fifty homers regularly, the answer

is that of course we should not, since none of the other people who have hit fifty homers have been able to do it consistently.

As to whether we would expect him to hit *forty* homers consistently, my answer is that I think he will if he stays healthy. Before last year he had 506 career at bats with 31 home runs, a rate of 35 home runs/season if he is a regular.

Why didn't anybody realize it before?

Primarily because major league organizations pay too much attention to their scouts, and too little attention to how players produce. Fielder was signed by the Royals in 1982, and in half a season at Butte in '82 he hit .322 with 28 doubles, 20 home runs and 68 RBI in 69 games. The Royals traded him to Toronto for Leon Roberts because they thought he wasn't very good defensively and would put on weight. The Blue Jays had a McCovey/Cepeda problem with both Fielder and McGriff, and they chose McGriff. The two players are exactly the same age, within a few weeks.

Should he have won the MVP Award?

No way. The argument for Fielder as the MVP is, simply stated, that playing for a championship team shouldn't matter, in that it's not Cecil Fielder's fault that the Tigers have no pitching. I will agree with this up to a point. I think contributing to a championship team should be considered because the idea of the game is to win, not to compile impressive individual stats. I don't think it should be given great weight, because I don't think any one player has a great impact on the performance of the team.

But the argument fails because there is no way in hell that Cecil Fielder, as an individual, was as valuable as Rickey Henderson as an individual. Henderson created an estimated 137 runs by his individual accomplishments; Fielder created

128. Fielder created 128 runs while making 435 outs; Henderson created 137 runs while making 457 outs. Henderson did this while playing in the Oakland Coliseum, one of the toughest parks for a hitter in baseball. Fielder played in Tiger Stadium, a hitter's park. Henderson has far more defensive value than Fielder.

Fielder had 51 home runs, but Henderson also hit 28. That's a difference of 23 homers. Henderson out-hit Fielder by almost fifty points (.325-.277), hit more doubles and more triples, drew more walks, struck out less than one-third as many times, grounded into fewer double plays and beat him in stolen bases 65 to nothing. You add it all up, and it's obvious that Henderson's package of accomplishments is bigger than Fielder's.

Another argument for Fielder is that he had a disadvantage of context in not having great hitters around him. A basic problem with this one is that the Tigers actually scored more runs than the A's did, 750-733.

Note: There were four major league players last year who averaged at least two bases per hit, Fielder leading the four at 2.13 bases/hit. In many seasons there aren't any such players. The four were Fielder, McGwire, Rob Deer and Jack Clark.

Tom FILER, Milwaukee
Will he ever land a job? What happened to him last year, after he had pitched so well in '89?

The same thing that happened to Jeff Ballard and Allan Anderson, only at a lower level. Filer turned 34 in December; the odds are that he will never pitch again in the major leagues.

Pete FILSON, Kansas City
Why's he still around?

He isn't. His career ended with rotator cuff surgery late last summer. He's signed for 1991 as a minor league pitching coach.

Chuck FINLEY, California
Where does he rank? Is he the best left-handed starter in the American League?

Finley is not only the best left-handed starting pitcher in the American League, but the only candidate for that distinction. All of the other guys who could have been ranked first either have slipped a notch (Langston, Higuera, Jimmie Key), been traded to the National League (Viola) or both (Danny Jackson).

Finley over the last two seasons has the best ERA of any major league starting pitcher (2.48). Hershiser is at 2.49.

Steve FINLEY, Baltimore
What's his future? Is he on the way up?

He's on the way up, but this train ain't bound for glory. He could be a .300 hitter, but

a. every year he doesn't do it makes it less likely that he will, and
b. even if he hit .300, he wouldn't be anything special.

If he hits .250 again this year, it will be time for the Orioles to give up on him. If he hits .275, .280 he's OK in center field because of his speed and defense, but even then he's not any kind of any offensive player.

Brian FISHER, Pittsburgh
What happened to him?

He got greedy with the medical help. In the off-season 1988–89 he had arthroscopic surgery on his left knee *and* his right shoulder (it's because of people like him that a national health program will never work.) He had a 6.80 ERA with Tucson last year, which probably indicates that his recovery is not yet complete.

Carlton FISK, Chicago
Can he go on forever?

When a player exceeds the normal parameters of performance it becomes al-

most impossible to predict by *how much* he will exceed the normal parameters. Fisk last year, at 42, was well over his lifetime batting average (.285; his lifetime average is .272), still hits with power and although he is certainly slow still swiped seven bases in nine attempts, and grounded into only twelve double plays.

I really have no idea how much longer he'll last, but let's assume that he'll start losing ten points a year off his batting average. He could last four more years as a regular, if he did that, and then a couple more years as a bench player. There is no precedent for a 47-year-old catcher playing a hundred games, but then, there is no precedent for a 42-year-old catcher hitting .285 with 18 homers, either. My guess is he'll last until his next major injury.

Is he still the best catcher in baseball?

He probably is, yes, or was in 1990. He created more runs than any other catcher, and more runs per out than any other catcher except Don Slaught, who isn't *really* a .300 hitter and isn't a match for Fisk defensively.

Mike FITZGERALD, Expos
How good is he? Is he a championship quality catcher?

He's bad. He drives in forty runs a year as a half-time player, plays good defense. He's not going to carry a team to a championship, but a lot of teams have won the World Series with worse catchers than Fitzgerald. Like in 1990, for instance.

Darrin FLETCHER, Philadelphia
Who is he?

Left-handed hitting catcher, looks good defensively and hit .291 with 13 homers at Albuquerque (AAA). He went to Philadelphia in the Dennis Cook deal.

If the Phillies had not re-signed Darren Daulton, Fletcher would have been

on my list of the top prospects to win the National League Rookie Of the Year award. I see him as being similar to the guy right above him (Fitzgerald) with the possibility of getting better. He should be a regular catcher somewhere within two or three years.

Scott FLETCHER, Chicago White Sox
Does he need to be replaced?

Fletcher's batting average has declined every year since 1986 (.300, .287, .276, .253, .242), with persistent declines in all other areas of his game as well. He stole only one base last year. It's clear that if he takes one more step along that road, he has to be replaced. He is still a very good defensive second baseman, and if it was up to me I'd give him another half-season to get his bat untracked before I started looking at other options.

Tom FOLEY, Montreal
What does he contribute to a team? Does it justify a roster spot?

Over a period of several years he has been one of the best utility infielders in the major leagues. Buck Rodgers uses a "professional bench"—players like Foley, Fitzgerald, Otis Nixon, Wallace Johnson, Mike Aldrete—as opposed to using low-salaried kids on the bench, as many managers do, or high-salaried veterans like Tommie Lasorda does. Rodgers' bench is composed of people who have had the same jobs for several years, aren't going to move into regular jobs if they get hot and aren't going to be released if they have a little slump. It's unusual—in fact, I don't think there is any other manager around who does that. Most organizations don't have more than one bench player who has been with them more than a year or two.

Foley would be a regular except that he lacks any selling points. He hits .250—enough for a shortstop—walks some, plays a decent shortstop and isn't terrible slow. He's as good a player as

Felix Fermin, Alvaro Espinosa or Greg Gagne.

It's hard for a player to stay in top shape if he doesn't play, and the development of Delino DeShields almost eliminated Foley's playing time. He may need to go to AAA and play a couple of months to get back in shape.

Tony FOSSAS, Milwaukee
Will he be around this year?

There's not much market for guys with 75 MPH fastballs even when they're effective. Fossas' ERA was 6.44.

John FRANCO, New York Mets
Who got the better end of the trade?

The Reds, obviously.

Why do you pay a guy like this $2.5 to $3 million a year, and then only pitch him 68 innings? Don't write—I know the answer. The Mets gave Franco a light workload because he had burnt out late in the season several times with Cincinnati. They thought this was a consequence of pitching him too much, so they would hold his workload down.

It didn't work; Franco still posted a 5.91 ERA in September, and was charged with his only three losses of the year in that month.

Julio FRANCO, Texas
Is he really as good as his numbers?

Asked to name the most under-rated player in baseball, I have taken to responding that it is Julio Franco. Franco:

a. is a lifetime .297 hitter.
b. has some line-drive power,
c. is one of the most consistent players in baseball.
d. is never hurt.
e. drew 82 walks last year.
f. drives in 70 to 90 runs a year.
g. steals some bases and is a good percentage base stealer.
h. plays a key defensive position.

i. is average or above-average at that position.
j. hit .336 last year with men on base. Nine of his eleven home runs were hit with men on base; the league average is less than 50%.
k. hits left-handers and right-handers equally well.

He has an estimated 32% chance to get 3000 hits in his career, and is certain to roll well past 2000. In fact, by the formula I use to estimate these things, there are two major league players who as of now have a chance to get 4000 hits—Kirby Puckett, who has a 2% chance, and Julio Franco, who has a ½ of one percent chance.

No, I don't *really* believe there is any way he's going to get 4,000 hits. I'm just using it to point out how impressive his career hit total is.

People tell me he's not as good as his numbers. OK, let's say he's not. If he's not as good as another guy hitting .300, is he as good as a .280 hitter? Is he as good as a guy missing thirty games a year with injuries, like most middle infielders? Is he as good as a guy who walks 65 times a year? There's no way that a guy with *that many* positives can avoid being listed as one of the best players in baseball.

Willie FRASER, Toronto
Is he going to stay in the bullpen or go back to starting?

He doesn't have the stuff to be a starter. I'm not sure he has good enough stuff to be a reliever. I don't know why Toronto wanted him.

Marvin FREEMAN, Atlanta
What's the holdup? Why isn't he progressing? Will he ever be any good?

Freeman, a six-foot-seven right-hander, started three games late in the 1986 season and was overpowering. Since then he has struggled with his control, and has bounced up and down.

You never know, but there are signs that Freeman is on the verge of a breakthrough, and could be the answer to Atlanta's bullpen problems in 1991. His major league strikeout to walk ratio before last year was 45/58—more walks than strikeouts. Last year it was 38/17, and in sixteen innings with Atlanta he walked only four men.

I recommend that you consider drafting him if he is on a roster at the end of spring training. I know you're going to be reluctant to take a chance on a guy who has floundered for four years, but there is extensive precedent for power pitchers struggling for years before they find their control, and then becoming dominating, going back to Dazzy Vance and beyond, and there is also abundant precedent for a pitcher struggling as a starter, and becoming dominant in relief. Freeman may not make it, but he's still a reasonable gamble.

Steve FREY, Montreal
Is he as good as his numbers?

Frey posted a 2.10 ERA in 51 games with the Expos. He's a left-handed spot reliever, but left-handers hit much better against him (.274) than did right-handers (.194).

The Expos have a right-handed closer who is not a superstar (Tim Burke), and Frey may well begin to share the closer role with him and Barry Jones this year. As such, he could gather 15-20 saves. He had nine saves last year, and Dave Schmidt, who had thirteen, probably isn't going to be back.

Frey isn't a coming star; I'm still not a hundred percent convinced he'll be effective. But if you're looking for a guy who could get you fifteen saves cheap, he could be the answer.

Todd FROHWIRTH, Philadelphia
Why wasn't he in the majors last year?

Frohwirth had a 3.59 ERA and a good strikeout/walk ratio in 45 games with

Philadelphia in '89, but spent 1990 at Scranton/Wilkes-Barre, where he was the closer, and was effective in the role.

Frohwirth lost his job to Darrel Akerfelds, who was purchased from Texas. Since

a. Akerfelds was no more effective than Frohwirth had been in the same role, possibly less effective, and
b. Frohwirth pitched well at AAA,

it would seem reasonably likely that Frohwirth will be back in the majors this year.

Travis FRYMAN, Detroit
How good is he going to be? What's his potential to be a big star?

a. Fryman hit .297 with nine homers in 66 games last year, making it pretty clear that he was a major league hitter.
b. He was 21 years old.
c. *Anybody* who is a major league hitter at the age of 21, regardless of how good he is, has a chance to eventually be a star. There are many examples of guys who were ordinary hitters at age 21 developing into major league stars, like George Brett and Robin Yount.
d. Travis is a shortstop, although he is playing third base right now to accommodate Trammell.

My best guess is that Fryman may not post impressive numbers in 1991, but has an excellent chance to be a star in the longer term. He is an *extremely* valuable property.

•G•

Gary GAETTI, Minnesota
Is he still helping his team? He's a free agent . . . do you want to sign him? Will he come back? Where does he rank now among third basemen?

You hate to say it, because Gaetti was a fine player for several years and is central to this team, but he really is *not* a good player anymore, or at least hasn't been for the last two years. Gaetti's premature decline is one of the key failures which has wiped the Twins out of the race. It's not *just* that he hit .229 last year (or .251 the year before) but also:

1. his strikeout/walk ratio, which wasn't good anyway, has gotten worse,
2. his speed, which wasn't much anyway, has gotten less. He grounded into 22 double plays and scored only 61 runs in 154 games.
3. his power, which is the strongest element of his offensive game, isn't what it used to be. Sixteen homers is an OK total, but it's not enough to keep you in the lineup if that's all you do.
4. he hit .197 from the first of August to the end of the season.

Gaetti's defense, which was always outstanding, still is. He is young enough, at 32, to come back strong. The divisive effects of his religious conversion have probably worn away by now; after a couple of years he's probably stopped talking about God, and his teammates have probably accepted his beliefs.

But if Gaetti's bat *doesn't* come back, the Twins are going to have to stop thinking of him as a team leader, and start thinking about replacing him. Regardless of what kind of a defensive player he is, it's tough to go with a slow .240 hitter at third base. And they *have* to get him out of the four-five spots of the batting order, where he has hit for several years, and did last year.

Incidentally, Gaetti's power figures are *not* inflated by playing in the Metrodome. In his career he has hit eleven more home runs on the road (106) than in Minnesota (95) . . . Gaetti last year was behind in the count 56% of the time, which is very high.

Greg GAGNE, Minnesota
Is he a quality shortstop? Is he underrated? Should he be a regular at all?

He could not be considered a quality shortstop, no. He's like a shortstop version of Gary Gaetti—a smart player and more power than your average shortstop, but he hits for a low average, has a poor strikeout/walk ratio and is slow. He's an average offensive shortstop, an average defensive shortstop, probably about the eighth-best shortstop in the American League.

In many ways the Minnesota Twins after their World Championship in 1987 have behaved like the Milwaukee Brewers after they were in the series in '82. Milwaukee's Gorman Thomas trade, an irrational expression of the impulse to do *something,* is paralleled by Minnesota's Tom Brunansky trade. In both cases a popular slugging outfielder was traded away for a singles-hitting defensive player who really wasn't very good. In both cases, the organization messed with the core of the team in a hasty, poorly thought out way.

Having been burned by that experience, the Milwaukee Brewers committed themselves to live or die with the old guard, and stood by as those players grew gracelessly old. The Brewers continued to play Cecil Cooper, Ted Simmons and Ben Oglivie every day for several years after 1982 even when they didn't hit a lick, as if refusing to believe that quality players could grow old so quickly. In 1982 Cecil Cooper hit .313 with 32 homers and 121 RBI; two years later he hit .275 with 11 homers, but batted more than 600 times anyway. In 1982 Ted Simmons hit 23 homers and drove in 97 runs; in 1984 he hit .221 with 4 homers in 497 at bats. In 1982 Ben Oglivie hit 34 homers and drove in 102 runs; in 1984 he hit 12 and drove in 60, but he continued to play.

The Twins are kind of the same. They dropped to 12th in the league in runs scored last year, but they refuse to consider that maybe some of these guys can't play anymore. It's a "we finished last BUT" syndrome.

Andres GALARRAGA, Montreal
Why isn't he playing as well as he used to? What's happened to him?

I was on a talk show in Montreal last spring when, as you might expect, Andres Galarraga's name came up. A caller asked me why I thought Andres had not hit well in 1989, and I said that my opinion was that in 1989 we had seen the *real* Andres Galarraga for the first time. Since Galarraga had had a Hall of Fame season in 1988 (.302, 42 doubles and 29 homers) and a less impressive year in 1989 (.257, 23 homers), this was not a popular thing to say in Montreal, and was regarded as borderline insulting to Galarraga.

I didn't mean it that way. What I was trying to say—I was spectacularly inarticulate on this particular evening—was that Galarraga was tremendous in 1988, but

1. His strikeout/walk ratio was 153-30, not counting intentional walks. There has probably never been a truly great hitter who had a strikeout/walk ratio that bad.
2. He was 27 years old, the age at which fluke years most often happen, and
3. He was performing at a level that was way above what he had done over the years, including the major league equivalents of his minor league performance. His MLEs showed him as a player who would hit about .260 with some power.

Yes, said a caller, but couldn't he have improved? Why do you say it was a fluke

year? Don't you think he could really have gotten better?

Maybe, I answered, but a hitter's level of ability doesn't change that much over a period of years—in fact, it changes amazingly little as a general rule, and normally in predictable ways.

Well, said another caller, what about Howard Johnson? When he came up with Detroit he wasn't any kind of a hitter, but look at him now. If Johnson can improve, Galarraga can improve.

My answer to this was that Johnson had hit 22 home runs as a rookie for Detroit in his first full season. This is

a. wrong—Johnson *never* hit 22 homers for Detroit, and
b. not exactly what I was trying to say anyway.

What I was trying to say is look, Howard Johnson and Andres Galarraga are the same age, within a few months. They both entered baseball in 1979. If you look at them in 1979, Johnson is ahead of Galarraga as a hitter. If you look at them *throughout* their minor league careers, Johnson is ahead of Galarraga. In 1982, when Galarraga was still in the Florida State League, Johnson came to the major leagues and, while he didn't hit 22 homers, did hit very well—.316 in 54 games. From 1983 through 1985, while Galarraga was slogging through the minors, Johnson was unimpressive—but he was in the major leagues.

From 1987 through 1989 Galarraga and Johnson were both regulars in the National League. While Galarraga hit much better in 1988, Johnson hit somewhat better in 1987, and *much* better in 1989.

If evaluated from 1980, 1981, 1982, 1983, 1984, 1985, 1986, 1987 or 1989, Howard Johnson appears to be the better hitter—not that he was necessarily better in every one of those seasons, but that, taking the whole picture, he was always ahead. Evaluated from 1988, Galarraga

appears to be ahead. This suggests, to me, that 1988 is an aberration.

The players being the same age, it is unrealistic to expect Andres Galarraga to develop *now*, when they are 30, the way that Howard Johnson developed several years ago, in his mid-twenties. It ain't going to happen.

Now, if you leave that one year out of the discussion entirely, you'll see that Galarraga's a fine player. He hits for a respectable average with power, he's a Gold Glove first baseman and he runs the bases well. In the last three seasons he has stolen 35 bases in 45 attempts. If he has a good year he can drive in a hundred runs. That's a good player. It's not a superstar, but it's good enough to help you win.

Dave GALLAGHER, Chicago
OK, we know now that he shouldn't be a regular, but how about a bench player? How's he stack up as a fourth outfielder?

Gallagher's OK as a bench player, but there are a million guys just like him—Cecil Espy, Nick Capra. He doesn't do any one thing well enough that you would want to put him in the game to let him do it. He doesn't steal bases or hit home runs or play wonderful defense in the outfield. He's OK all around. If it was my team, I'd rather have a guy on the bench who may be a terrible outfielder but can hit a home run, rather than a guy who's an OK hitter and an OK outfielder. There are different theories on the subject, and a player who is in possession of a job tends to stay around.

Mike GALLEGO, Oakland
Is he going to be a regular? Does his defense justify his offense?

In 1989 Gallego hit .256; last year, he hit .206. During the playoffs Jim Kaat said that he had "improved tremendously as a hitter."

Gallego is never going to be a regular, and the persistent talk about making him one is a perfect illustration of why championship teams have such a hard time staying on top. Gallego has *no* credentials to be a regular, and in fact it's questionable whether he should be playing as much as he is. Sure, he's a fine defensive second baseman, but he's a .220 hitter with no speed or power. His .206 average last year was the worst of any major league player going to the plate 400 or more times. Other than Alvaro Espinoza he was the least productive offensive player in the major leagues. He's thirty years old. Does that sound to you like a guy who should be a regular?

But when a team is successful for a period of years, they begin to make excuses for their shortcomings. Carney Lansford was pathetic last year—but you try to tell people that, and you get a lot of excuses:

1. He's a great team leader.
2. His batting average is still OK.
3. He's a terrific defensive third baseman (which he *isn't*.)
4. He's an integral part of the team.
5. He just had a bad back, he'll be better next year.
6. We won with him last year, didn't we?

A successful team inevitably begins to evaluate every player only by what he has contributed to their success, ignoring weaknesses and thereby allowing them to grow. Leaving a guy like Gallego on the roster, and pretending that he's good enough to play regularly if he has to, is just a part of that process.

Ron GANT, Atlanta
How much of what he did last year is for real? How close to the level of 1990 will he be able to stay?

1. The best predictor of future performance is *career* performance. Per 162 games in his career, Gant has hit 25 homers, stolen 27 bases, hit .262. When a player bounces dramatically up and down, the best thing to bet on is that he will stabilize in the middle.

2. I don't in any sense regard what Gant did last year as a fluke. If you take what Gant did in 1988 and project normal improvement, you can see him having a season like he had in 1990. He was 23 years old then, hit 19 homers and stole 19 bases.

3. Gant's agent, who is a good friend of mine, tells me that Gant is a very bright, motivated young man. Obviously he has a good deal of ability. Why wouldn't we expect him to succeed?

Jim GANTNER, Milwaukee
Should he still be a regular?

Probably not, although not having seen him every day I'd be reluctant to speak too loudly on the subject. I always liked Gantner, subjectively, but when he was 27 years old (ten years ago) he was a .275 hitter with a secondary average just over .100—no walks, no power, no stolen bases. You project even moderate decline from that level—one percent decline per year—and you've got somebody who has to be replaced in his early thirties. The fact that he stays in the lineup, at first blush, would seem to make him an example in support of Gary Sheffield's thesis that in Milwaukee, the white guys just have to show up.

But Gantner, although hurt quite a bit, is playing in several ways better than he ever has. Last year he was 18 for 21 as a base stealer, the best base stealing season of his career, although he played only 88 games (his previous best seasons in stealing bases were 1988 and 1989). His strikeout/walk ratio last year, 19/29, was also the best of his career, the first time since 1980 that he has had more walks than strikeouts. His batting average hasn't slipped significantly, and his defensive statistics at second base are still very good.

Still, you don't want to kid yourself about him. In 323 at bats last year he scored 36 runs and drove in 25. That

may be OK for a second baseman, but it ain't Lou Whitaker.

Another interesting thing about Gantner is that he has stayed so long with one team at one position, without being a star. The media tries to sell us on the notion that we live in the age of instability—the players move around a lot, and there's no "loyalty". It's a lot of hooey, as I've tried to show many times, but Jim Gantner may be one of the easiest ways to show that. Gantner has played 1,322 games at second base—for one team. How many players, in the entire history of baseball, do you think have played that many games at second base for one team?

I don't know exactly, but it would be less than ten. Several of those are active players—Frank White in Kansas City, Lou Whitaker in Detroit. Can you name *any* second baseman from the fifties or sixties who wasn't a star, but managed to play fifteen years with one team?

No, you can't—because there wasn't one.

Rich GARCES, Minnesota
Who is he?

The top prospect in the California League last summer. He pitched well for the Twins the last couple of weeks, and the Twins are talking about making him their bullpen ace.

Which is crazy. The comment about Andy MacPhail (see Rick Aguilera) should not be taken to say that it is not possible for Rich Garces to do the job as the Twins' closer if they decide to try that. There is plenty of precedent for very young kids with very little minor league experience stepping into a key role on a major league pitching staff and being successful right away, from Billy McCool (1964) to Steve Howe (1980) to Gregg Olson (1989). The problem is that:

a. while it is *possible* for this to happen, there is a great deal *more* precedent for kids like that being asked to do the job and *not* being able to,

b. even when 19- and 20-year-old pitchers are dramatically successful, the great majority of the time they will hurt their arms within a couple of years,

c. the Twins already have a quality closer in Rick Aguilera, and

d. if the Twins send Aguilera to the starting rotation, *Aguilera* will hurt his arm.

It's not that it *can't* work out. It's a question of loading the odds in your favor. One of Earl Weaver's "laws" was "The best place for a rookie pitcher is in long relief." Weaver's thinking was, let the kid watch and learn for a year or two. Let him build up his strength, let him mature physically a little more, and let him learn how to handle the job with as little pressure on him as possible. That way, he's got a better chance of slipping gracefully into the job, but also that way, when he succeeds, he'll be prepared to handle the success. Doesn't that make a lot more sense?

(**Late note:** the addition of Bedrosian obviously appears to mean that Garces is not being counted on to be the closer.)

Carlos GARCIA, Pittsburgh
Who is he?

A shortstop in the Pirates' system, a decent hitter and can steal some bases. He's young (23) and a Grade B prospect. He probably cannot dislodge Jay Bell as long as Bell is playing well, but Garcia probably will get a good shot at a major league job within two or three years.

I would not be reluctant to open the 1991 season with Carlos Garcia as my regular shortstop. I'd rather have him out there than several guys who have jobs.

Mike GARDELLA, New York
Who is he?

Left-handed reliever, regarded as a possible heir to Dave Righetti in New York. Short with a blocky build, Gardella was a low draft pick who shot through the minors by pitching well, and should be in the major leagues by the end of this season.

Mike GARDINER, Seattle
Who is he?

Right-handed starting pitcher with Seattle. The bad news in a nutshell: he's 25 years old, spent the season at AA, was called up late and in five games (three starts) posted an ERA of 10.66.

Despite which, I like him. Gardiner, who pitched for Canada in the 1984 Olympics, pitched brilliantly at Williamsport (1.90 ERA in 26 starts), and has pitched well for two years in a row. His arm has not been abused in the low minors, as so many pitchers are, and his strikeout/walk ratio last year was 149/29. His manager, Rich Morales, says that "He has tremendous poise and control. He has four major league pitches" (*Baseball America*, October 10, 1990.) He's a Grade B prospect in view of his slow progress to this point, but I like his chances.

★★★
Mark GARDNER, Montreal
★★★

Mike Gardella, Mike Gardiner, Mark Gardner . . . how are we supposed to keep all of these people straight?

Don't worry about it; if any of them turn out to be any good you'll figure it out.

Is he awfully good? Why did you mark him with asterisks?

Positive markers. He's 29, which is old for a pitcher to be developing as a star, but I think he could. He was great his last two years in the minor leagues, and good last year with Montreal. His strikeout ratio is very good (eight men per nine innings), and his control is decent. He pitched well last year, but his won-lost record doesn't reflect this because of poor offensive support. Playing for Buck Rodgers, who knows how to handle a pitcher, is certainly a positive. This is probably a pitcher's park, although it's hard to tell (varies from year to year more than usual. Also, the Expos reportedly are doing something to cut down on the foul territory, which may make it a better park for a hitter.) I think Gardner is going to be a terrific pitcher.

Wes GARDNER, San Diego
Will he ever get it together? How does he stay in the majors without getting people out?

They keep putting him on the mound because he's a big guy with a good fastball and a nasty slider.

Is there any precedent for a pitcher like this finally getting to be good?

Yes, quite a bit. Mike Cuellar struggled until he was about 30, and then won almost 200 games. Dazzy Vance didn't win a game until he was 31, and is in the Hall of Fame. Mike Scott, of course. There aren't many examples that dramatic, but there have been a lot of pitchers who struggled for years, but finally did turn it around and become good pitchers. Joaquin Andujar was almost 30 before he found any consistency. Stu Miller struggled until he was 30. Dave Stewart was almost 30 when he began to win.

I have always believed that the Red Sox have a special problem in developing pitchers in that the park distorts their statistics in a way that puts pressure on them to pitch at an almost impossible level. In the simplest form, a pitcher with an ERA of 4.10 in another park needs to make some adjustments, while a pitcher with an ERA of 4.10 in Fenway Park is doing a pretty good job.

What you have then is a pitcher who is actually pitching fairly well, but who is *perceived* as failing, not only by other people but by himself. Perceiving himself as failing, he will try to adjust, try to use his other pitches more, try to pitch inside more or pitch up in the strike zone more or whatever.

This makes it very difficult for a young pitcher to get his feet on the ground. It breeds confusion and self-doubt—if the pitcher is able to stay in the league at all. Whereas a pitcher might give up three runs in six innings in another park and be thought of as doing OK, in Fenway it might become five runs in six innings, at least sometimes, and that can easily lead to a trip to the bullpen. That, in my opinion, is why the Red Sox have had trouble developing starting pitchers, and have had much of their success with pitchers brought in after they had been successful somewhere else.

I think that to develop starting pitchers, the Red Sox need to work against the nature of the park. They need to *tell* young pitchers not to worry too much about their ERA, that their ERA is going to be a little higher here than it would be somewhere else. They need to *tell* young pitchers not to react emotionally when they give up runs in Fenway Park, because it's going to happen. They need to re-adjust their thinking as to when a starting pitcher comes out of the game. I don't know if you ever noticed this, but the normal rule for when a starting pitcher is yanked (in the first six innings) is "whenever he gives up four runs and is in danger of giving up a fifth." That's approximate, of course, but it works. It needs to be a run higher in Fenway Park—but it isn't.

Joe Morgan, of course, isn't going to do this, nor is any old baseball man. The Red Sox have had trouble developing starting pitchers for forty years, and they probably will for another forty, if the park lasts that long. Gardner, in San Diego, is released from the cycle, and gets another shot at getting people out. It may be his last one.

Scott GARRELTS, Giants
Can he bounce back? Which is the real Scott Garrelts, the Garrelts of 1989 (14-5, 2.28 ERA) or the Garrelts of 1990 (12-11, 4.15).

In 1987, as a reliever, Garrelts struck out 127 men in 106 innings—10.7 per game. As a starter in 1989 he struck out 119 in 193 innings—5.5 per game. In 1990 he struck out 80 in 182 innings—slightly less than four per game.

The kind of a decline in strikeout rates is more than surprising. It's alarming. It suggests to me that something is wrong with Garrelts' arm, and unless whatever it is goes away, he won't get back to where he was a year ago.

I also believe, despite his superb performance as a starter in 1989, that Garrelts would be most effective in relief.

Rich GEDMAN, Houston
What happened to him?

We could talk about that forever. I don't know what happened; ask somebody who was with the Red Sox.

Does he still deserve a major league job?

No. In the last four years he's hit .205, .231, .212 and .202. It's obvious to anybody that he is not a good enough defensive catcher to keep him in the lineup if he's going to hit .210. The only reason for keeping him around is to see if he can snap back as a hitter. After four years we have to assume that the change is permanent, that that's his level of ability.

Bob GEREN, Yankees
Does he belong in the major leagues?

I don't know, but I'd rather have him than Rich Gedman. He throws well and has some power, which may be enough to justify keeping him on a major league roster.

Geren is a classic illustration of how much major league teams cost themselves by refusing to accept that minor league statistics predict accurately what a player will hit in the majors. It took the Yankees two years to find out something that you and I knew all along—that Geren couldn't hit major league pitching consistently. And they may not be convinced yet.

Kirk GIBSON, Kansas City
Will he help the Royals?

The only good thing about the Royals signing Kirk Gibson, from their standpoint, is that it means they won't have Gerald Perry anymore. New General Manager Herk Robinson made a statement at the Gibson signing which reveals how astonishingly little the Royals understand of their own history:

The Royals' way of winning always has been with pitching, speed and defense, along with an aggressive attitude. Signing Kirk is one step toward getting back to that.

1. The Royals championship team of 1976–1980 was put together *entirely*, without any exception, of players who had had limited success or no success before coming to Kansas City. About half of that team was from the Royals' young farm system, and about half was composed of players who had failed trials with other teams. Those teams had *no* Mike Boddickers, Mark Davises or Kirk Gibsons who had been stars with other teams.
2. The success of those teams was based at least as much on hitting as on any other element of the team. The teams of 1977 and 1980 scored over 800 runs. In 1980 they had a team batting average of .286, the highest in the majors in the last forty years. They also hit .285 and .282 in two other seasons.
3. Those teams were built of *contact* hitters, *line drive* hitters. The Royals now have three players in the heart of the order—Jackson, Tartabull and Gibson—who if they were healthy would strike out 450–500 times.

Those teams were built initially by Cedric Tallis, and finished by Whitey Herzog. Those men understood something that the people running the Royals in recent years haven't understood: the organic component of a baseball team. They understood that if you took *young* players with ability but no history of success, and you told them that we want you to do this and this and this, those young men would bust their butt to do it because they wanted to make it as big league players. They understood that it is impossible to get the same degree of commitment from guys in their thirties. The Royals now are trying to *buy* leadership, trying to *buy* intensity.

Several Kansas City sportswriters wrote that Gibson, because of his speed, was perfect for Royals' Stadium. Gibson was 26 for 28 as a base stealer last year, the best percentage of any major league player with 25 or more tries, but Gibson is a power hitter who strikes out a lot, coming to a turf park which is the toughest home run park in the American League. Gibson is a player in his mid-thirties with a long history of leg problems, coming to play for the first time a full season on artificial turf. It seems unlikely to me that this will prove a perfect match.

Gibson's intensity, his professionalism—in my opinion these are real assets, and are things the Royals needed. Gibson's negotiating power was hurt by two seasons of injuries; if he's healthy, his salary will be very reasonable. Gibson is a better player than the man he will replace, Gerald Perry. The Royals were almost certain to have a better year in 1991 than they did in 1990, and signing Gibson won't change that.

But all the same, if the Royals want to get back where they were ten years ago, they've got to stop this crap. They've got to stop giving up draft picks to sign players in their mid-thirties, and start concentrating on finding young men that they can *build* with. Until they accept

that, the long-term trend of the Royals will continue downward.

Why are the Royals so successful in the free agent market all of a sudden?

Kansas City has always been regarded among ballplayers as a good place to play and a good organization, although whether or not it is still a good organization is questionable. In the early days of free agency the Royals made competitive offers to Catfish Hunter, Tommy John, Pete Rose, Goose Gossage and others, but never brought home the player primarily because at that time all that counted was the top dollar. Now, because the dollar figures are so huge, it's like monopoly money; whether you sign for $2.7 million or $2.9 million, after you have $4 million socked away, doesn't really have any impact on your life. There's a tendency now to choose among the three or four best offers the place where you would most like to play, and Kansas City does well in that situation.

The exception, of course, is a player like Steve Farr, who has never made any big money in baseball, and is therefore still in the position of trying to get what he can get.

Paul GIBSON, Tigers
Can he pitch consistently at the level of 1990?

Gibson posted a 3.05 ERA in 61 games last year, which is about as well as you can pitch with his heater. I don't believe he can stay at that level, but he has a 3.67 ERA over a three-year major league career. I can believe he he'll keep his ERA to 3.67.

Brett GIDEON, Montreal
Who is he?

Right-handed relief pitcher, pitched some for Pittsburgh in 1987.

I used to like him quite a bit, for the usual reasons that I cite when I like a young pitcher (see article on Norm

Charlton for a complete list.) He made the team last spring, but pitched only one inning and went on the disabled list with a sore elbow. He never came off; I don't know what happened to him. It's anybody's guess whether he'll be back.

Brian GILES, Seattle
Was that a game, or what?

Giles, who hit only four home runs all year, and hit only two in 400 at bats when he was with the Mets in 1983, hit two home runs and a double in one game at Toronto, May 17 (4 3 3 7). This is probably as remarkable a feat as Derek Lilliquist homering twice in one game—maybe more so, since Giles has proven in the course of 287 major league games that he *isn't* the kind of hitter who can do that.

That would be a fun list to do for a *Baseball Digest* article or something—the greatest games ever by lousy hitters. I remember Freddie Patek, who normally homered about four times a year, hitting three in one game at Fenway Park in 1980. He hit five during the season. I think Merv Connors, who hit only eight major league home runs, hit three in a game in 1938. Connors was probably a good hitter, but he got stuck in the minors, where he hit more than 400 home runs. I remember that Pat Seerey, a catcher who hit kind of like Rob Deer without quite as much power, hit four homers in a game in 1948 and also, what is less known, hit three homers and a triple in a game in 1945. I don't have time to research the topic right now, but it would be fun.

Bernard GILKEY, St. Louis
How good is he?

His opportunity is tremendous, with McGee, Coleman and Brunansky all leaving St. Louis, and his skills are right for the park. He is a major league hitter.

My best guess is that Gilkey will hit around .270, steal about 50 bases and have a strikeout/walk ratio about even, maybe a little better than even. No power. He certainly could be the NL Rookie of the Year if things break right for him (see Ray Lankford).

Tom GILLES, Toronto
Who is he?

Overage right-handed pitching prospect, had a 2.18 ERA for Syracuse, relief role. He's a finesse pitcher, good control. Grade D prospect.

Joe GIRARDI, Chicago Cubs
Who is the better catcher—Berryhill or Girardi?

Let's assume that Berryhill is healthy, because if he's not there's nothing to argue about. Offensively, they are as close as humanly possible. I estimate that Girardi (in his career) has created 3.44 runs/27 outs, and Berryhill 3.46.

Really, they're both pretty bad hitters. Girardi hit .270 last year, but believe it or not he walked less than half as often as Shawon Dunston, not counting intentional walks. (Girardi walked 17 times, eleven of them intentional.) He has no power (one home run) and not enough speed to be worth talking about. Berryhill has a little bit of power, but not much, he's a .250 hitter and he doesn't walk, either, in addition to which he is slow.

Defensively, Girardi throws better, but Berryhill makes fewer mistakes.

Girardi is one year younger.

Hm. If they're both healthy, I'll go with Girardi, but it's a 100-99 decision.

Can they platoon? Not really. Berryhill is a switch hitter, but in 1989 he hit .340 against left-handers, .224 against right-handers. Girardi also hit almost a hundred points better against left-handers than right-handers last year (.326-.241).

If they start out in a platoon arrangement, bet on Girardi to win the job. Girardi will be playing against left-handers, whom he hits well, and Berryhill against right-handers, whom he hits poorly.

Dan GLADDEN, Minnesota
How much longer will he last?

I'd be very surprised if he can last more than one more year as a regular. He's 33 years old, and not a great player. He grounded into 17 double plays last year, more than he had grounded into in any other two seasons. He's marginal. I mean, I know he's popular, but he batted 534 times last year with 64 runs scored and 40 RBI. For an outfielder/leadoff man, that's inadequate. Pedro Munoz may take his job.

Tom GLAVINE, Braves
Is he ever going to be good? What was the problem last year?

I like him better now than I ever have. A headline in the September 24 issue of *The Sporting News* read "Glavine's Mediocrity Reflects Braves' Staff." Sure, he was 10-12, 4.28 ERA, but 10-12 isn't bad with the Braves, a .400 team. A 4.28 ERA isn't bad in Fulton County Stadium.

There are two reasons I like him more now:

1. He has pitched in rotation for three years. That proves he can carry the load of being a major league starter without getting hurt—and not that many young pitchers can. *Most* young pitchers will develop sore arms after a year or two of starting.
2. His strikeout rates are going *up*—3.8 per game as a rookie, 4.4 in his second year, 5.4 last year. That indicates a pitcher who is learning and developing.
3. His team is going to be better.

I can see him as a good pitcher.

Jerry Don GLEATON, Detroit
Why did he pitch so well last year?

Gleaton, a ten-year major league veteran, pitched 57 games with a 2.94 ERA, 13 saves. He got regular work in a defined role for the first time in his career, and his control record improved because of it. He doesn't have a great arm anymore, as he did ten years ago, but he still has a major league fastball.

Can he pitch this well every year?

I don't see any reason that he couldn't.

Jerry GOFF, Montreal
How good is he? Can he play?

Goff is probably going to be in the majors for ten years as a backup catcher, never a regular. He was in the Seattle system for years, making slow progress because of a slow bat. Acquired by the Expos a year ago, he got off to an excellent start at Indianapolis—not only playing well on defense, but hitting well. Called up by the Expos in early June, he completed an excellent season by hitting .227 for the Expos—that's better than anybody thought he could hit—with a secondary average near .300.

If Goff plays consistently the way he played last year, majors and minors, then he has a chance to be a regular. My reading of it is that it was just a case of a player responding to an opportunity by playing a little over his head, but even so, Goff will probably stay around as part of Buck Rodgers' professional bench.

★★★
Leo GOMEZ, Baltimore
★★★

This guy can *hit,* not for average but for power. He led the International League in runs scored (97), RBI (97), and was second in walks (89) and home runs (26). He has a very good hitting record over a period of years—.326 with 110 RBI in A ball in 1988, .285 with 19 homers, 88 RBI in AA in 1989.

• I estimate that as a major leaguer, Gomez would hit about .260, with a slugging percentage close to .500 and a good many walks. He would be comparable as a hitter to Dwight Evans, for example, or a slow Howard Johnson, or Gary Gaetti with more walks.

- He is reported to have good work habits and a positive attitude.
- The problem, if there is one, is that he is very slow. The Orioles already have a young third baseman, Craig Worthington, who isn't too bad although he had an awful year. Gomez is a better hitter than Worthington, but Worthington is in possession of the job, and if he shows up in February in shape and ready to play, he won't be easy to move.
- The Orioles have first basemen coming out the kazoo, so neither Gomez nor Worthington is going to move to first.
- *Both* Gomez and Worthington are slower than a senile bureaucrat, so neither of them can move to right field, which would be the natural solution to the problem.

Gomez is two years younger than Worthington (24 to 26), and Worthington is a better third baseman. So unless a trade can be worked out, it is far from certain that Gomez will get a chance to show what he can do in 1991. But he can hit.

Rene GONZALES, Baltimore Orioles
Does he justify a roster spot? Should he be in the major leagues?

Not if you're going to play Cal Ripken every inning at shortstop, no. Gonzales, who is a shortstop and a good, consistent .217 hitter, might be alright as a backup shortstop. As a spare third baseman he doesn't hit enough, so that leaves him on the roster as a backup second baseman. Who devotes a roster spot to a backup second baseman who doesn't hit?

Jose GONZALEZ, Los Angeles
Will he ever get a chance to play regularly?

Yes, like Mickey Hatcher did and Joe Simpson and Candy Maldonado. If the Dodgers had intended to try him as a regular, they would have done it before now. The Dodgers obviously don't feel that he can hit and I've no reason to disagree with them, but eventually they'll have to send him somewhere to let him take his shot.

I don't know if you noticed this, but early last year the Dodgers had the worst defensive outfield in baseball playing, with the best defensive outfield in baseball on the bench. Playing, they had Kal Daniels in left, Juan Samuel or Kirk Gibson in center and Hubie Brooks in right—an awful defensive outfield. On the bench, however, they had Gonzalez, Stan Javier and John Shelby, three fine defensive center fielders.

★★★
Juan GONZALEZ, Texas
★★★
Is he going to be a superstar?

I don't believe in that. I don't believe in projecting a player three or four steps ahead of where he is. Let's find out whether or not he can play in the majors, *then* we'll consider whether he will be a star, *then* we'll consider whether he will be a superstar.

Is he going to be a regular?

Probably. I have mixed feelings about Gonzalez. In my fantasy league, where we can only protect seven players from year to year, I drafted Gonzalez and protected him, even though this meant that I had to cut loose players like Hal Morris and Randy Johnson. I did this in recognition that:

1. Gonzalez is obviously the one player most likely to win the American League Rookie of the Year Award in 1991, and
2. He does have a chance to be a big star. Gonzalez' MLEs from 1989 showed him as a .274 hitter with 17 homers, 72 RBI. In 1990 they showed him as a .240 hitter but with 24 homers, 85 RBI.

It seems obvious that a man who can hit that way when he is 19 and 20 years old figures to be pretty damn good when he gets to 27.

At the same time, he really isn't my type of player. His strikeout to walk ratios are going to be awful, and a .260 hitter with no stolen bases and a bad K/W . . . what is that, really? That's not a player who helps you win unless he hits at least 30 homers.

Gonzalez is a center fielder as of now, but is seen as being best suited to right field. He has a right fielder's arm; he may not have a center fielder's speed in a couple of years. If he develops into a star, he will develop along the lines of Jose Canseco or Bobby Bonilla, as opposed to the lines of Ryne Sandberg, Rickey Henderson or Barry Bonds. He probably looks more like Canseco than anyone has since Canseco came along.

He *is* the number one candidate to win the A.L. Rookie Award; that's just stating the obvious. I can also see the possibility of his hitting .188 through 45 games, striking out 51 times and earning another year in AAA. That's why it's a pre-season guide; we don't give guarantees.

Luis GONZALEZ, Houston Astros
Who is he?

Third base prospect; if he was in another system I might be raving about him. Gonzalez is young (23), has power (24 homers at Columbus) and speed (27 stolen bases.) He is a left-handed hitter.

One infers from the fact that he is a first baseman slash third baseman that he probably isn't much of a defensive third baseman—anyway, I've seen a thousand of those guys come up, and none of them yet has turned out to be a good third baseman. He's not going to run Glenn Davis off of first base. The Astrodome will eliminate a good portion of his power, so what are you left with? A poor defensive third baseman who is going to hit .235 with 15 home runs.

He needs another year in AAA—and Bagwell deserves the first shot at Caminiti's job.

Dwight GOODEN, New York Mets

Is he as good as he used to be?

Definitely not. People accepted his 19-7 won-lost record at face value because his name is Dwight Gooden—but he didn't pitch that well last year. He gave up almost a hit an inning. He was 19-7 only because he had the best offensive support of any major league pitcher (6.77 runs scored for him per nine innings. Doug Drabek was second, at 5.91.)

Maybe he'll pitch better this year. Maybe he won't.

Where does he rank among the all-time greats?

Well, he's only had one twenty-win season. His career winning percentage to this point in his career is .721, which would be the highest of all time, but that's misleading because almost every pitcher's career ends with a couple of records like 9-14 and 2-6. You'd have to compare Gooden's record to others in mid-career to have an honest comparison. I don't know where he would rank, but I know that Ron Guidry at a comparable point was 122-51, which isn't much different than Gooden (119-46). Clemens is 116-51. I suspect there are many other pitchers who have had records just as good.

So my answer to where Gooden ranks among the all-time greats is that he doesn't yet. A few more years of this, another twenty-win season, and he rates. Not now.

Tom GORDON, Kansas City

What's his problem? Why isn't he great?

Gordon was mechanically messed up all of 1990, which was one of the things which convinced me that the Royals pitching coach had to go. Frank Funk, the coach, was fired at season's end and replaced by Pat Dobson.

The fact that Gordon's mechanics were messed up is no particular condemnation of Funk, nor even the fact that Gordon *and* Mark Davis were messed up, nor the fact that Gordon and Davis were messed up and most of the other starters were hurt. Those things happen in baseball; you can't make the coach a scapegoat.

What got to me was that Funk insisted that Gordon's mechanics were fine, when any idiot could see they weren't. Gordon's delivery for most of the last year was entirely different than it was when he was on top of his game in early '89. Then Gordon was throwing three-quarters, swivelling his hips and throwing his arm out as if it were a lariat, a rope. It was a loose, relaxed delivery. Late in 1989 he began throwing straight overhand, driving off the mound with his legs and bending his torso to the left so he could get his arm up to twelve noon.

So what did Funk have to say about this? "There is nothing wrong with Tom Gordon's mechanics. His mechanics are fine." His mechanics are FINE? What about the fact that he's doing everything different than he did when he was pitching well? "His mechanics are fine."

I live in the Kansas City area. What was maddening about this was that the rest of us were supposed to say, "Well, OK, the expert has spoken, I guess it's not his mechanics." How can *I* try to convince somebody that his delivery is fouled up when his *pitching coach* says that it's fine?

The problem was that the expert either never looked at a video tape of Gordon while he was pitching well, or is blind as a bat. Gordon's still a good bet to be a dominating pitcher. He's still young, still has a good fastball and a great curve. If he can start putting it where it belongs, he'll be a winner.

Jim GOTT, Los Angeles

Can he come all the way back?

Gott, out almost all of 1989 with a bone spur and a "ruptured medial collateral ligament in his right elbow", posted a 2.90 ERA in 50 games last year. That's impressive, because you figure it will take him a year to get back up to strength. I wouldn't be surprised to see him have a real good year in '91.

Mauro GOZZO, Cleveland

Who is he?

Grade D prospect, kicked around the Toronto and Kansas City systems since 1984 before coming to Cleveland for Bud Black. Big right-hander; he will probably pitch very well for stretches of eight or ten starts at a time.

Mark GRACE, Chicago Cubs

Where'd he disappear to last year? How good is he going to be?

Grace had basically the same year last year as he did in 1989. He hit .309 and had career highs in hits, doubles, RBI and stolen bases. We just didn't hear anything about him because

a. the Cubs were out of the race, and
b. Grace got off to a slow start, creating the impression that he was heading for an off season.

Joe GRAHE, California

Who is he?

Right-handed starting pitcher, very young. He was a second-round draft pick in '89, didn't pitch the rest of that year, but worked his way through the minors in one year last year.

He doesn't have a long enough track record to evaluate how well he can pitch. I think he was probably brought along too quickly.

Mark GRANT, Atlanta

What's his role?

He's a middle relief guy, a set-up man. He has good K/W ratios, and you know how I like that in a pitcher, but it's hard to move a pitcher up to a better job when he has a lifetime ERA of 4.23.

Jeff GRAY, Boston
Can he help the Red Sox?

I think he's got a real chance to surprise people. He gets no respect—signed as an undrafted free agent, ignored in the minors even when he was tremendously effective (14-2 with a 2.35 ERA at Vermont in 1986.) He's always pitched well, and he's always been healthy. I like him—not as a Dennis Eckersley, of course, but as a Dale Mohorcic.

Craig GREBECK, Chicago White Sox
Who is he?

White Sox utility infielder, a rookie. He's not as bad a player as his rookie performance would suggest, particularly his .168 batting average. He's small, not exceptionally fast and 26 years old, which makes him a Grade C prospect at best. But he can hit as well as the average major league shortstop. If Guillen goes down with an injury, Grebeck will surprise some people.

Gary GREEN, Texas Rangers
Is he ever going to play?

He's not a major league hitter. He's very marginal even as a utility infielder, in that his only role appears to be to play second and short in the late innings.

Tommy GREENE, Philadelphia
Is he still a prospect?

His stock crashed last year as he finally got a chance to pitch and was pretty terrible. He was a Grade C prospect a year ago; he's a Grade D prospect now.

Greene is still being thought of as a starting pitcher. Almost uniquely for his generation, he has been in organized baseball for six years, and has never been tried as a reliever. He had 138 minor league appearances, 137 of them as a starter. But if he has any chance of being a successful pitcher now, it would appear that it's time to try him as a reliever.

Willie GREENE, Montreal
Who is he?

Nineteen-year-old shortstop, #1 draft pick in 1989 and generally thought to be the best long-range prospect in the Pittsburgh system before he was traded to Montreal as part of the Zane Smith package. I'm not high on him, although it is too soon to give up on him. His defense at short is marginal (he may wind up at third base or center field), and while they say they like his bat, he hasn't hit anything yet.

Mike GREENWELL, Boston
Can he come back?

He had one of the greatest off years you'll ever see—in fact, we had a bunch of those last year. Greenwell had an off year—he hit .297. Ruben Sierra had an off year—he drove in 96 runs. Will Clark had an off year—he drove in 95 runs. Robin Yount, he had a terrible year—yet he scored 98 runs. Wade Boggs had an off year—he hit .302. Tony Gwynn, too—he hit .309. Do you think we're starting to take ourselves too seriously? We're watching these guys so carefully that normal season-to-season fluctuations are acquiring an unnatural significance.

Among those players, Greenwell may be the most certain to come back. First, there is an obvious reason why he started poorly last year—an injury to his left ankle, which bothered him all year. Second, after a slow start he was his usual formidable self the last four months of the season. He hit .238 with little power the first two months of the season, .313 but still with no power in June, but .320 with twelve homers from July to the end of the season.

He'll be great this year. Hell, he could be the MVP.

Tommy GREGG, Atlanta
Has he found his role?

Gregg had a terrific year as a pinch hitter last year, getting 18 pinch hits including three doubles and four homers, a whopping .673 slugging percentage in that role. A poll of National League managers by Neil MacCarl named him the best pinch hitter in the National League (see *Baseball Digest*, January, 1991).

This is good news and bad news. The good news is that this gives Gregg a clean shot at a major league career; with any luck, his "proven" ability as a pinch hitter will keep him in the majors for ten years, and make him a moderately wealthy man. The bad news is that he is still battling for a regular job, and his "proven value" as a pinch hitter, combined with some other factors, will almost certainly mean that he is assigned to be a pinch hitter. The other factors are that:

1. Gregg, although he is a good line-drive hitter, does not have the power one expects of a first baseman.
2. Francisco Cabrera, who Gregg is competing with for the first base job, does.
3. The Braves have signed Sid Bream.

Gregg's a classic pinch hitter type—a left-handed line-drive hitter, doesn't strike out a lot and hits the first pitch a good percentage of the time. Denny Walling, Rance Mulliniks.

It is extremely likely that Gregg will now be type-cast as a pinch hitter, and will be around for several years in that role. Only by hitting .320 or better is he likely to re-establish himself as a regular.

Gregg's data on pitch counts is interesting:

1. he hit .419 when he hit the first pitch (18/43),
2. he was behind in the count 57% of the time, which is extremely high,
3. he hit *vastly* better when ahead in the count (.309) than when behind (.174). *All* of his power comes when he is ahead in the count.

All of this data is vaguely normal, but extreme.

Ken GRIFFEY, Sr., Seattle
Where do the Griffeys rank, as a father-son combo? Are they the best? Are they going to be the best?

There are four father-son combinations in which both father and son were good players—the Griffeys, the Bondses, the Bells and the Boones. Well, you can make arguments if you want for the Kennedys, the Bagbys and the Treshes.

As I see it, the players to rank must *both* be good. A situation where the father was great but the son was nothing, like the Walshes, doesn't stack up. Daddy with 3000 hits and junior with 105 isn't the same as two good players with 1500 each.

Among the four Daddies, I am inclined to think that Bobby Bonds was the best player. It is far from an easy choice, for Gus Bell was a terrific player, Ken Sr. was very good and had more hits than any of the others and Ray Boone, though clearly the weakest of the four, was a quality player. That's how I rank them— Bonds, Bell, Griffey and Boone.

As to the sons, Buddy Bell or Bob Boone ranks first so far. We often hear that Bob Boone will go into the Hall of Fame, but I'm not really sure why people say this or whether it is true or not. I don't think it's a consensus opinion.

Since it won't change the conclusion, let's say Boone ranks first and Bell second among the sons. Barry Bonds, on the basis of what has been accomplished so far, has to rank ahead of Griffey Jr, which makes the lists:

Fathers	Sons
1. Bonds	1. Boone
2. Bell	2. Bell
3. Griffey	3. Bonds
4. Boone	4. Griffey

The Griffeys rank third and fourth among the four. This makes it pretty clear that, pending the arrival of Ken Jr's incipient immortality, the Griffeys together rank fourth among the four, and the Bells rank first. The Griffeys to this point have 2,418 career hits; the Bells had 4,337. That suggests, again, that the Griffeys have a ways to go, and Junior has a lot yet to prove, before they can be considered the best of the group.

Ken GRIFFEY Jr., Seattle
Has he been over-hyped? Is he re-ally that good?

He hasn't been over-hyped; he's worth it. Griffey is the only major league player who has not yet established some reasonable limits for himself. He could be anything—he could be the greatest player there ever was, or he could be Cesar Cedeno.

Alfredo GRIFFIN, Dodgers
What's his role now? Is he going to be a regular anymore?

1. He's lost his job to Offerman.
2. In his three years with Los Angeles his average is .222.
3. He wasn't a very good player when he hit .250.
4. While he wasn't very good, what he could bring to a team was defense and baserunning intensity. He's pulled more kamikaze missions on the basepaths than any other player in twenty years.
   I am told by people in the LA area that Griffin at age 34 has neither the speed nor the intensity that he did two years ago.
5. He was involved in a mid-summer incident, a fight at a nightclub.
6. By the runs created formula he was the least productive offensive player batting 400 or more times in the National League last year.

Adding it all up, I'd say there's no way in hell he would ever be a regular again. You never know.

Ty GRIFFIN, Chicago Cubs
How's he coming along? Is he still a super-prospect?

He had a dismal year at AA, hit only .209. He has a history of bursitis in his shoulder, and his best position is second base, where the Cubs already have an adequate player. The Ty Griffin Express is seriously behind schedule.

Jason GRIMSLEY, Philadelphia
Is he going to be a rotation starter? Is he going to be good?

Grimsley, a 23-year-old right-hander, was called up in July and made eleven major league starts, going 3-2 with a 3.30 ERA. He's a six-foot-three right-hander.

I don't think he's ready to be an effective starter:

1. His control is terrible.
2. His strikeout rate isn't impressive.
3. The Phillies probably aren't going to be able to support him very well.

Marquis GRISSOM, Montreal
What's his star potential?

I think he's going to be a decent player. Given anything like normal progress, he does *not* project as a star. To become a star, he would have to show *unusual* development from where he is now—a .260 range hitter with no power.

Grissom's central skill is his speed. How long he lasts, and how high he rises, will depend primarily on how long he retains his speed, and how well he learns to use that speed within the game.

★★★
Kevin GROSS, Los Angeles
★★★
Will he help the Dodgers?

This could be a *great* free agent signing. Gross has always been a very underrated pitcher. Given better teams and better luck, he could be 95-75 in his career rather than 80-90. If he's healthy, he'll win fifteen games for the Dodgers.

Kip GROSS, Cincinnati
Who is he?

Right-handed reliever. He has as much chance of cracking the Reds' bullpen as Luis Polonia has of anchoring *Nightline*.

Kelly GRUBER, Toronto
Is this his real level of ability?

I was extremely surprised that Gruber played as well as he did last year and, not meaning to be stubborn about it, I do *not* believe that it is a real level of ability. I think he'll drop off significantly next year.

Was he helped by the change in parks?

Quite a lot, yes. Gruber actually hit fewer home runs on the road last year (8) than he had the previous two seasons (10 and 11). But he hit more home runs in Toronto last year than he had in his entire career previously (23-22). He hit .292 with 23 homers, 62 RBI in Toronto, .254 with 8 homers on the road.

Was he the best third baseman in baseball?

He was last year. There are other guys who have had good years.

Cecilio GUANTE, Cleveland
Is he still around?

He was last year. After posting a 5.01 ERA and giving up ten home runs in 46 innings, he'll be scrambling for a spot.

Mark GUBICZA, Kansas City
Will he come back from the injury?

He's a question mark. He's had surgery on his rotator cuff.

On September 12, 1989 (four days after signing his new contract) Gubicza felt tightness in the left side of his chest while pitching against Texas. He came out of the game in the fifth inning and had tests, which proved negative. Feeling the pressure of a pennant race *and* a new contract, Gubicza started again on Sep-

tember 16, but altered his throwing motion to relieve the discomfort, and developed soreness in his right shoulder. He was told that "he had a muscle strain behind his right shoulder, but was assured that it would not be a long-lasting problem." (*The Sporting News*, October 2, 1989).

Gubicza wasn't right all winter 1989, and wasn't able to throw hard when spring training opened. We heard all spring training that Gubicza was the one player who had needed a full spring, but after three shaky outings he began to pitch well, and Wathan and Funk began to ride him as if he were the horse he's always been. Despite knowing that Gubicza wasn't one hundred percent and despite the shortened spring training, Gubicza pitched eight innings with ten strikeouts on April 26, and then beginning on May 8 had a string of seven straight starts in which he pitched seven innings, seven innings, six and two thirds, eight, seven and a third, eight innings and seven and a third.

After that Gubicza became unable to stay in the game. He left for the disabled list at the end of June; a few weeks later it was announced that he was out for the season. On August second he underwent "successful arthroscopic surgery to repair a partial tear in the rotator cuff of his throwing shoulder." (*TSN*, August 13, 1990. The headline on the story is "Gubicza's Prognosis Encourages Royals.")

As to the surgery being "successful", the only good rotator cuff surgery is no rotator cuff surgery. I'd sink my life savings in junk bonds before I would put any stock in cheerful pronouncements about how he's going to be fine in January.

You can't say absolutely that the gamble of letting a pitcher who wasn't a hundred percent pitch 51 and a third innings in one month, May 8 to June 8, led to his rotator cuff injury. You *can* say absolutely that it was a gamble, and that Gubicza missed the rest of the year.

The signing of Boddicker was inter-

preted by some as a sign that Gubicza would not be able to return, although the Royals denied this. Reports in December are that he is throwing without pain from sixty feet, itchy to stretch it to ninety feet but sticking with the doctor's program. I don't believe that Gubicza has a mechanical problem which creates unusual ongoing stress, and would make it difficult for him to come back. After several years of struggle he's a smart veteran pitcher, and *will* be able to pitch effectively even if his velocity is not the same as it was.

Pedro GUERRERO, St. Louis
How long will he last? How will he be remembered?

Guerrero is 35 years old and very slow, and he's on a team caught in the grip of youth movement. It's unlikely he'll last more than another year as a regular with St. Louis, but may get a shot with an American League team as a DH.

I still feel that Guerrero was the best hitter of his generation, except maybe Jack Clark. Despite playing in terrible hitter's parks—he has lost about 36 home runs to the parks he played in—he has almost the same career batting average, slugging percentage and on-base percentage as George Brett. But he was never a good defensive player anywhere, couldn't stay healthy and had a reputation as a tough guy to manage. Whether it will be remembered that he could hit with anybody, it's tough to say.

Lee GUETTERMAN, New York Yankees
With Righetti gone, can he step into the role as the closer?

One assumes that, because he has done the job in the past, Steve Farr will get the first shot at the job as Yankee closer, with Guetterman setting him up.

Guetterman's been effective in three of the last four seasons, and has had a better ERA than Righetti the last two years. I think as long as nobody does anything stupid like ask him to throw more than thirty pitches in a game, he'll continue to be alright.

Ozzie GUILLEN, Chicago White Sox

Is he the White Sox' best player? Is he the best shortstop in the American League?

I know I'll get hammered for saying this, but I think he's an over-rated player. He's a good defensive shortstop, a .265 hitter and a very smart player, but with no power he's not going to drive in many runs, and with his on-base percentage (below .300) and baserunning (13 for 30 last year) he's not going to score many. His stolen base percentage was the worst in the major leagues among players with 25 or more attempts. With the retirement of Terry Francona he has the lowest career secondary average of any active player with 500 or more games (.135). His defense puts him a little ahead of the average shortstop, but offensively he's more like Felix Fermin than Alan Trammell.

Did he deserve his Gold Glove?

I'd have given it to Fernandez, who had a higher fielding percentage (.989-.977) and range factor (5.06 to 4.79).

Notes: The ten players with the lowest career secondary averages are Ozzie, Andrew Thomas, Curtis Wilkerson, Domingo Ramos, Mickey Hatcher, Scott Bradley, Alfredo Griffin, Rafael Ramirez, Jim Gantner and Donnie Hill.

Guillen was also the only major league player last year who saw less than three pitches per plate appearance. Guillen saw 1,604 pitches in 563 plate appearances, or 2.85 pitches per try. Teammate Lance Johnson was next-lowest, at 3.01.

Bill GULLICKSON, Houston

Did the Astros make a mistake in not re-signing him?

Gullickson made 32 starts last year with a 3.82 ERA, but the Astros elected not to pick up his option. Did they act correctly?

I think they did. It isn't that easy to find a starting pitcher who can stay healthy and post an ERA below four, but:

1. This is the Astrodome. ERAs have to be adjusted.
2. Gullickson struck out only 73 men, suggesting that he is living on the edge.
3. The Astros aren't likely to win in '91, anyway. They need to get serious about re-constructing a pitching rotation to get back in contention, and that means that they need to find the *stars*, not the ordinary pitchers. Searching for them can be a painful process, but the Astros need to go through it.

Eric GUNDERSON, San Francisco

Who is he?

Left-handed starting pitcher, 25 years old. A year ago *Baseball America* named him the #2 prospect in the Giants' system, citing his "mental toughness".

Is he a major league starter?

No. He might surprise as a reliever, but he's no better than a Grade C prospect, if that.

★★★
Mark GUTHRIE, Minnesota
★★★

How good is he?

As an individual, I like him *a lot*. He has the things you dream of seeing in a young pitcher—a left-hander who throws hard, has a breaking pitch and a good understanding of what he is doing. I have misgivings about the Twins' ability to help a young pitcher succeed, but if anyone can, I think Guthrie will.

Chris GWYNN, Los Angeles

Can he hit enough to play regularly?

He *has* made progress as a hitter, and has a better shot now than he did a cou-

ple of years ago. Time hasn't run out on him, as he's only 26. He still faces an uphill battle.

Tony GWYNN, San Diego

What was all that fuss about? Why are his teammates suddenly sniping at Tony Gwynn?

There was a big headline in the May 21, 1989 *Sporting News* which said "GWYNN: PADRES ARE TAKING ME FOR GRANTED." He meant, of course, that he was underpaid. In view of the fact that he was being paid less than six of his teammates, this seems eminently reasonable in its own distorted way, and Gwynn was speaking freely to reporters about the subject.

In mid-May Mike Pagliarulo told a New York writer about an unnamed teammate. "If we win and he goes 0 for 4, forget it," said Pagliarulo. "He's ticked. If he gets his hits and we lose, that's fine with him. He doesn't give a damn about this team, and that's weak."

Gwynn took the remarks to be directed at him, and fired back. This led to a closed-door, players-only clubhouse meeting on May 24. At that meeting, it was learned later, Gwynn "was blasted by teammates Jack Clark and Garry Templeton for caring more about his batting average than winning." (*Sports Illustrated*, October 1, 1990.)

The meeting was reported to have cleared the air, which would probably have lasted a week if the Padres had become monks, and taken a vow of silence. On September 8, Gwynn found a toy figurine of himself—I'm guessing a Kenner figure—hanging by a chain in the Padres' dugout. According to *The Sporting News* (September 24):

Gwynn assumed the prank was staged by one of his teammates. "It shocked me, absolutely shocked me," Gwynn said. "I can't believe someone would do that. It's like someone is testing me. This whole year has been like a test. People want to see me fail. They want to see me come down. Well, they can damn well do what they want; they're not bringing me down."

Before the figurine was discarded, Gwynn asked a photographer to take a picture of it. He then hung the photo in his locker. "I want it there so people who didn't see it can see what it looked like," Gwynn said. "I know I'm never going to forget about it."

A few days later it was revealed that the figure was placed there by an unidentified stadium worker, who meant it as a joke. This explanation is convenient enough to be regarded with just a dot of skepticism by those of us with suspicious minds.

On September 15 Gwynn fractured his right index finger in a collision with the wall in Atlanta; he underwent surgery September 19 to repair the finger.

Rather than remaining with the team, Gwynn cleaned out his locker and went home, triggering another round of criticism and controversy.

During this series of misadventures the public was generally behind Tony Gwynn. *Sports Illustrated* described Gwynn as "friendly, classy and accommodating." I do a radio show on Sunday nights, a call-in show with a national audience. George Will, who had spent a great deal of time with Tony Gwynn and made him a key figure in his book, *Men at Work*, was a guest on our show in late May. *"What* are these people *talking about?"* he asked. "What has any of these men ever done for the San Diego Padres that is comparable to what Tony Gwynn has done?" (Jim Bouton pointed out in *Ball Four* that in baseball, the value of what you say is universally assumed to depend on how good a ballplayer you are.) A caller late in the season went a step further, arguing that Tony Gwynn was such a wonderful guy that—this is a direct quote—"no matter what happened, it couldn't have been his fault."

A great deal of the action in this soap opera takes place off screen, and we have no way of knowing exactly what the truth is. Garry Templeton has become recognized as a clubhouse leader in San Diego, but in my own opinion Templeton is a dumb ballplayer who has wasted most of his talent because he had no idea what to do with it. One can't help but suspect that Garry Templeton's "leadership" has contributed to San Diego's disappointing play in the last few years.

Tony Gwynn is a smart, successful ballplayer who has turned what appear to be limited skills into a formidable talent.

The things that Templeton said about Gwynn—that he was greedy, more interested in his batting average than in winning—are the sorts of things that small-minded people will often say about those more successful than themselves.

But looking at the string of problems as a whole, not at any one incident, it is apparent that Gwynn not only *could* have been responsible for his own problems, but in fact *was* responsible for them.

It was Tony Gwynn who signed the contract which paid him $1,000,000 in 1990.

It was Tony Gwynn who decided that this wasn't enough money for a player of his quality.

It was Tony Gwynn who decided to complain about it to the newspapers, not once but several times.

When Pagliarulo spoke to a reporter, he didn't mention Tony Gwynn. Gwynn *assumed* that Pagliarulo was talking about him. Even if Pagliarulo *did* mean him, Gwynn didn't have to read it that way. He could have said to himself "I'm Tony Gwynn. I'm bigger than that."

Many people have access to a major league dugout—but when Gwynn found a figurine there, he assumed it was put there by another player.

It could have been intended as a harmless joke—we are told that it was—but Gwynn assumed that it was intended as an ugly message.

Tony Gwynn may well be "friendly, classy and accommodating"—but his statements *and* his actions in 1990 reflect insecurity and paranoia. Rather than taking the incidents and the criticism in stride, Gwynn savoured his hurts, tried to make the most of them. He took offense at an innocuous, obscure reference by Pagliarulo. He had a picture taken of the figurine so that we could all see what he was mad about.

If Tony Gwynn looks to his left he can see a good many players of lesser skill than himself who are earning more money than he is. But if he looks to his right he can see a vast number of people—a brother, a father, a cousin, a schoolmate—who are working just as hard as he is for two or three percent of his income. He chose to look to his left.

I'm all for ballplayers making big money, as opposed to the owners keeping it all. Hell, I not only *would* help them earn it, I *do*. If Tony Gwynn can make $4 million a year, I'm happy for him.

But if Tony Gwynn makes a million dollars a year and complains about it, that's another matter. What Pagliarulo, Clark and Templeton were telling Gwynn, in effect, was that his bitching and moaning about his salary was hurting the team, and it was time to shut up about it. I'm with them. Any ballplayer who makes a million dollars a year and complains about it deserves a good swift kick in the balls. Tony Gwynn got one. And Tony Gwynn must take the responsibility for stemming this tide of unfortunate events. If he doesn't, no one else can.

Stat notes: With the release of Bill Buckner, who was at 5.99 to 1, Tony Gwynn has by far the best ratio of career hits to strikeouts in the majors (5.98 to 1). Even last year, having a distressing season, he had easily the best ratio in the majors (7.7 to 1) He was followed on the 1990 list by Brian Harper, Don Mattingly, Felix Fermin and Greg Jeffries; he is followed on the career list by Mattingly, Johnny Ray, Marty Barrett and Wade Boggs . . . Gwynn also had the best strikeout/walk ratio in the major leagues last year.

•H•

John HABYAN,
New York Yankees
Is he a major league pitcher?

Habyan, now 27 years old, has had major league trials since 1985 without sticking. He's never really been great even in the minor leagues. At this point, it's questionable whether he is even a Grade D prospect.

Chip HALE, Minnesota
Could he be a regular this year?

I don't see any reason that Hale can't be a regular second baseman, but let's face facts. The Twins in the last few years have tried Wally Backman, Tommy Herr, Al Newman, Fred Manrique and Nelson Liriano at second base. If he doesn't get a chance to play in that environment, when his team is trying out new second basemen every week, he ain't going to get a chance to play. He could make it as a utility infielder.

Drew HALL, Montreal
Is he any closer to being what he was supposed to?

Hall, a big left-hander with a good fastball, was once the top pitching prospect in the Cubs' system, and has had trials now with Chicago, Texas and Montreal. Last year he pitched 40 games with Montreal, with a 5.09 ERA, which is still better than his career ERA.

He may have a pulse left, as a prospect, but it's getting weak. Unless he turns it around he is within one or two years of being out of baseball.

Mel HALL,
New York Yankees

There don't seem to be any basic questions to ask about Hall which don't have obvious answers. Does he justify the roster spot . . . obviously he does; he's a good hitter against right-handed pitching. He's consistent with the bat, and won't kill you if he has to play the outfield. Does he have a chance to be a regular (much less a star) . . . obviously not, since he can't hit left-handed pitching at all. He's not at an age at which his skills or his role on the team figure to change suddenly.

Daryl HAMILTON, Milwaukee
Is he as good as he was last year?
Is he going to be a regular?

Hamilton, a veteran minor leaguer with one previous half-season as a reserve outfielder (1988), was the pleasant surprise of the Brewer season in 1990. On the roster primarily as a pinch runner and defensive sub, Hamilton hit .295 for the season and, following the trade of Braggs and the poor performance of Vaughn, was able to earn some playing time.

Hamilton's major league career batting average, .251, is probably not too far from his true ability, which doesn't absolutely mean he can't play in the majors. Let's assume that he can hit a few points better than that, .270, steal some bases and draw 50–70 walks, which it appears he would. He could score enough runs to stay in the lineup.

I wouldn't bet on it.

Jeff HAMILTON, Los Angeles
How far back will he come?

Hamilton was the Dodgers' regular third baseman before his injury, which was to the rotator cuff. Obviously a 27-year-old player who was a regular in 1989 and is healthy in 1991 figures to be in the major leagues. There are four reasons to wonder if he will be able to regain a starting job:

1. he wasn't great anyway. As a regular third baseman he scored 45 runs and drove in 56.
2. his strongest asset was the one which is damaged, his throwing arm. With the exception of Dunston he had the best arm of any major league infielder,

and could throw a fastball in the mid-nineties.

3. the men who replaced him at third base in 1990, Lenny Harris and Mike Sharperson, were both very good.

4. see Dave Hansen.

Atlee HAMMAKER, San Diego
Is he going to keep doing this forever? Will he be around next year?

Hammaker had an ERA of 4.36 last year, ending a string of four years with almost identical ERAs around 3.70, and a string of three straight years with won-lost percentages exactly .500. Late in the season he was dropped by the Giants and picked up by the Padres. Actually, though, I don't think he pitched any worse last year than he had the previous years. His luck was just off. Since he didn't pitch well with the Padres and there is no history there, nothing to bind the Padres to him, he'll be lucky to make a roster in '91.

Chris HAMMOND, Cincinnati
Who is he?

Left-handed starting pitcher, worked through the minors with sensational won-lost records (composite 56-28), but didn't pitch well in three starts with Cincinnati.

Hammond is a *very* good prospect, a Grade A prospect. He has a super changeup, and throws hard enough to set it up. His control isn't real good, but it's always been good enough for him to win. He would probably have gotten a more thorough trial in '90 if the Reds weren't in a pennant race. He's a good prospect for the NL Rookie of the Year in 1991.

Dave HANSEN, Los Angeles
Who is he?

Third baseman, hit .316 with 92 RBI at Albuquerque and was named by *Baseball America* as the sixth-best prospect in the Pacific Coast League. MLEs show that as a regular he would hit about .270

with 8-10 home runs, but a strikeout/walk ratio better than even. He's only 22 years old, a left-handed hitter and said to be a good defensive third baseman.

Hansen is *going* to play regularly in the major leagues; it's just a question of when. With the Dodgers being stacked up at third base (Sharperson, Harris and Hamilton) he will probably not play a lot this year, 1991, but if the Dodgers don't want him, there are about twenty teams that would love to have him.

Erik HANSON, Seattle
Is he really that good?

Every bit that good. Hanson was 18-9 last year with 211 strikeouts. He's the number three right-handed starting pitcher in the American League, behind Clemens and Stewart. If he doesn't get hurt, he may be the best in a couple of years.

Mike HARKEY, Chicago Cubs
How good will he be?

Very good, I hope. There are three areas of concern in projecting Harkey to be an outstanding pitcher. Those are:

1. his health record—he missed most of the 1989 season with tendinitis in the shoulder.
2. he pitches in Wrigley Field, where only a few pitchers in forty years have had good careers.
3. his strikeout rate isn't as high as I would like it to be. He struck out 4.9 men per game last year.

In spite of those things, Harkey has a good chance to be among the best starting pitchers in the National League. He's young, he's big, he throws hard, and he's a competitor.

Pete HARNISCH, Baltimore
Will he ever become a quality starter?

He should. He's 24, has major league stuff and isn't a bad pitcher. If you figure a three percent gain in control and a

three percent gain in effectiveness due to experience, he comes in about 14-12 this year. Pitchers don't work that way, of course.

Brian HARPER, Minnesota
How can a guy who is this good spend so many years in the minor leagues?

First of all, he's not *that* good; he's a .286 hitter with doubles but not a home run hitter, and not great defensively.

That's not answering the question, though. Harper came up with the Angels at a time when

a. they were committed to trying to win with free agents, and
b. they simply didn't have the ability to make a good decision about a young player.

It's like a bad marriage; it casts a long shadow. The Angels made bad decisions about a lot of people in a few years Rance Mulliniks, Tom Brunansky, Dickie Thon. Harper is another one.

In 1981 Harper hit .350 with 28 homers, 45 doubles and 122 RBI in the Pacific Coast League; he was 21 years old. He should have been in the majors in 1982, but the Angels traded him to Pittsburgh for a sack of potpourri and a petrified starfish. I shouldn't make fun of the Angels; they did win the division in 1982, although the title was purchased at a terrible cost.

Anyway, the Pirates

a. didn't think Harper could catch, and
b. already had Tony Pena.

Harper became a pinch hitter/outfielder, and after hitting well enough for a couple of years fell into a slump, at which time it was decided that he didn't hit enough to play regularly in the major leagues. He became a journeyman, and it took almost ten years for him to regain his confidence and find his role in the major leagues.

Apart from the fact that he's a singles

hitter and Cliff Johnson was a power hitter, it's quite a bit like the Cliff Johnson epic.

Say, did you notice that Harper hit 42 doubles last year? Is that a record for a catcher? I didn't see it anywhere, but I can't remember another catcher hitting 42 doubles in a season, can you?

Note: Harper in his career has grounded into more double plays per at bat than any other active player, one every 26 at bats. His ratio last year was the fourth-worst, behind Tony Pena, Ivan Calderon and Jeff Leonard.

Gene HARRIS, Seattle
Is he a major league pitcher?

I think so, yes. He's a Grade C prospect, but I like him.

Greg A. HARRIS, Boston
Will he last the year in the Sox' rotation?

The Red Sox have had some success over the years with pitchers who arrived in Boston with no better credentials than Harris—Ellis Kinder, Ray Culp, Sonny Siebert. Luis Tiant arrived in Boston when he was 30 and his career was on the rocks, although he had been a great pitcher.

The departure of Boddicker and Andersen and the signing of Darwin and Matt Young throw the Boston staff into chaos. It's anybody's guess whether Harris will open the season as the Red Sox number three starter, number four starter, number five starter or long reliever. But for ten years, major league teams have given up on Harris the moment he began to struggle. There is no reason to think they'll stop now.

Greg W. HARRIS, San Diego
Should he be somebody's closer?

He's building a case. He's got a 2.40 ERA through two-plus major league seasons, which is better than Thigpen, Franco, Eckersley, Myers, Reardon, Lee

Smith . . . most anybody. He came to the majors with a good fastball, and has shown a surprising curve.

Lenny HARRIS, Los Angeles
Is he going to hit .300 consistently? How does he fit into the Dodgers third base picture?

Harris hit .236 as a rookie in 1989, but jumped to .304 last year. He has never done anything anywhere to suggest that he is a legitimate .300 hitter, or even a .280 hitter. He hit .246 in the Midwest League in 1984 (all of these averages are as a regular), .259 in the Florida State League in 1985, .253 in the Eastern League in 1986, and .248 and .277 in two years in the American Association. What is perhaps most interesting is that he continued to make steady progress through the minor leagues even though he didn't hit, which indicates that *somebody* saw *something* they liked.

I think it's very unlikely that Harris will hit .300 again. I suspect he's a .260 hitter. With the Dodgers' crowd at third base, it's likely that Harris will have to tear through a crowd of second basemen to get established as a regular. My guess is that he'll never be able to do it.

Reggie HARRIS, Oakland
Did the A's come up with anything here?

Probably not, but you never know. Harris, the Red Sox' number one draft pick in 1987, was unimpressive for three years in the Boston system, so the Sox didn't protect him on their winter roster. The A's drafted him under Rule 5, kept him on the roster for a year and spotted him into a few games. They received very favorable press notices for this; according to the November 25, 1990 *Baseball America*, Harris "has become one of the prizes of the organization, a pitcher who has the potential to step into a major league starting job only one season removed from a losing record in Double-A."

With the supervision of Dave Duncan and the advantage of pitching in the Oakland Coliseum, Harris has a chance to be a major league pitcher. Dave Stewart has taken him under his wing, and that's got to be a tremendous help.

But to be honest, there isn't a lot to like about him as a major league pitcher. He throws over ninety, but then so do a hundred other guys who can't pitch major league baseball. His career record in the minor leagues is 16-32, and that's about how well he's pitched. There have been pitchers with records like that who made it in the majors. He's a good athlete, was offered scholarships to play college basketball. He's a Grade C prospect.

Mike HARTLEY, Los Angeles
What's his role?

This sucker can *pitch*, that's his role. Anybody who can post a 0.80 ERA at Albuquerque (1988, 30 games, 45 innings) can pitch for me.

Hartley, in the minor leagues since 1982, took a long time to emerge as a prospect. He was signed by the Cardinals as an undrafted free agent, but was stuck in the low minors due to control problems. He was being used as a starter. Drafted by the Dodgers in December, 1986, he was converted immediately to the bullpen, and began to edge upward, reaching the majors last year and pitching well. He's a good reliever; in my opinion he could be a closer . . . In high school he was a championship wrestler.

Cullen HARTZOG, New York
Who is he?

Right-handed pitcher, said to have the best arm in the Yankee system. He pitched so-so at Prince William last year (A ball), fights his control and tends to put on weight, but the scouts like him, so you read about him sometimes. Grade C prospect in my opinion.

Bryan HARVEY, California
Where does he rank, among reliev- ers? Is he good enough for a cham- pionship team?

In the last two years he has struck out more men per nine innings than anyone except Dibble. His control is OK, but he has bad outings sometimes.

Harvey pitched only 64 innings last year, 55 in 1989, when he had a leg in- jury. I suspect he would benefit from pitching a few more innings. He's awfully strong to be working that few innings. He throws 92 MPH and throws a forkball.

There are four outstanding relievers in the American League—Eckersley, Olson, Henke and Thigpen. With the off season of Plesac, Harvey or Jeff Mont- gomery would rank as the fifth best.

Bill HASELMAN, Texas
Who is he?

A catcher who was at Double-A last year; he appears to be a hitter. He was a first-round draft pick in 1987, made slow progress for a couple of years before mak- ing a leap forward last year. He's a big guy (6-3, 200 pounds), average defensively and not a disciplined hitter, but probably has a major league future because of his bat—.270 range hitter with power to hit 12-20 homers in a season.

Ron HASSEY, Oakland
Will he be around?

I can't understand why an organiza- tion would want to keep *both* Ron Hassey and Jamie Quirk. Hassey hit .213 last year, .228 the year before, and he doesn't throw well enough to get by with that. There are an unusual number of good backup catchers trapped in AAA ball at the moment. I can't see any reason he would be on a major league roster.

Billy HATCHER, Cincinnati
Is he as good as he looked in Octo- ber?

No. He's just another in a long line of ordinary or less-than-ordinary players who got hot in September. In his case, less than ordinary. Hatcher batted 504 times last year and drove in 25 runs, the fewest of any major league player with more than 500 at bats. (In fact, every other major league player with 500 at bats drove in *at least* 50% more runs than Hatcher. Kevin Seitzer had the sec- ond-fewest RBI among regulars, with 38.) Hatcher's ratio of RBI to total bases was also the lowest in the major leagues.

He hit leadoff about half the time, which partially explains the low RBI count, but

a. every team has a leadoff hitter,
b. he also batted 291 times in spots 2, 5, 6, 7 and 8.
c. the Reds eighth-place hitter, Mariano Duncan, is a good hitter, hit .306.

Hatcher hit just .198 with men in scor- ing position (21/106), and all of his home runs were with the bases empty. Hatcher also scored only 68 runs, which is ex- tremely few for a leadoff man.

He was having one of his best years, hit .276 after hitting .231 the year before. He's not much of a player.

Mickey HATCHER, Los Angeles
Is his playing career over?

One would think so, but I wouldn't be too sure. His own poor performance and the exceptionally good season of Lenny Harris, who fills a similar role on the team, certainly places him in jeopardy. Still, Hatcher hit .293 in 1988 and .295 in 1989, and that might well be enough to get him a job in '91.

(**Late Note:** Hatcher has been offered salary arbitration by the Dodgers.)

Andy HAWKINS, New York Yankees
Will he ever be effective again?

He may, but he'll always be a bad risk. When he won 18 games in 1985, his ratio of strikeouts to wins was less than four to one, making it obvious that he could not sustain that level of performance (see Ron Robinson). His control went last year. If his control comes back he is capa- ble of doing again what he did in '85 or '88, but he's always going to be a bad risk.

Charlie HAYES, Philadelphia
Where does he rank? Is he one of the better third basemen in the league? Is he developing?

Hayes improved dramatically on de- fense last year, but still has to prove that he deserves a regular job. His perform- ance levels in all areas of the game are more that of a reserve than a regular. The Phillies are indulging him by keeping him in the lineup in the hope that he'll de- velop, and in their position—they don't have anybody better—that's the smart thing for them to do. But he can't go on as a regular hitting .260 with an on-base percentage below .300 and a slugging per- centage in the mid- three hundreds. That's tough even for Terry Pendleton, who has a Gold Glove rep.

Von HAYES, Philadelphia
Is he overrated?

No, he's a good player. When you play for a losing team, some people are going to brand you a loser. He's about like Kevin McReynolds.

Mike HEATH, Detroit
Will he play 122 games again this year? Could he have been a regular earlier in his career?

It is puzzling, in view of the perpetual demand for catchers, that he didn't become a regular earlier or remain one longer when he was one (1984–85 with Oakland.) He's a decent hitter, .250 range with a little power, a good defen- sive player now although he probably needed more games at catcher before he came to the majors. He's middle of the pack, not the catcher that Tony Pena is or the hitter that Lance Parrish is, but OK. He should remain a regular in '91.

Neal HEATON, Pittsburgh
Was his first half a fluke? Will he be successful again?

Heaton was 12-9 last year, with a 3.45 ERA. The statistical indicators of the ability to sustain success aren't quite screaming "FLUKE", but there are red flags:

1. When he has pitched well in the past, he has always flopped in the following season.
2. He pitched well the first half of the season last year, but didn't do anything the second half.

On the other hand, his performance last year wasn't significantly better than the year before. In 1989 he pitched 147 innings with a 3.05 ERA; last year he pitched 146 innings with a 3.45 ERA. Also, his ratio of strikeouts to wins (5.7-1) is low, but it isn't alarmingly low. His strikeout/walk ratio last year was pretty decent.

Danny HEEP, Boston
What happened to him?

He had surgery July 16 for removal of a herniated disc in his back, was in traction for a while. His position with the team wasn't safe anyway, and he'll probably have to go down and prove he can still hit to get a major league job in '91.

Scott HEMOND, Oakland
Is he eventually going to replace Carney Lansford?

Hemond, the A's number one draft pick in 1986, has reached the AAA level and begun to poke through into the majors. At this point he is no threat to Lansford or anybody else—a .220, .230 range hitter with some speed but little power. I don't expect him to have a major league career.

Dave HENDERSON, Oakland
Who's going to play center for the Athletics in 1991? Is this Henderson vital to their team?

The A's have signed Willie Wilson. Wilson, despite his age and lack of a throwing arm, is a better center fielder than Henderson, but Henderson is a much better hitter and better suited to play in Oakland. My guess is that Wilson will be a fourth outfielder/defensive sub/pinch runner, and Henderson will remain the regular center fielder.

Rickey HENDERSON, Oakland
Should he have been the MVP?

I wrote my argument about that under Cecil Fielder, and won't repeat it here. To me, it is obvious that he was the best player in the league. He led the majors in all of the basic offensive indicators—runs created, runs created per out and offensive winning percentage.

Is he the best leadoff man ever?

During the World Series somebody on ESPN referred to him as "Rickey Henderson, who some say is one of the best leadoff men in baseball." This is a landmark of understatement, like describing Nolan Ryan as "one of the better strikeout pitchers of the last few years." Rickey Henderson *is* the greatest leadoff man in baseball history, by a wide margin, and no one who knows anything would argue about that.

In the September 20, 1990 edition of *USA Today*, in an article by Tom Weir, Rickey Henderson is quoted as saying that the record he most wants to break is Ty Cobb's career record for runs scored, which is 2,245. "That's the No. 1 thing I look at now when I think about what I want to do," quotes Weir, who then adds, inexplicably, that "With Henderson just approaching 1,300 that record appears out of reach."

Why in the world would you think that record was out of reach? Here's a 31-year-old man (then) who has already accomplished 57% of a goal. If a baseball player accomplishes 57% of something by age 31, why would you not think he had a chance to accomplish the other 43% *after* age 31? Doesn't it seem like he's about where he ought to be?

Obviously, it is a very difficult goal—the record, which is one of the game's most important, has stood for a long time—and the odds are that Henderson will fall short. But since Henderson and Cobb were both born in late December, comparisons of them at the same age are close comparisons. Because Cobb started young and fast, Tyrus at one time was 150 runs ahead of Rickey at the same age. Now, comparing them at the same age, Henderson is just 33 runs behind, 1,323 to 1,290. My estimate is that Henderson has a 17% chance of breaking this record.

Note: Rickey led the majors in so many things, and so many important and basic things like runs created and offensive winning percentage, that it would be a considerable undertaking to list them all. One stat that you probably didn't hear was that Rickey hit .426 in the late innings of close games (26 for 61, also twenty walks). Henderson and Walt Weiss (.405) were the only American Leaguers over .400.

Tom HENKE, Toronto
Where does he rank?

Henke is one of the top three or four relievers in baseball, and the most unappreciated of the good ones. Pitching in a hitter's park, he has tremendous ERAs and strikeout rates. He's been extremely effective for five and a half seasons.

In my opinion, based on where they are *now,* Henke has to rate way ahead of guys like Righetti, Bedrosian, McDowell and Reardon, and safely ahead of the $3 million dollar class, the guys like Franco, Doug Jones and Burke. He rates with Myers, Dibble, Olson and possibly Thigpen in the class just behind Eckersley.

Mike HENNEMAN, Detroit
Is he a solid closer? Do the Tigers need to replace him?

He is not a solid closer, and the Tigers do need to find one, but it probably isn't their top priority. Henneman was sharing the closer role with Jerry Don Gleaton last year. Henneman's a good pitcher, but after four years as a closer his career high in saves is 22, and his ERA is around three. He blew six saves last year, which isn't a lot. Until the Tigers come up with some starting pitchers who can go seven, he's probably as good a closer as they need.

Randy HENNIS, Houston
Who is he?

Right-handed starting pitcher, a big horse with poor control and no breaking pitch. Grade C prospect.

Dwayne HENRY, Atlanta
Is he out of chances?

He has one hundred career game appearances, with an ERA of 5.43. Since 1986 his ERAs are 4.66, 9.00, 8.71, 4.26 and 5.63. He looks good on the mound, but what more do you need to see?

My comment about him last year was "with the Braves' abundance of pitching prospects will have to work his way back by pitching well at Richmond." He did. He pitched 13 games at Richmond with a 2.33 ERA, gave up twelve hits in 27 innings, and of course the Braves needed relief help, which is like saying you need a fly swatter in Calcutta. He bombed, and at 29 is pretty much indistinguishable from Wes Gardner except that he hasn't pitched as well.

Carlos HERNANDEZ, Los Angeles
Who is he?

Catching prospect, young, built like a catcher and has hit .300 at AA and AAA. A Venezuelan native, he was signed for the Dodgers in 1984 by two scouts, both of whom are now dead. He was just 17 then, and didn't begin to impress anybody until 1988. *Baseball America* ranked him last year as the top catching prospect in the Dodger system, and he didn't hurt that by hitting .315 at Albuquerque.

He should be on the roster this year, back up Scioscia for two or three years and then get a shot at the regular job. I think he'd hit .260–.270 in the majors at this point, and that could improve although a catcher doesn't normally improve his hitting very much after his mid-twenties.

Keith HERNANDEZ, Cleveland
Does he have any chance to go in the Hall of Fame?

He does have a chance to go in the Hall of Fame, yes, although the odds are that he will have a long wait.

Hernandez did 38 things which I recognize as being characteristic of a Hall of Fame type player. He hit .300 (six times), had two hundred hits in a season and drove in a hundred runs. He scored a hundred runs (twice), had 35 doubles twice and 45 doubles another year. He drew a hundred walks in a season, led the league at various times in batting average, runs scored (twice), and doubles. He had more than 2,000 hits in his career. He won an MVP Award, or actually shared one, played in five All-Star games, won eleven Gold Gloves and was a regular on two World Champion teams (the 1982 Cardinals and the 1986 Mets.) All of these are the sorts of things that Hall of Famers do.

As best I can evaluate it, Hernandez ranks in the bottom half of the gray area, meaning that *most* players with comparable credentials do *not* go in the Hall of Fame, but some have. But this is also the area in which a player's image, his charisma, is most important, and Keith certainly had a mystique about him. He played in New York, and was popular with the writers and the fans. He could go in the Hall of Fame, but the odds are that it will be a long time before he does.

Xavier HERNANDEZ, Houston
Is he a major league pitcher?

The only thing he has going for him is the Astrodome. Apart from that there

is *no* indication that he is a major league pitcher.

Tom HERR, New York Mets
Will he help the Mets?

As to the general proposition that a team needs to have a second baseman, I vote yes. Granting that Jefferies is a player of immense value and Herr is not, I would still rather start the year with Herr as my second baseman than Jefferies, simply because Herr is a second baseman. Herr, over the course of a season, would probably turn about thirty double plays that Jefferies would not.

I think Herr's signing is a good one. Herr is 35, which is a legitimate concern, but you can't use it against him. You can't evaluate a ballplayer by his birth certificate, independent of other information. Herr can still hit. He can still run. He can still play second base. Those are all things that the Mets have been needing at second base.

Orel HERSHISER, Los Angeles
Can he come back?

At the time of his rotator cuff surgery Dr. Jobe announced that Hershiser would miss the rest of the 1990 season, but "I look for him to be back next year and be as good as in 1988." Dr. Jobe is full of beans, don't you think? How many times have you seen a pitcher miss an entire season, and be fine the next spring? A broken leg or something, maybe, but a rotator cuff?

Setting aside the campaign promises (please), I have no idea what Hershiser's chance of making a comeback is. Let me tell you one thing which is useful. If Hershiser is pitching in April and posts a 1.17 ERA in April, this means nothing. We *know* that Hershiser is a good pitcher anyway. What is at issue here is whether his shoulder will stand up to the rigors of a major league schedule.

I think there is *no* likelihood, none, that Hershiser can resume pitching 260 innings a year, at least in the next two or three years. It is very likely that he will pitch well, when he pitches, early in the season. What must be tested is

1. whether he can carry a reasonable workload, and
2. whether Lasorda can recognize his limits and keep him within them until he regains his strength.

If Lasorda lets him pitch nine innings in a game in April or May, then the answer to the second question is clearly "no", and you'll want to dump him, even if he is pitching shutouts. The first question will simply remain open until mid-season.

Joe HESKETH, Boston
Can he help the Red Sox bullpen?
I doubt it. He has a good strikeout to walk ratio, which you all know I like to see, and he pitched well for the Sox. The problem is that

1. until last August he hadn't gotten anybody out for two years, and
2. he's no more effective against left-handed hitters than right-handers.

It's hard to use a left-handed spot reliever who doesn't get out left-handers.

Eric HETZEL, Boston
Is he a major league pitcher?
See "Wes Gardner" comment. Hetzel's career record, 3-7, is the same as Gardner's record in each of the last two years.

Hetzel has good stuff, but he walked 74 men in 109 innings at Pawtucket last year. That indicates that he lacks confidence in his ability to get people out with his basic pitches, and is probably trying to hit corners with impossible pitches. Fenway will tear up a pitcher like that.

Greg HIBBARD, Chicago
Can he win twenty games?
It's unlikely that Hibbard can pitch consistently at the level he reached in 1990 (14-9, 3.16 ERA.) Three things:

1. He has a limited history of sustained success. In 1988 he was 11-11, 4.12 ERA at Vancouver.
2. He struck out less than four men a game, while almost all successful pitchers strike out more than that.
3. He pitched more innings last year than ever before in his professional career, which often indicates a coming decline.

His strikeout rate *did* increase last year, and it isn't alarmingly low. His workload didn't increase dramatically; just slightly. My guess is he'll go 13-14 with an ERA around 4.00.

Kevin HICKEY, Baltimore
Was his '89 season a fluke?
Of course. It's nice to believe in Cinderella, but you've got to believe in midnight, too.

Ted HIGUERA, Milwaukee
Will he ever start 35 games in a season again?
He could. Higuera, who is a wonderful pitcher, has two problems which contribute to his injuries. First, he puts on weight, which may (or may not) have contributed to his trouble in 1989. Second, he completes his delivery balancing on his right foot in a somewhat awkward manner, which could put stress on his knee and lower back.

Don't misinterpret that comment. It is almost impossible to throw a baseball in such a way that, over a period of years, it doesn't put strain on some part of your body. Higuera has a beautiful, graceful delivery, except for a little bit of awkwardness at the end. Pitchers get hurt.

Last year Higuera was struck on his knee by a line drive from Henry Cotto, May 21. He pitched with the soreness, which probably contributed to his later injuries. On June 13 he went on the disabled list with a pulled groin. In August he was diagnosed with tendinitis in his left shoulder. Higuera very well could

come back and be an outstanding pitcher over the next five seasons.

Donnie HILL, California
Has he found his niche with the Angels? Will he be consistent at this level?
Hill, who had floated around for years as a fringe player, hit .217 for the White Sox in '88, was released, signed by the A's, played 1989 in the minor leagues, and was released by the A's. He landed a job with California last year and played well, hitting .264 in 102 games.

Hill's 1990 performance was a surprise, but it really was not far from his career performance norms. His batting average and slugging percentage were within six points of his career norms. In that sense, there is no reason to believe that he was over his head. On the other hand, this is exactly the same thing I said last year about Milt Thompson, and you know how that worked out . . .

Glenallen HILL, Toronto
Will he break through this year, with Bell and Felix gone? Did he see "Arachnaphobia"?
A year ago I had Hill marked with stars, meaning "draft him". Get him on your team, in your rotisserie league, your APBA league or whatever.

In retrospect, I don't know why the hell I did this. Hill has been a prospect since the early eighties, and I have always been skeptical about him. I have always categorized him as one of those guys with tremendous ability who simply didn't know how to play baseball—a guy who would hit about .235 in the major leagues.

In 1989 at Syracuse he did have a tremendous season, a season which would strongly indicate that he was capable of hitting major league pitching. I took that season way too seriously. I should have held it at arm's length, as I have the 1990 successes of Lenny Harris, Ron Robinson and a hundred other people, and said

"I'd like to see more." I over-reacted to limited information, and if I caused you to have him on your team, I apologize.

Now, is he helped by the departure of Junior Felix and George Bell . . . no, not really, because they've been replaced by Devon White and Joe Carter. It helps more that McGriff is gone, which probably keeps Olerud out of the outfield, and that Mookie Wilson will probably be released or on the bench, but Hill must still break through a crowd of outfielders. He's not a *bad* player and he could have a big year sometime, but he's always going to strike out.

★ ★ ★
Ken HILL, St. Louis
★ ★ ★

What?

Hill went to Louisville last year and mastered a forkball, a new pitch. His control record also improved dramatically, in the majors and minors. He could be a completely different pitcher this year than he was in '89.

Shawn HILLEGAS, Cleveland
Will he help the Indians?

Hillegas, once a prospect in the Dodger system as a starter, bombed with the White Sox in '89, but re-established himself by posting a 1.74 ERA with Vancouver last year.

When they film the series "Adventures with the White Sox" Hillegas will be another episode, like Kenny Williams or Lance Johnson. Hillegas, a starter all his life including five years in the minors, started six games for the White Sox late in '88, posting a 3.15 ERA. In '87 he had started ten times for the Dodgers, and done well enough there, too, 4-3, 3.57 ERA.

He started slowly with the White Sox in '89, so they sent him to the bullpen. Despite pitching well over the last four months of the '89 season (3.00 ERA in his last 37 games), the Sox sent him to Vancouver last year, and then included

him in the trade for Cory Snyder.

He can help the Indians. He's a major league pitcher—has been since 1987. The White Sox didn't seem to like him, for some reason, but he's as good a pitcher as Patterson or Peterson or Perez or any of those people. Radinsky and Rosenberg. The Indians can use him.

Howard HILTON, St. Louis
Who is he?

Big right-handed relief pitcher with the Cardinals. Stays healthy but doesn't have much else to recommend him. Grade D prospect.

Chris HOILES, Baltimore
Will he move Tettleton off the plate this season?

Hoiles, always regarded as having potential as a hitter, began to actually hit last summer, hitting .348 at Rochester with a .655 slugging percentage. Babe Ruth's stats, roughly speaking.

A year ago I didn't think that Hoiles would make it as a major league regular. Now I have no doubt that Chris Hoiles can hit major league pitching—hit it well enough to hold a regular job, maybe even belt his way into a few All-Star games. He can hit .280–.310 with power. He still faces an uphill battle to get a major league job. He has never impressed anybody as a catcher, and most people doubt that he will be able to play that position regularly in the major leagues. At first base/DH the Orioles already have:

1. One of their best players, Randy Milligan,
2. Sam Horn, who also can hit,
3. David Segui, who is probably not the hitter than Hoiles is, but a good hitter and a better fielder.

Dave HOLLINS, Philadelphia
Who is he?

Young third baseman, drafted by the Phillies from the San Diego system a year ago. Philadelphia had to keep him on the

major league roster or let San Diego have him back, but he needs a full season at AAA to be taken seriously.

I saw Hollins play at Wichita in '89. He's an excellent athlete, reminds me of a young George Brett with maybe a little more speed. He impressed me as having a major league attitude, and I mean that in the worst sense. He's too young to write off (24) and too good an athlete, but he still has a long way to go.

Brian HOLMAN, Seattle
Where's he rank, among the Mariner starters? Could he catch up to Hanson and Johnson?

Holman, the Mariners number three starter, pitched fairly well, 11-11 with a 4.03 ERA. He had a decent strikeout/walk ratio, 121-64.

He's a basic, old-style pitcher—nothing outstanding, nothing negative. He doesn't have a great fastball, but he does have a fastball. He changes speeds, throws two or three breaking pitches, mixes up his pitches well and has reasonably good location. I see no reason that he shouldn't be a consistently good pitcher over the next several years.

Darren HOLMES, Los Angeles
Who is he?

Right-handed relief pitcher, struck out 99 men in 93 innings at Albuquerque. He's been in the minors for a long time as a starting pitcher, in which role his career was going nowhere, but switched to the bullpen last year and was quite effective.

The Dodgers have relief pitchers, so the opportunity for Holmes isn't good. Holmes is in line behind Howell, Crews, Gott and Hartley, at least. The Dodgers almost certainly will be making an all-out push to win in 1991, so they're not going to go with him a long time if he doesn't pitch well. Still, put together two things—

1. 99 strikeouts in 93 innings at Albuquerque, and
2. Dodger Stadium,

and you've got a pitcher who can explode on the league. If he pitches 54 games with an ERA of 1.51, I'm not going to be shocked.

Rick HONEYCUTT, Oakland
How critical is he to the A's?

He's not critical. He's a good pitcher, but the A's could replace him if they needed to. Joe Klink or somebody. They shouldn't need to. One thing LaRussa does awfully well is keep pitchers within their limits.

John HOOVER, Texas
Who is he?

You remember "John Who?" The Giants one year had a kid named John Pregenzer who made the team out of nowhere, and some people decided to start a fan club for him, which they called the "John Who? Fan Club".

This is the new John Who, John Whoover. Like the original, he's a 28-year-old right-hander who has been kicking around the minor leagues for years—in fact, he was signed by the Rangers a year ago as a six-year free agent. No one, including me, expects him to be a major league pitcher.

Sam HORN, Baltimore
Could he play everyday?

I'd be awfully reluctant to say that he couldn't. Horn's career totals now are uncannily similar to Cecil Fielder's a year ago. Fielder before he went to the land of the Rising Sun had 506 major league at bats with 31 home runs, 84 RBI, a .243 average, but people had always kind of dismissed him by saying that he couldn't maintain that kind of power ratio if he played every day. Horn as of now has 519 at bats with 30 homers, 91 RBI and a .235 average, but people talk about his being inconsistent with the bat and just having a couple of hot streaks when he has hit home runs.

I'm certainly not suggesting that Horn would hit 50 home runs if you gave him a chance and a park, but there are many noticeable similarities. The two men are almost the same size (two of the biggest men in baseball) and almost the same age (separated by five weeks).

Ricky HORTON, St. Louis
Will he get another shot, or is this the end?

There is *no* reason to believe that Horton can pitch. His ERAs the last three years are 4.87, 4.85 and 4.93, which is consistent if nothing else. His strikeout/walk ratios are terrible—he doesn't strike anybody out, and he doesn't have great control.

Steve HOSEY, San Francisco
Who is he?

21-year-old outfielder, regarded a year ago as the top prospect in the San Francisco system. His stock has fallen sharply after he hit .232 at San Jose.

Charlie HOUGH, Chicago White Sox
How long can he keep pitching?

Hough is 43. The experience of previous knuckle-ball pitchers suggests that declines will be detectable, but not dramatic, for the next four years. I picked Phil Niekro, Hoyt Wilhelm and Dutch Leonard as the most-comparable pitchers. At age 42 the three of them pitched 302 innings with a 22-15 won-lost record. At age 44 they pitched 359 innings with a 17-17 record, and at age 46 they pitched 302 innings with a 22-17 record.

You have to be concerned about the steady degeneration of Hough's strikeout to walk ratio. In 1987 he struck out 223 men and walked 124, a ratio of 1.90-1. In 1988 the ratio declined to 1.38-1, in 1989 to .99-1 and in 1990 to .96-1. He's got to turn that around, or he may not get the chance to find out whether he can pitch when he's 46. But working with Fisk, as opposed to the Rangers' catcher-of-the-week program, has got to help.

Incidentally, what's the oldest battery in history?

Mike HOUSE, Minnesota Farm System
Who is he?

House is a first baseman who was the Twins 18th-round draft pick in 1989, drafted out of Hawaii Pacific. He went to Elizabethton in the Appalachian League in 1989, where he hit .376 and led the league in Slugging Percentage (.633) and On Base Percentage (.474) as well as several other things, like doubles and RBI. He had 68 RBI in 63 games.

When *Baseball America* polled the coaches and managers to rank the top prospects in the league, the number three prospect was an outfielder named Jeff Jackson, who had hit .227 with two homers and 66 strikeouts in 48 games. House? He wasn't listed.

Maybe they were right. House played at Visalia last year, and didn't do anything much (.266 with 10 homers.)

Tyler HOUSTON, Atlanta
Who is he?

Houston is a very young catcher, the Braves number one draft pick in 1989, in danger of dropping off the prospects list.

After signing for a nice bonus ($241,-500) he apparently developed an attitude, and had an off year in the Pioneer League in 1989. He started out better in the Sally League last year, but dropped off to .210, and was not listed by *Baseball America* as one of the top ten prospects in the league.

Steve HOWARD, Oakland
Who is he?

Outfielder, apparently has a throwing arm. No prospect.

Thomas HOWARD, San Diego
Who is he?

Switch-hitting outfielder who can run, hit .328 at Las Vegas. With the trade of Joe Carter, receiving no outfielder in return, he figures to get some playing time. In my opinion he'll prove to be comparable to Mike Felder of Milwaukee—a

.250–.275 range hitter with speed but no power. He's not quite good enough to be a regular in my opinion, but if they do decide to make him a regular he's good enough that it might take two years for him to play himself out of a job.

Jack HOWELL, California
Is he really bad?

No, he isn't. Howell, whose job is in jeopardy if it isn't gone, isn't a bad player. He hits for a low average (.239 career) but with enough defense, power and walks to be a decent third baseman. Two years ago he was very comparable to Kelly Gruber, but he's hit .228 the last two years, and not many players can survive that.

Jay HOWELL, Los Angeles
How solid is he? Is he getting old?

Howell, now 35, appears to be more solid now than he has been for several years:

1. He has had three straight outstanding years, the most consistent period of his career,
2. His strikeout rate is still high, 59 men in 66 innings,
3. The Dodgers no longer are looking for him to save 30 games. He is well backed up, beginning with Crews.

Howell had arthroscopic surgery on his left knee last April, and the bullpen was catastrophic while he was gone. I don't think that would happen now. Their bullpen has been fortified in the last year by the return of Gott, the development of Hartley, the development of Crews and the addition of Darren Holmes.

Ken HOWELL, Philadelphia
Can he come back from the injury?

Howell was pitching great, the best ball of his career, through June 17 last year (8-3, 2.48 ERA), when he had a series of poor starts which led to the disabled list, eventually to arthroscopic surgery on the shoulder. I think chances are good that he will come back and have his best year in 1991.

Dann HOWITT, Oakland
Who is he?

Left-handed hitting outfielder/first baseman. He hit 26 homers and drove in 111 runs at Huntsville in 1989, but didn't do anything at Tacoma last year. Grade D prospect, at best.

Kent HRBEK, Minnesota
How long will he last? Will he hit 400 home runs? 500 home runs? Is he still a good player?

Hrbek is still a good player, still helping the Twins. He's an excellent hitter, a good defensive first baseman and as good a baserunner as you can be when you run like William Conrad. (You remember that show "Cannon"? I think that was what it was called . . . this was fifteen or twenty years ago, before Jake and the Fat Man. I was in the Army in the middle of nowhere at the time, so we used to watch that stuff. For some reason, the producers of this show couldn't go an hour without having this middle-aged fat guy jump out of his Buick, chase a couple of 18-year-old thugs down an alley and beat the crap out of them.)

Anyway, Hrbek is a little unlikely to last long enough to hit 400 home runs, and extremely unlikely to last long enough to hit 500. My formula for estimating these things says that Hrbek has a 36% chance to hit 400 home runs, a five percent chance to hit 500. In view of his history of weight problems and lack of mobility, those estimates are on the high side.

Rex HUDLER, St. Louis
Can he help a team as a regular?

Apparently his defense was not up to being considered as a regular second baseman, and his offense, though very good for an infielder, is not going to make him a regular outfielder. He's thirty years old now, and you can count on your fingers and warts the number of players in each generation who become regulars after they're thirty. He's a hell of a bench player, though, because there are four ways to use him—backup infielder, backup outfielder, pinch hitter and pinch runner. With the market what it is he could become the first player to make a million dollars a year without ever being a regular.

Mike HUFF, Cleveland
Who is he?

Singles-hitting outfielder, hit .325 at Albuquerque with 82 walks and 27 stolen bases. The Dodgers left him off their 40-man roster and the Indians drafted him. He's no prospect but I kind of like him. He'd hit around .275 in the major leagues, maybe better in some parks. He's now 27 years old, and will compete for a job with Turner Ward, Joey Belle and Beau Allred.

Keith HUGHES, New York Mets
Will he get a shot with Strawberry gone?

Hughes is a minor league journeyman outfielder, now 27 years old. The departure of Strawberry probably doesn't help him, since nobody believes he could do Strawberry's job anyway. Hughes isn't a bad player, really—probably as good a hitter as Mark Carreon—but he just hasn't been able to catch a job. The acquisition of two players to replace Strawberry (Brooks and Coleman) suggests that they probably won't find a place for him in '91, either.

Tim HULETT, Baltimore
Could he play regularly? Is he a valuable sub?

He did play regularly for two years with the White Sox, but isn't likely to regain a regular role. With the development of Billy Ripken as a hitter Baltimore isn't looking for people who can do the things that he can do. He's a good backup infielder.

Todd HUNDLEY, New York Mets
Is he ready to start? Is he any good?

He is so young (21) that he should develop some and may develop enormously as a hitter. At this point, based on 1989–1990 performance, I have to conclude that his bat is so weak that even a Gold Glove couldn't keep him in the lineup. I don't think he could hit .250 or hit for any power in the major leagues.

He definitely has a future. If he doesn't develop (much) as a hitter, he'll spend ten years in the majors as a backup catcher. If he does develop, he'll be a regular. I doubt that he'll be a star.

Bruce HURST, San Diego
Is he losing anything? Is he still as good as ever?

He hasn't lost a thing—in fact, he may be pitching the best ball of his career now. He was 11-9 last year, but his run support was poor. From July first to the end of the season last year he had an ERA of 2.26. He was less effective when he pitched into the late innings last year (.291 batting average against him after the seventh inning, as opposed to .189 in 1989), but whether that was aging or just a statistical fluctuation, who knows. Last year was his fifth consecutive winning season, his fourth of 200 or more innings. How many major league pitchers have pitched 200 innings and had winning records each of the last four years?

(The question was rhetorical but I decided to check. The answer is that four pitchers have streaks of four consecutive seasons in which they have pitched 200 innings with winning records—Roger Clemens, who has five such seasons, Dave Stewart, Bob Welch and Bruce Hurst. Only six pitchers have streaks of three such seasons.

Earlier in his career Ron Darling had a streak of five such seasons, as did Mike Scott and Frank Viola. Five pitchers have had streaks of four straight earlier in their careers, but the most impressive performance in this area by any active pitcher was by Jack Morris, who had a streak of seven consecutive seasons with 200 innings and a winning record, and who missed by only four innings having a streak of ten such seasons. He threw 198 innings in 1979 and again in 1981, and had winning records both times.)

Jeff HUSON, Texas
Who will be the Rangers' shortstop in '91?

The candidates are Huson, Green, Kunkel and Monty Fariss, from AAA. Fariss is the best hitter of the four, but his future appears to be at second or third. Green is the defensive player, but he hits like Mark Belanger's little brother. Kunkel plays well for about two weeks at a time, but probably should have been a pitcher. I guess that leaves Huson in command of the job . . .

Huson as a shortstop could be described as a tall Wayne Tolleson—stretched defensively to play short, but above average at the position offensively. (Tolleson isn't anymore, of course.) Huson walks and can steal bases, but he has no power. He's only 26 and I'm not saying he can't play, just that there are eleven shortstops in the American League that I'd rather take a chance on.

●│●

Pete INCAVIGLIA, Texas
How do you balance his strengths and weaknesses? Does he help the Rangers?

Incaviglia's batting average has slipped for the last several years (.271, .249, .236, .233), making him marginal as a regular. Incaviglia created about 3.7 runs per 27 outs last year, which is not enough for a regular outfielder, let alone one as slow as Incaviglia. He grounded into a career-high 18 double plays, hit no triples and was three for seven as a base stealer.

Valentine has always stood by him as a defensive player, insisting that he was better than he looks. He even plays him some in center field (parts of 27 games last year, 148 innings.) Pete Incaviglia belongs in center field when Bea Arthur belongs in a bikini, if anybody wants my opinion.

Incaviglia apparently will be a free agent one year from now, and some players have good years in their free agent campaign. Incaviglia is a better hitter than his 1990 stats show, and 1990 isn't *all* that bad—24 homers, 85 RBI. Harold Baines has been traded, which opens up the DH slot for Incaviglia if Valentine doesn't need him to play center. All things considered, Incaviglia is probably a good player to take a chance on in a 1991 draft.

I don't know if this is useful to you, but Incaviglia does not play well in day games. Over the last two years (53 day games) he has hit .190 in day games with 5 homers and 21 RBI, a .354 slugging percentage. Take that out of his record and he'd look a lot better.

Alexis INFANTE, Atlanta
Does he have a role?

Utility infielder/strictly defense. He's no prospect.

Jeff INNIS, New York Mets
Is he ever going to break through?

1991 should be his year. Innis has been bouncing up and down between New York and Tidewater since 1987, despite pitching consistently well in the major leagues (ERAs of 3.16, 1.89, 3.18 and 2.39 in 12 to 29 games a year.) 1991 should be his year because:

1. Davey Johnson is gone. Johnson obviously didn't believe in him, but Harrelson might.
2. His major league success has gone on too long for anybody to say it's just luck. He's got 76 games now with a 2.77 ERA. Sooner or later you have to respect that.
3. He's got to be out of options, doesn't he?

The Mets have a deep staff, but sooner or later somebody's got to get hurt. If the Mets have room for Don Aase (1989) and Jeff Musselman, sooner or later they have to find a place for Jeff Innis.

Darryl IRVINE, Boston
Who is he?

If your last name was Irvine, wouldn't you name your kid "U.C." You don't need to, if he's a baseball player; Chris Berman will do it for you.

U.C. Irvine is a 26-year-old right-hander who probably goes to bed every night saying "Dear God, let Jeff Gray get raked over the coals." He's a similar pitcher to Gray and will get a long look if Gray fails. I like Gray better than Irvine.

•J•

Bo JACKSON, Kansas City
Putting aside all the hype, how good is he? Is he still getting better? Is he a star? Is he a superstar? Is he the fastest man in baseball?

A "20/20" segment last fall said that Bo had a chance to be the first player to go into both the pro football and the pro baseball Hall of Fame. They must have seen him play a few times when I was out of town.

Five years into his career, Bo remains a talented but erratic player. In 1989, for the first time, he helped the Royals. In 1990, as in the other years, he didn't.

Bo is unmistakeably still improving as a hitter, improving all across the board. Every year he hits for a better average with more power and strikes out less. Last year, despite missing nearly two months due to silliness, he drew a career-high 44 walks, demonstrating that he is learning to lay off the bad pitches. He has reached a point, as a hitter, that if he could stay in the lineup for 155 games—his career high is 135—he could pile up numbers that would make him an MVP candidate. His 1990 season, projected to 155 games: .272 with 39 homers, 109 RBI. A Darryl Strawberry season.

Last year was probably his most disappointing major league season, because the Royals decided after the season had started to break him in in center field. They knew he would make mistakes in center, but no one had guessed that he would make so many mistakes in center, or would show such an uncanny instinct for making them at the wrong time. His play in center field was one of the critical failings of the team, and cost them maybe five of the twenty or so games that the Royals finished below where they were expected. An ill-advised dive for a line drive took him out of action for several weeks in mid-summer. But this can't be held against him, because after all he wasn't the one who decided to turn the season into on-the-job training.

Bo is not a legitimate star or superstar in terms of performance on a baseball field. He is, by far, the most spectacular player I have ever seen, and this is not a press agent's creation. He does do amazing things quite regularly. Baseball is not a spectacle. Wrestling's a spectacle.

Bo can hit any pitcher, right-handed or left-handed, good or bad; he hits them all about the same. They can all strike him out, even if they don't strike people out. When he came up he used to live off of pitchers who had an 88-MPH fastball, but that's not true anymore.

Bo has not, to this point, found any way to make use of his speed on a baseball field. In the outfield he still gets a poor jump on everything. He still isn't on base a lot, and he still isn't a good baserunner. He rarely has any occasion to run full speed on the field. The American League managers, in a post-season poll, named Bo the fastest man in the league, but just watching them play I would have thought Willie Wilson was still the fastest man on the team.

In a sense, the problem with Bo is that he is a superstar, when he really isn't. Bo does some things very well, and other things very poorly. What does a manager do, when he has a ballplayer who does some things well and others poorly? He finds a way to use the good parts of the player, and minimize the weak parts.

But because Bo is regarded as a superstar, that's hard to do with him. If Wathan used Bo as a DH people would say "You're going to DH Bo Jackson? Don't you want that great speed and arm in the outfield?" If he pinch hit for Bo, which he should in some cases, people would raise quizzical eyebrows and start talking about how far Bo can hit a ball when he does hit one. If he lifted Bo for defense in the late innings, held him out of a few games and let him pinch run, or whatever he did, people would second-guess him. A manager doesn't want that, and he doesn't need that; he *needs* for everybody on his team to believe that he knows what he is doing and why. Having Bo on a team is a manager's dream—and a manager's nightmare.

Note: Bo has a career batting average when not striking out of .384, the highest in baseball. The top five are Bo (.384), Danny Tartabull (.383), Wade Boggs (.376), Andres Galarraga (.373) and Fred McGriff (.373).

Danny JACKSON, Chicago Cubs
How will he do in Wrigley Field?

The Cubs have normally been unable to attract pitchers to Wrigley Field because it is such a hitter's park. Jackson has always been a pitcher who didn't give up many home runs—I believe he has led both leagues in fewest home runs allowed per inning—and there is an intuitive logic which suggests that a pitcher who doesn't give up home runs should do well in a park where home runs are hit. You would have a difficult time demonstrating that this was true with the data, but it might be.

Jackson has pitched only three times in Wrigley Field. His first game there, in September, 1988, was a six-hit shutout, and he has split two decisions since, making him 2-1 with a 4.26 ERA at the park.

I haven't really answered the question . . . if Danny's on his game, he'll win anywhere. If he's off his game, he'll lose anywhere. I would worry less about the park in his case than in most others.

What I worry about with Danny is the home plate umpire. Danny throws a pitch—I call it a nuclear slider—right above the belt, breaks in on a right-handed hitter's hands. If the home plate umpire calls that pitch a strike, Danny has a tremendous advantage. If the umpire calls it a ball, Danny is in trouble. He doesn't have three other pitches to go to—he's got his fastball, and he's got that awesome slider. If he doesn't get the call on it, he's out of luck.

Darrin JACKSON, San Diego
Does he deserve more at-bats?

Jackson isn't a terrible player—a .250-range hitter with a little power and speed. In 487 major league at bats—a little less than one season—he has hit .248 with 22 doubles, 13 home runs and eight stolen bases.

He has two things going for him in 1990:

1. The Padres have traded Joe Carter without getting an outfielder in return, and
2. He's 27 years old, the age at which players tend to have their best years.

Even so, he must break through a crowd of outfielders (Jerald Clark, Thomas Howard, Shawn Abner) to earn playing time. My guess is that he'll play *more* and *better* in 1991 than he has in the past, but not dramatically more or better.

Jeff JACKSON, Philadelphia
Who is he?

Jackson is an eighteen-year-old outfielder with Eric Davis' body and Omar Vizquel's hitting stats in the low minors. You'll hear people rave about him because he is strong and fast, but whether he will ever learn to play baseball is anybody's guess.

Mike JACKSON, Seattle
Can he be the closer if Schooler can't come back?

There was a lot of talk about trading Jackson early last year, when he was coming off of two good years. Herzog reportedly was interested in him as the closer in St. Louis. He wasn't healthy at the time, though, so it didn't happen, and then he didn't have a good year. Toward the end of the year his control went, and he walked 21 men in his last 22 innings of pitching.

Jackson is only 26 years old—he came up early—and may yet develop into an outstanding pitcher. I've always liked his

arm and his delivery, and he hasn't pitched badly, even last year when his ERA was high. I'd be very concerned, at this point, if I had to count on him as a closer.

Brook JACOBY, Cleveland
Should the Indians trade him? Is he a good ballplayer? Where does he rank?

Jacoby's been a consistent player with the exception of the 1987–1988 years, when he bounced from very good to very bad. He hangs around .275 with medium range power and good enough defense at third base, although his range has slipped badly in the last two years. A player like that can help you win.

American League third basemen could be loosely sorted into three groups—The Good, the Decent, and the Bad and Unproven. The good ones are Wade Boggs and Kelly Gruber. The Bad and Unproven are Craig Worthington, Jim Leyritz, Robin Ventura, Steve Buechele and Associates (Texas), and whoever California has there.

That leaves seven players in the middle group—Jacoby, Tony Phillips, Gary Sheffield, Kevin Seitzer, Gary Gaetti, Carney Lansford and Edgar Martinez. Phillips and Seitzer, in my opinion, have to rank ahead of Jacoby, and Gaetti and Lansford have to rank behind him. Sheffield and Martinez are still somewhat unknown, but in view of the fact that they are years younger than Jacoby, one has to assume that with another year they should be ahead of him. So Jacoby would rank about seventh among American League third basemen.

Should the Indians trade him . . . in general I think that if you can't use a player to his fullest ability you should consider a trade. This is particularly true when you are short of talent, as the Indians are. The Indians are talking about playing Jacoby, who I think is a fairly decent third basemen, at first base or using him at DH, opening third base for

Carlos Baerga. Perhaps they should trade him before it comes to that.

The All Could-Be-Jewish team . . . C—Terry Steinbach, 1B—Sid Bream, 2B—Steve Sax, 3B—Brook Jacoby, SS—Walt Weiss, LF—Jim Eisenreich, CF—Keith Miller, RF—John Moses, SP—David Cone, Jeff Juden, RP—Craig Lefferts.

Chris JAMES, Cleveland
Is his 1990 performance level for real?

Of course not. James hit .299 last year after hitting .242 and .243 the previous two years. In the past James has murdered left-handed pitching but struggled against right-handed pitchers, but last year he was almost balanced (.302 vs. left-handers, .298 against right-handers.)

You can never be sure, but

a. the best predictor of what a player will do next year is *career* performance, not performance last year,

b. he was 27 years old last year, the age at which fluke seasons tend to happen, and

c. his strikeout/walk ratio was still bad. Three hundred hitters don't strike out two and a half times as often as they walk, as a rule.

Dion JAMES, Cleveland
Why did the Indians release him?

They're a ballclub; they don't have to explain these things.

What does he do for a lineup?

He gets on base. His career on-base percentage, .355, is good—better than any remaining Indians regular except Browne (.356) and Alex Cole (.357, but that's just 63 games.) On-base percentage is the most important individual offensive stat, and one would think a player who was near the team lead would qualify for a roster spot.

He's not a great player. He gets on base and runs OK, but he's inconsistent,

has no power and doesn't throw well. If his attitude was good I'd like to have him around to do R.J. Reynolds' job.

Stan JAVIER, Los Angeles
Who won the trade? Does he help the Dodgers? Will he ever be a regular?

I think Javier is a more valuable property at this point in his career than is Randolph, but I don't know why you trade for Javier if

a. you don't intend to play him, and

b. you already have two backup center fielders on your roster.

I like Javier, and I think he could be a regular. He hits for a decent average now, will take a walk, is a terrific base runner and outfielder and is still young enough to improve.

Mike JEFFCOAT, Texas
Does he have any future?

Probably none to speak of. He's 31 years old, doesn't have a great fastball, still hasn't established himself and is coming off a disappointing season. If he doesn't impress somebody early he is in a position to be released.

Gregg JEFFERIES, New York Mets
What position will he play? Is he still going to be a star?

He is going to be a star, yes. He's proven now that he can play, he has a variety of skills, and he's only 23. Unless something breaks, he's going to be a star.

I don't know where the Mets will play him, but I know what I would have done. With Strawberry leaving, I would have moved him to the outfield. I think that would have released the pressure on the infield alignment problem—put Jefferies in center, Boston in right and McReynolds in left. Then you can straighten out the infield by finding a true shortstop, and you have a *ballclub*, rather than a collection of mis-matched talent. I

wouldn't have signed Vince Coleman or traded for Hubie.

Stan JEFFERSON, Cleveland
Can he play?

No.

Chris JELIC, New York Mets
Who is he?

27-year-old outfield prospect, will battle for a job with Keith Hughes, Kelvin Torve, Keith Miller and others. The departure of Strawberry won't help him, but the loss of Pat Tabler probably will. In my opinion Hughes is the best player of the group. Jelic can hit for average about as well as Hughes, but not as much power.

Steve JELTZ, Kansas City
Why did the Royals trade for Steve Jeltz when they already had Bill Pecota?

It was just a mistake, one of about ten key mistakes which contributed to the Royals' miserable season. The Royals traded a young pitcher with a hellacious fastball (DeJesus) for Jeltz, because they thought that Frank White might not be able to play second base, and were afraid that a hole at second could wipe them out. In fact, White *couldn't* play second, but Jeltz couldn't, either . . . Jeltz has the lowest career batting average (.210) of any active player (500 or more games), and also the lowest slugging percentage (.268).

Doug JENNINGS, Oakland
Is he worth keeping around?

He's having trouble making contact in the major leagues—strikes out in about 30% of his at bats.

Jennings is very small but very strong, and that's a good combination for a baseball player, so he may be able to reach a late peak. He *looks* awfully good, as a hitter, but he really hasn't done anything since A ball, 1987. He was with the Angels then; the A's took him in the major league draft, gave him a season in the majors (1988), one in the minors (1989) and another one in the majors (1990). He didn't do anything impressive any of the three years, and at this point has to be counted among the A's weaknesses, rather than among their strengths. But you watch him in batting practice and you'll think he can hit.

Chris JOHNSON, Milwaukee
Who is he?

Johnson is a six-foot-eight right-hander in the Brewers system, a long-range prospect. After nine starts in A ball last year he was 9-0 with an 0.87 ERA, but slumped to finish 13-6. He is described as being similar in build to Mike Witt.

Dave JOHNSON, Baltimore
Can he continue to pitch well?

All of the indicators I would look at say loudly that Johnson *cannot* continue to pitch as well as he has. He won thirteen games last year but

1. his luck (his offensive support) was very good,
2. he struck out only 68 men, one of the lowest ratios of strikeouts to wins in the major leagues,
3. he has no history of consistent success,
4. he allowed 30 home runs, the most in the majors, while pitching only 180 innings,
5. he also surrendered 43 doubles, the most of any American League pitcher (Fernando Valenzuela allowed 51 in the National.)

I don't know if you know this . . . Johnson has allowed only one stolen base in his major league career, Only a few people have tried to steal on him, and they've mostly been thrown out. It's hard to evaluate the impact of a special skill like that; he just *eliminates* a part of the other team's offense.

Johnson is an archetype. Any time you run a list there are a handful of play-ers who are liable to turn up on one end of it or the other—Rob Deer, Ozzie Guillen, Alvaro Espinoza, Mickey Tettleton, Nolan Ryan, Sid Fernandez. Johnson is one of those: he's always at one end of the list or the other. His ratio of fly balls to ground balls last year was the highest in the American League. It's hard to know whether that makes him "special" in a meaningful sense, exceptional enough to be exempt from the ordinary rules of what makes a successful pitcher. But it's not going to cause me to change my recommendation to rotisserie owners: stay away from him.

Howard JOHNSON, New York Mets
Should he play shortstop or third base for the Mets?

What I originally believed, when I started doing this stuff professionally fifteen years ago, was that you should always play a player at the most demanding defensive position he can handle, because this maximizes your offense. Let's say Johnson creates 100 runs in a season. If he's at third base, an average third baseman in the NL will probably create 75 runs with the same number of plate appearances, so Johnson's net value is 25 runs. He is 25 runs better than an average third baseman.

On the other hand, if you play him at shortstop and he creates 100 runs, he might be 40 runs better than an average shortstop, who would create only 60. So his value is higher at shortstop than it would be at third base.

Over the years I have completely changed my thinking on this issue. What I described before is good APBA logic. If you've got Johnson's APBA card and can play him at short or third, you're probably going to put him at short.

But in a real world, there are other things to think about:

1. It is not characteristic of good organizations to stretch their defensive skills. You look at the Yankees in the fifties, the Orioles in the seventies, the Reds in the seventies, the A's today . . . did any of these teams normally try to position a player at his most demanding defensive position? No, they didn't. Clete Boyer, who could have played shortstop or third base for the Yankees, played third base. Don Buford, who could have been a bad second baseman or a good left fielder, played left field for the Orioles. Tony Perez, who could have played first base well or third base badly for the Reds, played first base well. Rickey Henderson, who could be a good left fielder or a poor center fielder, is a good left fielder. *Good organizations place their players where they have the best chance to succeed.*

2. Howard Johnson may be fifteen runs more valuable offensively at shortstop, but if he gives those fifteen runs back on defense, would you ever know? *In a judgment which involves tangible and intangible benefits, there is always a tendency to undervalue the intangible ones.*

Offensive skills in baseball are calibrated in great detail; we have not perfect knowledge, but extremely good knowledge about the offensive abilities of Howard Johnson and everybody else who plays shortstop. Defensive abilities are much less well measured, much more elusive. They are not truly intangible—you *could* measure them—but we don't know nearly as much about them. That doesn't mean they don't exist.

3. In a real world, Johnson probably will not hit as well if he plays shortstop as he would at third base. If he's uncomfortable in the field he may get hurt. Almost certainly he would decline as a hitter over a period of years.

There have been great sluggers who played shortstop in the major leagues—Rogers Hornsby, Vern Stephens, Ernie Banks, Arky Vaughn, Robin Yount—

and there have been shortstops who played well into their thirties, even into their forties. But not since Honus Wagner has there been a slugger who played shortstop more than a year or two past his thirtieth birthday.

Lance JOHNSON, Chicago White Sox
Now that he's here, what is he?

It's funny how this works. Johnson in the major leagues did pretty much what I thought he would do. He hit .285 with 36 stolen bases. But having seen him do it, he seems considerably less impressive than I had imagined. A center fielder who hits .285 with no power, not many walks, a 64% stolen base rate, and marginal defense in center field, isn't of much value. He's better than Dave Gallagher, the White Sox center fielder in '89, but not much better.

He may be able to do better than this. If he keeps his job, he might move up to .300 with a better stolen base percentage and a few more walks. I hope he's working on it, because where he is right now, the difference between him getting a tiny bit better and a tiny bit worse is $2 million a year.

Johnson led the American League in times caught stealing, 22. The trades for Cory Snyder and Tim Raines leave it unclear whether Johnson will have a regular job. The outfield now appears to be Raines, Sosa and Snyder.

Randy JOHNSON, Seattle
Was this his best year? Will he be able to sustain his success?

Johnson's star is still rising; he should be as good as he was last year, if not better, in 1991. All of the things which combined to make him a great draft pick in 1990 will still be working for him next year:

1. Last year the Mariners moved their fences out. This year they are moving them out again.

2. The team should be better, and might be dramatically better (as if I hadn't been saying that for ten years.)
3. Johnson is a young power pitcher with a strong, fluid motion whose control still needs to be refined.

A pitcher of this type can only get better. Well, that's not true, he can also get worse, but you know what I mean: with more experience, Johnson has the ability to succeed beyond what he has yet accomplished. He could strike out 250 men in a season.

Wallace JOHNSON, Montreal
Will he be back?

No. He was a one-dimensional player, a singles-hitting pinch hitter, who was released after hitting .163. He's 34 years old.

Barry JONES, Montreal
How valuable is a bullpen setup man? Is his talent being wasted?

Jones in Chicago was probably being utilized as well as any major league pitcher.

Jones has been in the majors for parts of five seasons, and has had an ERA below 3.00 four times—2.89 with Pittsburgh in '86, 2.37 with Chicago in 1989, 2.31 with Chicago in 1990 and 2.84 in a split season in 1988. Last year he was the major league leader with 30 "holds", meaning that 30 times he came in with a lead and passed the lead to another reliever. He also had an 11-4 won-lost record.

First of all, I don't believe that Jones could be a relief ace. I don't believe that he has either the stuff or the control to be effective in that role. But the interesting question here is, how valuable is a pitcher being used in this way? *Is* Dibble as valuable to the Reds as Myers, even if Myers is used in such a way that he gets credit for all the saves?

The best way to answer this would appear to be a simulation study. One could

1. construct identical teams,
2. vary the instructions guiding how relief pitchers are used, and
3. run the competing teams through hundreds of simulated seasons to see what the results are.

We're not asking here "is Rob Dibble a better pitcher than Randy Myers" or "is Barry Jones better than Bobby Thigpen". That's a different question. We are asking "what is the relative value of a setup man as opposed to a closer?"

For that, you need teammates of realistic but *different* calibre, one clearly better than the other. If you use the best reliever to save the games, as they are used now, how many games does the team win? If you use the best pitcher as a setup man, how many games do they win? Is there another way to use a relief pitcher which is better yet?

This wouldn't be an easy study to do, and there are only a few of us who would be able to write such a program. If we did, we might learn something, and we might not. As of yet, none of us has gotten around to doing it.

Incidentally, holds are much more numerous in the American League than in the National. Rob Dibble led the NL with 17 holds, while Honeycutt was second in the American League with 27. This would seem to be because of the designated hitter rule. National League middle relievers come into the game after the starter is lifted for a pinch hitter, and thus often come in with the score tied or the team behind. American League middle relievers come in as soon as the starter weakens, ahead or behind. This probably means—I'm guessing—that there are more come-from-behind wins in the National League.

Chipper JONES, Atlanta
Who is he?

The number one pick of the '90 draft, a shortstop taken by the Braves. He hit .229 in the Gulf Coast League, so we won't look for him to come up for a couple of years.

Doug JONES, Cleveland
Does he deserve more respect? How does a pitcher save 45 games with Cleveland?

1. Yes, it is true that Jones would get more respect if he pitched for a better team, but then, a better team would never have made Doug Jones their closer to begin with. The Indians took a chance on him because they were desperate.

2. There probably isn't as much difference as you might think between a bad team and a good team in terms of how many *close* games they win. A team that wins 60 games in a season might win 50 close ones and ten easy ones. A team that wins 100 games in a season might win 65 close ones and 35 easy ones.

Why did he take so long to get good?

1. He was a starting pitcher in the minor leagues, and he doesn't have the variety of pitches which characterizes an effective starter. He has two pitches—a fastball and a changeup. Like Eckersley, he is just better suited to relief.

2. He wasn't all that bad as a minor league starter; he just never got lucky. He had earned run averages of 3.04 and 2.97 in the Pacific Coast League, where anything under 4.00 is real good. He never had a big winning year, and the Brewers hopped him around a lot so that his records look garbagey. In 1980 he was 14-7, but if you look at him in the book you see 6-2, 3-2 and 5-3, because he did it in three different leagues.

3. He got hurt at a key time. He was just ready to break into the American League when he got hurt, and missed almost all of one season (1983). Then

it was back to point A, and he was a starting pitcher in the Texas League in 1984.

Jimmy JONES, New York Yankees
Does he still have a chance to be good?

Not that I can see.

Ron JONES, Philadelphia
Will he ever be healthy? Is he really this good?

Three years ago, before Jones started hurting himself, my opinion was that he wasn't all that good a hitter anyway, and would probably reveal this as soon as he got a chance to play. After three years of his hitting so well in limited play (.290, .290, and .276 with consistent power) I have to believe that I may have misjudged him as a hitter. On the other hand, he has only 213 major league at bats, and that's not enough to make a decision on a player.

The snapped tendons in the knee . . . I don't know how many times I have seen that in various sports, where if a player tears one of them then the next year he will tear the other one, too. I know of four cases where that's happened, and I have to think there is a genetic reason for it. The explanation of the doctors was that Jones was just too strong; when he stopped himself suddenly in mid-stride he tore the tendon. "If you've seen his thighs, you know what I mean when I say they are monstrous," said Dr. Phillip Marone. "The quadricep was stronger than the bone to which it's attached. It actually pulled the patella away from the bone . . . Everything being equal, he should be able to come back sometime next year."

Whether he will ever be healthy, I just don't know. It would seem obvious that if they want him to be healthy, they need to

1. get him out of the outfield, and
2. tell him to take it a little bit easy for a year or so.

Tim JONES, St. Louis
Is he a candidate to move up to a regular job?

No. He wasn't a candidate last year, when he hit .293, so he certainly isn't one now, when he has hit .219. He's a good utility infielder.

Tracy JONES, Seattle
What the hell happened to him? Is he a major league hitter or not?

a. Jones was never a power hitter in the minor leagues. He was a .300 hitter who hit singles.

b. His first season in the majors he hit .290 with 10 homers in part-time play—but this was 1987, when everybody was hitting home runs.

c. He's a great big guy—weighs about 230 pounds.

d. He hit .299 through his first 253 major league games, but with power that was considered disappointing.

e. Probably trying to pull the ball more than was good for him, he got messed up and went into a year-and-a-half slump, hitting almost nothing from the start of 1989 through most of 1990.

f. Traded to Seattle late last year, he resumed hitting singles, hitting .302 in 86 at bats with the Mariners.

This leaves two questions unanswered:

1. Is his resurgence for real, and
b. Does anybody really need a 230-pound singles hitter?

He's a weird case—it's like his statistics and his body don't fit together. Jones when he came up was not only a singles hitter but a base stealer, which if you've seen him in uniform you can hardly believe. Kind of like Steve Balboni with Tim Raines' numbers.

For what it is worth, I suspect the answers are that:

1. His resurgence is for real, but
2. He'll never be a regular.

I think if he stays in his role—hitting singles, pinch hitting and playing against left-handers—he can be a useful player.

Ricky JORDAN, Philadelphia
What happened to him last year?

He wasn't hitting well, and then he heard something pop in his left hand during a doubleheader against the Expos on June 11. The hand bothered him for two months.

A lot of people were suspicious of him anyway because he was a first baseman with no power and a real bad strikeout/walk ratio (in three major league seasons he has 30 walks, not counting intentional.) I was more optimistic about him; apparently I was wrong.

When a player bounces from very good to very bad, like Jacoby in '87–'88, the best thing to bet on is the mid-point. Jordan's lifetime batting average is .278, and that's probably about what he'll hit.

Will that keep him in the lineup?

Probably not. There's a lot of pressure on the first base spot because everybody who *can't* play another position but can swing the bat will get a chance to play first base. The Phillies have several candidates for first base—Von Hayes, Ron Jones, John Kruk. If Jordan doesn't hit better than .278 with limited power, he probably isn't going to play much.

A few notes about him . . . Veterans Stadium isn't helping him. Although he hit well enough at home in '88, his half-season, he has hit better on the road than in Philadelphia the last two years. I may be wrong, but when a young player struggles in his home park I tend to associate it with a crisis of confidence . . . Jordan has hit extremely well against the Cubs each of the last two years, a total of .321 with more RBI against the Cubs than

against any other team in each season . . . he has batted far more times in the cleanup spot than any other position in each of the last two years, which is strange in view of his performance . . .

I am hesitant to put too much weight on this kind of stuff over just a few years, but I note that Jordan has hit much better *late* in the season. In 1988 he was a surprise star when he was called up for the second half of the season. In 1989 he hit .244 in April and May, .292 in June and July and .310 in August and September. Last year, again, he showed some signs of coming out of his funk late in the year, hitting .274 after September first.

Felix JOSE, St. Louis
Will he help the Cardinals?

I like him better as a Cardinal than I did in Oakland, because I think he fits the park better. My comment on him last year concluded by saying "he's a .250 hitter with limited power and an awful strikeout/walk ratio. I think he's a real longshot to ever do anything interesting in the major leagues, and I strongly recommend that you *not* draft him."

Well, I'm not *that* negative on him for 1991. If he can hit .250 in Oakland he can probably hit .270 in St. Louis, and if he can hit .250 as a rookie he can probably hit .270 when he gets some experience. Put it together, maybe he can hit .300 and steal some bases. I still feel that he has limited if any star potential.

Why would the Oakland A's give up Felix Jose for a month worth of Willie McGee?

First, they may have concluded that Jose wasn't all that good. Second, they didn't get just Willie McGee out of this. Because McGee left *Oakland* as a free agent, the A's will get a draft pick as compensation. Although teams have been awfully slow to realize it, the draft pick is probably worth as much in the long run as Felix Jose.

Wally JOYNER, California
What happened to him last year?

He was hit in the knee by Chris Bosio on May 15, played in pain for two months and was diagnosed as having a stress fracture of the right kneecap. He should be fine in 1991.

Will he come back?

The Angels played badly with Joyner gone, so they probably will be happy to have him back in the lineup. Their only other first base candidate is Lee Stevens, who can't hit. Other than that, they were using people like Bill Schroeder and Donnie Hill at first base. They'll be thrilled to have him back, and he'll be back.

Jeff JUDEN, Houston
Who is he?

Juden is a huge right-handed pitcher, compared by some people to a young Rick Sutcliffe, although for some reason he reminds me more of Baby Huey. He went 10-1 at Osceola last year, earning a promotion to Columbus (Double A) at the age of 19. He wasn't throwing well at the end of the year, was examined by a physician and found to have a tired arm. Not likely to surface this year.

Dave JUSTICE, Atlanta
Did he deserve the Rookie of the Year award?

He probably did. I told everybody who asked me that I would have voted for Hal Morris, but I confess I was just being contrary, and don't have any *real* reason to object to the pick of Justice over Morris. Justice created more runs than any other NL rookie.

Is he going to be a big star?

Lou Piniella said in September that "Justice looks like a young Ted Williams", leaving us to wonder how Piniella, who wasn't *born* until after Williams hit .400 and had gone off to fight The War, knows what Ted Williams looked like when he was young. One sees the similarities that he is referring to. Justice is a tall, thin left-handed hitter, and the ball jumps off his bat.

Among the NL rookies in 1990, the one who has the best chance to be a big star is Delino DeShields. DeShields is three years younger than Justice, has more speed and is in a comparable range of value. Hal Morris' MLEs showed him to be a major league .300 hitter before last year, so I certainly think he will be consistent at that level.

Justice performed better in the major leagues than I would have thought he would based on his minor league stats—not tremendously better, but better. Given the number of at bats he had, I would have expected him to hit about .250 with 17 home runs, not .282 with 28 home runs. But his most recent MLE is 1988, when he was 22 years old; last year he was 24. Maybe he just improved. This is a great hitter's park, and that affects different players in different ways. Justice may have an unusual ability to take advantage of this park, as Bob Horner did (19 of Justice's 28 home runs were hit in Atlanta.)

Justice *isn't* going to be Ted Williams. Williams drove in 145 runs when he was twenty years old, and hit .400 at age 22. What Justice did isn't in the same league.

But Justice doesn't have to *improve* to be a superstar. He hit .282 and had a .535 slugging percentage last year. He doesn't have to jack up those levels; he just needs to prove that they're for real. If he can do over a period of years what he did last year, he's going to make $6 million a year.

•K•

Jeff KAISER, Cleveland
Who is he?
Kaiser, a thirty-year-old left-handed pitcher, pitched two games with the Indians in 1987, three games in 1988, six games in 1989 and five games last year—all in relief. You can tell the Indians really believe in him. Forty to one against his making arbitration rights.

Ron KARKOVICE, Chicago
Has he learned to hit? Is he ready to be a regular?
By acclamation, Karkovice has the best throwing arm in the American League. He hit just terrible in 1987 and 1988 (26 for 200, a .130 average) but his MLEs in 1986 were good, he hit well in 37 games with the White Sox in 1986, and he has hit well the last two years. Not "well", maybe, but well enough if you throw like he does—around .250 with power. He's a big strong guy.

My reading of him offensively is that he is a major league hitter who got confused for a couple of years and lost his confidence. He's going to be around for a good many years, probably will play regularly sometime, and I think he should hit alright.

Roberto KELLY,
New York Yankees
Where does he rank among AL center fielders? Does he have a chance to be truly outstanding, and rank with the great Yankee center fielders of the past?

1. Kelly ranks fourth or fifth among American League center fielders. The top three are Ellis Burks, Kirby Puckett and Ken Griffey Jr. Robin Yount ranks ahead of Kelly if his 1990 decline in batting average was just a fluke, and behind him if it was for real.

2. If you mean does Kelly have a chance to rank with Joe DiMaggio and Mickey Mantle, the answer is no, but he does have a chance to be a hell of a player. He has power and speed and he hits for average. He is young enough that he could get quite a bit better. He has shown steady progress over a period of several years.

Terry KENNEDY, San Francisco
Is he still a useful part-time player?
No. Kennedy hit .277 last year, his highest average in seven years, so a lot of people think he was fine. He wasn't. He hit two homers and is slow as hell, so offensively he's nothing. Steve Buechele hit .219 last year in fewer at bats than Kennedy—but drove in and scored more runs. Andres Thomas hit .219 with less playing time than Kennedy, but drove in and scored more runs. Mike LaValliere, who is also slow and has no power, hit just .258 in less at bats than Kennedy, but drove in and scored more runs.

Defensively, he never could throw. He can't play anymore.

Charlie KERFELD, Last seen
with Atlanta
Is his career over?
Is a pig fat? Is George Burns old? Does the FBI have fingerprints?

Jimmy KEY, Toronto
How much longer will he be effective?
Probably at least three more years. With his control and knowledge of how to pitch, he should be effective until his strikeout rate drops below four per game, and he's still above five per game.

How will he be affected by the changes in Toronto?
The only way he would be affected is if the Blue Jays wind up without a shortstop. Otherwise, he'll be about the same as he's always been.

Dana KIECKER, Boston
Was he a fluke? Can he pitch consistently at this level?

I don't think it was a fluke. I think he's going to surprise people over a period of years.

I don't know what it was, but something seems to have happened to him at Pawtucket in 1988. Suddenly his control improved, and at the same time his strikeout rate improved. He's been a consistent player in the minor leagues, and his record last year was about the same. I think he'll have a career.

Darryl KILE, Houston
What happened to him?

Kile, promoted a year ago as a super prospect, pitched at Tucson and pitched real bad (5-10, 6.64 ERA).

Eric KING, Cleveland
How good is he?

Apart from an inability to stay healthy, he's good. He has cut his walks per nine innings from 4.7 in 1987 to 4.5 (1988), 3.6 (1989) and 2.4 (1990). He has cut his ERA in those years from 4.89 to 3.28, and he has a better career winning percentage *and* ERA than Rick Sutcliffe or Jack Morris.

Will he ever *be* Rick Sutcliffe or Jack Morris? No. But for the next two or three years, he could help the Indians.

Jeff KING, Pittsburgh
Has he turned the corner? Will he be a regular in '91?

King, once the number one draft pick in the country, struggled in 1988 and 1989, but hit for some power last year. Actually, his career batting record isn't bad—586 major league at bats with 30 doubles, 19 homers, runs scored and RBI in the seventies but a .227 average.

King is a year older than Matt Williams, so at this stage there isn't much prospect of his developing into a star. He could be a regular, but

a. Backman can't hit left-handers, and
b. King hit fifty points higher against left-handers than right-handers (.264-.214).

For now, it seems like a natural platoon arrangement.

King also had the lowest batting average in the majors in 1990 in the late innings of a close game. He hit .117 in those situations (7 for 60). The worst in the NL were King, Kevin Elster, Dale Murphy, Alfredo Griffin and Jim Presley.

Mike KINGERY, San Francisco

No question about him. Nobody thinks he is going to be a regular, and he's not going to lose his job after hitting .295.

Kingery is one of my favorite players, which is not to say that I delude myself about his ability. Kingery is not *all* hustle, but that is the largest part of him. He runs well, and more to the point he runs hard. Last year he was six for seven stealing bases, and grounded into only one double play in 207 at bats. He's a good defensive outfielder and a good bunter. He's kind of a benchwarmer version of Brett Butler.

Bob KIPPER, Pittsburgh
How good is he?

Very good, in the role that he plays. Kipper bombed as a starter in 1986–1987, but has had two straight good years as a reliever. Leyland uses him almost exactly as LaRussa uses Honeycutt, a few batters at a time, and for the last two years he has gotten both left-handers and right-handers out.

Ron KITTLE, Baltimore
What will the Orioles do with him?

The signing of Dwight Evans eliminates his position with the Orioles, but he should land a job. Kittle is still an effective power hitter. In the last two

years he has 497 at bats with 29 home runs, 83 RBI. (Late note—the Orioles have announced that they will not re-sign Kittle. He is unsigned.)

Note: In his career Kittle has accounted for an estimated 47% of his career runs created with home runs, the highest such percentage in the major leagues . . . the most-comparable player to Ron Kittle is Steve Balboni.

Joe KLINK, Oakland
Is he really all that good?

Klink, a journeyman, pitched 40 times for the A's last year with a 2.04 ERA. He allowed only 13% of inherited runners to score, the lowest percentage in the American League (Randy Myers was better.) The A's have put together an entire staff of castoff pitchers (Honeycutt, Eckersley, Stewart, Sanderson, etc.) and Klink could be the next one, but you can't take an ERA in 39 innings seriously, no matter what it is. He has pitched well in the A's system for two years since the Twins gave up on him.

Brent KNACKERT, Seattle
Who is he?

Right-handed relief pitcher. The Mets drafted him out of the White Sox system under Rule 5, then put him on waivers. He was claimed by Seattle. The Mariners had to keep him on the roster all year or offer him back to Chicago. He has *no* experience at AA or AAA, and probably won't be back in the major leagues for at least two years.

Bob KNEPPER, San Francisco
Is his career over?

Yes, but he has a job lined up as a PR man for Molly Yard. It's funny, I can't even remember what it was he said that got him in trouble with women's groups, but here I am making feeble jokes about it. Shows you how unfair we all are . . .

★ ★ ★
Chuck KNOBLACH, Minnesota
★ ★ ★
Who is he?

Second base prospect. Let me tell you why I marked him:

1. His MLEs show that with Minnesota he should hit about .270, steal about 20 bases, hit doubles and have a strikeout/walk ratio better than even.
2. *Baseball America* says that he is the #7 prospect in the Southern League.
3. An opposing manager says that "He can do everything defensively, he knows how to play and he's going to hit."
4. The Twins regard him as their second baseman of the future.

As you know, I like Liriano; I think he's a good player—but his position is not solid. The Twins have been running through second basemen for fifteen years, and if Liriano doesn't hold the job Knoblach will be the next guy who gets a shot.

Mark KNUDSON, Milwaukee
Will he remain a rotation starter?

Almost certainly not. He's a big guy with good control, best pitch is a mediocre fastball. He turned down a chance to go to Japan a couple of years ago, believing he could pitch in the majors, and has won the gamble so far. He's gone 8-5 and 10-9 with the Brewers.

I still don't believe in him. He's thirty, has no history of consistent success, his ERA was high last year for a pitcher with a winning record (4.12), the Brewers are a bad organization and he's on the Ron Robinson list. He might be the last pitcher I would want on my team in 1991.

Brad KOMMINSK, Baltimore (released)
Is he out of chances? Is he out of baseball?

It probably depends on how badly he wants to keep going. Komminsk is only thirty, and there are worse outfielders around. He's never going to be a regular, but if he wants to go to Peoria and wait for a hamstring to snap he can probably add another year or two to his pension time.

Joe KRAEMER, Chicago Cubs
Can he pitch in the majors?

Not if history means anything, no. Kraemer, a left-hander who reached AAA in 1987 and will probably be there for several more years, shows none of the signs of being an effective pitcher. He's been used as a starter; the only way he could fool us might be if he moves to relief and learns a new pitch or something.

Randy KRAMER, Chicago Cubs
Is he going to land on his feet?

No. He's one percent better than Joe Kraemer.

Jimmy KREMERS, Atlanta
Who is he?

Catching prospect in the Braves' system, got called up as much out of desperation as anything else. Despite his .110 batting average (8 for 73) he probably isn't a terrible hitter. It's too early to tell but I suspect that he *does* have a major league future. but not in 1991.

Chad KREUTER, Texas
Have the Rangers given up on him?

He's hit .169 through 125 games, and the Rangers have a couple of catching prospects. Mark Parent has probably taken his job.

Bill KRUEGER, Seattle
Where's his career going?

Krueger is a tall left-hander with a degree in business administration. He failed an extended trial as a starter with the A's back in the Steve Boros era, went down and re-established himself by leading the PCL in wins and ERA in 1988. Now 33 years old (in April), he has pitched well with the Brewers the last two years, and signed with Seattle as a free agent.

Krueger started 17 times last year, but wasn't effective as a starter (4.40 ERA as a starter, 3.07 as a reliever.) Given the strength of the Seattle starting rotation, Krueger probably will remain in the bullpen. On the other hand, the batting average against him last year was .305 in his first 45 pitches, but dropped to .231 after that.

John KRUK, Philadelphia
Where do you play him?

It took us a few years to figure out what we had in Kruk because, like a lot of people, he had a misleading season in 1987, hitting twenty home runs (he hasn't hit more than nine in any other year.) His production has stabilized now. He's a .290 hitter with line-drive power, walks a lot and runs the bases well for a guy who runs like a wind-up toy. If it was my decision I'd leave him in left field. He's not going to hit enough to have a long career as a first baseman.

Jeff KUNKEL, Texas
Can he play?

As a utility infielder, yes. Kunkel hit .270 in 1989, .170 in 1990, the midpoint being .220, which is about his career average, and also about what you expect a backup infielder to hit. He's a good defensive shortstop, but the Rangers have been wasting at bats on him in the ill-fated hope that he was going to become a hitter.

Randy KUTCHER, Boston
Will he be on a roster?

He might. He's hit .225 and .230 the last two years, and ordinarily there's not too much call for outfielders who hit .230. On the other hand:

1. he had a secondary average of .338, and
2. Morgan seems to like him.

Jerry KUTZLER, Chicago White Sox
Who is he?

Right-handed starting pitcher, pitched well for Tampa in 1988. I don't expect him to be a major league starting pitcher, ever.

•L•

Mike LaCOSS, San Francisco
Can he still pitch?

As well as ever, yes. LaCoss tore the cartilage in his left knee during a rundown play on April 26, had a scope on May 14 and returned in August. He started four times in September, going 2-1 with a 3.51 ERA in 26 innings, so he can still pitch. He's been consistent for five years, with ERAs all in the threes. He's a good, safe player to have on your team.

Steve LAKE, Philadelphia
Why isn't this guy a regular?

He took too long to show people that he could hit. Lake, who is regarded as one of the best defensive catchers in baseball, hit just .151 in 58 games in 1985, pushing his career batting average so low that it took years to recover. He hasn't hit less than .250 since then, but he doesn't have any power and is now 34 years old, so he's not going to break through as a regular. In fact, with the acquisition of Darrin Fletcher he may have to move on to stay in the majors.

An interesting statistical fluke about Lake is that he hit .211 last year in April (4 for 19), May (4 for 19 again) and June (4 for 19 once again.) Then he got hot in July, boosted his average to .250 and went out of the lineup with an injury first reported as "sprained fingers". I don't know what happened to him after that, but he didn't play.

Dennis LAMP, Boston
Will he pitch in the majors this year?

Lamp, who had a 2.32 ERA in '89, doubled it last year (4.68) with accompanying increases in hits, walks and home runs and a decline in strikeouts. He'll probably be on the roster until they find out whether last year was a fluke, but

he'll have to pitch well the first two months.

Tom LAMPKIN, San Diego
Could he catch regularly for somebody?

When Benito Santiago was out last summer and San Diego was dropping further out of the pennant race each minute, the Padres traded Alex Cole to Cleveland for Lampkin, a 27-year-old (then 26-year-old) catching prospect. He's not a major league hitter, and it didn't work out great for him, but if his defense is good enough he may hang around as a backup. The Padres have traded Mark Parent, their other backup catcher.

Les LANCASTER, Chicago Cubs
What's his role? Is he a starter, middle reliever, closer, or what?

He pitched well as a starter last year (3-1, 3.66 ERA in six starts), but then he also pitched great as a reliever in 1989 (1.36 ERA for the season.) My general belief is that the only reliever who can be as valuable as a starter is probably the closer, so if the Cubs don't intend to make him the closer, which they obviously don't, they probably should give him a shot as a starter. Wrigley Field kind of got to him last year, as he had a 5.37 ERA in Wrigley, 3.81 on the road. He also had a 5.98 ERA in day games, 3.21 at night.

Rick LANCELLOTI, Boston
Could he have played in the major leagues, if he'd gotten a chance earlier? What would he have done?

Lancelloti, now 33 years old, has hit nearly three hundred home runs in his professional career, only two of them in the majors. He signed with the Pirates in 1977, and hit 41 homers for Buffalo in 1979. The Pirates sent him back to Buffalo the next year. He drove in 95 runs for Hawaii in 1982, hit 29 homers and drove in 131 runs for Las Vegas (PCL) in 1984, hit 31 homers and drove in 106 runs for Phoenix in 1986, hit 39 home runs in Japan in 1987, and played a few games with the Red Sox last year. He's a big left-handed batter, not huge or obscenely slow.

Of course Lancelloti could have played in the major leagues. I doubt that he could have been a player of much note. While he would have had good seasons—seasons in which he hit .270 with power—I think on balance he would have hit no higher than .240 as a major league player, with around twenty homers a year, poor K/W ratio but not terrible. There have been worse players who got better chances.

Bill LANDRUM, Pittsburgh
How much will he pitch? Should he be the Pirates' closer?

Landrum, a journeyman until he came to Pittsburgh at the age of 31, has been the most effective pitcher in the Pirate bullpen the last two years, posting ERAs of 1.67 and 2.13. Leyland didn't use a closer last year, using all five relievers in save situations. Actually, eight pitchers had saves for the Pirates last year.

I like Leyland's arrangement, and wouldn't suggest that Landrum should be a closer. Leyland is telling all five of his relievers, in effect, "I have confidence in you. I'm not afraid to use you when the game is on the line." By using all five men in this way, he isn't making any one of them a star, as he would if he gave somebody forty saves. This way, they're all working together toward a common goal, rather than one guy doing the dirty work and one guy getting the glamour job. There's less jealousy and backbiting, less reason for it. There's less *pressure* on each pitcher. I like it.

Despite his superb pitching for two years, I'm not convinced that Landrum could be an effective closer.

Mark LANGSTON, California
Why'd he have an off season?

Langston didn't pitch well, but he didn't pitch as badly as his won-lost record would suggest. His offensive support was very poor. He suffered nine tough losses, tying Matt Young for the most in the major leagues. (A tough loss is any game in which a pitcher has a game score of 50 or above but is charged with the defeat.)

As is often true of power pitchers, Langston was dramatically more effective in night games (3.85 ERA) than in day games (6.55).

Will he come back this year?

Absolutely. You can be as sure of that as you ever can, which is maybe 80% sure. First, his strikeout rate remains very high, 7.9 per game, so we know he still has the arm. Second, he's been successful in the past, so we know he can pitch a little. Third, he's come back from off seasons in the past, so we know he can do that. Fourth, the Angels are going to have a better team in '91 than they did in '90, so that should help him. Fifth, he won four games in August and pitched well in September (2-1, 3.47 ERA). He'll be back on top in '91.

Ray LANKFORD, St. Louis
Will he be Rookie of the Year in '91?

A year ago I had him marked with stars, meaning that I liked him. He did not have a good season last year at Louisville, but then played in the majors (39 games) exactly the way I would have thought he would.

He definitely has a chance to be the National League Rookie of the Year. He's one of the top candidates.

Carney LANSFORD, Oakland
Is he still helping the A's? Is he still among the better third basemen in the league?

Carney Lansford last year was a very poor player. If the back continues to bother him and he can't come back, the A's will have to replace him in 1992:

1. Lansford has limited range at third base. He always has had, because he dives for everything. I've been writing about this for ten years, but it happened several times in the World Series: balls were hit four feet from him, and he dived for them.
2. He has no power. He has hit five home runs in the last two years.
3. He's not fast. He stole 37 bases two years ago, but he wasn't fast then, and he wasn't running as well last year as he did in '89.

In '89 he hit .336, and if he hits .336 you can live with the other things. If he hits .268, like he did last year, he ain't gettin' the job done.

* * * * *

Jim Kaat said during the playoffs that Lansford "hits very well in the fifth spot. He is *not* a good hitter in the number two spot." He said this so confidently that I assumed he had some data to back it up, but if he did he apparently had it confused. Lansford hit .285 last year while hitting second, but .176 while hitting fifth (9 for 51). In '89 he hit .362 while hitting second, .312 while hitting fifth.

Dave LAPOINT, New York Yankees
Why are the Yankees starting this man?

Because

a. he won fourteen games in 1988, and
b. they're the Yankees.

Anything to avoid taking a look at a kid.

Will he start in '91?

Even for the Yankees, you'd think he'd be out of chances now. Steinbrenner is gone, and the Yankees have several young pitchers begging for a look. The Yankees may have Sanderson.

Barry LARKIN, Cincinnati
Is he the best shortstop in baseball?

It will be interesting to see Fernandez and Larkin going head to head next year; I've got to get to a Cincinnati/San Diego series just to compare the two of them.

Larkin is probably the best shortstop in baseball. He's a good defensive player, an excellent baserunner and his average over the last three years is over three hundred. It's not an empty three hundred; there are other plusses. I don't know that he's the best in any one area.

Is he going to be a Hall of Famer?
It's too early to talk about it.

Gene LARKIN, Minnesota
Does he help the Twins? Does he deserve a job?

He does *not* deserve a job, no; he's the kind of mediocre slow white guy that the Twins and Brewers have fallen in love with over the last few years.

He has been extremely consistent, perhaps the most consistent player in baseball for the last four years. His batting averages are .266, .267, .267 and .269. His slugging percentages are .382, .382, .368 and .392.

This makes it even more puzzling that the Twins keep playing him. If he had bounced up and down you could understand the Twins figuring that he was a good hitter who was just having some problems. But when you *know* what kind of a hitter he is, and his production is clearly below the standards of his position, why do you keep playing him?

Mike LAVALLIERE, Pittsburgh
Where's he rank? Should he be the full-time catcher?

LaValliere, who won a Gold Glove in 1987, slipped into a platoon arrangement with Don Slaught last year.

A healthy LaValliere is a good catcher, certainly good enough to be a regular. Before Mike Scioscia began to

hit for power, I used to write that LaValliere and Scioscia were two of the most identical talents in baseball. Both players:

1. Are excellent defensive catchers, throw well and block the plate well.
2. Are left-handed, line-drive hitters with no power.
3. Are slow as hell, and
4. Don't hit left-handers.

Last year LaValliere hit .375 against left-handers. He may have been challenged by the platoon arrangement to prove that he could, too, hit them people. That's only 56 at bats, so it doesn't mean a whole lot. The only thing it really affects is his APBA card.

He's a good player, but I'd platoon. First, you don't expect a catcher to play 162 games anyway, right? So you might as well get the platoon advantage while you are resting your catcher. Second, LaValliere (like Scioscia when he was young) has been hurt several times, on the disabled list in '84, '85, '87 and '89, so if you did expect a catcher to play every day, he wouldn't be the catcher.

If you asked him to be the everyday catcher, you're leaving yourself vulnerable during his next injury. If you platoon two catchers and one of them gets hurt, you're protected.

Note: LaValliere in his career has been on base by hit, walk or hit batsman 608 times (not counting home runs), but has scored only 108 runs (again, not counting homers.) That's the lowest ratio of runs scored per time on base of any major league player; he is followed on that list by Scioscia, Steve Balboni, Mike Fitzgerald and Jody Davis . . . he also has the highest career ratio of RBI to runs scored of any active player.

Tim LAYANA, Cincinnati
What's his role going to be?
The Reds' bullpen is unusually deep. Layana pitched well enough last year (3.49 ERA) to move up a slot when there is an injury ahead of him, but not well

enough to push somebody aside. He'll probably continue to work a batter here and a batter there in the middle innings until Dibble or Myers gets hurt or Dibble kills somebody and goes to jail or something.

Rick LEACH, San Francisco
Would you want him on your team?

In my opinion, it's alright to have a head case on your team as long as:

1. He isn't a key player,
2. You don't have too many of them, and
3. He doesn't do certain specific types of things which affect the rest of the team.

If an organization has a key player who has psychological problems—Dick Allen, Alex Johnson—then I think you've got to get rid of him. Everybody will be watching him, talking about him, seeing what he can get by with, and it will destroy the team. A minor player, if he does things like demand special favors, deride his teammates, start fights, whine about his place on the team, you need to get rid of that, too. But as long as he's just a little screwy, has a job to do and doesn't always do it right, I think you can live with that. It's just a negative factor that you throw into the mix of positives and negatives when you're evaluating him.

Terry LEACH, Minnesota
What's his role? How would you use him?

Leach is one of the few non-strikeout pitchers that I like, because he throws ground balls. Leach, Billy Swift, Don Carman. Not that any of these people are setting the world on fire.

Leach is now 37 years old, which pretty much rules out the idea of putting him in the starting rotation. If pressed for a closer, I wouldn't be reluctant to use him in that role for a short period of time.

Leach has very good control, which means that he can start an inning. He gets ground balls, which means that he is valuable with a runner on first and less than two out. I would be reluctant to let him face a left-handed hitter with a runner in scoring position when the run means anything.

Tim LEARY, New York Yankees
Is he worth the money?

In 1989 Leary had a very good excuse for finishing 8-14. His offensive support was terrible, the worst of any major league pitcher. Remarkably enough, again last year he had the weakest offensive support of any American League pitcher. The Yankees scored only 71 runs for him in 208 innings, or 3.1 a game. The bottom five: Leary, Allan Anderson (3.4), Greg Hibbard (3.8), Matt Young (3.8) and Mark Langston (3.9).

He also didn't pitch great:

1. He threw 23 wild pitches, one short of the major league record of 24.
2. Although he didn't walk a lot of people, he was behind the hitters more often than he was ahead.

As to whether he is worth the money, I think he is a reasonable gamble.

1. Leary throws hard.
2. He is healthy. He has proven that he can pitch two hundred innings a year without getting hurt. Not that many pitchers can.
3. His strikeout/walk ratio is still pretty good.
4. His bad luck can't last forever. Danny Jackson had bad luck for three years in a row with the Royals, but when his luck turned he went 23-8.
5. His salary, $2 million a year, isn't inflationary. That's basically the same deal the Yankees gave Pascual Perez a year ago, and Leary's a lot better risk than Perez. I'd rather have Leary at his reported salary than Tom Browning at his.

Why'd the Yankees pull him from the rotation just to avoid his twentieth loss? Does that make sense?

Not wishing to be vulgar, the appropriate term for this strategy is chickenshit. Sorry for the language, but that's the term we use for a decision which implies both pettiness and weak knees.

What did the Yankees gain by this? Nothing. I think this is another of Chuck Tanner's contributions to the game. The first time I ever heard of a pitcher being ashamed of losing twenty games was in 1985, when DeLeon was pulled from the Pirate rotation so he wouldn't lose twenty. I despise the tactic for 28 reasons. A lot of fine pitchers have lost twenty games in a season, including Steve Carlton, Walter Johnson, Luis Tiant, Mickey Lolich and Mel Stottlemyre. I never thought that any of these people were ashamed of losing twenty games or had any reason to be.

It's the wrong message. It's another step toward saying that "personal statistics are important." The manager's job is to say "I don't care about your personal stats. We do what is best for the team." Pulling the pitcher from the rotation to avoid his twentieth loss says that a pitcher should be *ashamed* of losing twenty—but if he's ashamed of losing twenty, then what about nineteen?

In 1962 Dick Farrell lost twenty games for Houston. His attitude was "It takes a hell of a pitcher to lose twenty games." There was an article about him in the *Saturday Evening Post*; that was the title. Isn't that a lot better attitude than Merrill's?

Manny LEE, Toronto
Will he do the job at short?

The Blue Jays traded Tony Fernandez for a second baseman last December, apparently on the belief that Lee could play shortstop. I have no reason to believe that he can't. I'm not a scout, but he's always looked good there to me, with the exception of one inning in '87. The Blue Jays also traded Sojo, their other shortstop candidate, but probably have three guys hiding in Florida who will emerge next year. They usually do, anyway.

Mark LEE, Milwaukee
Who is he?

An interesting pitcher; he might surprise us. Lee is a left-handed reliever, started in the Tiger system and failed a trial with Kansas City in '88. He's been given up on by two organizations and has an unimpressive minor league record until last year, when he went to Denver and suddenly turned tiger. At Denver he had 35 strikeouts and six walks in 28 innings; in eleven games with Milwaukee he had a 2.11 ERA and walked only four men. I'll try to make room for him on my list of American League Rookie of the Year candidates.

Terry LEE, Cincinnati
Who is he?

Based on 1990, he's a tremendous hitter. He started last year at AA, where his MLE (major league equivalent) showed .309 with a .513 slugging percentage. After 43 games he moved up to AAA, where he hit at the same level, a .293 average with a .539 slugging percentage. His composite MLE is .299 with 21 homers, 76 RBI in 115 games.

Now, the bad news. Lee is a 29-year-old first baseman. He started his career in 1984, played OK but not great, developed a chronic ankle problem in 1986 and missed most of two years. He's not fast or a defensive player, and never impressed anyone as a hitter until 1990. He reminds me of Champ Summers, the old A's farmhand who was close to 30 when he came up, failed two trials but eventually had a couple of good years with Detroit. Lee probably will make an impact somewhere, sometime, as a first baseman or DH. His struggles probably are not over yet.

Craig LEFFERTS, San Diego
How was he as the stopper? Are there any young Padres waiting to take his job?

He was fine as a closer, saved 23 games in 30 chances. He wasn't Mark Davis but he wasn't the reason the Padres flopped, either.

A short essay on converting statistics into moral judgments. Statistics carry certain limited, defined information about how well players do things. Nothing interferes with understanding what the statistics are and what they mean more often than the omnipresent tendency to convert certain statistical categories into measures of moral worth. Saves are one example.

Craig Lefferts has pitched effectively in the major leagues for eight years. He has pitched at least 56 games every year, with a career ERA of 2.95. His *worst* ERA ever is 3.83. He has always been effective, although he doesn't have a knockout fastball or anything.

Despite this, there has been this persistent idea that "he's not a closer". What does that mean, exactly? Does that mean that he can pitch in the seventh inning but can't pitch in the ninth? Does it mean that he's had chances as a closer and has failed? What does it mean?

What it means, precisely, is that he doesn't have a lot of career saves. That's it.

Charlie LEIBRANDT, Atlanta
Was last season for real? Can he continue to pitch this well?

Leibrandt is a lot like Bud Black, another ex-Royals pitcher who was a teammate a few years ago. The Royals have had many of this type over the years—Larry Gura, Paul Splittorff. They don't have one right now, which is part of their problem.

Leibrandt works on the margins. He can't afford to make a mistake, but if everything is right for him he can pitch inning after inning without ever making a mistake. He did that last year, and my guess is he will do it again next year.

Leibrandt last year gave up only nine home runs while pitching in Atlanta, which is about half what his home run rate used to be when he pitched in Kansas City. His control was very sharp last year, the best of his career, but it would be interesting to talk to him and ask if he made some adjustment which made that possible. When he was in Kansas City and had a good defensive outfield he could throw fly balls all night; maybe last year he decided to keep the ball away from the hitters more, or maybe he was throwing down in the strike zone more.

In any case, I seriously doubt that he can keep his ERA at 3.16 in Atlanta. He doesn't have to.

John LEISTER, Boston
Who is he?

Thirty-year-old right-hander, has pitched thirty-six innings with the Sox and has an 8.50 ERA. He played quarterback at Michigan State, and was honorable mention on the All-Big Ten football team in 1980. At thirty, he hasn't yet found his control.

Al LEITER, Toronto
Will he ever come back from the injury?

Leiter, a talented left-hander, has been plagued for two years by blisters on his fingertips. The Blue Jays have tried everything to stop it from happening, but it's been a battle. He has also had control troubles, walking 68 men in 78 innings at Syracuse last year.

I still like him. He's only 25 years old. Of course he has control troubles after not pitching for most of two years; that's to be expected. The inability to pitch has kept his arm from being abused at an age when many young pitchers' arms are wasted, and may actually help him in the long run. As soon as he finds his control and works out some sort of agreement with the blisters, he'll probably be back in the majors.

Mark LEITER, New York Yankees
Can he pitch in the major leagues?

He's certainly entitled to try, as opposed to another year of Dave LaPoint. At Columbus last year he struck out 115 and walked only 27 in 123 innings.

Originally signed by the Orioles, Leiter had three shoulder operations and didn't pitch in 1986, 1987 or 1988. He was released by the Orioles in June, 1988 and signed by the Yankees. He isn't regarded as a hot prospect, and the Yankees have split his work between starting and relief.

Both Leiters, incidentally, are listed at six foot three, 210 pounds.

Scott LEIUS, Minnesota
Who is he?

Second base/shortstop prospect, hits more like a shortstop. He hit .303 at Orlando in 1989, but hasn't hit anywhere else. Will probably have to hit more than .229 at Portland, which he did in 1990, before he gets a long look.

Mark LEMKE, Atlanta
What was his problem last year? Will he ever be good?

I had him marked with stars last year, but with a curiously reserved comment "Don't release Ryne Sandberg to pick him up, but I think he's a major league player."

That's still what I think. I should never have marked him with stars last year; it was a dumb decision. While Lemke *is* a major league player, there is no job waiting for him. Treadway is a major league player, too, a good one, and Treadway is in possession of the job. I think Lemke can play, but who knows how long it will be before he gets 400 at bats in a season?

Chet LEMON, Detroit
How long can he go on? Does he still help a team at 36?

He's not helping the team. The productive phase of his career ended three years ago; he's just hanging around soaking up at bats and collecting paychecks. Nothing against him, but he's the kind of player that an organization has got to get rid of.

Note: Lemon still has the worst career stolen base record of any active player, 43%. Among players with a hundred or more attempts the only players under 50% are Lemon and Tim Wallach. Lemon also has been hit by the pitch more times (151) than any other active player.

Jeff LEONARD, Seattle (released)
Why is he still around?

The essential lesson of Jeffrey Leonard, I think, is that you've got to be very careful who your leaders are. Leonard has been a mediocre player all of his career. I remember one time about 1985 I went through his skills and concluded that he should be a platoon player, which was being pretty generous. In San Francisco it was regarded as heresy.

I went to the city to promote the book. "But what about his leadership?" asked a reporter, or was it twenty. There is an assumption in the media that all leadership is positive. There is an assumption that if you have a veteran player asserting his influence in the clubhouse that's got to be a good thing—but very often it *isn't* a good thing. If you have a mediocre player asserting himself at the expense of developing stars, is that a good thing? Was it a good thing last summer in San Diego, when veteran players took it upon themselves to cow Tony Gwynn?

As time passes we see what kind of "leadership" Leonard provided—ex-teammates ripping into him in San Francisco and Milwaukee, a fight with a coach in the dugout in Seattle. Yeah, he was a leader alright—but did they win? San Francisco didn't win until they came up with players like Will Clark, Brett Butler and Rick Reuschel, who were better players and stronger personalities than Leonard.

It is a harsh reality of sports that the stars *have* to be the leaders. In football the quarterback has to be the leader; in baseball, it's the cleanup hitter. Maybe I don't mean that but this: that in all sports, the *best* leadership is the leadership of stars. Everyone is *watching* the stars; everyone is thinking about what they are doing. People admire them. That makes it possible for the star to have an impact that goes beyond what a Jeffrey Leonard can accomplish. If the star works hard, everyone will be aware of it. If the star gets lazy, everybody gets lazy. That's why Casey Stengel rode Mickey Mantle harder than he rode anybody else. That's why LaRussa offered to take on Canseco when Canseco didn't run out a ground ball, why Martin wanted to punch out Reggie when Reggie didn't want to bunt. It's a rule in baseball that I've never known to fail: if your star loafs, you lose.

I think it is very dangerous for a team to have mediocre players as leaders. You can't have a leader who is afraid that somebody else is going to turn into a better player than he is.

Jeff Leonard post-1985 has been an awful player. What he is is a one-dimensional power hitter who doesn't have much power. They bat him fourth and then tell you that he's an RBI man (he did hit .306 with men in scoring position last year—his one good stat. On the other hand, he hit .141 in the late innings of close games, the worst average in the American League.) So what you have here is an awful player who has stayed in the league five years after his abilities because he's a clubhouse leader, and what is the consequence of that? Was Seattle over-achieving last year because of his great leadership? Show me the team that he led to victory.

Note: The American League's worst hitters of 1990 in the late innings of a close game: Leonard, Carney Lansford (.152), Chet Lemon (.156), Junior Felix (.160) and Al Newman (.161).

Mark LEONARD, San Francisco
Who is he?

My favorite minor league player. He faces an uphill battle because he can't run, and on the Giants the two spots he would have to play one of are occupied by Will Clark and Kevin Mitchell. This obscures the fact that he is tremendous hitter, nearly as good a hitter as Clark or Mitchell. If he ever gets a chance to play in the majors he'll hit .290–.310 with a lot of walks, 18-25 home runs and more doubles than homers. No defensive value or speed, and it may be a couple of years before he gets a chance to play.

Darren LEWIS, San Francisco
Why did the A's trade him? Is he going to be a good player?

Lewis, regarded as the number one prospect in the A's system, was traded to San Francisco for Ernest Riles. There's no reason yet to think that Lewis will hit major league pitching, although he is young enough to improve. He'll probably hit .240–.270 for the Giants, speed but poor K/W. He'll need to improve to hold a job.

Mark LEWIS, Cleveland
Who is he?

A shortstop, the second player taken in the 1988 draft. *Baseball America* rated him the best prospect in the Eastern League last year.

Lewis is a better player right now than Felix Fermin, and will take his job within a year. He has a chance to be very, very good.

Scott LEWIS, California
Who is he?

Right-handed starting pitcher with the Angels. He had a 3.90 ERA last year with Edmonton, which is damn good for the Pacific Coast League, and a strikeout/walk ratio almost four to one. He'll be on my Rookie of the Year list.

Jim LEYRITZ, New York Yankees
Is he a major league third baseman?

Leyritz looked better at third than Blowers or Velarde, and the Yankees should stay with him until they have a definitive answer as to whether he can play the position. He still has a large number of things to prove, which can be basically summarized as offense and defense. Offensively, he has to prove that he has either the power one expects of a third baseman, or something else to compensate for it. In the minors his career high in homers was ten.

Offensively, I suspect Leyritz will be OK for a third baseman but no better. I think he'll hit .270–.300 with a slugging percentage around .400. If he was a Gold Glove that would be great, but he's a converted catcher who is still learning how to play the position. He's got work to do.

Dave LIDDELL, New York Mets
Who is he?

25-year-old catcher, took him five years to get out of A ball. He was given one at bat by the Mets last year, it is difficult to say whether from kindness or desperation.

Derek LILLIQUIST, San Diego
When he stops bouncing up and down, how good will he be?

Obviously he has a better chance of succeeding in San Diego than he had in Atlanta. In San Diego last September he walked only two men in five starts, 33 innings. To be successful he almost has to do that, because he doesn't have great stuff.

I am skeptical about his *long-range* future. I am *quite* optimistic about how he

will do in 1991. I expect Derek Lilliquist to be one of the most improved pitchers in the National League in 1991.

Jose LIND, Pittsburgh
Does his glove justify his bat?

The information to accurately balance offensive and defensive assets still does not exist, although we are closer than we were five years ago. Lind is certainly a wonderful second baseman, but we simply do not *know* how many hits Lind takes away from the opposition, or how many double plays he turns that another second baseman might not. The fact that Ryne Sandberg won the Gold Glove Award over Lind *and* Oquendo, to me, seems like one of the more obvious examples of a player winning a Gold Glove with his bat.

There is no doubt that Lind's defensive plusses more than balance his offensive shortcomings, if one is merely asking whether he deserves to keep his job.

There is no doubt that they do *not* balance if one is trying to argue that he is really a better player than Ryne Sandberg.

In between there, one must use subjective judgment. I would encourage you not to put *too much* weight on the performance of his team, because after all the Mets won the same division in 1988 with Wally Backman at second base.

My opinion—just take it for what it's worth—is that the top class of NL second basemen is a class of one. The second-best second baseman in the NL, Roberto Alomar, is now in the American League. The third-best is Jose Oquendo.

Then you get the group of good ones who are hard to distinguish—Lind, Treadway, Doran, Thompson and DeShields. Let's suppose I'm drafting a team and the top three guys are gone, who do I draft?

It would depend on the team. If I'm worried about my pitching, I have to pick Lind because he'll save the pitcher once in awhile. If I'm choosing a real team for

the long run, I have to take DeShields. If the team already has a non-hitting glove man, then I have to pick Treadway or Doran, because I don't think you can win with two non-hitters in the lineup.

Nelson LIRIANO, Minnesota
Will he be the Twins second baseman in 1991?

Liriano, who I marked with stars a year ago, lost his job and wound up in Minnesota. I don't think he was in shape at the start of the year—he looked heavy and slow.

After joining Minnesota he played well over the last two months. After August first he hit .261 with seven triples, five stolen bases and twenty walks.

Minnesota has been going through second basemen like Mike Tyson punching his way through the League of Women Voters, and they (the Twins) may decide to punch out Liriano and try Chuck Knoblach at any moment. Since they won the World Championship in 1987 they have gone through Steve Lombardozzi, Tommy Herr, Al Newman and Fred Manrique, none of whom is really all that bad except maybe Lombardozzi. I still think Liriano could be and should be among the best in the league.

In fact, now that I think about it the Twins haven't seen a second baseman they liked since Gene Mauch moved Carew to first base in 1976. The odd thing is that *many* of the second basemen they have used weren't really bad, but the Twins for some reason gave up on them after a year or so. They started with Bob Randall, who was brilliant on the double play and hit .267 his first year, but then he got hurt and they dumped him for Rob Wilfong. Wilfong hit .313 his first year as a regular and was projected as a star, but then dropped to the .240s and went off to finish his career in California, doing Gene Mauch's laundry or something. He was replaced by John Castino, a brilliant defensive third baseman and 1979 Rookie of the Year, moved over so that Gaetti could play third. Castino's career was ended by a congenital back problem, but Tim Teufel won the International League Player of the Year Award in '83, and seemed to be the answer to the problem.

Teufel had a very good rookie season, finishing fourth in the Rookie of the Year voting behind three guys who now make about $10 million a year among them. Ray Miller, however (you remember Ray Miller?) didn't like Teufel, and decided to give the second base job to Steve Lombardozzi. This brings us back to the championship year, where we started the story.

One of the things which most characterizes unsuccessful organizations, like unsuccesful people, is the habit of making major decisions in a casual, off-hand way. What the Twins have done at second base is to get down on the man they had, and then get rid of him before asking the question "Who do we have that's going to be any better in the long run?" They've got *two* good second basemen now, Liriano and Knoblach, maybe three with Chip Hale. They need to make it work.

Greg LITTON, San Francisco

No open questions about him . . . he obviously is good enough to be a major league backup infielder, and obviously is not good enough to take anybody's job. What you've seen is what you're going to get.

Bill LONG,
Chicago Cubs (Released)
Can he pitch?

Long is now 31 years old, and will celebrate his eighth birthday in 1992 (he was born February 29.) He isn't a great pitcher, so needs to have conditions working *for* him, rather than against him. He didn't have that last year in Wrigley Field with Walton and Berryhill out, and the Cub defense in some disarray. He had a 6.41 ERA in Wrigley Field, as opposed to 3.12 on the road. (His Day/

Night split was even worse—6.83 in day games, 2.51 at night.)

Long was released by the Cubs in late December. If he can get a shot somewhere else, being released by the Cubs could be the best thing that ever happened to him. With luck, he could move into the class of guys like Dennis Lamp and Frank DiPino, who hang around forever and are good sometimes.

Luis LOPEZ, Los Angeles
Who is he?

A first baseman who hit .353 at Albuquerque. He's 26 years old, doesn't have great power and doesn't have a *consistent* hitting record in the minor leagues. He's not going to take Eddie Murray's job, is what I'm saying. He could probably do a good job as a right-handed pinch hitter, and obviously doesn't have much left to prove at Albuquerque.

Vance LOVELACE, Seattle
Who is he?

235-pound left-handed pitcher, has a creative interpretation of the strike zone. He had the best ERA of anyone at Calgary last year (3.47).

Is he going to be in the majors?

He's not on the forty-man mid-winter roster.

Rick LUECKEN, Toronto
Can he pitch in the majors?

He probably can, at least a little. He was terrible last year—the league hit .339 against him—but pitching for the Braves isn't exactly a recommended way to break in a rookie. Steve Avery was terrible, too, and nobody is giving up on him.

Luecken's not a prospect. He's a six-foot-six, thirty-year-old right-hander who was a starting pitcher in the minors from 1983 to 1987 and was never effective. Converted to relief at Memphis in 1988, he pitched his way to the major leagues. He's working against time.

Urbano LUGO, Detroit
Was this his last shot?

Oh no, of course not. Urbano pitched thirteen times with the Tigers last year and posted a handsome 7.03 ERA. This might shake up a lesser man, but Urbano's been through this before. He knows how to handle failure. He didn't give up when he had a 9.32 ERA for California in 1987, or a 9.00 ERA in 1988. His career didn't end when he had a 6.75 ERA for Montreal in 1989. Why should it end now?

Scott LUSADER, Detroit
Could he play regularly?

Not bloody likely, as the British say. Lusader, a fifth outfielder, hits around .250 with an occasional home run, and shares a major league record by having committed three errors in the outfield in one inning. Lusader has a degree in marketing from the University of Florida, which probably means that he has a future in marketing.

Fred LYNN, San Diego
Is his career over?

Apparently not. He's still on the roster.

Why?

Curiosity. Lynn had 79 RBI in 1984, then successive totals of 68, 67, 60, 56, 46 and 23. The Padres are curious to know how long he can continue this.

Does he have any chance to get in the Hall of Fame?

It is possible, yes, when enough time has passed and he has been forgiven for not living up to expectations. Lynn has done 33 things which would be characteristic of a Hall of Famer. He has hit .300 (four times), driven in 100 runs (twice) and scored a hundred (twice). He has hit 35 doubles in a season (twice), and once hit 45. He has led the league in batting, runs scored, and doubles. He has 300 career home runs. He has won an MVP

Award and a Rookie of the Year Award, played in nine All-Star games and won five Gold Gloves. He was the regular center fielder on one league champion team (the 1975 Red Sox) and one division champion (the 1982 Angels.)

Altogether, it adds up to 86 points, which puts him in the bottom half of the gray area. Most players with comparable credentials are not in the Hall of Fame, but some are.

Barry LYONS, Los Angeles
Can he make it as Scioscia's backup?

It's the right job for him. He can hit against left-handers and take the day off against the Cardinals. It's the job he was born to do. The Dodgers also have Carlos Hernandez, a young right-handed hitting catcher, and may decide not to carry both of them.

Steve LYONS, Chicago White Sox
If you had him on your team, what would you do with him?

He's a utility infielder. He's not a bad utility infielder; he just had to play regularly for a couple of years when the Sox didn't have anybody else.

•M•

Kevin MAAS, New York Yankees
How good is he, really?

He's a good hitter, at least against right-handed pitching. He's a God-awful defensive player, and no, he's not going to hit 40 homers if he plays regularly. My guess is that as a regular he could hit .260 with around thirty homers, or hit for a higher average if he sacrifices power. He is *not* a potential superstar, but he can hit.

The big question yet to be decided about him is whether he will be a regular, and thus a star, or a platoon player. As well as he hits, if he can play 155 games he'll have totals that will earn him some big money. He hit .164 against left-handers last year, and as many lefties as the Yankees see, he's going to lose half of his income if he has to sit down.

Bob MacDONALD, Toronto
Who is he?

Left-handed relief pitcher, will probably spend the year at Syracuse. He's pitched well at Knoxville for two years in a row, but has yet to prove himself at AAA.

Mike MacFARLANE, Kansas City
Is he a potential All-Star?

Probably not a legitimate one. You know how they do that, if you hit .325 the first half of the season they'll put you on the All-Star team. Macfarlane could certainly hit .325 for half a season, but he's very slow, has no power and can't throw. That's a lot to overcome on the way to stardom.

Is his grip on the job safe?

For the time being. He hits pretty decent, and the Royals apparently won't re-sign Bob Boone. They don't have anybody else pushing him except Brent Mayne, who isn't ready.

Macfarlane is probably a good draft in a rotisserie league. He is 27 years old this year, and goes to camp with a job for the first time. His defense won't count against you in rotisserie league, and there's a good chance he'll have his best year with the bat.

Note: Macfarlane last year threw out only fourteen of 82 runners who attempted to steal, the lowest percentage of any major league catcher (75 or more attempts.) This statement is normally followed by a disclaimer to the effect that this is actually the pitching staff's fault, but don't buy it: the Royals' pitchers, as a whole, do a pretty good job of holding runners. Macfarlane just doesn't throw well . . . the catchers with the worst percentages were Macfarlane, Jeff Reed, Mike Fitzgerald, Greg Olson and Gary Carter.

★ ★ ★
Julio MACHADO, Milwaukee
★ ★ ★
Why did the Mets give him up for Charlie O'Brien?

Machado is a small right-hander, which in the thinking of some baseball men automatically disqualifies him from being a good pitcher.

Is he a good pitcher?

He's a terrific pitcher. The Mets have chopped up his career so much that he's never been able to post impressive numbers anywhere, but if you add together his 1989 numbers at Peninsula, St. Lucie, Jackson, Tidewater and New York you have to reach the conclusion that he was too good for his competition, some of which was major league. The Mets made a mistake in letting him get away.

Shane MACK, Minnesota
Was last season a fluke? Can he really hit?

Mack, who played with San Diego in 1987–1988 and hit .241 for them, hit

.326 last year for Minnesota. A few thoughts:

1. Mack obviously is better suited to the Minnesota park than he was to San Diego. In San Diego in 1987 Mack hit .225 at home, .252 on the road. In Minnesota last year he hit .369 at home, .291 on the road. He was up 39 points on the road, 144 points at home.

2. Playing more late in the season, Mack's batting average did *not* falter. Playing 28 games after September first, Mack hit .432 (38 for 88).

3. Projected to 600 at bats last year, Mack would have had 132 strikeouts and 54 walks. Not too many guys can hit .326 with that kind of a strikeout/walk ratio.

4. Mack was also *behind* the pitcher 56% of the time last year, but overcame this by hitting .492 (30 for 61) when he hit the first pitch and an unbelievable .566 (30 for 53) when he hit the second pitch. If he didn't get a resolution on the first two pitches he hit .211.

5. Mack is a right-handed hitter, and he hits much better against left-handed than right-handed pitching. However, he was *not* extensively platooned last summer. He hit .370 against left-handers and .287 against right-handers, but *most* of his at bats were against right-handers.

Adding it all up, I think it's likely that Mack has shown some real improvement as a hitter from his San Diego experience, and can be expected to continue to hit well enough to play. He's a better hitter than the people he would drive to the bench (Gene Larkin and Randy Bush). He's not a .326 hitter, and should not be expected to contend for the batting title as a regular.

When the league gets to know him a little better, the pitchers will learn not to give him anything good to hit early in the count. He'll probably get anxious, start chasing bad pitches, and his batting average will drop.

Greg MADDUX, Chicago Cubs
Where's he rank? Is he one of the top ten starters in the National League?

Maddux *is* one of the top ten starting pitchers in the National League, possibly one of the top five:

1. He can pitch 240 innings a year, half of them in Wrigley Field, without being destroyed by it. Not many pitchers can.

2. While his ERAs are always better on the road than they are in Wrigley, he deals fairly well with the park. He doesn't let it destroy his confidence.

3. His won-lost record over the last three years is 52-35. No other pitcher has won 52 games in the National League in the last three years (Drabek is second with 51; no one else has more than 48.) Maddux' winning percentage is better than that of his team all three years.

Mike MADDUX, Los Angeles
Is his career over?

Probably not. He's not old. He still has a major league fastball, and his control is very good. He'll get some more trials.

Dave MAGADAN, New York Mets
Was 1990 a career year? Is he really this good? Can he contend for the batting title regularly?

I doubt that Magadan is a legitimate .328 hitter, but then who is? I do think he is a legitimate .310–.315 hitter, and if he is that then he'll have some more chances to win a batting title.

Two reasons to think Magadan isn't a true .328 hitter:

1. He was 27 years old last year, the age at which people tend to have their best seasons, and

2. His lifetime batting average is .305, not .328.

Shea Stadium, of course, is a very tough place to hit for average. No Met has ever won the batting title, and Magadan's home/road splits show why: he hit .372 on the road, but .278 in Shea Stadium. In another park, I think Dave Magadan would win a few batting titles. In Shea Stadium, he may not.

Joe MAGRANE, St. Louis
Will he be back? Will he ever be consistently good?

His chance of being a *great* pitcher seems to be evaporating. There's always some reason he's not winning; after four years he has an excellent career ERA (3.07), but he's a .500 pitcher (42-42). His strikeout rate is declining; last year it was a career-low 4.4 per nine innings. The Cardinals no longer appear to be one of the better organizations in the league; it may be two or three years before they are back in contention.

I still like Magrane; I'm just cautioning that we can't be as optimistic about his future as we were a year or two ago. He's bright, throws strikes and has a good arm. After starting badly last year he posted an ERA of 2.98 over the last three months. I think he'll continue to pitch well, but at the moment he is *not* a top candidate for a Cy Young season.

Rick MAHLER, Cincinnati (Released)
Have we seen the last of him?

Mahler was not offered arbitration by the Reds, making him a free agent. Mahler's ERAs were under four in '88 and '89. Although his ERA jumped over four last year his ratios of hits/innings and walks/innings weren't bad. I think he could still help some teams in middle relief. He'll probably have a job in '91. Hell, he'll probably have a job in '96.

Candy MALDONADO, Cleveland
Will he ever have another season like 1990? Is he a good free agent risk?

I certainly don't expect him to have another year like 1990, but then, I didn't expect him to have another year like 1987. Maldonado actually wasn't that far ahead of his career batting average or slugging percentage last year (.273-.256 in batting average, .446-.418 in slugging percentage.) Those are normal deviations, so in that sense it is certainly possible for him to have another season like this.

Is he a good free agent risk?

Not in my opinion. If Maldonado hits .273 and slugs .446 you can justify his spot in the lineup, but what if he hits 17 points *under* his career batting average (.239) with a slugging percentage 28 points *under* his career norm (.390)? Do you want him then?

Why'd he drive in 95 runs last year? Did he hit well with men in scoring position?

No. Maldonado hit .268 with men in scoring position, five points under his batting average. He drove in the runs simply because he got hot early in the season, was put in the cleanup slot and had a lot of RBI opportunities.

Carlos MALDONADO, Kansas City
Who is he?

Right-handed reliever, very good medium-range prospect. He was rushed to the majors ahead of his time last year because of the injuries to the Royals' pitching staff, and should spend 1991 at Omaha.

Bob MALLOY, Montreal
Who is he?

Six-foot-five right-hander out of the Rangers' system. He was a 19th-round draft pick in 1986 who vaulted to a major league trial in 1987, then began to strug-gle. He pitched his way back to a trial with Montreal by pitching well in Indianapolis. Good control/so-so stuff. He's a Grade D prospect, but given Rodgers' ability to work with pitchers you have to think he has a chance.

Chuck MALONE, Philadelphia
Who is he?

Six-foot-seven right-hander; wilder than M.C. Hammer with a bee in his pants. Don't draft him for at least a couple of years.

Kelly MANN, Atlanta
Who is he?

Catching prospect, came over to the Braves for Paul Assenmacher. He hit .202 at Richmond last year, despite which I think he will eventually hit. In fact, he could wind up as the NL Rookie of the Year this year let's just imagine—and then people will say "See, minor league hitting stats don't mean anything. Kelly Mann hit .202 in the minors, but then he was the NL Rookie of the Year." But the fact is that Mann's minor league batting record, *as a whole*, suggest that he *can* hit major league pitching.

Mann's a well-regarded defensive catcher, excellent arm, who could probably hit around .250 in the major leagues with some power, 12-15 home runs. That's based on what he's done at ages 21 and 22; when he gets to 25, there's a real good chance he's going to be a major league hitter. He's definitely a prospect.

Ramon MANON, Texas
Who is he?

Long-range pitching prospect; has no control and minor league ERAs around six. I've no idea why the Rangers decided to take a look at him.

Fred MANRIQUE, California
Does he deserve a full-time job? Will he help the Angels?

The Angels have added Manrique as a free agent and Sojo by trade. I think either one of these men is a decent second baseman, of comparable skill. I would make Sojo my second baseman because he is four years younger.

I think the Angels would be making a mistake if they keep both of them on the roster, because that would lead to the same sort of confusion that the Angels have suffered from for years, like last year when they used six right fielders. They need to choose *one* second baseman, not collect several of them.

Jeff MANTO, Cleveland
Is he a major league player?

I think so, yes, but it's going to be close. Offensively, I see him as a .250–.270 range hitter with 12-17 homers a season. He's a first baseman/third baseman.

As a third baseman, that offense is good enough, but his defense probably isn't. I doubt that he will be able to play third base in the major leagues.

As a first baseman, he could be outstanding defensively, but can you live with the bat?

If it's .270 with 17 homers and the defense *is* good, yes, you can live with it. If it's .250 with 12 homers and the defense is average, that's another story. So he's on the line; he needs to hit as well as he is capable of hitting if he's going to have a major league career.

Kirt MANWARING, San Francisco
Will he be on a major league roster this year?

Manwaring, who played 85 games with the Giants in their 1989 championship season, went back to Phoenix last year and struggled, hitting .235. The odds are that he will *not* be in the major leagues this season.

Paul MARAK, Atlanta
Who is he?

Right-handed pitching prospect, Grade D prospect but could surprise.

You can tell that his organization doesn't believe in him because they use him as a starter/reliever. In 1989 he had 15 starts in the minors and thirty relief appearances; last year he had 16 of each.

He pitched brilliantly last year at Richmond (2.49 ERA) and has pitched well for the last four years. He pitched well in seven major league starts, posting a 3.69 ERA. In the majors his control wasn't good, but in the minors he has been a control pitcher. The late Bobby Cox had been quoted as saying that "With the action on his pitches, you've got to find a spot for him on your staff."

Given that he pitched well last year, and given that the Braves need pitching, it seems obvious that he should continue to start for them. I think in the short run he's a very good prospect. It's easy to see him going 14-11 this year with a 3.60 ERA in Atlanta, although obviously the odds are that he won't do that well. In the long run, he has little if any star potential.

Mike MARSHALL, Boston
Does he help a team? Now that we have finally disposed of the notion that he is going to be a star, would you want to have him around?

The dominant facts about Marshall in the eighties were that

1. he wasn't as good as he was supposed to be, and
2. he gets hurt a lot.

The attention drawn by these points, the criticism, obscures the facts that

1. he's a very *consistent* hitter, and
2. he does hit enough to help you win.

His slugging percentages have been in the .400s in eight of the last nine years, the other one being over .500.

I would not want Mike Marshall as my cleanup hitter. I wouldn't want him if people still thought he was a star. First, you want a cleanup hitter with a .500

slugging percentage. More importantly, if you're counting on him to be a key to your team and his back acts up and he's out for an indefinite period of time, you've got a problem. You have to shuffle the team, and it creates uncertainty and self-doubt.

But as a part-time player hitting fifth to seventh, Marshall is fine; he'll help the team. If he's there it's a plus; if he's not somebody else does the job. At that level, I'd like to have him on my team.

Incidentally, Marshall may be one of the very few players, one of two or three in the majors, who actually hits better the wrong way. A right-handed hitter, he hit .279 last year against right-handers, .219 against left-handers. In 1989 he hit .267 against right-handers, .246 against left-handers, and in 1988 he hit .301 against right-handers, .231 against left-handers. The 1989 *Elias Analyst* reported that at that time his career average was .280 against right-handers, .258 against lefties. So you don't want to platoon him, or if you do you want do it backwards, platoon him with another right-handed hitter. He could platoon with Jack Clark, not that there are going to be three weeks during the year that both Clark and Marshall will be healthy.

Carlos MARTINEZ, Chicago White Sox
Will he get another chance as a regular?

In view of his youth (he's only 25) and history of having hit, he probably will. He's like Jeff Manto in that he's a good hitter for a third baseman, but can't *quite* do the job defensively, and a good fielder for a first baseman but doesn't hit quite enough. He's also the only player in the American League that you can drive a Toyota between his legs.

Carmelo MARTINEZ, Pittsburgh
Does he justify a roster spot?

Certainly. Martinez is a .248 hitter and slow, but his secondary offensive

skills are good, and he's not a bad outfielder. You wouldn't willingly trade Wes Chamberlain for him, but he's a good bench player.

Dave MARTINEZ, Montreal
Should he be a regular?

Martinez got a chance as a regular when he was very young (22) and hit .292 for the Cubs. That was 1987 and everybody hit, and after that he began to struggle and lost his job.

At the moment, he is one of Buck Rodgers' professional non-regulars, like Otis Nixon and Mike Fitzgerald. With Marquis Grissom and Larry Walker around, not to mention Ivan Calderon, it will be very difficult for him to get back to being a regular. But you have to think, on the basis of how he played last year, that he may have a chance to do it. Start counting the positives:

1. he's still young (26).
2. he's hit .274 and .279 the last two seasons, a decent average.
3. he can steal a base, about twenty a year.
4. he's a good center fielder.
5. he hit eleven homers last year in 118 games.

Martinez is small, but some players are still developing power in their mid-twenties. If Martinez' 1990 increase in power turns out to be a real change in ability, rather than a one-year fluke, he's got a good argument to be somebody's everyday center fielder when his free agency comes at the end of the 1992 season.

Dennis MARTINEZ, Montreal
Where's he rank? Is he one of the better starting pitchers in the league?

Martinez is a better pitcher now than he's ever been, and one of the best starting pitchers in the National League. His strikeout to walk ratio last year, 156 to 40, shows that he can still get ahead of you with the fastball and still carve you up with that devastating curve.

Martinez is like Bert Blyleven—been

around forever, has great control, wonderful curveball. Like Blyleven, he's bounced up and down a lot, but like Blyleven he's won a lot more than he's lost.

Edgar MARTINEZ, Seattle
Is he really this good?

Martinez' .300 batting average last year was misleading, not that he's not a legitimate .300 hitter (he is), but that there were lizards hiding in the cellar. He didn't hit much with men in scoring position (.244) and was disappointing defensively, committing 27 errors, which I think was the most of any major league player at any position. As a hitter, though, he's for real. He'll hit close to .300 lifetime, with an on-base percentage up around .400.

Ramon MARTINEZ, Los Angeles
Can he continue to pitch at this level?

All of the statistical indicators a year ago were that Martinez would be an outstanding pitcher. All of the indicators now are that he will remain an outstanding pitcher.

I have been told that Martinez has poor mechanics, but I got out a videotape to study it, and I don't see the problem. I don't see anything mechanically that's going to cause an injury.

I see two problems for him. One is that because of his ability he's going to pitch a lot of innings before his arm is fully mature, and this will probably prevent him from having a long career. The second is that he is very thin. Most of the outstanding pitchers that I have seen who were very thin were not consistent, and most of the consistent pitchers I have seen were solidly built, medium build. But looking at right now, he's as good a pitcher as there is.

Tino MARTINEZ, Seattle
How good is he?

I'm very cool toward him. As I see him, he's likely to hit around .260 with 15–18 home runs.

USA *Today* named Martinez the Minor League Player of the Year for 1990, which I think is nuts. Because of his buildup, Martinez will probably play regularly from opening day, and he will be one of a handful of rookies to do that. If he has a season which is near the top of his range—let's say he hit .275 with 22 home runs—he will be a strong candidate for the American League Rookie of the Year. But if you ask me is this a player to get excited about, my answer is that he definitely is not. He is the most overrated rookie of the 1991 crop.

John MARZANO, Boston
Could he be an effective platoon catcher?

Marzano is one of the puzzles of the game. When Gedman held out in '87 Marzano caught 52 games and played well, hitting .244 with a little power and catching well. When Gedman came back he was awful, but Marzano apparently alienated the Red Sox management by popping off, and the Red Sox refused to bring him up even when they were desperate for a catcher.

There is no reason to think that Marzano couldn't be a good platoon catcher or backup catcher.

Greg MATHEWS, St. Louis
Is he ever going to be back?

Probably not. He was a marginal pitcher when he was on top of his game. If he's lost three miles an hour, I doubt that he'll get anybody out.

Don MATTINGLY, New York Yankees
Will his bat come back? Will they really put him in right field?

1. Mattingly's bat will be back. Mattingly's back was bothering him last year, but he also hit in tough luck. He was still making contact. He struck out only 20 times last year. His batting average when the ball was in play (no strikeout or home run) was just .260 last year, and everybody hits better than that.

2. The mid-winter trade of Azocar obviously seems like a signal that the Yankees intend to use Mattingly in the outfield. If Barfield is still with the team, then Mattingly will probably play left field, Barfield in right.

Will it work?

Mattingly asked to play the outfield because he thinks the bending and stretching at first base is hard on his back, and the Yankees were receptive to the idea because of Kevin Maas.

It doesn't seem like good reasoning to me. Mattingly is very slow for a modern outfielder. He played the outfield for years in the minors—when his back was good. When he tries playing it with a bad back he may be surprised at how much bending and stretching there is out there, too. Mattingly is a good defensive first baseman; Maas isn't. I suspect that Mattingly will wind up at designated hitter until he makes some progress on getting his back healthy, and then will return to first base.

Derrick MAY, Chicago Cubs
Can he hit major league pitching?

Before the signing of George Bell, May was being touted as a 1991 regular. May is young (22), big (six foot four) and a decent hitter, but he has yet to do anything which shows me that he can hit what is expected of a major league outfielder. I think he could hit .270–.280 in Wrigley Field, which is OK, but he needs to add some power. My guess is he'll spend the season at Iowa.

Brent MAYNE, Kansas City
Who is he? Will he be in the major leagues this season?

Mayne was the Royals' first-round draft pick in 1989, played well at Memphis (AA) and got a look. His game is more defense than offense. He throws well but has no power, and has yet to prove he can hit for average.

He *should* spend the season at Omaha, but the Royals as of now (January) don't have a capable backup catcher on their roster. If they don't find one Mayne may be forced to stay in the majors.

Randy McCAMENT, San Francisco
Who is he?

Right-handed relief pitcher, extremely marginal prospect in the Giants system. He'll never play a key role on any team, and needs to catch a break if he's going to have a career.

I was on the air last year with Joe Garagiola when a caller called in asking some advice about his "cousin". His cousin, he said, was a 28-year-old pitcher who had been in AAA for three years, pitching fairly well but never getting a look by the major league team. He wanted to know what we thought: should he stick it out and hope for a chance, or should he find something else to do with his life?

From the information given we figured out who the caller probably was. It wasn't Randy McCament, but it was somebody *like* Randy McCament, a AAA pitcher hanging on and hoping for a break.

Joe and I split completely on it, and argued about it for twenty minutes after the show was over. What Joe said is "Give it up. Get on with your life. There is nothing sadder than some forty-year-old guy saying 'I coulda done this. I coulda been a major league player.' "

I suspect that the caller had more interest in Joe's opinion than he did in mine, and he should have, because after all Joe's been there. Joe had to decide how long he could stay with the game, and Joe makes *good* career decisions. Like most people, that decision was made for me the first time I tried to hit a good high-school curve ball.

But what *I* think is, hang in there. First, you're a professional, so think of it as an economic decision. Twenty years ago Joe's advice would have been the smart thing to do—but not now. Now, if this pitcher catches just a little tiny break, it means big dollars. If he has two years in the majors as a bit player, he'll make more money in those two years than he'll make any other way in the next ten years. If, like Dale Mohorcic, he is somehow able to hang around for *five* years . . . well, that's a lot of money. It's not enough money to retire on, but it will put the kids through Harvard.

It used to be that you weren't in the pension plan until you had played six years. Now you're in the pension plan the day you're called up—at a low level, but it mounts up rapidly. Two years in the major leagues is enough to create a nice little supplement to your income when you reach retirement age. And if you don't get those two years, what difference does it make if you start your next career at age 28 or 31?

On the larger issue, of course it is sad to see a guy saying "I coulda been somebody." But do you wind up that way because you follow your dreams all the way, or do you wind up that way because you give up on them too quickly? I guess that's the real key to the argument, but as I see it, if this guy gives up now and goes home, *that's* how he winds up saying "I coulda." I say, if you can't play in the majors let them *tell* you you can't. Then you know.

Kirk McCASKILL, California
Will this be the year he wins twenty games?

Probably not. There are two negative indicators about him for 1991, and one positive. The two negative indicators are:

1. his strikeout rate nose-dived last year. His 1990 strikeout/walk ratio (78-72) is definitely *not* characteristic of a quality pitcher.

2. he has yet to prove that he can pitch 200 innings in a year and remain healthy.

The positive indicator is that the Angels will be a better team this year than they were last year. On balance, I'm leery of him for the time being.

Paul McCLELLAN, San Francisco
Who is he?

Right-handed pitching prospect for the Giants. He looks like nothing, but then so did Brantley and Burkett.

Lloyd McCLENDON, Pittsburgh
Is there room for him on this team?

If McClendon can hit .240 he'll have a job, because he saves the team from having to waste a roster spot on a number three catcher.

I don't know if you're aware of this, but teams are carrying more pitchers than they used to, and making more pitching changes in the middle innings. Ten years ago nine pitchers on a 25-man roster was standard; now, the decision is "do we want to carry ten or eleven"? The inevitable consequence of this is that you'll see more multi-position players, and those players will get more playing time. One thing we haven't seen yet, but probably will, is minor league players being *groomed* to play multiple positions.

In 1989 McClendon hit .286 with 12 homers in 259 at bats. I don't know what I wrote about him, but I'm sure it was negative because I knew he wasn't that good a hitter.

But last year he hit .164, and he's a better hitter than that. He should be able to hit .240 with an occasional home run and play defense at two or three positions. You can use a guy like that.

Rodney McCRAY, Chicago White Sox
Will he be the Herb Washington of the '90s?

Actually, managers have been using professional pinch-runners for a long time; for some reason we talk about Herb Washington, probably because he wasn't a real baseball player. As teams keep more pitchers (see previous comment) it becomes more difficult to find roster space for a pinch runner.

McCray is not a major league hitter, not close. Never going to be one; he's a .160 hitter. His career, if he has one, will be as a pinch runner.

Lance McCULLERS, Detroit
What's been his problem?

If you graph his major league ERAs there is a spike in the middle, which is the time he was in New York (1989 and early 1990). Other than that period he's always been an effective pitcher.

The Yankees are a tough team to pitch for, and in the last ten years many pitchers who have succeeded other places have failed there. My reading of McCullers is that he is a fine pitcher who simply didn't handle New York.

Could he be the Tigers' closer this year?

The Tigers are talking about making him a starter. Coming off a period of his career when he has struggled, it wouldn't seem to be a good idea to push him into a pressure job. The Tigers had three other relievers who pitched well last year (Gibson, Gleaton and Henneman). The best idea would appear to be not to push their luck.

Ben McDONALD, Baltimore
How good will he be?

I know as much about it as you do. He's a big Mother with a great arm and a 2.43 ERA. That's a good place to start.

Although McDonald is a right-handed pitcher, he held left-handed batters to a .181 batting average last year, the lowest in the American League.

Jack McDOWELL, Chicago White Sox
Is he for real? Are his troubles over?

He's still learning his job, but I think he's a terrific pitcher. A first-round draft pick out of Stanford in '87, McDowell struggled through 1988 but won fourteen games last year.

The White Sox are moving into a new park in 1991, and it is believed to be a better park for a hitter, a worse park for a pitcher. McDowell's ERA was 3.82 last year, which isn't great.

Still and all, I love him. I say he's going to win 17 games this year, and be the Sox' best pitcher during the 1990s.

Oddibe McDOWELL, Atlanta
How does he fit into the Braves' outfield?

I've been stubborn about Oddibe, continuing to believe that he was better than he is. His numbers have never been great, but there was always something about him that I liked.

As of now there is no place for him in the Braves' outfield, and I'm not sure whether there will be a place for him anywhere else, either. Certainly he would be a useful player as a fourth outfielder, pinch runner and defensive sub, but would he accept the role? Oddibe was supposed to be a star. It remains to be seen how he will handle the challenge of *not* being a star.

Roger McDOWELL, Philadelphia
Will he bounce back this year?

He might, but I'd sure hate to bet on it.

McDowell over the last two years has an ERA of 1.76 on grass fields (67 innings), but 3.29 on artificial turf (82 innings). It was much better on grass than turf both years.

Craig Wright and I have a long-standing argument over whether ground-ball pitchers are more effective or less effective on artificial turf. He thinks they are

more effective on turf; I think they're less effective. We argued about this for a year one time in letters back and forth, but we couldn't really resolve it because at that time the data was limited. If I was still doing that stuff I'd go back and study the issue with the good data we have now.

Chuck McELROY, Philadelphia
Who is he?

Young left-hander in the Phillies' system, was being used as a garbage man at Scranton (AAA) but pitched so well that he'll probably be on the major league roster. I like him—decent fastball, good breaking pitch, good control.

Andy McGAFFIGAN, Kansas City
What role, if any, will he have this season?

McGaffigan washed out in Montreal and San Francisco, came to Kansas City and was forced into the starting rotation by the injuries to Saberhagen, Gubicza, Storm Davis and others. He pitched well as a starter, to everyone's surprise. He isn't on the KC mid-winter roster, but has a minor league contract and almost certainly will be on the major league team, pitching middle relief and being used as an emergency starter. He'll inherit Steve Farr's job.

Willie McGEE, San Francisco
How will he do with the Giants?

Willie McGee is *not* the ballplayer that Brett Butler is. They're comparable in that they're both small, both fast, both center fielders and singles hitters with no power. Butler had salary requests that the Giants felt were out of line, and I'm sure the Giants felt that there was no justification for going higher for Butler than they would for McGee, a former MVP and the reigning batting champion.

They're wrong; this guy isn't the player that Butler is. I'm confident that a year from now, 90% of the fans in the Bay area will agree with me about that.

1. McGee is less likely to win a batting title in San Francisco than he would be in St. Louis. He's a lifetime .297 hitter mostly in St. Louis; he might hit .285 here, over a period of years.
2. McGee isn't the center fielder that Butler is.
3. McGee isn't the fundamental player that Butler is.

Did anything like this ever happen before? The batting title, I mean—McGee winning the National League title while he was in the American League.

The closest historical parallel is Carl Furillo's batting title in 1953. Furillo was hitting .344 on September 6, 1953, when he broke his left hand in a fight with Leo Durocher of the Giants. He was leading the league in hitting, and had already qualified for the batting title, which at that time required 400 at bats. Unable to play, he became a stationary target for the other hitters, as McGee did last year.

Furillo won the title in a close battle. Red Schoendienst closed strong to finish at .342, and Stan Musial hit .430 in his last thirty games to get up to .337, similar to Eddie Murray's closing flourish last year (Eddie hit .410 in his last thirty games to close at .330.) Duke Snider and Don Mueller, the same two players who would battle Willie Mays to the last day in 1954, also finished close, at .336 and .333, but no one could catch Furillo.

Note: McGee hit .387 last year when the ball was in play (that is, neither a strikeout nor a home run). That was the highest average in the major leagues, ahead of Luis Polonia (.372) and Dave Magadan (.364).

Fred McGRIFF, Toronto
Why doesn't he drive in more runs? Does he get a bad rap as an RBI man?

It's not a bad rap. McGriff has the best career slugging percentage of any active player (.530), but hasn't driven in as many runs as you would expect for a hit-

ter who hits .280 with 35 homers a year. In 1989, when he hit .269, he hit .252 with runners in scoring position (34 for 135) but took 45 walks. Last year, when he hit .300, he hit .264 with runners in scoring position (34 for 129) with 33 walks.

It's easy to see what has happened: with runners in scoring position, they don't give him anything to hit, which results in many walks and a slightly lower batting average.

There is an old theory which jumps from here to "McGriff needed somebody to hit behind him, to protect him." I don't care for the theory as a general rule. I doubt that having Babe Ruth hitting behind Freddie McGriff would have significantly changed McGriff's batting average or home run count—but it would have changed his RBI count. I don't really understand why the Blue Jays hit George Bell fourth and McGriff fifth, but I guess it's a silly thing to argue about now.

How will he hit in San Diego? Will it hurt his stats?

1. The SkyDome is a much better hitter's park than Jack Murphy Stadium, so there is an initial presumption that his stats will decline somewhat in the move.
2. McGriff did *not* hit well in Toronto. Last year he hit .277 with 14 home runs in Toronto, .321 with 20 homers on the road. Only 46% of his career home runs have been in Toronto. His stats are in no sense a creation of the park(s) he leaves behind.
3. I don't know if you've noticed this, but the American League is a left-handers league. There are several American League parks which favor a left-handed hitter (Yankee Stadium, Tiger Stadium, the Metrodome, the Kingdome) and none which distinctly favor a right-hander, although you can argue about Fenway.

4. McGriff has always hit best in warm weather. He's done his best hitting in July and August. He may like San Diego.
5. McGriff has often been compared to Willie McCovey, so that makes it a natural question "How did McCovey do here?"

In his two full seasons with the Padres (1974–1975) McCovey was 36 and 37 years old, and hit .252 with 45 home runs. Full home/road breakdowns from that era aren't available, but in the two seasons McCovey hit 21 home runs in San Diego, 24 on the road. I'm not sure if they've moved any fences since then or not.

On balance, there is little reason to expect a significant change in McGriff's production based on locale.

Mark McGWIRE, Oakland
Is he a good player, even hitting .235? Does he need to get his batting average up?

This guy is a *great* player hitting .230. He'd be a good player hitting .210. Even hitting .230, he still brings you:

1. Gold Glove defense at first base,
2. A hundred walks a year, for a .370 on-base percentage,
3. More power than any other current major league player. With the passing of Ken Phelps he is the only major league player who has averaged two bases per hit throughout his major league career (2.02).

He also has the best career ratio of RBI to total bases of any active player. McGwire has hit 153 home runs in his four seasons as a regular, more than any other major league player. That's impressive enough, but what people don't realize is that he is also *losing* more home runs a year to the park he plays in than any other player. In his career he has lost about 36 home runs to the park he played in (he has hit 60 home runs in

Oakland, 96 on the road.) If he plays in Oakland all his career he will lose more home runs to the park than any other player in baseball history. The record now is 71, by Joe DiMaggio.

How many home runs will he hit in his career?

A lot, but at this point he can't be taken seriously as a threat to any records. The guys who hit the most home runs in their twenties are the big, strong horses like McGwire, Jimmie Foxx and Eddie Mathews, but the guys who hit the most home runs in their thirties are the lean, strong athletes, like Aaron and Musial. It's a generalization, of course.

Tim McINTOSH, Milwaukee
Who is he?

Catching prospect, now 26 years old. His batting stats in the minors are good, and they are consistent—.302 with 20 homers, 85 RBI at Beloit, .283 with 15 homers, 92 RBI at Stockton, .300 with 17 homers, 93 RBI at El Paso, .288 with 18 homers, 74 RBI at Denver. At the time of the Charlie O'Brien trade it was announced that McIntosh was to replace him as the Brewers' backup catcher.

The Milwaukee farm teams play in such tremendous hitter's parks, and County Stadium is such a poor hitter's park, that their hitters are often very disappointing when they arrive in the majors. If they expect McIntosh to hit .290 with 18 homers in The Show, they're in for another disappointment. He's more likely to hit around .250 with 12–15 home runs, if he were to play regularly in Milwaukee (there's the question of B.J. Surhoff to be dealt with.) He is not regarded as an outstanding defensive catcher.

Jeff McKNIGHT, Baltimore
Who is he?

First base prospect, doesn't hit enough to be a major league first baseman. He's a .260 hitter with no power.

Mark McLEMORE, Cleveland (Released)
Is it too late for him?

McLemore is only 26, but he will probably never re-establish himself as a regular. If he had impressed someone as a hitter *or* a fielder, he might get another shot, but the perception is that he's a .230 hitter who wasn't very good at second base. With his speed and experience, I would think he'd be a heck of a sixth infielder.

Craig McMURTRY, Texas
Why is he still around?

To prove that hope does spring eternal within the human breast.

Brian McRAE, Kansas City
Can he play?

1. Despite limited experience and a so-so throwing arm he is a wonderful center fielder. He's fast, but also he reads the ball and glides toward it as well as any young center fielder I've ever seen. He can turn side-saddle and run as fast as anybody else can run forward, and without looking awkward. Reminds you of Garry Maddox.
2. A year ago I would never have believed that he would hit major league pitching, but I'm beginning to believe. I've seen him do a lot of things with the bat—go with an outside pitch and slap it to the opposite field, time an off-speed pitch and drive it. The pitchers are searching for a weakness and they may find it, but it's not obvious.
3. McRae's Daddy was the most aggressive baserunner of his time. If you're wondering, Brian *did* get the gene for it. Twice last year I saw him hit a double *in front of* the right fielder. You can do it on artificial turf if you run hard because the right fielder has to wait for the hop to come down, but as a rule nobody does it.

Kevin McREYNOLDS, New York Mets
How will the loss of Strawberry affect his role on the team?

McReynolds has taken some silly criticism in the last couple of years for not being a superstar, but either McReynolds or HoJo is going to have to move into the number four spot and drive in a hundred runs if the Mets are going to win. McReynolds is more consistent than Johnson—he is more consistent than a good many rocks—but Johnson is a more potent hitter. Let's guess the regular lineup will go Coleman, Magadan, Jefferies, HoJo, McReynolds and Brooks.

My reading of McReynolds is that he is not somebody who is going to convince himself that with Strawberry gone he needs to hit .400 to make up for him. As long as he doesn't do that, his position on the team probably won't change much.

McReynolds hit .295 last year with men in scoring position . . . McReynolds has been ordered by Bud Harrelson to lose some weight.

Louie MEADOWS, Philadelphia
What does he do, exactly?

Meadows, who turns 30 in April, has now hit .190, .176 and .107 in three major league trials. There is nothing in his background which would make anyone think that he can hit, but he is fast and a good outfielder, and you can always convince yourself that he might hit better in the majors than he did in the minors, right? The only way he'd ever stick would be as a pinch runner and backup center fielder.

Scott MEDVIN, Seattle
Does that name ring a bell?

You probably remember him from the transactions list. Medvin was signed by the Tigers in 1983, loaned to the Mariners in 1984, returned to Detroit, traded to San Francisco as part of a multi-player deal in 1985, traded to Pittsburgh in the

Rick Reuschel trade, drafted by Houston, returned to Pittsburgh and is now with Seattle.

It would be interesting to know why a pitcher who is in so much demand, and who has generally pitched brilliantly in the minor leagues, has never received a real trial in the major leagues. He is 29 years old, on the other hand, and something tells me we are about to lose interest in the subject.

Jose MELENDEZ, Seattle
Who is he?

Right-handed pitcher, been around a long time and received his first look last fall. He has pitched well in AA and AAA, but no one treats him as if he was a prospect. I've never seen him.

Bob MELVIN, Baltimore
Is he any good? Does he deserve his playing time?

Melvin is a good defensive catcher who has set career highs in both at bats and batting average in 1988 (.234), 1989 (.241) and 1990 (.243). His playing time actually has been consistent over the last five years, although trending upward- 246 to 301 at bats every year.

Melvin's batting record is full of wild and contradictory splits, many of which I don't know what to make of.

- Although he has hit better the last two years than he ever had before he came to the Orioles he has *not* hit well in Baltimore. His average in Baltimore the last two years is .207; on the road it is .273.
- Although he is very slow he has hit extremely well in turf parks, .333 over the last two years (29 for 87).
- Although he is *not* platooned, at least regularly, Melvin has a huge platoon differential. Over the last three years he has hit .286 against left-handed pitching (111/388) and .200 against right-handers (93/464).

It is a strange thing to note that a half-time player with a huge platoon differential has nonetheless batted more times over a three-year period against right-handers than the people he hits well. Melvin alternates at catcher with a switch-hitter, Mickey Tettleton, who hits about as well one way as the other.

I don't in any sense mean this as criticism of Frank Robinson, but obviously Robinson is passing up a platoon advantage to get some other advantage. Apparently he prefers to have Melvin work with certain pitchers.

- Melvin has hit well the last two years with men in scoring position, .283 (49/173). However, as do many players with poor strikeout/walk ratios, he has hit *very* poorly when leading off an inning.

Orlando MERCADO, Mets
How many teams has this guy played for? Is he getting near a record?

Mercado has now played in the majors for seven teams—Seattle, Detroit, Los Angeles, Oakland, Minnesota, New York and Montreal. It isn't near the record, but it is pretty remarkable for a guy who has only 562 major league at bats. Almost half of those were with his first team. Since he left Seattle he's been averaging 45 at bats with each team . . . he's back in the Mets' system now, having signed a minor league contract.

Orlando MERCED, Pittsburgh
Who is he?

Line drive hitting first baseman, Grade D prospect.

Kent MERCKER, Atlanta
What are the Braves going to do with him?

The Braves' starting staff isn't bad— Leibrandt, Glavine, Smoltz, Avery. Well, it isn't terrible. Their bullpen is terrible. Mercker pitched in relief last year, and

wasn't as terrible as everybody else, posting a 3.17 ERA with seven saves.

The decision whether to start him or leave him in the pen may be dictated by something out of view. The Braves are under new management, and Mercker may have his own thoughts on the subject. If the decision is made on the basis of what we can see, Mercker will stay in relief.

Jose MESA, Baltimore
Can he pitch in the major leagues?

Can a bear perform heart surgery? I guess you never know unless you give him a scalpel and stand back.

Hensley MEULENS, New York Yankees
Is he finally ready? Is he a Rookie of the Year candidate?

Yes. Yes, he's ready, and yes, he's a candidate. The trade of Azocar and the possible trade of Barfield is partially intended to clear room for Meulens, as well as Mattingly, and Meulens can hit. My guess is that if he is a regular he'll hit about .265 with more than 20 home runs. He will strike out a lot, though.

Brian MEYER, Houston
Who is he?

Right-handed reliever, 28 years old, a candidate to move into Larry Andersen's old job.

Can he pitch?

He ain't Nolan Ryan, but he has a long history of getting people out in the minor leagues. He didn't enter baseball until he was 23 years old, I don't know why. He has never been hit hard anywhere, and the Astrodome will help him a little. He had a 2.97 ERA last year in the Pacific Coast League (64 games, 100 innings), and that's a tough place to pitch. My guess is he'll have an ERA of 2.70 for Houston and be around for ten years.

Gary MIELKE, Texas
Will he be a middle reliever all of his life?

Mielke has pitched well for two years in a protected role, facing three or four batters at a time. The Rangers probably know that if he gets out of that role he's going to get beat up.

Bob MILACKI, Baltimore
Can he come back?

Milacki went on the DL in late July with a strained right shoulder. He pitched well after coming back, but it's not enough innings (13 innings, 2.77 ERA) to mean very much.

Milacki doesn't like to make a good pitch on the first pitch, and usually pitches behind the hitters because of that. Whereas for most pitchers the batting average when the first pitch is hit is very high, for Milacki it isn't (.267 in 1989, .280 last year.) But Milacki was behind 52% of the hitters in 1989, which is dangerous, and was behind 56% of the hitters last year, which is deadly. The slugging percentage against him when he was behind in the count was over .500.

Milacki also wears out. The batting average against him in his first sixty pitches was .251 last year. After sixty pitches it went up to .316 (56/177). He may have a role in the major leagues, but he's going to have to be used carefully.

Keith MILLER,
New York Mets
Is he a good enough player to be a regular?

No. He's not terrible—a .250 hitter, a fine baserunner. That's not enough to be a regular outfielder in the major leagues.

Could he be a regular second baseman?

He hits enough to be a regular second baseman, but obviously the Mets don't feel he can do the job with the glove.

Is he worth the roster spot?

An infielder *and* outfielder who can pinch run or pinch hit? I'd sure think he was worth a roster spot.

Randy MILLIGAN, Baltimore
What could he do over a full season? Is he going to be a big star?

Milligan has a career secondary average of .449, so you know I like him. He's a guy who will put runs on the scoreboard if he hits .235, and he hits .260. He walks about as often as anyone in baseball, has power and even runs well for a 225-pound first baseman.

You have to be realistic about him. He spent a long time in the minor leagues, and he's not Ken Griffey Jr. He doesn't have a big variety of skills to build a star on. I don't think he's going to be a superstar, but he is a good player.

Alan MILLS, New York Yankees
Who is he?

Right-handed relief pitcher; the Yankees are doing their best to ruin him. They jumped him from A ball to AAA, gave him 29 innings of AAA ball and declared him ready for the majors. He wasn't, but maybe he'll be better next year.

Does he have any star potential?

Not that you can see from here. His rapid advancement from A ball to the majors indicates that the scouts like him.

Gino MINUTELLI, Cincinnati
Who is he?

Left-handed starting pitcher, now 26 years old. Undrafted, he was signed by an independent team (Tri-Cities) in 1985, and purchased by the Reds after his first season. He made very slow progress through the minor leagues until last year, when he pitched well for both Chattanooga (AA) and Nashville (AAA).

The Reds aren't short of pitchers. If Minutelli can pitch well for another year he'll force somebody to take a major league look at him.

Paul MIRABELLA, Milwaukee
Can he still pitch?

He's very marginal. He had a 3.97 ERA last year, but his stats are a lot worse than that if you look carefully. The batting average against him was .281. He gave up nine homers in 59 innings, whereas the league average would be five homers per 59 innings. His control record was poor, twenty percent more walks than the average pitcher. His strikeout rate was poor. He's a left-handed spot reliever, and he *did* get out left-handers (.235 batting average, no power), but right-handed hitters beat the crap out of him, with a slugging percentage over .500.

John MITCHELL, Baltimore
Isn't he getting up in years for a prospect? Did he pitch well for Baltimore? Will he stay in the rotation?

1. He is *not* getting old for a prospect, no. He started 19 games for the Mets in '87, but he was only 21 years old then, so he's 25 now.
2. He did not pitch particularly well for Baltimore, although his record was 6-6. The league batting average against him was .300, and his strikeout/walk ratio was less than even.
3. It is very unlikely that he will be able to stay in the rotation for Baltimore. The only positive thing about him is that he doesn't give up many home runs. He'll probably bounce around the league for several years as an emergency starter/long reliever.

Kevin MITCHELL, San Francisco
How many home runs will he hit?

In all probability Mitchell will hit around 400 home runs in his career. His career projected by computer from this moment produces 2,284 games with 400 home runs, 1,256 RBI and a lifetime .264 batting average.

After Mitchell's rookie season, 1986, I did a study in which I constructed a data base of rookie records, and then searched the data base for comparable players. I concluded that the most-comparable rookie to Kevin Mitchell in the last thirty years was Lee May, who came up with the Cincinnati Reds in 1967.

While I am sure that many of these "best comps" would look silly in retrospect, this one has proven accurate; Mitchell, as a hitter, has developed to be extremely similar to Lee May. Both players had similar second seasons, hitting 22 home runs each. May improved dramatically in his third season, which Mitchell didn't, but Mitchell exploded on the league in his fourth season. May then stabilized, and Mitchell last year had a season which would fit in almost perfectly with Lee May's career—35 homers, 93 RBI, .290 average.

At the same age and point in his career, Lee May had career totals of 761 games played, 147 home runs, 449 RBI and a .274 average. Mitchell's totals are similar—688 games, 135 homers, 412 RBI and a .278 average.

Given that the two have had parallel accomplishments to this point in their careers, it seems a reasonable guess that they might continue to travel along the same path. Lee May reached career totals of 354 home runs, 1244 RBI and a .267 average. I project Mitchell to exceed these totals somewhat, but that seems reasonable in view of the fact that Mitchell has more mobility than May, a better strikeout/walk ratio and a slightly higher batting average.

Has he had his best year?

Probably but not certainly. Mitchell has a career batting average of .278 and a slugging percentage of .517; the figures in his 1989 season were .291 and .635. If we assume that his career figures represent his true ability, then it is *likely* that he will at some time hit for a higher batting average than .291, and *unlikely but possible* that he would have a higher slugging percentage than .635.

Dale MOHORCIC, Montreal
Why did he pitch better last year?

He got out of New York. Like a dozen other guys—he pitched well before he came to the Yankees, pitched poorly with the Yankees and pitched well after he left the Yankees.

Paul MOLITOR, Milwaukee
What are his Hall of Fame chances?

If you mention Paul Molitor's name to the average baseball fan, it will be about four seconds until he mentions the word "injuries". Because there is a perception that Molitor is usually hurt; it may come as a surprise that he has already played more games in his career than some Hall of Famers (Fred Lindstrom, Chick Hafey, Jackie Robinson), and within a couple of years will pass many more (Joe DiMaggio, Travis Jackson, Bill Terry).

Actually, Molitor still has a reasonably good chance to get three thousand hits in his career. If he happens to do that, of course he will go in the Hall of Fame.

Molitor has done 19 things which would be characteristic of a Hall of Famer, which is not enough to make him a serious Hall of Fame candidate at this point. I credit him with 51 Hall of Fame "points", in a system I introduced years ago. You need at least 70 to have any chance, and a hundred to be a solid candidate.

Note: Molitor's career totals, projected by computer, show 2,843 hits, 190 home runs, 502 doubles and 1,519 runs scored.

Rich MONTELEONE, New York Yankees
Will he ever make it?

Monteleone, now 28, has one of the ugliest minor league records you'll ever see, with a career won-lost record of 58-80. His won-lost records look like Mike Morgan's, only he's been in the minor

leagues, and his ERAs are often in the fives.

He didn't have any control for several years, and then he was pitching in the Pacific Coast League, where ERAs are high. Based on the last two or three years, you'd conclude that he could pitch. In AAA last year he had an ERA around 2.00 and a good strikeout/walk ratio. In my opinion he *will* eventually land a job as a middle-inning reliever in the major leagues.

Jeff MONTGOMERY, Kansas City
Has he earned the job as closer? Where does he rank among the closers?

Depending on Mark Davis' performance, the Royals will probably either use Montgomery as the closer or split the work between Montgomery and Davis.

Montgomery had 24 saves last year and ten blown saves, which is not a good percentage (71%). This is misleading, however, because early in the year Montgomery was often brought into the game in the seventh inning with a theoretical chance to earn a save, but no real chance. If Montgomery gave up a run in those games he would be charged with a blown save, but if he pitched well he would pass the baton to Mark Davis, who would place-kick it toward right field. This is why, in figuring "save percentage" in the data in Section II, I counted "holds" as successes. Montgomery's save efficiency was 76%, which still isn't great.

Montgomery wasn't ahead of the hitters as much last year as the year before. He was great against right-handed hitters, but not good enough against left-handers to stay in the closer role. Still, Montgomery over the last two years has struck out 188 men in 186 innings and has an ERA of 1.88, so you have to consider him a proven pitcher. I would rank him sixth among AL closers, behind Eckersley, Henke, Thigpen, Olson and Jones. Aguilera, Harvey and Schooler are in the same range, but all three come with question marks.

Brad MOORE, Philadelphia

Who is he?

Right-handed relief pitcher with a Peggy Lee fastball, has hacked his way through the minors by pitching well at every level. He *didn't* have a good year in 1990, and since he's not the kind of pitcher who gets any favors he will probably not be in the majors in '91.

Mike MOORE, Oakland

What happened to him last year?

I have to wonder if he wasn't trying to pitch through an injury last year. His strikeout rate has had a truly alarming decline in the last two years, from 7.2 strikeouts per game with Seattle in 1988 to 6.4 in 1989 to 3.3 in 1990. His strikeout/walk ratio has declined from three to one in 1988 to two to one in 1989 to less than even (73-84) last year. That's extremely unusual, and obviously doesn't represent just normal aging.

If he was trying to pitch through an injury, and if he didn't permanently ruin something in the process, and if the injury goes away this year, I suppose he could be effective again. It's a bad risk. I frankly doubt that he will make it through the season in the A's rotation.

Mickey MORANDINI, Philadelphia

Can he play? Will he last a full season as the Phils' second baseman? Could he be Rookie of the Year?

I think he *will* make it through the year as the Phillies' second baseman, and could be Rookie of the Year. What Morandini hit in his late trial (.241) is probably a reasonable but conservative estimate of his hitting ability; I suspect he will hit .250–.270 with about 50 walks and a few stolen bases. The reports on his defense are positive, even glowing.

Mike MORGAN, Los Angeles

Morgan is the new Milt Gaston. Gaston was a pitcher in the twenties and thirties who, after posting winning records his first two seasons (5-3, 15-14) rung up nine straight losing records, most of them ghastly. His records from 1926 to the end of his career were 10-18 (leading the league in losses), 13-17, 6-12, 12-19, 13-20 (leading in losses again), 2-13, 7-17, 8-12 and 6-19. In his career he was 67 games under .500 (97-164), which if memory serves me is the record.

Morgan will have to get lucky to break that record—in his career he is only 41 games under .500 (53-94)—but in some respects he has even out-Gastoned Gaston, set a new standard for a pitcher of the type. Morgan has *never* had a winning record, while Gaston did have the two winning records early in his career. Morgan's career winning percentage, .361, is even worse than Gaston's. Gaston had nine straight losing seasons; Morgan has now had ten straight nonwinning seasons, although he did go 1-1 (with an ERA of 12.00) in 1985.

Gaston had terrible records, but compared to his teams he wasn't that bad. He was ten games worse than the teams he pitched for in his career, and his winning percentage was 39 points worse than his team (.411 to .372). Morgan is sixteen games worse than his teams, with a winning percentage 110 points off the team pace (.471 to .361).

Russ MORMAN, Kansas City

Can he help a major league team?

It's a close call. He's a good defensive first baseman, a left-handed line-drive hitter who could probably hit .270–.280, but hasn't yet. I'd say this. If you have a team which meets three conditions, Morman would be a good player to have. The three conditions are:

1. The regular first baseman is a right-handed batter.

2. The regular first baseman is either a bad defensive player or an older player who needs rest.
3. The team needs a left-handed pinch hitter.

Who does that fit? St. Louis, probably. Possibly Houston and Detroit and Boston maybe if Jack Clark is the first baseman. Even then, though, you have to answer this question: is this the *best* player of the type that we could find?

Hal MORRIS, Cincinnati

Is he really that good?

Morris hit .340 last year. I don't believe he's a .340 hitter—nobody is—but I do believe he is an outstanding hitter. I think he'll be in the race for the NL batting title as often as not.

Jack MORRIS, Detroit

Is he back as far as he's going to come? Will he have better years? Where does he stand in the battle for the Hall of Fame? Does he have any chance to get 300 wins?

Morris is still capable of having better years than 1990, when he was 15-18. Sparky leaves him in the game an awful long time, lets him get beat on unnecessarily. He can still throw fairly hard, changes speeds well and still has a wicked slider. If he wound up on a good team, which he won't in 1991, he could still win eighteen or even twenty games.

Hall of Fame?

There are certainly pitchers in the Hall of Fame who have done no more in their careers than Jack Morris has already done. Pitchers pitch longer now, so there's been a change in standards; more pitchers get to 300 wins and reach other career milestones than has ever been the case before, at least since 1920. This makes it extremely unlikely that Morris would be selected to the Hall of Fame on the basis of what he has done through 1990.

Morris has done 31 things which would be characteristic of a Hall of Famer. He has pitched in the All-Star game (four times), has two twenty-win seasons, two more seasons of eighteen or nineteen wins and six more seasons of fifteen to seventeen wins. He has struck out two hundred men three times, had a .700 winning percentage twice, thrown a no-hitter and led the league in wins, innings, strikeouts and shutouts. He has almost 200 career wins and a winning percentage over .550. He has started games in the World Series and won them. He has a win in the playoffs.

All of these things are characteristic of a Hall of Fame pitcher—but as of yet, the package isn't large enough.

Does he still have a chance to win 300 games?

He does, yes. Morris has 198 career wins. At the same age Gaylord Perry had the same number, 198, and Perry won 300. At the same age Phil Niekro had only 130 career wins, and Nolan Ryan had 205; they were able to win 300.

Of course Morris has struggled in the last couple of years, but many pitchers go through periods of ineffectiveness on the way to 300 wins. Early Wynn at the age of 37 was 14-17 with a 4.31 ERA, but he came back to win a Cy Young Award two years later. Don Sutton at 38 was 8-13 with a 4.08 ERA, but he came back to pitch well for three more years.

Notes . . . did you ever realize how many wild pitches Morris throws? He's in double figures every year, and has thrown 155 in his career, more than any other active pitcher except Nolan. Morris holds the single-season record, with 24 wild pitches in '87 . . . Morris is still one of the easiest pitchers in baseball to run against. Last year there were 45 stolen bases against him in 51 attempts, an 88% success rate.

John MORRIS, St. Louis
What's his status? Will he be back?

Morris, a free agent, isn't receiving any offers because of a chronic back problem, and his career may be over. If he doesn't sign a contract somewhere he will probably go to camp with the Cardinals without a contract.

Lloyd MOSEBY, Detroit
Is this as well as he is capable of playing? Should the Tigers let Milt Cuyler have center field?

When a player's productivity bounces up and down it will normally stabilize somewhere in the middle, and this appears to be what has happened to Moseby. Moseby's 1990 batting average, slugging percentage and on-base percentage were all within ten points of his career norms.

Moseby should be a platoon player. He hit .182 against left-handed pitching last year, .196 in 1989. It's hard to see how you can justify keeping Lloyd Moseby in center field at .190.

I think Moseby is probably a better player than Milt Cuyler. Moseby, although he is not a great player, is a legitimate power/speed combination, with career totals of 163 home runs and 272 stolen bases. I doubt that Cuyler would produce as many runs or play defense any better.

John MOSES, Minnesota
Can he help anybody?

The Twins do not intend to re-sign Moses, which is understandable due to the emergence of Shane Mack and the addition of Pedro Munoz.

Moses hit .316 in '88 and .281 in '89, and at that level he's a fine reserve outfielder. On the other hand:

1. He is a career .258 hitter.
2. He has no power.
3. Although he has stolen some bases, his career stolen-base percentage is at or below the break-even point.

4. He is now 33 years old, and probably not the player he was a few years ago.

He may find a job, but it's not going to be easy.

Jamie MOYER, Texas
Will he land a job?

In his five-year major league career Moyer's winning percentage has gone constantly downward: .636, .444, .375, .308 and .250. He's a free agent and the Rangers have announced that they won't re-sign him, probably figuring that they don't know exactly what will come after .250 but they also don't know exactly what might be living in the bottom of the Arlington sewer system, and sure as hell don't want to find out.

Unless he impresses somebody tremendously in spring training, Moyer will have to go back to the minor leagues and work his way back. I think he still has a major league arm, and with regular work and no help from Tom House has a good chance to get the gears to mesh.

Terry MULHOLLAND, Philadelphia
Will he get any better?

Mulholland pitched well enough last year to win fifteen to seventeen games if he was in the rotation with a better team. He is not going to be a great pitcher, but he could be a good one for the next two or three years.

Rance MULLINIKS, Toronto
Does he help the Blue Jays? Was it a good decision, to resign a 35-year-old fringe player for two more years?

Mulliniks was one of the most effective bench players in the league last year, hitting .289 with a secondary average of .351. Mulliniks had a poor year in 1989, but that was the only time since 1983 that he hasn't been a very effective player. He hits for a good average, walks and hits doubles. Sure, at his age if you sign him to a two-year contract you might be wasting a year, but what's that in today's market? It was a good move.

In the January, 1991 issue of the *Baseball Digest* there is an article by Neil MacCarl, a Toronto sportswriter, no less, entitled "Managers Rate Major League Players with the Best Skills". According to MacCarl, who I think does this survey annually, the managers named Scott Bradley of Seattle as the best pinch-hitter in the American League.

Why in the world would anyone rather have Scott Bradley pinch hitting for them than Rance Mulliniks? Mulliniks hit .289 last year and is a career .274 hitter. Bradley hit .223 last year and is a career .263 hitter. Bradley hits almost all singles; Mulliniks hits doubles. Mulliniks in 1990 was eight for twenty-two as a pinch hitter (.364), while Bradley was ten for thirty-five (.286).

Mike MUNOZ, Los Angeles
Who is he?

Left-handed reliever, had a 1.00 ERA in 56 games at San Antonio in 1988. He is not regarded as one of the top prospects in the organization, but has pitched very well in the minors for the last three seasons.

Pedro MUNOZ, Minnesota
Can he play?

You bet your bippy. Minnesota fans were impressed with him in 22 games last year, when he hit .271, and with some luck he could hit better than .271. His 1989 season at Knoxville translates to the majors as .253 but with 18 home runs. His 1990 season, at Syracuse, Portland and Minnesota, becomes .297 with 11 homers and 74 RBI. His strikeout/walk ratio isn't great and he doesn't have Otis Nixon speed, but he could certainly win the AL Rookie of the Year award if he starts out well.

Dale MURPHY, Philadelphia
What are his Hall of Fame chances? What's the best year he's going to have from now on?

Murphy probably will go into the Hall of Fame without much of a fight. He is not overwhelmingly qualified, like Pete Rose or Mike Schmidt or George Brett, but he is in the strong part of the gray area, and likely to annex enough career totals to push him even higher. Murphy has done more than 40 things which would be characteristic of a Hall of Famer.

Murphy has a huge platoon differential. Last year against left-handers he hit .311 with a .617 slugging percentage, whereas against right-handers he hit .214 with a .324 slugging percentage Although less than one-third of his at bats were against left-handers, most of his home runs (14 of 24) were against lefties. His 1989 data is less dramatic, but even in the 1989 data there is a striking feature, which is that Murphy had a strikeout/walk ratio almost four to one against right-handers, but better than even against left-handers.

Murphy probably should be platooned at this stage of his career, and probably would be a much more effective hitter if he played 130 games a year, half of them against left-handers. It probably hasn't been done simply because he is still The Great Dale Murphy.

Note: Murphy has led the NL in grounding into double plays in two of the last three years (24 in 1988, 22 last year), so you may be wondering whether he is a threat to the career GIDP record. The answer is no, there's no way he'll break the record.

Rob MURPHY, Boston
Will he bounce back?

A year ago, Murphy was still being talked about (by me, among others) as a possible relief closer. He will never bounce back to that level; he'll never be a thirty-save man now.

On a lower level, it seems most likely that he will recover, and save his job. He has a good arm and has been a successful pitcher; he just had an absurdly frustrating season. Right-handed hitters hit .404 against him in 1990, with a .677 slugging percentage. That's your *average* right-handed batter, so think what the percentages would have been with, say, Rickey Henderson or Cecil Fielder at the plate.

There was a Red Sox series in Kansas City last July, a four-game series. I happened to see all four games. Rob Murphy had a record of 0-6 at the time and an ERA over six, but he pitched in the first game. I thought "that's nice. Even though he is having an awful year, Morgan wants to show that he hasn't lost confidence in him."

Well, the Royals pounded him around a little more, although the runs were unearned, and I was back at the game the next day. Key moment of the game, Morgan goes to the mound. We were talking about who was going to come in, and I said to the guy with me, "Well, I think we can safely assume that it ain't going to be Rob Murphy."

Shows you what I know. I checked after the series, and sure enough, Rob Murphy was leading the American League in games pitched. Hadn't won a game, right-handed hitters hitting four hundred against him, and at the end of July he was leading the league in pitching appearances. Doesn't that strike you as a little peculiar?

Eddie MURRAY, Los Angeles
How do you compare him to Dale Murphy? Who has been a better player, over the course of his career?

I have been asked this question twice on the air, so I assume there is some general interest in it. Murphy and Murray were both born in 1956, have almost exactly the same career home run total (and have had for several years) and because of their names they are on facing pages in many reference books, so it is natural to link them.

To state what I think cannot be denied, Murray is a distinctly better hitter than is Murphy, although circumstances have disguised this. Murray has out-hit Murphy by 26 points, and 26 points over the course of fifteen years is a substantial margin.

Murray has a better strikeout to walk ratio—more walks, and fewer strikeouts. A lot fewer strikeouts. Per at bat, Murphy has struck out 65% more often, a difference of fifty strikeouts a season.

Their home run totals are almost the same, but this is misleading because Murphy has spent almost all of his career in the best home run park in baseball, and Murray has played in poor home run parks. Murphy has hit about 34 more home runs than he would have hit in a normal park, while Murray has hit 27 *fewer* home runs at home than on the road. Playing in the same park—any park—it is likely that Murray would have out-homered Murphy by a small but consistent margin, about five home runs a season.

So adding together the power, the batting average and the strikeout/walk ratio, it is clear that Murray has been (and is) a significantly better hitter than Dale Murphy.

They're comparable in some other areas. Both players have shown exceptional durability. Neither has suffered a major injury in the last eleven years. They are comparable baserunners. Murphy has stolen more often, but Murray more successfully, and it isn't a central part of either player's game.

Defensively, both players have been outstanding, at different positions. Both have won several Gold Gloves, but Murphy has been a Gold Glove outfielder, which has a greater value.

As clubhouse leaders, "intangibles", I don't know what to think. Murphy certainly has been an admirable player and

person, but his teams haven't won, either. Murray in his early years had a mystique about him, and was a tremendously *respected* player. In later years the press turned on him, and began to portray him as moody and difficult to be around.

Balancing it all out, I have to believe that Eddie Murray has been the more valuable player over the course of his career. Murphy has won two Most Valuable Player awards because he concentrated his hitting into a few big seasons, but he's also had some seasons at both the beginning and end of his career when he was pretty useless. Murray has never had an off season; he has been outstanding every year of his career except 1989. Murray's advantages are tangible, provable, *real*; Murphy's advantages are speculative. Murphy's been a great player, but I have to choose Eddie.

What are his Hall of Fame chances?

Not as good as Dale Murphy's, at the moment. Murphy's two MVP awards will mean a lot when they get around to voting, and put him up into the strong part of the gray area. Murray is still in the bottom half of the gray area.

On the other hand, Murray probably will do more in the rest of his career than will Murphy, and that may make him the stronger candidate. Murray outhit Murphy by 85 points last year. Murray has a chance to hit 500 home runs, while Murphy may be forced into retirement within a couple of years.

I don't know if anybody has mentioned this, but did you realize that Eddie Murray had the highest batting average of any major league player last year, but did not win a batting title? Murray hit .330, while Willie McGee, the NL batting champion, hit .324, and George Brett, the AL batting champion, hit .329. Strange, isn't it? It's never happened before, and will probably never happen again.

Jeff MUSSELMAN, New York Mets
Will there be room in the bullpen for him?

Musselman left the Blue Jays in April 1989 to go to an alcohol abuse treatment program. During the winter he filed for arbitration. What the hell is wrong with a guy like that? I think everybody in the business knew he'd lose that case. Probably his agent did, too. If he didn't know he should have.

In theory, alcoholism is just an illness like a broken toe or something, and the player deserves to be evaluated on the basis of what he does while he is with the team. It's fine to tell yourself that while you're getting ready for the case, but in the real world nineteen out of twenty arbitrators are going to rule against you on the face of it, and with the twentieth one you're going to lose half the time, anyway. Musselman is a Harvard graduate, too. Apparently they don't teach any classes in "Taking your medicine when you have it coming."

Greg MYERS, Toronto
Is he wasting at bats that should be going to Borders?

I would have platooned them last year, and I would continue to platoon them early in 1991 because:

1. I think Myers is a better hitter than his 1990 hitting record shows.
2. Borders' hitting record is deceptive—obvious plusses covering gaping holes.
3. You need two catchers, anyway. Borders isn't going to play 162 games.

They're not *truly* platooned; they're just *sort of* platooned. Myers doesn't play at all against left-handers, and plays some of the time against right-handers. Borders plays all of the time against left-handers, and some of the time against right-handers. Simply platooning them would give Myers most of the at bats, while Borders is probably the better player, so Gaston has developed this system, using Borders against the lefties and alternating them against the right-handers.

It's a good system, but you don't want to be stubborn. If Borders shows signs of developing into a star, you have to let him do it.

Randy MYERS, Cincinnati
Why did the Mets trade him?

You figure it out. It doesn't make any sense to me.

Who should be the closer here, Dibble or Myers?

There has been a reluctance to make Dibble the closer because he's a hothead, and managers understandably prefer not to have a hothead on the mound when the game is on the line.

As a closer, Myers has probably the best credentials of any National League pitcher right now—except Dibble. Given a choice of all the relievers in the National League, I would probably choose Dibble number one, and Myers number two.

•N•

Chris NABHOLZ, Montreal
Is he really this good?

Nabholz, who pitched brilliantly for the Expos in August and September, was nonetheless 0-6 with a 4.83 ERA at Indianapolis before being called up.

Nabholz has all of the basic things you look for in a young pitcher—good arm, good motion, good strikeout rate, good control, and shot through the minors like a rocket. Buck Rodgers obviously knows how to handle a pitcher. He probably will bounce up and down some and isn't a good bet to win the Cy Young Award in the next ten minutes, but he does look good.

Tim NAEHRING, Boston
Will he be the Sox' regular shortstop? Does he have a chance to be Rookie of the Year?

There is some question yet as to whether Naehring is a major league shortstop, but his MLEs look almost too good to be true, and he did nothing in 24 major league games to dispel the notion that he is a major league hitter. I think I'll place him second on my list of possible AL top rookies, with this comment:

1. *If* he can play shortstop, and
2. *If* Juan Gonzalez doesn't hit thirty homers, and
3. *If* his back doesn't bother him,

then Naehring will be the Rookie of the Year.

Charles NAGY, Cleveland
Is he ready to pitch in the majors?

He hasn't tried AAA yet, and didn't look good in eight major league starts, one of which I saw. He looked to me like a Bud Black-type left-hander, which is to say that

a. it will take him a little while to find himself in the majors, and
b. he will need a defense behind him.

The acquisition of King and Hillegas probably means that he will start the year in AAA, and he probably should.

Jaime NAVARRO, Milwaukee
Why was he off his game last year? Will he back this year?

Navarro started the year in the Brewers' rotation, and pitched just awful through ten starts, posting a 6.65 ERA. Moved to the bullpen, he pitched ten times in relief and pitched brilliantly; back in the starting rotation, he struggled through August and closed the year going well. In between switches he made two trips to Denver.

I'm not sure that this is an absolute answer, but there are many hints in the data that Navarro may be miscast as a starter, and might emerge as an extremely effective reliever. Those are:

1. Last year he had a 4.99 ERA as a starter (22 games), as opposed to 1.57 in relief (10 games). In 1989 he pitched only once in relief, but allowed no runs in two-plus innings.
2. The batting average against him last year in the seventh, eighth and ninth innings was .336. In 1989 it was .385. Obviously, it is much lower than this in the first six innings, or he wouldn't be in the league.
3. Last year the batting average against him was .260 in his first 30 pitches, .305 in the next 30 pitches, .296 in the third 30 pitches and .365 after that.

The 1989 data is similar: .237 in his first 30 pitches, .281 in his next 30 pitches, .286 in his third 30 pitches and .354 after that.

Very clearly, Navarro loses effectiveness quickly within the game; the data leaves no doubt of that. I would suggest that this means one of three things:

1. he needs to go to the bullpen, or
2. he needs to come out of the game earlier, or
3. he needs to get stronger, which he may do as he matures.

Note: Navarro has pitched poorly on artificial turf. Last year his ERA was 6.12 on turf (32 innings); in 1989 he pitched only once on turf, but pitched poorly.

Jim NEIDLINGER, Los Angeles
Was he for real?

I think he's for real; I think he's going to win fifteen or more games this year. His minor league records are superficially unimpressive, but they look exactly like Orel Hershiser's. Hershiser at Albuquerque went 9-6 with a 3.71 ERA, then 10-8 with a 4.09 ERA. Neidlinger in his two years there went 8-6 with a 4.06 ERA, then 8-5 with a 4.29. Both were being used in a mixed role, starter/reliever, and both had impressive strikeout/walk ratios despite mediocre records otherwise.

Pitching for the Dodgers is a tremendous asset, just as pitching for the Yankees is a tremendous disadvantage.

Neidlinger walked only 15 men in 74 innings.

His arm has always been healthy.

His mechanics are beautiful.

I don't like him as much as I did Martinez a year ago, but almost as much. I think he's the new Rick Rhoden—a pitcher who'll be around for fifteen years and win 150 games.

Gene NELSON, Oakland
Could he be a quality closer on another team?

Probably at some level. Nelson is extremely effective pitching for Tony LaRussa in this park. In another park with another defense for another manager he wouldn't be as effective, but he probably could do the job as well as Craig Lefferts.

Rob NELSON, San Diego
Who is he? Why does he pop up every season?

He's a former first base prospect. In 1987 Rob Nelson and Mark McGwire battled for the A's first base job in spring training—and Nelson won. Then he hurt himself about opening day, McGwire got the job and has held it so far.

Nelson can't play. He wouldn't hit .220 in the major leagues. He's Rob Deer without the defense and with eighty percent of the power.

Jim NEWLIN, Seattle
Who is he?

Relief pitcher. I love this guy. He was a member of the Wichita State team which won the College World Series in '89, and should have been drafted in the third or fourth round, but the Mariners got him in the 12th round because he has a funny delivery, kind of short-arms the ball, and scouts hate non-conformists. He has good control, moves the ball in and out and can zip it in there pretty good with a quick, deceptive delivery. He should be up in a year or two.

Al NEWMAN, Minnesota
Should he have kept the second base job?

Newman, a utility infielder for Minnesota since their championship year, had a shot as the Twins' regular second baseman between Backman and Manrique, or somewhere in there. He's a good infielder, a smart player and a lot of fun to watch, but he doesn't hit enough to be a regular.

Newman doesn't strike out, but the problem is that he just punches at the ball, and almost never hits it hard. When *not* striking out his career batting average is only .259, which is the lowest among all major league players (500 or more games.) He also has the lowest average of bases per hit of any major league player, both in 1990 (1.15) and in his career

(1.20). Basically he hits *no* triples or homers, and only a few doubles. (An average hitter, not a pitcher, will average almost exactly 1.5 bases per hit.)

Another of Newman's non-power distinctions is the lowest home run rate among major league players with 500 or more games. With one career home run in 1,615 at bats Newman has homered less than one-third as often as any other major league player.

Neil MacCarl's poll of the managers named Newman as the best utility player in the American League.

Warren NEWSOM, San Diego
Who is he?

Outfielder who looks like Walter (No Neck) Williams. He's kind of a minor league Gary Redus, terrific secondary averages. He has some power, walks a lot and steals bases. At Riverside in 1988 he hit .297 with a secondary average of .562. At Wichita in 1989 he hit .304 with a secondary average of .489. At Las Vegas last year he hit .304 with a secondary average of .399.

.304 at Las Vegas isn't very good, really. I shouldn't create the impression that Newsom would be a star if somebody would let him play. He's a 26-year-old left-handed batter, and probably should be a major league platoon player. He'd be about like Mike Devereaux, only I think a little better. He's fun to watch, too (I saw him several times at Wichita.)

Carl NICHOLS, Houston
Who is he?

Third-string catcher, came up with Baltimore several years ago. Couldn't hit a baby in the butt with a fly swatter.

Rod NICHOLS, Cleveland
Can he pitch?

He's like a lot of guys Cleveland has—I'd like him if he was with another team. After posting a five-plus ERA at Colorado Springs in '90 he probably isn't due for a long look by the Indians this year.

Tom NIEDENFUER, St. Louis
Has he come back?
Not at all. He had a 3.46 ERA in 1990, but pitching middle relief in Busch Stadium with the best double-play combination in the league behind him and the fastest outfield in baseball behind them. Give him a *real* job, and his ERA would be back to 5.28 before you can say "Don't throw Jack Clark a fastball".

Al NIPPER, Cleveland
Is his career over?
Never bet against a knuckle-ball pitcher. He may be ten years away from his prime.

Donell NIXON, Baltimore
Why is there a major league job for Otis Nixon but not for Donell?
Luck. Donell is basically the same player as his brother, maybe a little better than his brother. Otis has an advantage in being a switch hitter (Donell bats right), but Otis also has a lifetime batting average of .228. Donell is at .275, granted that that is only in 396 at bats, and nobody really believes he is a .275 hitter.

There are a lot of guys who can run but not do anything else, and there are a limited number of jobs for them. Otis has one, Donell doesn't.

Otis NIXON, Montreal
How many bases would he steal as a regular?
Let's figure it out . . . what percentage of the time does he steal when he is on?

It isn't easy to figure that, actually, because of his frequent pinch running appearances. Nixon was on first base by hit or walk 77 times, and let's guess that he pinch-ran another 40 times. That means he was on first 117 times and attempted 63 stolen bases, or 54% of the times he was on first.

Let's assume he went to the plate 700 times as a regular. His career on-base percentage is .302, which would mean that he would be on base about 211 times.

If he attempted to steal 54% of the time this would mean about 114 stolen base attempts.

His career stolen base percentage is .75, so that would mean he would steal about 85 bases a year.

Would that make him a valuable player?
Twenty-six major league managers feel that it wouldn't. Who am I to argue?

Note: In his career, 85% of Nixon's hits have been singles, which ties him with Alvaro Espinoza as the major league players who get the fewest extra base hits (each has exactly two extra base hits for each thirteen hits.) Following Nixon and Espinoza on that list are Jose Oquendo, Domingo Ramos and Curtis Wilkerson.

Junior NOBOA, Montreal
Has he found his role? Will he break through as a regular? Could he help another team?
Noboa, who has probably been a major league player for five years, made some progress in getting established last year, playing 81 games and hitting .266.

There is no way Noboa is going to take a job away from Delino DeShields, or for that matter from most any good second baseman. Ryne Sandberg is safe, should Junior be traded to Chicago. But I don't feel that Noboa has gone as far as he is capable of going, either. At worst, he's going to be one of the few reserve middle infielders in the league who can also pinch hit.

Paul NOCE, Cincinnati
Who is he?
31-year-old infielder/outfielder, has hit well at times in the minors. After hitting .218 at Nashville last year he has a good chance to be working in the plastics industry by this time next year.

Matt NOKES, New York Yankees
Does his bat justify his glove? Should he be a regular?
Since his rookie season in 1987 he has declined annually in both batting average and slugging percentage, pretty much obliterating his argument to be a regular. He can't throw, so he has to have a slugging percentage of *at least* .400 to compensate. He hasn't had the last two years.

Mike NORRIS, Oakland
How is his comeback coming?
Norris pitched well the first half of the year, but not very much—27 good innings in 14 games. He was cut loose in mid-season because the A's needed pitchers who could work harder. He did nothing in his half-season to show that he couldn't pitch.

Is there any precedent for this?
Norris hadn't pitched in the majors since 1983, hadn't pitched at all since 1986. In our own time this is unique, but in the first half of the century there were many cases where players dropped out of the majors for long periods of time, then came back. Perhaps the most perfect parallel is Vean Gregg, who won 23 games as a rookie in 1911, but developed arm trouble after two more twenty-win seasons. He dropped out of the league after the 1918 season, was out of baseball for a year or two, but came back to pitch 26 games for Washington in 1925. Other similar stories include Randy Gumpert and Huck Betts.

A note in the May 7 *Sporting News* said that "The Elias Bureau unearthed data that two pitchers, Jim Bouton and Fred (Cactus) Johnson went longer between major league victories than the A's Mike Norris, who had a seven-year gap from May 16, 1983 to April 17 this year." I don't know why the Elias Bureau missed this or if somebody mixed up the message, but Gumpert went ten years between wins. He won one game in 1936, and didn't win again until 1946.

Were any of those guys any good after they came back?

Several of them were, yes. Gregg didn't really make it back, but Gumpert and Betts became successful pitchers after a long absence.

Randy NOSEK, Detroit
Have the Tigers seen enough? Is he getting ready to turn a corner?

No one more clearly illustrates the problems of the Detroit organization than Nosek, a so-so prospect who was brought to the majors years before he was ready. Anyone can see immediately that he has no idea what he is doing out there. They ought to send him to the minors and look in on him in about three years. There is *no* chance that this guy is going to be a successful pitcher in the next year or two.

Rafael NOVOA, San Francisco
Is he ready to help the Giants?

A number nine draft selection in 1989, Novoa has been extremely impressive at every level below AAA, was brought to the majors for a couple of starts and stunk. He's a 23-year-old left-handed pitcher, almost certain to start the year with Phoenix.

Ed NUNEZ, Milwaukee
Can he help the Brewers?

Nunez pitched brilliantly last year (2.24 ERA), but he was a major disappointment the two previous seasons, and something of a disappointment for eight straight years. Common sense dictates that we make him have two straight good years before we place much confidence in him.

Jose NUNEZ, Chicago Cubs
Why can't he pitch?

I'm puzzled. He always looks good on the mound, but he doesn't get people out.

The batting average against him last year was .207 in his first 45 pitches (31 for 150), but .395 after that (30 for 76). Granted, it isn't a large sample, but that's got to be the biggest discrepancy like that I've ever seen, and it does suggest that he might be better off in the bullpen.

Nunez' ERA last year was 7.71 as a starter (47 innings), but 2.57 in relief (14 innings).

•O•

Charlie O'BRIEN, New York Mets
Why did the Mets trade a prospect to get this guy?

For the same reason the Royals traded Jose DeJesus for Steve Jeltz. It's one of the irrational things an organization will do when they start thinking about "losing" the pennant race, rather than about winning it.

Let's be honest: it's a stupid trade. O'Brien's been around for years, and he's a lifetime .209 hitter with no power. He is a good defensive catcher, but it's silly to trade a prospect for a player like this, because you don't have to. A good organization can pick up a defensive catcher—Carl Nichols, Larry Owen, somebody—without paying a big penalty in talent. What did the A's give away to pick up Jamie Quirk?

The Mets problem was that they didn't do anything about the need for a catcher who could actually catch until they were in the middle of a pennant race. Then they had to solve the problem right *now*, immediately, so they had to pay a price for a quick fix. But if they'd worried about their catching in the middle of the winter, when all their fans were worrying about it, they could have found a better solution at a lower price.

Pete O'BRIEN, Seattle
What happened to him? Can he bounce back?

He got off to a slow start, then broke his thumb making a diving catch on May 3. He just never got his bat going.

He'll surely have a better season in '91, but he is 33 years old. Put it this way: he's the same age as Floyd Rayford, Gene Roof, Bob James, George Wright and Darryl Sconiers. Remember them? He should come back, but at 33 you wouldn't want to bet too much on it.

Tom O'MALLEY, New York Mets
Should he be in the majors?

He probably *won't* be, after hitting .223, but he's not a bad player. He can play third base better than HoJo or Jefferies, and he's not a .223 hitter. He's Ken Oberkfell, basically.

Randy O'NEAL, San Francisco
What is he?

Thirty-year-old reliever, right-handed, been around for seven years and still making $155,000 a year. He's a staff filler. No star potential, isn't going to play a key role on the staff, probably won't be on the roster out of spring training. He's a guy who can step in when you have an injury and control the damage.

Paul O'NEILL, Cincinnati
Where does he rank? Is he one of the better outfielders in the National League? Is he still getting better?

He's a decent player, and probably as well suited to his park as anyone around. He's a good defensive outfielder with a good arm, which is important in Riverfront Stadium, where a small error can easily turn a single into a triple. Also, for some unknown reason, he hits exceptionally well there. He has hit more than twice as many home runs in Cincinnati (37) as on the road (17), although it is not a big home run park.

It would be wrong to leave the impression that O'Neill ranks with Andre Dawson and Darryl Strawberry; he doesn't. It would be wrong to suggest that O'Neill's defense means as much to his team as Bobby Bonilla's offense, because I don't believe that it does. O'Neill is a solid, middle-of-the-pack outfielder who has some nice assets. There is no reason to expect him to get better.

Ken OBERKFELL, Houston
Why did the Astros want him?

Baseball organizations are not run by geniuses. A record of having had good batting averages still has a peculiar power with a lot of people.

Ron OESTER, Cincinnati
Will he have a job in '91?

Oester hit .299 last year, so surely will land on his feet somewhere. With Doran and Duncan in Cincinnati, it probably won't be there.

Jose OFFERMAN, Los Angeles
How good is he?

Very good, the number two candidate for National League Rookie of the Year. Dodger Stadium is a tough place to hit, but I believe Offerman will hit better than .260 with a decent strikeout to walk ratio. If you add that to his speed (he can steal bases) and defense (which is reportedly sensational), you've got a serious Rookie of the Year candidate.

Bobby OJEDA, Los Angeles
Is he more valuable in the bullpen or the rotation?

There is some evidence that he would be better in relief. His ERA in relief last year was 2.19 (49 innings). As a starter it was 4.72 (69 innings). The batting average against him last year after he threw more than 75 pitches was .350, although that is limited data (21 for 60).

Also, his platoon differential is huge (.168 vs. .307 last year), and although all left-handed pitchers face mostly right-handed batters (see Orosco), a reliever can be spotted to face *more* left-handed batters.

The Dodgers announced at the time of the trade that they intended to use Ojeda as a starter—but they also released Ray Searage, a left-handed spot reliever, a couple of days later.

How good is he, really?

With a bad organization in a tough park—with Atlanta, for example, or the Yankees or Cleveland—his ERA would skyrocket, and he'd be out of the league very quickly. It was a questionable decision to give Ojeda starts early last year rather than Darling. With organizations like the Mets and Dodgers, he looks like he's doing OK.

John OLERUD, Toronto
Could he succeed as a hitter and a pitcher?

There is no real evidence that he could be a major league pitcher. The attention directed to it is disproportionate.

What's his role on the team in 1991?

One would assume, with the trade of McGriff, that Olerud becomes the first baseman. Offensively, his role is harder to figure out. He batted sixth most of the time last year, but in that

a. he is now a more established hitter, and

b. the Blue Jays' team on-base percentage is going to drop precipitously,

it might be advisable to move him up to the second spot, ahead of Gruber and Carter. He had a .364 on-base percentage last year; so he needs to be on when the RBI men come up. Because of his power potential, however, he may stay down in the five and six spots.

Steve OLIN, Cleveland
Is he the next Dan Quisenberry?

This is the Cleveland Indians for you. Steve Olin got a trial as a starter last year, late in the season. He started on Monday, September 17, and he pitched well—7 6 2 2 1 3. He got the win.

Three days later, he's pitching garbage relief. With a five-run lead and two innings to go, Olin was called in to finish up. He was great again—2 0 0 0 0 4. The next day, Friday, he's pitching middle relief again, third pitcher of five who was used.

Obviously, it is difficult for any pitcher to succeed when he is used in this erratic way. Apart from that, I like Olin an awful lot. He uses a sidearm delivery, like Quisenberry and Tekulve, which I think is a plus. He throws harder than Quiz or Tekulve. His control is good. With a little luck and maybe a little better management, he's got a chance to be a hell of a pitcher.

Omar OLIVARES, St. Louis
Will he start for the Cardinals this year?

Olivares started for the Cardinals six times late in the year and posted a 2.92 ERA, which is surely enough to put him in the rotation in April. I'm not optimistic about his chances to succeed. He has no real history of minor league success, other than a good ERA at Louisville. His strikeout to walk ratio will probably be bad enough to make it difficult for him to stay in the rotation.

Joe OLIVER, Cincinnati
Is that all there is?

Oliver, promoted last year as an outstanding young catcher, hit just .231, and his playing time decreased down the stretch. Oliver's .231 batting average isn't as bad as all that, because he did hit 23 doubles in 364 at bats, and he can throw. He threw out 40% of opposing base stealers, the best percentage in the National League. The basic problem was that he didn't hit right-handers (.179 against them, 104 points better against lefties), and there are a *lot* of right-handers.

I think he is capable of playing better than this. He wasn't the worst catcher in the league last year, and he will have better years.

Francisco OLIVERAS, San Francisco
Did Roger Craig turn him around?

Oliveras is a small right-hander who reached the AA level in 1981 (he was 18 at the time) and AAA in 1984. He has been pitching AA and AAA ball in several organizations since then, mostly getting the bejeezus beat out of him. He pitched well for Portland the first half of the 1989 season, was called up by the Twins and was ineffective, then pitched with the Giants last year and was quite good in a minor role. I doubt that he is ever going to be more than two bad outings away from AAA, but sometimes they'll surprise you.

Greg OLSON, Atlanta
Was he really an All-Star?

Of course not; that was a joke.

1. The All-Star game is supposed to be for the *stars,* not for some guy who has a hot streak early in the year.
2. Olson was hitting .299 through the end of June, but what does that mean? He had 45 major league hits at that time, 44 of them in 1990. If he had four less hits he would have been hitting .272. So the information bank which showed that he was a "star" catcher was four hits.
3. Even if he was a .299 hitter, which everyone should have known he wasn't, he wouldn't be an All-Star anyway. Catching is a key defensive position; a .299 hitter who is weak defensively is not an All-Star.

Will he stay around?

He can probably help a team as a platoon player. He hit .312 with power against left-handed pitching last year. He can probably hit left-handers well enough to stay in the league. Kelly Mann, who will fight for the Atlanta catcher's job, is also a right-handed hitter.

Gregg OLSON, Baltimore
Where does he rank among major league relievers? Will he end up with the career saves record?

Olson posted an ERA in the zeroes for the last five months of 1989, then started out 1990 as if intent on proving this was his true level of ability. Through July of last year he had a 1.01 ERA then was hit hard over the last two months of the season.

Eckersley is the best reliever in the majors; Olson ranks with Henke and Dibble right behind him. It would be hard to choose among those three, but I would probably pick Dibble because I think he can pitch more innings without losing any effectiveness than the other two.

My ordinary assumption is that a pitcher who is a star in his early twenties will not last, since this has been the most common pattern. Pitchers who rely on a big curve ball, like Blyleven, have sometimes been an exception to this rule.

Steve ONTIVEROS, Philadelphia
Will he ever recover from his injuries? Will he come back and pitch well if he does?

Ontiveros had the Tommy John surgery on July 20, 1989, and is just launching his comeback. He made five appearances in relief last year, beginning September 13, and pitched well.

Ontiveros has always been a decent pitcher, but never able to stay healthy. The year off may be good for his arm. John was a better pitcher after the surgery than he was before, surely not because of the surgery, but still it shows that it is possible. I think Ontiveros will be back in 1991, and probably pitching well.

Jose OQUENDO, St. Louis
Was he still helping the team last year?

Yes. Oquendo, who has become one of the most underrated players in the game, dropped to .252 last year after hitting .277 or better the previous four years. He drove in only 38 runs and scored only 37. Look pretty bad, don't it?

It isn't. He had a slump in May, when he may have been playing hurt, and hit .159 in that month; his batting average for the other five months of the season was more like his normal .280. His strikeout/walk ratio is still super (74/46). His RBI rate is low because he batted very few times with men in scoring position (118), but his rate of RBI in those chances was as good as the next guy's. He doesn't score many runs because the Cardinals for some odd reason insist on batting him eighth most of the time, rather than second, which is where he should hit. He made only three errors all year at second base, and his range is good. With the exception of Sandberg he's the best second baseman left in the National League.

Jesse OROSCO, Cleveland
Why was he off his form last year?

I was talking about Orosco with Dan Quisenberry. Quisenberry suggested that Orosco might bounce up and down because he is tough on left-handers, and some managers do a lot better job than others of spotting a left-handed reliever against left-handed batters. We were talking about this, and it occured to me that there was a basic question here that I didn't know the answer to, which is: How often does a pitcher like this normally have the platoon edge?

There are a lot of pitchers now who are brought in to get out a left-hander—Rick Honeycutt, Mirabella, Guetterman, Agosto, Ken Dayley. Almost every team has one, and some managers will carry two. But working like that, how many left-handed batters do they actually face, and how many right-handers?

The answer is that all of those pitchers, no matter how carefully they are used by their managers, still wind up facing more right-handed than left-handed hitters. Pinch-hitting is probably one reason for it, and although we think of them as being called in to get one man out, that really doesn't happen all *that* often. Here's the data on a few of them: Orosco faced 72% right-handed hitters, which is high, so Quisenberry did have a point. Agosto last year faced 70% right-handed hitters, Keith Comstock faced 64% right-handed hitters, Dayley faced 62% right-handed hitters (and incidentally was

more effective against right-handers than left-handers) and Honeycutt faced 63% right-handers.

A left-handed starting pitcher can face 80% right-handed hitters or more, depending on whether he is perceived as tough on lefties. Mark Langston last year faced 84% right-handed hitters. I don't believe there was any left-handed pitcher in the majors who faced more left-handed than right-handed hitters.

Joe ORSULAK, Baltimore
Will he keep his playing time?

Orsulak was the Orioles *best* hitting outfielder last year. He hit .269 with 11 homers. No other Oriole outfielder hit .269, and the only one who hit more than 11 homers was Devereaux, with 12. The Orioles have added Dwight Evans and are trying to add a left-handed hitting outfielder, but one would think Orsulak would be safe.

Javier ORTIZ, Houston
Who is he?

Big right-handed hitting outfielder, hit well at Tucson last year and hit .273 in a thirty-game trial with Houston.

Ortiz is 28 years old, meaning that his best years are probably already behind him, and he doesn't have either speed or power. His minor league hitting record, although it has its bright spots, is generally unimpressive. The one positive is that he could hit .270 to .300 in the majors, which may be enough to keep him around as a pinch hitter. If the Astros open the season with Ortiz in left field, take it as a sign that they don't know what they're doing.

Junior ORTIZ, Minnesota
What happened to him last year? Why'd he hit .335?

For the same reason he hit .336 in 1986. He's a line-drive singles hitter, and a decent one. If a .275 hitter bats 150 times, there is a 1% chance he will hit .360 by pure luck.

Ortiz is a good journeyman catcher. My problem with him for the Twins is that he is too much the same as their number one catcher, Harper. Both of them are right-handed, line-drive hitters, good hitters but slow and don't throw well. If your two catchers do *different* things then you have opportunities to exploit an advantage or avoid a disadvantage. The Twins number two catcher should be a left-handed power hitter who throws well, understanding that to get that you'd have to accept some weaknesses.

John ORTON, California
Will he ever hit major league pitching?

Never. What he hit last year—.190—is what he hits. He shouldn't be in the majors. It's almost unbelievable that the Angels a year ago regarded him as the top prospect in their organization.

Al OSUNA, Houston
Who is he?

Left-handed reliever, struck out 82 men in 69 innings at AA last year. With the Astros losing Schatzeder, Agosto, Darwin, Anderson and Dave Smith to trades and free agency there is a tremendous opportunity for a young relief pitcher. Osuna hasn't yet pitched at AAA, but despite that probably will nail a spot in the Astros' new bullpen, with Dan Schatzeder's old job (left-handed spot reliever) being the best bet.

Dave OTTO, Oakland
Who is he?

Huge left-hander. He's always been a starting pitcher in the minors, but his records aren't impressive and the A's have limited demand for starting pitchers, so he's been in the bullpen for his major league trials. I saw him play college ball seven or eight years ago, and thought he was a better hitter than a pitcher. At this point the best chance for him is that he and Mark Salas will wind up on the same team, and we'll have the first palindrome battery in major league history.

Incidentally, the word palindrome comes from the greek "palindromos", which means "running back". So he should have been a running back . . .

Spike OWEN, Montreal
Can he help a team, hitting .230? Is he threatened by any Expo prospects?

He's a decent player, even hitting .230. He's one of the few shortstops whose secondary average is higher than his batting average, and his defense is good. The Expos thought enough of him to move Delino to second.

Owen probably won't last more than maybe two more years. He's 30, and he's lost a step at shortstop. The Expos' top shortstop prospect is Will Cordero, a teenager who hit .234 in AAA ball last year.

•P•

Mike PAGLIARULO, San Diego (Unsigned)
What the Sam Hill happened to him, anyway?

Pagliarulo hit 32 homers in 1987 when

a. he was 27 years old, and
b. a whole lot of people like Larry Sheets and Matt Nokes also hit thirty homers.

I think it created unrealistic expectations for him, and set up a frustration cycle. He started trying to pull everything. Contributing to this, he has always had trouble hitting a breaking ball, and after his big season this became known. He never could hit a left-hander. He had surgery to repair the ulna nerve in his right elbow. His production just drifted away among these various problems.

Pagliarulo hit .254 last year, which was the best average of his career—but he still had a nothing year. In 1986–87 he hit a loud .235; last year he hit a quiet .254. It won't keep him in the league unless he gets some of his power back.

Tom PAGNOZZI, St. Louis
Will he start this season?

If the Cardinals keep Todd Zeile at third base, Pagnozzi becomes the catcher by default. The Cardinals AAA catcher was Ray Stephens, a glove man but no prospect.

Pagnozzi, despite a .277 average last year, isn't going to set the world on fire. He could probably hit .270 in 110 games, but he wouldn't drive in or score as many runs as Zeile would hitting .240.

Rey PALACIOS, Kansas City
Will he have a job?

Probably not. The Royals could make excuses for him a year ago because they were coming off a good season. Now,

coming off a bad year, the pressure is on them to fix the things that are wrong with the team.

Palacios isn't on the Royals' roster at mid-winter—but then, neither is anybody else you would want as your number two catcher. This is an area the Royals need to fix before April first; Palacios will be back on the roster if they don't.

Vince PALACIOS, Pittsburgh
Will he be in the majors? What will his role be?

Palacios pitched extremely well as a starter at Buffalo last year (13-7, 3.43 ERA, good strikeout/walk ratio). He has had good AAA seasons before, and he deserves a chance in the major leagues.

With Drabek, Zane Smith, Smiley and Tomlin the Pirates starting pitching is pretty well set (I haven't mentioned Neal Heaton.) Giving up only four hits in 15 innings in September, Palacios made a good argument for a place in the bullpen, which may have opened up for him when Ted Power went to Cincinnati.

Donn PALL, Chicago White Sox
Has he reached his limit?

Pall, who has ERAs the last three years of 3.45, 3.31 and 3.32, has the least glamorous job in the White Sox bullpen, pitching in lost causes and facing a batter or two while Thigpen is warming up. With the trade of Barry Jones, one would assume that he would move up to Jones' old job.

He'll be fine in that role, but I wouldn't want to see him as a closer or a starting pitcher. He is vulnerable to a left-handed hitter, and wasn't an effective starter in the minor leagues.

Rafael PALMEIRO, Texas
Will he ever win a batting title?

I don't know if you noticed this, but all of the contenders for the American League batting title hit much better on the road than they did in their home parks. George Brett, who won it, hit .319 with three home runs in Kansas City, but .340 with eleven homers on the road. Rickey Henderson, who finished second, hit .305 with eight homers in Oakland, but .342 with twenty homers on the road. Palmeiro, the third contender, hit .288 in Texas, and .350 on the road.

Palmeiro, who turned 26 late in the year, has now contended for the batting title in both leagues. Intuitively, one would think that a player who contends for a batting title in his early twenties and isn't a fluke ought to win one sooner or later.

A look at players in the past who have contended for a batting title at an early age suggests that it's something less than a fifty-fifty proposition. Tim Raines made a run at the batting title in 1985 (age 25); he won it in 1986. Ralph Garr, who was second in the NL in batting in 1971, his first full season, won the title in 1974. Al Oliver, who hit .312 in 1972, won a batting title ten years later. Fred Lynn, second in the league in batting as a rookie in 1975, won the title four years later. George Brett, who hit .308 the same season (1975), won the title in 1976.

On the other hand, Cal Ripken hit .318 in 1983, when he was 22 years old and .306 in 1984, but wasn't a contender when he matured. Garry Templeton, who contended for the batting title with .322 in 1977, .314 in 1979 and .319 in 1980, dropped off in later years, and hasn't been able to smell a batting title since 1981. Lonnie Smith, who hit .339 at age 24 without enough at bats to qualify, never did win a batting title. Manny Sanguillen, who contended for the batting title his first two years in the league, never won one. Cesar Cedeno, who hit .320 at ages 21 and 22, never won a title. Bobby Murcer, who missed a title by six points at age 25, never won one, but one can argue that the .331 season didn't represent his true ability.

So what's my conclusion? I think Palmeiro will win a batting title. Among the people I listed, the player he is most like is Al Oliver. Ripken, Templeton and Sanguillen played demanding defensive positions which divided their energies. It has been established that if you take a young catcher or middle infielder and a young outfielder who is a comparable hitter, over time the outfielder is likely to become a better hitter.

Palmeiro should develop more as a hitter because that is the only option he has to further his career. What's more, with the age and decline of Boggs, the fight for the American League batting title is wide open. Palmeiro will win it within a couple of years.

Johnny PAREDES, Expos
Could he play in the majors?

I liked him a couple of years ago. He's a decent prospect; the Expos just came up with a better one in DeShields. Paredes could hit in the .250 range and do a few other things well. 28 years old; faces an uphill battle at this time.

Mark PARENT, Texas
Does he justify the roster spot?

When your number one catcher gets hurt, you would hope that your number two catcher can step in without hurting the team. That didn't happen last year for San Diego. When Santiago suffered a fractured forearm on June 14, Parent stepped in and the Padres went down the tubes.

This, however, is not necessarily a fair test for Parent:

1. Santiago isn't your average catcher. A backup who was an inch behind Mike Fitzgerald might be a yard behind Santiago.
2. No one player makes a team go or slump; it only *appears* that way at times.

Still, the experience of having to play regularly doesn't encourage you about Parent's ability to step in. We knew he couldn't hit; he's a .197 hitter through almost 500 at bats. .197 hitters who disappoint defensively have short careers. Parent has been traded to Texas, where he will be part of a squad of catchers (Geno Petralli, John Russell, Mike Stanley) marking time until the *real* catchers, who are in the minor leagues, are ready to come up. He probably will replace Chad Kreuter.

Clay PARKER, Detroit
Will he help the Tigers?

He should. I don't know why the Yankees gave up on him so quickly. He pitched well for them in '89, seventeen starts and solid work, but they gave him only two starts last year, one of which he won. You'd think a team desperate for pitching would want to see more.

Dave PARKER, Milwaukee
Did he help the Brewers? Is he the best DH in the league? Does he have a chance to get in the Hall of Fame?

Thank God for the Brewers. What other organization, after all, brings in a 39-year-old designated hitter to help them through the year, finishes 74-88 and pats themselves on the back because the old fart drives in 92 runs. Well, OK, there is Cleveland.

Let's do this by the numbers:

1. Parker is, on one level, still a better hitter than his stats show, because he has played for several years in poor hitter's parks. Last year he hit .303 with 12 homers on the road.
2. On another level, Parker isn't really all that much of a hitter. He had 92 RBI last year because he batted 610 times, hit cleanup and wasn't terrible, but he also wasn't all that good. 21 homers in 610 at bats . . . what is that? That's about the same rate as Darryl Boston, Glenallen Hill or Lloyd Moseby, none of whom is considered a cleanup hitter. Parker hit .261 with men in scoring position.

3. The Brewers are one of the few teams in the American League which uses a regular designated hitter, and what Parker does is still better than the normal DH production. One of the curious things about the designated hitter rule is how reluctant most of the teams are to use it to get somebody in the lineup who can really *hit*.

Does he have a chance to get in the Hall of Fame?

Let's look at that first of all as if the drug thing had never happened.

If he was considered on the basis simply of what he has accomplished on the field, Parker would probably go into the Hall of Fame. He has done forty things which would be characteristic of a Hall of Famer, worth a total of 121 points, which is near the top of the gray area.

He could move higher. For one thing, he still has an outside shot at 3,000 career hits—only a six percent shot, but he's still alive.

So let's say he's a Hall of Famer without the drug rap. How will that affect his chances?

My guess is he gets in anyway.

Rick PARKER, San Francisco
Can he hit major league pitching?
Probably not. He's a right-handed Pat Sheridan.

Jeff PARRETT, Atlanta
What happened to him last year? Could he be the Braves' closer?

As to what happened to him, I honestly don't know. He started out the year badly, and gradually got going (ERA of 5.71 the first two months, 4.60 the middle two months, 3.48 the last two months.)

I wouldn't want to bet that Parrett couldn't be a closer. For one thing, he's never been used the way that a lot of modern relievers are used—two or three hitters at a time. Many pitchers are dramatically more effective if used for just a few batters at a time, and there is some evidence that Parrett might also be. The batting average against him in his first fifteen pitches last year was .259, in the next fifteen pitches .279, and after that .365 (35 for 96).

Lance PARRISH, California
Is he still the best catcher in the league?

He was certainly one of the best catchers last year. Fisk was probably the best, followed by Parrish. A few other catchers hit well (Brian Harper, Tettleton), but none of them can throw. Parrish threw out 47% of opposing base stealers, the highest percentage in the majors.

The previous three years, Parrish really wasn't much of an offensive player. He hit no more than .245 any of the three years, with slugging percentages under .400. When you don't walk and are one of the four or five slowest players in the league, you need to hit .250.

What are Parrish's chances for the Hall of Fame?

Parrish probably is not a Hall of Famer, unless he continues to play at the level of 1990. Catchers are hard to figure because they get voted in on the basis of defense and leadership, but as best I can calculate it Parrish hasn't yet reached the gray area.

Note: The highest percentage of runners caught: Parrish, 47%, Bob Geren, 43%, Pat Borders, 43%, Joe Oliver, 40%, and Geno Petralli, 38%.

Dan PASQUA, Chicago White Sox
Is he too good to play part-time?
Pasqua batted only 325 times last year, but batted cleanup almost always when he was in the lineup. When you think about it that seems strange, doesn't it, that a man would be good enough to be the center of the offense half the time, but not good enough to play the other half the time.

But he really doesn't hit left-handers—.194 against them in 1990, .224 in '89. If he don't hit 'em, you can't DH him for his defense.

Bob PATTERSON, Pittsburgh
Does he deserve a shot at the closer role?

No. One good year in a protected role doesn't balance out against ten years of frustration.

Patterson has super control—walked only fourteen men last year in 95 innings. He held left-handers to a .204 batting average. He struggled for years to establish himself as a starter, and still started five times last year (2-2, 4.10 ERA as a starter). The batting average against him after he threw more than 45 pitches was .368.

Ken PATTERSON, Chicago White Sox
What's his role?
Left-handed spot reliever for the White Sox, who seem to have a fourteen-man bullpen. He held left-handers to a .194 batting average, which will keep him in the league if he can continue to do it. Nothing else about him is impressive.

Dave PAVLAS, Chicago Cubs
Who is he?
28-year-old candidate for a notch in the Cub bullpen, pitched well in thirteen games.

Pavlas was once a starting pitcher in the Rangers' system. After posting a 2-14 record as a starter at Oklahoma City in 1989 he was released by the Rangers and signed by the Cubs, who moved him to the bullpen. He pitched his way to the majors in one year. He'll never be a star, but he could stick around a few years.

Bill (I-29) PECOTA, Kansas City
Could he be a regular?
Pecota's a lifetime .235 hitter, and it's hard to put a .235 hitter in the lineup. What you hear is that John Wathan likes

Pecota, but departed General Manager John Schuerholz didn't believe in him. This difference of opinion resulted in Pecota being shuttled to the minors again and again, hence his nickname (I-29 is the highway between Kansas City and Omaha.) A year ago Schuerholz traded Jose DeJesus to Philadelphia for Steve Jeltz, which was certainly a spectacular vote of no-confidence for Pecota. Jeltz was supposed to provide backup at second base in case White couldn't play, but White couldn't play and it was Pecota who wound up with most of the work at second base.

You hear this about a lot of people, but in Pecota's case it really is true, that he does the little things well. Pecota does the little things awfully well—takes an extra base when it's there, throws behind the runner when the runner rounds the bag, all that stuff.

You can't argue that a 30-year-old .235 hitter should be promoted to regular status, but in retrospect the Royals would have been better off last year if they had simply appointed Pecota as their regular second baseman, rather than straggling through the season with White, Pecota, Jeltz, Shumpert and Seitzer.

Alejandro PENA, New York Mets
Is he any good?

He's an under-rated player, in the peculiar way that New York makes underrated players in the modern age, focusing attention on the failures of their players and ignoring the successes. Alejandro's a hell of a pitcher, certainly a better pitcher than Roger McDowell, for whom he was in a sense traded.

Is he back as far as he can come?

He might not be. I wouldn't bet that he couldn't start. He was an effective starter at one time. His record shows no evidence that he loses effectiveness at any pitch limit. He can get out left-handers as well as right-handers, and gets ahead of the hitters a very high percentage of the time.

Geronimo PENA, St. Louis
Who is he?

Second base prospect, switch hitter. He's very fast (stole eighty bases one year) and they tell me he's a terrific second baseman, but he isn't yet a good enough hitter to threaten Oquendo, or even provide *really* attractive trade bait.

Tony PENA, Boston
How much credit does he deserve for the Red Sox' title?

Pena was certainly much better than the people he replaced on the Red Sox, Rick Cerone and Rich Gedman. In my peculiar analytical structure he doesn't receive extra credit because the guys he replaced were terrible. Pena is an average offensive catcher, better than average defensively. He hit .299 with men in scoring position.

Four Red Sox regulars had off years. Boggs was hurt, Greenwell was battling a foot injury, Evans grew old and Brunansky was by and large a disappointment.

What off-set these disappointments was that the Red Sox pitching was better than one would have expected. Clemens had his career-best ERA. Bolton, a disappointment in previous trials, was very good. Boddicker had his best season in six years. Jeff Reardon cut a run off his ERA.

Did Pena help to make these pitchers better than they were? I don't know that, and I'm not going to say it. But people who are associated with successful seasons deserve reasonable credit for that success—not deification, not to be stamped with a magical label "winner" which hides all of their shortcomings, but reasonable credit. Pena deserves his share of the credit for the Red Sox success in 1990.

Terry PENDLETON, Atlanta
If he's a free agent, do you want him? Is he any good?

I don't want him. He's thirty years old, a .250 hitter with little power. In the last three years he's a 59% base stealer, which is well below the break-even point. If he wasn't a switch hitter, and equally bad from both sides, you could maybe use him as a platoon player.

Will he help the Braves?

He's not any worse than Jim Presley, but he's not any better.

Melido PEREZ, Chicago White Sox
Will he ever make good on his promise of 1988?

Sure. His numbers are kind of a puzzle, in that he posted a 4.61 ERA with peripheral numbers which shouldn't add up to that. He gave up only 177 hits in 197 innings, only fourteen home runs. His control was bad, but not *that* bad. He must have been effective for stretches and then just lost it.

Perez has excellent stuff, and has a record of throwing strikes in the past. His effort to get back on the horse may not be helped by the White Sox move to a new park, which is supposed to be better for hitters.

Mike PEREZ, St. Louis
Who is he?

Right-handed relief pitcher, bearing no obvious resemblance to a major leaguer.

Pascual PEREZ, New York Yankees
Will he pitch well again?

Perez started three times at the beginning of the season, then left the rotation with a sore shoulder. In June it was determined that he was suffering from "chronic inflammation in the lining of his right shoulder joint", and would be out the rest of the year.

Later in the season, while still on the disabled list, Perez got into a shouting match with Stump Merrill when Merrill told him he didn't belong in the dugout.

Perez hasn't pitched 200 innings in a season since 1984, and it is unrealistic to think he is going to start now. He is one of the those pitchers, like Candelaria, who is going to be hurt half the time and effective the rest of the time, and a pain in the behind all of the time. Whether or not you want him around depends on how desperate you are for a pitcher.

Tony PEREZCHICA, San Francisco
Who is he?

Middle infielder, still young enough to have a career. Perezchica tore through the minor leagues until 1988, hitting .306 at Phoenix in 1988. He led two minor leagues in triples and also hit a few out of the park.

After a brief major league trial in 1988 he stopped hitting. He hasn't hit a lick for two years, and we have to wonder if he will again. But on the basis of age (25) and known offensive and defensive ability, there appears to be no certain reason that he can't have a major league career.

Gerald PERRY, St. Louis
Did he help the Royals?

Not really, no; not as much as I thought he would, anyway. Perry hit .300 the first month of the season, and led the team in RBI for two and a half months while Tartabull was hurt and Brett and Bo weren't hitting. He was a very popular acquisition, and Royals' announcer Denny Trease said in early June that "the acquisition of Gerald Perry has just entirely changed this Royal ballclub." This was intended as a compliment, but considering the changes in the Royal ballclub it came perilously close to slander.

The problem is that Perry isn't *really* a .300 hitter, and on top of that he isn't much else, either. He's a poor defensive player, and about the dumbest baserun-

ner the Royals have ever had. A game in Boston on July 14 illustrates the problem. Perry went four-for-four that day, leading the CBS crew which was telecasting the game to select him as the player of the game. It was 4 0 4 0—four for four, but no production. Perry could have cost the Royals the game with two baserunning blunders. In the second inning Willie Wilson grounded to second, and Perry went three yards out of the baseline to take out the pivot man. The Red Sox had no chance of getting Wilson, but the second base umpire called interference on Perry (correctly) and called Wilson out at first base anyway, completing the double play. That cost the Royals a run.

Eighth inning, same game. Perry was on third, Wilson on first when the ball was tapped to the pitcher. Perry, trying to score, was a dead duck, which is OK. At the end of the rundown, however, Tony Pena dropped the ball; it came loose as he tagged Perry out. Before the umpires could realize this, however, Perry slammed Pena to the ground with a shot from his elbow, and the third base umpire immediately called interference, freezing Wilson at second base. Wilson could easily have made third.

The fans loved it; Perry was showing that great "aggressiveness" as a baserunner. There is a fine line between aggressiveness and stupidity, and this was over the line: this was stupid. A *calculated* risk, yes; an indiscriminate risk, no. This was an indiscriminate risk.

And that's Perry. I thought before the Royals got him that Perry was a fast runner, but he really isn't. He has stolen quite a few bases, but if you look at the other five "speed indicators", you'll note that they are all below average. Perry never hits triples, grounds into an awful number of double plays, and has never scored very many runs. He's a first baseman, and his stolen base percentages are poor. So his "speed score", 5.0 being the norm, is around four; he is *below* average.

Making this worse, with the hot streak

early in the season Wathan fell in love with him, and had him in the lineup at times when he shouldn't have been. Perry and Pat Tabler are similar players, a natural platoon combination. Both are line-drive hitters, playing similar offensive and defensive roles. Tabler isn't much of a hitter against a right-handed pitcher, but he can annihilate a left-hander. Wathan, preferring to play Perry, left Tabler on the bench to rust while the Royals were scrambling for runs. (Perry had 134 at bats against left-handers and was absolutely terrible against them, hitting .209 against left-handers with on-base and slugging percentages barely over .250. At least half of those at bats came at the expense of Tabler, who hit .333 against left-handed pitchers, about his normal figure.) Gerald Perry in his natural role isn't a very good player, but he's OK. Outside his natural role, he's dead weight.

Adam PETERSON, Chicago White Sox
Is he a major league starter?

I have concerns about him, which are probably similar to the concerns of the White Sox which kept him in the minors for an extra year and a half of AAA, a year and a half after he had already proven he could win there.

Peterson gave up 90 hits in 85 innings last year; he struck out only 29 men. Left-handed hitters hit .354 against him, although he was very effective against right-handers. What that is telling us, in combination with the fact that they left him in AAA after he went 14-5, is that he doesn't have a fastball.

Pitchers of this type rarely succeed for a long period of time—but that doesn't justify prejudice against them in awarding opportunity. Peterson wasn't bad last year, in eleven starts. Finesse pitchers rarely succeed—but sometimes. Often they're good for a year or two. Peterson deserves his shot.

Geno PETRALLI, Texas
Is his career on the decline?

What probably happened to Petralli last year is that he was exposed to a workload beyond his limits. Petralli hit .300 in 1987, when he batted 202 times, and in 1989, when he batted 184 times. He set a career high in games played last year, 133, and was near a high in at bats.

Texas players, especially catchers, have a long history of wilting in the Dallas heat. Petralli hit .289 last April—but .216 in June, and .189 in July.

He hit *no* home runs last year, after hitting 18 the previous three years.

In the late innings (seventh inning or later) he hit .243, and drove in only three runs all year (103 at bats).

The conclusion *I* draw from these facts is that Petralli's bat was dragging in the summer heat. He hit better late in the year. I think if he is kept in his role—200, 250 at bats a year—he'll be as effective in 1991 as he has ever been.

Dan PETRY, Detroit
How long will the Tigers put up with him?

Petry was pretty bad last year, but the Tigers also have bigger problems, and they have a long history of having been loyal to Petry. They'll probably go with him another year.

Does he have any chance to come back?

Yes. There is a long anecdotal history of pitchers saying that their arm suddenly snapped back several years after an injury. What is hard for a pitcher is to survive, to stay in the game, long enough to find out if it will come back. I'm not betting that it will; just acknowledging the possibility.

Gary PETTIS, Texas
Is there going to be room for him in Arlington?

At 33, Pettis is going to have to accept a backup role, whether in Texas or somewhere else. Juan Gonzalez will start the year in center, and it is unlikely that Pettis will ever play regularly again.

Neil MacCarl's poll of the managers picked Pettis over Devon White as the best defensive outfielder in the American League. He is still awfully good, although I think most people would rather have White.

Tony PHILLIPS, Detroit
Where will he play?

The development of Travis Fryman, who will play third, probably pushes him back to the utility role that he played with the A's. Whitaker is 34 and misses some time every year, Trammell is 33 and the same, so Phillips could play 140 games without having a regular spot.

Phillips is a good player—99 walks last year, 97 runs scored. He's a good player—but not as good as Trammell or Whitaker, and not as young as Fryman. He'll get some work as a DH or maybe in the outfield.

Jeff PICO, Chicago Cubs
Can he pitch?

If he can he has kept the fact exceptionally well hidden. The league hit .321 against him last year.

Phil PLANTIER, Boston
Who is he?

Minor league power hitter. Asked by a reporter in November to name the top home run hitter of the 1990s, I offered Plantier. Granting that it was a capricious choice, it has as good a chance of being right as anybody else I can think of.

Plantier is a 22-year-old first baseman, signed for Boston by Bob Boone's father as an eleventh-round draft pick in 1987. He is not large (six foot, 175 pounds), but he hit 27 homers and drove in 105 runs at Lynchburg in 1989 (.300 average). Jumping to AAA, Plantier was unimpressed; he dropped to .253 but hit 33 home runs in 123 games. It was the most home runs by a AAA player, not counting the Mexican League, since Danny Tartabull hit 43 in 1985.

Apparently the Red Sox have reservations about Plantier, or else why would they want Jack Clark? He does strike out quite a bit, and there is a natural fear that major league pitchers would be able to exploit his weaknesses, and drive his batting average into Rob Deer territory. He was *not* named by International League managers as one of the top ten prospects in the *Baseball America* poll because "most managers feel that he has too many holes in his swing and [is] a defensive liability."

He's a "mistake hitter", you see. Minor league managers tend to mythologize major league pitchers as people who don't make any mistakes. I have heard those suspicions about many players who later turned out to be major league stars, although I suppose it could always prove true. I'd like to be his agent.

Dan PLESAC, Milwaukee
Can he bounce back?

I doubt that he'll ever be a dominant closer again, but, like Jeff Reardon, he could pitter along in the role for any number of years. Last year he pitched well through April, but had an ERA of 4.80 from May 1 to the end of the season. He held left-handed hitters to a .161 batting average, but right-handers hit .286 against him. He was never on the disabled list, and spoke mostly about a lack of confidence, which doesn't mean that he wasn't hurt.

Eric PLUNK, New York Yankees
Is he being well used as a middle reliever?

Plunk had a 2.72 ERA last year, and has three straight years with winning records and good ERAs. He doesn't have the control you would want to see in a closer. When he started early in his career he got the tar beat out of him. He was effective where he was last year, and I wouldn't want to try him on anything stiffer, so I guess he's well used.

Luis POLONIA, California

Just how good is he?

Polonia hit .335 last year. People seem to have trouble taking that in—.335. He is a lifetime major league .304 hitter, and a minor base stealer.

Polonia isn't a good outfielder and can't throw. He has no power and doesn't walk, a secondary average last year of .191. We all know he has embarrassed his teams in the past.

Still—.335. There aren't a lot of guys around who can hit .335. I don't know if you can hit .335 and run, and still be so bad all-around that there isn't some way you can be used to help the team.

Jim POOLE, Texas

Who is he?

Left-handed relief prospect with phenomenal strikeout rates at A ball and AA (77 strikeouts in 64 innings at San Antonio). He got a look by the Dodgers, and was traded to Texas in late December for two minor leaguers.

The Dodgers are filthy with pitching prospects and middle relievers—Crews, Searage, Gott, Hartley, Munoz, Walsh, Cook—and so Poole was crowded out. He looks good, and should help Texas.

Mark PORTUGAL, Houston

Has he found a home in the rotation? Is he an effective starter?

Portugal was very effective last year in the Astrodome (8-2, 1.78 ERA) but equally ineffective on the road (3-8, 5.57). Although a right-handed pitcher he got left-handers out consistently (.227, .333 slugging) but had trouble with right-handers (.281, .431 slugging). He struggled at the start of games, allowing a .311 batting average in his first fifteen pitches, but improved dramatically after that, and held up for seven innings.

Basically I think Portugal can pitch. His chances of remaining a rotation starter for several years are good.

Dennis POWELL, Milwaukee

I've had concerns about the Brewer organization for several years, but I didn't realize how far they had fallen until last summer, when I noticed that Dennis Powell was in their starting rotation. Here's a pitcher who has been with the Seattle Mariners, one of the most pitching-poor teams in baseball, for several years. With the Mariners he was pitching middle relief, the bottom of the staff. He was ineffective in the role, posting ERAs of 8.68 and 5.00 his last two years.

Powell was assigned to Calgary by the Mariners, refused the assignment, became a free agent and signed with the Brewers. The Brewers not only signed him, but gave him seven starts. He didn't win any, and posted a 6.86 ERA.

There are maybe six or seven things you look for before you put a pitcher in your starting rotation, which are outlined in the Norm Charlton comment. Let's say there are seven. You almost never find all seven, so you are happy when you find a pitcher who has five or six things going for him. If you need a starting pitcher you'll try a guy who has four things going for him. Pitchers who have two or three things going for them—let's say maybe they have good control, are thought to be intelligent and have a record of some success two or three years ago—pitchers like that are released and picked up by other organizations all the time, and if they pitch well in middle relief maybe they'll earn a couple of starts.

But think about how far down an organization has to fall before they give a spot in the *starting rotation* to a pitcher that there is *no* reason to believe will be successful.

Ted POWER, Cincinnati

Jim Leyland started Ted Power, who had not started a game all year, in the sixth and final game of the NL playoff. What do you think of that strategy? If it works, why don't they do it more often?

Power pitched well, but gave up a run due to a defensive mistake, and left with the Pirates behind 1-0 in the third.

This was an interesting thing to me, and I'm sure to many of you, because it was an old table-game strategy come to life. The idea is to start a right-handed pitcher, use him for a couple of innings, force the opposition manager to use his left-handed hitters, then put in a left-hander and claim the platoon advantage. I've seen managers do that in table game leagues for years—the strategy is not well thought of—and I've *heard of* managers doing it in the majors. Leo Durocher supposedly did it a few times, but I've never actually seen it done, and certainly never seen it done in the final game of a championship series.

Let's break it down into smaller questions:

Is that a fair strategy, or is it kind of chickenshit?

If it is a fair strategy to claim the platoon advantage by using a pinch hitter, then why isn't it a fair strategy to try to claim the platoon advantage by starting a right-hander and switching to a left-hander?

I wouldn't do it, in a table game, for several reasons. In almost all table games the number of games a player can play are regulated somehow, and so a strategy like this forces the opposition manager to waste precious games to counter the strategy. Table game strategies which take advantage of the flaws in the game are looked down on, for good reason. Also, there is a kind of gentleman's agreement on the subject. If one manager starts using the strategy then the next manager will and the next one, and the end result is no advantage for anyone, but everyone's life is more complicated.

But a professional manager has an obligation to win a critical game at all costs. There are rules of sportsmanship which are still in effect—you never try to hurt anyone, that sort of thing—but a gentleman's agreement not to complicate the other fellow's life isn't one of them. Leyland's responsibility was to win, not to be a nice guy.

Does it make sense to do it?

What Leyland was thinking, no doubt, is that while one might observe convention the rest of the time, the decisive game of the playoff is a special case. I agree with him about that.

But the down side of that argument is that it leaves you in the position of *experimenting* with an untried strategy in the sixth game of the Championship series. I wouldn't want to do that.

In 1985 a similar thing happened in the Kansas City/Toronto series, when the Royals started a right-hander (Bret Saberhagen), switched to a left-hander (Leibrandt) and then back to a right-hander (Quisenberry), whipsawing Bobby Cox and depriving him of the platoon advantage at the key moments of the game. The strategy worked brilliantly then, but the situation was different in several ways:

1. The Royals took out Bret Saberhagen, their best starting pitcher, not because they wanted to but because the Blue Jays kept pounding line drives off his person.
2. The Blue Jays were a platoon team, platooning at catcher, first, third and DH. This made them especially vulnerable to the strategy.
3. The Royals' relief ace, Dan Quisenberry, was right-handed, and two of the Blue Jays platoon left-handers, Rance Mulliniks and Al Oliver, could hit him at will. It was especially important, for that reason, that Dick How-

ser get Oliver and Mulliniks out of the game so Quiz could come in. Leyland uses no relief ace, but a mixture of left- and right-handers, so the same need was not there.

4. The Blue Jays could not have foreseen that Kansas City would do this before the game, and thus had limited ability to guard against it. Because this was Ted Power starting rather than Bret Saberhagen, Lou Piniella saw it as a gambit and declined to go for it.

My conclusion on the strategy? I wouldn't do it; I wouldn't criticize it. Power is a decent pitcher; he could have pitched shutout ball for two innings just as easily as not. The Pirates lost the game 2-1, which means that *defensively* they accomplished what they needed to.

Will Power help Cincinnati?

He's as good a pitcher as the man he replaces (Rick Mahler), or maybe a little better. If he fails the Reds have pitchers at AAA who can plug the gap.

Jim PRESLEY,
Atlanta (free agent)
Can he help anybody? Did he help the Braves?

He can't help anybody, and he was a fool not to stay with the Braves. He's a slow, .240-hitting third baseman with a terrible strikeout/walk ratio. If he can't succeed in Atlanta, he can't succeed anywhere.

Joe PRICE,
Baltimore (free agent)
Could he help somebody?

You'd think so. It's hard to see why the Orioles didn't choose to re-sign Price, who certainly wasn't any worse than your average left-handed spot reliever and maybe a little better. He has bounced around because teams have insisted on starting him, and he pitches well for two weeks and then gets hurt and flounders for a year. The uncertainty about his

health apparently made it difficult for him to work out a deal with Baltimore (the Orioles didn't want to guarantee his contract). But pitching 65 innings a year, he ought to be useful.

Tom PRINCE, Pittsburgh
Who is he?

26-year-old catching prospect, has hit .159 through 58 major league games. He's like Tony Perezchica, a good defensive prospect with a good minor league hitting record until 1988, then a bad one the last two years. He's not going to have a career unless he starts hitting again pretty soon.

Kirby PUCKETT, Minnesota
Is he the best player in baseball? Is he still a candidate? Is he going to be a Hall of Famer?

Two years ago it was common to hear that Kirby was the best player in the game. If one passionately believed that he was *not* the best player in the game, there were two arguments that you could use:

1. His batting stats are inflated by playing in Minnesota. His career average is about a hundred points higher in Minnesota than it is on the road.
2. The most important offensive statistic in baseball is on-base percentage. Puckett's on-base percentage, though above average, isn't outstanding.

In the last two years Kirby's batting average has slipped from .356 to .298, his power has been cut in half and he has lost some speed. This makes it no longer a question of whether he is the best player in the game. There is no way to argue that he is more valuable than Sandberg or Rickey Henderson or Bonds.

Is he a Hall of Famer?

Kirby is still an awfully good player. His positives include:

• terrific durability,
• a .320 lifetime batting average,

• 40 doubles a year, and

• some defensive skills in center field.

Last year he hit .341 with men in scoring position, and he walks more often than he used to.

Kirby is *clearly* a Hall of Fame type player, and unquestionably will go into the Hall of Fame if he continues to play well. Even if the rest of his career was nothing much, if he just hung around for six years as a .280 hitter, he would probably go in the Hall of Fame.

Terry PUHL, New York Mets
Will he help the Mets?

Puhl will probably bat a hundred times, and there's no way to guess who will have a good year in that role, because the at bats don't give a true read on ability. For Puhl, who doesn't have power, Shea may be a worse park than the Astrodome. Shea would give him home runs, which he won't hit anyway, but the poor visibility may drive down his batting average.

•Q•

Tom QUINLAN,
Toronto
Who is he?

Third base prospect, struck out 157 times at Knoxville last year. One cannot see him threatening Kelly Gruber for a decade or so.

Luis QUINONES,
Cincinnati
Is he a good backup?

Quinones' position with the Reds may be threatened by the re-signing of Bill Doran, which pushes Mariano Duncan into a utility role. Quinones is a decent backup infielder, and will land on his feet somewhere.

Carlos QUINTANA,
Boston
Will he lose his job this spring?

The Red Sox have talent backed up at the left end of the defensive spectrum—Quintana, Moe Vaughn, Plantier, Jack Clark—and are reportedly trying to unload Quintana in a trade.

Would I do that? If I was the Red Sox I wouldn't have signed Jack Clark, but I would try to unload Quintana. I like Quintana, as a hitter. What he hit last year (.287 with 7 home runs) is a little less than I expected him to hit. I expected him to hit .290 but with more power, and I still think he will if he stays in Boston. In another park, of course, he won't hit quite as well, but he can hit.

But so can Mo Vaughn and Plantier, probably better than Quintana. Quintana is a pretty awful first baseman, but then he has no experience there. People who have seen him in the minors say that he looks much better in the outfield. If that's true he's a valuable player, and it makes sense to try to convert that value into something the Red Sox need, like a quality starting pitcher.

Jamie QUIRK, Oakland
Why did he play so well with Oakland?

There are some pitchers that Jamie can hit, and there are some pitchers he can't hit. How well he will hit depends to a degree on how good a job his manager does of spotting him against the pitchers he can hit. LaRussa did that well, and the results were impressive—a .281 average, and a slightly better RBI rate (per plate appearance) than Cecil Fielder. He hit .448 with men in scoring position. Also, LaRussa had him bunt more than he ever had before, which kept him out of the double play.

•R•

Scott RADINSKY, Chicago White Sox
Will he move up? Has he found his role?

Let's say that Bobby Thigpen was hurt. Although Radinsky did not pitch as well last year as Barry Jones, Wayne Edwards, Don Pall or Ken Patterson, Radinsky might be the best bet to step into the closer role. He is younger than the other guys, and throws harder. He wasn't real effective last year because he jumped from A ball at age 22, but given a little more experience he could be a Grade A reliever.

Rock RAINES, Chicago White Sox
Is he still a good player? Is he still one of the best players in the league? Should he hit leadoff?

Raines is still a good player, but hasn't been a great one for the last three years. Raines created about 75 runs last year with 359 outs, or about 5.6 runs per game. This is still above the norm for a major league left fielder (5.1 runs per game), which is an important starting point in discussing Raines. Some people, including his manager, have tended to compare him not to other left fielders but to his own past, and regard him as a disappointment.

With the White Sox he'll move back to the leadoff spot, which is his natural offensive role. Even last year, off his game, he had a .379 on-base percentage and stole 49 bases. That would make him a hell of a leadoff man. But his slugging percentage was below .400, and he hit only eleven doubles and nine homers. That means he is of limited value in the middle of the order.

Delino DeShields is also a leadoff man, but DeShields had neither a .379 on-base percentage nor 49 stolen bases last year. Raines' stolen base percentage, the worst of his career, was still better than DeShields'.

I also believe, for what it is worth, that being taken out of the leadoff spot and asked to drive in runs has been confusing to Raines. I think it has caused him to make adjustments in his approach to hitting which have been ineffective, even counter-productive. Three years ago, Rickey Henderson and Tim Raines were comparable players. They're not now. I think Raines has a better chance of getting back to that level if he goes back to his familiar role.

Rafael RAMIREZ, Houston
Does he justify his job? Should he be a starting shortstop?

Whether or not he should be a regular depends first of all on whether the Astros have anybody better at short, which apparently they don't. Ramirez isn't a shortstop that you can be happy with. He doesn't make as many mistakes as he used to at short, but then he doesn't have the range that he used to, either. He doesn't make as many mistakes on the bases as he used to, but then he doesn't have the speed that he used to, either. He was a marginal shortstop four years ago, and he's a little bit better all-around player now.

Domingo RAMOS, Chicago Cubs
Why is he hitting so much better than he used to?

Ramos has had batting averages below .200 six times in his major league career, and what you don't realize at a glance is that five of those are in less than a hundred at bats, the other one being in 168 at bats. All six of his sub-.200 seasons, taken together, add up to 370 at bats.

When Ramos got more at bats, his batting record wasn't all that bad—.283 in 127 at bats with Seattle in 1983, .311 in 103 at bats in 1987.

So my understanding of why Ramos is hitting better than he used to is:

1. We probably all over-estimated how bad a hitter he was, because of the long line of ones in his record,
2. He is playing in Wrigley Field, one of the best parks in baseball to hit for average, and
3. He has probably worked hard and become a somewhat better hitter.

Ramos has certainly, the last two years, been one of the best backup infielders in baseball. I still wouldn't want to have to use him as a regular.

Willie RANDOLPH, Oakland
Can he still be a regular?

He's not a *good* regular at this point, but there are guys around who are worse. He's not fast, but he is still a good baserunner. He doesn't get on base a lot any more, but he is still on base more than your average second baseman. He is no longer durable, and he never did have power. He doesn't make mistakes in the field, and still turns the double play very well.

Among American League second basemen, Randolph would now rank *below* Jody Reed, Jerry Browne, Lou Whitaker, Steve Sax, Roberto Alomar, Harold Reynolds and Julio Franco. He would rank clearly *ahead* of Johnny Ray and whoever Kansas City puts out there, and in a group with Jim Gantner and Scott Fletcher. Billy Ripken and Nelson Liriano might be better than those three guys or worse, depending on whether they play the way they did last year or the way they have in the past, so that would make Randolph about the tenth best second baseman in the league.

Dennis RASMUSSEN, San Diego
Is he in danger of losing his spot in the rotation?

Rasmussen declined arbitration with the Padres, and is a free agent at this writing.

I've always defended Rasmussen, and

I still would on the basis of past performance. His career won-lost record is 80-60, which is damned good. But Rasmussen wasn't very good in 1989, and last year he was a step below that—11-15, 4.51 ERA, only 86 strikeouts in 188 innings. You can't keep pitching a guy like that. If he wants to stay in the rotation, he *has* to come out in April pitching better than he has the last two years.

Johnny RAY, California
Does he deserve more respect?

Despite a .290 career batting average, Ray isn't any kind of an offensive player. He doesn't walk or run or have any power, although he used to hit doubles. He's not going to drive in or score a whole lot of runs, and he is now 34 years old.

Defensively, he may have been underrated but I wouldn't want to bet on it. He had a good range factor at second, but then so did everybody else who played second for the Angels, including Rick Schu, Kent Anderson and Donnie Hill, so that may be some sort of illusion of circumstance. The habit of trying to make an outfielder out of him doesn't encourage you to believe he is a good second baseman.

Randy READY, Philadelphia
How good would he have been?

The question which can never be answered about Ready is what kind of career he would have had if the Brewers had put him in the lineup in 1984, rather than deciding to do everything backward for five years. I'm still inclined to think that he would have been pretty good. His major league batting average is .265, with 33 doubles, seven triples and 13 homers per six hundred at bats, also 84 walks. That's enough offense to be a major league third baseman, and certainly more than you need to play second.

Would he have done *less* than this if he had been a regular? Perhaps, but isn't it as likely that he would have done

more? They used to rip his defense, but you don't hear that much anymore. I think Buck Rodgers, under pressure to get his team in the pennant race, just made a bad decision on him, and then followed through on that bad decision by trying to prove it was right. Given a full shot, Ready could have had a career.

Jeff REARDON, Boston
Is he still good enough for the role?

He was last year, but he's been up and down. Last year he was good, but missed some time with the back. In 1989 he pitched 65 games but wasn't good. He's only had one season since 1985 that doesn't have a big "but" attached to it, and I don't really imagine he'll have any more as long as he is in that role.

Gary REDUS, Pittsburgh
Is he still a good backup?

He's still a super backup player. He doesn't steal quite as often as he used to, but he basically matched his career norms in batting average, slugging percentage and on base percentage last year. Add the last two years together and you'll see what kind of an offensive player he really is—506 at bats, 33 doubles, 10 triples, 12 homers, 36 stolen bases. He'll never hit .300—but he can still do the things that generate runs.

Darren REED, New York Mets
Who is he?

Center field prospect, was acquired by the Mets in the Rafael Santana trade with the Yankees three years ago, and has been playing for Tidewater ever since. He had a good enough year last year to earn a look. If he happened to break through he should hit in the .240s with a little speed, showed some power last year for the first time since the Mets got him. He's only 25, so if he can continue to hit an occasional homer (he hit 17 last year) he could make the majors as a fifth outfielder.

Jeff REED, Cincinnati
Could he play more? Could he play regularly for somebody?

Reed, once a prospect, had his best year with the bat last year, hitting .251, but had his worst year throwing, as he threw out only 15 of 82 opposition baserunners, probably the worst record in the majors (Mike Macfarlane was 14 for 82, but Macfarlane allowed 68 stolen bases in 911 innings. Reed allowed 67 stolen bases in about half as many innings behind the plate.) The emergence of Oliver reduced Reed's playing time to its lowest level in four years, but he's still one good slump away from AAA.

Jerry REED, Boston
Can he still pitch? Could he ever pitch?

It was a puzzle last spring why Jim Lefebvre released Reed after four straight years with ERAs in the threes. Apparently he knew something we didn't; Reed's ERA skyrocketed, and he struck out only nineteen men in 52 innings. He may get one more shot, but he'd better impress somebody quickly if he does.

Jody REED, Boston
Does his bat justify his glove?

As a shortstop, that may be a fair question; as a second baseman, it is obvious that Reed's bat *will* carry his glove. He doesn't quite have a shortstop's arm, and as a second baseman could be quicker on the DP, but then, how many second basemen hit forty doubles a year, anyway?

How many doubles would he hit if he wasn't playing in Fenway?

Almost forty, maybe more. In the last two years he has hit 49 doubles in his home parks, and 38 on the road.

Could he win an MVP Award?

It's not likely. The type of player he is, he'd have to hit .320 with 50 doubles to be a serious MVP candidate. I doubt that he will.

Rick REED, Pittsburgh
Who is he?

Right-handed starting pitcher candidate, excellent control but hasn't yet been able to control the number of line drives rocketing back at him. He had a trial in '89, then was called up last June and was in the Pirates' rotation until Randy Tomlin came along.

Will he be a major league pitcher?

Probably not. He's a Grade C prospect. There's no reason he *can't* pitch in the majors, but he'll need exactly the right combination of opportunity, development and luck.

Kevin REIMER, Texas
Will he get a real chance to play this season? Does he deserve one?

Time is working against Reimer. He's 27, already at his peak, and a big guy who probably won't run well when he's 32. I think what he hit last year (.260) is a good estimate of what he would hit with more playing time. It isn't enough to make him a regular, but he could make it as a pinch hitter/fifth outfielder.

Rick REUSCHEL, San Francisco
Will he come back?

Reuschel will be 42 in May. There haven't been a lot of successful 42-year-old starting pitchers in history, and most of those were knuckleball pitchers.

There is evidence to be introduced on Reuschel's behalf. He pitched some good games last year, after coming back. His 3.93 ERA wasn't bad, and his control was great. If he could win when he was 40, why not 42?

But let's not kid ourselves. He was 3-6 and gave up 102 hits in 87 innings. The league hit .297 against him. Perhaps the best parallel is Warren Spahn in 1964, one year after he was 23-7. He finished 6-13 in 1965, but what the record doesn't

show is that he did have a lot of good starts, starts when he was that close to having a shutout. People kept thinking he would get it started one more time, but he never could.

Harold REYNOLDS, Seattle
How good is he, really? Is he an acceptable leadoff man? Is he the best leadoff man in the American League? Is he the best player on the Mariners?

His value is *defensive*, rather than offensive. Let us look at Reynolds as a collection of abilities:

1. He is very durable.
2. He has excellent range at second base.
3. He can steal bases.
4. He hits for as good an average as the next second baseman, or a little better.
5. He has no power.
6. He turns the double play very well.

Reynolds steals bases, but not with a success rate that has any value, so we can throw that one out. He has no power, but then about twelve of the fourteen second basemen in the league have no power, so that has no real impact, either. Although he hit .300 in 1989 he's really average in that respect, so his ability to hit for average is no real factor. That leaves us:

1. He is very durable.
2. He has excellent range at second base.
3. He turns the double play very well.

See; his value is *defensive*, rather than offensive. He's a little better than an average offensive second baseman, but a very good defensive one.

As an offensive player, you have to give him credit for having improved tremendously. His walk totals since 1984: 0, 17, 29, 39, 51, 55 and 81. Whereas he used to be an anxious hitter, he is now a rather selective hitter, which is reflected in his runs scored total last year (100).

He is probably the best player on the Mariners year-in and year-out.

Note: Reynolds led the majors in plate appearances last year, with 737. Reynolds, Joe Carter and Jay Bell were the only major league players to make 500 outs, Reynolds leading the way with 516. He had 480 hitless at bats, was caught stealing sixteen times, grounded into nine double plays, had five sacrifice bunts and six sac flies.

R.J. REYNOLDS, Pittsburgh
How much will his loss hurt the Pirates?

If there's an impact it's in the clubhouse. He's a replaceable talent. Shifting a hundred of his at bats to Gary Redus would probably add three or four runs to the Pirate offense. No big deal.

The combined loss of Reynolds, Bream, Cangelosi, Chamberlain and Alou reduces the Pirates' ability to withstand an injury.

Arthur RHODES, Baltimore
Who is he?

Left-handed pitcher, Vida Blue model. He probably has the best fastball in the Baltimore system other than Ben McDonald. With Joe Price not returning he has an outside shot to make the Orioles in '91 as a middle reliever, but probably won't appear until 1992.

Karl RHODES, Houston
Who is he?

Outfield prospect who walks and steals bases. The Astros have a whole bunch of guys like this; it clearly seems to be some sort of development program. At Osceola in 1988 Rhodes drew 81 walks and stole 65 bases. At Columbus in 1989 he drew 93 walks, but apparently had an injury which limited him to 18 stolen bases. At Tucson last year in 107 games he drew 47 walks and stole 24 bases.

As a major league hitter Rhodes would hit about .240 with no power, and at that level he's going to have to have a whole bunch of walks and stolen bases in order to have a career.

Other Astros candidates in the same general group include Willie Ansley, Rafael Castillo, Arthur Frazier, Harry Fuller, Lawrence Lamphere and David Silvestri. Sometime one of those guys is going to walk a hundred times and steal a hundred bases in the major leagues.

Rusty RICHARDS, Atlanta
Who is he?

Right-handed pitching prospect, or non-prospect. He is probably the only prospect I could find who has *nothing* to make you think he could succeed in the major leagues.

Jeff RICHARDSON, Cincinnati
Who is he?

Right-handed reliever, overage for a prospect (27) because of several years spent struggling as a starter in the low minors. He had a 1.86 ERA in the Pacific Coast League last year, which will get your attention even though everything else about him is marginal. I haven't seen him, but from his record he looks like he must have come up with a specialty pitch or started throwing underhanded or something.

Dave RIGHETTI, San Francisco
Will he do the job for the Giants?

Righetti is perhaps the worst example of the recent tendency to stamp certain pitchers as "proven closers", and having so endowed them with special properties, exalting their abilities and excusing their failures. He hasn't had an ERA below 3.00 for four years, and for a relief pitcher coming in in the middle of the inning most of the time that really ain't very damn good. Craig Lefferts has a better record, but the Giants will pay Righetti a hell of a lot of money to try to do what they wouldn't give Lefferts the opportunity to do a year ago for half as much money or less.

Whether Righetti will be effective in San Francisco, all indications are that he might pitch better here than New York.

1. The Yankees don't help *anybody* reach their maximum performance level.
2. Roger Craig has a good record working with pitchers, although the press has at times made more of this than the record justifies.
3. Righetti pitched only 53 innings last year. I wonder if that is enough to keep him sharp, or if perhaps the practice of protecting Righetti with setup relievers hasn't run amok, and left Righetti with fewer innings than he needs to throw to remain sharp. Righetti faced only 235 batters in 1990.

Jose RIJO, Cincinnati
Can he win twenty this year?

He's about ready to do that. His stuff is as good as anybody's. He pitched only 197 innings last year, which was a career high, his career having been broken up by injuries and stinkbombs. He's been highly effective for three years now, and he's still getting better.

Ernest RILES, Oakland A's
Will he bounce back? Will he help the A's?

Riles was one of the best reserve infielders in baseball for several years before 1990, and his 1990 season wasn't as bad as you might think at first. He hit just .200, but homered more often (per at bat) than Eddie Murray or Andre Dawson, and also had almost as many walks as hits. He's becoming the Ken Phelps of middle infielders.

If you watch Riles in batting practice he pulls *everything* right down the first base line. I watched him in batting practice a half hour one day and I swear he never hit a ball the shortstop or third baseman would have fielded, and only a few the second baseman would have gotten to. Of course in a game you can't do that, so I don't know what's the use of it.

As to whether he will help the A's, he should. If Lansford continues to slip,

Riles could wind up playing quite a bit at third base.

Billy RIPKEN, Baltimore
Did he finally learn to hit? Is 1990 for real?

It probably is *not* for real, no. He's a lifetime .253 hitter; that's probably about what he'll hit. He is young enough that the improvement could be real, but it would be rare.

This Ripken is a terrific defensive player, a better second baseman than his brother is a shortstop. Having maintained regular status for two years when he *wasn't* hitting, he probably can play forever with a .250 batting average.

Cal RIPKEN, Baltimore
Should he have won the Gold Glove?

Give me a break. He shouldn't even be at shortstop anymore. Just because the Baltimore official scorers have decided that Ripken is incapable of committing an error does not mean that the rest of us have to take them seriously.

Should he take a rest?

There are two questions to consider about Cal Ripken's streak, which are the question of probability and that of wisdom. *Can* he, and *should* he?

As to the question of whether he *can* break Lou Gehrig's record, I have for several years estimated his chances of breaking the record by assuming

a. that his chance of getting through next year without being forced out of the lineup was about 80%, and
b. that this would decrease slightly in the following years.

By this logic, it has been apparent for several years that the record *could* be broken. Sportswriters and people like Chuck Tanner will often say that the record is unbreakable, because the players of today don't have the desire and determination to stay in the lineup like they did in Gehrig's day. This is an obviously fatuous argument, because it assumes that Lou Gehrig was typical of his generation—obviously he was not—and that the player who would threaten his record would have an attitude which was typical of our generation. We're dealing with individuals, not prevailing norms.

What *I* have argued is that the record, while it represents a monumental accomplishment, was somewhat vulnerable precisely because it was within the domain of determination. Human beings have very distinct limits in terms of physical capacity, but are capable of amazing feats of endurance and determination. No matter how we develop ourselves, we cannot learn to fly like a bird, nor run like a cheetah, nor punch like a gorilla; we simply are not capable of it. But people *can* learn to run thirty miles without stopping, swim long distances or do three thousand situps. If you can do one, you can learn to do three thousand if you want to badly enough.

Anyway, I would now estimate that Ripken's chance of beating Gehrig's record of 2,130 consecutive games played is about one in three, about 33%.

As to whether he *should* stay in the lineup . . . well, as anyone can tell you, I am stronger on probability than wisdom. It is hard for me to see how this stunt is helping the team. Ripken's records are exceptional for their consistency: every year he's a little bit worse than he was the year before. While other players in his age group are still setting career highs, Ripken every year sets several career lows—his worst batting average, his worst slugging percentage, his lowest range factor at shortstop. The reality is, although I hate to say it, that at this point Ripken just isn't that good a ballplayer. He's a .250 hitter with no speed and not a lot of power.

I don't believe in making demi-Gods of ballplayers. I don't believe in setting some ballplayers aside and making special rules for them. Robin Yount takes a day off or two every year, and in recent years he has played almost the best ball of his career. Eddie Murray takes off a couple of days a year, and he's several years older than Ripken, and he's playing great. Ripken's playing every game, and it's not working, but he keeps on doing it.

I don't get it.

Kevin RITZ, Detroit
Can he pitch?

His control, which was suspect anyway, disappeared completely in 1990. There is no other reason he can't pitch in the major leagues, but unless his control returns as inexplicably as it departed his chance of having a career is slim.

Luis RIVERA, Boston
Does it make sense to play Rivera, rather than Marty Barrett?

Not to me. See article on Marty Barrett.

Will he be replaced by Naehring?

Of course. Nobody but Joe Morgan thought he could play, anyway. *Nobody* is going to look at the two of them and choose Rivera.

Bip ROBERTS, San Diego
Where should he play? Should he be the regular third baseman?

It is not uncommon to see a major league player who hits well but can't find a position on defense. It *is* uncommon, however, when a player hits well, runs well and is a quick, agile athlete and can't find a position on defense. Roberts is the odd case where that happens. With a .300 batting average two years in a row, 46 stolen bases and a better-than-average strikeout to walk ratio, Roberts is one of the best leadoff men in the National League.

But in 1989 he was the only major league player to start games at six positions, and last year he played four positions—611 innings in left field, 400 innings at third base, 121 innings at shortstop, and 65 innings at second base. This probably isn't very good for his career. The Padres' moves this winter could be read to mean that he will wind up anywhere. The trade of Alomar could mean he will play second, but then Pagliarulo is also gone, which could mean he will play third, and the Padres traded a big outfielder (Carter) without getting one in return, which could mean that he will play left or center.

With some misgivings, I would put Roberts at second base. First, I would be reluctant to put him in left field, because left field is one of the positions at which players who hit for power are relatively available. The Padres already have one of the three top power positions (right field) occupied by a singles hitter. To have two of the top three occupied by singles hitters would make it difficult to construct an offense with a sufficient power center.

Second, I would not want to play him either at third base or in center field, because I don't think he has the arm for either position.

Third, his position in the minor leagues was second base. That's what he was trained to do. That's probably where he should play.

Note: Roberts hit .401 on artificial turf last year (39 games).

Billy ROBIDOUX, Boston
Can he play? Why do they keep giving him chances?

Robidoux is a square, heavy player, turrible slow and with no defensive position, so there is pressure on him to hit. He has failed to hit in the major leagues, but mostly in very quick looks—.182 in 44 at bats in 1990, .128 in 39 at bats in 1989, etc. His MLEs suggest that he eventually would hit in the major leagues, but he is probably out of chances to prove it. He is another example of the curious reluctance of American League teams to take a young player who can hit and make him a career designated hitter.

Don ROBINSON, San Francisco
How long is he going to last?

I'd be surprised if he lasts two more years. Robinson has battled his way back from rotator cuff surgery to have four straight years with winning records (11-7, 10-5, 12-11, 10-7), but his ERA has shot through the roof in the last two years, and his strikeout rate has declined sharply.

After September first last year Robinson had a 10.29 ERA and gave up 43 hits in 21 innings, which is clearly a sign that either a) something is seriously wrong with him, or b) he was very tired, and needed to get the season over. Either way, I suspect he is getting near the end.

Jeff D. ROBINSON, New York Yankees
How the hell do you tell these two guys apart? How can anyone remember which Robinson is which?

Maybe we could think of this one as Jeff, Dee Reliever. Although both Jeff Robinsons are right-handed pitchers, Jeff Dee Reliever over the last two years has been tougher on left-handers. Right-handers hit 53 points higher against him in 1989, and 46 points higher in 1990. This could be giving him an edge in his battle to stay in the league, because it would mean that people were pinch hitting left-handers against him and hurting themselves.

Even so, Robinson is fighting for his professional life. In 1987 and 1988 he appeared to be inches away from breaking through as a relief ace. In those two years he pitched 156 games, the most of any major league pitcher, with an ERA below three, a winning record and about seven strikeouts per nine innings. In the last two years he has been used a little as a starter, ineffectively, has a won-lost record of 10-19 and an ERA around four, striking out around five men per game.

Jeff M. ROBINSON, Detroit
Was his 1988 season an anomaly? Will he never have another good year?

I doubt that he will ever have another good year. His strikeout/walk ratio last year was 76/79, about the same in 1989. I don't think you can win with a strikeout/walk ratio like that unless you're a groundball pitcher, which Robinson is not.

Ron ROBINSON, Milwaukee
Can he sustain the success he had in 1990?

This is a companion article to the Steve Searcy piece, which if you haven't read you should go read now, or read it as soon as you finish this comment if you want to make sense of what I'm saying.

Battling his way back from elbow operations from 1987 through 1989, Robinson won 14 games last year, including a 12-5 record for the Brewers in 22 starts. On the other hand, he struck out only 71 men, a very low total for a pitcher with 14 wins. If it is logical that pitchers who have a very high ratio of strikeouts to wins in one year would tend to improve dramatically in the next year, wouldn't it also seem logical that pitchers who had a very *low* ratio of strikeouts to wins in any season would tend to decline in the next season? When I went back to the base year 1987 to see which pitchers had the highest ratios, I also looked for the pitchers with the lowest ratios.

In 1987 there were sixteen major league pitchers with ten or more starts who had a ratio of less than eight strikeouts for each win. Of those sixteen pitchers, *all sixteen* had worse won-lost records in 1988 than they had had in 1987. In the aggregate, they declined from 185 wins and a .636 winning percentage to 126 wins and a .490 winning percentage. Interestingly, only a couple of the sixteen pitchers were really poor the next season. They were mostly just a little less effective than they had been.

I didn't do a 1988 sample for this side

of the study, but in 1989 there were thirty-four major league pitchers with less than eight strikeouts per win (don't ask me why there were twice as many as in 1987.) Of these thirty-four pitchers, six did improve their records in 1990. Still, twenty-seven of the thirty-four pitchers declined in 1990, with one pitcher (Dave Stewart) posting a record which was not identical, but which was considered as being of the same quality.

As a group, the thirty-four pitchers who had ratios of less than eight strikeouts per win in 1989 won 408 games with a .590 winning percentage. In 1990 they won 262 games with a .501 winning percentage. Again, most of the pitchers in this group, with the exception of those with ratios lower than five to one, did not decline precipitously.

The record of those with ratios lower than five strikeouts per win is truly awful. In 1987 there were only two of these— Tommy John, who declined in 1988 from 13-6 to 9-8, and Lee Guetterman, who declined from 11-4 to 1-2.

In 1989 there were seven pitchers who had less than five strikeouts per win. All seven drove off a cliff in 1990.

Storm Davis, who was 19-7 in 1989 with 91 strikeouts (4.8 strikeouts per win), dropped to 7-10.

Dave Schmidt, who won ten games with 46 strikeouts (4.6), dropped to 3-3 last year.

Jerry Reuss, who was 9-9 with 40 strikeouts in 1989 (4.4), had no decisions in 1990.

Don August, who was 12-12 in 1989 with 51 strikeouts (4.3), was winless in three decisions last year.

Allan Anderson, who was 17-10 in 1989 with 69 strikeouts (4.1), dropped to 7-18 last year.

Jeff Ballard, who was 18-8 with 62 strikeouts (3.4), dropped to 2-11.

Tom Filer, who was 7-3 with 20 strikeouts (2.9), dropped to 2-3.

As a group, the nine pitchers who had ratios of less than five strikeouts per win in 1987 or 1989 dropped from 115-72, a .615 percentage, to 31-58, a .348 percentage. On the *average*, they dropped from 14-9 to 4-7.

So then, there is *no* doubt that a low ratio of strikeouts to wins does indicate a pitcher who cannot sustain his performance in terms of wins and losses. Who are the pitchers that we should stay away from for 1991?

I used a cutoff here of 7.5 to 1. There were twenty-six major league pitchers in 1990 who had ratios of less than 7.5 strikeouts per win. In all likelihood, at least twenty of these pitchers will be *less* effective in 1991 than they were in 1990:

Pitcher	W-L.	SO	Ratio
Kevin Brown	12-10	88	7.3-1
Dan Petry	10-9	73	7.3-1
Gullickson	10-14	73	7.3-1
John Mitchell	6-6	43	7.2-1
Dennis Cook	9-4	64	7.1-1
Dave Stieb	18-6	125	6.9-1
Jimmie Key	13-7	88	6.8-1
Scott Garrelts	12-11	80	6.7-1
Scott Erickson	8-4	53	6.6-1
Tom Browning	15-9	99	6.6-1
Greg Hibbard	14-9	92	6.6-1
Kirk McCaskill	12-11	78	6.5-1
Tom Bolton	10-5	65	6.5-1
Mike LaCoss	6-4	39	6.5-1
Curt Young	9-6	56	6.2-1
Doug Drabek	22-6	131	6.0-1
Eric King	12-4	70	5.8-1
Neal Heaton	12-9	68	5.7-1
Mark Knudson	10-9	56	5.6-1
Mike Moore	13-15	73	5.5-1
John Cerutti	9-9	49	5.4-1
John Tudor	12-4	63	5.3-1
Dave Johnson	13-9	68	5.2-1
Ron Robinson	14-7	71	5.1-1
Bob Tewksbury	10-9	50	5.0-1
Bob Welch	27-6	127	4.7-1

I listed this comment with Ron Robinson, because that's where it seems most germane. Bob Welch has a ratio of 4.7 to 1, but then, nobody in his right mind expects Welch to go 27-6 again, anyway. Tweksbury is at 5 to 1, but probably not that much is expected of him, either, and you never know, he might fool us.

But Robinson—he went 14-7 last year, 12-5 after coming over to the American League, and a lot of people are going to look at that and figure with 35 starts, he could have a big year. I don't think it's likely. I think he's a lot more likely to go 12-14.

There are quite a few people on this list that I *wouldn't* encourage you to avoid. Dave Stieb is on the list, but he's high on the list, where the declines are moderate. He was 18-6 last year; if he declines to 16-10, that's no big deal. Same with Browning, Hibbard, Drabek and Jimmy Key; they can *decline,* and still help you. They probably will.

But the guys between Drabek and Tewksbury—I'd be very leery of drafting any of those. As a group, they went 95-66 last year. They'll be 55-68 next year. If you knew the stock market was going to go down that much next year, would you buy stocks?

Mike ROCHFORD, Boston
Who is he?

Big left-hander, Grade D prospect. Rochford and Bolton had been "paired" by the Red Sox for several years, both regarded as good minor-league pitchers who we hope will be major leaguers someday. Rochford began the season on the Red Sox roster, pitched a couple of times, was sent to Pawtucket, where he had been for years. He pitched nine times for Pawtucket (and pitched well), and was sold by Pawtucket to the Yakult Swallows in Japan, where he pitched poorly (0-3, 8.61 ERA). The success of Bolton, in a sense, squeezed Rochford out of the picture, but as recently as the spring of 1990 the Red Sox liked Rochford better than Bolton, so there must be something there.

Rich RODRIGUEZ, San Diego
Who is he? Is he as good as his 1990 stats?

Rodriguez is a left-hander with a deceptive motion; I saw him pitch several times at Wichita in '89. At the time he wasn't regarded as much of a prospect, but here he is in the majors just a year later.

He won't continue to pitch the way he did last year (2.83 ERA in 32 games). I just don't think he has anything that would make him that effective.

Rick RODRIGUEZ, San Francisco
Why does he keep getting trials when he doesn't get anybody out?

He's probably out of trials; I just put him in here to tell you not to confuse him with Rich Rodriguez. This is the guy who pitched with Oakland a few years ago. He's had four trials, with ERAs of 6.61, 2.96, 7.09 and 8.10. With Oakland in '87 it was 2.96, but even then the league hit about .330 against him and he walked 15 in 24 innings, but somehow escaped without giving up runs. He can't pitch.

Rosario RODRIGUEZ, Pittsburgh
Who is he? Can he pitch?

21-year-old left-hander, claimed from Cincinnati in the winter draft. He's a young guy with a great arm who hasn't yet got any idea of the strike zone. As I understand it the Pirates will have to keep him on the roster, but he's probably a couple of years away from being ready to contribute.

Mike ROESLER, Pittsburgh
Who is he?

Right-handed veteran minor league reliever, Grade D prospect if that. Extremely unlikely to have a career.

Kenny ROGERS, Texas
Will he be the Rangers' closer this season?

In 1989 Rogers was the Rangers' left-handed spot reliever, and very effective in the role. With the injury to Jeff Russell he had to become the relief ace, and wasn't brilliant. He had eight blown saves in 29 chances, a poor percentage. This may be unfair to him because early in the year he was coming into the game in the seventh inning, and at least a couple of times he blew the save but got the win when he stopped the other team at a tie.

Still, he wasn't terrific. He was very effective against left-handers, very ordinary against right-handers. I suspect that if Russell isn't able to do the job the Rangers will look for somebody else, maybe Jim Poole, and fall back on Rogers if they don't find anybody better.

David ROHDE,
Houston

Can he fill Bill Doran's shoes?

Rohde, a 26-year-old middle infielder (27 in May) was regarded as the player most likely to take Doran's place when Doran was traded to Cincinnati in late August. He didn't play very well, and at season's end the Astros were talking more about Eric Yelding or even Casey Candaele as the new second baseman.

Rohde, despite a .184 batting average last year, is probably a better hitter than Yielding and a better defensive second baseman than Candaele. If it was my team, I'd play Rohde at second.

Mel ROJAS, Montreal
Who is he?

Right-handed pitcher, a starter in the minors but a reliever last year with Montreal. 24 years old, a little on the small side, Grade C prospect.

Ed ROMERO, Detroit
Will he be back?

Probably not. He was 32 years old last year, and played only a little for one of the worst teams in the league. He is not on the mid-winter roster.

Kevin ROMINE, Boston
What's his role? Will he ever move up?

He turns thirty in May, so he is beyond time of moving up, even if he plays well. He's a good defensive outfielder who has hit around .270 the last two years, which is enough to keep you around.

Romine is the kind of player who may be endangered by the salary structure. Last year he was two-plus (not eligible to arbitrate) and earned $260,000. This year he's three-plus and will earn somewhere in the fours, probably; next year, if he has a good year in 1991, he'll be over half a million as a part-time player. Then let's say he has an off year, and hits .209 in 120 at bats, which could happen to Willie Mays if he was used the way Romine is used. What's the team going to do? They're going to see a $400,000 gap between what they would have to pay Romine and what they would have to pay a rookie to do the same job—and they're likely to gamble on the rookie.

Rolando ROOMES, Montreal
Can he help a major league team?

Sure. Roomes didn't do a bad job for Cincinnati in 1989—.263 average, a little power and a little speed. He's not Lou Piniella's kind of player, and Piniella didn't know him, so it was natural for Piniella to replace his marginal players, like his fourth outfielder, with players of his own choosing. Roomes will swing at anything that doesn't hit him first, but in the right park for the right manager he could be a solid spare outfielder.

Victor ROSARIO, Atlanta
Who is he?

24-year-old shortstop, came to Atlanta as the player to be named in the Dale Murphy trade. He's kind of a poor man's Rafael Ramirez, won't get a shot unless Blauser makes about seventy errors and doesn't hit.

Bobby ROSE, California
Could he start at third this season?

Bobby Rose has a future. Rose is a third baseman, and the Angels are unhappy with their third base arrangement, Howell and Schu backed by Anderson and Donnie Hill. Rose may win the third base job out of spring training. My guess is that as a regular he would hit in the .250s or .260s with some power—enough to keep him in the job. He's only 24.

Steve ROSENBERG,
Chicago White Sox

Will he be back in the majors this year?

Probably not. The White Sox aren't crying for pitchers and he hasn't done anything impressive to earn another look. The trades of Hillegas and Barry Jones help his chances.

Mark ROSS, Pittsburgh
Will he make the Pirate roster this spring?

Ross is a journeyman/fringe player. He has had six major league trials, beginning with the Astros in 1982, with a total of 42 innings. He pitched well in nine games with the Pirates late last year, but is unlikely to survive the inevitable numbers crunch at the end of spring training. He could re-appear in June, once the injuries hit.

Rick ROWLAND, Detroit
Who is he?

24-year-old catcher, reached AAA last year. I believe he will hit enough to be a major league regular, but he has only half a season of AAA and the Tigers' number one catcher is a right-handed hitter coming off one of his best seasons. I expect Rowland to wait a year before he gets a major league job.

Bruce RUFFIN, Philadelphia
Will he ever get it turned around?

Of course not. We've seen enough; hell, we've seen too much. Since going

9-4 (2.46 ERA) as a rookie he has a major league record of 29-47. His ERA has gone up every year of his career; his winning percentage has gone down every year except one time it held steady at .375. What do *you* think the trend is? Where do *you* think he's going?

Note: Did you know that Ruffin didn't throw to first base all last year? Not once. To show you how unusual this is, Greg Maddux, who is one of the pitchers who throws to first *least* often per baserunner, still threw to first 91 times during the course of the season. The leader among pitchers who pitched at least 162 innings was Jose DeLeon, who threw to first only 13 times. But Ruffin never threw over at all.

Scott RUSKIN, Montreal
Who is he?

Left-handed relief pitcher, converted outfielder. He spent three years in the Pirate system as an outfielder, switched to pitching in 1989 and worked his way through the minors in one year. In 67 games last year with Pittsburgh and Montreal he had a 2.75 ERA.

Can he become the Expos' closer if Burke doesn't come back?

He could, but it might be pushing your luck. He gave up 75 hits in 75 innings last year, not the ratio you are looking for in a closer.

In the long run, I like him a lot. His years in the outfield kept his arm from being abused until it was mature. Several pitchers have had Hall of Fame or near-Hall of Fame careers after taking up pitching at an advanced age, so that's not a big problem. You have to like the fact that he can succeed in the majors with so little experience. I just think it would be rushing him a little to make him a closer at this point. (With the acquisition of Barry Jones there appears to be no chance of this, anyway.)

Jeff RUSSELL, Texas
Will he bounce back?

Russell pitched poorly in the early part of the season, and underwent surgery to remove bone chips and a bone spur from his right elbow on May 30. Dr. James Andrews announced that the surgery was a success, but then, did you ever hear of a doctor announcing that the operation was a failure? He didn't pitch again until mid-September.

Instinctively, I doubt that he can come back all the way. I don't know why, but Russell has always reminded me of Jim Kern, the scrambled reliever who had a monster year for Texas in 1979, one of the best years ever by a reliever. Kern hurt himself early in 1980. He hung on for six years but was never effective again, and I doubt that Russell will be, either. He did pitch well in September, however.

John RUSSELL, Texas

No questions about him. Russell, a catcher who can't throw and strikes out a lot, hit .273 last year. With that average and the Rangers' need for catching he'll be back on the roster, and nobody thinks he'll ever be a regular. Don't bet on him to hit .273 again.

Nolan RYAN, Texas
Is he a Hall of Famer?
Of course; don't be silly.

How many men will he strike out before he retires?

I have said this too many times already in different forms, but a pitcher's strikeout rate is the best indicator of how long he will last. If you take a 35-year-old pitcher with seven strikeouts a game and a 25-year-old pitcher with four strikeouts a game, same won-lost record and ERA, it is extremely likely that the 35-year-old will still be around and pitching after the 25-year-old is gone.

There are other things which you can use to build a "power index" or whatever. You can also consider walks per nine innings and hits per nine innings. These things don't indicate simply how hard the man throws, but also how much he knows about what he is doing, his ability to change speeds, etc. Sid Fernandez, for example, has a very high power index although he doesn't throw exceptionally hard because he changes speeds extremely well and has a deceptive motion, not that I would want to bet on Sid to last a long time.

However you figured a "power index," and I don't have a formula for it, Ryan would be off the charts. He is the most extreme power pitcher in baseball history, and it is thus to be expected that he would have lasted a long time.

Power index always declines as a player ages. It goes up for two or three years after a pitcher enters the league, and then begins to decline. I don't know of any case in the history of baseball where this hasn't happened, although once in a while there may be a sharp uptick in mid-career because of recovery from an injury, shifting roles, learning a new pitch or some other factor.

The decline in power index has certainly happened to Ryan, although at a significantly slower rate than normal. At age 25 he struck out 10.4 men per nine innings, walked 5.0 and allowed 5.3 hits. Last year he struck out fewer (10.2), walked many fewer (3.3) and allowed more hits (6.0). But his power index was so high then that even after eighteen years of decline, it remains the highest in baseball. Incidentally, Ryan had the best strikeout to walk ratio of his career last year, 3.14 to 1; the previous years when he was over 3-1 were 1987 and 1989.

What I am saying is that all pitchers are skiing down a slope. How long it will take any one pitcher to reach the bottom depends on how high up the slope he is. Nolan Ryan is, at 43, still higher up on the slope than anybody else in baseball.

Does that mean he is still going to be pitching when he is 50? Probably not, but it does mean that I would hate to bet against it. People ask me on the radio how long I think Nolan Ryan can pitch. When he turned forty I started using a joke answer: I don't think he can possibly last more than another ten years or so. It's less of a joke now than it was three years ago.

In 1986 Dr. Frank Jobe examined Ryan's elbow, and announced that it was hanging by a thread. He said then that Ryan needed immediate elbow surgery, but Ryan refused to have the surgery, and decided to pitch some more no-hitters instead. So far, Dr. Jobe's medical opinion looks pretty inane, but who knows? In two years the tendon may suddenly snap.

There are other ways that this could end. Ryan could drift into ineffectiveness, post a couple of 9-13 records and decide that he's seen all the hotel rooms he can take. But if you want me to say that Nolan Ryan *can't* strike out 6,000 men or 7,000 or even 8,000, I'm not going to say it. Ryan is a one of a kind, an absolutely unique historical figure. Common sense tells us to let him find his own limits.

Will his strikeout record ever be broken?

I can't imagine it being broken in my lifetime. There are two things to note:

1. Because more batters are using whip-handled bats, strikeout rates are still going up. They went down for several years, in the mid-seventies, but they're going back up now, have been for several years.
2. Despite reports to the contrary, more pitchers than ever are having long careers.

These things could make the record vulnerable. Certainly we will see other pitchers strike out 4,000 men and more. Still, Ryan combines two features which make it difficult to imagine anyone catching him:

1. He is the most extreme power pitcher in baseball history, and
2. He has had exceptional durability over time.

Also, he pitched 320 innings a year in his prime, which managers (wisely) are unwilling to risk now. I just don't believe that we are likely to see anyone else who has this *combination* of attributes.

My basic belief is that all records are more vulnerable than you think they are. But Ryan's strikeout record, I think, would be much, much more difficult to break than Aaron's home run record, Rose's hit record or Joe DiMaggio's hit streak. It may be more difficult to break than Cy Young's win record. It's going to be around awhile.

Is there some systematic way to determine that?

Well, yes, now that you mention it, I do have a method. What I do is to look at what a normal league-leading figure is in a performance category, and then look at the all-time record in terms of how many seasons worth of league-leading performance it represents. For example, since the all-time record for his is 4,256 and a normal league-leading hit total in our time is 212, Pete Rose's hit record represents twenty seasons worth of league-leading performance—twenty times 212 is 4,240.

Normal league-leading figures change dramatically over time; in the 1950s you could lead the league in stolen bases with 30. As these norms change, records become more vulnerable or less vulnerable.

I have always believed that if a record represented *less than* 18 years worth of league-leading performance, then that record was vulnerable. If the record represents *more than* 21 years of league-leading performance, then the record is, for now, not in any danger.

I looked up the all-time career records in fourteen categories—runs, hits, dou-

bles, triples, home runs, RBI, walks, batter's strikeouts, stolen bases, wins, innings pitched, complete games, pitcher's strikeouts and saves. Then I figured the normal league-leading total in each of these categories from 1985 through 1990, and put the two together to see how vulnerable the current record is.

Two of the category records are ridiculously vulnerable, those being the career record for saves, which represents only a little more than eight seasons worth of league-leading performance, and the career record for stolen bases, which represents eleven seasons of league-leading performance, a typical league-leading figure being 84. The stolen base record, of course, will be broken in April, and the career save record, 341 by Rollie Fingers, will probably be broken by Jeff Reardon and several other active pitchers.

Other than those, three records are somewhat vulnerable, those being Reggie Jackson's career record for batter's strikeouts, which represents 15.8 seasons of league-leading performance, Tris Speaker's record for doubles (17.6) and Henry Aaron's home run record (17.8 seasons).

The most *in*vulnerable of these records, by far, is Cy Young's record of 750 complete games, which represents just short of fifty seasons of league-leading performance, the normal league-leading figure being 15.1. Following that are Cy Young's record for innings pitched, 7,356, which represents 27.1 seasons of modern league-leading performance, and Cy Young's record for wins, 511, which represents 22.8 seasons of league-leading performance.

Ryan's strikeout record represents 20.9 seasons of league-leading performance, just short of the "safe" level of 21. This, however, fails to consider two things:

1. that Ryan is still active and still building his total, and

2. that Ryan himself is still leading the league in strikeouts almost every year, so the "normal league-leading performance" is based not on what other people do, but to a large degree on what Ryan himself does.

The record clearly should be considered safe—not safe for all time, perhaps, but safe for now.

Notes: Ryan at 42 still led the league in all kinds of things, some of which you may have missed. He led the league in fewest hits/nine innings (6.04) by a margin of more than one full hit per game. He held opponents to the lowest batting average of any major league starter (.188), allowed the fewest baserunners per nine innings in the American League (9.62), held right-handers to a .158 batting average (the lowest in the majors by 36 points), got the leadoff man out 77% of the time (best in the league), and held opponents to a .157 batting average when there was a runner in scoring position, the best in baseball.

I have a "game score" system which sums up a pitcher's game line. It's intended to be a zero-to-a-hundred scale, but it is theoretically possible to break a hundred, and every five years or so a pitcher will. In a typical season the best game by any major league starting pitcher will score at 96 to 98.

The top three game scores in the majors last year were by Nolan Ryan on August 17th (101), Nolan Ryan on April 26 (99) and Nolan Ryan on June 11 (99). Erik Hanson also had a 99, actually. These are the game lines:

Date	IP	H	R	ER	BB	SO	Game Score
8-17	10	3	0	0	0	15	101
4-26	9	1	0	0	2	16	99
6-11	9	0	0	0	2	14	99

•S•

Bret SABERHAGEN, Kansas City

Is he due for a good year? This being an odd-numbered year, is he going to go 22-7 or something?

Saberhagen now has a career record of 61-22 in odd-numbered years, but 36-48 in even-numbered years.

I didn't believe in that stuff a year ago, and I don't believe in it now. Most phenomena which can be put on a graph will show the graph going up/down/up/down much of the time. This is true of pitchers' records as it is true of the stock market, the price of gold and the ratio of girls to boys at your local McDonald's.

Sometimes that up/down pattern will be so regular and so forceful that it will draw attention, and seem to embody some profound truth but it doesn't. It's just a natural phenomenon, emphasized by random chance.

Saberhagen will probably be good this year because

a. he's a very good pitcher, and
b. the injury shouldn't have any lingering effects.

Chris SABO, Cincinnati

Is his power surge for real? Can he hit 25 home runs again? Is he one of the best third basemen in the league?

Sabo probably will have *some* ongoing increase in power. He hit 16 homers the first three months last year, only 9 the second three—but even nine homers in half a season is more than he has hit in the past. I would expect him to hit fifteen to twenty home runs this year.

Sabo is probably the fourth-best third baseman in the National League, an evaluation which, oddly enough, probably won't change whether he hits ten homers this year or twenty. If Matt Williams proves that what he did in 1990 is for real, which I think we all believe it is,

then Williams is the best third baseman in the National League. Tim Wallach and Howard Johnson, if he stays at third, are also better players than Sabo. But Sabo would rank *well* ahead of anyone else in the league.

Mark SALAS, Detroit

Can he help a team?

When a player bats only one hundred or two hundred times a season, you can't place any faith in his stats in that season. You have to evaluate him by his career performance norms.

Salas has a lifetime batting average of .254, with a slugging percentage of .399. Those figures are normal for a catcher, actually a little above normal (the average slugging percentage for a catcher is around .375). His strikeout to walk ratio is decent, and he's not any slower than the average catcher.

Salas is not a good defensive catcher, and for that reason can't be a regular. But as a second-string or third-string catcher, to play against right-handed pitchers when the opposition can't run or in the day game following a night game, Salas is a solid player.

Luis SALAZAR, Chicago Cubs

Should he be a regular? Would he be useful in a more limited role?

He would be a *good* bench player, but it's a disgrace to have him in the lineup on a regular basis. He's a good bench player because

1. he can hit left-handed pitching,
2. he runs well enough to pinch-run if needed, and
3. he can play the infield or outfield, which gives his manager some maneuverability.

Also, he is well-liked, said to be a good guy in the clubhouse. But he's a terrible player for an everyday third baseman because

1. he can't hit right-handers,
2. his strikeout/walk ratio is terrible, and
3. he's not a *good* defensive player at any position.

On balance, he doesn't put enough runs on the scoreboard to justify a regular job if he was a good third baseman, and he's not a good third baseman.

Roger SALKELD, Seattle
Who is he?

20-year-old right-handed pitcher, regarded as the top prospect in the Seattle system. He's big (6-5, 215) and throws very hard, 94 MPH. He is said to be a classic power pitcher with a textbook delivery, and struck out 167 men in 153 innings in the Eastern League. Grade A prospect.

Bill SAMPEN, Montreal
Could he move into the Expos' rotation?

Sampen, a 12th-round draft pick of the Pirates in 1985, was picked by the Expos in the winter draft a year ago, and had to spend the season on the Expos' roster. To the surprise of everyone he pitched well, pitching 59 times with a 12-7 record and a 2.99 ERA, and actually led the Expos in wins. He was used by Rodgers mostly when the Expos were a run or two behind in the middle innings.

With the departure of Kevin Gross the Expos will need another starting pitcher, but there are other candidates, and probably better candidates, to do that job. The Expos' rotation will probably be Martinez, Boyd, Gardner, Nabholz and Brian Barnes, with the possibility of Scott Anderson, Kevin Bearse, Ruskin and/or another reclamation project crashing in there somewhere.

Sampen, however, should move up in the bullpen, ahead of Schmidt, who had thirteen saves but was hammered, as well as Mohorcic and Rojas. He may get some saves, but the Expo bullpen is still very deep.

Juan SAMUEL, Los Angeles
What do you do with him?

Juan Samuel has become a cornerstone of my philosophy. Looking around me, I see Juan Samuels everywhere. Walter Matthau, for example, is a Juan Samuel: He's a great actor, but *what do you do with him?* He's not a leading man, obviously. His persona doesn't have the depth or resonance that would enable him to play, let's say, the Henry Fonda part in *On Golden Pond* or the part of Sam in *Avalon*. He's a character actor, but it's hard to cast him in a minor role because

a. he's a star, or was a star,
b. one generally prefers that character actors not carry in such a strong identity that it becomes hard for them to get lost in the part, and
c. he'll start doing Walter Matthau schtick, and it gets in the way of the story.

So he's a great actor, but he winds up in generally awful movies because *what can you do with him?* Nothing. Or there's this woman I know—a very pretty young woman, extremely bright and well-organized, but *what do you do with her?* She's not like somebody you would marry, because for one thing you'd never know who she was sleeping with. She's not somebody you can just be friends with, because she's not capable of dropping the flirtatious front. She's not somebody you would want to be in business with, because she has this compulsion to mind everybody else's business as well as her own. So she's a great woman and I really do like her, but *what the hell do you do with her?* She's a Juan Samuel.

Juan Samuels have *obvious attributes* but a collection of *varied liabilities* which prevent them from fitting in wherever you put them. Juan Samuel can run, but he doesn't get on base enough to bat leadoff. Juan Samuel has power, but not enough power to hit cleanup or third. Juan Samuel hits well for a second baseman, but isn't a good second baseman. Look around; you'll find people like that all over your life.

Izzy (Zip) SANCHEZ, Kansas City
Can he pitch?

Sanchez, signed as a teen-ager, made steady progress through the Royals system for years, finally emerging as one of the top pitching prospects in the organization in 1988. He suffered a devastating ankle injury in the spring of 1989, and hasn't yet gotten back where he was. He's a six-year free agent, and thought to be leaving the organization.

I think Sanchez eventually will have at least one good season in the major leagues. His strengths—quickness around the mound, good control and an average fastball—are enough to provide the basis of a career. His weaknesses basically amount to the fact that he hasn't been able to get his feet on the ground in the major leagues. I've never been able to see any reason that he couldn't pitch.

Ryne SANDBERG, Chicago Cubs
Where does he rank among all-time second basemen? Could he be the greatest second baseman of all time?

With his magnificent 1990 season, Ryne Sandberg has to be considered a serious candidate for the position as the greatest second baseman of all time.

Let's deal with the negative stuff first:

1. Sandberg is *not* as good a hitter as his basic hitting stats would suggest. Wrigley Field is a great hitter's park, despite what the people who play there will tell you, and it does inflate Sandberg's stats, and make them look better than they are. In his career he has hit 40% more home runs in Wrigley Field than on the road, meaning

that his power totals are inflated by twenty percent, and you can see his home/road breakdowns for 1990 in Section II.

2. Although Sandberg wins the Gold Glove every year, I've never been convinced that he didn't win it at least a little bit with his bat. I think Jose Oquendo and Jose Lind are every bit as good as Sandberg defensively, and maybe a little better.

None of that disqualifies Sandberg from being considered the greatest second baseman of all time. The three greatest second basemen of all time are Joe Morgan, Eddie Collins and Rogers Hornsby. Compared to Morgan, Sandberg is comparable but much more durable. Compared to Collins, Sandberg has much more power. Compared to Hornsby, Sandberg is a much better defensive second baseman.

No player is perfect, but Sandberg ranks with Willie Mays as the closest thing I have ever seen to a perfect player. Let's list the basic things we evaluate a second baseman on:

1. *Offense*
   a. Hitting for average
   b. Hitting for power
   c. Strike zone judgment
   d. Speed and baserunning
   e. Bat Control
2. *Defense*
   a. Range
   b. Arm
   c. Reliability
   d. Ability to turn the double play
3. *Overall*
   a. Durability
   b. Consistency
   c. Judgment

Where's his weakness? None. He is the only major league player who, if evaluated in this way, wouldn't show at least one weakness. Well, Will Clark maybe, but Clark doesn't play a key defensive position.

There are other things that one looks at, such as contributions to a winning team. Eddie Collins and Joe Morgan led many teams into the World Series, but they also played for great teams. Sandberg has led two teams with serious shortcomings to division titles. Which is more impressive?

Sandberg needs to play another thousand games or so before we can really know what to do with him. If he has a few more seasons like 1984, 1985 and 1990 there will be no doubt: he'll go to the top of the list.

Should Sandberg have been the MVP in 1990?

Not in my opinion, no. Sandberg and Bonds' numbers, taken at face value, are of essentially the same worth—actually, Bonds' are a little bit better. Sandberg has an additional value, in that he plays second base, but he also has an additional quibble, in that he plays in Wrigley Field, which makes him look like a better hitter than he is. I trade the two off, and that makes them even. Bonds, though not a second baseman, is a wonderful defensive left fielder. Bonds led his team to the division title; Sandberg's team did not contend. Sandberg has won an MVP Award before, when his team won the division. Sandberg's an all-time great, but 1990 was Barry Bonds' year.

Deion SANDERS
What's the big deal about this guy?

I see the Sanders fiasco as symptomatic of the problems of a despotic ownership.

Steinbrenner was obsessed with publicity, as measured in quantity.

Steinbrenner saw the tremendous publicity generated by Bo Jackson.

Steinbrenner determined to re-create this on his own team.

Deion Sanders gave the appearance of being a major league player, but on closer examination turned out not to be.

The basic elements of the Bo phenomenon simply were not there. Bo has a mystique; Deion Sanders has trinkets. Bo can play major league baseball; Sanders cannot.

Steinbrenner, refusing to recognize that his plan wasn't working, forced it ahead just as if it were.

If Sanders would go to the minor leagues and put in his time, he probably could be a good major league player. Unless he does that, he won't.

Steinbrenner's determination to make Sanders a star reinforced Sanders' inherent arrogance, and thus insured that he would fail as a major league player.

Scott SANDERSON,
Oakland or New York
Can he pitch more than 200 innings again?

Sanderson's 3.88 ERA last year in the Oakland Coliseum is not nearly as impressive as his 3.94 ERA the year before in Wrigley Field, but his season was better because, for the first time in eight years, he was able to stay healthy and stay in the rotation all year. This is naturally interpreted as a tribute to Tony LaRussa and Dave Duncan's judgment and attention to detail, that they were able to monitor Sanderson's workload in such a way as to keep him healthy. One's intuitive logic is that if they did that last year, there is no reason why they can't do it again. If he winds up in New York, the Yankees had better keep a spot on the DL warm for him.

Andres SANTANA,
San Francisco
Who is he?

Shortstop prospect, expected to take Jose Uribe's job in a year or two. He was the number one prospect in the Giants' organization until he broke his fibula (leg) on April 25, 1989. He came back last year at Shreveport (AA) to hit .292 with 31 stolen bases. My belief is that he will be a major league player, and a good one.

Benito SANTIAGO, San Diego
Did his injury cost the Padres the division?

No, it did not; that's just an excuse. Santiago's injury cost the Padres only two or three games; the Padres finished sixteen games behind.

- Santiago was hurt on June 14; on that date the Padres were already in trouble, with a record of 30-28, seven games behind Cincinnati (36-20).
- The Padres played poorly while Santiago was out (21-31), and dropped an additional five and a half games behind Cincinnati—but a great many things went wrong during that period of time, other than just Santiago's injury.
- The Padres didn't play much better after Santiago returned (24-28), and dropped an additional three and a half games behind.

Is he the best catcher in the National League?

Definitely.

In baseball?

Probably, but you can still make an argument for Fisk or Parrish.

Note: Santiago hit .433 last year in the late innings of close games (29 for 67). This was the highest average in baseball. The only other National Leaguer over .400 was Randy Ready, who hit .407.

Nelson SANTOVENIA, Montreal
Is his job safe? Will the Expos give up on him?

He'll probably keep about the same share of the job. Santovenia may have suffered from the misguided belief that he was a young star. He's 29, just a year younger than Mike Fitzgerald, four years old than Benito Santiago. He's got no

star potential, probably didn't a year ago, but he's a good defensive catcher and has some power.

Mackey SASSER, New York Mets
Is he the Mets' catcher? Will he have any competition this season?

Sasser's "competition" comes not from his competition, but from his own apparent shortcomings, which are probably not going to go away. With a .292 lifetime batting average through almost 250 games, Sasser has by now convinced the Mets that his one legitimate strength—his ability to hit for average—isn't going to disappear with more playing time. He still has a secondary average below .200 (no power, speed *or* walks) and he still isn't Johnny Bench behind the plate.

The Mets paid a fair price to get Charlie O'Brien, and will probably play him some. Todd Hundley will get a look if he hits anything at Tidewater. My guess is that Sasser isn't going to bat more than 400–425 times, but will hit .285–.300.

Jack SAVAGE, Minnesota
Who is he?

Right-handed pitcher; no prospect.

Steve SAX, New York Yankees
Is he still a valuable player?

Sax had his best year as a base stealer last year, stealing 43 in 52 tries (83%). Unless Sax hits somewhere near .300 he *isn't* a good leadoff man. Because there are a lot of good-hitting second basemen around now, Sax last year was *less* productive with the bat than the average major league second baseman. He is a very under-rated defensive second baseman, and obviously in a good year he hits more than the average pivot man.

Jeff SCHAEFER, Seattle
Who is he?

Journeyman infielder, now thirty years old. He's supposed to be a brilliant short-

stop, but as an offensive player he makes Alvaro Espinoza look like Rod Carew. He may or may not stay on the Seattle roster.

Dan SCHATZEDER, Kansas City Royals
Will he help the Royals?

The Royals needed a left-handed spot reliever and he may fill the bill, but signing Schatzeder was a stupid and pathetic move. First, the Royals had announced just days earlier that they were going to get away from going out and purchasing veteran ballplayers, and get back to building from within—then they signed Schatzeder, a fourteen-year veteran who has pitched for everybody in both leagues.

Second, left-handed spot reliever is the one position at which talent is *most* available. How many times have I said in these pages that "here's another candidate for the job of left-handed spot reliever, neither better nor worse qualified than most of the others." There's a hundred guys like that, and here's another one—yet the Royals signed him to a good salary based on a 2.20 ERA in the Astrodome.

Third, he has *no* history of consistent success—a 4.45 ERA in 1989, 6.49 in '88, 5.31 in '87.

So what kind of sense does it make to wait until somebody in this group of guys has a good year, and then pay him $700,-000 to see if he can repeat it? None. The Royals simply don't believe anymore in their ability to spot talent or develop talent, so they try to buy talent.

Curt SCHILLING, Baltimore
Is he ready to start for the Orioles?

Schilling, a starter in the minor leagues, had a 2.54 ERA in 35 relief appearances as a rookie.

The Orioles have three sure starters—Ben McDonald, Dave Johnson and Pete Harnisch. They'll choose their other two starters from among Milacki, Mitchell, Ballard, Telford and Curt Schilling.

Schilling is the dark horse, but he would be high on my list, within that group. The rap on him is that he has only two pitches, a fastball about 89 MPH and a good slider. He needs a third pitch, but he's young. He was a successful starter in the minors; he pitched well in the majors last year.

The Orioles have two proven right-handers in the bullpen, Olson and Williamson. The third right-hander in the bullpen has limited value. I'm not saying it will do Schilling any harm to let him spend a full season in middle relief, but I'd want to make sure he stayed on track to be a starter.

Calvin SCHIRALDI, San Diego
Does he have any value?

I may be dead wrong, but I think that Schiraldi has a chance to be one of those pitchers who has his best years in his thirties, and I wouldn't rule out his chance of being the Mike Scott of the 1990s, Mike Scott being a pitcher who struggled through his twenties and became outstanding at age thirty.

Schiraldi has carried the burden of being a potential star. He was a college teammate of Roger Clemens at Texas, and he and Clemens were thought to be about even coming out of college. Both were first-round draft picks, Clemens being the 19th player taken, Schiraldi the 27th. In 1986, when Clemens took the league by storm, Schiraldi joined him in August and was equally dominant for two months, posting a 1.41 ERA and a fearsome strikeout to walk ratio.

Schiraldi pitched well in the playoffs and early part of the World Series, but flopped in the sixth and seventh games of the World Series, and has never recovered from that. Since then he has battled both the stigma of the 1986 World Series failure, and the perception that he had the ability to be outstanding.

But it's been four years now, and all

that has to be wearing out, doesn't it? Nobody thinks that he's going to be a superstar anymore. People have forgotten about '86, not Schiraldi but most other people. It's OK for him just to be another pitcher now. I still think he could thrive in that role.

Note: This is Schiraldi's career. He got hot last summer as a reliever. In a string of 14 relief appearances in June and early July he had more than a strike-out an inning and an ERA below 1.00. The Padres had a double-header so they needed a starter, and Schiraldi filled in and was OK, winning the game.

Well, you know what happened. They made a spot for him in the starting rotation, and he got his liver beat out for two months, ruining his season. As a starter he was 1-5 with a 5.40 ERA, overpowering decent numbers in relief. For the year the batting average against him was .253 for his first 45 pitches, but .291 after that.

Schiraldi needs a *manager*. He needs a Tony LaRussa or Buck Rodgers, somebody who knows better than to pitch him in relief for half a season, and then see if they can push him into a starting role in August. That's another thing he hasn't had yet.

Dave SCHMIDT, Montreal
Where does he go from here?

Schmidt is entering the difficult years at the end of his career. Schmidt was a marginal prospect who caught a couple of breaks and turned it into a career, but after a 5.69 ERA as a starter in 1989 he tried relief last year, and the league hit .301 against him. There are a hundred pitchers trapped in AAA that I'd rather have on my roster.

★ ★ ★
Dick SCHOFIELD, California
★ ★ ★
Where's he rank? Should he keep his job? Should the Angels look for somebody else?

Over his last 55 games last year Schofield hit .312 (53 for 170), and also drew

31 walks in there, giving him an on-base percentage well over .400. I saw him play during that period, and I was quite impressed. Schofield was using a heavy bat, waiting for a good pitch and slapping at the ball. He looked nothing at all like he has looked over the years.

I am on record as being extremely skeptical about whether anyone can learn to hit in the major leagues. If Schofield were to suddenly become a .300 hitter, this would be almost without historical precedent, so certainly I would not predict that.

But I *do* believe that Schofield is going to have his best major league season in 1991.

Mike SCHOOLER, Seattle
How good is he?

He's been awfully good for two years, but I would be concerned about whether he'll be able to stay healthy. I've already run down the pecking order among American League relief pitchers a couple of times (see "Bryan Harvey" and "Gregg Olson") so I won't do that again, but Schooler is near the top. He had 30 saves in 34 opportunities last year, the third-best percentage among major league relief pitchers, (behind Eckersley and Righetti, but ahead of Thigpen, Olson, Henke, Franco, Randy Myers and Lee Smith. Thigpen blew eight saves.) He's only been healthy for one full season and has never pitched for a good team, but if he's healthy he'll have some good years.

Schooler's season ended on August 24, when he suffered a shoulder injury. He tried to throw on the sidelines September 13, but it still hurt. He was told to wait until next year. The party line is that his injury was due to a lack of strength in the shoulder, and he is on an exercise program this winter to strengthen the muscles in the shoulder.

Don't sound too great, does it?

Bill SCHROEDER, California
Could he play regularly? Could he play more?

He's a weak defensive catcher who strikes out about a third of the time. He has real good power, but nothing else to recommend him.

Rick SCHU, California
Was last season representative of his abilities?

After struggling through the first two months of the season with a .214 average Schu hit almost .300 the last four months, and finished at .268 in a limited role. Schu could probably play regularly if he could maintain his 1990 batting and slugging percentages (.433 slugging), but unfortunately those were his best in four years.

Schu's been tried by four teams now, but it's kind of curious that he's never really been looked at as a platoon player. In 1989 he hit a hundred points better against left-handers (.261 to .161), but split his at bats between the two. Last year he again split his at bats and hit for about the same average each way, but all the power was against left-handers, a slugging percentage near .500.

There are a lot of teams with third base problems right now—as many teams as have problems at any position.

Q: *What do you do if you can't find a regular at a position?*
A: Try to build a platoon combination.

Schu's an OK defensive player who can hit left-handers. You'd think that would get him a job.

Jeff SCHULZ, Kansas City
Who is he?

Right fielder, minor league veteran regarded as strong defensively but suspect as a hitter. Schulz was a high school teammate of Don Mattingly, and after entering baseball hit .300 in Rookie ball (.327 at Butte, 1983), A ball (.336 at Charleston and .314 at Fort Myers,

1984), AA ball (.305 at Memphis, 1985) and AAA (.303 at Omaha, 1986.)

Rather than calling up Schulz, however, the Royals traded for Danny Tartabull and sent Schulz back to Omaha, where he stopped hitting. He's been at Omaha ever since, and is still trying to prove he could play in the major leagues.

Mike SCHWABE, Detroit
Is he a major league pitcher?

He could fill a role in middle relief. Schwabe is a big right-hander with amazing control, walks consistently less than two men per game in the minor leagues. He isn't a hot prospect, but he's got a chance.

Mike SCIOSCIA, Los Angeles
Why's he hitting for more power now? How long will he last?

The mystery about Scioscia is not why he is hitting for power now, but why he *didn't* hit for any power for so many years. He's a horse. Having learned to pull the ball occasionally, he may well be able to increase those occasions in the next few years, and may hit as many as twenty homers.

A catcher normally begins to burn out after catching 1200–1400 games. Scioscia is nearing that level. Although we have had some notable exceptions to this rule in recent years, it would be wrong to conclude that the general rule no longer applies. In fact, most of the best catchers of recent years—Gary Carter, Terry Kennedy, Tony Pena, Darrell Porter, Jim Sundberg—*have* burned out in the normal time frame. Some, like Fisk and Boone, have been able to escape that by training exceptionally hard, but Scioscia certainly doesn't *look* like a man who takes training seriously. He looks fat.

Mixed forecast—possible continued increases in power, offset by probable decline onsetting within two or three years.

Mike SCOTT, Houston
Is his decline irrevocable, or can he come back?

1. The *most* comparable historical pitcher to Scott is Dazzy Vance, a Dodger of the twenties. Vance did have a couple of years like this and bounce back. In 1926, when he was 35, Vance went 9-10 with a 3.89 ERA, but he came back two years later to go 22-10 with a 2.09 ERA.
2. Scott's strikeout totals have declined with unusual regularity. In 1986 he struck out 306, in 1987, 223, in 1988, 190, in 1989, 172, and in 1990, 121.

  Many pitchers are quite effective with the kind of strikeout/walk data that Scott had last year—but if he doesn't stop that erosion, obviously he's not going to come back.
3. Scott's ERA last year was 5.04 in the first two months of the year (11 starts), 3.48 the middle two months (also 11 starts), and 3.00 the last two months (10 starts.)
4. Scott's offensive support in 1990 was very poor.
5. Scott had a scope on his right shoulder in December to shave some loose cartilage.
6. Whereas in the past Scott has been supported by a very good bullpen, he may not be in 1991.

There are a couple of things you ought to check out in the data section—his home/road split, and his stolen bases allowed/caught stealing. He is perhaps the easiest pitcher in baseball to run on.

I haven't given you a clear answer here, have I? In my opinion, Scott may come back somewhat as a starter—maybe to 14-11 or something—but probably won't again be a top-flight pitcher except possibly as a reliever.

Scott SCUDDER, Cincinnati
Is he ready to pitch in the majors?

Over the last three years Scudder has a minor league record of 27-6. He was 7-3 with Cedar Rapids in 1988, 7-0 with Chattanooga the same year, 6-2 with Nashville in 1989 and 7-1 with Nashville in 1990. This doesn't leave much doubt about his ability to win in AAA, so there's no point in sending him back there.

The problem is that, at least as much as I can see, he's probably never going to do much as a major league pitcher. He's young (23) and has a 90 MPH fastball, which is a good start. He doesn't have any kind of a breaking pitch, he doesn't change speeds effectively and he's lucky to hit the plate, never mind hitting spots. He doesn't field his position particularly well, and he is very easy to run on. It's an ugly combination, and there are a lot of things that need work.

My guess is that Scudder will probably have a good year or two, somewhere along the road. I can't see any reason to believe that he will ever be a consistently good pitcher.

Rudy SEANEZ, Cleveland
What is he doing in the major leagues?

In 1989 Seanez walked 111 men in 113 innings of A ball, after which the Indians gave him one inning of AAA ball and brought him to the major leagues. It doesn't make any sense, and any of you reading this book would know better, but then since when did we start expecting the Indians to make sense? They'll probably let him fight his control for four years, and then get mad at him because he's not developing.

Ray SEARAGE,
Los Angeles (Released)

Searage was released by the Dodgers right after the Brooks/Ojeda trade, but I wouldn't bet that he won't be back with LA this year anyway. Searage will be 36 years old in May. After floundering for ten years he finally slipped into the slot as left-handed spot reliever for the Dodgers the last two years, and has pitched well. He seems to be doing a good-guy routine for the Dodgers, hiding on the disabled list whenever they don't feel that they need him for awhile. Based on his 2.78 ERA in 1990 (32 innings) he may receive an offer from somebody else.

★ ★ ★
Steve SEARCY, Detroit
★ ★ ★
Will he ever make it in the majors? What's the holdup?

In this section of the book I mark a few players, about twenty, with stars to indicate that they are good pickups in a rotisserie league, a fantasy league, or an APBA or Strat-O-Matic league where you keep players over the years.

In looking back at the players I tagged with stars last year, I was generally pleased with my picks among position players, but felt that I should have done better in picking pitchers. I'm not bragging about my record in picking players, because after all I recommended that you draft Nelson Liriano and Rob Richie (WHO?), nor am I apologizing for my picks with pitchers, because among the eleven pitchers I tagged were Erik Hanson and Ramon Martinez. The eleven pitchers that I named had a combined major league record of 47-48 in 1989, and improved to 93-83 last year. I felt that I should have done better than that.

In reviewing the selections and how they were made, I felt that I had made two fundamental errors in tagging pitchers:

1. I named too many rookies. Six of the eleven pitchers that I named were either rookies or near-rookies like Andy Benes. Since rookie pitchers rarely make much of an impact, that doesn't make any sense.
2. I had not been systematic in my approach. I had played too many hunches, just naming guys that I liked for some reason, rather than looking for systematic biases which would balance the odds in favor of the group.

This leads to the question, then, of how do you *systematically* identify a group of pitchers who figure to improve substantially in the next season?

Thinking about it, I decided that the simplest formula which should target pitchers who are due for improvement is strikeouts divided by wins. This simple formula should indicate pitchers who were likely to improve (or decline) because it combines three biases:

- the randomness of won-lost records. Won-lost records are very important, but not a truly reliable indicator of how well someone has pitched.
- the law of competitive balance.
- the power pitcher bias, which I've discussed many times in this section.

I stepped backward to 1987, and located a list of pitchers with the highest (and lowest) ratios of strikeouts to wins. I studied only pitchers with ten or more starts, since this eliminates relievers and flukey stats. My theory was that the pitchers with the highest ratios of strikeouts to wins in 1987 should pitch much better in 1988 than they had in 1987, and vice versa.

Well, it worked better than I would have believed. An extremely high ratio of strikeouts to wins proved to be 20 to 1, which we'll extend in a moment to 16 to 1. Looking at three years of data (1987, then 1988 and 1989) virtually one hundred percent of the pitchers who had strikeout/win ratios of 20 to 1 or greater posted better records in the following season than in the base year, and many of the improvements were dramatic.

In 1987 there were sixteen pitchers with extremely high ratios of strikeouts to wins. These pitchers had an aggregate 1987 record of 57 wins, 141 losses, a .288 percentage. In 1988 they improved to 117-96, a .549 percentage. They had twice as many wins, many fewer losses and a 261-point improvement in aggregate winning percentage.

In 1988 there were nine pitchers who were in this extreme group, with a combined base year (1988) won-lost record of 27-82, a .248 percentage. In 1989 they improved to 77-49, a .611 percentage.

In 1989 there were eight pitchers in the group, with a combined won-lost record of 20-77, a .206 percentage. In 1990 they improved to 29-29, or .500.

The only pitchers in the group who failed to improve their won-lost records were four pitchers who didn't pitch at all in the following season, and two pitchers who posted exactly the same won-lost records. Bobby Witt, 8-10 in 1987, was 8-10 again in 1988—*then* began to improve. Wes Gardner, 3-7 in 1989, was 3-7 again in 1990. With those exceptions, every pitcher in the study improved his won-lost record in the next season.

Many of the pitchers in the group showed dramatic rises, including several pitchers who were not young in the base year. Greg Swindell, 3-8 with 97 strikeouts in 1987—at the time his major league won-lost record was 8-10—won 18 games in 1988.

Jose Rijo, 2-7 with 67 strikeouts in 1987, won 13 games and led the NL in ERA in 1988.

Paul Kilgus, 2-7 with 42 strikeouts in 1987, was 12-15 in 1988.

Mark Birkbeck, 1-4 with 25 strikeouts in 1987, was 10-8 in 1988.

Nolan Ryan, 8-16 with 270 strikeouts in 1987, was 12-11 in 1988, although it is hardly fair to include him in this group.

Tim Leary, 3-11 with 61 strikeouts in 1987, was 17-11 in 1988.

Rick Honeycutt, 3-16 with 102 strikeouts in 1987, improved to 3-2 in 1988, and has retained his effectiveness.

Jay Tibbs, 4-15 with 82 strikeouts in 1988, was 5-0 in 1989.

Mike Moore, 9-15 with 182 strikeouts in 1988, was 19-11 in 1989.

John Dopson, 3-11 with 101 strikeouts in 1988, was 12-8 in 1989.

Joe Magrane, 5-9 with 100 strikeouts in 1988, was 18-9 in 1989.

Zane Smith, 1-13 with 93 strikeouts in 1988, was 12-9 in 1989.

Now, I'm not proposing this as an entire policy of how to spot pitchers who will improve dramatically in the next season. I am proposing it as AN indicator, to be used in combination with other types of knowledge.

Also, it would not be accurate to say that this method spotlights a group of pitchers who are going to be brilliant next year. What it does, actually, is spotlight a group of pitchers who were terrible last year, and who will be, as a group, somewhat above average next year.

Most people in rotisserie leagues, I would assume, go into the draft looking for a combination of safe picks and gambles, with each of you having his own idea about what the right ratio is. This method will not help you find the safe picks. It *will* help you find the good gambles, the guys you can pick up cheap who might have an impact.

I later expanded the concept to cover a broader range of strikeout/win ratios. If your ratio of strikeouts to wins is about 20-1, your chance of having a better year next year is about 85%. The chart below gives estimates like this for the whole spectrum:

Ratio	Chance of Improving
20-1	85%
18-1	80%
16-1	72%
14-1	60%
12-1	50%
10-1	45%
9-1	38%
8-1	33%
7-1	25%
6-1	20%
5-1	15%

Now, the list. The 1990 pitchers with very high ratios of strikeouts to wins were:

Pitcher	W-L	SO	Ratio
Greg Mathews	0-5	18	inf
Marty Clary	1-10	44	44 -1
Steve Searcy	2-7	66	33 -1
Jamie Moyer	2-6	58	29 -1
Steve Avery	3-11	75	25 -1
Jeff Ballard	2-11	50	25 -1
Steve Wilson	4-9	95	23.8-1
Jose DeLeon	7-19	164	23.4-1
Chuck Cary	6-12	134	22.3-1
Matt Young	8-18	176	22 -1
Jim Clancy	2-8	44	22 -1
Sid Fernandez	9-14	181	20.1-1
Mark Langston	10-17	195	19.5-1
Chris Bosio	4-9	76	19.5-1
Mark Gardner	7-9	135	19.3-1
Mark Gubicza	4-7	71	17.8-1
Nolan Ryan	13-9	232	17.8-1
Saberhagen	5-9	87	17.4-1
Roy Smith	5-10	87	17.4-1
Jim Deshaies	7-12	119	17 -1
Mike Walker	2-6	34	17 -1
David Cone	14-8	233	16.6-1
Rick Reuschel	3-6	49	16.3-1

Notes:

1. There are 23 pitchers on this list, with a 1990 aggregate record of 120-232, .341. History suggests that their 1991 aggregate record will be about 213-174.

2. On this particular list there are a large number of veteran pitchers who were having off years, like Langston, DeLeon and Sid Fernandez. That's not really the normal pattern; it's just what happened in this case.

3. These 23 pitchers can be sorted into four general groups, which are

the guys who probably won't even have jobs (4),
the guys who will probably be better but who cares (1),

the ones who were hurt and may still be (4), and

the guys we are really interested in (14).

Four guys on this list probably won't even be in the majors in 1991, those four being Mathews, Clary, Clancy and Walker.

Jeff Ballard will certainly be better in 1991 then he was in 1990, but after all, 3-7 is better than 2-11. I'm not sure that Ballard is a good draft pick.

Four guys on this list are established quality pitchers who were hurt—Bosio, Saberhagen, Gubicza and Reuschel. You will want to listen to the reports on them in March, and see if they're throwing OK, but even if they are they won't go real cheap.

That leaves the fourteen guys we are really interested in, who are Steve Searcy, Jamie Moyer, Steve Avery, Steve Wilson, Jose DeLeon, Chuck Cary, Matt Young, Sid Fernandez, Mark Langston, Mark Gardner, Nolan Ryan, Roy Smith, Jim Deshaies and David Cone. If you can pick up four or five of those guys—say, Steve Avery, Steve Wilson, Chuck Cary, Mark Gardner and Jim Deshaies—you will probably have at least one player who takes the league by storm in 1991.

Bob SEBRA, Milwaukee
Will he pitch in the majors?

The Brewers signed him as a free agent last summer, originally to send him to Denver. Pitching coach Ray Burris, however, watched him and decided that "he has a good fastball, probably one of the best curveballs on the club and a good change-up, so he has three pitches he can throw for strikes." Unfortunately, major league hitters could apparently hit all of them, and he was back in Denver very quickly.

David SEGUI, Baltimore
Will the Orioles find a spot for him?

Segui is an *extremely* good defensive first baseman, and a good line-drive hitter. He hit .336 at Rochester last year; my guess is that he could hit .300 or better in the major leagues, although he didn't in 40 games last year.

This may sound better than it is—a .300 hitter with great defense sounds like an All-Star, but he may not be. He has no power, and he's slow. The Orioles have a full-time first baseman, Milligan, and several candidates for the DH job—Sam Horn, Dwight Evans, Chris Hoiles, Leo Gomez. Still, what is likely to happen is that Segui will be wedged in at first base, with Milligan as the DH and both losing some playing time.

Kevin SEITZER, Kansas City
What's this stuff about Seitzer moving to second base . . . does that have any chance of working?

I am of two minds about the experiment of playing Kevin Seitzer at second. As an analyst I know that right-ward shifts along the defensive spectrum attempted in mid-career almost always fail, and in particular third-to-second attempts have an appalling record. There is something seductive about the idea in this case. Seitzer *looks* like a second baseman, more than a third baseman—narrow shoulders, spindly legs, the whole bit. His batting record looks like a second baseman's record. He hits like Steve Sax, loosely speaking.

Seitzer is a very under-rated defensive third baseman, in my opinion, but he looks awkward at third base because of an odd throwing motion. The motion looks more natural at second base than it does at third.

This is probably the logic of being too close to the situation. The Royals would like to move Seitzer to second because they could replace him at third easier than they could find a second

baseman. My official position is that moves of this nature fail the great majority of the time.

What's happened to his bat?

Seitzer hit 15 homers as a rookie, but that was 1987 when lots of people who don't hit homers were hitting homers. His batting average has dropped off, and I'll give you two theories about why:

1. *The Bo Jackson Theory.* Bo hates Seitzer, as is well known. Think about what this means. Bo is a pivotal figure on the Royals, a dominant figure. Even though he's really not all that good, everyone is always watching Bo, paying attention to him. He is also, in his own way, an extremely strong personality. It is possible that Seitzer has simply been intimidated by Jackson, and his self-confidence undermined because of that.

2. *The Fatigue Theory.* Seitzer plays almost every game, and might be better off if he didn't. Last year he hit .302 the first half the season, but .251 after July 1. In 1989 he hit .298 the first two months of the season, but dropped off to finish at .281. Maybe he simply shouldn't be batting 600 times a year.

Seitzer also became a born-again Christian in 1988, and hasn't hit .300 since. He is still an intense player, still takes an extra base whenever he can and goes into second base hard.

Mike SHARPERSON, Los Angeles
OK, what took them so long?

There are good players trapped in AAA—not a huge number of them, but some. Sharperson was one of them. He got a brief shot in Toronto at a time when the team was under pressure to win, and for no better reason than that he was the rookie, took the fall when the team didn't perform. He wound up back on the treadmill, and it took him until

1990 to get another shot. He's always been a good player.

Jeff SHAW, Cleveland
Is he ready to slide into the Tribe's rotation?

He's a joke. He can't pitch. There is no way in the world to explain why an organization would give up on Kevin Bearse, but invest nine starts in Jeff Shaw, except that the organization is run by old-time baseball men with the intellectual self-discipline of Pee Wee Herman.

Larry SHEETS, Detroit
Will he ever hit 31 home runs again? Will he ever hit 11 home runs again?

Sheets hit 31 homers in 1987, when he was 27 years old, so it's sort of a compound fluke—the 1987 lively ball, and the prime age for fluke years. If you leave that season out of his career he's about as good a hitter as Mark Salas, which isn't good enough to keep you in the league if you're a 236-pound designated hitter. He really should be released.

Gary SHEFFIELD, Milwaukee
Is he the next Dick Allen? Will he ever help the Brewers? Will he ever help anybody?

Sheffield is an extremely talented player, although his talents may not quite be in the Dick Allen class. At the age of 21 he hit .294 with 30 doubles, ten homers and 25 stolen bases. Given normal development from ages 21 to 27, Sheffield projects as one of the best players in baseball throughout the 1990s.

Frankly, I doubt that he'll ever help anybody, but I guess we'll see. Sheffield often says and does things which alienate the people around him, and while there is a natural tendency to ascribe this to immaturity, one should also consider the possibility that he's just a jerk.

Sheffield last summer said that on the Brewers the black guys have to earn everything they get, but all the white boys have to do is just show up and collect their paychecks. The odd thing is that he's at least eighty percent right. I have no idea whether the Brewers consider race in making silly decisions; racism is often hard to distinguish from ordinary mediocrity. But certainly it is true that the Brewer organization since 1983 has been overrun by mediocre white boys who just show up and collect their paychecks. What better description could you give of Rick Manning, Greg Brock, Rob Deer, Jim Gantner, Dale Sveum and Charlie O'Brien? None of them really *does* anything, but they keep their jobs forever.

Sheffield obviously has emotional problems. I hate to say it, but baseball isn't kind to people with emotional problems. People often imagine that playing baseball for a living must be an easy job, but it isn't. The pressure is incredible, the working conditions often difficult. Talented players with emotional problems rarely come around in that environment.

It's probably off the subject, but did you ever think about this: that psychology is the great failure of the twentieth century. Psychology, it seems to me, has made us all grand promises, which it has been manifestly unable to fulfill. We have placed in psychology the faith that our fathers placed in God, in country, in *doing what was right.* Psychology has largely supplanted the concepts of manhood and honor and eaten into literature and manners, but what has it done for us? We were all supposed to gain insight into ourselves, to understand why we are who we are and what we can do about it. We're more confused about who we are then we've ever been. "Criminal" psychology—remember that idea? It was going to teach us how to deal with criminals. Forty years later criminals are taking over the world, and we don't have any idea how to deal with them. Nobody can get through college without a class in developmental psychology—but tell me the truth: are we doing a great job with our children? If Educational Psychology is such a wonderful thing, how come our educational system is such a mess? We confess to psychologists what we used to confess to priests, but is their absolution worth any more?

I'm not suggesting that we should get rid of psychology, only that maybe we should begin to ask it to pay the rent. Anyway, back to baseball . . . when a young player exhibits the signs of emotional instability, don't bet on a handy psychologist to pull him out of it. It's probably a good idea just to stay away from him.

Note: STATS, Inc. produces two primary measures of clutch performance, which are hitting with runners in scoring position and batting in the late innings of close games. Sheffield was the *only American League* player who was among the *best* in the league in both areas. He hit .336 with men in scoring position, sixth-best in the league, and hit .397 in the late innings of close games, third-best in the league. One National League player, Len Dykstra, did comparably well.

John SHELBY, Detroit
Will he be in the majors?

Sure. If he didn't lose his job when he hit .183, why would he lose it when he hits .248?

Tim SHERRILL, St. Louis
Who is he?

Left-handed reliever, skipped AA and pitched for Louisville last year. He looks great; I think he'll help the Cardinals as a left-handed spot reliever.

Sherrill will probably join the Cardinals this year although he was *not* the relief ace for Louisville. This is another tiny little marker in the ever-growing development of the modern bullpen. Twenty years ago, relievers were failed starters, but for some time now relief pitchers have been groomed in the minors to play the role. Now, however, pitchers are being groomed in the minors to be *role players* in the bullpen—almost like grooming players in the minors to be pinch hitters or pinch runners. This is a very recent development.

(**Note:** This was written before the signing of Juan Agosto. Agosto's signing makes it less likely that Sherrill will open the season in the major leagues.)

Eric SHOW, Oakland
Can he come back? Is there room for him in the rotation?

If anyone other than Oakland had signed Show I would have written that he was a poor risk. Even though it's the A's and they have performed a Lazarus on Eckersley, Honeycutt, Stewart, Sanderson and others, I'm not convinced they can turn Show around. One has to figure that they saw something in Show that convinced them he could bounce back. They've done it a lot of times, and we have to respect that.

Terry SHUMPERT, Kansas City
Who is he?

Young second baseman, played some for the Royals because he started well at Omaha and the Royals were desperate. He hit .275 before damaging his thumb diving for a ball in infield drills.

I wouldn't be drafting him. It's extremely unlikely that he's really a .275 hitter—more likely that he'd hit .240. That may be optimistic. He never hit over .255 in the minors, not since he left Eugene in the Northwest League anyway. His strikeout/walk ratio in the majors was 17/2, and not too many .275 hitters have that kind of a ratio.

Also, the Royals are afraid that the injury is very serious, even career-threatening. He was sent to Omaha on a rehabilitational assignment, but didn't play well and re-injured the thumb. He is extremely fast, and looks good at second base.

Ruben SIERRA, Texas
What happened to his power?

Sierra was great last year; it's just that the expectations for him were so high. People think he should be an MVP candidate every year.

Sierra strained the ligaments in his left ankle on May 14 chasing his three-year-old girl, who had made a run for the escalator at a shopping mall. The injury ended his string of consecutive games at 325, and he hit just .184 for the month of May, whereas he hit over .300 in three of the other five months, no worse than .274 in any of them. He drove in 96 runs, hit 37 doubles and was nine for nine as a base stealer; like Will Clark (see Clark comment) he has become a sensational percentage base stealer, 35 for 41 over the last three years. His strikeout to walk ratio continues to improve every year. He was on a Hall of Fame path a year ago, and he's on a Hall of Fame path now.

Mike SIMMS, Houston
Who is he?

Young first baseman; he hit 39 homers at Asheville in 1987. In the right park I might take a liking to him. He's buried behind Glenn Davis in a league with no DH rule. The Astrodome will kill his power. He's young and probably not a bad player, but I wouldn't expect him to do anything in the majors in the next two or three years.

Matt SINATRO, Seattle
Is this guy still hanging around?

Hanging around and hit .300 in fifty at bats last year. He might be like Jamie Quirk—a decent defensive catcher who can hit some pitchers if his manager can find them. The Mariners are talking about using Scott Bradley at positions other than catcher this year, which may help Sinatro stay in the majors. He'll probably be on a roster, but I wouldn't bet on him to bat a hundred times or hit .300 again.

Joel SKINNER, Cleveland
How long can he last as Alomar's backup?

As a number one catcher Skinner was a washout, but as a backup he's above average. His defense is good, and he is pushing his lifetime batting average up a little. It would help if he was left-handed so he could spell Alomar *and* get the platoon advantage.

Don SLAUGHT, Pittsburgh
How do he and LaValliere rank among recent catching platoons?

It's probably too early to rank them based on one season, but the Pirates' catching was among the best in the majors last year. Slaught and LaValliere hit .277 with 33 doubles, 7 homers, 71 walks and good defense. Neither player was way over his head.

Should Slaught, who hit .300, get more playing time?

No. Slaught's not a .300 hitter, although he is a good hitter; their career batting averages are about the same. LaValliere is a better defensive catcher. Platooning them makes sense.

John SMILEY, Pittsburgh
Will he bounce back?

He should. Smiley's injury (he slammed his pitching hand in a taxi door on May 19) shouldn't effect his ability to pitch. He returned from the injury in early July and did not pitch well the rest of the year (3.35 ERA before the accident, 5.21 after) but that's probably due to being out of sync. I don't see any reason he wouldn't be back this year.

Bryn SMITH, St. Louis
Is he too old, or might the Cards still get a return on their investment?

He also should be able to bounce back. Smith pitched very well the first two months of the season, but got hit through June and July. In late July he went on the disabled list with a sore shoulder.

He pitched very well in September, after his return. He's still a good pitcher.

Daryl SMITH, Kansas City
Who is he?

Minor league veteran, thirty years old, has been with several organizations. He pitched well at Omaha (6-2, 3.09 ERA) while the Royals' pitching staff was struck by serial injuries, so he got a few innings.

Dave SMITH, Chicago Cubs
Will he help the Cubs?

Smith moves from the best pitcher's park in baseball, the Astrodome, to the worst. His ERA has got to jump, in all likelihood, by at least a run. Smith has been the most consistent relief pitcher in baseball, and despite his age and weight there is no sign that he is losing his effectiveness—but don't bet on him to have a 2.39 ERA in Wrigley Field.

What would you all think of a rule requiring a pitcher to pitch one full inning to get credited with a save? Would you go for that? In 1986 Smith pitched just 56 innings in 54 games, but was credited with 33 saves. At the time I thought this was an extraordinary ratio, but as time passes it becomes more and more ordinary. Thigpen had a higher ratio last year, with more innings. It's almost becoming a farce.

There is an article under Bobby Thigpen's name on where this will all lead if we don't change the rules, but let's think about this: *should we?* Maybe the save rule just needs a little fine-tuning. What about this:

A pitcher should be credited with a save whenever he finishes a win for another pitcher and meets any of the following conditions:

1. He pitches one-third of an inning with the potential tying run in scoring position,
2. He pitches two-thirds of an inning with the potential tying run on base.

3. He pitches one full inning with the potential tying run at the plate.
4. He pitches *more* than one inning with the potential tying run on base, at the plate or on deck, or
5. He pitches the last three innings.

A pitcher cannot make himself eligible for a save by putting runners on base. The save situation must exist when he enters the game.

The notion that a relief pitcher who pitches three innings needs to be designated as "pitching effectively" by the official scorer—that's a dead letter anyway. It's in the rules, but as a practical matter it has been several years since a relief pitcher pitched three innings and was denied a save because the official scorer thought he wasn't effective enough.

How many saves would this take away from Thigpen? I haven't studied it; my guess is about fifteen. This rule would just force a pitcher to earn a save a little bit more, and thus control the explosion in save totals.

The down side is, think how long it would take the public to understand this. The save rule hasn't changed in more than a decade, but the one thing that radio talk show hosts are asked most often is to define the save rule.

Dwight SMITH, Chicago Cubs
Will he play?

With the signing of George Bell, Smith is out of a job, and will probably be traded. He's a perfect example of the kind of player American League teams *should* be looking for to be a designated hitter—a young player who is a good hitter but has no defensive position. Smith has a batting average for his two seasons of .295, with some speed and some power. That's about his true level of ability, I think—but he's an awful outfielder, and consequently out of a job. You'd think an American League team would be after him, but for some reason they don't seem to want to do it.

Greg SMITH, Los Angeles
Why did the Dodgers want him?

One of the surprise trades of the winter was the Dodgers' trade of Jose Vizcaino, a bright long-term prospect, for Greg Smith. This is another sign that the Dodgers regard 1991 as a year that they can win, and don't want to leave any bullets in the warehouse. Vizcaino is a better prospect somewhere down the road, but Greg Smith is a much better player *right now.* The Dodgers want Greg Smith so that, if Samuel starts acting like Juan Samuel, they'll have a major league second baseman. If he has to play, Smith will hit .250–.270 with four or five stolen bases a month (25 to 30 a year). On the other hand, Vizcaino is only a year younger than Smith, so maybe it's just a case of the Dodger prospects being over-promoted.

Lee SMITH, St. Louis
Has he lost anything?

As much as you can tell, Smith is as effective now as he has ever been, despite his knees and his weight. He has struck out more than a man per inning every year since 1984, with improving control. He has pitched 62 to 69 games every year since 1983. My guess is he'll still be saving thirty games a year five years from now.

Lonnie SMITH, Atlanta
Should the Braves hang on to him?

Lonnie led the Braves in batting (.305) and on-base percentage (.384), despite which the Braves seem determined to trade him. He's not a great player even if he hits .305—a bad left fielder, not as fast as he used to be and makes mistakes on the bases. He hit .221 through the end of May, then saved his season by hitting .364 in June, .337 in July, .318 in August and .327 after September 1.

I suppose, to be honest, that if I were John Schuerholz I would be doing the same thing Schuerholz is doing—trying to trade Lonnie. A veteran ballplayer on a bad team is useful only if he helps the younger players in some way. Lonnie doesn't have that reputation, so he's just using up at bats that the Braves need to find the next Dave Justice.

Michael SMITH, Baltimore
This is Texas Mike Smith. He got three innings in the big leagues; the other one didn't get any. He's a Grade D prospect. There's nothing that makes you think he's going to be a pitcher.

Ozzie SMITH, St. Louis
Is he still a good player? Should the Cardinals dump him while they can? Would anyone want him?
Ozzie is still one of the best shortstops in the National League. He started slowly with the bat last year and a lot of people wrote him off, but he came back strong the second half (.219 through the end of June, .285 after July first). Apparently his conflicts with Herzog were influencing his play to some degree. He won the Gold Glove, as always, and maybe still deserved it. He certainly is not the defensive player he was three years ago, but he still walks twice as often as he strikes out, and still steals thirty bases a year without being caught much. He rarely misses a game.

Pete SMITH, Atlanta
Is he healthy?
His injury, a tear to the rotator cuff, has a good chance of putting his career out of its misery. Smith really isn't a bad pitcher, but you'll never convince anybody of that. His won-lost record is ugly because he's been an unlucky pitcher on a bad team, and his ERA is ugly because of the park and defense, but if he was healthy on a good team, he could win.

Roy SMITH, Minnesota
Why did the Twins release him?
He didn't pitch well—4.81 ERA—and the Twins never did like him. He had to win almost a hundred games in the

minors and pitch well in several trials in the majors before they would give him a shot. He had a good year, then a bad year and he's gone.

He did get hit hard last year, allowing a .369 batting average to left-handed pitchers. .313 overall. I wouldn't be surprised if he were to bounce back strong with another team, perhaps in middle relief.

Zane SMITH, Pittsburgh
Did the Pirates give up too much?
It was a reasonable trade. I don't think Moises Alou is going to be a superstar. I doubt very much that he'll ever be as good as any of the three Pirate outfielders. Ruskin is a good prospect, but he is a prospect as opposed to a pitcher, and nearly as old as Smith.

Will he be a consistent winner for Pittsburgh?
I think he will be, yes. His 2.55 ERA last year is misleading because a lot of the runs he gave up were scored as unearned, but he's a ground-ball pitcher who throws fairly hard, changes speeds well and has good control, and that's a hell of a combination.

Smith is a member of the Tommy John family of pitchers. There were more double plays turned behind Smith last year (34) than behind any other major league pitcher. A peculiarity of the Tommy John family of pitchers is that they'll pitch .350 ball on a .400 team, but .650 ball on a .600 team. Put Smith on a good team, and he'll win.

John SMOLTZ, Atlanta
Where does he rank?
He's one of the best starting pitchers in the National League, and probably will remain so for many years if he isn't pushed too hard. In 1989 he was 12-11 with a team that lost 97 games, meaning that he was 141 points better than the rest of his team. Last year, while the team failed to improve, he moved up to 14-11,

188 points better than the rest of the team.

How many better starting pitchers are there in the National League? Well, there's Gooden, Viola, Cone, Ramon Martinez, Maddux and Drabek . . . I'd take those six guys over Smoltz, with some misgivings. There are three guys I *might* take ahead of him, those being Dennis Martinez, Bruce Hurst and Jose Rijo. I can't think of any others. Smoltz would appear to rank somewhere between seventh and tenth among NL starting pitchers.

Cory SNYDER, Chicago White Sox
Will he help the Sox? Did they give up too much for him? Why has his career gone into eclipse?
My initial reaction to the trade was that the White Sox had given up way too much for Snyder (Eric King and Shawn Hillegas). On reflection, I don't think it's such a bad trade:

1. Snyder is almost certain to hit more home runs for Chicago than he did for Cleveland, for two reasons:
   a. What goes down generally comes back up.
   b. Snyder in the last three years has hit almost twice as many home runs on the road (38) as in Cleveland (20). We're dealing with an unknown park here (new Comiskey) but it can't be much worse for him, and the odds are it will be better.
2. Snyder isn't a great player, but neither of the pitchers acquired by Cleveland is likely to be a great player, either.
   a. King has won 60% of his decisions, but his ERA isn't impressive, his strikeout/walk ratio is ordinary and he's never started more than 25 times in a season.
   b. Hillegas has yet to prove that he can pitch in the majors.

I wouldn't have made the trade just because I wouldn't want Cory Snyder, but he's more likely to have a big year than anybody else in the trade.

Snyder, once regarded as a coming star, spent 1990 embroiled in a battle with Cleveland batting coach Jose Morales. The courthouse gossip is that Snyder's father is his batting coach; he listens to what Daddy says, and no one else. His father doesn't really know anything about hitting, so this is sort of like asking Tammy Faye Bakker for makeup tips.

Note: You remember the concept of run element ratio? A player with a high run element ratio is a player who is much more valuable *early* in an inning than *late* in an inning; a player with a low run element ratio is the opposite. Both in 1990 and for his career as a whole, Snyder's run element ratio is the lowest of any major league player.

Luis SOJO, California
How good is he? Is he a Rookie of the Year candidate?

Sojo, acquired by the Angels in the White/Felix trade, is a second baseman. Let's assume that he plays regularly. How will he do?

He's not Ryne Sandberg, but he does look good. He should hit over .250, possibly as high as .285. His offense is in the traditional model of a second baseman—no power, not many walks, a little speed. Defensively, he's a converted shortstop—very good tools, good range but it may take him a couple of years to learn the mechanics of the double play. He's working with one of the best, in Schofield.

★★★
Paul SORRENTO, Minnesota
★★★
Will they find a spot for him this year?

Sorrento is a designated hitter/first baseman, a good hitter despite bad numbers so far. He drove in 112 runs for Orlando in 1989, then hit .302 with great power at Portland. He's 25, good sized but not huge, slow but not Lance Parrish. My best guess is that he will hit .250–.275 with more than twenty homers if he gets the playing time. Tom Kelly, God bless his patient little heart, is still talking about Randy Bush bouncing back, as if Randy Bush was ever more than a shrub. They should give Sorrento the job and let him run with it.

Sammy SOSA, Chicago White Sox
Is he still a potential superstar? How good is he going to be?

Sosa is probably a very good player to have on your team in 1991:

1. He is very young, and young players will sometimes show dramatic improvement in one season,
2. The White Sox are moving to a new park, which will probably give a break to all of their hitters, and particularly their right-handed hitters.
3. His 1990 season probably doesn't represent fully even his current offensive ability.

The acquisition of Snyder also gives the White Sox two terrific outfield arms, Snyder and Sosa.

Sosa has a chance to be very good, but you want to be careful. He has a lot of things in common with Juan Samuel. He has speed, but his on-base percentage is very low and he's really not a good baserunner, so his speed is of little offensive value. He has power, but not enough overall offense to hit in the middle of the lineup. The White Sox would be doing themselves a disservice if they promoted him as a star.

Bill SPIERS, Milwaukee
Will he hit enough to stay in the lineup?

Yes, because he's a good shortstop. The 1991 season will be the pivotal year of his career. If he's going to be a *good* player he's going to have to cork up his batting totals right now. If he doesn't he'll be Greg Gagne, a guy who keeps his regular job for three or four years and hits the bench as soon as he loses a step at short.

Steve SPRINGER, Cleveland
Who is he?

Thirty-year-old catcher, was a prospect with the Mets years ago. Springer has played more than a thousand games of minor league baseball, more than seven hundred games at AAA. He's regarded as having Grade D offensive skills, Grade C defensive skills—not quite enough to cut it.

Mike STANLEY, Texas
Where's he going? Is he ever going to be a regular?

Three years ago I thought Stanley was going to be an outstanding hitter. He didn't have a defensive position, however; he was a bad catcher and a worse third baseman. He couldn't get any playing time, got tied up and stopped hitting.

Stanley is now in the difficult process of coming to grips with the fact that he is not going to be a star. If he can do that, he can still be a very good bench player as a pinch hitter, DH and emergency defensive sub at several positions. He has 806 at bats and an unimpressive hitting record, but I still believe he's a better hitter than he has shown yet. He'll never be a regular.

Mike STANTON, Atlanta
How serious was the injury? Can he come back?

Stanton, a young reliever who looks like Joe Sambito, was being promoted a year ago as the Braves' relief ace. I liked him; I thought he'd be great. He was ineffective early in the year, and placed on the disabled list with an inflamed rotator cuff. He went to Greenville on a rehabilitational assignment, but had surgery on his left shoulder June 13 for a "torn labrum". Russ Nixon said that "losing him has been the biggest loss of all," meaning that his injury cost the Braves even more than the illness of Esasky.

In all likelihood, it will take Stanton two years to get back where he was.

Matt STARK, Chicago White Sox
Who is he?

26-year-old DH/Catcher. He was a first-round draft pick of the Blue Jays in 1983 and has always hit well in the minors, but didn't make any progress because of a couple of major injuries and the fact that the Blue Jays played him at catcher.

I don't know why they have him catching—it's one of those things that when you see him it makes you scratch your head and say "They want this guy to be a *catcher?*" He looks like a slightly-larger version of Bob Horner, if you can imagine Bob Horner in a face mask—blond hair, thick wrists, thick neck, thick waist. Other than being huge and slow, he doesn't look anything like a catcher. He also had surgery on his shoulder in the spring of '88.

But now the good news—he also reminds you of Bob Horner at the plate. The only thing quick about him is his bat. He only hit one double last year, and maybe I'm over-reacting, but it was impressive. He took a pitch that was by him down and in and slapped it about 370 feet. It wasn't something you see a lot.

Stark drove in 109 runs last year at Birmingham, in part because he was batting behind Frank Thomas, and Thomas had an on-base percentage around .500. Stark's MLEs show him hitting .287 with 14 homers, 88 RBI. That's projected into old Comiskey; he's going into what is probably a *better* hitter's park.

I think Stark is a hitter. I think he's as good a hitter as Ivan Calderon, maybe a little better. The White Sox have four outfielders right now (Snyder, Sosa, Raines and Lance Johnson), so one of them may be used at DH. I think Stark

is a better hitter than any of the four except Raines.

Terry STEINBACH, Oakland
Is he a championship quality player? Is he one of the best catchers in the league?

There are a lot of catchers in the American League who are roughly of the same quality—Steinbach, Surhoff, Macfarlane, Pena, Harper, Heath, probably Alomar and Borders. Some of them have more offense and some of them have more defense, some of them have more experience and some of them have more potential, but fundamentally there's not a lot of difference among them. Steinbach's right in the middle of the group, offensively and defensively.

Ray STEPHENS, St. Louis
Who is he?

Backup catcher from Louisville. 28 years old, no future. Like Steve Springer—could make a roster somewhere if a manager takes a liking to him.

Phil STEPHENSON, San Diego
Will he get another chance?

He should, but probably won't. Stephenson wasn't awful last year—a .209 average, but a .302 secondary average and good defense at first base. That's my definition of an under-rated player—low average, good secondary average, good defense.

He probably won't be in the majors, my guess is. He had an advantage last year in that he was backing up Jack Clark, who

a. is right-handed (Stephenson bats left),
b. gets hurt a lot, and
c. is kind of an oaf around first base.

They needed Stephenson. In '91 the Padres will have McGriff at first, who is left-handed, never gets hurt and isn't a bad first baseman. Stephenson's job has evaporated.

Also, the Padres had an off year. In

economics it is a truism that a recession always hits hardest on the poor and minorities. Last hired, first fired. In baseball there's a parallel rule: an off year always hits hardest on the marginal players. An off year doesn't hurt Joe Carter or Tony Gwynn; it just re-arranges their opportunities a little. It *hurts* Phil Stephenson. If the Padres had had a good year, they would see Phil Stephenson as having contributed to it. They had an off year, so they'll see Stephenson as having contributed to that.

Lee STEVENS, California
Can he play?

He has made some progress in the last year. My synopsis of Stevens a year ago was that "he would hit in the low .200s with 12-20 home run power, very poor K/W ratio, no speed and marginal defense." All of this proved to be precisely correct, but Stevens could hit somewhat better than he did as a rookie. He looks kind of like a left-handed Rob Deer, but he doesn't have quite as much power.

Dave STEWART, Oakland
Is he the best starting pitcher in baseball?

No, he isn't. See the Roger Clemens comment for argument.

Does he have any chance to get in the Hall of Fame?

Yes, he does, despite his late start. Twenty-win seasons are the basis of a Hall of Famer's career. A pitcher with not much more than 200 wins but several twenty-win seasons, like Bob Lemon or Catfish Hunter, will normally go in the Hall of Fame, while a pitcher with 250 wins but only one or two twenty-win seasons normally will have a long wait.

Stewart now has 59 Hall of Fame "points", if you understand that system, so he's not yet even in the gray area, which starts at 70. He will be in the gray area with one more year like the last four, though.

Will he win twenty again this year?

It's fifty-fifty. If you look up a group of pitchers who have had four straight twenty-win seasons—Spahn, Roberts, Jenkins, Palmer, Hunter, McNally, etc.—you'll find that about half of them made it five in a row, and half didn't.

My impression of Stewart, frankly, is that he is just hitting his stride. In '87 and '88, although he won twenty games, he would still fight his control from time to time. He doesn't any more; he makes it look easy. 1990 was probably his best year—but 1991 may be better.

Stewart's age isn't a factor, to me, because

a. he's not that old, and
b. he's in such great shape.

I doubt that the A's will be as dominant in '91 as they have been the last three years, but Stewart won twenty for them in 1987, when they were a .500 team.

Note: Remember that crazy balk rule in '88? Everything else in Stewart's record is perfectly consistent, but his balk totals in his four twenty-win seasons read zero, sixteen, zero, and zero.

Dave STIEB, Toronto
Where does he rank among the pitchers of his generation? Does he have a chance for Cooperstown? Could he win 300 games?

Dave Stieb is to this generation of pitchers exactly what Don Sutton was to the last generation. In Sutton's time there were the Grade A pitchers—Carlton, Palmer, Seaver, Hunter—and Sutton wasn't one of them. But he was the *best* of the pitchers who weren't on the cover of the magazine. He lasted. Randy Jones would be better one year and J.R. Richard would be better the next, but Sutton would always be there.

That's Stieb. He's not Clemens or Gooden or Stewart or Viola, but he's the best of the rest of them, him and Jack Morris.

Does he have a chance for the Hall of Fame?

Some, but not much. Stieb and Stewart are the same age and Stieb has a much better career record (166 wins as opposed to 123), but Stewart is much closer to the Hall of Fame, because he wins twenty. To make himself a serious Hall of Fame candidate Stieb would either have to win twenty a couple of times, or he would have to go on like he has until he's 40. Neither one of those is impossible.

Could he win 300?

He could, yes.

Stieb has 166 career wins. The last six pitchers to win 300 were Nolan Ryan, Sutton, Niekro, Carlton, Seaver and Gaylord Perry. At Stieb's age they had an average of 161 wins. Seaver, Carlton and Sutton were well ahead of him, but Ryan had 167 wins, Perry had 134 and Niekro had only 81.

I don't think he *will* win 300. It's an immensely difficult goal. Stieb's strikeout rate, 5.4 per game, is not high enough to suggest that he will last the roughly nine more years that he would need to last.

Kurt STILLWELL, Kansas City
Is he still developing? How good is he?

He's a Generic shortstop (Notice: This Shortstop may crumble on the field. He may display a slight inconsistency under certain conditions. This Shortstop is suitable for most ballclubs.) He is not developing in any way; he has stalled at the level of being almost an exactly average shortstop. In Kansas City he takes a lot of criticism for not being durable, which is misguided because

a. it's unfair to criticize people for getting hurt, and
b. he's more durable than most shortstops.

He misses some playing time, but then so do most middle infielders. He plays as much as Trammell or Schofield or Gagne or Uribe or Larkin or Walt Weiss or whoever; they all get hurt, except for a few guys like Ripken, Franco and Sandberg.

As an offensive player he hits .250, hits some doubles and doesn't drive you batty swinging at pitches over his head, but he's not a good hitter and not getting any better. As a defensive player he looks OK, not brilliant, but his range factors are very low.

Jeff STONE, Boston
Will he make a roster? Will he ever play in the majors again?

He'd make the Red Sox roster if it wasn't for his baserunning mistakes. He's very fast and not a bad hitter, so if he could pinch run as well as pinch hit and spell Burks as well as Greenwell, he'd have to make the roster ahead of Heep or Kutcher, maybe even Romine. But he can't pinch run because he leans the wrong way off first base, so he's very marginal.

Mel STOTTLEMYRE, Kansas City
Can he pitch?

It's almost impossible to evaluate his record because his usage has been so inconsistent. He's been used as a starter and reliever, switched from team to team and has missed large blocks of time with injuries, so his record is garbled.

I've seen him pitch, and he's not impressive. He does look like his Dad, and his Dad wasn't impressive, either. He's a Grade D prospect, but I'm not convinced that he can't be a major league pitcher.

Todd STOTTLEMYRE, Toronto
Does he have any business in the rotation?

None. He's had 67 starts in the last three years, and he's eight games under .500 with a 4.51 ERA. Last year he had a losing record although the Blue Jays scored 5.81 runs per nine innings in support of him, the best offensive support for any American League pitcher except Bob Welch. That's enough; it's time to pull the plug on him.

There used to be a saying in baseball that "a .500 pitcher will kill you in a pennant race." This was true at the time, but it isn't true now for three reasons:

1. There's more competitive balance. In the fifties you didn't win unless you played .600 ball; now you might win at .550.
2. In the fifties the starting pitchers were counted on to get the decisions. Now, more of the wins go to the bullpen.
3. In the fifties everybody used four starters; now they use five.

Think about it. In the fifties, you wanted four starters to be thirty games over .500, maybe 35 over. If one guy was at .500, that put a load on the other three starters.

But now, you want five starters to be fifteen games over .500. If one guy is at .500, that's nothing; everybody has one .500 pitcher. Even Oakland has a .500 pitcher in the rotation.

Under .500 though, that's another matter. Stottlemyre *loses*. He puts the other four guys in the hole. You can't have that on a contending team. The Blue Jays have shuffled their roster all winter to give them a better "chemistry", but they haven't done anything to improve the depth of their starting pitching, which is probably their biggest weakness.

Darryl STRAWBERRY, Los Angeles
How will he hit in Dodger Stadium? How will his loss effect the Mets?

1. When Strawberry signed, Tony Kubek was quoted as saying that Strawberry could hit 40 homers a year in LA. In fact, Strawberry has never

hit well in Dodger Stadium. We went through the box scores and figured his career batting record in LA. In 43 games, 178 at bats, he's hit .230 there with five homers, 21 RBI, a .343 slugging percentage. It is probably his poorest hitting record in any park.
2. Strawberry never hit great in Shea Stadium, so if Dodger Stadium isn't good for him, this won't be big news. The parks aren't greatly different. Both are pitchers' parks, fair for the home run but very tough on the batting average. Dodger Stadium is tougher.
3. A typical Darryl Strawberry season is .263 with 37 home runs. My guess is that in Dodger Stadium that will be more like .255 with 34 home runs.

How will his loss effect the Mets?

1. Darryl Strawberry is a great player.
2. The impact of a great player on the performance of the team as a whole is vastly less than people expect it to be.
3. Darryl Strawberry creates about 105 runs a year if he's healthy; Hubie Brooks creates about 80. That's a difference of 25 runs, or maybe three games.
4. Many pennant races are decided by less than three games.
5. Looking ahead at the season, one can project the Mets to perform within a certain range. If that range was 85 to 100 wins with Strawberry, it's probably 82 to 97 wins without him.
6. Staring at the *center* of that range, one can see the importance of Darryl Strawberry. With Straw, they might expect to win 92 games, which is probably enough to win the division. Without him, they might expect to win 89, which probably isn't.

But the implication that they *cannot* win without Strawberry is silly. They damn well *can* win the race anyway.

Many times, I've seen teams facing the loss of their best player pull together and

win. If the loss of Strawberry challenges the other Mets to play their best, they'll still win the NL East.

How many home runs will he hit in his career?

Right around 500. My guess is that he'll be holding on at the end to clear 500, but could get to 550.

Should he have been the MVP last year?

No; Bonds deserved it. Strawberry was incredibly hot for short stretches, but he didn't play as well wire to wire as Bonds did.

Note: 46% of Strawberry's hits in his career have been for extra bases, the highest percentage in the major leagues. He is followed on that list by Steve Balboni (45%), Mark McGwire, Rob Deer and Ken Phelps.

Franklin STUBBS, Milwaukee
Will he help the Brewers?

On the simplest level—is Stubbs a better player than the man he replaces—the answer is yes if Stubbs is at first base, and maybe if he is in right field. Stubbs is a better player than Greg Brock, and might be better than Deer. Stubbs has worked in the two toughest hitter's parks in the National League, Dodger Stadium and the Astrodome, yet he has compiled reasonable batting stats. He should hit .250–.270 for the Brewers with 20–25 home runs and some stolen bases.

Let's give the Brewers the benefit of the doubt, and assume that Stubbs will play first base. On another level, you have to ask if Stubbs is a championship quality player, one of the *best* first basemen around. The answer is that he isn't. Several teams in the league have new first basemen—Toronto has Olerud, Chicago has Frank Thomas, the Yankees have Kevin Mass, Seattle has Tino Martinez, etc. Stubbs will never do for Milwaukee what Olerud will do for Toronto or what Frank Thomas will do for Chicago.

In a sense, anytime you fill a hole with a player who isn't of championship quality, you lose ground to the other teams. Stubbs is a decent player, but trying to patch holes with decent players is a second-division strategy. Good teams must be able to fill holes with good players.

B.J. SURHOFF, Milwaukee
Will he lose some playing time to McIntosh?

McIntosh is only a few months younger than Surhoff, and I doubt that he will be good enough to eat into Surhoff's playing time significantly.

Surhoff threw out only 31 of 120 opposition base stealers last year, the second-worst percentage in the league (Macfarlane was worse.) He's a very *consistent* offensive player, but not terribly good—a .265 hitter with no power.

I'm not sure why you make a man who runs well and doesn't throw real well a catcher. It seems likely to me that had he been put in left field rather than Glenn Braggs he would have developed more as an offensive player, and would be a more valuable player than he is. It's too late now.

He's not a bad player, but he's not a good player. Like Stubbs, he typifies the Brewer malaise.

Rick SUTCLIFFE, Chicago Cubs
Can he come back from the injury?

Sutcliffe had shoulder surgery, pitched poorly in September but was throwing without pain. He is lifting weights this winter, and expects to be ready to open the season.

Sutcliffe has battled his way back from near-oblivion twice already. With LA in '80 he was 3-9 with a 5.56 ERA, but he came back to star with Cleveland and then the Cubs. In 1986 he was 5-14 with a 4.64 ERA, but he came back to win 47 games in three years. A pitcher who can do that, like Reuss or Reuschel, can probably do it until time runs out on him. I think Sutcliffe will be back, although not necessarily this year.

Glenn SUTKO, Cincinnati
Who is he?

Long-range catching prospect in the Reds' system. They got him one at bat so he could say he was part of a championship team, but he won't be in the majors for real until 1993, if then.

Dale SVEUM, Milwaukee
Is his career over?

The Brewers feel that Sveum is healthy and has regained all of his ability, which as far as I'm concerned is like announcing that Strom Thurmond is as sharp as he's ever been. He's another Milwaukee Brewer. He really doesn't do anything very well, a .243 hitter with no speed, not much power and a terrible strikeout/walk ratio. For some reason, they keep putting him out there.

Russ SWAN, Seattle
Can he help the Mariners? In what role?

Swan is a left-handed pitcher who has always been a starter in the minor leagues, every game. He's 27 years old, so-so fastball, changes speeds a little and throws strikes.

Swan started eight times for the Mariners last year and pitched OK, so I assume that he will open the year in their starting rotation. The departure of Matt Young probably insures this.

The Kingdome has been modified so that it is

a. better for pitchers, and
b. better for left-handers.

I still wouldn't bet on Swan to make it through the year in the rotation. First, I think it's unlikely that he'll pitch well, although he might. Second, Swan has never pitched more than 158 innings in a professional season. If he pitches well they'll just keep running him out there, and after about 180 innings he'll probably pull up with a sore arm. That's what normally happens to a pitcher like this, anyway. I'd say it's five to one against

Swan lasting the season as a rotation starter.

Billy SWIFT, Seattle
Has he finally found himself?

Swift was the second player taken in the 1984 draft, behind Shawn Abner. He is now 29 years old, and his career has had more bumps than speed, but he was 6-4 with a 2.39 ERA last year (128 innings), so hope arises once more. In 1989 he was effective as a reliever (3.02 ERA), but got kicked around as a starter. Last year he was effective both as a starter (3-2, 2.10 ERA in eight starts) and a reliever (2.58 ERA in 47 games). He started in July and August, then went back to the bullpen when Schooler got hurt.

It is against my nature to say anything good about a pitcher who strikes out three men a game, but I've always liked Swift. The reason I don't like non-strikeout pitchers, as a rule, is that they don't throw hard, and because they don't throw hard they are forced to throw *as hard as they can* most of the game, which destroys their arms in a year or two.

Swift, however, *does* have a good fastball, but rather than throwing a strikeout pitch he throws a hard, sinking fastball that yields ground balls. I don't think there's a lot of strain on his arm the way there is on, say, Greg Hibbard. A hard sinking fastball is a great pitch because it's the only pitch in baseball, other than a knuckleball, that you can throw pitch after pitch for 200 innings a year and still be effective.

Swift has improved his control tremendously, from 4.1 walks per game in 1986 to 1.05 (!) in 1990.

I like his mechanics.

I'll tell you the real reason I've always liked him. I was at a game in Fenway Park in '86, and Swift was pitching. At the time he was inches away from making another trip to Calgary. The Red Sox were hitting him, and I noticed the woman in the next seat cringing with every hit. I asked her about it, and sure enough it was Swift's wife. I thought, "Well, hell, I can't sit here and root for her husband to get sent to Calgary," so I switched sides and started rooting for him. And, in that context, I noticed that although he wasn't effective he did do a lot of things well. I've rooted for him ever since—but he's never been as close to being over the hump as he is now.

Greg SWINDELL, Cleveland
Could he still become a star?

He's a heck of a pitcher. He's got three straight winning years with the Cleveland Indians, and how easy is that? He eliminates the running game and works efficiently, throws very few pitches per batter despite a good strikeout rate. (Incidentally, over the three years Swindell and Candiotti have almost the same record. Swindell is 43-29, Candiotti 42-29.)

I don't think Swindell is in great shape, and he hasn't benefitted from having a collection of numbnuts for managers. Despite a history of elbow problems his managers seem incapable of letting him pitch six innings a start in April and May, then lengthening him out as the summer goes longer; for some reason it is important to them that he pitch nine innings in April. Put him on the Oakland A's or the Dodgers, and I'll guarantee you he'll be one of the best starting pitchers in the league.

Note: As the manuscript for this book was near completion, the Cleveland Indians revealed that they were considering moving their fences further out in '91. If they do follow through on this, our expectations for *all* Cleveland pitchers would improve substantially.

•T•

Pat TABLER, Toronto
Can he help a club?

Yes. Tabler is an excellent line-drive hitter against a left-handed pitcher. The Blue Jays are good with platoon players, so they should be able to keep him in his role. Also, he has a deceptively good arm as an outfielder, although he's not quick enough to play the outfield on artificial turf.

Frank TANANA, Detroit
Can he come back?

After September first last year Tanana was 3-1 with a 2.04 ERA (six starts, 40 innings), suggesting that he still has something left. He's very strong, and still strikes out some people by changing speeds, although he doesn't have much left in the way of a fastball.

You probably think I'm crazy for mentioning this, but Tanana isn't very far off a 300-win pace. He has 207 career wins. At the same age Nolan Ryan had 219, Gaylord Perry 216 and Phil Niekro only 145.

Kevin TAPANI, Minnesota
How good is he?

Vic Voltaggio said last summer than Tapani reminded him of Catfish Hunter. There are obvious problems with the comparison. By the time Hunter was as old as Tapani is he had 115 major league wins, and a history of pitching 250 innings a year for six years. Hunter never missed a start, and would have rolled along until about 300 wins if his kindly managers hadn't decided to let him pitch 328 innings in a year, thirty complete games. Tapani missed starts last year after a line drive off his shin and with pulled muscles in the rib cage.

He's not Catfish Hunter and he's not going to be, but he is good. He can throw 90 and hit spots. He's the best of the pitchers that the Mets got for Viola, and

should be the Twins' top starter for the next five years.

Danny TARTABULL, Kansas City
Should the Royals get rid of him?

Tartabull is not popular with Royals' fans, and is a frequent target of trade speculation. He has gotten tired of hearing about being traded for three years, and has sounded off on the subject. He is also regarded by the fans as being a bad apple in the clubhouse, although I don't know how much truth there is in this.

Tartabull is heading into his free agent year; he'll be eligible to leave a year from now. My own feeling basically is that the Royals should let him have his free agent year, which will probably be a good year with the bat, and then should let him leave.

Tartabull is a frustrating player. He truly is a tremendous hitter, better than most people realize. Tartabull and Jose Canseco came up the same year and have played almost the same number of games (699 for Canseco, 691 for Tartabull). Tartabull has a better batting average (.281–.270) and on-base percentage (.367–.345) and is only a few points behind in slugging percentage (.510–.498). He has a better strikeout/walk ratio than Jose—more walks, and fewer strikeouts. He is not as good an RBI man as Canseco, but his career RBI rate is still very good, one of the best in baseball. Last year his RBI rate—and most of his statistics—were almost exactly the same as Bobby Bonilla's, but with half the playing time. Bonilla had 625 at bats; Tartabull had half as many (313). Bonilla had 120 RBI; Tartabull had half as many (60). Bonilla had 39 doubles; Tartabull had half as many (19). Bonilla had 32 homers, Tartabull had almost half as many (15).

And yet, to hear the talk shows, you'd have thought Tartabull didn't have a hit all year. Think about it: here's a guy producing, at bat per at bat, at a rate comparable to Jose Canseco and Bobby

Bonilla—and yet the whole town wants to get rid of him.

I don't particularly want to get rid of him, but he is an exceptionally frustrating player. He's a great hitter with a good throwing arm, but he is a poor defensive outfielder, a poor baserunner and he gets hurt. You throw in the attitude rap, and it's a tough call what you want to do with him.

Dorn TAYLOR,
Baltimore (released)
Who is he?

Longtime Pirates' farmhand, reached AAA in 1986. He's had three straight outstanding seasons at Buffalo. In 1988 he was 10-8 with a league-leading 2.14 ERA, in 1989 10-8 with a 2.58, and last year 14-6 with a 3.02. He was traded to Baltimore as the player to be named for Jay Tibbs, but the Orioles took a quick look and shot him.

He's 32, so the odds aren't in favor of his having a career. He's earned a chance, but he's not on anyone's roster right now.

Anthony TELFORD, Baltimore
Who is he?

Telford was a 1987 All-American from San Jose State, drafted by the Orioles in the third round. His shoulder more or less exploded in early 1988, and required some big surgery which was done in August. He didn't pitch again until the middle of '89.

Telford started 1990 at A ball, but after carving up hitters at Frederick and then Hagerstown (AA, Eastern League) he skipped AAA and into the Oriole rotation. His stats in the majors are unimpressive but may be misleading, because he had a tired arm his last start and was hammered, knocking his ERA for eight starts from the mid-threes to 4.95.

Telford has a fastball in the mid-eighties and a good curveball, which he can throw for strikes and is not afraid to throw when he is behind in the count.

He will probably start the season as the Orioles' fourth starter. I make him a Grade B or C prospect. I don't love him, but he has some markers.

Garry TEMPLETON,
San Diego
What becomes of him after the Fernandez trade?

Let's see, who's desperate for a shortstop . . . the Yankees, Mariners, Rangers and Mets. The Mets are desperate but probably not *this* desperate, so rule them out. Bobby Valentine likes kids, so he wouldn't fall. It looks like his one chance to be a regular would be with the Yankees.

Can he play?

No, but then he hasn't been able to play for five years, so why should that stop him? He's a clubhouse leader, if you like the direction he leads you in.

Maybe the Mariners. If you liked Jeff Leonard, you'll *love* Garry Templeton.

Walt TERRELL, Detroit
What is he doing in the majors?

Sparky has a thing about the guys who have been good to him. Terrell's 33 years old in May and had a 5.24 ERA, so he fits in perfectly with Morris, Tanana and Petry. Say, you don't happen to have a phone number for Milt Wilcox, do you?

Scott TERRY, St. Louis
Is he ever going to find a role?

My comment about him a year ago was "you put this guy on a bad team, and he'd have a record that would curl your toes. But in St. Louis, carefully handled by Herzog, he looks like he's doing fine."

Herzog left last year and the Cardinals were a bad team, and Terry's record showed the effects: 2-6, 4.75 ERA. He's 31, beyond time of stepping into a key role. I don't necessarily know that he's as bad a pitcher as he looked last year, but he's definitely not as good as he looked the previous two years. My guess is that

he'll be around the league for two or three more years.

Mickey TETTLETON,
Baltimore
Isn't he taking the concept of plate discipline a bit too far?

He is, yes. He's Gene Tenace all over again. He takes pitches, good ones as well as bad ones. In 559 plate appearances last year Tettleton saw 2,482 pitches, or 4.4 per at bat. This was the highest average in the major leagues, edging out a couple of pretty good hitters (Wade Boggs, 4.3, and Rickey Henderson, 4.3. Kal Daniels sees the most pitches in the National League.)

The problem is that with men in scoring position he becomes so tentative that he never gets anything done. He hit .155 with men in scoring position last year, the lowest of any major league regular, and .190 the year before. He does walk a lot with a man on second, but that's not really what you're looking for in a cleanup man.

Why does he hit cleanup?
Do I look like Frank Robinson?

Will he ever have another big year?

My guess is that, like Gene Tenace, he will be extremely consistent at a level between 1989 and 1990—somewhere around .240 with 18 homers, 55 RBI.

Tettleton's a good player. He's not a *good* cleanup man, but how many catchers are cleanup men, anyway? He doesn't throw well, but he does work well with the pitchers. He's not somebody the Orioles need to replace. They just need to find a cleanup hitter.

Note: Tettleton had 160 strikeouts last year and 99 hits, the worst ratio of strikeouts to hits in the major leagues. He edged out Rob Deer (1.60 to 1), who normally leads the majors; they were followed by Jesse Barfield, Sammy Sosa and Devon White.

Tim TEUFEL, New York Mets
Could he start for another team?

The Mets need a second baseman badly, so if he can't start for them, his chances with somebody else wouldn't be good. He hits well for a second baseman, but not as well as Jefferies. He's not a good defensive second baseman, although he may not be as bad as Jefferies. He's probably in the right role, fifth infielder.

Bob TEWKSBURY, St. Louis
Can he keep pitching this way?

Tewksbury, a starting pitcher candidate for five years, won ten games in two-thirds of a season for the Cardinals, including two shutouts.

I don't think his performance in 1990 was in any sense a fluke. I think his 1990 performance—10-9, 3.47 ERA—is a real level of ability, maybe even a conservative estimate thereof.

The question is, can he *sustain* it. He has no fastball, so he has to be almost perfect to be effective. Any little thing—a groin pull, a twisted ankle—will throw him off his game just enough to make him ineffective.

I like to watch him pitch. He's a real professional, moving the ball around, in and out, working ahead of the hitters. He's not the kind of pitcher I would bet on to be consistently successful.

Bobby THIGPEN, Chicago White Sox
How high will the save record eventually go? Fifty years from now, what will the record be for saves in a season?

Jim Kaat said during the World Series that Thigpen's record for saves in a season was "a record that may *never* be broken." More likely, Thigpen's record is merely a step in a process which has been going on for half a century, and probably will continue for many more years.

Kaat was reacting to the fact that Thigpen's record represents an impressive stride forward from the previous record, which was 46. Thigpen broke the old record by eleven, saving 57. That's impressive, but it has very little to do with whether the record will or will not be broken. That's looking *backward*, comparing Thigpen's performance to the *past*. The record, if it is to be broken, will be broken in the *future*, so the question is how this will compare to future performance norms.

I would argue that the more stunning an individual performance is, the greater the likelihood that the record will be broken. Consider, for example, the home run record. When Babe Ruth hit 59 home runs in 1920 this was a shattering event—more than twice the previous record, which Ruth himself had set the previous year. But did that mean that the record could never be broken, or did that merely mean that the game of baseball had changed in some way so that more home runs would be hit? When Ruth himself hit 60 home runs in 1927 no one paid much attention, because by that time seasons of 40 or more homers were no longer shocking, and so no one really thought that the record of 60 would stand—but it did, lasting for 34 years.

Think about it. If you *edge* past an existing record, then it may be that the previous standards still apply, and the record was broken simply by a superb individual performance. If the record is *smashed*, however, it *must be* because the performance norms in this category have changed. Bobby Thigpen is a fine reliever, but there have been fine relievers before, right? If the performance standards for saves remained the same, would it be possible for him to be 25% better than *anybody else* ever has been, in his best season?

Of course it would not. Obviously, Thigpen's record was brought about in part because of a change in the way that relief pitchers are used—a generalized change, operating thoughout baseball.

From 1925 through 1960—Firpo Marberry through Elroy Face, loosely speaking—a relief ace's job was *to pitch in the late innings of any game after the starter got tired.* Not to "save" the game, but to pitch whenever it was close. Johnny Murphy, Joe Heving, Joe Page, Hoyt Wilhelm—these guys were *often* brought into the game with their teams one or two runs behind or with the score tied.

There are three historical markers which have brought about this change, which can be identified as

1. Jerome Holtzman,
2. Bruce Sutter, and
3. Ron Davis.

Jerome Holtzman in the 1950s developed the concept of the "save". A relief pitcher's effectiveness could be measured in many ways, but a count of the number of saves became the standard measure, and this had a tremendous impact on the way that people *thought* about relief pitching. A relief pitcher's job was to save the game.

The second thing that happened—for some reason, this is a Chicago story—also happened in Chicago. For two seasons in a row, 1977 and 1978, Bruce Sutter was unhittable, truly an astonishing pitcher, for the first half of the season. On June 28, 1977, Sutter had pitched 37 games, 67 innings. He had given up only 37 hits, struck out 78 men and walked 10, most of those probably intentional. He had saved 21 games and had an ERA of 0.67. In early 1978 he wasn't quite as phenomenal, but at the All-Star break in 1978 he had an ERA of 1.77, and put an exclamation mark behind it by making the American League All-Star team look like a bunch of little leaguers.

Both seasons, however, Sutter faded badly in the second half, carrying his team out of the pennant race (or, more accurately, allowing a team which should never have been in the pennant race to find its own level.) Because of that, Herman Franks decided in the winter of 1978–1979 that he would use Sutter *only* in save situations, to avoid burning him out. Sutter saved 37 games the next year—a record at the time.

From 1925 to 1975, standards for *how much* a relief pitcher could pitch had moved upward time and time again. Johnny Murphy, relief ace of the New York Yankees in the Joe McCarthy era, would pitch 35–40 times a season, a total of maybe sixty to seventy-five innings a season. Contrary to what many people think, he *was* one of the key pitchers on that team. Elroy Face, a generation later, would pitch 55–65 times a year, about ninety innings a season. Rollie Fingers, a generation after him, would pitch 75 times a year, pitching 130 innings a season. Other pitchers, like Jim Konstanty and Mike Fornieles and Dick Radatz and John Wyatt and Ted Abernathy and Wayne Granger and Mike Marshall, were breaking the records for games pitched in a season one after another after another, although most of the pitchers who broke these records were ineffective a year or two later.

This trend toward asking relief pitchers to do more and more stopped abruptly in the late seventies. In my mind, the experience of the Cubs with Bruce Sutter was the turning point. After Sutter, the idea changed from asking the relief ace to pitch in *any* critical situation, pitch as much as he could, to asking him to pitch *only* when he had a chance to save the game.

At the time, I didn't know—and in a sense, I still don't know—whether it was a good idea to define a relief pitcher's job in this way. Would a relief pitcher be more valuable, perhaps, if he pitched when the score was tied or when his team was one run behind, rather than when his team is two or three runs ahead? I don't know the answer to that, and I don't think anyone knows.

But at the same time, it must now be said that this change has unquestionably

been successful in accomplishing its intended purpose. Before Sutter, relief aces were noted for their extreme unreliability from season to season. They often were brilliant one year and useless the next, and were famous for this—in fact, you will still sometimes hear old baseball people say that relief pitchers are not consistent from season to season, although it is no longer true. Even the best relievers before 1970 (Roy Face and Hoyt Wilhelm) had dramatic ups and downs in their career, for which reason baseball men were somewhat in awe of Rollie Fingers, who was the first relief ace to stay at the top of his form for longer than about three years.

That simply isn't the way it is anymore. Now the best relievers—Lee Smith, Reardon, Franco, Righetti, Eckersley, Thigpen—are as consistent from year to year as the best starting pitchers, if not more so. This was the reason for making the change, to stop relievers from burning out after a couple of good years, and it has happened.

But if you don't use your relief ace except when he has a chance to save the game, then what do you do with the rest of those innings? Do you ask starting pitchers to go longer into the game?

The man who came up with a good answer to that question was Bob Lemon. Lemon divided the former duties of the relief ace into two jobs, the Goose Gossage job and the Ron Davis job. The Goose Gossage job was to save the game. The Ron Davis job was

a. to come into the game when it was close but the Yankees didn't have the lead,

b. to save the game when Gossage wasn't available, and

c. to set up Gossage by pitching the sixth and seventh innings when needed.

Davis was very successful in this role. All successful strategies are imitated, and this was more than a successful strategy: this was a successful strategy which an-

swered a question that major league managers were asking themselves: how do we hold back our relief aces to pitch only in save situations?

In the last ten years, this strategy has gone from an experiment to a commandment. *All* good teams now try to set up their relief ace with another pitcher. The effect of these changes has been to concentrate the relief ace's innings more and more into save situations. In 1977 Sparky Lyle won the Cy Young Award with 26 saves. You can't imagine that happening today. Now, 40 saves in a season is nothing in particular, and the trend toward higher and higher totals is still powerfully in motion.

The record for saves in a season will settle somewhere above 80, possibly as high as 90.

Why? Because there is nothing to stop the trends which are in motion from continuing in motion before that point is reached. In 1985 Dan Quisenberry saved 45 games—but he pitched 139 innings to do it. Quisenberry pitched primarily in save situations, but he was normally called into the game in the seventh or eighth inning. Only on occasion would he pick up a save by getting one or two outs, and his ratio of innings pitched to saves was about 3 to 1.

When Dave Righetti saved 46 games in 1986 he pitched 107 innings, so his ratio was more like 2 to 1. He was being called into the game later than Quisenberry was. When Jeff Russell saved 38 games in 1989 he pitched only 73 innings, a ratio of less than 2 to 1. Last year Thigpen picked up 57 saves while pitching 89 innings, a ratio about one and a half to one.

In theory, a relief pitcher could save 60 games while pitching only 20 innings. That's not going to happen, of course, but the ratio between saves and innings pitched has been flattening out for fifty years. It is nowhere near its theoretical limit. Is there any reason why it would *stop* flattening out right now?

None at all—none that I can see any way. Next there's going to be a pitcher who pitches 80 games, 80 innings and saves 60 games, or some combination like that. Then there's going to be a pitcher who pitches 85 games, 75 innings and saves 62 games, and so on.

What *is* the limit? Where does it *have* to stop?

Well, think about it. Pitching less than an inning a game, as some relief aces already are, how much can a pitcher pitch? Maybe 110 games, 90 innings a season? That would certainly seem to be possible, wouldn't it? Mike Marshall in 1974 pitched 106 games, 208 innings, and major league pitchers have told me that while they wouldn't want to try that, they could certainly pitch 110 games if it was just a couple of hitters a game.

How many games could a pitcher save if he was used in that way?

All records tend to be set in a combination of near-optimal circumstances. Home run records are set in home run parks, etc. Let's assume near-optimal conditions for some un-named relief pitcher, at some un-named point maybe twenty years from now. That means:

a. pitching for a great team, a team winning more than a hundred games,
b. in a season when they have a lot of close games—say, 80% close games,
c. and having a great season himself.

This is more likely to occur in a pitcher's park than in a park like Wrigley, where scores are higher and one-run margins therefore less common, but really, no team wins all that many games by more than three runs. Most games are won by less than three runs.

Anyway, how many saves would this create? I don't know exactly, but the answer is *clearly* over seventy, and could be as high as the low nineties. In the year 2025, if the save rule isn't changed, the record for saves in a season will be about 83.

Andres THOMAS, Atlanta
Should he be a regular?

He has no assets. I can't find *anything* that he does well. Blauser does everything better than Thomas.

Should he be a bench player?

Not on my team. What do you use him for? He doesn't run well enough to pinch run. He doesn't hit well enough to pinch hit. He's too erratic at short to be the man you would want to come in for defense. His career on-base percentage (.255) is the lowest of any major league player by more than 25 points. Why would you even want him around?

★★★
Frank THOMAS,
Chicago White Sox
★★★
How good can he be?

Thomas has been heralded long in advance, so I'm not placing the stars here to indicate a "sleeper". I'm placing the stars to indicate my concurrence.

Thomas is a giant of a man who is light on his feet, has tremendous bat speed and won't swing at a ball. In my opinion, he will rank as a hitter with Canseco, McGriff, Eddie Murray—the very best in the game. His on-base percentage through sixty games last year was .454, and that's really what it's going to be. There is no telling how good he could be.

The best offensive players in the majors last year batting 100-400 times: 1. Frank Thomas, 2. Hal Morris, 3. Glenn Davis, 4. Kevin Maas, 5. Dan Pasqua.

Milt THOMPSON, St. Louis
What happened to him last year? Who is the real Milt Thompson—the Milt Thompson of 1989, or that of 1990?

It's a mystery to me what happened to him. The Cardinals had him in right field, which was a new position to him, and sometimes that will effect a player's

hitting. That's not much of an explanation.

I thought a year ago Thompson was for real. Oddly enough, Thompson last year *improved* his strikeout/walk ratio, *improved* his stolen base percentage, and *increased* his isolated power. All of that, taken together, doesn't begin to compensate for a 72-point drop in batting average.

Robbie THOMPSON,
San Francisco

There are no obvious questions about him, other than "Where does he rank?", and I've already ranked the NL second basemen two or three times (see Oquendo, Lind). To state what I take to be obvious, Thompson is a very good player but not a star, a good hitter but not an outstanding one, an outstanding second baseman but not quite a Gold Glove. There is no reason to expect his role on the team to change in 1989, or his contribution within that role.

Here's an odd thought: traditional baseball often has the second baseman hitting second in the lineup. For several years, three of the NL's best second basemen have batted second although they obviously do *not* fit the position, and one second baseman has not batted there although he obviously does:

1. *Ryne Sandberg* has batted second for years although he looks to everybody else in the world like a cleanup hitter. The only intelligible reason that Zimmer bats Sandberg second and Grace third or fourth is that first basemen usually hit third or fourth, and second basemen normally hit second—or if you don't believe that, give me another one.
2. *Jose Lind* batted second in '88 and '89 although he never gets on base and isn't a great hit-and-run man.
3. *Robbie Thompson* batted second for years, and even part of last year, although he isn't anything like a tradi-

tional number two hitter. His strike-out/walk ratio is about three to one and he hits .250, but he does have a little power.

On the other hand, *Jose Oquendo*, who defines the traditional number two hitter about as well as anybody you could find, has hit eighth for years. I'm not saying it *matters*; I'm just saying it's curious.

Dickie THON, Philadelphia
Is he a championship quality shortstop?

Thon was a championship quality shortstop in '89, probably wasn't in '90, but wasn't too bad, either. He played more last year (552 at bats) than he had since the accident, and hit .210 after September first. He could probably use a day off once in awhile against a right-hander.

Gary THURMAN, Kansas City
Can he hit major league pitching?

Yes. Thurman, still only 26 years old, has had trials with the Royals since 1987. He's a base stealer, and won the American Association batting title in 1990 with a .331 batting average. The major league equivalent is .314, but

a. it was not a *loud* .314—no power, bad K/W, and

b. that probably is not his true level of ability.

I doubt that he's a consistent .314 hitter.

I *do* believe that he belongs in the majors, and has for several years. He's a comparable player to Willie Wilson, and I think has been a better player for at least two years.

Wilson is gone from the Royals now, but his place has been taken by Brian McRae, so Thurman is still up against a wall. He's not going to be a star, but he's a better player than Steve Finley or Dave Gallagher.

Mark THURMOND, San Francisco
Is his job safe? Is middle relief the best role for him?

Thurmond's season was ended in early September with an inflamed nerve running from his neck to his left shoulder. He's a left-handed ground-ball pitcher, reasonable fastball and good control but the league has been known to hit .320 against him. He had a 3.34 ERA last year, his best in six years, so he will obviously be back for another year. The signing of Righetti may push him on to another team.

Jay TIBBS, Pittsburgh
Is he a major league pitcher?

Tibbs was assigned to Buffalo in July and didn't report; his career is apparently over.

Wayne TOLLESON, New York Yankees
Why is this man on a roster?

For precisely the same reason that John Sununu is in the White House: because the Boss has the only vote that counts. You can't defend it logically, or even explain it. Over two years and 152 games he's hit .159. In 1989 he hit .164 in 79 games, and earned a $25,000 incentive bonus. His career RBI rate, one RBI for each 17.5 at bats, is easily the worst in the major leagues.

He'll be useful to us in '91, as a test. If Tolleson is still on the roster, that means that Steinbrenner is still running things behind the scenes.

Randy TOMLIN, Pittsburgh
Can he pitch over a period of years the way he pitched the last two months of 1990?

Yes. The easiest parallel that comes to mind is Harvey Haddix, another small left-hander who came up late in 1952, made six starts and pitched about as well as Tomlin did last year (Haddix 2-2, 2.79, Tomlin 4-4, 2.55.) Haddix won twenty

games the next year, and while he didn't go on to be a great pitcher he was a rotation starter for the next ten years. That's about what I expect of Tomlin—a career like Haddix's.

Kelvin TORVE, New York Mets
Is he a major league player? What's his role?

Torve is 31 years old, has a bachelor's degree in marketing from Oral Roberts University. He's been in the minors since 1981, with the Giants, Orioles and Twins, plus maybe another organization or two. He was almost ready to break through as a major league player in 1986, but had a miserable season at Rochester (.242 with four homers), and got derailed.

He's as good a player as a lot of guys who have five years in the pension fund. I'd compare him to Dave Bergman, except he wears his glove on the left hand.

Alan TRAMMELL, Detroit
How many more good years will he have? Does he have a chance to get into the Hall of Fame?

Trammell should have several years left as a regular player, somewhere between four and eight. He's still a good shortstop, although like most shortstops his age he doesn't throw as well as he used to. The Tigers may use Trammell at short and Fryman at third or the other way around . . . I don't know that it will make a lot of difference.

Does he have a chance to get into the Hall of Fame?

Yes. In fact, he is already in the gray area, the bottom part of it.

Note: Trammell hit .379 with men in scoring position last year, the best in the American League. The top five were Trammell (55 for 145), Brett (.360), Lance Johnson (.345), Kirby Puckett (.341) and Wade Boggs (.338).

Brian TRAXLER, Los Angeles

Who is he?

Left-handed power hitter, 23 years old, built like a nose guard. He hasn't rung up impressive numbers in pro ball, but everybody who has seen him hit, including me, is impressed anyway. I don't know what the missing element is, but he's very strong and takes a quick, vicious, level cut at the ball, looks like a thirty-homer swing.

Jeff TREADWAY, Atlanta

How good is he? Is he one of the better second basemen in the league? Is he still getting better?

Treadway always misses some playing time. Last year he bruised his left knee in a collision at first base, July 15; the injury nagged him the rest of the year, and kept him from having better numbers than he did (11 homers, 59 RBI, .283). Incidentally, Benito Santiago's injury probably kept Treadway from making the All-Star team last year. Greg Olson went representing the Braves, but Treadway was a better player having a better season. If Santiago hadn't been hurt Santiago and Treadway would probably have been All-Stars; instead, it was Olson and Alomar.

Treadway has a career high of 474 at bats. This makes it almost impossible to say that he is one of the best in the league, but other than that there isn't any reason why he shouldn't be. He has three weaknesses—he hasn't been durable, he's not fast and he doesn't walk—but he has about a dozen things you like. He's hit consistently around .280 with some pop, which makes him one of the better hitters at the position. He's a good second baseman, not bad on the double play and still improving. He hit .341 with men in scoring position last year. He hits left-handers and right-handers well and isn't prone to slumps.

Alex TREVINO, Cincinnati

Will he be on a major league roster this year?

It's probably more a question of *where* than *if*. He's a known quantity, an OK defensive catcher who can hit around .250. Somebody will need him.

John TUDOR

Tudor is a free agent, and may retire. Over the last four years, since he started having serious arm trouble, he's won 32 games, lost only 14 and posted a 2.69 ERA. Given that record, somebody will probably offer him a guaranteed million just to come to spring training and see if he can throw, plus a couple million in incentives. I don't know about you, but if it was me, I wouldn't retire.

•U•

Jose URIBE, San Francisco

Is he in any danger of losing his job?

Uribe's job is under pressure from several sources:

1. He has been cleared in ugly incidents in the Dominican Republic the last two winters. One more of those, and his career will skid to a halt.
2. He hasn't played his best ball the last two seasons, hitting .221 in 1989 and .248 last year.
3. He is 31 years old. Light-hitting defensive infielders rarely play regularly much past thirty.
4. The Giants have three young shortstops—Andres Santana (excellent but probably not ready), Mike Benjamin (ready but not very good) and Greg Litton (a good enough young player, but not a true shortstop).

Uribe probably won't be a regular by the end of 1992.

•V•

Efrain VALDEZ, Cleveland
Who is he?

Left-handed reliever. He's pitched very well in the Dominican Republic since he was a kid, but seemed to have trouble adjusting to the states until 1989. He was signed by the Padres, sold to the Rangers, and drafted by the Indians before clearing AA, but has pitched well the last two years at AA, AAA and in the majors.

He's aggressive, as Dominican pitchers almost always are, likes to throw strikes and take his chances. He's only 24. I think at a minimum he'll have a career as a left-handed spot reliever.

Rafael VALDEZ, San Diego
Isn't this the guy in the coffee commercials?

Valdez has belonged to the Padres since 1985, but is only 22 years old. He was signed as an infielder, and played the infield through 1987. He wasn't impressive, but then he wasn't awful, either (.264 in the Sally League), and he was quite young. In 1988 it was decided that his throwing arm was more impressive than his bat, and he moved to the mound. He throws in the mid-90s. In a year and a half he blew away the Sally League, the California League and the Texas League, reaching the Pacific Coast League last year. Slowed by shoulder and elbow problems, he didn't pitch well for Las Vegas, but earned a late look and remains a Grade B prospect.

Sergio VALDEZ, Cleveland
No, this is the guy in the coffee commercials.

Sergio and Efrain Valdez are cousins. Efrain is I think a better pitcher, but Sergio isn't a bad prospect, either. I think he must have been hurt the first half of the season. I saw him pitch in June, and didn't think he had any chance to be a pitcher, but he was gone for a while, came back and pitched well in August. Let me give you the good news:

1. With West Palm Beach in 1986 he was 16-6, 2.47 ERA, led the Florida State League in wins.
2. With Indianapolis in 1987 he had a 5.12 ERA but led the league in strikeouts, with 128.
3. In 1988 and 1989 he pitched very well with Indianapolis.
4. Last year, despite an ugly ERA, he pitched well at the end of the season, and his strikeout/walk ratio was good.

Now, the bad news:

1. This is still the Cleveland Indians.
2. They just traded for two starting pitchers, Eric King and Shawn Hillegas.
3. Valdez has pitched 165 major league innings with a 5.39 ERA.

He's a Grade C prospect.

Fernando VALENZUELA, Los Angeles
Does he have anything left? Did the screwball destroy his arm?

The notion that the screwball destroys a pitcher's arm is silly. It isn't the *pitch* that damages the arm; it's the *motion*. The only thing the screwball does is make him "reverse platoon"—left-handers hit him better than right-handers.

The Dodgers offered Valenzuela arbitration, and he apparently will return to the Dodgers in 1991. Let's face the facts: he's thirty, he's overweight, and he's been ineffective for four years. Since 1987 he is 42-48, 4.05 ERA in Dodger Stadium, which would be about 4.50 in a normal park. His arm was used awfully hard from 1981 to 1986, while he was still young. His ERA on the road last year was 5.73. If the Dodgers are serious about winning in '91, they can't afford to keep Fernando in the rotation unless he starts pitching better.

Julio VALERA, New York Mets
Were the Mets right to stick him into the rotation in the middle of the pennant race?

The Mets, who have not been short of starting pitching for several years, brought up Valera at the end of Tidewater's season and started him on September 1, using Ojeda and Darling to relieve him. He won, so they started him twice more, and he was hammered both times. According to *Baseball America* (October 25) "Although no one questioned Valera's talent, his mission put him to the test immediately. He was asked to take Ron Darling's spot in the rotation. That set off a heated political war in the Mets clubhouse. The pro-Darling, anti-management sentiment peaked at the worst possible time, during a three-game sweep by the Pittsburgh Pirates."

It would be unfair for us to second-guess the move, because after all, who is second-guessing the Pirates for doing exactly the same thing with Randy Tomlin, or the Expos for bringing up Chris Nabholz? The Mets were just trying to counter their phenom with *our* phenom. It didn't work.

I wouldn't say it was a good percentage move. If you studied the performance of pitchers in their first ten major league starts, even *great* pitchers in their first ten starts, I'm sure you'd find it was lousy. The Mets, who had six starting pitchers anyway, started Valera hoping he'd be an exception. That's not bright in retrospect, but it's all of us; that's how we make decisions.

Can Valera pitch?

Definitely. Only 22 years old, he's worked his way through the Mets system one step a year. He's always had control. He's a pitcher, and a Rookie of the Year candidate.

Dave VALLE, Seattle
Why is he called the "Beltin' Backstop"?

Probably because he'd belt you if you called him the Rickety Receiver. Valle's first year in the league he hit 12 homers and drove in 53 runs in 324 at bats, which we all took to be his true level of ability. That was 1987, and a lot of people did things that don't represent their true level of ability.

On the good side, Valle has steadily improved his strikeout/walk ratio, from 46/15 in 1987 to 38/18, 32/29 and 48/45 (playing time basically constant). On the down side is everything else. His slugging percentage, which of course sums up his singles, doubles, triples and homers, has gone down in the same years from .435 to .400 to .354 to .331. Like most catchers, he gets hurt more years than not.

At 30, Valle certainly has no chance of being a star, and may continue as a semi-regular only for one or two more years if he doesn't reverse the trend. He could last indefinitely as a part-time catcher.

Andy VAN SLYKE, Pittsburgh
How good is he? Is he the best center fielder in the National League?

Almost all the good center fielders are in the American League—Burks, Griffey, Puckett. Van Slyke is the best center fielder in the National League.

There are four players that one could rank first among the National Leaguers —Van Slyke, Dykstra, Gant and Van Slyke.

Gant was amazing last year, but I don't see how we can rank him first after one good year. He will rank first if he does it again.

Dykstra has the same problem but worse. Dykstra has twenty-six hundred at bats to prove that he *isn't* that good.

Brett Butler I love, but I would have a tough time arguing that he's a better player than Van Slyke. Van Slyke has power; Butler doesn't. Van Slyke has a better arm. Butler steals bases more often, but Van Slyke is a better percentage base stealer—in fact, he's one of the best in baseball at 80%.

Van Slyke was platooned by Herzog in St. Louis, and for several years had one big weakness, in that he didn't hit left-handers. He's put that behind him now, though, and has a normal platoon differential.

Gary VARSHO, Chicago Cubs
Will he ever stick?

Well, he's thirty in June. He's a decent left-handed line drive hitter, which is the traditional model of a pinch hitter. He'll never be a regular, so the best-case scenario for him is that he'll have Jim Dwyer's career, or Denny Walling's. More likely, he'll bounce up and down for three or four more years.

Jim VATCHER, Atlanta
Who is he?

Outfielder, acquired from Philadelphia in the Dale Murphy trade. He's small but strong, fast but not a burner, a line drive hitter. His strike zone judgment is good, despite what he did in the majors last year. He's a Grade C prospect—probably not going to be a regular, but still young enough to surprise.

Who won the trade?

You hate to say it, but the Murphy trade is almost nothing for nothing. Murphy's just another player now, and none of the guys the Braves got for him are likely to be stars. Vatcher may be the player most likely to make the trade for the Braves.

Greg VAUGHN, Milwaukee
Does he still have a chance to be a star? Should we write him off now?

I didn't think Vaughn was star material a year ago, so naturally I don't now. He's probably a good player to pick in a rotisserie league this year, for several reasons:

1. What he did last year is *less* than he is capable of. He should hit .240–.250; he hit .220.
2. Highly touted rookies who fall on their face will sometimes break through in their second season.
3. Vaughn has both power and speed, which makes him more valuable in rotisserie than in real life.
4. He hit very well in September—six homers, 15 RBI.
5. Vaughn hit only .220 last year but was the only major league regular or near-regular with more extra base hits (45) than singles (39).

Don't write him off, in other words; just forget the idea that he's going to be Darryl Strawberry. He isn't.

Mo VAUGHN, Boston
Can he hit?

My belief is that he will hit around .300 with a slugging percentage around .500. He's going to be a cleanup hitter.

Randy VELARDE, New York Yankees
Where's his career go now?

In all likelihood, he's had his last good shot. With the emergence of Leyritz he'll have to earn everything he gets from now on.

Here's another perfect illustration of how a fouled-up organization destroys a young player. You know how many at bats Velarde has in the majors? 466. He's been up and down and up and down for four years, and the organization he plays for has been looking for a third baseman almost all of that time, and he's got 466 at bats.

He hasn't been good in those 466 at bats, but he hasn't been terrible. He's hit .221 with 12 homers, 43 RBI. Poor as it is, that's better than the other Yankee third basemen have done in the same period, Pagliarulo and Blowers and Luis Aguayo.

I thought Velarde was going to be a good player, but looking back on it that opinion was based to a large degree on 1987 MLEs, and you can't base anything on 1987 stats. I'm not saying he would have been a good player. I'm saying he *might* have been a good player. The Yankees set up an obstacle course in front of him, on the theory that if he was *really* a good player he would be able to overcome all the obstacles. He wasn't, so they congratulate themselves on having known all along that he wasn't real good—but they're still looking for a third baseman.

Max VENABLE,
California
Why is he hitting so much better in his old age?

Venable, now 34, has hit .281 over the last two years, with a good on-base percentage and slugging percentage. Considering that he is fast and throws well, one would figure that if he could have gotten started sooner he could have had an impressive career, so why didn't he?

Venable was a third-round draft pick of the Dodgers in 1976. In 1978 he hit .318 with 134 runs scored and 101 RBI in the California League, but the Dodgers inexplicably failed to protect him, and the Giants drafted him. This meant he had to spend the 1979 season in the majors, without a day of prior experience above A ball. He couldn't handle it, hit .165 and got messed up. Because he couldn't hit, he kept getting sent back to the minors—but because he could run and field, he kept getting called back to the majors to be a role player. The consequence was that he never did get 500 at bats in a season at any level—hasn't to this day—and his development as a hitter was very slow.

Given proper handling and better luck, he could have been a good player.

Robin VENTURA,
Chicago White Sox
Is that all there is?

Ventura's 1990 major league season was virtually identical to his MLEs from Birmingham the previous year, so I certainly don't think his rookie performance was misleading. I do think that he figured out a lot of things as the season went on, and will be a better player next year—maybe a .270 hitter with eight to ten homers. What I wrote about him a year ago was "there is nothing about him that says STAR", and that's still true.

Randy VERES, Milwaukee
Who is he?

He's another one of these hopeless pitchers the Brewers keep bringing up. I can't really see that he has any chance to be good.

Hector VILLANUEVA,
Chicago Cubs
Who is he?

Catcher/first baseman, a lot of fun to watch. They list him at 6'1", 210 pounds, but he looks more like 6'0", 225. He has a blacksmith's arms and used them to hit seven homers in 114 at bats last year, despite which he has no real chance to be a regular. He's not a good enough catcher to catch every day or a good enough hitter to take first base away from Grace, and he's too slow to play the outfield. You remember Carl Sawatski, who I think is now President of the Texas League? This is a right-handed hitting Carl Sawatski.

Frank VIOLA, New York Mets
How long can he keep doing this?

Almost unlimited. I wouldn't be surprised if he kept on like he is until he's 40. You watch him pitch and you'd swear he's got three elbows in each arm.

Is he the best starting pitcher in the National League?

He's certainly not as dominant as Doc or Ramon Martinez or for that matter Rijo, but on the theory that in baseball consistency counts for more than flash, he's probably got the best argument to be number one. He's started 35 to 37 games and pitched 246 to 261 innings every year since 1984, numbers which are so consistent that it seems silly even to check and see if anyone else has equalled them. He's had a winning record with sixteen or more wins every year but once.

Could he be a Hall of Famer?

It's too early to speculate, because it depends entirely on how long he lasts. If he's as durable as I think he will be in the next ten years, he'll go right in. If he stopped now, he wouldn't get a vote.

Could he win 300?

He has 137 wins. The last six pitchers to win 300 had an average of 127 at the same age. Only one of the six, Seaver with 168, was more than one year ahead of Viola's pace.

Jose VIZCAINO, Chicago Cubs
Why did the Dodgers dump him?

Vizcaino was regarded as the Dodgers' second baseman of the future until he was traded to Chicago for Greg Smith. Vizcaino has been primarily a shortstop in the minor leagues, but doesn't rival Offerman as a prospect. He could play second base, but his bat probably won't be much for a second baseman, and it may take him a couple of years to learn the position. The Dodgers are making a big push for 1991.

The trade was a surprise when it was announced, but when you look at Vizcaino and Smith side by side, they balance. Vizcaino is just one year younger. Both were at AAA last year. Smith hit .291, Vizcaino .279. Neither has power; Smith had similar edges in on-base percentage and slugging percentage. Smith did this for Iowa in the American Association; Vizcaino did it for Albuquerque in the Pacific Coast League, a vastly easier place to hit. Vizcaino was 13 for 19 as a base stealer, Smith 26 for 40. If anything, Smith may be a little better prospect than Vizcaino.

Vizcaino probably will not make the Cubs this year, as the Cubs have a second baseman, a shortstop and two good reserve infielders (Ramos and Wilkerson). If he does play, he can be expected to hit around .250, no power but some speed and a reasonable on-base percentage. He can be expected to hit about the way that Omar Vizquel hit with Seattle last year.

Omar VIZQUEL, Seattle
Can the Mariners live with his bat?

Vizquel spent the first half of the 1990 season at Calgary, came back in July and wasn't too bad the second half the season, hitting .247 with almost as many walks as strikeouts. His glove is very good, but there is still some question about whether he will hit enough to survive:

1. Although he hit well with the Mariners the second half, he didn't do anything with Calgary the first half. If you add together his major league performance with his equivalency from Calgary, it's not much better than his 1989 season, which was awful.
2. Even though he was better last year, neither his slugging percentage nor his on-base percentage reached even .300.

In view of his youth (he's 24), his defense and signs of progress as a hitter, he'll be around for several years. I don't anticipate his moving into the top rank of American League shortstops.

Ed VOSBERG, San Francisco
Who is he?

Left-handed relief pitcher, one of the 107 pitchers used by Roger Craig last summer. No prospect; unlikely ever to pitch in the major leagues again.

•W•

Hector WAGNER, Kansas City
Who is he?

Right-handed pitcher, very athletic. He throws a major league average fastball, maybe a little bit above average, and has excellent control, but he doesn't have a breaking pitch. He has a little sinker/slider that he uses as his breaking pitch, but it won't get the job done. He had a 2.40 ERA at Memphis last year (AA, Southern League), but I'm not sure he's that close to pitching in the majors. He has to come up with a breaking pitch *and* learn to change speeds more effectively.

Jim WALEWANDER, New York Yankees
Is he out of chances?

Probably. Actually, I wouldn't mind having Walewander on my team as a backup infielder. He's a pretty good second baseman who draws lots of walks and steals some bases, but his batting average is so low that teams are reluctant to make a spot for him. He could probably hit around .230 with a little more playing time, no power.

Bob WALK, Pittsburgh

Jim Leyland's strong point is his handling of his pitching staff, and Walk is another example of what he does right. As a rotation starter in '89 Walk was 13-10, but showed signs of dropping off the face of the earth. He pitched well the first two months of 1989 (3.38 ERA) but then had an ERA around five the rest of the year.

Leyland's reaction to this was to shave his workload. Walk started the year pitching just five or six innings a start. On May 13 he stretched it to seven, but never went more than seven innings until August 25, when he pitched eight. Walk wound up the year pitching his best ball in the last two years.

Larry WALKER, Montreal
How good is he going to be?

There is something curiously episodic about Walker's talents. He has power, he has speed and he has a throwing arm, but my impression of him is that these talents are unconnected one to another. I guess what I'm saying is that I have difficulty visualizing how he will develop because his talents don't seem organic. Maybe he'll develop tremendously in one area, but not develop much in others. I'm not sure if he's really fast, or if he steals bases because he's determined to steal bases.

It is very unlikely that Walker will ever be a .300 hitter, because he strikes out so much. He didn't drive in runs last year because he didn't hit with men in scoring position, but that's probably just a one-year thing, and he'll probably drive in 80 runs this year. I think it's clear that Walker as a player will fit in somewhere between Rob Deer and Jose Canseco—better than Deer, not as good as Canseco, but the same type of player.

Note: Walker went 0-for-29 last year when hitting on an 0-2 count, the worst of any major league player. The three guys who didn't get a hit on an 0-2 count all year were Walker, Jeff King (0 for 23) and Steve Lyons (0 for 21). Everybody else got at least one hit on 0-2.

Mike WALKER, Cleveland
Who is he?

Young starting pitcher, looks really awful.

It is truly puzzling to me how the Cleveland Indians make decisions. The Indians have many young pitchers who look good—Kevin Bearse, before they got rid of him, Olin, the Valdezes, maybe some others. Walker pitched at Colorado Springs in 1989, where he was 6-15 with a 5.79 ERA. He walked 93, struck out 97 and gave up 193 hits in 168 innings.

He started 1990 at Colorado Springs and was just as bad—2-7, 5.58 ERA. The Indians decided to call him up.

How do you do that? Can anybody

explain that to me? How do you look over the pitchers available to the Cleveland Indians, and decide that the guy you want to take a chance on is Mike Walker?

This is probably irrelevant, but I'll tell you what I thought of when I saw him pitch. Do you remember a couple of years ago some company was advertising microwave milk shakes? Maybe they're still selling them. It sounds kind of disgusting, but I figured what the hell, maybe it'll be good.

The instructions were clear, and the "milk shake" turned out with just the right temperature and consistency. It *looked* and *felt* just like a milk shake, but it tasted exactly like chocolate refrigerator frost. I remember holding my forehead in one hand and the "milk shake" in the other, looking stupidly at the cup and wondering how anybody could have the gall to push this stuff off as a commercial product. That's what I thought of when I saw Mike Walker: how does anybody have the gall to push this man off as a major league pitcher?

Tim WALLACH, Montreal
Is he still the best third baseman in the National League?

I'd think you'd have to take Matt Williams, wouldn't you?

What about Sabo?
I'd still choose Wallach.

Did he still deserve the Gold Glove?

Probably not. It takes a couple of years for defensive reputation to catch up with the facts. Wallach won the Gold Glove in 1990 because the other traditional competitor, Terry Pendleton, wasn't playing regularly, but at 33 Wallach probably isn't any better third baseman than Williams or Sabo.

A good quick indicator of a third baseman's defense is the ratio between his *double plays* started and his *errors*. Third basemen have about as many DPs

as Errors, and while either category can be thrown off by a variety of factors, generally speaking the ratio between the two is a good indicator of what kind of a defensive player you're dealing with.

Wallach in his time has had very good ratios—29-21 in 1984 (29 double plays, 21 errors), 34-18 in 1985, 26-16 in 1986, 31-18 in 1988. Last year Matt Williams had the best ratio among NL third basemen, 33 to 19. Charlie Hayes was second (31-20), Sabo third (17-12). Wallach was fifth, at 23-21, which is pretty much average. Of course, Delino DeShields isn't Bill Mazeroski.

Denny WALLING, St. Louis
Is his career over?

Probably. A .220 batting average in 127 at bats doesn't provide any *real* evidence that Walling has lost it, but he's 37 in April, and the new manager in St. Louis will probably want to pick his own role players. Walling may not have enough to sell to get him another job.

David WALSH, Los Angeles
Can he get major league hitters out?

Walsh is a minor league veteran, a left-handed pitcher who was taken in the 9th round of the 1982 draft, and was in the Toronto system from 1982 through 1987. He was wall to wall awful for Toronto in the low minors, posting ERAs in the fives, and almost all of Toronto's minor league teams play in pitcher's parks.

Walsh was released by Toronto in 1987. He went to Mexico, and dominated the Mexican League as a starter, with a 14-1 record and a 1.73 ERA, more than a strikeout an inning.

In *The Miracle at Coogan's Bluff*, by Thomas Kiernan, Sal Maglie attributed his improved pitching later in life to his time in the Mexican League. According to Maglie, "Pitchin' in that thin air really improved my curve ball. You really had to break it off to get any action on it.

When I came back to sea level I could bend it like a hoop." Maglie may be the only historical precedent for it, but apparently the same thing happened to Walsh: he came back from Mexico with a lot better curveball than he had before.

Anyway, the Dodgers signed him in January, 1989. Since signing with the Dodgers he has been a completely different pitcher than he was with Toronto—many more strikeouts, better control, and better ERAs with San Antonio and Albuquerque, which are tough places to pitch. Called up by the Dodgers in August, he pitched well in the majors.

The Dodgers' bullpen seems infinite. You get the impression that the bullpen charters its own airplane. The release of Searage in December and the trade of Jim Poole a week later may be a signal that the Dodgers intend to use Walsh as the left-handed spot reliever, but even so Walsh has to compete with Mike Munoz, Dennis Cook and possibly Bob Ojeda. Still, Walsh probably will be in the majors for at least part of the season, pitching in a limited role.

Jerome WALTON, Chicago Cubs
What happened to him last year? Was he over his head in 1989? Will he be back in 1990?

I think Walton just had an off year in 1990. I think he is not only as good a player as he was in 1989, but possibly a better one, and will probably be back in 1991 unless he is concealing a problem or something.

An interesting thing to note is that although Walton's batting average went down last year, his strikeout/walk ratio improved dramatically, from 77-27 to 70-50, so that his on-base percentage, which is the critical stat for a lead-off man, actually *improved* last year. I still believe in Jerome Walton.

Note: Walton last year had 63 runs scored with only 21 RBI, a three-to-one ratio. That's the highest in the major leagues.

Steve WAPNICK, Detroit
Who is he?

Right-handed reliever, a 30th-round draft pick from Fresno State (1987) who was blazing his way through the Toronto system a year ago. The Blue Jays didn't put him on their roster, so the Tigers drafted him, looked at him in April and let him go back to Toronto. He went to Syracuse but got hurt, throwing his future into doubt. Grade C prospect if healthy.

Colby WARD, Cleveland
Is he a major league pitcher?

Ward is a 27-year-old right-hander, formerly in the California system, who has always been considered no prospect until he was the best pitcher on the Colorado Springs team last year, as a middle reliever. Grade D prospect. I've seen pitchers like this break through once or twice, but it's certainly rare.

Duane WARD, Toronto
Could he move up?

Yes.

Ward, who throws very hard, is one of the hardest-working relievers in baseball today—73 games, 128 innings last year, which was his third straight season with a similar load. He does Rob Dibble's job, and he's the closest thing there is to Rob Dibble in the American League.

He's not going to displace Henke because Henke's a better pitcher, but Ward quite certainly could be a closer for someone. He'll be eligible for free agency after 1993, and if his arm is still sound he'll become somebody's ace.

Gary WARD, Detroit
Why is he still in the league?

The Detroit Tigers: the organization that kept Gary Ward and got rid of Ernie Harwell. Ward was originally signed by Minnesota as an undrafted free agent, and took nine years to work his way through the Twins' system. He's gotten an extra year or two out of his career on

the other end because he's a good guy, and also he's not the kind of guy who is going to give up and go home until *everybody* tells him they don't want him, but at 37 you really can't justify a roster spot for him.

Incidentally, Ward's son, Agee, is a forward on the Fullerton State basketball team.

Turner WARD, Cleveland
Is he a real prospect?

No. Ward hit .348 in fourteen games late in the season, creating a nice APBA card and a natural expectation that he's a prospect, but he isn't.

The Indians have gotten rid of several outfielders—traded Cory Snyder, released Dion James. Maldonado hasn't resigned and apparently won't. There is an opening here for an outfielder, and the Indians may not be able to distinguish between a guy who hits .348 in a late-season look and a real prospect. But even if he plays, Ward is a .260 hitter with no power who will probably be back at Colorado Springs by mid-summer.

(Late Note: The December 31, 1990 *Sporting News,* column by Moss Klein, referred to Ward as the Indians' "promising left fielder", and suggested that he was central to the Indians' plans for '91. The guy is older than Manny Lee or Stan Javier, and he was 22 for 37 as a base stealer at Colorado Springs.)

Claudell WASHINGTON, New York Yankees
Is his career over?

Logically yes, but probably not. He hit .167 last year in 45 games, and it's never been *quite* clear whether he helps you if he hits .280. On the other hand, he has a 1991 contract for a guaranteed $875,000, so you know the Yankees will want to bring him to spring training to *see* whether he can still play. They'll figure it doesn't cost them anything to look. Once in camp he's still an impressive athlete at 36, can still run. He'll be compet-

ing for a job with a kid, and the kid will be feeling all the pressure, so my guess is that Claudell will wind up with a job. He'll probably hit .260 with 11 home runs.

Gary WAYNE, Minnesota
Is he a major league pitcher?

Wayne, a left-hander with a funny motion, was the surprise of the Twins' camp in 1989, pitched fairly well in 1989 but not so well last year, and made a trip to Portland.

Wayne is a left-handed pitcher, which is something that teams are always looking for. He is in possession of a major league job. The organization is notably short of pitching prospects, so short that they traded for Steve Bedrosian to be their closer. His manager likes him. All of these things suggest that he will be in the major leagues in 1991.

He's not the worst pitcher in the league. He's not one of those yahoos that Cleveland runs out there, Mike Walker or Rudy Seanez or somebody. He has no chance to move up into a bigger role. He's in the survival game, but he'll survive.

Lenny WEBSTER, Minnesota
Who is he?

Catching prospect, a Grade D prospect if that. He's 26 years old, hasn't played AAA ball yet but has gotten a couple of looks by the Twins. He might make it as a light-hitting defensive backup.

Mitch WEBSTER, Cleveland
Has he been under-rated?

Webster is a switch hitter, but really should be used as a right-handed platoon player and bench player. He hits left-handed pitchers well, last year .292 with a slugging percentage almost .500. In 1989 he hit .311 against left-handers. Starting against left-handers, going into the outfield for defense and pinch running, he'd be a valuable man. He doesn't hit right-handers, though (.220 last year), so he's not much of an everyday player.

Webster used to be a selective hitter. In 1987 he drew seventy walks, but he's gone steadily backward in this area, putting him in line with the Cleveland Indians, who normally like their players to strike out three or four times as often as they walk.

Bill WEGMAN, Milwaukee
Does he have a snowball's chance in hell of ever coming back?

Roughly, yes. He wasn't very good to start with, and then had shoulder surgery in 1989 and was scheduled for surgery on his right elbow after the 1990 season. His best chance of having a career is probably to apply for a waiver and see if he can't get into the Senior's League a few years early.

Walt WEISS, Oakland
How much did his absence in October cost the A's?

Unless he was planning to hit six or seven homers in the series, I don't see how he could have made any difference. I didn't notice Gallego having a lot of trouble at shortstop or anything. That would be a weak excuse.

Is he ever going to be a star? Is he one of the best shortstops in the league?

He's just another shortstop, as good as Gagne or Stillwell or Schofield, but not any better. I don't see him as having any star potential.

Bob WELCH, Oakland
Did he deserve the Cy Young Award?

No one *really* believes that Bob Welch is the best pitcher in the American League. If you surveyed a hundred baseball writers and ask them "Who is the best pitcher in the American League" you'd get votes for Clemens, Stewart,

Eckersley, Saberhagen if he's healthy, and maybe a couple of other guys, but it is doubtful that *anybody* would vote for Welch.

If he isn't the best pitcher in the league, why would you want to give him the award which is designed for the best pitcher in the league?

You give him the award because, even though he isn't the best pitcher, "he had the best year". But what does that mean? Did he have the best ERA? Did he lead the league in strikeouts or walks or strikeout/walk ratio? Did he lead the league in starts or innings? Did he have the best combination of these accomplishments? Obviously he did not.

What it *really* means to say that he had the best "year" of any pitcher is that he had the best won-lost record. Is that a good reason?

If his won-lost record represented an outstanding individual accomplishment, then it would be reasonable to predicate the award on that accomplishment. Of course it does not. No one *really* believes, do they, that Bob Welch went 27-6 because *he* pitched so well?

The Oakland A's scored, for Bob Welch, 5.9 runs per nine innings. More runs were scored for Welch than for any other American League pitcher, which resulted in his winning 27 games rather than his usual seventeen.

Also, his support from the bullpen, in Dennis Eckersley and others, was exceptionally good. If he left with a 3-2 lead after six innings, his team would hold the lead for him.

The inevitable conclusion is that Bob Welch won the Cy Young Award because his team happened to score a lot of runs on the days that he pitched.

That doesn't make any sense.

The award to Welch *is* consistent with the tradition of the Award, which has normally gone to the pitcher with the best won-lost record. It is tradition in the worst sense, continuing to do things in a certain way even though you know they

are wrong, just because that's the way they have always been done.

The reporters of fifteen years ago had an excuse: they didn't know any better. The reporters of fifteen years ago really *believed* that the won-lost record indicated how a man had pitched. They believed that luck evens out over the course of the year, and that the won-lost record indicated how well the man had pitched at key moments of the game. This was a reasonable thing for them to believe because even though it could be theoretically demonstrated that luck would not even out that quickly, the actual *facts* on the matter had never been studied or published.

But we know better now, don't we? We *know* that luck does not even out. *No one really believes that Welch's won-lost record truly indicates how he pitched*; that argument has been lost to history. We *know* that Bob Welch did not pitch better than Dave Stewart. So what kind of sense does it make to give him the Cy Young Award and pretend that he did?

Does Welch have any chance at the Hall of Fame?

Welch did more to help himself in that respect last year than any other major league player. Before last year, Welch was a pitcher who had the nuts and bolts of a Hall of Fame career, but none of the chrome and leather. Big seasons, star-type seasons, are tremendously important in making a man a Hall of Famer.

A starting pitcher with less than 150 wins has no chance of getting into the Hall of Fame. Above 250 wins, the career win total becomes a positive factor, pushing the pitcher rapidly along. Between 150 and 250, and we look at the complete circle of the pitcher's accomplishments.

Welch was just poised to enter the circle: he had 149 wins before last year. His 27-win season pushed him into the area where his win total ceases to work strongly against him, and it also gave him a portfolio of star-type accomplishments.

A year ago, he was a long shot. Now, he's not.

Could he win 300?

He is on a 300-win pace. He has 176 wins; the last six pitchers to win 300 had an average of 178 at the same age.

You can't really be upset about Welch winning the Cy Young Award. He's a good guy, and he's been a quality pitcher for a long time. You like to see a player like that get a break. I just think that you should vote for the man that you really believe has been the best pitcher in the league.

★ ★ ★
David WELLS, Toronto
★ ★ ★

How good will he be as a full-time starter? Could he win 18 or 20 games?

He could, yes. Wells, who had a fine year as a reliever in '89, started last year in the bullpen but moved to the rotation because the Blue Jays had three good relief pitchers but only two good starters, which is the wrong ratio.

The Blue Jays did it right—they gave him four innings, then six innings, gradually stretching him out until he could pitch seven or eight innings a start.

He was very good, as a starter. He had 18 quality starts in 25 tries, including eight in a row at one stretch and seven in a row at another. Of his seven non-quality starts, two were early starts when he was pulled before pitching six innings, although he had pitched well, and three more were consecutive starts in a stretch when something was bothering him. On the whole, he did an exceptional job as a starting pitcher, and I see no reason to believe that he won't be as good as Stieb or Key this year.

Terry WELLS, Los Angeles
What was he doing in the majors?

It beats me. Wells, who had a 4.72 ERA and a strikeout/walk ratio less than

even at Albuquerque, was given five starts by Lasorda late in the year. The Dodgers were probably planning to let Valenzuela get away, were out of the race and wanted to take a look at a left-handed starter to see if there was anything there. There isn't any reason to believe that Wells is a major league pitcher.

David WEST, Minnesota
Is he ever going to develop?

West's 1990 season ended when he pulled a hamstring on September 4. He wasn't pitching any better when that happened than he has before. Last year he pitched well in April, but poorly the rest of the year.

I don't see West as a star, but I still see him as someone who can probably pitch. The Metrodome isn't helping him. He had 6.03 ERA in Minnesota last year, 4.41 on the road (the 1989 data was even worse, in limited innings—7.68 ERA in Minneapolis.) He has first-inning troubles. The batting average against him is over .300 for his first fifteen pitches, and he has poor control early in the game. These are little nagging things. I don't think he's a long way from turning a corner and being a guy who can win twelve or fifteen games.

Mickey WESTON, Baltimore
Is he a major league pitcher?

It is becoming absurd to keep sending him to the minors. Weston in 1988 was 10-4, 2.09 ERA while splitting his time between Jackson (AA) and Tidewater (AAA) in the Mets system. In 1989 he was 8-3, 2.09 ERA at Rochester (AAA) in the Baltimore system. In 1990 he was 11-1, 1.98 ERA at Rochester. What is that, 29-8 over a three-year period? There's not too much doubt that he can pitch AAA ball.

Weston has no fastball. He changes speeds from slow to slower and throws strikes. There is, to say the least, a prejudice against pitchers of this type. Major

league scouts want to see your heater, and the prejudice is well-founded to this extent: that pitchers without a good fastball rarely are consistently successful in the majors.

I think the prejudice is mis-applied in Weston's case. I've seen major league pitchers who were successful without a fastball, and I'm betting you have, too. They have trouble sustaining success because they try to pitch at their limits, which causes arm injuries—but that won't apply to Weston, who knows better than to try to get out hitters by loading up and blowing it in there at 81 MPH.

I can't see how a pitcher could be *that* good at AAA, unless he had enough ability to be adequate in the majors. It doesn't make sense to me. Yes, he'll need a couple of trips around the league to figure out what he is doing, and no, he'll probably never be a star—but not even to give him a chance? He's got 34 major league innings. Why not let him fail before you turn loose of him?

★ ★ ★
John WETTELAND, Los Angeles
★ ★ ★

What happened?

Sometimes you have to stick with a player. Wetteland, who I had marked with stars a year ago, had a miserable season, winning only two games with a 4.81 ERA. His year had four parts:

a. He began the year in the bullpen, pitching five times, five innings with a 10.80 ERA, but he got hammered once and was OK the other four times.

b. After the injury to Hershiser he moved into the starting rotation and was terrible. Between April 30 and June 1 he started five times and relieved twice, posting an 0-3 record with a 7.08 ERA.

c. Moved back to the bullpen, he pitched very well in four outings between June 5 and June 12, allowed no earned runs in seven innings. Then he was sent to Albuquerque, where he didn't pitch too well and pulled a muscle in his rib cage.

d. Returning to the Dodgers in mid-September, he pitched six times in the closing weeks and was very good, allowing only one earned run in ten and two-thirds innings.

Wetteland throws a slider or split-fingered fastball which gets away from him sometimes, goes in the dirt and back to the screen. In 146 major league innings it has gotten away from him—and the catcher—24 times, which is an unacceptable rate.

On the other hand:

1. He still has a great arm,
2. He still has a great strikeout/walk ratio,
3. He still pitches in Dodger Stadium,
4. He still works for the Dodgers, and
5. He had a 0.51 ERA from June second until the end of the year.

He may not get another shot at a major role on the staff this year—but I'm still betting on him to be an outstanding pitcher.

Lou WHITAKER, Detroit
Is he still a good player?

Whitaker hit .237 last year, but is still one of the best-hitting second basemen in baseball, and is still an above-average defensive second baseman.

Black athletes sometimes complain that when a white player does something the press always talks about how hard he works and how smart he is and what great character he shows, but when a black player does the same thing it's just "great natural talent." Perhaps the most appalling example of this is the treatment of Alan Trammell and Lou Whitaker by the Detroit media. You couldn't name two players of more nearly identical accomplishments. Playing side by side for

thirteen years (in the majors) they have played almost the same number of games (Trammell leads 1,835-1,827), scored almost the same number of runs (Whitaker leads 1,040-1,009) and driven in almost the same number (Trammell, 810-781). They have the same on-base percentage (.355) and almost the same slugging percentage. One year one of them will be a little better than the other, and the next year the other one will have the better season.

In spite of this, there is, believe it or not, a widespread belief among the Detroit public that Trammell is a tough, aggressive player who has built himself up to this level by working hard, while Lou is just . . . well, a kind of a shiftless black guy who has a lot of ability but hasn't done much with it. This appalling attitude, as close to overt racism as you can get without ruining your linen, is expressed freely in the Motor City media. Joe Falls, while exalting Trammell, wrote that Whitaker has watched a Hall of Fame career drift away from him, and a couple of radio guys stand right behind him, one holding the gasoline and the other the match.

I was in Detroit last spring, doing radio shows. The third time this was put to me I challenged the caller on it. You know what he said? He said, "Yeah, they have about the same totals now, but when they came up Whitaker was already a .300 hitter. Trammell was a .220 hitter. He's worked hard to become the player he is now." In fact, of course, they were as even when they came into the league as they are now. In their rookie season Whitaker hit .285 with 3 homers, Trammell .268 with 2 homers. Trammell, not Whitaker, was the first one to hit .300 and the first one to drive in or score a hundred runs, which he did in 1980.

Of course there are *individual* differences between them, which contribute to (or more likely, justify) the racist preference. Trammell is a visible on-field "leader", a holler guy; Whitaker is quiet,

laid back. Sometimes he's a little bit of a space cadet. But the survival of this blatant supremacist stereotype into the 1990s is shocking and unseemly. Lou Whitaker may not be the player you dreamed he would—but who's been better? What American League second baseman would you rather have had these last thirteen years? Give the man credit for what he is.

Devon WHITE, Toronto
Can he come back?

I saw White play several times after his return from the minors last year, and it *seemed* to me that he was showing greatly improved plate discipline. I saw him take several pitches just outside the strike zone, pitches I was sure he would swing at. Twice I saw him go with the pitch and take it to the opposite field. I have never seen him do this before. None of it shows up in the stats, however. He hit just .222 after being recalled.

White has never really been a very good offensive player. He hit 24 home runs as a rookie, but that was 1987. On the other hand:

1. He is probably the best defensive outfielder in the majors.
2. He's a bad hitter, but not really a .217 hitter.
3. He'll hit better in Toronto than he did in California.

The Angels got frustrated with him, as they did with Gary Pettis, because they wanted him to shorten up on the bat and slap at the ball, and he wouldn't or couldn't. They could have saved themselves the frustration: no one learns to hit in the major leagues, so forget about that. It's not going to happen. If you try to make the player 1% better you might accomplish something; if you try to make him 40% better you're just going to set up a cycle of failure and frustration. The Angels got the better end of the trade, but White should be a better player this year because he has escaped the cycle of failure and frustration that the Angels created with their unrealistic expectations for him.

Frank WHITE, Kansas City (released)
Can he still play?

White hasn't yet accepted that he can't play anymore. If he would agree to be a bit player he might be alright in that role, playing a little second base against left-handers. He's not fast anymore but he's not slow, still a pretty good second baseman. I wouldn't want to play him more than two games a week.

Wally WHITEHURST, New York
Will he make the Mets? Is he being mis-cast as a middle reliever?

Whitehurst is a good pitcher, good enough to be a starter. His strikeout/walk ratio last year, in the major leagues, was 46 to 7. There's probably never in baseball history been a pitcher who had a strikeout to walk ratio of six to one and wasn't effective, granting that he probably won't sustain that.

The Mets, despite the trade of Ojeda, still have six starting pitchers (Viola, Gooden, Cone, Fernandez, Darling and Valera), so Whitehurst is going to have to stay in the bullpen. He'll be one of the best long relievers in baseball.

Mark WHITEN, Toronto
Is he ready to play? How good is he?

He is ready, and he's good. Whiten, now 24 years old, is a switch hitter with power, speed, and a throwing arm. He's not a Grade A prospect because of his age, his strikeout rate and his inconsistent batting record before 1990. But he's a good Grade B prospect, and could be the Rookie of the Year.

The opportunity for him still isn't great, despite the trade of Junior Felix, who played his position, and the departure of George Bell. The Jays traded Felix for another outfielder, and acquired an outfielder without giving one up in the big trade with San Diego, so Whiten still is in the group of young outfielders trying to fight their way past Mookie Wilson. My guess is that Whiten is roughly a .270 hitter with a slugging percentage in the low .400s, meaning that he probably *won't* win the Rookie of the Year award, but very well could.

Ed WHITSON, San Diego
Is he really one of the best pitchers in the National League?

Yes, believe it or not, he really is. Whitson pitched so poorly in New York that people have trouble believing that his .600 winning percentages and 2.60 ERAs aren't some sort of legerdemain. He was hurt in the American League because it's a left-handers league, and his platoon differential is larger than normal. Left-handed hitters get a good line on him, but his control is terrific and he knows what he is doing. Last year he threw an average of only 3.2 pitches per batter, the fewest of any major league pitcher (162 innings or more.)

Is he a safe pick for 1991?

No one is *certain* to retain his effectiveness. Whitson is 35 years old and coming off his best season, so he's probably not going to match it. But he's pitched 200 innings for four years in a row, and his ERA for the last two seasons combined is 2.63. How many guys can match that?

Ernie WHITT, Atlanta (released)
Will anybody give him a job?

He might come back. He had a hand injury that cost him the first half of the season, but prior to that he showed *no* signs of decline. I doubt that he'll ever bat 400 times a year again, but I wouldn't be surprised if he could stay around three or four more years as a pinch hitter/backup catcher. He doesn't have a contract for '91.

Kevin WICKANDER, Cleveland
Who is he?

Left-handed pitching prospect, was used as a spot reliever at Colorado Springs, and also by the Indians. Good arm, no control, needs another pitch . . . you've probably heard that story more times than TV stations have broadcast *It's a Wonderful Life*. Grade C prospect.

Curt WILKERSON, Chicago Cubs
Could he start for somebody?

He is correctly cast as a backup infielder. His speed, quickness and versatility make him valuable in that role; his .250 batting average, no power and tendency to lunge at everything would prevent him from being a regular.

Dean WILKINS, Houston
Who is he?

Grade D prospect, a right-handed pitcher who the Cubs got as one-third of Steve Trout. The Astros, struck by a Holocaust in the bullpen, grabbed him from the Cubs under Rule 5. There's not a lot to like about him as an individual, but his opportunity is fantastic. The Astros have no relievers, and the Astrodome will cut a half-run or more off his ERA. The combination gives him a good chance to surprise.

Jerry WILLARD, Chicago White Sox
Can he hit major league pitching?

You bet. Willard is basically the same story as Brian Harper, except that he's a power hitter rather than a line-drive hitter. He caught for the Indians in 1984–1985, lost his job to Andy Allanson and dropped out of the league. He was released by Oakland in 1987, and was working construction in Southern California, which gave him a renewed appreciation for the life of a baseball player. He decided to get serious about conditioning, and try to get back in the game.

He is in his prime as a hitter now, and is actually one of the best *hitting* catchers in baseball, major leagues or minors. If you were in a decent hitting park and needed catching help, you could do a lot worse than just pick up Willard and decide to live with his defense. That's probably not going to happen, but he can help somebody as a third catcher/DH/pinch hitter.

Bernie WILLIAMS, Yankees
Who is he?

The top prospect in the Yankee system. According to the January 25, 1990 issue of *Baseball America*, "scouts say Williams compares favorably to Roberto Kelly as a hitter and center fielder, and [is] the fastest player in the organization."

He's a switch hitter, now 22 years old, born in Puerto Rico. *Baseball America* also says that "Williams has a superb swing from both sides of the plate, but is a stronger lefthanded hitter. Scouts think he can be a 20-homer man. And 50-stolen-base seasons are in his future once he learns technique . . . Williams tracks fly balls as well as Kelly and makes a solid, accurate throw." Later in the season, in mid-1990, he was rated the second-best prospect in the Eastern League. In that article Butch Hobson, a rival manager, wondered why Williams wasn't already in the majors, and an unidentified coach said "he's better than 75 percent of the center fielders in the majors."

Despite what scouts say, it is unlikely that Williams will ever be an outstanding base stealer. Most great base stealers are effective base stealers from the time they enter professional baseball. By the time Rickey Henderson was Bernie Williams' age he had already had his first 100-stolen base season in the major leagues, and by the same age Tim Raines had stolen 71 and 78 in the majors. Vince Coleman was still in the minors at this age, but he was stealing a hundred bases a year in the minors.

If he is in the major leagues in 1991, Williams will probably hit about .265 with less than ten homers and about 30 stolen bases. Given his age, he could improve substantially.

Eddie WILLIAMS, San Diego
Will he ever get a real shot?

Williams is the same player as Darnell Coles, except a little worse third baseman and a little better hitter. Basically the same player.

Originally out of the Mets system, then Cincinnati, then Cleveland, Williams in 1989 played 66 games at third base for the White Sox, and he wasn't half bad—hit .274 with a little power and a respectable strikeout/walk ratio. He didn't do the job defensively, however, and went back to the minors. After the year he was a six-year free agent, so he signed with the Padres, who needed a third baseman.

Pagliarulo struggled and Williams was hitting the hell out of the ball for Las Vegas, so they called him up. In 14 games he hit .286 with a .571 slugging percentage, after which they sent him back to Vegas.

Williams isn't old—he's only 26. He's certainly not out of chances. He's a pretty awful third baseman, I grant you, but it's hard to see why there isn't any way to figure out a job for him. His MLEs from Las Vegas suggest that as a hitter he is comparable to Chris Sabo—that is, he would hit about .270 with a slugging percentage in the mid-fours. If he's that good a hitter, why doesn't somebody find a spot for him as a designated hitter/pinch hitter/backup outfielder/emergency infielder?

Ken WILLIAMS, Toronto
Does he have a career left?

I think Williams needs to go to Japan or Mexico or Tidewater or Outer Mongolia or something and just start over. He's a great athlete and a wonderful outfielder, and a few years ago it looked like he would hit at least a little. But he played for two teams last year, and he hit .133 for Detroit, and .194 for Toronto. He hit .146 at home and .182 on the road. He hit .196 in day games and .141 at night. He hit .156 on grass fields and .169 on artificial turf. He hit .186 against left-handers and .095 against right-handers. He hit .169 with men on base, .143 with runners in scoring position and .171 when leading off an inning. He hit .178 in the first six innings of the game, .138 in the late innings. He hit .182 as a left fielder, .163 as a center fielder, .185 as a right fielder, .077 as a pinch hitter and .091 as a designated hitter, which brings up the question, why in holy hell would you use him as a pinch hitter or designated hitter, anyway?

Everybody's record has a bright spot, and I'll give you Williams'. When he hit the first pitch—not when he swung at it, but *assuming* he hit it—he hit .231. When he got behind in the count, however, he hit .139, and when he got ahead in the count he hit .158.

Williams' batting average the two previous years, 1988 and 1989, was .184. This is in almost 500 at bats—more than 600, if you throw in 1990. There is no realistic hope anymore that he is going to hit.

Matt WILLIAMS, San Francisco
Should he have been the MVP?

He's got an argument, probably as good an argument as Sandberg. His RBI count *isn't* a function of his batting order position, but of his production. He hit .331 with men in scoring position, and hit sixteen homers with men on base.

Players who have poor strikeout/walk ratios normally hit very poorly when leading off an inning, and this is also true of Williams. When leading off an inning, which is also a very important "clutch" situation, he hit only .206 with a .245 on-base percentage. But with men on base he hit .330, with men in scoring position .331; his slugging percentage in both those categories was up near .600.

I wouldn't have voted for Williams as MVP. Offense is two-sided, and *scoring* runs is as important as driving them in. Williams' poor performance leading off an inning is an important liability. But he was still one of the half-dozen best players in the league.

Mitch WILLIAMS, Chicago Cubs
What happened to him?
It was an injury season. Williams opened the season pitching brilliantly. Through May 6 he had pitched 11 times, saved six games and allowed *no* earned runs in fourteen innings. He had a series of four rocky outings in mid-May, and Zimmer, being Zimmer, stopped using him as the closer. The Cubs were struggling as a team, which made Williams' four-game slump more noticeable. Williams came back to allow only one run in a series of fourteen outings from mid-May to mid-June, but wasn't getting saves.

On June 11 Williams was hurt while covering first base on a play against the Mets; he had surgery to repair a torn ligament in his right knee two days later, and went on the 21-day. He was ineffective after his return.

Will he bounce back?
Williams wasn't a great prospect to sustain success a year ago, when he was on top. He's still very wild, and he's been up and down his whole career. If you're asking "Will he go up again?" the natural answer is "Yes". If you're asking "Will he ever be a pitcher you can depend on?" my answer is "Probably Not".

Mark WILLIAMSON, Baltimore
Could he play a more important role?
Williamson was having a nice season last year (8-2, 2.21 ERA) until stopped on August 18 by a broken middle finger on his right hand. He was also extremely good in 1989, and you have to think that if circumstances forced him into the closer role, he'd be alright. He's 31 years old and has been a reliever virtually all of his pro career, so moving him to the rotation seems to be out. He's not going to bump Gregg Olson. He appears to have arrived where he is going, and he's doing great there.

Frank (Whoosh) WILLS, Toronto
What do they see in this guy?
He's got the best pitch in baseball. Wills throws a slider that's unhittable, but that's his only pitch, and he's not consistent enough with it to keep him ahead of the game. Of course, as he ages (he's 32 now) he doesn't throw as hard and the slider doesn't break as sharply, so in about two more years he'll have nothing.

Craig WILSON, St. Louis
Can he take over for Pendleton?
Opinion is divided over whether the Cardinals will move Todd Zeile to third base and try to find somebody to help Pagnozzi, or whether they will give third base to Wilson and try to teach Zeile to get rid of the ball in less time than it takes a gorilla to figure out Rubik's cube.

Wilson is really a middle infielder type—small, not real fast, a dedicated singles hitter who could hit anywhere from .240 to .280. He looks a great deal more like Larry Bowa than Mike Schmidt, but the Cardinals have tried to make a third baseman out of him, perhaps only because it will make him a more valuable utility man. I doubt that he'll ever play regularly.

Glenn WILSON, Houston
Can he help anybody?
Wilson had arthroscopic surgery on his right knee on September 4. He's a free agent, and may have to go to spring training and play himself into a job.

After bouncing up and down early in his career Wilson has become a very *consistent* player, hitting .245 to .275 every year with an occasional show of power. He's a great defensive outfielder, wonderful arm, slow and not a good baserunner. He was slow *before* the scope; I don't imagine he's any faster now. He hits left-handers OK, but his overall offensive skills are such that he shouldn't get ten at bats a year against a right-hander. He does, somehow.

A SHORT ESSAY ON OUTFIELD ASSISTS
There's an old saw about outfield assist totals which holds that outfield assist totals don't indicate how well a guy throws because if the baserunners know a guy has a good arm they won't run on him. You've heard that one? It makes as much sense as saying that home run totals don't indicate how much power a hitter has, because if pitchers know a guy has good power they won't pitch to him. The two statements are equally well supported by the facts. If you're ever tempted to believe in this theory, look up the outfield assist totals of Cory Snyder, Jesse Barfield and Glenn Wilson. Everybody in baseball has known for years that Wilson was in the league because of his throwing arm, but he still throws out a huge number of opposition baserunners. Or, on the other hand, look up *Willie* Wilson, who has no throwing arm, and is credited with a good, consistent two assists per year.

Why then do people believe this? Because the data isn't in circulation. Even I don't have a source which lists career fielding statistics in an intelligible form, and if I don't have a source like that, I know you don't have one. With the bulk of the data not in circulation, the occasional fluke that pops up in the category (Kirby Puckett threw out only six runners last year) has a disproportionate impact on the discussion. People see the fluke, so to try to explain the fluke they'll come up with a generalized explanation, which is this "reverse fields" crap.

Outfield assists are a fairly important statistic, but largely ignored. If you can take twenty runners a year off the bases, like Jesse Barfield does, that's a big deal. That's equivalent to thirty points on your batting average. I think the problem is that outfield assists have such a wimpy name. "Assists"—what is that? It sounds like you were being a good little boy, helping mommy around the house. You "assist" an old lady across the street.

What they should be called is BASE-RUNNER KILLS. Which sounds more natural: "Glenn Wilson gunned down Vince Coleman going first to third in the fourth inning", or "Glenn Wilson 'registered an outfield assist' on a play against Vince Coleman in the fourth inning."

"Registered an outfield assist" sounds like he was scoring brownie points, earning gold stars from the teacher. Summarizing the game, the announcer could say "Glenn Wilson hit a two-run double in the third inning, and also killed a base-runner in the fourth, cutting down a rally." That's descriptive, and it makes sense. As it is now the announcer says "Glenn Wilson hit a two-run double in the third, and was credited with an assist on a play at third in the fourth, preventing a rally from developing." What's that sound like, he "was credited with an assist"? It's passive; not he *did* something, but he *was credited* with it. It sounds like he was just in the right place, sort of standing around being helpful, so the official scorer said, "Gee, let's *credit* him with an assist."

The same problem exists only more so in season totals. If you say that Jesse Barfield hit only .246 last year but was credited with 17 outfield assists, it sounds like you're apologizing for him. If you say he hit only .246 last year but shot down 17 baserunners, it sounds like he *did* something.

Baserunner kills. I'm serious about this.

Mookie WILSON, Toronto
Will he be a regular this year?

Hell, he shouldn't have been a regular last year. Wilson lost his job with the Mets, who needed a center fielder, so what the Sam Hill is he doing playing regularly for the Blue Jays, who have out-fielders oozing out of the carpet? He has a one-month hot streak with the Blue Jays in '89, so they take an airbrush to all of his flaws, pronounce him a team leader and put him in center field for the whole season. Jesus, these people will drive you crazy sometimes. Then they finish second instead of running away from the division like they should have, and the media talks about "clubhouse chemistry". OK, I'll buy clubhouse chemistry, but how about talking a little bit about idiotic personnel decisions? There are eleven million baseball fans who knew damn well a year ago that Mookie Wilson had no business being a regular center fielder on a contending team. If Cito Gaston didn't, why not? What do we know that he doesn't?

Steve WILSON, Chicago Cubs
What's his future? Can he pitch?

Apart from the fact that he pitches in Wrigley Field, which is the professional equivalent of selling life insurance to kamikaze pilots, I like almost everything about him. He's a left-hander, he's been healthy, his arm hasn't been abused, he throws hard, his strikeout/walk ratio is good. You don't want Cub pitchers on a rotisserie league team, but if the Cubs ever trade him he'll be a bargain.

Trevor WILSON, San Francisco
Will he get any better?

Wilson ended the 1990 season pitching poorly, and is penciled in as a middle reliever. You know, I would guess, that Roger Craig casually shifts pitchers from starting to relief throughout the season, so the current plans won't mean much in May.

Giant fans like to compare Wilson to a young Sandy Koufax, an analogy the exact basis of which is lost to the rest of us. He's a wild left-hander with dark hair. He's much smaller than Koufax, and doesn't have the same kind of breaking pitch.

Wilson started last year at Phoenix. After being called up he had two stretches of pitching brilliantly, from June 9 to July 14 and from July 30 to August 8. In the first stretch he started seven times, 49 innings with a 1.29 ERA, including a one-hit shutout in which he got the first 24 men out, struck out nine and walked no one (Game Score: 94) and another shutout, a five-hitter.

After that he got hammered three times, and then had three more superb starts, giving up two hits in eight innings once and pitching a two-hit complete game. At this point he pulled a muscle in his rib cage and went to the fifteen-day disabled list. After he came off the list he went to the bullpen.

Wilson has proven that he can pitch tremendously well for a short period of time. That certainly has to be considered among the things you look for in spotting a young star. Pitching great half the time shows a lot more than pitching fairly well most all the time.

For all of his reputation as a genius with pitchers, Roger Craig has yet to prove that he can bring along a young pitcher and make him a star. He has managed the Giants since late 1985, and very successfully, yet his staff has remained in a kind of static disarray. The other pitchers he has had who had a chance to be outstanding—Garrelts, Downs, Mark Davis, Mulholland—for one reason or another didn't develop for him. Wilson may be the best shot he has had.

Willie WILSON, Oakland
Can he still help a team?

I can't imagine why Oakland signed him, and I won't wash over it by saying that this is Oakland so they have to know what they're doing. Let's do a balance sheet:

Positives
1. Wilson hit .290 last year.
2. He is still extremely fast, possibly still the fastest man in the league.
3. He is a fine baserunner.
4. Apart from his throwing arm, he's a topnotch center fielder—good instincts, very few mistakes.
5. He walks more than he used to—thirty times last year as a half-time player. His on-base percentage last year (.354) was his best since 1982.

Negatives
1. No power.
2. 35 years old.
3. No throwing arm.
4. Pain in the butt to be around most of the time.
5. Question whether he will hit in Oakland the way he did in Kansas City.

Hm. I guess it's not as bad a gamble as I thought at first. Wilson probably will be easier to get along with in Oakland than he was in Kansas City, where he was inclined to act as if he had inherited the clubhouse. It's unfair to use the fact that he's 35 to balance off his skills, since I listed what his skills are at this time. It's still easier for me to see him failing in Oakland than succeeding.

Dave WINFIELD, California
Is he still a good player?

He was still a terrific player last year—an amazing thing, for a 39-year-old who had missed an entire season. He's lost something in the outfield, but I wouldn't wager anything I was afraid to lose that he won't drive in a hundred runs this year.

Is he in the Hall of Fame yet?

No. He's still in the gray area, albeit in the strong part. I have him at 108 points. Winfield has created more runs in his career than any active player except George Brett. He's about 130 behind Brett.

Herm WINNINGHAM, Cincinnati
Does he deserve more playing time?

He's well cast as a fifth outfielder. He's a .250 hitter with no power, good speed, good center fielder. He's about what Willie Wilson will be in Oakland.

★★★
Bobby WITT, Texas
★★★
Has he turned the corner for good?

He has, yes. That's not to say that he won't turn another corner, or an ankle or a rotator cuff. He could. But other than Ryan and Clemens, he is the most dominating pitcher in the American League when he is on his game, and he has finally reached the point at which his good games outnumber his bad.

Many young pitchers are compared to Sandy Koufax. Although he is a right-hander, Witt is more comparable to Koufax than any other pitcher has ever been. Like Koufax, he came to the majors with almost no experience, and has had to pitch his way through a long learning process. Witt's 1989 season was very comparable to Koufax' 1960. Witt's 1990 season is Koufax' 1961. Koufax took over the league in '62, although a circulatory problem kept him from winning the Cy Young Award until '63.

Witt started out last year 3-8. He finished up 17-10. You think you can take it from there?

Mike WITT, New York Yankees
Can he still pitch?

I think he can. In early May there were rumors that Mike Witt would be traded to the Yankees. George Steinbrenner was quoted as saying that "As long as I own the Yankees, Witt will never pitch for this team," and went on to explain that Witt was someone who would have trouble dealing with New York.

I think this must be what the Commissioner was referring to when he wrote

that Steinbrenner's managerial style bordered on the bizarre. It was bizarre enough that Steinbrenner would berate a veteran pitcher and question his makeup, only to trade for him a few days later. But who would believe anyway that Steinbrenner was capable of making a judgment about whether a pitcher could stand up to New York or not? I mean, isn't he the guy that brought in Doyle Alexander and Ed Whitson and Shane Rawley and Bob Shirley and Mike Armstrong and Neil Allen? Where did he get to be an expert on who could pitch in New York?

Witt went on the disabled list June 8 because of a strained right elbow, and went to California in early July to have the Angels' team physician take a look at it. After coming back he was 5-5 in eleven starts, ERA in the high fours.

The Yankees have succeeded in creating conditions in which it is almost impossible for any pitcher to be successful. If Witt can get things going the right way for him, I think he can still have a good year.

Todd WORRELL, St. Louis
Will he ever come back?

"Ever" is a long time. It's unlikely he'll be highly successful in 1991.

Craig WORTHINGTON, Baltimore
What happened to him last year? Is he in danger of losing his job?

He didn't report to camp in good shape last year; he was a little chubby. He didn't play with much intensity or enthusiasm. If he shows up in better shape and with a better attitude this year, he'll probably have a better year. If not, the Orioles have a super third base prospect in Leo Gomez, and they'll be just as happy to let Gomez have the position.

Rick WRONA, Chicago Cubs
Where is he now?

He was released by the Cubs, and signed a AAA contract with the Brewers.

He's a natural Brewer—a slow white guy who hits singles. He'll probably be up for part of the season as a third-string catcher or when Surhoff or McIntosh is on the DL.

Marvell WYNNE, Chicago Cubs

Has been sold to Japan. Without comment, the Cub lineup of July 23:

1. Dascenzo, rf
2. Sandberg, 2b
3. Grace, 1B
4. Wynne, cf
5. Clark, rf
6. Salazar, 3b
7. Dunston, ss
8. Girardi, c
9. Maddux, p

Eric YELDING, Houston
What's his best position? What do you do with him?

Yelding was a shortstop in the minor leagues, moved to center field last year because

a. Gerald Young was struggling, and
b. Yelding had the speed to play center.

It is very unlikely that he will prove to be a major league shortstop, which leaves him with center field and second base. My guess is that he will start the season at second base.

Notes: Yelding had only 15 extra base hits last year among 130 hits, or 12%. That's the lowest percentage of extra base hits of any major league regular. The bottom five were Yelding, Luis Polonia, Carney Lansford, Jose Uribe and Jeff Huson.

Yelding also was caught stealing 25 times, the most of any major league players.

Rich YETT, Minnesota
Will he pitch in the majors again?

Yett had a 6.17 ERA as a starting pitcher for Portland (twenty starts), but the Twins called him up for a look, anyway. If I was trying to find a pitcher I'd put "taking a look at Rich Yett" on my list somewhere between "converting Tim Laudner to a pitcher" and "trying to talk Ed Halicki out of retirement."

Mike YORK, Pittsburgh
Who is he?

A starting pitcher, signed by the White Sox in 1983 (apparently undrafted), released by the Sox in '86, signed by Pittsburgh and has picked his way through the minors. He's a Grade D prospect, but he's always gotten better in his second year at each level. Last year was his first year at AAA. He's 26.

Cliff YOUNG, California
Who is he?

A left-handed relief pitcher, a big guy and a great athlete. Young was the first-round draft pick of the Blue Jays in 1983, but was never dominant even in the low minor leagues. The Blue Jays traded him to California for DeWayne Buice in '89.

Toronto had him as a starter. California moved him to the bullpen, and his effectiveness improved dramatically. In 30 games at Edmonton (Pacific Coast League) last year he had a 2.42 ERA, then pitched so-so with the Angels in 17 games.

He's a Grade C prospect. He throws hard and has very good control, and also is almost impossible to run on. He doesn't have a breaking pitch or a specialty pitch, and he's not going to have a career unless he learns one.

Curt YOUNG, Oakland
Is he a suitable fifth starter?

His 9-6 record last year will probably earn him three or four more chances, but he can't pitch any more. He's had constant arm injuries. They usually call it "tendinitis", which is coach-speak for "something hurts but we're not going to operate." If he wasn't in Oakland last year he'd have been 4-11 with a six-plus ERA.

Gerald YOUNG, Houston
What the hell happened to him?

Young hit .321 in half a season in '87, .257 in a full season in '88, .233 in '89 and .175 last year, when he slipped back to the minors.

Young is only 26 years old, and I don't think there is anything seriously wrong with him. I think he's just incredibly messed up as a hitter. Young's minor league batting record would lead you to believe he was a .250-range hitter, which isn't terrible in the Astrodome if you walk and steal bases, which he does. But he hit .321 in '87 (the fluke year, remember) in enough games to make people think he could do that. When he didn't do it in '88 the Astros began to tinker with him to try to get him "back where he was in '87". The result was that he got so messed up—trying to drive one pitch, trying to punch at the next one—that he couldn't do anything.

Will he come back?

Probably not with the Astros. Before long the Astros will give up on him and send him along, and another organization will probably have better luck with him. He just needs a fresh start. He's one of the best defensive outfielders in baseball.

Strangest comment by a friend, 1990: *The Scouting Report: 1990* says that Young "was rushed to the big leagues and is still learning his profession." That book is written by John Dewan and Don Zminda, who are my buddies and it's a real good book, but hey, guys, you ought to double-check that one. Young played 592 minor league games, which puts him in the upper third of major league players.

Matt YOUNG, Red Sox
Will he help the Red Sox?

The signing of Matt Young for a reported $6.4 million for three years was attacked by the media. Dave Nightingale of *The Sporting News* wrote that "Red Sox General Manager Lou Gorman was the winner of the convention's 'I'd Like to Get You on a Slow Boat to China . . . and Bring a Deck of Cards' award for 1990."

I don't really understand the criticism. $2 million a year was established as the going rate for a run-of-the-mill starting pitcher a year ago, when Pascual Perez, Storm Davis and Sid Fernandez signed at that level. Young pitched 225 innings with a 3.51 ERA. Surely that puts him in a class with Pascual Perez and Storm Davis?

Young pitched well last year for Seattle after stinking up the league with Los Angeles (1987) and Oakland (1989). This is weird, because LA and Oakland are the two easiest places in baseball for a pitcher to succeed—great pitchers' parks, and organizations which know how to handle a pitcher. Ordinarily you would figure that if Young couldn't pitch for them there is no way in hell he's going to succeed in Seattle.

As to whether he will help the Red Sox, I'm skeptical. Young is a left-handed pitcher. He throws a fastball that tails in on left-handed hitters, which makes him tough for a left-hander to hit, but he doesn't have any consistent history of getting out right-handers. His control wasn't good, even last year. Seattle is a left-hander's park and not a hitter's park anymore; Young had a 2.69 ERA there, but 4.73 on the road.

Even though his ERA was good last year he was 8-18, but that's mostly just poor offensive support. He was the fourth worst-supported starting pitcher in the league, with 3.75 runs/nine innings, and tied Mark Langston for the major league lead with nine tough losses. His career record, 51-78, is pretty awful. I can't think of a lot of left-handers with poor control who were successful in Fenway Park. I'm guessing he'll go 10-13, and be taken out of the rotation down the stretch.

Robin YOUNT, Milwaukee
Will he bounce back?

I think he will, yes. Although the perception is that Yount had a terrible year, he still scored 98 runs, hit 17 homers and drove in 77. There was no *generalized* degeneration of his record, as would result from aging; there was merely a sharp drop in his batting average. He ended the season hitting well (.327 after September 1). He was still ahead in the count, still runs well and still hits the ball hard. The hits just didn't fall.

Milwaukee County Stadium has the characteristics of a hitting park, but as John Rickert discovered several years ago, it functions as a pitcher's park because of the weather. In mid-summer it *is* a hitter's park, but in April and October it's a pitcher's park because of the cold weather, and on balance the package favors the pitcher more than the hitter.

1990 was a cool summer, and Yount did not hit well at home. He hit .272 on the road, but .222 in Milwaukee.

Does he still have a chance to get 4,200 hits?

That was a long shot a year ago; his off season makes it almost impossible. In fact, Rose's record, which was never really *endangered*, is now almost entirely safe from this generation of players. *All* of the players who could conceivably have broken that record had off years to one degree or another in 1990. Yount was healthy at 34 but didn't hit. Don Mattingly had back trouble at 29, and it is now inconceivable that he could last long enough or play well enough to get 4,000 hits. Tony Gwynn had a miserable year. Wade Boggs failed to get his usual 200 hits. Kirby Puckett, who had 220 hits a year for the previous four years, slipped to 164. It is now a 100-1 shot that any active player could break Rose's record.

•Z•

Todd ZEILE, St. Louis
Should he move to third base?

Let's list the reasons he should and the reasons he shouldn't.

He should because:

1. He doesn't throw great.
2. He could improve his release, but how often does that *really* work?
3. If he stays at catcher it is unlikely that he will develop much as a hitter.

He shouldn't because

1. The major leagues are not a tryout camp.
2. He doesn't throw great, but he's not as bad as all that. His percentage of baserunners thrown out *wasn't* one of the worst in the league.
3. A good catcher is hard to find.
4. He wants to stay behind the plate.

Hm. Looks like a tough call. If it was my team, I'd leave him at catcher, just because I've seen so many guys mess up their careers with ill-advised position switches. If the Cardinals made a bad decision four years ago about where he should play that's very unfortunate, but there's a real risk of ruining the player by trying to straighten it out now. The Cardinals don't seem to have another good catcher *or* another good third baseman, so that's no factor.

Note: The Cardinals often had Zeile hitting cleanup as a rookie, usually fifth. He hit just .163 with runners in scoring position, the worst average in the National League. I wouldn't expect this to happen again, but it does suggest that there may be a lack of underlying confidence, which could be aggravated by asking him to play an unfamiliar position.

Eddie ZOSKY, Toronto
Who is he?

Shortstop prospect, one of the factors behind the trade of Fernandez. His arm is compared to Shawon Dunston's. They say he's a wonderful shortstop and he'll hit above .250, but with a poor strikeout/walk ratio, and he's not a base stealer. He'll come up if Manny Lee doesn't work out at short.

BASIC DATA

INTRODUCTION TO PLAYER DATA

In the first section of this book we focused on the basic questions about each player. In this section we have tried to present a cross-section of basic information. Our goal was to take the mountains of player data, and identify those things which, as a rule, the reader would most benefit from knowing. We tried to leave out anything which would be speculative or of uncertain meaning. We tried not to include any information which would not be significant for the normal player.

The problem with the statistical breakdowns in some guides is that they include information that you don't know what to do with. Basic statistics are broken down into groups so small that no significance can be attributed, or could if the material were accumulated for a hundred years. One guide publishes lists of what players hit with men in scoring position in late-inning pressure situations. This category combines the two most-commonly cited elements of "clutch" performance—but the combination of the two happens only fifteen to twenty-five times a year, for an everyday player, so a record of what the player hit in that situation has *no* significance, and would have none even if the material was accumulated over a player's career.

The other evil of modern statistics is categories combined in obscure ways the exact purpose of which is uncertain. I have evaluative stats, too, but I tried to make the purpose of them clear. There are three types of data blocks, one for a hitter, one for a starting pitcher and one for a reliever.

Regular Players

The data block for a regular player runs eighteen lines, most of which don't require any explanation. The "age" given is the player's age as of April 15, 1991. The defensive position is the position at which the player played the most innings in 1990.

There are three pieces of "formula information" about each player. "Runs created" is something I've attempted to measure for years. The theory is that a hitter's job isn't to hit singles, or to hit doubles, or to hit triples, specifically, but to put runs on the scoreboard. Runs created attempts to take the elements of the player's record, and tell you how many *runs* resulted from his individual accomplishments. The scale is just the same as the scale for runs scored or RBI. A hundred runs created represents an exceptional accomplishment, like 100 runs or 100 RBI. 120 runs created will lead the league, 80 is a good total for a second baseman, 70 isn't too good for an outfielder with 600 at bats, 50 is terrible for a regular outfielder, etc. The formula for runs created has evolved a little bit since the last time I published it.

"Offensive winning percentage" puts runs created in the context of opportunities. Fifty runs created with 200 outs is an exceptionally good rate; 50 runs created with 400 outs is poor.

Fifty runs created in Busch Stadium, where runs are relatively scarce, are worth more than 50 runs created in Fenway Park. Offensive winning percentage considers these things, and asks this question: if everybody on the team hit the way that this man hits, and if the team were average defensively, what would the team's winning percentage be? The highest in the majors was .868, by Rickey Henderson, which means that if everybody on a team was Rickey Henderson offensively and the team was average defensively, that team could expect to win 87% of their games. The scale for offensive winning percentage is the same as the scale for a pitcher's winning percentage: .500 is average, .600 is good, .700 exceptional.

The things that a player does offensively can be divided into two roughly equal halves: batting average and secondary offensive skills. Secondary offensive skills include hitting for power, stealing bases and taking a walk. If a player does many of these things, he will have a high secondary average; if he does few of them, he'll have a low one. The "norm" for secondary average is the same as the norm for batting average, about .250. But while everybody has a batting average between .200 and .350, secondary averages swing from .100 to .500. It's a way of making a general statement about the *other* things that a player does to create runs, other than hit singles.

"Most often bats" just tells you in what position in the batting order the man had the most at bats last year. "Hits first pitch" means the percentage of the time the player hits the first pitch *fair*, actually; foul balls don't count. "Gets ahead of the hitter" and "gets behind the hitter" also refer to the first pitch—how often the guy went 1-0 as opposed to 0-1. The batting average with men in scoring position is a 1990 figure, not a career average.

The bottom line, where it says "Life," is the player's career record in seasonal notation, which means what the player has done *per 162 games.* Eddie Murray has played 2,135 games in his career, which is equivalent to 13.2 years of 162 games each. For each 162 games, he has hit 29 homers and driven in 104 runs.

I included all players with 300 or more plate appearances, and a few other guys who were below 300. I understand that some of you would like to have information about the part-time players, but if you take 250 at bats and start breaking them into sub-groups, the data becomes meaningless pretty quick. I don't want to encourage that. This was also the standard for pitchers—300 batters faced.

Starting Pitchers

The information given for a starting pitcher includes Offensive Support and Double Play Support. Offensive support is the number of runs scored, per nine innings, while this man is in the game. Double Play support is the number of ground-ball double plays, per nine innings, while the pitcher is in the game.

"First Pitch is Hit", "Gets Ahead of the Hitter" and "Gets Behind the Hitter" are the mirror images of the same stats for hitters. "Gets Leadoff Man Out" is self-explanatory, I would think. We didn't present winning percentages at home and on the road because you don't need them and they're not significant. If a guy goes 7-2 in his home park and 1-7 on the road you know what this means; presenting ".778" and ".125" doesn't help, and also falsely implies that the percentage is of some significance.

The "Life" line for pitchers is based on 37 starts as a full season, with each relief appearance counting as one-half of a start. If a guy has never pitched in relief, his typical season will be based on 37 starts; if he has never started a game, his season will be based on 74 relief appearances. If he has a mix of starts and relief appearances over the years, he'll be somewhere between 37 and 74.

What I wanted to do was find stats which describe the pitcher's skills in a meaningful way. To print what the guy has done in April or May or June—that doesn't tell you what kind of a pitcher the man is. To present the batting average with men in scoring position and two out might be interesting once in awhile, but if a pitcher had an ability to pitch in that situation which was distinct from his ability to pitch in another situation, this would be unique and inexplicable.

Does a pitcher work behind the hitters, or ahead of them? I believe this measures an ability. Is a pitcher easy to run on, or hard? I believe this measures an ability.

Relief Pitchers

For relief pitchers, I printed saves, blown saves and holds. "Save efficiency" considers a save or a hold to be a success, and a blown save to be a failure.

I cut the home/road lines from the relief pitchers' data, and I'm sure some of you will be unhappy about this, but the fact remains that it is *not* meaningful information. A relief pitcher in our time typically pitches less than a hundred innings a season, and normally gives up runs in only ten to fifteen games. This small sample places us in danger of presenting statistically insignificant data in several areas. Splitting the work in half greatly increases that risk. If a player gives up runs in ten games during a year, it can easily happen that eight of those games will be at home or eight on the road. The pitcher can wind up with an 0.57 ERA on the road but 4.06 at home by simple chance. This not only could happen, but very commonly does happen. To present this data would cause people to make unjustified and misleading inferences about how pitchers perform in their home parks, and how they might do in another park. More than that, the conclusions that we would draw from this data, if I presented it, would *normally* be misleading. All conclusions that one would tend to draw from that data would tend to be erroneous. It is better to leave it out.

I did present left/right splits, which also reduce the samples to dangerously small groups, but there are several differences. Presenting left/right data tells you *how* the pitcher is used, whether he is and to what extent he is spotted to gain the platoon advantage. Left/right splits are normally presented in details—doubles, triples, and home runs allowed—while home/road splits are normally presented in collective terms (wins, losses and ERA.)

The failure to present saves as a part of the career record in seasonal notation was an oversight.

I am not in the business of compiling statistics. This information was compiled for me by STATS, Inc., 7366 N. Lincoln, Lincolnwood, Illinois, 60646. STATS compiles a vast array of statistical information about baseball, and I have an on-going relationship with them (for example, they run *Bill James Fantasy Baseball.*) My contribution to these stats was only to pick and choose among that information those things which I thought you might like to see. More information of the same type is available from them in their publications, including *STATS 1991 Major League Handbook* and *The STATS Baseball Scoreboard.*

•A•

Jim ABBOTT

CALIFORNIA STARTING PITCHER 23 Years Old
10-14 4.51 ERA

Opponents Batting Average: .295
Offensive Support: 4.08 Runs Per Nine Innings
Double Play Support: 1.15 GDP Per Nine Innings

First Pitch is Hit: 16%
Gets Ahead of the Hitter: 51%
Gets Behind the Hitter: 49%
Gets Leadoff Man Out: 65%

1990 On Base Pct Allowed: .353 Slugging Percentage: .401
Stolen Bases Allowed: 15   Caught Stealing: 4

Pitches Left	AB	H	2B	3B	HR	RBI	BB	SO	AVG
Vs. RHB	723	211	32	2	13	76	57	85	.292
Vs. LHB	110	35	4	0	3	20	15	20	.318

	G	IP	W-L	Pct	SO	BB	ERA
At Home	17	110	4-7		46	31	4.75
On the Road	16	102	6-7		59	41	4.25
1990 Season	33	212	10-14	.417	105	72	4.51
Life 1.7 Years	37	235	13-16	.458	131	87	4.24

Jim ACKER

TORONTO RELIEF PITCHER 32 Years Old
4-4 3.83 ERA 1 SAVES

Blown Saves: 1   Holds: 7   Save Efficiency: 89%
Inherited Runners who Scored: 39%
Opponents Batting Average: .281
Double Play Support: .59 GDP Per Nine Innings

First Pitch is Hit: 14%
Gets Ahead of the Hitter: 49%
Gets Behind the Hitter: 51%
Gets First Batter Out: 58%

1990 On Base Pct Allowed: .340 Slugging Percentage: .418
Stolen Bases Allowed: 6   Caught Stealing: 7

Pitches Right	AB	H	2B	3B	HR	RBI	BB	SO	AVG
Vs. RHB	217	60	11	0	7	37	16	41	.276
Vs. LHB	149	43	10	1	2	16	14	13	.289

	G	IP	W-L	Pct	SO	BB	ERA
1990 Season	59	92	4-4	.500	54	30	3.83
Life 5.7 Years	69	137	5-8	.405	75	49	3.78

Juan AGOSTO

HOUSTON RELIEF PITCHER 33 Years Old
9-8 4.29 ERA 4 SAVES

Blown Saves: 4   Holds: 16   Save Efficiency: 83%
Inherited Runners who Scored: 17%
Opponents Batting Average: .261
Double Play Support: .49 GDP Per Nine Innings

First Pitch is Hit: 16%
Gets Ahead of the Hitter: 49%
Gets Behind the Hitter: 51%
Gets First Batter Out: 70%

1990 On Base Pct Allowed: .345 Slugging Percentage: .350
Stolen Bases Allowed: 5   Caught Stealing: 1

Pitches Left	AB	H	2B	3B	HR	RBI	BB	SO	AVG
Vs. RHB	239	66	12	2	3	24	32	26	.276
Vs. LHB	110	25	3	0	1	15	7	24	.227

	G	IP	W-L	Pct	SO	BB	ERA
1990 Season	82	92	9-8	.529	50	39	4.29
Life 5.8 Years	74	84	6-5	.559	42	34	3.62

Rick AGUILERA

MINNESOTA RELIEF PITCHER 29 Years Old
5-3 2.76 ERA 32 SAVES

Blown Saves: 7   Holds: 0   Save Efficiency: 82%
Inherited Runners who Scored: 21%
Opponents Batting Average: .224
Double Play Support: 1.10 GDP Per Nine Innings

First Pitch is Hit: 10%
Gets Ahead of the Hitter: 56%
Gets Behind the Hitter: 44%
Gets First Batter Out: 66%

1990 On Base Pct Allowed: .291 Slugging Percentage: .322
Stolen Bases Allowed: 3   Caught Stealing: 0

Pitches Right	AB	H	2B	3B	HR	RBI	BB	SO	AVG
Vs. RHB	131	30	7	0	5	21	7	32	.229
Vs. LHB	114	25	2	0	0	5	12	29	.219

	G	IP	W-L	Pct	SO	BB	ERA
1990 Season	56	65	5-3	.625	61	19	2.76
Life 3.4 Years	53	181	13-10	.563	138	51	3.44

Darrel AKERFELDS

PHILADELPHIA   RELIEF PITCHER   28 Years Old
5-2   3.77 ERA   3 SAVES

Blown Saves: 0   Holds: 7   Save Efficiency: 100%
Inherited Runners who Scored: 26%
Opponents Batting Average: .201
Double Play Support: .77 GDP Per Nine Innings

First Pitch is Hit: 13%
Gets Ahead of the Hitter: 49%
Gets Behind the Hitter: 51%
Gets First Batter Out: 78%

1990 On Base Pct Allowed: .316 Slugging Percentage: .346
Stolen Bases Allowed: 14   Caught Stealing: 4

Pitches Right	AB	H	2B	3B	HR	RBI	BB	SO	AVG
Vs. RHB	169	34	6	1	3	18	29	23	.201
Vs. LHB	155	31	7	1	7	30	25	19	.200

	G	IP	W-L	Pct	SO	BB	ERA
1990 Season	71	93	5-2	.714	42	54	3.77
Life 1.5 Years	65	126	5-6	.438	67	69	5.04

•

Roberto ALOMAR

SAN DIEGO   SECOND BASE   23 Years Old

Runs Created: 77   Offensive Winning Percentage: .549
Batting Average: .287   Secondary Average: .217

Most Often Bats: 2nd
Hits First Pitch: 8%
Gets Ahead of the Pitcher: 52%
Hits Behind the Pitcher: 48%

1990 On Base Percentage: .340   Career: .339
1990 Slugging Percentage: .381   Career: .379
Batting Avg with Men in Scoring Position: .338

Switch Hitter	AB	R	H	2B	3B	HR	RBI	BB	SO	SB	AVG
Vs. RHP	382	58	115	14	4	3	43	27	34	21	.301
Vs. LHP	204	22	53	13	1	3	17	21	38	3	.260
At Home	76	298	43	85	9	4	4	36	23	37	12	.285
On the Road	71	288	37	83	18	1	2	24	25	35	12	.288
1990 Season	147	586	80	168	27	5	6	60	48	72	24	.287
Life	2.8 Years	634	89	180	28	4	8	57	54	84	33	.283

Sandy ALOMAR JR

CLEVELAND   CATCHER   24 Years Old

Runs Created: 60   Offensive Winning Percentage: .529
Batting Average: .290   Secondary Average: .193

Most Often Bats: 8th
Hits First Pitch: 18%
Gets Ahead of the Pitcher: 52%
Hits Behind the Pitcher: 48%

1990 On Base Percentage: .326   Career: .325
1990 Slugging Percentage: .418   Career: .417
Batting Avg with Men in Scoring Position: .307

Bats Right-Handed	AB	R	H	2B	3B	HR	RBI	BB	SO	SB	AVG
Vs. RHP	328	41	85	21	2	7	48	17	33	3	.259
Vs. LHP	117	19	44	5	0	2	18	8	13	1	.376
At Home	70	227	33	68	12	0	5	30	13	22	3	.300
On the Road	62	218	27	61	14	2	4	36	12	24	1	.280
1990 Season	132	445	60	129	26	2	9	66	25	46	4	.290
Life	0.9 Years	538	71	154	31	2	12	83	32	58	5	.286

•

Larry ANDERSEN

BOSTON   RELIEF PITCHER   37 Years Old
5-2   1.79 ERA   7 SAVES

Blown Saves: 4   Holds: 8   Save Efficiency: 79%
Inherited Runners who Scored: 37%
Opponents Batting Average: .227
Double Play Support: .56 GDP Per Nine Innings

First Pitch is Hit: 9%
Gets Ahead of the Hitter: 61%
Gets Behind the Hitter: 39%
Gets First Batter Out: 77%

1990 On Base Pct Allowed: .283 Slugging Percentage: .273
Stolen Bases Allowed: 16   Caught Stealing: 3

Pitches Right	AB	H	2B	3B	HR	RBI	BB	SO	AVG
Vs. RHB	183	33	4	0	0	15	10	68	.180
Vs. LHB	165	46	4	1	2	23	17	25	.279

	G	IP	W-L	Pct	SO	BB	ERA
1990 Season	65	96	5-2	.714	93	27	1.79
Life 7.2 Years	74	113	4-4	.516	81	35	3.15

Allan ANDERSON

MINNESOTA	STARTING PITCHER	27 Years Old
	7-18 4.53 ERA	

Opponents Batting Average: .289
Offensive Support: 3.43 Runs Per Nine Innings
Double Play Support: .91 GDP Per Nine Innings

First Pitch is Hit: 18%
Gets Ahead of the Hitter: 52%
Gets Behind the Hitter: 48%
Gets Leadoff Man Out: 70%

1990 On Base Pct Allowed: .325 Slugging Percentage: .433
Stolen Bases Allowed: 10   Caught Stealing: 11

Pitches Left	AB	H	2B	3B	HR	RBI	BB	SO	AVG
Vs. RHB	632	186	39	3	18	84	32	71	.294
Vs. LHB	109	28	2	0	2	13	7	11	.257

	G	IP	W-L	Pct	SO	BB	ERA
At Home	18	111	4-12		51	25	4.77
On the Road	13	77	3-6		31	14	4.19
1990 Season	31	189	7-18	.280	82	39	4.53
Life 3.0 Years	39	225	14-14	.506	95	56	3.05

•

Kevin APPIER

KANSAS CITY	STARTING PITCHER	23 Years Old
	12-8 2.76 ERA	

Opponents Batting Average: .252
Offensive Support: 4.61 Runs Per Nine Innings
Double Play Support: 1.02 GDP Per Nine Innings

First Pitch is Hit: 15%
Gets Ahead of the Hitter: 49%
Gets Behind the Hitter: 51%
Gets Leadoff Man Out: 72%

1990 On Base Pct Allowed: .307 Slugging Percentage: .334
Stolen Bases Allowed: 13   Caught Stealing: 1

Pitches Right	AB	H	2B	3B	HR	RBI	BB	SO	AVG
Vs. RHB	399	98	8	0	6	27	19	77	.246
Vs. LHB	311	81	9	1	7	32	35	50	.260

	G	IP	W-L	Pct	SO	BB	ERA
At Home	15	84	7-4		59	18	2.77
On the Road	17	101	5-4		68	36	2.75
1990 Season	32	186	12-8	.600	127	54	2.76
Life 0.9 Years	42	229	14-13	.520	151	73	3.43

Jack ARMSTRONG

CINCINNATI	STARTING PITCHER	26 Years Old
	12-9 3.42 ERA	

Opponents Batting Average: .242
Offensive Support: 4.66 Runs Per Nine Innings
Double Play Support: .49 GDP Per Nine Innings

First Pitch is Hit: 16%
Gets Ahead of the Hitter: 48%
Gets Behind the Hitter: 52%
Gets Leadoff Man Out: 73%

1990 On Base Pct Allowed: .311 Slugging Percentage: .352
Stolen Bases Allowed: 14   Caught Stealing: 6

Pitches Right	AB	H	2B	3B	HR	RBI	BB	SO	AVG
Vs. RHB	238	52	9	2	3	18	19	59	.218
Vs. LHB	386	99	21	4	6	46	40	51	.256

	G	IP	W-L	Pct	SO	BB	ERA
At Home	14	71	6-4		46	29	3.93
On the Road	15	95	6-5		64	30	3.03
1990 Season	29	166	12-9	.571	110	59	3.42
Life 1.4 Years	38	203	13-14	.486	132	87	4.17

•

Paul ASSENMACHER

CHICAGO	RELIEF PITCHER	30 Years Old
	7-2 2.80 ERA 10 SAVES	

Blown Saves: 10   Holds: 10   Save Efficiency: 67%
Inherited Runners who Scored: 29%
Opponents Batting Average: .239
Double Play Support: .79 GDP Per Nine Innings

First Pitch is Hit: 15%
Gets Ahead of the Hitter: 52%
Gets Behind the Hitter: 48%
Gets First Batter Out: 75%

1990 On Base Pct Allowed: .305 Slugging Percentage: .351
Stolen Bases Allowed: 6   Caught Stealing: 4

Pitches Left	AB	H	2B	3B	HR	RBI	BB	SO	AVG
Vs. RHB	255	63	6	1	9	23	30	65	.247
Vs. LHB	121	27	2	1	1	19	6	30	.223

	G	IP	W-L	Pct	SO	BB	ERA
1990 Season	74	103	7-2	.778	95	36	2.80
Life 4.3 Years	74	90	6-4	.605	80	34	3.37

Steve AVERY

ATLANTA   STARTING PITCHER   21 Years Old
3-11   5.64 ERA

Opponents Batting Average: .302
Offensive Support: 3.45 Runs Per Nine Innings
Double Play Support: .45 GDP Per Nine Innings

First Pitch is Hit: 15%
Gets Ahead of the Hitter: 44%
Gets Behind the Hitter: 56%
Gets Leadoff Man Out: 61%

1990 On Base Pct Allowed: .372 Slugging Percentage: .431
Stolen Bases Allowed: 20   Caught Stealing: 8

Pitches Left	AB	H	2B	3B	HR	RBI	BB	SO	AVG
Vs. RHB	340	105	24	2	7	55	40	56	.309
Vs. LHB	61	16	1	1	0	12	5	19	.262

	G	IP	W-L	Pct	SO	BB	ERA
At Home	11	59	3-4		43	27	4.25
On the Road	10	40	0-7		32	18	7.71
1990 Season	21	99	3-11	.214	75	45	5.64
Life 0.6 Years	38	179	5-20	.214	135	81	5.64

•B•

Wally BACKMAN

PITTSBURGH   THIRD BASE   31 Years Old

Runs Created: 49   Offensive Winning Percentage: .651
Batting Average: .292   Secondary Average: .257

Most Often Bats: 1st
Hits First Pitch: 10%
Gets Ahead of the Pitcher: 56%
Hits Behind the Pitcher: 44%

1990 On Base Percentage: .374   Career: .351
1990 Slugging Percentage: .397   Career: .343
Batting Avg with Men in Scoring Position: .358

Switch Hitter		AB	R	H	2B	3B	HR	RBI	BB	SO	SB	AVG
Vs. RHP		284	53	86	20	3	2	25	35	44	6	.303
Vs. LHP		31	9	6	1	0	0	3	7	9	0	.194
At Home	53	154	30	43	12	1	0	12	21	28	4	.279
On the Road	51	161	32	49	9	2	2	16	21	25	2	.304
1990 Season	104	315	62	92	21	3	2	28	42	53	6	.292
Life 5.9 Years	505	77	141	21	3	2	37	57	73	19	.279

Carlos BAERGA

CLEVELAND   THIRD BASE   22 Years Old

Runs Created: 37   Offensive Winning Percentage: .449
Batting Average: .260   Secondary Average: .186

Most Often Bats: 3rd
Hits First Pitch: 16%
Gets Ahead of the Pitcher: 51%
Hits Behind the Pitcher: 49%

1990 On Base Percentage: .300   Career: .300
1990 Slugging Percentage: .394   Career: .394
Batting Avg with Men in Scoring Position: .264

Switch Hitter		AB	R	H	2B	3B	HR	RBI	BB	SO	SB	AVG
Vs. RHP		209	31	56	13	2	5	31	15	35	0	.268
Vs. LHP		103	15	25	4	0	2	16	1	22	0	.243
At Home	51	150	27	45	10	1	3	28	9	22	0	.300
On the Road	57	162	19	36	7	1	4	19	7	35	0	.222
1990 Season	108	312	46	81	17	2	7	47	16	57	0	.260
Life 0.7 Years	468	69	122	26	3	11	71	24	86	0	.260

Harold BAINES

OAKLAND   DESIGNATED HITTER   32 Years Old

Runs Created: 68   Offensive Winning Percentage: .665
Batting Average: .284   Secondary Average: .318

Most Often Bats: 5th
Hits First Pitch: 16%
Gets Ahead of the Pitcher: 50%
Hits Behind the Pitcher: 50%

1990 On Base Percentage: .378   Career: .344
1990 Slugging Percentage: .441   Career: .461
Batting Avg with Men in Scoring Position: .262

Bats Left-Handed	AB	R	H	2B	3B	HR	RBI	BB	SO	SB	AVG
Vs. RHP	324	39	95	12	1	13	50	55	58	0	.293
Vs. LHP	91	13	23	3	0	3	15	12	22	0	.253
At Home	67	200	28	56	4	0	9	40	28	40	0	.280
On the Road	68	215	24	62	11	1	7	25	39	40	0	.288
1990 Season	135	415	52	118	15	1	16	65	67	80	0	.284
Life	9.6 Years	599	76	173	30	5	21	93	53	92	3	.288

•

Steve BALBONI

NEW YORK   DESIGNATED HITTER   34 Years Old

Runs Created: 33   Offensive Winning Percentage: .481
Batting Average: .192   Secondary Average: .346

Most Often Bats: 4th
Hits First Pitch: 9%
Gets Ahead of the Pitcher: 47%
Hits Behind the Pitcher: 53%

1990 On Base Percentage: .291   Career: .292
1990 Slugging Percentage: .406   Career: .450
Batting Avg with Men in Scoring Position: .179

Bats Right-Handed	AB	R	H	2B	3B	HR	RBI	BB	SO	SB	AVG
Vs. RHP	105	5	17	2	0	3	7	5	38	0	.162
Vs. LHP	161	19	34	4	0	14	27	30	53	0	.211
At Home	56	123	10	26	5	0	8	17	18	40	0	.211
On the Road	60	143	14	25	1	0	9	17	17	51	0	.175
1990 Season	116	266	24	51	6	0	17	34	35	91	0	.192
Life	5.9 Years	527	59	120	21	2	31	84	46	144	0	.228

Jeff BALLARD

BALTIMORE   RELIEF PITCHER   27 Years Old
                    2-11   4.93 ERA   0 SAVES

Blown Saves: 0   Holds: 7   Save Efficiency: 100%
Inherited Runners who Scored: 19%
Opponents Batting Average: .290
Double Play Support: 1.01 GDP Per Nine Innings

First Pitch is Hit: 15%
Gets Ahead of the Hitter: 45%
Gets Behind the Hitter: 55%
Gets First Batter Out: 81%

1990 On Base Pct Allowed: .344 Slugging Percentage: .480
Stolen Bases Allowed: 8   Caught Stealing: 6

Pitches Left	AB	H	2B	3B	HR	RBI	BB	SO	AVG
Vs. RHB	390	112	30	0	18	52	33	27	.287
Vs. LHB	136	40	4	0	4	15	9	23	.294

	G	IP	W-L	Pct	SO	BB	ERA
1990 Season	44	133	2-11	.154	50	42	4.93
Life 2.8 Years	42	202	11-14	.435	64	62	4.42

•

Jesse BARFIELD

NEW YORK   RIGHT FIELD   31 Years Old

Runs Created: 84   Offensive Winning Percentage: .675
Batting Average: .246   Secondary Average: .391

Most Often Bats: 5th
Hits First Pitch: 9%
Gets Ahead of the Pitcher: 49%
Hits Behind the Pitcher: 51%

1990 On Base Percentage: .359   Career: .340
1990 Slugging Percentage: .456   Career: .473
Batting Avg with Men in Scoring Position: .264

Bats Right-Handed	AB	R	H	2B	3B	HR	RBI	BB	SO	SB	AVG
Vs. RHP	314	38	75	14	2	12	53	49	99	1	.239
Vs. LHP	162	31	42	7	0	13	25	33	51	3	.259
At Home	74	239	34	52	10	0	12	35	33	79	2	.218
On the Road	79	237	35	65	11	2	13	43	49	71	2	.274
1990 Season	153	476	69	117	21	2	25	78	82	150	4	.246
Life	8.1 Years	540	83	141	25	4	27	81	62	139	8	.261

Steve BEDROSIAN

SAN FRANCISCO   RELIEF PITCHER   33 Years Old
         9-9   4.20 ERA   17 SAVES

Blown Saves: 5   Holds: 2   Save Efficiency: 79%
Inherited Runners who Scored: 23%
Opponents Batting Average: .241
Double Play Support: 1.02 GDP Per Nine Innings

First Pitch is Hit: 17%
Gets Ahead of the Hitter: 46%
Gets Behind the Hitter: 54%
Gets First Batter Out: 69%

1990 On Base Pct Allowed: .341 Slugging Percentage: .341
Stolen Bases Allowed: 14   Caught Stealing: 1

Pitches Right	AB	H	2B	3B	HR	RBI	BB	SO	AVG
Vs. RHB	134	28	4	0	2	14	18	20	.209
Vs. LHB	165	44	6	1	4	22	26	23	.267

	G	IP	W-L	Pct	SO	BB	ERA
1990 Season	68	79	9-9	.500	43	44	4.20
Life 8.1 Years	68	122	8-9	.481	96	54	3.31

•

Tim BELCHER

LOS ANGELES   STARTING PITCHER   29 Years Old
         9-9   4.00 ERA

Opponents Batting Average: .240
Offensive Support: 4.18 Runs Per Nine Innings
Double Play Support: .65 GDP Per Nine Innings

First Pitch is Hit: 13%
Gets Ahead of the Hitter: 53%
Gets Behind the Hitter: 47%
Gets Leadoff Man Out: 72%

1990 On Base Pct Allowed: .299 Slugging Percentage: .382
Stolen Bases Allowed: 11   Caught Stealing: 7

Pitches Right	AB	H	2B	3B	HR	RBI	BB	SO	AVG
Vs. RHB	268	69	8	3	9	41	18	47	.257
Vs. LHB	298	67	11	2	8	26	30	55	.225

	G	IP	W-L	Pct	SO	BB	ERA
At Home	10	75	6-3		45	22	2.77
On the Road	14	78	3-6		57	26	5.17
1990 Season	24	153	9-9	.500	102	48	4.00
Life 2.6 Years	41	231	15-11	.580	185	72	3.12

George BELL

TORONTO   LEFT FIELD   31 Years Old

Runs Created: 70   Offensive Winning Percentage: .485
Batting Average: .265   Secondary Average: .219

Most Often Bats: 4th
Hits First Pitch: 7%
Gets Ahead of the Pitcher: 54%
Hits Behind the Pitcher: 46%

1990 On Base Percentage: .303   Career: .325
1990 Slugging Percentage: .422   Career: .486
Batting Avg with Men in Scoring Position: .275

Bats Right-Handed		AB	R	H	2B	3B	HR	RBI	BB	SO	SB	AVG
Vs. RHP		413	47	112	19	0	16	64	17	63	3	.271
Vs. LHP		149	20	37	6	0	5	22	15	17	0	.248
At Home	70	274	36	70	12	0	11	41	16	41	0	.255
On the Road	72	288	31	79	13	0	10	45	16	39	3	.274
1990 Season	142	562	67	149	25	0	21	86	32	80	3	.265
Life 7.3 Years	621	88	178	33	4	28	102	35	77	8	.286

•

Jay BELL

PITTSBURGH   SHORTSTOP   25 Years Old

Runs Created: 73   Offensive Winning Percentage: .468
Batting Average: .254   Secondary Average: .237

Most Often Bats: 2nd
Hits First Pitch: 12%
Gets Ahead of the Pitcher: 50%
Hits Behind the Pitcher: 50%

1990 On Base Percentage: .329   Career: .312
1990 Slugging Percentage: .362   Career: .348
Batting Avg with Men in Scoring Position: .281

Bats Right-Handed		AB	R	H	2B	3B	HR	RBI	BB	SO	SB	AVG
Vs. RHP		332	47	79	15	3	5	35	31	67	7	.238
Vs. LHP		251	46	69	13	4	2	17	34	42	3	.275
At Home	80	287	42	75	14	4	1	17	31	56	2	.261
On the Road	79	296	51	73	14	3	6	35	34	53	8	.247
1990 Season	159	583	93	148	28	7	7	52	65	109	10	.254
Life 2.2 Years	553	76	136	26	6	6	54	53	112	10	.246

Andy BENES

SAN DIEGO   STARTING PITCHER   23 Years Old
10-11   3.60 ERA

Opponents Batting Average: .242
Offensive Support: 4.02 Runs Per Nine Innings
Double Play Support: .66 GDP Per Nine Innings

First Pitch is Hit: 13%
Gets Ahead of the Hitter: 48%
Gets Behind the Hitter: 52%
Gets Leadoff Man Out: 70%

1990 On Base Pct Allowed: .306 Slugging Percentage: .374
Stolen Bases Allowed: 23   Caught Stealing: 5

Pitches Right	AB	H	2B	3B	HR	RBI	BB	SO	AVG
Vs. RHB	302	71	8	3	9	31	29	72	.235
Vs. LHB	428	106	16	6	9	40	40	68	.248

	G	IP	W-L	Pct	SO	BB	ERA
At Home	15	89	6-4		74	33	3.93
On the Road	17	103	4-7		66	36	3.32
1990 Season	32	192	10-11	.476	140	69	3.60
Life 1.1 Years	37	231	14-12	.533	184	89	3.58

•

Todd BENZINGER

CINCINNATI   FIRST BASE   28 Years Old

Runs Created: 38   Offensive Winning Percentage: .428
Batting Average: .253   Secondary Average: .146

Most Often Bats: 6th
Hits First Pitch: 15%
Gets Ahead of the Pitcher: 51%
Hits Behind the Pitcher: 49%

1990 On Base Percentage: .291   Career: .300
1990 Slugging Percentage: .340   Career: .391
Batting Avg with Men in Scoring Position: .252

Switch Hitter	AB	R	H	2B	3B	HR	RBI	BB	SO	SB	AVG
Vs. RHP	204	20	46	7	2	3	29	13	54	2	.225
Vs. LHP	172	15	49	7	0	2	17	6	15	1	.285
At Home	62	190	21	49	8	1	4	23	10	30	2	.258
On the Road	56	186	14	46	6	1	1	23	9	39	1	.247
1990 Season 118	376	35	95	14	2	5	46	19	69	3	.253
Life 2.9 Years	560	68	142	28	2	15	81	37	106	4	.254

Juan BERENGUER

MINNESOTA   RELIEF PITCHER   36 Years Old
8-5   3.41 ERA   0 SAVES

Blown Saves: 2   Holds: 9   Save Efficiency: 82%
Inherited Runners who Scored: 27%
Opponents Batting Average: .232
Double Play Support: .72 GDP Per Nine Innings

First Pitch is Hit: 12%
Gets Ahead of the Hitter: 50%
Gets Behind the Hitter: 50%
Gets First Batter Out: 72%

1990 On Base Pct Allowed: .338 Slugging Percentage: .346
Stolen Bases Allowed: 12   Caught Stealing: 6

Pitches Right	AB	H	2B	3B	HR	RBI	BB	SO	AVG
Vs. RHB	208	43	4	0	6	21	35	43	.207
Vs. LHB	159	42	7	2	3	19	23	34	.264

	G	IP	W-L	Pct	SO	BB	ERA
1990 Season	51	100	8-5	.615	77	58	3.41
Life 6.6 Years	60	162	10-8	.538	133	83	3.88

•

Dante BICHETTE

CALIFORNIA   RIGHT FIELD   27 Years Old

Runs Created: 42   Offensive Winning Percentage: .480
Batting Average: .255   Secondary Average: .238

Most Often Bats: 5th
Hits First Pitch: 11%
Gets Ahead of the Pitcher: 49%
Hits Behind the Pitcher: 51%

1990 On Base Percentage: .292   Career: .274
1990 Slugging Percentage: .433   Career: .394
Batting Avg with Men in Scoring Position: .253

Bats Right-Handed	AB	R	H	2B	3B	HR	RBI	BB	SO	SB	AVG
Vs. RHP	203	26	49	7	0	10	32	9	49	5	.241
Vs. LHP	146	14	40	8	1	5	21	7	30	0	.274
At Home	50	159	21	41	6	0	8	26	6	33	1	.258
On the Road	59	190	19	48	9	1	7	27	10	46	4	.253
1990 Season 109	349	40	89	15	1	15	53	16	79	5	.255
Life 1.1 Years	485	49	118	22	1	16	69	20	100	7	.244

Mike BIELECKI

CHICAGO   STARTING PITCHER   31 Years Old
                 8-11   4.93 ERA

Opponents Batting Average: .287
Offensive Support: 4.23 Runs Per Nine Innings
Double Play Support: .59 GDP Per Nine Innings

First Pitch is Hit: 12%
Gets Ahead of the Hitter: 45%
Gets Behind the Hitter: 55%
Gets Leadoff Man Out: 62%

1990 On Base Pct Allowed: .359 Slugging Percentage: .428
Stolen Bases Allowed: 17   Caught Stealing: 9

Pitches Right	AB	H	2B	3B	HR	RBI	BB	SO	AVG
Vs. RHB	258	80	15	4	5	36	25	42	.310
Vs. LHB	396	108	20	5	8	51	45	61	.273

	G	IP	W-L	Pct	SO	BB	ERA
At Home	18	76	2-7		54	31	4.88
On the Road	18	92	6-4		49	39	4.97
1990 Season	36	168	8-11	.421	103	70	4.93
Life 3.4 Years	42	198	11-11	.507	122	86	4.12

●

Craig BIGGIO

HOUSTON   CATCHER   25 Years Old

Runs Created: 68   Offensive Winning Percentage: .554
Batting Average: .276   Secondary Average: .213

Most Often Bats: 3rd
Hits First Pitch: 11%
Gets Ahead of the Pitcher: 54%
Hits Behind the Pitcher: 46%

1990 On Base Percentage: .342   Career: .330
1990 Slugging Percentage: .348   Career: .369
Batting Avg with Men in Scoring Position: .297

Bats Right-Handed		AB	R	H	2B	3B	HR	RBI	BB	SO	SB	AVG
Vs. RHP		337	31	103	18	1	2	29	26	52	14	.306
Vs. LHP		218	22	50	6	1	2	13	27	27	11	.229
At Home	76	277	28	76	11	1	2	21	25	39	15	.274
On the Road	74	278	25	77	13	1	2	21	28	40	10	.277
1990 Season	150	555	53	153	24	2	4	42	53	79	25	.276
Life 2.1 Years		544	64	142	25	2	10	52	53	83	25	.261

Bud BLACK

TORONTO   STARTING PITCHER   33 Years Old
                 13-11   3.57 ERA

Opponents Batting Average: .233
Offensive Support: 4.27 Runs Per Nine Innings
Double Play Support: .39 GDP Per Nine Innings

First Pitch is Hit: 16%
Gets Ahead of the Hitter: 52%
Gets Behind the Hitter: 48%
Gets Leadoff Man Out: 74%

1990 On Base Pct Allowed: .290 Slugging Percentage: .350
Stolen Bases Allowed: 12   Caught Stealing: 8

Pitches Left	AB	H	2B	3B	HR	RBI	BB	SO	AVG
Vs. RHB	633	140	26	2	12	49	50	94	.221
Vs. LHB	145	41	4	0	7	20	11	12	.283

	G	IP	W-L	Pct	SO	BB	ERA
At Home	16	104	8-5		53	27	3.13
On the Road	16	103	5-6		53	34	4.02
1990 Season	32	207	13-11	.542	106	61	3.57
Life 6.7 Years	45	218	12-12	.503	111	64	3.70

●

Willie BLAIR

TORONTO   RELIEF PITCHER   25 Years Old
                 3-5   4.06 ERA   0 SAVES

Blown Saves: 0   Holds: 1   Save Efficiency: 100%
Inherited Runners who Scored: 30%
Opponents Batting Average: .250
Double Play Support: .26 GDP Per Nine Innings

First Pitch is Hit: 15%
Gets Ahead of the Hitter: 48%
Gets Behind the Hitter: 52%
Gets First Batter Out: 86%

1990 On Base Pct Allowed: .320 Slugging Percentage: .383
Stolen Bases Allowed: 5   Caught Stealing: 2

Pitches Right	AB	H	2B	3B	HR	RBI	BB	SO	AVG
Vs. RHB	138	35	9	2	2	18	14	25	.254
Vs. LHB	126	31	6	2	2	14	14	18	.246

	G	IP	W-L	Pct	SO	BB	ERA
1990 Season	27	69	3-5	.375	43	28	4.06
Life 0.4 Years	61	154	7-11	.375	96	63	4.06

Jeff BLAUSER

ATLANTA   SHORTSTOP   25 Years Old

Runs Created: 54   Offensive Winning Percentage: .533
Batting Average: .269   Secondary Average: .238

Most Often Bats: 7th
Hits First Pitch: 16%
Gets Ahead of the Pitcher: 48%
Hits Behind the Pitcher: 52%

1990 On Base Percentage: .338   Career: .327
1990 Slugging Percentage: .409   Career: .400
Batting Avg with Men in Scoring Position: .241

Bats Right-Handed	AB	R	H	2B	3B	HR	RBI	BB	SO	SB	AVG
Vs. RHP	250	23	64	12	2	5	22	19	50	2	.256
Vs. LHP	136	23	40	12	1	3	17	16	20	1	.294
At Home	52	172	25	51	12	2	3	21	19	25	1	.297
On the Road	63	214	21	53	12	1	5	18	16	45	2	.248
1990 Season 115	386	46	104	24	3	8	39	35	70	3	.269
Life 2.0 Years	534	63	141	28	4	12	53	46	107	7	.264

•

Bert BLYLEVEN

CALIFORNIA   STARTING PITCHER   40 Years Old
8-7   5.24 ERA

Opponents Batting Average: .303
Offensive Support: 4.84 Runs Per Nine Innings
Double Play Support: .67 GDP Per Nine Innings

First Pitch is Hit: 18%
Gets Ahead of the Hitter: 53%
Gets Behind the Hitter: 47%
Gets Leadoff Man Out: 68%

1990 On Base Pct Allowed: .339 Slugging Percentage: .463
Stolen Bases Allowed: 4   Caught Stealing: 9

Pitches Right	AB	H	2B	3B	HR	RBI	BB	SO	AVG
Vs. RHB	268	79	20	1	7	38	11	42	.295
Vs. LHB	270	84	13	3	8	35	14	27	.311

	G	IP	W-L	Pct	SO	BB	ERA
At Home	11	71	4-2		30	10	3.82
On the Road	12	63	4-5		39	15	6.82
1990 Season	23	134	8-7	.533	69	25	5.24
Life 17.9 Years	37	269	16-13	.540	202	72	3.28

Mike BODDICKER

BOSTON   STARTING PITCHER   33 Years Old
17-8   3.36 ERA

Opponents Batting Average: .258
Offensive Support: 5.41 Runs Per Nine Innings
Double Play Support: .83 GDP Per Nine Innings

First Pitch is Hit: 12%
Gets Ahead of the Hitter: 51%
Gets Behind the Hitter: 49%
Gets Leadoff Man Out: 75%

1990 On Base Pct Allowed: .319 Slugging Percentage: .368
Stolen Bases Allowed: 13   Caught Stealing: 10

Pitches Right	AB	H	2B	3B	HR	RBI	BB	SO	AVG
Vs. RHB	409	104	18	1	9	33	36	92	.254
Vs. LHB	464	121	20	4	7	44	33	51	.261

	G	IP	W-L	Pct	SO	BB	ERA
At Home	20	136	11-5		83	36	2.97
On the Road	14	92	6-3		60	33	3.93
1990 Season	34	228	17-8	.680	143	69	3.36
Life 7.2 Years	38	249	16-13	.554	163	84	3.66

•

Wade BOGGS

BOSTON   THIRD BASE   32 Years Old

Runs Created: 102   Offensive Winning Percentage: .679
Batting Average: .302   Secondary Average: .257

Most Often Bats: 1st
Hits First Pitch: 2%
Gets Ahead of the Pitcher: 50%
Hits Behind the Pitcher: 50%

1990 On Base Percentage: .386   Career: .436
1990 Slugging Percentage: .418   Career: .472
Batting Avg with Men in Scoring Position: .338

Bats Left-Handed	AB	R	H	2B	3B	HR	RBI	BB	SO	SB	AVG
Vs. RHP	389	60	124	30	3	5	33	66	29	0	.319
Vs. LHP	230	29	63	14	2	1	30	21	39	0	.274
At Home	80	309	51	111	30	1	3	32	52	42	0	.359
On the Road	75	310	38	76	14	4	3	31	35	26	0	.245
1990 Season 155	619	89	187	44	5	6	63	87	68	0	.302
Life 8.3 Years	624	110	216	43	5	8	71	102	49	2	.346

Tom BOLTON

BOSTON   STARTING PITCHER   28 Years Old
                10-5   3.38 ERA

Opponents Batting Average: .251
Offensive Support: 5.49 Runs Per Nine Innings
Double Play Support: 1.20 GDP Per Nine Innings

First Pitch is Hit: 13%
Gets Ahead of the Hitter: 49%
Gets Behind the Hitter: 51%
Gets Leadoff Man Out: 70%

1990 On Base Pct Allowed: .323 Slugging Percentage: .339
Stolen Bases Allowed: 7   Caught Stealing: 5

Pitches Left	AB	H	2B	3B	HR	RBI	BB	SO	AVG
Vs. RHB	344	87	17	1	5	36	41	54	.253
Vs. LHB	99	24	2	0	1	9	6	11	.242

	G	IP	W-L	Pct	SO	BB	ERA
At Home	8	54	6-1		32	16	1.99
On the Road	13	65	4-4		33	31	4.55
1990 Season	21	120	10-5	.667	65	47	3.38
Life 1.4 Years	59	166	9-9	.500	104	71	4.21

•

Barry BONDS

PITTSBURGH   LEFT FIELD   26 Years Old

Runs Created: 128   Offensive Winning Percentage: .818
Batting Average: .301   Secondary Average: .543

Most Often Bats: 5th
Hits First Pitch: 11%
Gets Ahead of the Pitcher: 55%
Hits Behind the Pitcher: 45%

1990 On Base Percentage: .406   Career: .358
1990 Slugging Percentage: .565   Career: .479
Batting Avg with Men in Scoring Position: .377

Bats Left-Handed	AB	R	H	2B	3B	HR	RBI	BB	SO	SB	AVG
Vs. RHP	279	58	83	18	1	16	56	62	42	36	.297
Vs. LHP	240	46	73	14	2	17	58	31	41	16	.304
At Home	76	239	50	66	9	3	14	46	50	43	26	.276
On the Road	75	280	54	90	23	0	19	68	43	40	26	.321
1990 Season 151	519	104	156	32	3	33	114	93	83	52	.301
Life 4.4 Years	588	106	155	35	6	26	76	85	101	38	.265

Bobby BONILLA

PITTSBURGH   RIGHT FIELD   28 Years Old

Runs Created: 104   Offensive Winning Percentage: .666
Batting Average: .280   Secondary Average: .317

Most Often Bats: 4th
Hits First Pitch: 17%
Gets Ahead of the Pitcher: 51%
Hits Behind the Pitcher: 49%

1990 On Base Percentage: .322   Career: .350
1990 Slugging Percentage: .518   Career: .467
Batting Avg with Men in Scoring Position: .282

Switch Hitter	AB	R	H	2B	3B	HR	RBI	BB	SO	SB	AVG
Vs. RHP	345	64	102	20	5	18	72	25	71	1	.296
Vs. LHP	280	48	73	19	2	14	48	20	32	3	.261
At Home	81	310	47	81	19	2	13	52	17	44	3	.261
On the Road	79	315	65	94	20	5	19	68	28	59	1	.298
1990 Season 160	625	112	175	39	7	32	120	45	103	4	.280
Life 4.7 Years	578	87	161	33	7	21	91	65	92	6	.279

•

Pat BORDERS

TORONTO   CATCHER   27 Years Old

Runs Created: 48   Offensive Winning Percentage: .547
Batting Average: .286   Secondary Average: .263

Most Often Bats: 7th
Hits First Pitch: 17%
Gets Ahead of the Pitcher: 50%
Hits Behind the Pitcher: 50%

1990 On Base Percentage: .319   Career: .303
1990 Slugging Percentage: .497   Career: .439
Batting Avg with Men in Scoring Position: .225

Bats Right-Handed	AB	R	H	2B	3B	HR	RBI	BB	SO	SB	AVG
Vs. RHP	160	14	46	8	0	5	22	3	28	0	.287
Vs. LHP	186	22	53	16	2	10	27	15	29	0	.285
At Home	63	164	24	45	13	1	10	28	12	23	0	.274
On the Road	62	182	12	54	11	1	5	21	6	34	0	.297
1990 Season 125	346	36	99	24	2	15	49	18	57	0	.286
Life 1.7 Years	437	43	120	24	4	14	58	19	74	1	.274

Chris BOSIO

MILWAUKEE STARTING PITCHER 28 Years Old
4-9 4.00 ERA

Opponents Batting Average: .258
Offensive Support: 4.27 Runs Per Nine Innings
Double Play Support: .68 GDP Per Nine Innings

First Pitch is Hit: 16%
Gets Ahead of the Hitter: 51%
Gets Behind the Hitter: 49%
Gets Leadoff Man Out: 70%

1990 On Base Pct Allowed: .311 Slugging Percentage: .411
Stolen Bases Allowed: 7 Caught Stealing: 4

Pitches Right	AB	H	2B	3B	HR	RBI	BB	SO	AVG
Vs. RHB	235	53	12	1	5	23	19	51	.226
Vs. LHB	273	78	11	4	10	37	19	25	.286

	G	IP	W-L	Pct	SO	BB	ERA
At Home	12	81	2-7		46	25	5.11
On the Road	8	52	2-2		30	13	2.26
1990 Season	20	133	4-9	.308	76	38	4.00
Life 3.3 Years	44	228	11-14	.446	155	56	3.94

•

Shawn BOSKIE

CHICAGO STARTING PITCHER 24 Years Old
5-6 3.69 ERA

Opponents Batting Average: .265
Offensive Support: 4.15 Runs Per Nine Innings
Double Play Support: .65 GDP Per Nine Innings

First Pitch is Hit: 13%
Gets Ahead of the Hitter: 48%
Gets Behind the Hitter: 52%
Gets Leadoff Man Out: 70%

1990 On Base Pct Allowed: .322 Slugging Percentage: .397
Stolen Bases Allowed: 6 Caught Stealing: 6

Pitches Right	AB	H	2B	3B	HR	RBI	BB	SO	AVG
Vs. RHB	160	41	6	0	6	17	3	26	.256
Vs. LHB	213	58	15	2	2	16	28	23	.272

	G	IP	W-L	Pct	SO	BB	ERA
At Home	9	60	2-5		27	16	4.07
On the Road	6	38	3-1		22	15	3.08
1990 Season	15	98	5-6	.455	49	31	3.69
Life 0.4 Years	37	241	12-15	.455	121	76	3.69

Daryl BOSTON

NEW YORK CENTER FIELD 28 Years Old

Runs Created: 52 Offensive Winning Percentage: .578
Batting Average: .272 Secondary Average: .294

Most Often Bats: 7th
Hits First Pitch: 9%
Gets Ahead of the Pitcher: 51%
Hits Behind the Pitcher: 49%

1990 On Base Percentage: .327 Career: .302
1990 Slugging Percentage: .439 Career: .400
Batting Avg with Men in Scoring Position: .276

Bats Left-Handed	AB	R	H	2B	3B	HR	RBI	BB	SO	SB	AVG
Vs. RHP	307	60	85	19	2	12	37	21	39	18	.277
Vs. LHP	60	5	15	2	0	0	8	7	11	1	.250
At Home	62	186	32	50	12	1	4	17	16	27	9	.269
On the Road	58	181	33	50	9	1	8	28	12	23	10	.276
1990 Season	120	367	65	100	21	2	12	45	28	50	19	.272
Life 3.8 Years	452	64	111	22	4	13	44	36	76	18	.246

•

Oil Can BOYD

MONTREAL STARTING PITCHER 31 Years Old
10-6 2.93 ERA

Opponents Batting Average: .234
Offensive Support: 4.20 Runs Per Nine Innings
Double Play Support: .42 GDP Per Nine Innings

First Pitch is Hit: 17%
Gets Ahead of the Hitter: 52%
Gets Behind the Hitter: 48%
Gets Leadoff Man Out: 65%

1990 On Base Pct Allowed: .288 Slugging Percentage: .376
Stolen Bases Allowed: 25 Caught Stealing: 6

Pitches Right	AB	H	2B	3B	HR	RBI	BB	SO	AVG
Vs. RHB	273	67	17	1	9	29	17	46	.245
Vs. LHB	430	97	22	1	10	31	35	67	.226

	G	IP	W-L	Pct	SO	BB	ERA
At Home	14	90	6-3		61	19	2.91
On the Road	17	101	4-3		52	33	2.94
1990 Season	31	191	10-6	.625	113	52	2.93
Life 4.9 Years	38	249	14-13	.530	141	64	3.96

Phil BRADLEY

CHICAGO	LEFT FIELD	32 Years Old

Runs Created: 51   Offensive Winning Percentage: .494
Batting Average: .256   Secondary Average: .230

Most Often Bats: 1st
Hits First Pitch: 13%
Gets Ahead of the Pitcher: 49%
Hits Behind the Pitcher: 51%

1990 On Base Percentage: .349   Career: .369
1990 Slugging Percentage: .327   Career: .421
Batting Avg with Men in Scoring Position: .263

Bats Right-Handed	AB	R	H	2B	3B	HR	RBI	BB	SO	SB	AVG
Vs. RHP	261	36	70	7	0	2	22	28	37	12	.268
Vs. LHP	161	23	38	7	2	2	9	22	24	5	.236
At Home	55	190	31	45	8	0	4	16	25	28	7	.237
On the Road	62	232	28	63	6	2	0	15	25	33	10	.272
1990 Season	117	422	59	108	14	2	4	31	50	61	17	.256
Life	6.3 Years	586	90	168	28	7	12	60	68	114	25	.286

Sid BREAM

PITTSBURGH	FIRST BASE	30 Years Old

Runs Created: 64   Offensive Winning Percentage: .651
Batting Average: .270   Secondary Average: .329

Most Often Bats: 6th
Hits First Pitch: 9%
Gets Ahead of the Pitcher: 53%
Hits Behind the Pitcher: 47%

1990 On Base Percentage: .349   Career: .336
1990 Slugging Percentage: .455   Career: .421
Batting Avg with Men in Scoring Position: .288

Bats Left-Handed	AB	R	H	2B	3B	HR	RBI	BB	SO	SB	AVG
Vs. RHP	293	31	80	15	1	13	55	42	49	8	.273
Vs. LHP	96	8	25	8	1	2	12	6	16	0	.260
At Home	74	181	19	50	11	1	8	36	21	26	3	.276
On the Road	73	208	20	55	12	1	7	31	27	39	5	.264
1990 Season	147	389	39	105	23	2	15	67	48	65	8	.270
Life	4.4 Years	487	57	128	31	2	14	70	55	72	9	.263

Jeff BRANTLEY

SAN FRANCISCO	RELIEF PITCHER	27 Years Old
5-3	1.56 ERA	19 SAVES

Blown Saves: 5   Holds: 8   Save Efficiency: 84%
Inherited Runners who Scored: 24%
Opponents Batting Average: .240
Double Play Support: .83 GDP Per Nine Innings

First Pitch is Hit: 7%
Gets Ahead of the Hitter: 47%
Gets Behind the Hitter: 53%
Gets First Batter Out: 67%

1990 On Base Pct Allowed: .315 Slugging Percentage: .293
Stolen Bases Allowed: 7   Caught Stealing: 4

Pitches Right	AB	H	2B	3B	HR	RBI	BB	SO	AVG
Vs. RHB	135	26	1	0	2	9	13	34	.193
Vs. LHB	186	51	7	0	1	13	20	27	.274

	G	IP	W-L	Pct	SO	BB	ERA
1990 Season	55	87	5-3	.625	61	33	1.56
Life 1.7 Years	73	121	7-3	.706	83	45	3.17

George BRETT

KANSAS CITY	FIRST BASE	37 Years Old

Runs Created: 106   Offensive Winning Percentage: .736
Batting Average: .329   Secondary Average: .305

Most Often Bats: 3rd
Hits First Pitch: 15%
Gets Ahead of the Pitcher: 53%
Hits Behind the Pitcher: 47%

1990 On Base Percentage: .387   Career: .378
1990 Slugging Percentage: .515   Career: .502
Batting Avg with Men in Scoring Position: .360

Bats Left-Handed	AB	R	H	2B	3B	HR	RBI	BB	SO	SB	AVG
Vs. RHP	357	59	120	34	4	9	59	40	37	6	.336
Vs. LHP	187	23	59	11	3	5	28	16	26	3	.316
At Home	75	288	40	92	18	5	3	46	27	27	4	.319
On the Road	67	256	42	87	27	2	11	41	29	36	5	.340
1990 Season	142	544	82	179	45	7	14	87	56	63	9	.329
Life	14.1 Years	618	98	192	40	9	20	99	69	50	13	.311

Greg BRILEY

SEATTLE   RIGHT FIELD   25 Years Old

Runs Created: 41   Offensive Winning Percentage: .507
Batting Average: .246   Secondary Average: .267

Most Often Bats: 2nd
Hits First Pitch: 11%
Gets Ahead of the Pitcher: 56%
Hits Behind the Pitcher: 44%

1990 On Base Percentage: .319   Career: .329
1990 Slugging Percentage: .356   Career: .402
Batting Avg with Men in Scoring Position: .274

Bats Left-Handed		AB	R	H	2B	3B	HR	RBI	BB	SO	SB	AVG
Vs. RHP		304	36	76	17	2	5	26	33	41	16	.250
Vs. LHP		33	4	7	1	0	0	3	4	7	0	.212
At Home	62	166	20	41	8	1	4	17	17	23	9	.247
On the Road	63	171	20	42	10	1	1	12	20	25	7	.246
1990 Season	126	337	40	83	18	2	5	29	37	48	16	.246
Life	1.6 Years	489	63	126	27	4	12	54	52	87	17	.257

Huble BROOKS

LOS ANGELES   RIGHT FIELD   34 Years Old

Runs Created: 71   Offensive Winning Percentage: .494
Batting Average: .266   Secondary Average: .220

Most Often Bats: 5th
Hits First Pitch: 9%
Gets Ahead of the Pitcher: 48%
Hits Behind the Pitcher: 52%

1990 On Base Percentage: .307   Career: .318
1990 Slugging Percentage: .424   Career: .409
Batting Avg with Men in Scoring Position: .267

Bats Right-Handed		AB	R	H	2B	3B	HR	RBI	BB	SO	SB	AVG
Vs. RHP		351	46	99	16	1	11	57	16	67	0	.282
Vs. LHP		217	28	52	12	0	9	34	17	41	2	.240
At Home	76	275	36	69	8	1	9	44	21	49	0	.251
On the Road	77	293	38	82	20	0	11	47	12	59	2	.280
1990 Season	153	568	74	151	28	1	20	91	33	108	2	.266
Life	8.3 Years	609	67	167	30	4	15	84	38	103	7	.274

Greg BROCK

MILWAUKEE   FIRST BASE   33 Years Old

Runs Created: 46   Offensive Winning Percentage: .457
Batting Average: .248   Secondary Average: .248

Most Often Bats: 5th
Hits First Pitch: 9%
Gets Ahead of the Pitcher: 55%
Hits Behind the Pitcher: 45%

1990 On Base Percentage: .324   Career: .336
1990 Slugging Percentage: .368   Career: .399
Batting Avg with Men in Scoring Position: .245

Bats Left-Handed		AB	R	H	2B	3B	HR	RBI	BB	SO	SB	AVG
Vs. RHP		281	32	73	18	0	5	33	33	33	4	.260
Vs. LHP		86	10	18	5	0	2	17	10	12	0	.209
At Home	63	176	21	42	9	0	3	28	23	22	2	.239
On the Road	60	191	21	49	14	0	4	22	20	23	2	.257
1990 Season	123	367	42	91	23	0	7	50	43	45	4	.248
Life	6.1 Years	518	68	128	23	1	18	75	69	76	7	.247

Kevin BROWN

TEXAS   STARTING PITCHER   26 Years Old
12-10   3.60 ERA

Opponents Batting Average: .255
Offensive Support: 5.20 Runs Per Nine Innings
Double Play Support: 1.20 GDP Per Nine Innings

First Pitch is Hit: 16%
Gets Ahead of the Hitter: 48%
Gets Behind the Hitter: 52%
Gets Leadoff Man Out: 68%

1990 On Base Pct Allowed: .315 Slugging Percentage: .365
Stolen Bases Allowed: 7   Caught Stealing: 4

Pitches Right	AB	H	2B	3B	HR	RBI	BB	SO	AVG
Vs. RHB	348	91	16	0	7	36	30	41	.261
Vs. LHB	337	84	18	1	6	35	30	47	.249

	G	IP	W-L	Pct	SO	BB	ERA
At Home	12	87	6-4		44	28	2.58
On the Road	14	93	6-6		44	32	4.56
1990 Season	26	180	12-10	.545	88	60	3.60
Life 1.6 Years	37	250	16-13	.565	130	87	3.52

Jerry BROWNE

CLEVELAND   SECOND BASE   25 Years Old

Runs Created: 72   Offensive Winning Percentage: .512
Batting Average: .267   Secondary Average: .269

Most Often Bats: 1st
Hits First Pitch: 12%
Gets Ahead of the Pitcher: 58%
Hits Behind the Pitcher: 42%

1990 On Base Percentage: .353   Career: .356
1990 Slugging Percentage: .372   Career: .363
Batting Avg with Men in Scoring Position: .260

Switch Hitter		AB	R	H	2B	3B	HR	RBI	BB	SO	SB	AVG
Vs. RHP		374	67	98	17	2	6	36	46	38	9	.262
Vs. LHP		139	25	39	9	3	0	14	26	8	3	.281
At Home	70	250	48	68	12	4	2	22	40	20	5	.272
On the Road	70	263	44	69	14	1	4	28	32	26	7	.262
1990 Season	140	513	92	137	26	5	6	50	72	46	12	.267
Life	3.1 Years	573	86	158	27	5	4	49	72	62	19	.276

Tom BRUNANSKY

BOSTON   RIGHT FIELD   30 Years Old

Runs Created: 72   Offensive Winning Percentage: .552
Batting Average: .255   Secondary Average: .301

Most Often Bats: 4th
Hits First Pitch: 12%
Gets Ahead of the Pitcher: 52%
Hits Behind the Pitcher: 48%

1990 On Base Percentage: .338   Career: .330
1990 Slugging Percentage: .419   Career: .441
Batting Avg with Men in Scoring Position: .213

Bats Right-Handed		AB	R	H	2B	3B	HR	RBI	BB	SO	SB	AVG
Vs. RHP		339	39	81	16	2	10	44	50	83	2	.239
Vs. LHP		179	27	51	11	3	6	29	16	32	3	.285
At Home	71	252	43	84	19	5	13	52	27	47	3	.333
On the Road	77	266	23	48	8	0	3	21	39	68	2	.180
1990 Season	148	518	66	132	27	5	16	73	66	115	5	.255
Life	8.5 Years	582	78	144	27	3	26	84	71	106	7	.248

Tom BROWNING

CINCINNATI   STARTING PITCHER   30 Years Old
15-9   3.80 ERA

Opponents Batting Average: .266
Offensive Support: 3.83 Runs Per Nine Innings
Double Play Support: .24 GDP Per Nine Innings

First Pitch is Hit: 19%
Gets Ahead of the Hitter: 54%
Gets Behind the Hitter: 46%
Gets Leadoff Man Out: 70%

1990 On Base Pct Allowed: .309 Slugging Percentage: .412
Stolen Bases Allowed: 12   Caught Stealing: 10

Pitches Left	AB	H	2B	3B	HR	RBI	BB	SO	AVG
Vs. RHB	720	194	36	6	19	73	39	69	.269
Vs. LHB	162	41	8	0	5	15	13	30	.253

	G	IP	W-L	Pct	SO	BB	ERA
At Home	20	128	8-8		52	30	4.64
On the Road	15	100	7-1		47	22	2.71
1990 Season	35	228	15-9	.625	99	52	3.80
Life 5.9 Years	37	243	16-10	.604	130	66	3.73

Tim BURKE

MONTREAL   RELIEF PITCHER   32 Years Old
3-3   2.52 ERA   20 SAVES

Blown Saves: 5   Holds: 6   Save Efficiency: 84%
Inherited Runners who Scored: 27%
Opponents Batting Average: .247
Double Play Support: .84 GDP Per Nine Innings

First Pitch is Hit: 15%
Gets Ahead of the Hitter: 52%
Gets Behind the Hitter: 48%
Gets First Batter Out: 67%

1990 On Base Pct Allowed: .300 Slugging Percentage: .345
Stolen Bases Allowed: 5   Caught Stealing: 1

Pitches Right	AB	H	2B	3B	HR	RBI	BB	SO	AVG
Vs. RHB	143	30	0	1	3	21	11	28	.210
Vs. LHB	144	41	8	0	3	17	10	19	.285

	G	IP	W-L	Pct	SO	BB	ERA
1990 Season	58	75	3-3	.500	47	21	2.52
Life 5.3 Years	74	105	8-4	.645	70	33	2.48

John BURKETT

SAN FRANCISCO STARTING PITCHER 26 Years Old
14-7 3.79 ERA

Opponents Batting Average: .257
Offensive Support: 5.60 Runs Per Nine Innings
Double Play Support: .62 GDP Per Nine Innings

First Pitch is Hit: 15%
Gets Ahead of the Hitter: 49%
Gets Behind the Hitter: 51%
Gets Leadoff Man Out: 69%

1990 On Base Pct Allowed: .313 Slugging Percentage: .374
Stolen Bases Allowed: 18 Caught Stealing: 7

Pitches Right	AB	H	2B	3B	HR	RBI	BB	SO	AVG
Vs. RHB	328	84	14	1	8	28	25	56	.256
Vs. LHB	453	117	19	1	10	50	36	62	.258

	G	IP	W-L	Pct	SO	BB	ERA
At Home	16	104	6-2		67	33	3.98
On the Road	17	100	8-5		51	28	3.60
1990 Season	33	204	14-7	.667	118	61	3.79
Life 0.9 Years	39	229	15-8	.667	134	70	3.81

•

Ellis BURKS

BOSTON CENTER FIELD 26 Years Old

Runs Created: 92 Offensive Winning Percentage: .637
Batting Average: .296 Secondary Average: .287

Most Often Bats: 4th
Hits First Pitch: 10%
Gets Ahead of the Pitcher: 48%
Hits Behind the Pitcher: 52%

1990 On Base Percentage: .349 Career: .350
1990 Slugging Percentage: .486 Career: .470
Batting Avg with Men in Scoring Position: .306

Bats Right-Handed	AB	R	H	2B	3B	HR	RBI	BB	SO	SB	AVG
Vs. RHP	400	56	118	23	6	16	65	28	56	8	.295
Vs. LHP	188	33	56	10	2	5	24	20	26	1	.298
At Home	78	297	44	91	20	4	10	48	23	39	4	.306
On the Road	74	291	45	83	13	4	11	41	25	43	5	.285
1990 Season	152	588	89	174	33	8	21	89	48	82	9	.296
Life 3.2 Years	642	107	187	37	6	22	93	58	99	25	.291

Todd BURNS

OAKLAND RELIEF PITCHER 27 Years Old
3-3 2.97 ERA 3 SAVES

Blown Saves: 1 Holds: 9 Save Efficiency: 92%
Inherited Runners who Scored: 35%
Opponents Batting Average: .263
Double Play Support: 1.03 GDP Per Nine Innings

First Pitch is Hit: 13%
Gets Ahead of the Hitter: 48%
Gets Behind the Hitter: 52%
Gets First Batter Out: 53%

1990 On Base Pct Allowed: .331 Slugging Percentage: .428
Stolen Bases Allowed: 1 Caught Stealing: 2

Pitches Right	AB	H	2B	3B	HR	RBI	BB	SO	AVG
Vs. RHB	170	44	11	0	5	23	15	32	.259
Vs. LHB	127	34	6	4	3	13	17	11	.268

	G	IP	W-L	Pct	SO	BB	ERA
1990 Season	43	79	3-3	.500	43	32	2.97
Life 1.7 Years	64	161	10-6	.630	86	54	2.79

•

Brett BUTLER

SAN FRANCISCO CENTER FIELD 33 Years Old

Runs Created: 108 Offensive Winning Percentage: .668
Batting Average: .309 Secondary Average: .302

Most Often Bats: 1st
Hits First Pitch: 13%
Gets Ahead of the Pitcher: 54%
Hits Behind the Pitcher: 46%

1990 On Base Percentage: .397 Career: .368
1990 Slugging Percentage: .384 Career: .379
Batting Avg with Men in Scoring Position: .279

Bats Left-Handed	AB	R	H	2B	3B	HR	RBI	BB	SO	SB	AVG
Vs. RHP	377	59	118	14	7	2	24	57	34	33	.313
Vs. LHP	245	49	74	6	2	1	20	33	28	18	.302
At Home	81	312	59	105	12	1	3	25	50	28	27	.337
On the Road	79	310	49	87	8	8	0	19	40	34	24	.281
1990 Season	160	622	108	192	20	9	3	44	90	62	51	.309
Life 8.4 Years	596	101	170	23	10	5	43	78	63	43	.285

•C•

Greg CADARET

NEW YORK   RELIEF PITCHER   29 Years Old
      5-4   4.15 ERA   3 SAVES

Blown Saves: 1   Holds: 8   Save Efficiency: 92%
Inherited Runners who Scored: 29%
Opponents Batting Average: .268
Double Play Support: .74 GDP Per Nine Innings

First Pitch is Hit: 10%
Gets Ahead of the Hitter: 43%
Gets Behind the Hitter: 57%
Gets First Batter Out: 64%

1990 On Base Pct Allowed: .359 Slugging Percentage: .405
Stolen Bases Allowed: 6   Caught Stealing: 17

Pitches Left	AB	H	2B	3B	HR	RBI	BB	SO	AVG
Vs. RHB	328	90	22	5	5	42	49	63	.274
Vs. LHB	119	30	5	0	3	15	15	17	.252

	G	IP	W-L	Pct	SO	BB	ERA
1990 Season	54	121	5-4	.556	80	64	4.15
Life 2.8 Years	67	127	8-5	.618	91	65	3.90

•

Ivan CALDERON

CHICAGO   LEFT FIELD   29 Years Old

Runs Created: 76   Offensive Winning Percentage: .517
Batting Average: .273   Secondary Average: .285

Most Often Bats: 3rd
Hits First Pitch: 18%
Gets Ahead of the Pitcher: 47%
Hits Behind the Pitcher: 53%

1990 On Base Percentage: .327   Career: .332
1990 Slugging Percentage: .422   Career: .451
Batting Avg with Men in Scoring Position: .328

Bats Right-Handed	AB	R	H	2B	3B	HR	RBI	BB	SO	SB	AVG
Vs. RHP	380	53	99	25	0	8	47	30	54	18	.261
Vs. LHP	227	32	67	19	2	6	27	21	25	14	.295
At Home	77	284	45	87	24	2	6	40	30	37	19	.306
On the Road	81	323	40	79	20	0	8	34	21	42	13	.245
1990 Season	158	607	85	166	44	2	14	74	51	79	32	.273
Life 4.1 Years		597	87	163	38	4	20	79	54	107	15	.273

Ken CAMINITI

HOUSTON   THIRD BASE   27 Years Old

Runs Created: 50   Offensive Winning Percentage: .403
Batting Average: .242   Secondary Average: .172

Most Often Bats: 5th
Hits First Pitch: 15%
Gets Ahead of the Pitcher: 49%
Hits Behind the Pitcher: 51%

1990 On Base Percentage: .302   Career: .301
1990 Slugging Percentage: .309   Career: .334
Batting Avg with Men in Scoring Position: .259

Switch Hitter	AB	R	H	2B	3B	HR	RBI	BB	SO	SB	AVG
Vs. RHP	301	29	72	11	1	2	28	35	62	6	.239
Vs. LHP	240	23	59	9	1	2	23	13	35	3	.246
At Home	81	285	34	82	15	0	2	31	27	47	4	.288
On the Road	72	256	18	49	5	2	2	20	21	50	5	.191
1990 Season	153	541	52	131	20	2	4	51	48	97	9	.242
Life 2.5 Years		562	55	137	24	2	7	61	46	100	5	.244

•

Casey CANDAELE

HOUSTON   SECOND BASE   30 Years Old

Runs Created: 38   Offensive Winning Percentage: .651
Batting Average: .286   Secondary Average: .256

Most Often Bats: 2nd
Hits First Pitch: 14%
Gets Ahead of the Pitcher: 49%
Hits Behind the Pitcher: 51%

1990 On Base Percentage: .364   Career: .317
1990 Slugging Percentage: .397   Career: .338
Batting Avg with Men in Scoring Position: .303

Switch Hitter	AB	R	H	2B	3B	HR	RBI	BB	SO	SB	AVG
Vs. RHP	136	13	32	5	4	1	12	17	30	2	.235
Vs. LHP	126	17	43	3	2	2	10	14	12	5	.341
At Home	61	126	18	36	3	5	1	12	17	18	4	.286
On the Road	69	136	12	39	5	1	2	10	14	24	3	.287
1990 Season	130	262	30	75	8	6	3	22	31	42	7	.286
Life 2.2 Years		439	51	112	20	5	2	26	39	47	8	.256

Tom CANDIOTTI

CLEVELAND STARTING PITCHER 33 Years Old
15-11 3.65 ERA

Opponents Batting Average: .263
Offensive Support: 5.30 Runs Per Nine Innings
Double Play Support: .76 GDP Per Nine Innings

First Pitch is Hit: 12%
Gets Ahead of the Hitter: 44%
Gets Behind the Hitter: 56%
Gets Leadoff Man Out: 74%

1990 On Base Pct Allowed: .315 Slugging Percentage: .388
Stolen Bases Allowed: 18 Caught Stealing: 7

Pitches Right	AB	H	2B	3B	HR	RBI	BB	SO	AVG
Vs. RHB	385	104	17	0	14	48	23	76	.270
Vs. LHB	403	103	13	0	9	38	32	52	.256

	G	IP	W-L	Pct	SO	BB	ERA
At Home	18	112	7-6		74	38	4.10
On the Road	13	90	8-5		54	17	3.10
1990 Season	31	202	15-11	.577	128	55	3.65
Life 4.7 Years	38	247	15-14	.522	150	82	3.69

•

Jose CANSECO

OAKLAND RIGHT FIELD 26 Years Old

Runs Created: 98 Offensive Winning Percentage: .758
Batting Average: .274 Secondary Average: .457

Most Often Bats: 3rd
Hits First Pitch: 9%
Gets Ahead of the Pitcher: 50%
Hits Behind the Pitcher: 50%

1990 On Base Percentage: .371 Career: .345
1990 Slugging Percentage: .543 Career: .510
Batting Avg with Men in Scoring Position: .260

Bats Right-Handed		AB	R	H	2B	3B	HR	RBI	BB	SO	SB	AVG
Vs. RHP		358	57	98	11	1	25	73	57	117	16	.274
Vs. LHP		123	26	34	3	1	12	28	15	41	3	.276
At Home	64	217	40	56	7	0	18	43	45	71	10	.258
On the Road	67	264	43	76	7	2	19	58	27	87	9	.288
1990 Season	131	481	83	132	14	2	37	101	72	158	19	.274
Life	4.3 Years	613	98	166	29	2	38	122	68	166	22	.270

Don CARMAN

PHILADELPHIA RELIEF PITCHER 31 Years Old
6-2 4.15 ERA 1 SAVES

Blown Saves: 1 Holds: 8 Save Efficiency: 90%
Inherited Runners who Scored: 27%
Opponents Batting Average: .218
Double Play Support: .62 GDP Per Nine Innings

First Pitch is Hit: 12%
Gets Ahead of the Hitter: 49%
Gets Behind the Hitter: 51%
Gets First Batter Out: 74%

1990 On Base Pct Allowed: .307 Slugging Percentage: .396
Stolen Bases Allowed: 5 Caught Stealing: 1

Pitches Left	AB	H	2B	3B	HR	RBI	BB	SO	AVG
Vs. RHB	213	51	12	1	6	24	28	39	.239
Vs. LHB	103	18	3	0	7	22	10	19	.175

	G	IP	W-L	Pct	SO	BB	ERA
1990 Season	59	87	6-2	.750	58	38	4.15
Life 5.6 Years	56	158	9-9	.505	104	64	4.06

•

Joe CARTER

SAN DIEGO CENTER FIELD 31 Years Old

Runs Created: 72 Offensive Winning Percentage: .456
Batting Average: .232 Secondary Average: .270

Most Often Bats: 4th
Hits First Pitch: 11%
Gets Ahead of the Pitcher: 47%
Hits Behind the Pitcher: 53%

1990 On Base Percentage: .290 Career: .304
1990 Slugging Percentage: .391 Career: .456
Batting Avg with Men in Scoring Position: .266

Bats Right-Handed		AB	R	H	2B	3B	HR	RBI	BB	SO	SB	AVG
Vs. RHP		431	57	107	20	1	17	83	31	66	17	.248
Vs. LHP		203	22	40	7	0	7	32	17	27	5	.197
At Home	81	322	35	71	11	0	12	53	18	49	14	.220
On the Road	81	312	44	76	16	1	12	62	30	44	8	.244
1990 Season	162	634	79	147	27	1	24	115	48	93	22	.232
Life	6.3 Years	623	86	163	30	4	28	102	34	100	24	.262

Chuck CARY

NEW YORK   STARTING PITCHER   31 Years Old
    6-12   4.19 ERA

Opponents Batting Average: .260
Offensive Support: 3.16 Runs Per Nine Innings
Double Play Support: .40 GDP Per Nine Innings

First Pitch is Hit: 12%
Gets Ahead of the Hitter: 46%
Gets Behind the Hitter: 54%
Gets Leadoff Man Out: 70%

1990 On Base Pct Allowed: .321 Slugging Percentage: .437
Stolen Bases Allowed: 14   Caught Stealing: 10

Pitches Left	AB	H	2B	3B	HR	RBI	BB	SO	AVG
Vs. RHB	484	122	28	3	17	58	45	118	.252
Vs. LHB	113	33	5	2	4	12	10	16	.292

	G	IP	W-L	Pct	SO	BB	ERA
At Home	14	92	4-3		82	26	3.04
On the Road	14	65	2-9		52	29	5.82
1990 Season	28	157	6-12	.333	134	55	4.19
Life 2.0 Years	55	170	6-10	.375	141	58	3.83

John CERUTTI

TORONTO   STARTING PITCHER   30 Years Old
    9-9   4.76 ERA

Opponents Batting Average: .297
Offensive Support: 5.01 Runs Per Nine Innings
Double Play Support: 1.41 GDP Per Nine Innings

First Pitch is Hit: 16%
Gets Ahead of the Hitter: 50%
Gets Behind the Hitter: 50%
Gets Leadoff Man Out: 61%

1990 On Base Pct Allowed: .356 Slugging Percentage: .489
Stolen Bases Allowed: 6   Caught Stealing: 3

Pitches Left	AB	H	2B	3B	HR	RBI	BB	SO	AVG
Vs. RHB	434	131	21	3	20	59	43	42	.302
Vs. LHB	112	31	5	2	3	14	6	7	.277

	G	IP	W-L	Pct	SO	BB	ERA
At Home	16	71	5-5		27	20	5.32
On the Road	14	69	4-4		22	29	4.17
1990 Season	30	140	9-9	.500	49	49	4.76
Life 4.0 Years	47	191	11-9	.554	91	63	3.87

Tony CASTILLO

ATLANTA   RELIEF PITCHER   28 Years Old
    5-1   4.23 ERA   1 SAVES

Blown Saves: 1   Holds: 3   Save Efficiency: 80%
Inherited Runners who Scored: 42%
Opponents Batting Average: .302
Double Play Support: .70 GDP Per Nine Innings

First Pitch is Hit: 17%
Gets Ahead of the Hitter: 51%
Gets Behind the Hitter: 49%
Gets First Batter Out: 71%

1990 On Base Pct Allowed: .342 Slugging Percentage: .399
Stolen Bases Allowed: 16   Caught Stealing: 3

Pitches Left	AB	H	2B	3B	HR	RBI	BB	SO	AVG
Vs. RHB	213	66	13	0	3	32	14	39	.310
Vs. LHB	95	27	2	0	2	18	6	25	.284

	G	IP	W-L	Pct	SO	BB	ERA
1990 Season	52	77	5-1	.833	64	20	4.23
Life 1.3 Years	72	90	5-2	.700	70	27	4.40

Norm CHARLTON

CINCINNATI   RELIEF PITCHER   28 Years Old
    12-9   2.74 ERA   2 SAVES

Blown Saves: 1   Holds: 9   Save Efficiency: 92%
Inherited Runners who Scored: 20%
Opponents Batting Average: .231
Double Play Support: 1.11 GDP Per Nine Innings

First Pitch is Hit: 18%
Gets Ahead of the Hitter: 48%
Gets Behind the Hitter: 52%
Gets First Batter Out: 69%

1990 On Base Pct Allowed: .319 Slugging Percentage: .326
Stolen Bases Allowed: 17   Caught Stealing: 4

Pitches Left	AB	H	2B	3B	HR	RBI	BB	SO	AVG
Vs. RHB	451	105	14	2	6	27	53	92	.233
Vs. LHB	116	26	6	0	4	19	17	25	.224

	G	IP	W-L	Pct	SO	BB	ERA
1990 Season	56	154	12-9	.571	117	70	2.74
Life 2.2 Years	62	143	11-8	.585	117	60	3.04

Jim CLANCY

HOUSTON	RELIEF PITCHER	35 Years Old
2-8	6.51 ERA	1 SAVES

Blown Saves: 1   Holds: 1   Save Efficiency: 67%
Inherited Runners who Scored: 27%
Opponents Batting Average: .322
Double Play Support: .71 GDP Per Nine Innings

First Pitch is Hit: 15%
Gets Ahead of the Hitter: 48%
Gets Behind the Hitter: 52%
Gets First Batter Out: 83%

1990 On Base Pct Allowed: .387 Slugging Percentage: .463
Stolen Bases Allowed: 8   Caught Stealing: 5

Pitches Right	AB	H	2B	3B	HR	RBI	BB	SO	AVG
Vs. RHB	149	41	9	3	3	26	12	31	.275
Vs. LHB	162	59	9	4	1	32	21	13	.364

	G	IP	W-L	Pct	SO	BB	ERA
1990 Season	33	76	2-8	.200	44	33	6.51
Life 10.8 Years	39	225	13-15	.458	127	85	4.24

•

Jack CLARK

SAN DIEGO	FIRST BASE	35 Years Old

Runs Created: 83   Offensive Winning Percentage: .808
Batting Average: .266   Secondary Average: .590

Most Often Bats: 4th
Hits First Pitch: 10%
Gets Ahead of the Pitcher: 51%
Hits Behind the Pitcher: 49%

1990 On Base Percentage: .441   Career: .380
1990 Slugging Percentage: .533   Career: .483
Batting Avg with Men in Scoring Position: .278

Bats Right-Handed	AB	R	H	2B	3B	HR	RBI	BB	SO	SB	AVG
Vs. RHP	220	36	46	8	0	16	41	63	62	1	.209
Vs. LHP	114	23	43	4	1	9	21	41	29	3	.377
At Home	61	176	34	45	5	1	16	39	50	53	2	.256
On the Road	54	158	25	44	7	0	9	23	54	38	2	.278
1990 Season 115	334	59	89	12	1	25	62	104	91	4	.266
Life 10.9 Years	558	92	151	28	3	28	97	101	112	7	.270

Will CLARK

SAN FRANCISCO	FIRST BASE	27 Years Old

Runs Created: 101   Offensive Winning Percentage: .660
Batting Average: .295   Secondary Average: .270

Most Often Bats: 3rd
Hits First Pitch: 16%
Gets Ahead of the Pitcher: 53%
Hits Behind the Pitcher: 47%

1990 On Base Percentage: .357   Career: .375
1990 Slugging Percentage: .448   Career: .507
Batting Avg with Men in Scoring Position: .291

Bats Left-Handed	AB	R	H	2B	3B	HR	RBI	BB	SO	SB	AVG
Vs. RHP	351	55	98	18	1	10	48	40	62	3	.279
Vs. LHP	249	36	79	7	4	9	47	22	35	5	.317
At Home	77	296	42	94	14	2	8	44	37	49	6	.318
On the Road	77	304	49	83	11	3	11	51	25	48	2	.273
1990 Season 154	600	91	177	25	5	19	95	62	97	8	.295
Life 4.5 Years	594	99	179	33	6	26	98	70	111	7	.302

•

Martin CLARY

ATLANTA	RELIEF PITCHER	29 Years Old
1-10	5.67 ERA	0 SAVES

Blown Saves: 0   Holds: 1   Save Efficiency: 100%
Inherited Runners who Scored: 63%
Opponents Batting Average: .308
Double Play Support: .71 GDP Per Nine Innings

First Pitch is Hit: 14%
Gets Ahead of the Hitter: 47%
Gets Behind the Hitter: 53%
Gets First Batter Out: 53%

1990 On Base Pct Allowed: .364 Slugging Percentage: .442
Stolen Bases Allowed: 11   Caught Stealing: 3

Pitches Right	AB	H	2B	3B	HR	RBI	BB	SO	AVG
Vs. RHB	180	55	11	1	2	22	18	25	.306
Vs. LHB	236	73	10	3	7	29	21	19	.309

	G	IP	W-L	Pct	SO	BB	ERA
1990 Season	33	102	1-10	.091	44	39	5.67
Life 1.2 Years	48	185	4-12	.263	67	61	4.48

Roger CLEMENS

BOSTON   STARTING PITCHER   28 Years Old
                    21-6   1.93 ERA

Opponents Batting Average: .228
Offensive Support: 4.49 Runs Per Nine Innings
Double Play Support: .43 GDP Per Nine Innings

First Pitch is Hit: 13%
Gets Ahead of the Hitter: 53%
Gets Behind the Hitter: 47%
Gets Leadoff Man Out: 70%

1990 On Base Pct Allowed: .278 Slugging Percentage: .306
Stolen Bases Allowed: 14   Caught Stealing: 14

Pitches Right	AB	H	2B	3B	HR	RBI	BB	SO	AVG
Vs. RHB	404	86	15	3	0	18	27	112	.213
Vs. LHB	443	107	20	2	7	28	27	97	.242

	G	IP	W-L	Pct	SO	BB	ERA
At Home	15	112	11-2		95	31	1.53
On the Road	16	117	10-4		114	23	2.31
1990 Season	31	228	21-6	.778	209	54	1.93
Life 5.6 Years	37	272	21-9	.695	256	77	2.89

•

Alex COLE

CLEVELAND   CENTER FIELD   25 Years Old

Runs Created: 37   Offensive Winning Percentage: .623
Batting Average: .300   Secondary Average: .357

Most Often Bats: 1st
Hits First Pitch: 11%
Gets Ahead of the Pitcher: 55%
Hits Behind the Pitcher: 45%

1990 On Base Percentage: .379   Career: .379
1990 Slugging Percentage: .357   Career: .357
Batting Avg with Men in Scoring Position: .320

Bats Left-Handed		AB	R	H	2B	3B	HR	RBI	BB	SO	SB	AVG
Vs. RHP		175	29	55	5	3	0	9	18	27	27	.314
Vs. LHP		52	14	13	0	1	0	4	10	11	13	.250
At Home	35	121	24	37	2	3	0	9	18	23	22	.306
On the Road	28	106	19	31	3	1	0	4	10	15	18	.292
1990 Season	63	227	43	68	5	4	0	13	28	38	40	.300
Life 0.4 Years		584	111	175	13	10	0	33	72	98	103	.300

Vince COLEMAN

ST. LOUIS   LEFT FIELD   29 Years Old

Runs Created: 74   Offensive Winning Percentage: .634
Batting Average: .292   Secondary Average: .334

Most Often Bats: 1st
Hits First Pitch: 16%
Gets Ahead of the Pitcher: 51%
Hits Behind the Pitcher: 49%

1990 On Base Percentage: .340   Career: .326
1990 Slugging Percentage: .400   Career: .339
Batting Avg with Men in Scoring Position: .259

Switch Hitter		AB	R	H	2B	3B	HR	RBI	BB	SO	SB	AVG
Vs. RHP		306	49	95	5	5	1	21	26	51	49	.310
Vs. LHP		191	24	50	13	4	5	18	9	37	28	.262
At Home	63	259	44	77	10	6	5	21	22	48	50	.297
On the Road	61	238	29	68	8	3	1	18	13	40	27	.286
1990 Season	124	497	73	145	18	9	6	39	35	88	77	.292
Life 5.4 Years		652	104	173	20	10	3	40	58	116	101	.265

•

Pat COMBS

PHILADELPHIA   STARTING PITCHER   24 Years Old
                    10-10   4.07 ERA

Opponents Batting Average: .257
Offensive Support: 4.96 Runs Per Nine Innings
Double Play Support: .69 GDP Per Nine Innings

First Pitch is Hit: 14%
Gets Ahead of the Hitter: 47%
Gets Behind the Hitter: 53%
Gets Leadoff Man Out: 64%

1990 On Base Pct Allowed: .339 Slugging Percentage: .375
Stolen Bases Allowed: 11   Caught Stealing: 10

Pitches Left	AB	H	2B	3B	HR	RBI	BB	SO	AVG
Vs. RHB	561	144	33	4	7	61	70	83	.257
Vs. LHB	135	35	3	1	5	20	16	25	.259

	G	IP	W-L	Pct	SO	BB	ERA
At Home	13	83	4-2		47	33	3.05
On the Road	19	101	6-8		61	53	4.92
1990 Season	32	183	10-10	.500	108	86	4.07
Life 1.0 Years	37	219	14-10	.583	136	91	3.73

David CONE

NEW YORK	STARTING PITCHER	28 Years Old
	14-10 3.23 ERA	

Opponents Batting Average: .226
Offensive Support: 4.72 Runs Per Nine Innings
Double Play Support: .38 GDP Per Nine Innings

First Pitch is Hit: 11%
Gets Ahead of the Hitter: 56%
Gets Behind the Hitter: 44%
Gets Leadoff Man Out: 68%

1990 On Base Pct Allowed: .284 Slugging Percentage: .364
Stolen Bases Allowed: 23   Caught Stealing: 9

Pitches Right	AB	H	2B	3B	HR	RBI	BB	SO	AVG
Vs. RHB	317	77	9	1	7	34	27	109	.243
Vs. LHB	467	100	22	6	14	35	38	124	.214

	G	IP	W-L	Pct	SO	BB	ERA
At Home	16	108	7-6		114	35	3.85
On the Road	15	104	7-4		119	30	2.60
1990 Season	31	212	14-10	.583	233	65	3.23
Life 3.2 Years	41	246	17-8	.663	227	87	3.14

•

Dennis COOK

LOS ANGELES	RELIEF PITCHER	28 Years Old
	9-4 3.92 ERA 1 SAVES	

Blown Saves: 1   Holds: 4   Save Efficiency: 83%
Inherited Runners who Scored: 49%
Opponents Batting Average: .262
Double Play Support: .58 GDP Per Nine Innings

First Pitch is Hit: 14%
Gets Ahead of the Hitter: 48%
Gets Behind the Hitter: 52%
Gets First Batter Out: 58%

1990 On Base Pct Allowed: .325 Slugging Percentage: .413
Stolen Bases Allowed: 16   Caught Stealing: 4

Pitches Left	AB	H	2B	3B	HR	RBI	BB	SO	AVG
Vs. RHB	456	115	15	1	16	56	40	49	.252
Vs. LHB	135	40	8	2	4	20	16	15	.296

	G	IP	W-L	Pct	SO	BB	ERA
1990 Season	47	156	9-4	.692	64	56	3.92
Life 1.5 Years	49	198	12-9	.581	95	69	3.76

Henry COTTO

SEATTLE	RIGHT FIELD	30 Years Old

Runs Created: 38	Offensive Winning Percentage: .436
Batting Average: .259	Secondary Average: .211

Most Often Bats: 2nd
Hits First Pitch: 14%
Gets Ahead of the Pitcher: 51%
Hits Behind the Pitcher: 49%

1990 On Base Percentage: .307	Career: .299
1990 Slugging Percentage: .349	Career: .366

Batting Avg with Men in Scoring Position: .223

Bats Right-Handed		AB	R	H	2B	3B	HR	RBI	BB	SO	SB	AVG
Vs. RHP		163	15	42	7	1	2	14	9	27	11	.258
Vs. LHP		192	25	50	7	2	2	19	13	25	10	.260
At Home	61	173	21	45	7	2	2	15	13	21	10	.260
On the Road	66	182	19	47	7	1	2	18	9	31	11	.258
1990 Season	127	355	40	92	14	3	4	33	22	52	21	.259
Life 3.7 Years	395	52	102	17	2	8	37	21	64	20	.258

•

Steve CRAWFORD

KANSAS CITY	RELIEF PITCHER	32 Years Old
	5-4 4.16 ERA 1 SAVES	

Blown Saves: 1   Holds: 7   Save Efficiency: 89%
Inherited Runners who Scored: 36%
Opponents Batting Average: .254
Double Play Support: .45 GDP Per Nine Innings

First Pitch is Hit: 14%
Gets Ahead of the Hitter: 51%
Gets Behind the Hitter: 49%
Gets First Batter Out: 65%

1990 On Base Pct Allowed: .310 Slugging Percentage: .379
Stolen Bases Allowed: 9   Caught Stealing: 2

Pitches Right	AB	H	2B	3B	HR	RBI	BB	SO	AVG
Vs. RHB	187	36	5	0	4	23	11	43	.193
Vs. LHB	124	43	11	1	3	20	12	11	.347

	G	IP	W-L	Pct	SO	BB	ERA
1990 Season	46	80	5-4	.556	54	23	4.16
Life 3.5 Years	69	147	8-6	.563	80	48	4.01

Tim CREWS

LOS ANGELES	RELIEF PITCHER	30 Years Old
4-5	2.77 ERA	5 SAVES

Blown Saves: 4   Holds: 5   Save Efficiency: 71%
Inherited Runners who Scored: 34%
Opponents Batting Average: .238
Double Play Support: .50 GDP Per Nine Innings

First Pitch is Hit: 13%
Gets Ahead of the Hitter: 54%
Gets Behind the Hitter: 46%
Gets First Batter Out: 75%

1990 On Base Pct Allowed: .280 Slugging Percentage: .358
Stolen Bases Allowed: 8   Caught Stealing: 3

Pitches Right	AB	H	2B	3B	HR	RBI	BB	SO	AVG
Vs. RHB	193	41	6	0	6	22	13	44	.212
Vs. LHB	218	57	10	3	3	15	11	32	.261

	G	IP	W-L	Pct	SO	BB	ERA
1990 Season	66	107	4-5	.444	76	24	2.77
Life 2.4 Years	73	115	4-3	.563	84	30	2.94

•

Chuck CRIM

MILWAUKEE	RELIEF PITCHER	29 Years Old
3-5	3.47 ERA	11 SAVES

Blown Saves: 5   Holds: 19   Save Efficiency: 86%
Inherited Runners who Scored: 33%
Opponents Batting Average: .261
Double Play Support: .74 GDP Per Nine Innings

First Pitch is Hit: 18%
Gets Ahead of the Hitter: 51%
Gets Behind the Hitter: 49%
Gets First Batter Out: 66%

1990 On Base Pct Allowed: .309 Slugging Percentage: .371
Stolen Bases Allowed: 5   Caught Stealing: 0

Pitches Right	AB	H	2B	3B	HR	RBI	BB	SO	AVG
Vs. RHB	206	55	6	2	6	26	16	23	.267
Vs. LHB	131	33	6	0	1	15	7	16	.252

	G	IP	W-L	Pct	SO	BB	ERA
1990 Season	67	86	3-5	.375	39	23	3.47
Life 3.7 Years	73	120	7-7	.490	58	34	3.22

•D•

Kal DANIELS

LOS ANGELES	LEFT FIELD	27 Years Old

Runs Created: 95   Offensive Winning Percentage: .755
Batting Average: .296   Secondary Average: .396

Most Often Bats: 3rd
Hits First Pitch: 10%
Gets Ahead of the Pitcher: 57%
Hits Behind the Pitcher: 43%

1990 On Base Percentage: .389   Career: .402
1990 Slugging Percentage: .531   Career: .514
Batting Avg with Men in Scoring Position: .292

Bats Left-Handed	AB	R	H	2B	3B	HR	RBI	BB	SO	SB	AVG
Vs. RHP	299	62	90	17	1	21	64	43	71	3	.301
Vs. LHP	151	19	43	6	0	6	30	25	33	1	.285
At Home	67	231	38	67	10	1	12	43	35	48	3	.290
On the Road	63	219	43	66	13	0	15	51	33	56	1	.301
1990 Season 130	450	81	133	23	1	27	94	68	104	4	.296
Life 3.1 Years	532	101	160	32	2	26	84	89	103	26	.300

•

Ron DARLING

NEW YORK	STARTING PITCHER	30 Years Old
7-9	4.50 ERA	

Opponents Batting Average: .273
Offensive Support: 4.79 Runs Per Nine Innings
Double Play Support: .21 GDP Per Nine Innings

First Pitch is Hit: 14%
Gets Ahead of the Hitter: 49%
Gets Behind the Hitter: 51%
Gets Leadoff Man Out: 69%

1990 On Base Pct Allowed: .336 Slugging Percentage: .451
Stolen Bases Allowed: 24   Caught Stealing: 4

Pitches Right	AB	H	2B	3B	HR	RBI	BB	SO	AVG
Vs. RHB	212	62	9	4	11	27	14	43	.292
Vs. LHB	283	73	9	1	9	40	30	56	.258

	G	IP	W-L	Pct	SO	BB	ERA
At Home	14	54	4-2		41	19	3.52
On the Road	19	72	3-7		58	25	5.23
1990 Season	33	126	7-9	.438	99	44	4.50
Life 6.3 Years	38	242	15-10	.595	174	93	3.48

Danny DARWIN

HOUSTON   RELIEF PITCHER   35 Years Old

11-4   2.21 ERA   2 SAVES

Blown Saves: 2   Holds: 0   Save Efficiency: 50%
Inherited Runners who Scored: 30%
Opponents Batting Average: .225
Double Play Support: .44 GDP Per Nine Innings

First Pitch is Hit: 16%
Gets Ahead of the Hitter: 59%
Gets Behind the Hitter: 41%
Gets First Batter Out: 90%

1990 On Base Pct Allowed: .266   Slugging Percentage: .331
Stolen Bases Allowed: 17   Caught Stealing: 6

Pitches Right	AB	H	2B	3B	HR	RBI	BB	SO	AVG
Vs. RHB	242	40	9	0	4	20	8	41	.165
Vs. LHB	363	96	22	0	7	24	23	68	.264

	G	IP	W-L	Pct	SO	BB	ERA
1990 Season	48	163	11-4	.733	109	31	2.21
Life 9.4 Years	52	203	12-12	.505	134	62	3.40

•

Jack DAUGHERTY

TEXAS   LEFT FIELD   30 Years Old

Runs Created: 48   Offensive Winning Percentage: .647
Batting Average: .300   Secondary Average: .206

Most Often Bats: 2nd
Hits First Pitch: 18%
Gets Ahead of the Pitcher: 56%
Hits Behind the Pitcher: 44%

1990 On Base Percentage: .347   Career: .346
1990 Slugging Percentage: .435   Career: .423
Batting Avg with Men in Scoring Position: .272

Switch Hitter	AB	R	H	2B	3B	HR	RBI	BB	SO	SB	AVG
Vs. RHP	233	29	72	17	2	6	37	15	29	0	.309
Vs. LHP	77	7	21	3	0	0	10	7	20	0	.273
At Home	62	164	20	51	9	1	5	25	13	24	0	.311
On the Road	63	146	16	42	11	1	1	22	9	25	0	.288
1990 Season	125	310	36	93	20	2	6	47	22	49	0	.300
Life 1.2 Years	367	45	109	22	3	6	50	28	63	2	.296

Darren DAULTON

PHILADELPHIA   CATCHER   29 Years Old

Runs Created: 76   Offensive Winning Percentage: .654
Batting Average: .268   Secondary Average: .320

Most Often Bats: 2nd
Hits First Pitch: 13%
Gets Ahead of the Pitcher: 55%
Hits Behind the Pitcher: 45%

1990 On Base Percentage: .367   Career: .332
1990 Slugging Percentage: .416   Career: .359
Batting Avg with Men in Scoring Position: .282

Bats Left-Handed	AB	R	H	2B	3B	HR	RBI	BB	SO	SB	AVG
Vs. RHP	346	47	94	22	1	11	48	50	49	6	.272
Vs. LHP	113	15	29	8	0	1	9	22	23	1	.257
At Home	71	224	26	56	15	0	5	24	34	31	3	.250
On the Road	72	235	36	67	15	1	7	33	38	41	4	.285
1990 Season	143	459	62	123	30	1	12	57	72	72	7	.268
Life 2.9 Years	461	50	105	21	1	12	54	73	93	5	.227

•

Alvin DAVIS

SEATTLE   DESIGNATED HITTER   30 Years Old

Runs Created: 87   Offensive Winning Percentage: .705
Batting Average: .283   Secondary Average: .318

Most Often Bats: 3rd
Hits First Pitch: 7%
Gets Ahead of the Pitcher: 56%
Hits Behind the Pitcher: 44%

1990 On Base Percentage: .387   Career: .391
1990 Slugging Percentage: .429   Career: .468
Batting Avg with Men in Scoring Position: .278

Bats Left-Handed	AB	R	H	2B	3B	HR	RBI	BB	SO	SB	AVG
Vs. RHP	326	40	97	14	0	11	39	57	44	0	.298
Vs. LHP	168	23	43	7	0	6	29	28	24	0	.256
At Home	72	252	42	70	11	0	12	40	47	38	0	.278
On the Road	68	242	21	70	10	0	5	28	38	30	0	.289
1990 Season	140	494	63	140	21	0	17	68	85	68	0	.283
Life 6.3 Years	583	83	168	31	1	23	95	98	75	1	.289

Chili DAVIS

CALIFORNIA   DESIGNATED HITTER   31 Years Old

Runs Created: 59   Offensive Winning Percentage: .565
Batting Average: .265   Secondary Average: .284

Most Often Bats: 4th
Hits First Pitch: 14%
Gets Ahead of the Pitcher: 50%
Hits Behind the Pitcher: 50%

1990 On Base Percentage: .357   Career: .340
1990 Slugging Percentage: .398   Career: .422
Batting Avg with Men in Scoring Position: .219

Switch Hitter	AB	R	H	2B	3B	HR	RBI	BB	SO	SB	AVG
vs. RHP	286	44	77	12	1	8	38	43	60	1	.269
Vs. LHP	126	14	32	5	0	4	20	18	29	0	.254
At Home	59	216	38	66	9	1	10	39	30	46	0	.306
On the Road	54	196	20	43	8	0	2	19	31	43	1	.219
1990 Season	113	412	58	109	17	1	12	58	61	89	1	.265
Life	8.0 Years	589	81	157	27	3	19	82	67	111	13	.267

Glenn DAVIS

HOUSTON   FIRST BASE   30 Years Old

Runs Created: 62   Offensive Winning Percentage: .753
Batting Average: .251   Secondary Average: .437

Most Often Bats: 4th
Hits First Pitch: 13%
Gets Ahead of the Pitcher: 51%
Hits Behind the Pitcher: 49%

1990 On Base Percentage: .357   Career: .337
1990 Slugging Percentage: .523   Career: .483
Batting Avg with Men in Scoring Position: .263

Bats Right-Handed	AB	R	H	2B	3B	HR	RBI	BB	SO	SB	AVG
Vs. RHP	204	21	51	9	4	11	37	25	43	5	.250
Vs. LHP	123	23	31	6	0	11	27	21	11	3	.252
At Home	50	175	19	38	7	2	4	22	21	35	7	.217
On the Road	43	152	25	44	8	2	18	42	25	19	1	.289
1990 Season	93	327	44	82	15	4	22	64	46	54	8	.251
Life	5.1 Years	592	83	155	29	2	32	101	61	96	4	.262

Eric DAVIS

CINCINNATI   CENTER FIELD   28 Years Old

Runs Created: 81   Offensive Winning Percentage: .714
Batting Average: .260   Secondary Average: .404

Most Often Bats: 4th
Hits First Pitch: 12%
Gets Ahead of the Pitcher: 55%
Hits Behind the Pitcher: 45%

1990 On Base Percentage: .347   Career: .364
1990 Slugging Percentage: .486   Career: .522
Batting Avg with Men in Scoring Position: .252

Bats Right-Handed	AB	R	H	2B	3B	HR	RBI	BB	SO	SB	AVG
Vs. RHP	303	52	75	15	2	16	50	41	68	15	.248
Vs. LHP	150	32	43	11	0	8	36	19	32	6	.287
At Home	58	193	38	45	8	1	13	34	32	42	7	.233
On the Road	69	260	46	73	18	1	11	52	28	58	14	.281
1990 Season	127	453	84	118	26	2	24	86	60	100	21	.260
Life	4.7 Years	543	109	148	23	4	35	105	79	140	49	.272

Mark DAVIS

KANSAS CITY   RELIEF PITCHER   30 Years Old
2-7   5.11 ERA   6 SAVES

Blown Saves: 4   Holds: 7   Save Efficiency: 76%
Inherited Runners who Scored: 40%
Opponents Batting Average: .259
Double Play Support: .66 GDP Per Nine Innings

First Pitch is Hit: 7%
Gets Ahead of the Hitter: 46%
Gets Behind the Hitter: 54%
Gets First Batter Out: 70%

1990 On Base Pct Allowed: .383 Slugging Percentage: .423
Stolen Bases Allowed: 15   Caught Stealing: 0

Pitches Left	AB	H	2B	3B	HR	RBI	BB	SO	AVG
Vs. RHB	219	60	13	1	9	42	41	54	.274
Vs. LHB	55	11	3	0	0	7	11	19	.200

	G	IP	W-L	Pct	SO	BB	ERA
1990 Season	53	69	2-7	.222	73	52	5.11
Life 7.3 Years	64	126	6-10	.368	113	53	3.86

Storm DAVIS

KANSAS CITY   STARTING PITCHER   29 Years Old
                     7-10   4.74 ERA

Opponents Batting Average: .281
Offensive Support: 5.71 Runs Per Nine Innings
Double Play Support: .64 GDP Per Nine Innings

First Pitch is Hit: 14%
Gets Ahead of the Hitter: 54%
Gets Behind the Hitter: 46%
Gets Leadoff Man Out: 66%

1990 On Base Pct Allowed: .330 Slugging Percentage: .407
Stolen Bases Allowed: 3   Caught Stealing: 0

Pitches Right	AB	H	2B	3B	HR	RBI	BB	SO	AVG
Vs. RHB	224	60	13	0	5	26	13	30	.268
Vs. LHB	235	69	14	2	4	29	22	32	.294

	G	IP	W-L	Pct	SO	BB	ERA
At Home	15	80	5-7		45	22	4.50
On the Road	6	32	2-3		17	13	5.34
1990 Season	21	112	7-10	.412	62	35	4.74
Life 6.6 Years	40	218	15-11	.579	127	80	3.93

•

Andre DAWSON

CHICAGO   RIGHT FIELD   36 Years Old

Runs Created: 101   Offensive Winning Percentage: .707
Batting Average: .310   Secondary Average: .335

Most Often Bats: 4th
Hits First Pitch: 14%
Gets Ahead of the Pitcher: 54%
Hits Behind the Pitcher: 46%

1990 On Base Percentage: .358   Career: .328
1990 Slugging Percentage: .535   Career: .490
Batting Avg with Men in Scoring Position: .297

Bats Right-Handed	AB	R	H	2B	3B	HR	RBI	BB	SO	SB	AVG
Vs. RHP	348	49	110	18	3	19	75	28	46	13	.316
Vs. LHP	181	23	54	10	2	8	25	14	19	3	.298
At Home	77	266	31	84	10	3	14	51	27	26	9	.316
On the Road	70	263	41	80	18	2	13	49	15	39	7	.304
1990 Season 147	529	72	164	28	5	27	100	42	65	16	.310
Life 12.5 Years	625	91	177	32	7	28	99	40	96	24	.283

Ken DAYLEY

ST. LOUIS   RELIEF PITCHER   32 Years Old
                     4-4   3.56 ERA   2 SAVES

Blown Saves: 5   Holds: 14   Save Efficiency: 76%
Inherited Runners who Scored: 43%
Opponents Batting Average: .233
Double Play Support: .61 GDP Per Nine Innings

First Pitch is Hit: 14%
Gets Ahead of the Hitter: 47%
Gets Behind the Hitter: 53%
Gets First Batter Out: 67%

1990 On Base Pct Allowed: .305 Slugging Percentage: .337
Stolen Bases Allowed: 3   Caught Stealing: 2

Pitches Left	AB	H	2B	3B	HR	RBI	BB	SO	AVG
Vs. RHB	164	33	8	1	2	23	22	29	.201
Vs. LHB	106	30	3	0	3	15	8	22	.283

	G	IP	W-L	Pct	SO	BB	ERA
1990 Season	58	73	4-4	.500	51	30	3.56
Life 5.5 Years	68	103	6-8	.423	73	30	3.62

•

Rob DEER

MILWAUKEE   RIGHT FIELD   30 Years Old

Runs Created: 64   Offensive Winning Percentage: .531
Batting Average: .209   Secondary Average: .373

Most Often Bats: 6th
Hits First Pitch: 9%
Gets Ahead of the Pitcher: 49%
Hits Behind the Pitcher: 51%

1990 On Base Percentage: .313   Career: .327
1990 Slugging Percentage: .432   Career: .446
Batting Avg with Men in Scoring Position: .218

Bats Right-Handed	AB	R	H	2B	3B	HR	RBI	BB	SO	SB	AVG
Vs. RHP	300	31	51	10	1	11	35	39	107	1	.170
Vs. LHP	140	26	41	5	0	16	34	25	40	1	.293
At Home	67	214	24	40	7	0	11	30	35	67	1	.187
On the Road	67	226	33	52	8	1	16	39	29	80	1	.230
1990 Season 134	440	57	92	15	1	27	69	64	147	2	.209
Life 4.7 Years	539	80	122	20	2	32	87	78	193	7	.225

Jose DeJESUS

PHILADELPHIA   STARTING PITCHER   26 Years Old
                      7-8   3.74 ERA

Opponents Batting Average: .211
Offensive Support: 4.15 Runs Per Nine Innings
Double Play Support: .97 GDP Per Nine Innings

First Pitch is Hit: 12%
Gets Ahead of the Hitter: 46%
Gets Behind the Hitter: 54%
Gets Leadoff Man Out: 62%

1990 On Base Pct Allowed: .321 Slugging Percentage: .320
Stolen Bases Allowed: 10   Caught Stealing: 6

Pitches Right	AB	H	2B	3B	HR	RBI	BB	SO	AVG
Vs. RHB	161	40	7	0	6	28	20	30	.248
Vs. LHB	298	57	9	2	4	20	53	57	.191

	G	IP	W-L	Pct	SO	BB	ERA
At Home	11	71	2-5		49	34	3.68
On the Road	11	59	5-3		38	39	3.81
1990 Season	22	130	7-8	.467	87	73	3.74
Life 0.7 Years	39	204	10-13	.438	132	125	4.22

•

Jose DeLEON

ST. LOUIS   STARTING PITCHER   30 Years Old
                   7-19   4.43 ERA

Opponents Batting Average: .246
Offensive Support: 2.96 Runs Per Nine Innings
Double Play Support: .39 GDP Per Nine Innings

First Pitch is Hit: 14%
Gets Ahead of the Hitter: 46%
Gets Behind the Hitter: 54%
Gets Leadoff Man Out: 68%

1990 On Base Pct Allowed: .331 Slugging Percentage: .370
Stolen Bases Allowed: 20   Caught Stealing: 12

Pitches Right	AB	H	2B	3B	HR	RBI	BB	SO	AVG
Vs. RHB	282	54	8	0	7	30	28	96	.191
Vs. LHB	401	114	22	5	8	56	58	68	.284

	G	IP	W-L	Pct	SO	BB	ERA
At Home	16	84	3-9		74	43	5.55
On the Road	16	98	4-10		90	43	3.48
1990 Season	32	183	7-19	.269	164	86	4.43
Life 6.1 Years	38	234	11-16	.415	202	105	3.79

Jim DESHAIES

HOUSTON   STARTING PITCHER   30 Years Old
                 7-12   3.78 ERA

Opponents Batting Average: .245
Offensive Support: 3.53 Runs Per Nine Innings
Double Play Support: .34 GDP Per Nine Innings

First Pitch is Hit: 15%
Gets Ahead of the Hitter: 45%
Gets Behind the Hitter: 55%
Gets Leadoff Man Out: 67%

1990 On Base Pct Allowed: .322 Slugging Percentage: .386
Stolen Bases Allowed: 21   Caught Stealing: 9

Pitches Left	AB	H	2B	3B	HR	RBI	BB	SO	AVG
Vs. RHB	645	151	27	3	20	69	61	99	.234
Vs. LHB	115	35	7	2	1	14	23	20	.304

	G	IP	W-L	Pct	SO	BB	ERA
At Home	15	98	4-3		51	32	2.75
On the Road	19	111	3-9		68	52	4.70
1990 Season	34	209	7-12	.368	119	84	3.78
Life 4.1 Years	37	229	13-12	.538	154	86	3.50

•

Delino DeSHIELDS

MONTREAL   SECOND BASE   22 Years Old

Runs Created: 75   Offensive Winning Percentage: .643
Batting Average: .289   Secondary Average: .321

Most Often Bats: 1st
Hits First Pitch: 11%
Gets Ahead of the Pitcher: 53%
Hits Behind the Pitcher: 47%

1990 On Base Percentage: .375   Career: .375
1990 Slugging Percentage: .393   Career: .393
Batting Avg with Men in Scoring Position: .283

Bats Left-Handed	AB	R	H	2B	3B	HR	RBI	BB	SO	SB	AVG
Vs. RHP	306	45	93	19	3	2	28	40	48	29	.304
Vs. LHP	193	24	51	9	3	2	17	26	48	13	.264

		AB	R	H	2B	3B	HR	RBI	BB	SO	SB	AVG
At Home	59	226	36	71	15	2	3	27	32	41	24	.314
On the Road	70	273	33	73	13	4	1	18	34	55	18	.267
1990 Season	129	499	69	144	28	6	4	45	66	96	42	.289
Life 0.8 Years	627	87	181	35	8	5	57	83	121	53	.289

Mike DEVEREAUX

BALTIMORE CENTER FIELD 28 Years Old

Runs Created: 38 Offensive Winning Percentage: .380
Batting Average: .240 Secondary Average: .264

Most Often Bats: 7th
Hits First Pitch: 14%
Gets Ahead of the Pitcher: 52%
Hits Behind the Pitcher: 48%

1990 On Base Percentage: .291 Career: .300
1990 Slugging Percentage: .392 Career: .366
Batting Avg with Men in Scoring Position: .239

Bats Right-Handed	AB	R	H	2B	3B	HR	RBI	BB	SO	SB	AVG
Vs. RHP	207	29	51	11	1	5	27	18	33	8	.246
Vs. LHP	160	19	37	7	0	7	22	10	15	5	.231
At Home	51	150	23	35	7	0	6	21	16	25	7	.233
On the Road	57	217	25	53	11	1	6	28	12	23	6	.244
1990 Season	108	367	48	88	18	1	12	49	28	48	13	.240
Life 1.7 Years	496	66	121	21	2	12	59	40	74	22	.244

•

Rob DIBBLE

CINCINNATI RELIEF PITCHER 27 Years Old
8-3 1.74 ERA 11 SAVES

Blown Saves: 6 Holds: 17 Save Efficiency: 82%
Inherited Runners who Scored: 35%
Opponents Batting Average: .183
Double Play Support: .73 GDP Per Nine Innings

First Pitch is Hit: 8%
Gets Ahead of the Hitter: 52%
Gets Behind the Hitter: 48%
Gets First Batter Out: 78%

1990 On Base Pct Allowed: .255 Slugging Percentage: .254
Stolen Bases Allowed: 20 Caught Stealing: 3

Pitches Right	AB	H	2B	3B	HR	RBI	BB	SO	AVG
Vs. RHB	166	30	6	0	2	19	10	67	.181
Vs. LHB	173	32	7	1	1	19	24	69	.185

	G	IP	W-L	Pct	SO	BB	ERA
1990 Season	68	98	8-3	.727	136	34	1.74
Life 2.4 Years	74	106	8-4	.679	139	39	1.90

Frank DiPINO

ST. LOUIS RELIEF PITCHER 34 Years Old
5-2 4.56 ERA 3 SAVES

Blown Saves: 2 Holds: 4 Save Efficiency: 78%
Inherited Runners who Scored: 57%
Opponents Batting Average: .294
Double Play Support: .56 GDP Per Nine Innings

First Pitch is Hit: 14%
Gets Ahead of the Hitter: 46%
Gets Behind the Hitter: 54%
Gets First Batter Out: 61%

1990 On Base Pct Allowed: .352 Slugging Percentage: .447
Stolen Bases Allowed: 4 Caught Stealing: 2

Pitches Left	AB	H	2B	3B	HR	RBI	BB	SO	AVG
Vs. RHB	180	53	13	2	6	40	19	31	.294
Vs. LHB	133	39	5	1	2	18	12	18	.293

	G	IP	W-L	Pct	SO	BB	ERA
1990 Season	62	81	5-2	.714	49	31	4.56
Life 6.8 Years	73	100	5-5	.479	74	38	3.80

•

Billy DORAN

CINCINNATI SECOND BASE 32 Years Old

Runs Created: 81 Offensive Winning Percentage: .769
Batting Average: .300 Secondary Average: .387

Most Often Bats: 2nd
Hits First Pitch: 13%
Gets Ahead of the Pitcher: 60%
Hits Behind the Pitcher: 40%

1990 On Base Percentage: .411 Career: .356
1990 Slugging Percentage: .434 Career: .377
Batting Avg with Men in Scoring Position: .226

Switch Hitter	AB	R	H	2B	3B	HR	RBI	BB	SO	SB	AVG
Vs. RHP	261	42	83	17	1	5	25	44	39	16	.318
Vs. LHP	142	17	38	12	1	2	12	35	19	7	.268
At Home	60	199	32	66	14	2	4	18	38	26	14	.332
On the Road	66	204	27	55	15	0	3	19	41	32	9	.270
1990 Season	126	403	59	121	29	2	7	37	79	58	23	.300
Life 7.3 Years	592	85	159	26	5	10	56	81	71	27	.269

Brian DOWNING

CALIFORNIA   DESIGNATED HITTER   40 Years Old

Runs Created: 59   Offensive Winning Percentage: .677
Batting Average: .273   Secondary Average: .345

Most Often Bats: 1st
Hits First Pitch: 6%
Gets Ahead of the Pitcher: 51%
Hits Behind the Pitcher: 49%

1990 On Base Percentage: .374   Career: .368
1990 Slugging Percentage: .467   Career: .424
Batting Avg with Men in Scoring Position: .291

Bats Right-Handed	AB	R	H	2B	3B	HR	RBI	BB	SO	SB	AVG
Vs. RHP	211	19	49	10	1	9	35	25	31	0	.232
Vs. LHP	119	28	41	8	1	5	16	25	14	0	.345
At Home	48	162	28	49	9	0	11	26	24	14	0	.302
On the Road	48	168	19	41	9	2	3	25	26	31	0	.244
1990 Season	96	330	47	90	18	2	14	51	50	45	0	.273
Life	13.0 Years	546	81	145	25	2	19	75	83	77	4	.266

Doug DRABEK

PITTSBURGH   STARTING PITCHER   28 Years Old
22-6   2.76 ERA

Opponents Batting Average: .225
Offensive Support: 5.91 Runs Per Nine Innings
Double Play Support: .43 GDP Per Nine Innings

First Pitch is Hit: 15%
Gets Ahead of the Hitter: 49%
Gets Behind the Hitter: 51%
Gets Leadoff Man Out: 76%

1990 On Base Pct Allowed: .274 Slugging Percentage: .331
Stolen Bases Allowed: 18   Caught Stealing: 9

Pitches Right	AB	H	2B	3B	HR	RBI	BB	SO	AVG
Vs. RHB	314	60	8	0	5	18	21	62	.191
Vs. LHB	532	130	29	4	10	47	35	69	.244

	G	IP	W-L	Pct	SO	BB	ERA
At Home	16	120	11-3		72	28	3.00
On the Road	17	111	11-3		59	28	2.51
1990 Season	33	231	22-6	.786	131	56	2.76
Life 4.1 Years	38	243	17-11	.605	140	66	3.21

Tim DRUMMOND

MINNESOTA   RELIEF PITCHER   26 Years Old
3-5   4.35 ERA   1 SAVES

Blown Saves: 1   Holds: 1   Save Efficiency: 67%
Inherited Runners who Scored: 47%
Opponents Batting Average: .295
Double Play Support: 1.19 GDP Per Nine Innings

First Pitch is Hit: 14%
Gets Ahead of the Hitter: 48%
Gets Behind the Hitter: 52%
Gets First Batter Out: 52%

1990 On Base Pct Allowed: .357 Slugging Percentage: .419
Stolen Bases Allowed: 6   Caught Stealing: 1

Pitches Right	AB	H	2B	3B	HR	RBI	BB	SO	AVG
Vs. RHB	204	59	7	1	3	21	22	34	.289
Vs. LHB	149	45	9	1	5	28	14	15	.302

	G	IP	W-L	Pct	SO	BB	ERA
1990 Season	35	91	3-5	.375	49	36	4.35
Life 0.7 Years	68	158	4-7	.375	88	66	4.29

Mariano DUNCAN

CINCINNATI   SECOND BASE   28 Years Old

Runs Created: 69   Offensive Winning Percentage: .670
Batting Average: .306   Secondary Average: .255

Most Often Bats: 7th
Hits First Pitch: 17%
Gets Ahead of the Pitcher: 45%
Hits Behind the Pitcher: 55%

1990 On Base Percentage: .345   Career: .298
1990 Slugging Percentage: .476   Career: .363
Batting Avg with Men in Scoring Position: .257

Bats Right-Handed	AB	R	H	2B	3B	HR	RBI	BB	SO	SB	AVG
Vs. RHP	247	36	56	5	7	6	28	14	45	8	.227
Vs. LHP	188	31	77	17	4	4	27	10	22	5	.410
At Home	66	230	31	71	12	5	5	30	13	30	6	.309
On the Road	59	205	36	62	10	6	5	25	11	37	7	.302
1990 Season	125	435	67	133	22	11	10	55	24	67	13	.306
Life	3.4 Years	571	74	143	23	6	10	48	35	110	35	.251

Shawon DUNSTON

CHICAGO   SHORTSTOP   28 Years Old

Runs Created: 66   Offensive Winning Percentage: .458
Batting Average: .262   Secondary Average: .237

Most Often Bats: 7th
Hits First Pitch: 17%
Gets Ahead of the Pitcher: 43%
Hits Behind the Pitcher: 57%

1990 On Base Percentage: .283   Career: .287
1990 Slugging Percentage: .426   Career: .393
Batting Avg with Men in Scoring Position: .230

Bats Right-Handed	AB	R	H	2B	3B	HR	RBI	BB	SO	SB	AVG
Vs. RHP	357	40	89	16	4	8	43	12	63	18	.249
Vs. LHP	188	33	54	6	4	9	23	3	24	7	.287
At Home	72	268	39	67	12	4	7	25	7	46	11	.250
On the Road	74	277	34	76	10	4	10	41	8	41	14	.274
1990 Season 146	545	73	143	22	8	17	66	15	87	25	.262
Life 4.7 Years	592	73	152	28	6	13	62	24	108	24	.257

•

Lenny DYKSTRA

PHILADELPHIA   CENTER FIELD   28 Years Old

Runs Created: 121   Offensive Winning Percentage: .776
Batting Average: .325   Secondary Average: .322

Most Often Bats: 1st
Hits First Pitch: 15%
Gets Ahead of the Pitcher: 54%
Hits Behind the Pitcher: 46%

1990 On Base Percentage: .418   Career: .359
1990 Slugging Percentage: .441   Career: .408
Batting Avg with Men in Scoring Position: .427

Bats Left-Handed	AB	R	H	2B	3B	HR	RBI	BB	SO	SB	AVG
Vs. RHP	390	80	134	29	2	8	43	60	28	22	.344
Vs. LHP	200	26	58	6	1	1	17	29	20	11	.290
At Home	74	280	56	95	15	1	6	27	52	23	13	.339
On the Road	75	310	50	97	20	2	3	33	37	25	20	.313
1990 Season 149	590	106	192	35	3	9	60	89	48	33	.325
Life 4.8 Years	544	89	153	33	5	9	48	64	60	34	.281

•E•

Dennis ECKERSLEY

OAKLAND   RELIEF PITCHER   36 Years Old
4-2   0.61 ERA   48 SAVES

Blown Saves: 2   Holds: 0   Save Efficiency: 96%
Inherited Runners who Scored: 14%
Opponents Batting Average: .160
Double Play Support: .37 GDP Per Nine Innings

First Pitch is Hit: 13%
Gets Ahead of the Hitter: 66%
Gets Behind the Hitter: 34%
Gets First Batter Out: 79%

1990 On Base Pct Allowed: .172 Slugging Percentage: .226
Stolen Bases Allowed: 1   Caught Stealing: 2

Pitches Right	AB	H	2B	3B	HR	RBI	BB	SO	AVG
Vs. RHB	138	21	5	0	1	2	2	51	.152
Vs. LHB	119	20	4	1	1	10	2	22	.168

	G	IP	W-L	Pct	SO	BB	ERA
1990 Season	63	73	4-2	.667	73	4	0.61
Life 13.0 Years	46	216	13-11	.547	149	51	3.49

•

Tom EDENS

MILWAUKEE   RELIEF PITCHER   29 Years Old
4-5   4.45 ERA   2 SAVES

Blown Saves: 0   Holds: 2   Save Efficiency: 100%
Inherited Runners who Scored: 31%
Opponents Batting Average: .262
Double Play Support: .61 GDP Per Nine Innings

First Pitch is Hit: 12%
Gets Ahead of the Hitter: 52%
Gets Behind the Hitter: 48%
Gets First Batter Out: 76%

1990 On Base Pct Allowed: .331 Slugging Percentage: .374
Stolen Bases Allowed: 9   Caught Stealing: 6

Pitches Right	AB	H	2B	3B	HR	RBI	BB	SO	AVG
Vs. RHB	198	50	8	0	6	27	19	24	.253
Vs. LHB	142	39	4	1	2	15	14	16	.275

	G	IP	W-L	Pct	SO	BB	ERA
1990 Season	35	89	4-5	.444	40	33	4.45
Life 0.6 Years	61	160	7-8	.444	72	61	4.64

Wayne EDWARDS

CHICAGO   RELIEF PITCHER   27 Years Old
5-3   3.22 ERA   2 SAVES

Blown Saves: 0   Holds: 4   Save Efficiency: 100%
Inherited Runners who Scored: 31%
Opponents Batting Average: .234
Double Play Support: 1.23 GDP Per Nine Innings

First Pitch is Hit: 12%
Gets Ahead of the Hitter: 48%
Gets Behind the Hitter: 52%
Gets First Batter Out: 60%

1990 On Base Pct Allowed: .319 Slugging Percentage: .329
Stolen Bases Allowed: 9   Caught Stealing: 5

Pitches Left	AB	H	2B	3B	HR	RBI	BB	SO	AVG
Vs. RHB	253	64	13	0	5	28	27	47	.253
Vs. LHB	93	17	0	1	1	12	14	16	.183

	G	IP	W-L	Pct	SO	BB	ERA
1990 Season	42	95	5-3	.625	63	41	3.22
Life 0.7 Years	67	140	7-4	.625	99	60	3.25

•

Mark EICHHORN

CALIFORNIA   RELIEF PITCHER   30 Years Old
2-5   3.08 ERA   13 SAVES

Blown Saves: 3   Holds: 4   Save Efficiency: 85%
Inherited Runners who Scored: 29%
Opponents Batting Average: .289
Double Play Support: .64 GDP Per Nine Innings

First Pitch is Hit: 11%
Gets Ahead of the Hitter: 59%
Gets Behind the Hitter: 41%
Gets First Batter Out: 69%

1990 On Base Pct Allowed: .341 Slugging Percentage: .354
Stolen Bases Allowed: 4   Caught Stealing: 3

Pitches Right	AB	H	2B	3B	HR	RBI	BB	SO	AVG
Vs. RHB	184	53	10	0	1	31	13	40	.288
Vs. LHB	155	45	4	1	1	19	10	29	.290

	G	IP	W-L	Pct	SO	BB	ERA
1990 Season	60	85	2-5	.286	69	23	3.08
Life 4.2 Years	72	128	7-7	.525	100	42	3.17

Jim EISENREICH

KANSAS CITY   LEFT FIELD   31 Years Old

Runs Created: 64   Offensive Winning Percentage: .513
Batting Average: .280   Secondary Average: .226

Most Often Bats: 6th
Hits First Pitch: 19%
Gets Ahead of the Pitcher: 53%
Hits Behind the Pitcher: 47%

1990 On Base Percentage: .335   Career: .321
1990 Slugging Percentage: .397   Career: .402
Batting Avg with Men in Scoring Position: .239

Bats Left-Handed	AB	R	H	2B	3B	HR	RBI	BB	SO	SB	AVG
Vs. RHP	340	46	104	20	5	4	35	32	33	8	.306
Vs. LHP	156	15	35	9	2	1	16	10	18	4	.224
At Home	70	236	30	61	12	5	2	29	25	19	5	.258
On the Road	72	260	31	78	17	2	3	22	17	32	7	.300
1990 Season	142	496	61	139	29	7	5	51	42	51	12	.280
Life 2.8 Years	510	62	139	31	6	8	58	38	57	18	.273

•

Kevin ELSTER

NEW YORK   SHORTSTOP   26 Years Old

Runs Created: 33   Offensive Winning Percentage: .391
Batting Average: .207   Secondary Average: .258

Most Often Bats: 8th
Hits First Pitch: 9%
Gets Ahead of the Pitcher: 52%
Hits Behind the Pitcher: 48%

1990 On Base Percentage: .274   Career: .280
1990 Slugging Percentage: .363   Career: .343
Batting Avg with Men in Scoring Position: .256

Bats Right-Handed	AB	R	H	2B	3B	HR	RBI	BB	SO	SB	AVG
Vs. RHP	195	27	38	13	1	7	37	20	38	2	.195
Vs. LHP	119	9	27	7	0	2	8	10	16	0	.227
At Home	47	163	17	32	11	1	2	24	15	30	1	.196
On the Road	45	151	19	33	9	0	7	21	15	24	1	.219
1990 Season	92	314	36	65	20	1	9	45	30	54	2	.207
Life 2.6 Years	474	52	104	23	2	11	54	40	73	3	.219

Scott ERICKSON

MINNESOTA STARTING PITCHER 23 Years Old
8-4 2.87 ERA

Opponents Batting Average: .256
Offensive Support: 5.10 Runs Per Nine Innings
Double Play Support: 1.12 GDP Per Nine Innings

First Pitch is Hit: 16%
Gets Ahead of the Hitter: 47%
Gets Behind the Hitter: 53%
Gets Leadoff Man Out: 65%

1990 On Base Pct Allowed: .342 Slugging Percentage: .367
Stolen Bases Allowed: 6 Caught Stealing: 3

Pitches Right	AB	H	2B	3B	HR	RBI	BB	SO	AVG
Vs. RHB	198	53	7	1	5	17	24	37	.268
Vs. LHB	224	55	9	1	4	27	27	16	.246

	G	IP	W-L	Pct	SO	BB	ERA
At Home	13	78	7-2		44	24	3.45
On the Road	6	35	1-2		9	27	1.56
1990 Season	19	113	8-4	.667	53	51	2.87
Life 0.5 Years	39	232	16-8	.667	109	105	2.87

•

Alvaro ESPINOZA

NEW YORK SHORTSTOP 29 Years Old

Runs Created: 29 Offensive Winning Percentage: .207
Batting Average: .224 Secondary Average: .089

Most Often Bats: 9th
Hits First Pitch: 24%
Gets Ahead of the Pitcher: 37%
Hits Behind the Pitcher: 63%

1990 On Base Percentage: .258 Career: .279
1990 Slugging Percentage: .274 Career: .301
Batting Avg with Men in Scoring Position: .187

Bats Right-Handed	AB	R	H	2B	3B	HR	RBI	BB	SO	SB	AVG
Vs. RHP	294	19	62	10	1	1	11	7	41	0	.211
Vs. LHP	144	12	36	2	1	1	9	9	13	1	.250
At Home	74	219	14	47	7	2	0	9	9	21	0	.215
On the Road	76	219	17	51	5	0	2	11	7	33	1	.233
1990 Season	150	438	31	98	12	2	2	20	16	54	1	.224
Life 2.3 Years	458	40	116	17	1	1	31	14	58	2	.253

Dwight EVANS

BOSTON DESIGNATED HITTER 39 Years Old

Runs Created: 60 Offensive Winning Percentage: .531
Batting Average: .249 Secondary Average: .299

Most Often Bats: 5th
Hits First Pitch: 10%
Gets Ahead of the Pitcher: 56%
Hits Behind the Pitcher: 44%

1990 On Base Percentage: .349 Career: .369
1990 Slugging Percentage: .391 Career: .473
Batting Avg with Men in Scoring Position: .268

Bats Right-Handed	AB	R	H	2B	3B	HR	RBI	BB	SO	SB	AVG
Vs. RHP	298	43	72	8	1	10	47	42	44	3	.242
Vs. LHP	147	23	39	10	2	3	16	25	29	0	.265
At Home	60	218	41	55	10	2	7	31	30	42	3	.252
On the Road	63	227	25	56	8	1	6	32	37	31	0	.247
1990 Season	123	445	66	111	18	3	13	63	67	73	3	.249
Life 15.5 Years	564	93	153	31	5	25	87	86	106	5	.272

•F•

Steve FARR

KANSAS CITY   RELIEF PITCHER   34 Years Old

13-7   1.98 ERA   1 SAVES

Blown Saves: 1   Holds: 7   Save Efficiency: 89%
Inherited Runners who Scored: 20%
Opponents Batting Average: .220
Double Play Support: .92 GDP Per Nine Innings

First Pitch is Hit: 14%
Gets Ahead of the Hitter: 55%
Gets Behind the Hitter: 45%
Gets First Batter Out: 76%

1990 On Base Pct Allowed: .301 Slugging Percentage: .295
Stolen Bases Allowed: 8   Caught Stealing: 3

Pitches Right	AB	H	2B	3B	HR	RBI	BB	SO	AVG
Vs. RHB	247	53	6	1	4	24	21	60	.215
Vs. LHB	204	46	6	1	2	14	27	34	.225

	G	IP	W-L	Pct	SO	BB	ERA
1990 Season	57	127	13-7	.650	94	48	1.98
Life 4.7 Years	68	133	8-7	.514	109	53	3.33

•

John FARRELL

CLEVELAND   STARTING PITCHER   28 Years Old

4-5   4.28 ERA

Opponents Batting Average: .286
Offensive Support: 5.12 Runs Per Nine Innings
Double Play Support: .93 GDP Per Nine Innings

First Pitch is Hit: 14%
Gets Ahead of the Hitter: 47%
Gets Behind the Hitter: 53%
Gets Leadoff Man Out: 64%

1990 On Base Pct Allowed: .344 Slugging Percentage: .446
Stolen Bases Allowed: 6   Caught Stealing: 4

Pitches Right	AB	H	2B	3B	HR	RBI	BB	SO	AVG
Vs. RHB	172	51	13	2	6	21	14	25	.297
Vs. LHB	205	57	11	1	4	23	19	19	.278

	G	IP	W-L	Pct	SO	BB	ERA
At Home	5	28	1-2		13	4	3.54
On the Road	12	69	3-3		31	29	4.59
1990 Season	17	97	4-5	.444	44	33	4.28
Life 2.4 Years	37	246	13-13	.516	124	81	3.93

Junior FELIX

TORONTO   RIGHT FIELD   23 Years Old

Runs Created: 69   Offensive Winning Percentage: .579
Batting Average: .263   Secondary Average: .302

Most Often Bats: 9th
Hits First Pitch: 16%
Gets Ahead of the Pitcher: 50%
Hits Behind the Pitcher: 50%

1990 On Base Percentage: .328   Career: .322
1990 Slugging Percentage: .441   Career: .419
Batting Avg with Men in Scoring Position: .292

Switch Hitter		AB	R	H	2B	3B	HR	RBI	BB	SO	SB	AVG
Vs. RHP		311	48	90	15	6	6	43	30	58	12	.289
Vs. LHP		152	25	32	8	1	9	22	15	41	1	.211
At Home	67	236	35	58	13	6	6	29	24	50	6	.246
On the Road	60	227	38	64	10	1	8	36	21	49	7	.282
1990 Season	127	463	73	122	23	7	15	65	45	99	13	.263
Life 1.5 Years		600	92	157	25	10	16	76	53	137	21	.261

•

Felix FERMIN

CLEVELAND   SHORTSTOP   27 Years Old

Runs Created: 36   Offensive Winning Percentage: .286
Batting Average: .256   Secondary Average: .118

Most Often Bats: 9th
Hits First Pitch: 23%
Gets Ahead of the Pitcher: 47%
Hits Behind the Pitcher: 53%

1990 On Base Percentage: .297   Career: .304
1990 Slugging Percentage: .304   Career: .282
Batting Avg with Men in Scoring Position: .254

Bats Right-Handed		AB	R	H	2B	3B	HR	RBI	BB	SO	SB	AVG
Vs. RHP		284	36	72	10	2	1	25	17	18	3	.254
Vs. LHP		130	11	34	3	0	0	15	9	4	0	.262
At Home	74	205	27	57	12	1	1	24	8	13	1	.278
On the Road	74	209	20	49	1	1	0	16	18	9	2	.234
1990 Season	148	414	47	106	13	2	1	40	26	22	3	.256
Life 2.3 Years		461	49	115	10	2	0	29	35	30	5	.249

Alex FERNANDEZ

CHICAGO   STARTING PITCHER   21 Years Old
5-5   3.80 ERA

Opponents Batting Average: .265
Offensive Support: 4.52 Runs Per Nine Innings
Double Play Support: .51 GDP Per Nine Innings

First Pitch is Hit: 13%
Gets Ahead of the Hitter: 53%
Gets Behind the Hitter: 47%
Gets Leadoff Man Out: 68%

1990 On Base Pct Allowed: .338 Slugging Percentage: .360
Stolen Bases Allowed: 1   Caught Stealing: 4

Pitches Right	AB	H	2B	3B	HR	RBI	BB	SO	AVG
Vs. RHB	160	41	4	1	3	21	17	32	.256
Vs. LHB	176	48	6	1	3	12	17	29	.273

	G	IP	W-L	Pct	SO	BB	ERA
At Home	4	27	2-1		17	11	3.67
On the Road	9	61	3-4		44	23	3.86
1000 Season	13	88	5-5	.500	61	34	3.80
Life 0.4 Years	37	250	14-14	.500	174	97	3.80

●

Sid FERNANDEZ

NEW YORK   STARTING PITCHER   28 Years Old
9-14   3.46 ERA

Opponents Batting Average: .200
Offensive Support: 4.22 Runs Per Nine Innings
Double Play Support: .20 GDP Per Nine Innings

First Pitch is Hit: 14%
Gets Ahead of the Hitter: 53%
Gets Behind the Hitter: 47%
Gets Leadoff Man Out: 68%

1990 On Base Pct Allowed: .277 Slugging Percentage: .340
Stolen Bases Allowed: 20   Caught Stealing: 6

Pitches Left	AB	H	2B	3B	HR	RBI	BB	SO	AVG
Vs. RHB	524	102	19	5	15	46	51	137	.195
Vs. LHB	126	28	6	1	3	22	16	44	.222

	G	IP	W-L	Pct	SO	BB	ERA
At Home	15	105	8-5		99	34	2.41
On the Road	15	75	1-9		82	33	4.94
1990 Season	30	179	9-14	.391	181	67	3.46
Life 5.3 Years	38	229	15-11	.569	218	93	3.26

Tony FERNANDEZ

TORONTO   SHORTSTOP   28 Years Old

Runs Created: 88   Offensive Winning Percentage: .540
Batting Average: .276   Secondary Average: .268

Most Often Bats: 2nd
Hits First Pitch: 16%
Gets Ahead of the Pitcher: 54%
Hits Behind the Pitcher: 46%

1990 On Base Percentage: .352   Career: .338
1990 Slugging Percentage: .391   Career: .399
Batting Avg with Men in Scoring Position: .311

Switch Hitter	AB	R	H	2B	3B	HR	RBI	BB	SO	SB	AVG
Vs. RHP	433	63	127	21	15	3	53	40	52	21	.293
Vs. LHP	202	21	48	6	2	1	13	31	18	5	.238
At Home	81	321	46	99	17	12	2	38	31	36	12	.308
On the Road	80	314	38	76	10	5	2	28	40	34	14	.242
1990 Season 161	635	84	175	27	17	4	66	71	70	26	.276
Life 6.3 Years	623	80	180	30	10	6	64	45	54	22	.289

●

Mike FETTERS

CALIFORNIA   RELIEF PITCHER   26 Years Old
1-1   4.12 ERA   1 SAVES

Blown Saves: 0   Holds: 1   Save Efficiency: 100%
Inherited Runners who Scored: 44%
Opponents Batting Average: .287
Double Play Support: .93 GDP Per Nine Innings

First Pitch is Hit: 13%
Gets Ahead of the Hitter: 47%
Gets Behind the Hitter: 53%
Gets First Batter Out: 58%

1990 On Base Pct Allowed: .341 Slugging Percentage: .418
Stolen Bases Allowed: 6   Caught Stealing: 3

Pitches Right	AB	H	2B	3B	HR	RBI	BB	SO	AVG
Vs. RHB	140	35	1	0	2	14	14	22	.250
Vs. LHB	128	42	5	1	7	26	6	13	.328

	G	IP	W-L	Pct	SO	BB	ERA
1990 Season	26	68	1-1	.500	35	20	4.12
Life 0.4 Years	69	181	3-3	.500	100	54	4.31

Cecil FIELDER

DETROIT	FIRST BASE	27 Years Old

Runs Created: 128　　Offensive Winning Percentage: .747
Batting Average: .277　　　Secondary Average: .471

Most Often Bats: 4th
Hits First Pitch: 10%
Gets Ahead of the Pitcher: 52%
Hits Behind the Pitcher: 48%

1990 On Base Percentage: .377　　　　Career: .346
1990 Slugging Percentage: .592　　　　Career: .536
Batting Avg with Men in Scoring Position: .265

Bats Right-Handed		AB	R	H	2B	3B	HR	RBI	BB	SO	SB	AVG
Vs. RHP		395	63	93	14	1	26	78	53	135	0	.235
Vs. LHP		178	41	66	11	0	25	54	37	47	0	.371
At Home	80	271	47	76	13	0	25	60	52	81	0	.280
On the Road	79	302	57	83	12	1	26	72	38	101	0	.275
1990 Season	159	573	104	159	25	1	51	132	90	182	0	.277
Life	2.3 Years	461	73	121	19	1	35	92	58	139	0	.261

Steve FINLEY

BALTIMORE	RIGHT FIELD	25 Years Old

Runs Created: 48　　Offensive Winning Percentage: .392
Batting Average: .256　　　Secondary Average: .188

Most Often Bats: 1st
Hits First Pitch: 15%
Gets Ahead of the Pitcher: 46%
Hits Behind the Pitcher: 54%

1990 On Base Percentage: .304　　　　Career: .302
1990 Slugging Percentage: .328　　　　Career: .325
Batting Avg with Men in Scoring Position: .255

Bats Left-Handed		AB	R	H	2B	3B	HR	RBI	BB	SO	SB	AVG
Vs. RHP		350	41	97	14	4	2	28	30	38	19	.277
Vs. LHP		114	5	22	2	0	1	9	2	15	3	.193
At Home	75	247	24	57	9	3	1	14	15	31	11	.231
On the Road	67	217	22	62	7	1	2	23	17	22	11	.286
1990 Season	142	464	46	119	16	4	3	37	32	53	22	.256
Life	1.4 Years	495	59	126	15	4	4	45	34	60	28	.254

Chuck FINLEY

CALIFORNIA	STARTING PITCHER	28 Years Old
	18-9　2.40 ERA	

Opponents Batting Average: .243
Offensive Support: 4.54 Runs Per Nine Innings
Double Play Support: .88 GDP Per Nine Innings

First Pitch is Hit: 13%
Gets Ahead of the Hitter: 50%
Gets Behind the Hitter: 50%
Gets Leadoff Man Out: 72%

1990 On Base Pct Allowed: .308　Slugging Percentage: .351
Stolen Bases Allowed: 15　　　　Caught Stealing: 18

Pitches Left	AB	H	2B	3B	HR	RBI	BB	SO	AVG
Vs. RHB	743	179	34	3	17	57	67	162	.241
Vs. LHB	121	31	2	0	0	6	14	15	.256

	G	IP	W-L	Pct	SO	BB	ERA
At Home	17	132	11-4		98	42	1.63
On the Road	15	104	7-5		79	39	3.39
1990 Season	32	236	18-9	.667	177	81	2.40
Life 3.3 Years	46	230	14-12	.539	163	93	3.22

Carlton FISK

CHICAGO	CATCHER	43 Years Old

Runs Created: 79　　Offensive Winning Percentage: .705
Batting Average: .285　　　Secondary Average: .316

Most Often Bats: 5th
Hits First Pitch: 12%
Gets Ahead of the Pitcher: 55%
Hits Behind the Pitcher: 45%

1990 On Base Percentage: .378　　　　Career: .344
1990 Slugging Percentage: .451　　　　Career: .464
Batting Avg with Men in Scoring Position: .221

Bats Right-Handed		AB	R	H	2B	3B	HR	RBI	BB	SO	SB	AVG
Vs. RHP		287	40	77	11	0	9	35	40	50	4	.268
Vs. LHP		165	25	52	10	0	9	30	21	23	3	.315
At Home	69	219	28	63	13	0	5	37	33	30	2	.288
On the Road	68	233	37	66	8	0	13	28	28	43	5	.283
1990 Season	137	452	65	129	21	0	18	65	61	73	7	.285
Life	14.1 Years	573	87	156	28	3	25	88	56	89	9	.272

Mike FITZGERALD

MONTREAL   CATCHER   30 Years Old

Runs Created: 51   Offensive Winning Percentage: .662
Batting Average: .243   Secondary Average: .367

Most Often Bats: 7th
Hits First Pitch: 14%
Gets Ahead of the Pitcher: 53%
Hits Behind the Pitcher: 47%

1990 On Base Percentage: .365   Career: .327
1990 Slugging Percentage: .393   Career: .353
Batting Avg with Men in Scoring Position: .277

Bats Right-Handed	AB	R	H	2B	3B	HR	RBI	BB	SO	SB	AVG
Vs. RHP	175	21	45	14	1	4	21	30	39	4	.257
Vs. LHP	138	15	31	4	0	5	20	30	21	4	.225
At Home	54	134	12	33	10	0	2	14	27	23	4	.246
On the Road	57	179	24	43	8	1	7	27	33	37	4	.240
1990 Season	111	313	36	76	18	1	9	41	60	60	8	.243
Life 4.2 Years	458	44	110	21	2	9	59	59	86	6	.241

•

Scott FLETCHER

CHICAGO   SECOND BASE   32 Years Old

Runs Created: 49   Offensive Winning Percentage: .386
Batting Average: .242   Secondary Average: .161

Most Often Bats: 8th
Hits First Pitch: 15%
Gets Ahead of the Pitcher: 54%
Hits Behind the Pitcher: 46%

1990 On Base Percentage: .304   Career: .338
1990 Slugging Percentage: .312   Career: .339
Batting Avg with Men in Scoring Position: .268

Bats Right-Handed	AB	R	H	2B	3B	HR	RBI	BB	SO	SB	AVG
Vs. RHP	336	29	74	14	3	3	43	24	47	0	.220
Vs. LHP	173	25	49	4	0	1	13	21	16	1	.283
At Home	77	265	31	64	9	1	1	29	20	32	1	.242
On the Road	74	244	23	59	9	2	3	27	25	31	0	.242
1990 Season	151	509	54	123	18	3	4	56	45	63	1	.242
Life 7.1 Years	533	69	141	23	4	3	51	56	57	8	.264

John FRANCO

NEW YORK   RELIEF PITCHER   30 Years Old
5-3   2.53 ERA   33 SAVES

Blown Saves: 6   Holds: 0   Save Efficiency: 85%
Inherited Runners who Scored: 34%
Opponents Batting Average: .252
Double Play Support: .67 GDP Per Nine Innings

First Pitch is Hit: 13%
Gets Ahead of the Hitter: 49%
Gets Behind the Hitter: 51%
Gets First Batter Out: 73%

1990 On Base Pct Allowed: .306 Slugging Percentage: .347
Stolen Bases Allowed: 6   Caught Stealing: 1

Pitches Left	AB	H	2B	3B	HR	RBI	BB	SO	AVG
Vs. RHB	205	53	9	0	4	19	13	40	.259
Vs. LHB	57	13	2	1	0	9	8	16	.228

	G	IP	W-L	Pct	SO	BB	ERA
1990 Season	55	68	5-3	.625	56	21	2.53
Life 6.1 Years	74	98	8-5	.587	70	38	2.49

•

Julio FRANCO

TEXAS   SECOND BASE   29 Years Old

Runs Created: 95   Offensive Winning Percentage: .661
Batting Average: .296   Secondary Average: .301

Most Often Bats: 2nd
Hits First Pitch: 7%
Gets Ahead of the Pitcher: 54%
Hits Behind the Pitcher: 46%

1990 On Base Percentage: .383   Career: .354
1990 Slugging Percentage: .402   Career: .403
Batting Avg with Men in Scoring Position: .299

Bats Right-Handed	AB	R	H	2B	3B	HR	RBI	BB	SO	SB	AVG
Vs. RHP	403	65	119	18	1	8	50	51	58	20	.295
Vs. LHP	179	31	53	9	0	3	19	31	25	11	.296
At Home	81	303	52	96	16	0	4	27	41	37	17	.317
On the Road	76	279	44	76	11	1	7	42	41	46	14	.272
1990 Season	157	582	96	172	27	1	11	69	82	83	31	.296
Life 7.5 Years	626	90	186	29	5	9	79	56	72	24	.297

Willie FRASER

CALIFORNIA   RELIEF PITCHER   26 Years Old

5-4   3.08 ERA   2 SAVES

Blown Saves: 3   Holds: 5   Save Efficiency: 70%
Inherited Runners who Scored: 38%
Opponents Batting Average: .241
Double Play Support: .83 GDP Per Nine Innings

First Pitch is Hit: 17%
Gets Ahead of the Hitter: 52%
Gets Behind the Hitter: 48%
Gets First Batter Out: 75%

1990 On Base Pct Allowed: .297 Slugging Percentage: .336
Stolen Bases Allowed: 4   Caught Stealing: 2

Pitches Right	AB	H	2B	3B	HR	RBI	BB	SO	AVG
Vs. RHB	165	44	8	1	3	23	10	16	.267
Vs. LHB	121	25	5	0	1	12	14	16	.207

	G	IP	W-L	Pct	SO	BB	ERA
1990 Season	45	76	5-4	.556	32	24	3.08
Life 2.9 Years	55	186	11-12	.477	93	65	4.26

•G•

Gary GAETTI

MINNESOTA   THIRD BASE   32 Years Old

Runs Created: 56   Offensive Winning Percentage: .349
Batting Average: .229   Secondary Average: .220

Most Often Bats: 5th
Hits First Pitch: 17%
Gets Ahead of the Pitcher: 44%
Hits Behind the Pitcher: 56%

1990 On Base Percentage: .274   Career: .307
1990 Slugging Percentage: .376   Career: .437
Batting Avg with Men in Scoring Position: .263

Bats Right-Handed	AB	R	H	2B	3B	HR	RBI	BB	SO	SB	AVG
Vs. RHP	411	40	95	19	5	11	67	22	73	3	.231
Vs. LHP	166	21	37	8	0	5	18	14	28	3	.223
At Home	77	286	38	68	15	3	7	43	16	40	1	.238
On the Road	77	291	23	64	12	2	9	42	20	61	5	.220
1990 Season 154	577	61	132	27	5	16	85	36	101	6	.229
Life 8.4 Years	594	77	152	30	3	24	90	43	104	9	.256

•

Greg GAGNE

MINNESOTA   SHORTSTOP   29 Years Old

Runs Created: 38   Offensive Winning Percentage: .357
Batting Average: .235   Secondary Average: .209

Most Often Bats: 9th
Hits First Pitch: 19%
Gets Ahead of the Pitcher: 48%
Hits Behind the Pitcher: 52%

1990 On Base Percentage: .280   Career: .292
1990 Slugging Percentage: .361   Career: .390
Batting Avg with Men in Scoring Position: .182

Bats Right-Handed	AB	R	H	2B	3B	HR	RBI	BB	SO	SB	AVG
Vs. RHP	264	25	54	10	2	4	20	14	49	5	.205
Vs. LHP	124	13	37	12	1	3	18	10	27	3	.298
At Home	69	182	20	45	13	2	3	20	13	37	7	.247
On the Road	69	206	18	46	9	1	4	18	11	39	1	.223
1990 Season 138	388	38	91	22	3	7	38	24	76	8	.235
Life 5.3 Years	481	66	119	26	6	10	48	27	99	12	.247

Andres GALARRAGA

MONTREAL	FIRST BASE	29 Years Old

Runs Created: 72   Offensive Winning Percentage: .549
Batting Average: .256   Secondary Average: .240

Most Often Bats: 6th
Hits First Pitch: 12%
Gets Ahead of the Pitcher: 52%
Hits Behind the Pitcher: 48%

1990 On Base Percentage: .306   Career: .334
1990 Slugging Percentage: .409   Career: .450
Batting Avg with Men in Scoring Position: .266

Bats Right-Handed		AB	R	H	2B	3B	HR	RBI	BB	SO	SB	AVG
Vs. RHP		362	42	99	20	0	11	52	29	107	10	.273
Vs. LHP		217	23	49	9	0	9	35	11	62	0	.226
At Home	78	286	31	76	20	0	6	42	21	82	6	.266
On the Road	77	293	34	72	9	0	14	45	19	87	4	.246
1990 Season	155	579	65	148	29	0	20	87	40	169	10	.256
Life	4.6 Years	593	79	164	34	3	21	88	44	154	11	.276

Ron GANT

ATLANTA	CENTER FIELD	26 Years Old

Runs Created: 109   Offensive Winning Percentage: .687
Batting Average: .303   Secondary Average: .381

Most Often Bats: 3rd
Hits First Pitch: 14%
Gets Ahead of the Pitcher: 51%
Hits Behind the Pitcher: 49%

1990 On Base Percentage: .357   Career: .316
1990 Slugging Percentage: .539   Career: .456
Batting Avg with Men in Scoring Position: .257

Bats Right-Handed		AB	R	H	2B	3B	HR	RBI	BB	SO	SB	AVG
Vs. RHP		371	64	113	19	3	22	52	29	66	23	.305
Vs. LHP		204	43	61	15	0	10	32	21	20	10	.299
At Home	77	288	57	90	15	1	18	47	22	37	13	.313
On the Road	75	287	50	84	19	2	14	37	28	49	20	.293
1990 Season	152	575	107	174	34	3	32	84	50	86	33	.303
Life	2.4 Years	609	93	160	30	6	25	73	48	114	27	.262

Mike GALLEGO

OAKLAND	SECOND BASE	30 Years Old

Runs Created: 29   Offensive Winning Percentage: .240
Batting Average: .206   Secondary Average: .170

Most Often Bats: 9th
Hits First Pitch: 14%
Gets Ahead of the Pitcher: 50%
Hits Behind the Pitcher: 50%

1990 On Base Percentage: .277   Career: .303
1990 Slugging Percentage: .272   Career: .298
Batting Avg with Men in Scoring Position: .202

Bats Right-Handed		AB	R	H	2B	3B	HR	RBI	BB	SO	SB	AVG
Vs. RHP		261	28	57	8	2	2	25	26	31	3	.218
Vs. LHP		128	8	23	5	0	1	9	9	19	2	.180
At Home	69	187	14	40	4	1	1	14	24	20	4	.214
On the Road	71	202	22	40	9	1	2	20	11	30	1	.198
1990 Season	140	389	36	80	13	2	3	34	35	50	5	.206
Life	3.5 Years	358	43	81	14	1	3	32	37	53	4	.226

Jim GANTNER

MILWAUKEE	SECOND BASE	37 Years Old

Runs Created: 35   Offensive Winning Percentage: .397
Batting Average: .263   Secondary Average: .201

Most Often Bats: 2nd
Hits First Pitch: 20%
Gets Ahead of the Pitcher: 55%
Hits Behind the Pitcher: 45%

1990 On Base Percentage: .328   Career: .321
1990 Slugging Percentage: .319   Career: .352
Batting Avg with Men in Scoring Position: .237

Bats Left-Handed		AB	R	H	2B	3B	HR	RBI	BB	SO	SB	AVG
Vs. RHP		235	24	58	6	5	0	16	17	13	10	.247
Vs. LHP		88	12	27	2	0	0	9	12	6	8	.307
At Home	44	158	22	44	5	0	0	12	17	9	12	.278
On the Road	44	165	14	41	3	5	0	13	12	10	6	.248
1990 Season	88	323	36	85	8	5	0	25	29	19	18	.263
Life	9.6 Years	561	67	154	23	3	5	52	36	47	13	.274

Mark GARDNER

MONTREAL   STARTING PITCHER   29 Years Old
7-9   3.42 ERA

Opponents Batting Average: .230
Offensive Support: 3.66 Runs Per Nine Innings
Double Play Support: .59 GDP Per Nine Innings

First Pitch is Hit: 13%
Gets Ahead of the Hitter: 48%
Gets Behind the Hitter: 52%
Gets Leadoff Man Out: 78%

1990 On Base Pct Allowed: .312 Slugging Percentage: .351
Stolen Bases Allowed: 16   Caught Stealing: 6

Pitches Right	AB	H	2B	3B	HR	RBI	BB	SO	AVG
Vs. RHB	243	56	11	0	4	24	14	65	.230
Vs. LHB	318	73	10	4	9	32	47	70	.230

	G	IP	W-L	Pct	SO	BB	ERA
At Home	13	80	5-3		79	28	1.91
On the Road	14	73	2-6		56	33	5.08
1990 Season	27	153	7-9	.438	135	61	3.42
Life 0.9 Years	39	207	8-14	.368	180	83	3.67

●

Wes GARDNER

BOSTON   RELIEF PITCHER   29 Years Old
3-7   4.89 ERA   0 SAVES

Blown Saves: 2   Holds: 0   Save Efficiency: 0%
Inherited Runners who Scored: 28%
Opponents Batting Average: .259
Double Play Support: .81 GDP Per Nine Innings

First Pitch is Hit: 15%
Gets Ahead of the Hitter: 55%
Gets Behind the Hitter: 45%
Gets First Batter Out: 76%

1990 On Base Pct Allowed: .339 Slugging Percentage: .370
Stolen Bases Allowed: 12   Caught Stealing: 2

Pitches Right	AB	H	2B	3B	HR	RBI	BB	SO	AVG
Vs. RHB	148	35	6	1	5	16	14	33	.236
Vs. LHB	149	42	7	0	1	20	21	25	.282

	G	IP	W-L	Pct	SO	BB	ERA
1990 Season	34	77	3-7	.300	58	35	4.89
Life 2.9 Years	59	151	6-10	.383	119	70	4.84

Scott GARRELTS

SAN FRANCISCO   STARTING PITCHER   29 Years Old
12-11   4.15 ERA

Opponents Batting Average: .272
Offensive Support: 3.66 Runs Per Nine Innings
Double Play Support: 1.09 GDP Per Nine Innings

First Pitch is Hit: 16%
Gets Ahead of the Hitter: 42%
Gets Behind the Hitter: 58%
Gets Leadoff Man Out: 66%

1990 On Base Pct Allowed: .339 Slugging Percentage: .404
Stolen Bases Allowed: 18   Caught Stealing: 5

Pitches Right	AB	H	2B	3B	HR	RBI	BB	SO	AVG
Vs. RHB	311	77	13	2	8	35	29	47	.248
Vs. LHB	387	113	21	3	8	43	41	33	.292

	G	IP	W-L	Pct	SO	BB	ERA
At Home	18	103	6-7		54	42	3.83
On the Road	13	79	6-4		26	28	4.58
1990 Season	31	182	12-11	.522	80	70	4.15
Life 5.8 Years	59	162	12-9	.567	120	70	3.23

●

Bob GEREN

NEW YORK   CATCHER   29 Years Old

Runs Created: 23   Offensive Winning Percentage: .285
Batting Average: .213   Secondary Average: .159

Most Often Bats: 8th
Hits First Pitch: 13%
Gets Ahead of the Pitcher: 51%
Hits Behind the Pitcher: 49%

1990 On Base Percentage: .259   Career: .288
1990 Slugging Percentage: .325   Career: .374
Batting Avg with Men in Scoring Position: .229

Bats Right-Handed	AB	R	H	2B	3B	HR	RBI	BB	SO	SB	AVG
Vs. RHP	163	10	30	3	0	4	21	6	48	0	.184
Vs. LHP	114	11	29	4	0	4	10	7	25	0	.254
At Home	57	143	10	31	5	0	4	15	5	41	0	.217
On the Road	53	134	11	28	2	0	4	16	8	32	0	.209
1990 Season	110	277	21	59	7	0	8	31	13	73	0	.213
Life 1.1 Years	431	41	104	11	1	15	51	24	105	0	.242

Kirk GIBSON

LOS ANGELES	CENTER FIELD	33 Years Old

Runs Created: 50   Offensive Winning Percentage: .621
Batting Average: .260   Secondary Average: .346

Most Often Bats: 2nd
Hits First Pitch: 15%
Gets Ahead of the Pitcher: 53%
Hits Behind the Pitcher: 47%

1990 On Base Percentage: .345   Career: .355
1990 Slugging Percentage: .400   Career: .469
Batting Avg with Men in Scoring Position: .290

Bats Left-Handed	AB	R	H	2B	3B	HR	RBI	BB	SO	SB	AVG
Vs. RHP	213	40	56	13	0	5	23	27	35	21	.263
Vs. LHP	102	19	26	7	0	3	15	12	30	5	.255
At Home	43	157	24	39	8	0	2	19	20	29	16	.248
On the Road	46	158	35	43	12	0	6	19	19	36	10	.272
1990 Season	89	315	59	82	20	0	8	38	39	65	26	.260
Life	7.4 Years	582	98	159	26	5	26	86	71	128	32	.273

Joe GIRARDI

CHICAGO	CATCHER	26 Years Old

Runs Created: 41   Offensive Winning Percentage: .350
Batting Average: .270   Secondary Average: .134

Most Often Bats: 8th
Hits First Pitch: 28%
Gets Ahead of the Pitcher: 40%
Hits Behind the Pitcher: 60%

1990 On Base Percentage: .300   Career: .301
1990 Slugging Percentage: .344   Career: .340
Batting Avg with Men in Scoring Position: .276

Bats Right-Handed	AB	R	H	2B	3B	HR	RBI	BB	SO	SB	AVG
Vs. RHP	278	21	67	9	1	0	22	14	39	7	.241
Vs. LHP	141	15	46	15	1	1	16	3	11	1	.326
At Home	66	202	21	55	11	1	1	25	7	26	2	.272
On the Road	67	217	15	58	13	1	0	13	10	24	6	.267
1990 Season	133	419	36	113	24	2	1	38	17	50	8	.270
Life	1.2 Years	486	43	128	29	2	2	44	24	64	8	.264

Paul GIBSON

DETROIT	RELIEF PITCHER	31 Years Old
5-4	3.05 ERA	3 SAVES

Blown Saves: 3   Holds: 9   Save Efficiency: 80%
Inherited Runners who Scored: 24%
Opponents Batting Average: .269
Double Play Support: .65 GDP Per Nine Innings

First Pitch is Hit: 15%
Gets Ahead of the Hitter: 51%
Gets Behind the Hitter: 49%
Gets First Batter Out: 68%

1990 On Base Pct Allowed: .344 Slugging Percentage: .427
Stolen Bases Allowed: 7   Caught Stealing: 3

Pitches Left	AB	H	2B	3B	HR	RBI	BB	SO	AVG
Vs. RHB	250	68	19	2	8	31	33	45	.272
Vs. LHB	118	31	5	0	2	15	11	11	.263

	G	IP	W-L	Pct	SO	BB	ERA
1990 Season	61	97	5-4	.556	56	44	3.05
Life 2.2 Years	68	149	6-6	.481	85	62	3.67

Dan GLADDEN

MINNESOTA	LEFT FIELD	33 Years Old

Runs Created: 60   Offensive Winning Percentage: .450
Batting Average: .275   Secondary Average: .197

Most Often Bats: 1st
Hits First Pitch: 18%
Gets Ahead of the Pitcher: 51%
Hits Behind the Pitcher: 49%

1990 On Base Percentage: .314   Career: .331
1990 Slugging Percentage: .376   Career: .384
Batting Avg with Men in Scoring Position: .280

Bats Right-Handed	AB	R	H	2B	3B	HR	RBI	BB	SO	SB	AVG
Vs. RHP	371	46	103	19	6	3	24	21	49	20	.278
Vs. LHP	163	18	44	8	0	2	16	5	18	5	.270
At Home	69	263	36	79	15	5	2	17	14	27	11	.300
On the Road	67	271	28	68	12	1	3	23	12	40	14	.251
1990 Season	136	534	64	147	27	6	5	40	26	67	25	.275
Life	5.4 Years	610	91	168	29	5	9	55	47	84	36	.275

Tom GLAVINE

ATLANTA   STARTING PITCHER   25 Years Old
10-12   4.28 ERA

Opponents Batting Average: .281
Offensive Support: 4.28 Runs Per Nine Innings
Double Play Support: .97 GDP Per Nine Innings

First Pitch is Hit: 14%
Gets Ahead of the Hitter: 46%
Gets Behind the Hitter: 54%
Gets Leadoff Man Out: 67%

1990 On Base Pct Allowed: .343 Slugging Percentage: .410
Stolen Bases Allowed: 22   Caught Stealing: 9

Pitches Left	AB	H	2B	3B	HR	RBI	BB	SO	AVG
Vs. RHB	676	200	42	4	16	83	58	96	.296
Vs. LHB	151	32	3	0	2	11	20	33	.212

	G	IP	W-L	Pct	SO	BB	ERA
At Home	16	104	5-8		65	31	4.86
On the Road	17	111	5-4		64	47	3.74
1990 Season	33	214	10-12	.455	129	78	4.28
Life 2.8 Years	37	228	12-14	.446	114	75	4.29

●

Jerry Don GLEATON

DETROIT   RELIEF PITCHER   33 Years Old
1-3   2.94 ERA   13 SAVES

Blown Saves: 3   Holds: 7   Save Efficiency: 87%
Inherited Runners who Scored: 30%
Opponents Batting Average: .213
Double Play Support: .98 GDP Per Nine Innings

First Pitch is Hit: 12%
Gets Ahead of the Hitter: 47%
Gets Behind the Hitter: 53%
Gets First Batter Out: 72%

1990 On Base Pct Allowed: .279 Slugging Percentage: .289
Stolen Bases Allowed: 3   Caught Stealing: 4

Pitches Left	AB	H	2B	3B	HR	RBI	BB	SO	AVG
Vs. RHB	200	40	5	0	4	22	22	43	.200
Vs. LHB	91	22	2	0	1	16	3	13	.242

	G	IP	W-L	Pct	SO	BB	ERA
1990 Season	57	83	1-3	.250	56	25	2.94
Life 3.4 Years	69	100	3-6	.344	58	41	4.28

Dwight GOODEN

NEW YORK   STARTING PITCHER   26 Years Old
19-7   3.83 ERA

Opponents Batting Average: .258
Offensive Support: 6.77 Runs Per Nine Innings
Double Play Support: .46 GDP Per Nine Innings

First Pitch is Hit: 16%
Gets Ahead of the Hitter: 51%
Gets Behind the Hitter: 49%
Gets Leadoff Man Out: 65%

1990 On Base Pct Allowed: .315 Slugging Percentage: .345
Stolen Bases Allowed: 60   Caught Stealing: 16

Pitches Right	AB	H	2B	3B	HR	RBI	BB	SO	AVG
Vs. RHB	368	94	9	3	4	36	26	93	.255
Vs. LHB	519	135	24	4	6	58	44	130	.260

	G	IP	W-L	Pct	SO	BB	ERA
At Home	18	126	9-3		119	31	3.56
On the Road	16	106	10-4		104	39	4.15
1990 Season	34	233	19-7	.731	223	70	3.83
Life 5.7 Years	37	268	21-8	.721	245	79	2.82

●

Tom GORDON

KANSAS CITY   STARTING PITCHER   23 Years Old
12-11   3.73 ERA

Opponents Batting Average: .258
Offensive Support: 5.02 Runs Per Nine Innings
Double Play Support: .88 GDP Per Nine Innings

First Pitch is Hit: 14%
Gets Ahead of the Hitter: 45%
Gets Behind the Hitter: 55%
Gets Leadoff Man Out: 62%

1990 On Base Pct Allowed: .346 Slugging Percentage: .387
Stolen Bases Allowed: 8   Caught Stealing: 10

Pitches Right	AB	H	2B	3B	HR	RBI	BB	SO	AVG
Vs. RHB	381	100	19	5	11	49	44	100	.262
Vs. LHB	365	92	12	2	6	30	55	75	.252

	G	IP	W-L	Pct	SO	BB	ERA
At Home	15	93	7-5		90	45	3.10
On the Road	17	102	5-6		85	54	4.31
1990 Season	32	195	12-11	.522	175	99	3.73
Life 1.8 Years	47	204	16-12	.569	188	104	3.75

Jim GOTT

LOS ANGELES   RELIEF PITCHER   31 Years Old
3-5   2.90 ERA   3 SAVES

Blown Saves: 2   Holds: 6   Save Efficiency: 82%
Inherited Runners who Scored: 27%
Opponents Batting Average: .257
Double Play Support: .73 GDP Per Nine Innings

First Pitch is Hit: 7%
Gets Ahead of the Hitter: 50%
Gets Behind the Hitter: 50%
Gets First Batter Out: 72%

1990 On Base Pct Allowed: .347 Slugging Percentage: .370
Stolen Bases Allowed: 2   Caught Stealing: 2

Pitches Right	AB	H	2B	3B	HR	RBI	BB	SO	AVG
Vs. RHB	98	21	2	0	4	17	14	22	.214
Vs. LHB	132	38	7	1	1	8	20	22	.288

	G	IP	W-L	Pct	SO	BB	ERA
1990 Season	50	62	3-5	.375	44	34	2.90
Life 5.4 Years	56	149	7-10	.418	105	63	4.07

•

Mark GRACE

CHICAGO   FIRST BASE   26 Years Old

Runs Created: 94   Offensive Winning Percentage: .629
Batting Average: .309   Secondary Average: .229

Most Often Bats: 3rd
Hits First Pitch: 22%
Gets Ahead of the Pitcher: 56%
Hits Behind the Pitcher: 44%

1990 On Base Percentage: .372   Career: .382
1990 Slugging Percentage: .413   Career: .424
Batting Avg with Men in Scoring Position: .329

Bats Left-Handed	AB	R	H	2B	3B	HR	RBI	BB	SO	SB	AVG
Vs. RHP	404	50	125	20	1	6	49	39	33	11	.309
Vs. LHP	185	22	57	12	0	3	33	20	21	4	.308
At Home	79	308	38	102	18	0	4	46	29	24	4	.331
On the Road	78	281	34	80	14	1	5	36	30	30	11	.285
1990 Season	157	589	72	182	32	1	9	82	59	54	15	.309
Life 2.7 Years	593	79	182	31	3	11	82	74	52	12	.307

Mike GREENWELL

BOSTON   LEFT FIELD   27 Years Old

Runs Created: 94   Offensive Winning Percentage: .633
Batting Average: .297   Secondary Average: .257

Most Often Bats: 3rd
Hits First Pitch: 22%
Gets Ahead of the Pitcher: 52%
Hits Behind the Pitcher: 48%

1990 On Base Percentage: .367   Career: .385
1990 Slugging Percentage: .434   Career: .490
Batting Avg with Men in Scoring Position: .228

Bats Left-Handed	AB	R	H	2B	3B	HR	RBI	BB	SO	SB	AVG
Vs. RHP	408	53	129	22	4	11	51	48	24	6	.316
Vs. LHP	202	18	52	8	2	3	22	17	19	2	.257
At Home	81	306	39	95	21	2	6	41	34	24	2	.310
On the Road	78	304	32	86	9	4	8	32	31	19	6	.283
1990 Season	159	610	71	181	30	6	14	73	65	43	8	.297
Life 3.9 Years	576	83	180	35	5	19	99	64	45	11	.313

•

Tommy GREGG

ATLANTA   FIRST BASE   27 Years Old

Runs Created: 30   Offensive Winning Percentage: .485
Batting Average: .264   Secondary Average: .226

Most Often Bats: 5th
Hits First Pitch: 16%
Gets Ahead of the Pitcher: 43%
Hits Behind the Pitcher: 57%

1990 On Base Percentage: .322   Career: .306
1990 Slugging Percentage: .389   Career: .369
Batting Avg with Men in Scoring Position: .286

Bats Left-Handed	AB	R	H	2B	3B	HR	RBI	BB	SO	SB	AVG
Vs. RHP	220	14	61	13	1	5	32	17	33	4	.277
Vs. LHP	19	4	2	0	0	0	0	3	6	0	.105
At Home	60	122	8	30	5	0	2	19	8	17	0	.246
On the Road	64	117	10	33	8	1	3	13	12	22	4	.282
1990 Season	124	239	18	63	13	1	5	32	20	39	4	.264
Life 1.6 Years	352	31	90	16	1	7	38	25	57	4	.256

Ken GRIFFEY JR

SEATTLE   CENTER FIELD   21 Years Old

Runs Created: 103   Offensive Winning Percentage: .703
Batting Average: .300   Secondary Average: .313

Most Often Bats: 3rd
Hits First Pitch: 14%
Gets Ahead of the Pitcher: 49%
Hits Behind the Pitcher: 51%

1990 On Base Percentage: .366   Career: .350
1990 Slugging Percentage: .481   Career: .454
Batting Avg with Men in Scoring Position: .313

Bats Left-Handed	AB	R	H	2B	3B	HR	RBI	BB	SO	SB	AVG
Vs. RHP	378	57	112	14	6	17	58	46	36	10	.296
Vs. LHP	219	34	67	14	1	5	22	17	45	6	.306
At Home	80	305	45	89	17	4	8	45	34	33	11	.292
On the Road	75	292	46	90	11	3	14	35	29	48	5	.308
1990 Season	155	597	91	179	28	7	22	80	63	81	16	.300
Life	1.7 Years	604	87	172	29	4	22	81	61	94	18	.284

Marquis GRISSOM

MONTREAL   CENTER FIELD   23 Years Old

Runs Created: 37   Offensive Winning Percentage: .561
Batting Average: .257   Secondary Average: .264

Most Often Bats: 2nd
Hits First Pitch: 11%
Gets Ahead of the Pitcher: 55%
Hits Behind the Pitcher: 45%

1990 On Base Percentage: .320   Career: .328
1990 Slugging Percentage: .351   Career: .345
Batting Avg with Men in Scoring Position: .257

Bats Right-Handed	AB	R	H	2B	3B	HR	RBI	BB	SO	SB	AVG
Vs. RHP	107	18	30	3	0	1	13	7	20	10	.280
Vs. LHP	181	24	44	11	2	2	16	20	20	12	.243
At Home	52	146	20	36	5	2	2	17	16	22	12	.247
On the Road	46	142	22	38	9	0	1	12	11	18	10	.268
1990 Season	98	288	42	74	14	2	3	29	27	40	22	.257
Life	0.8 Years	473	76	121	21	3	5	41	51	80	30	.257

Alfredo GRIFFIN

LOS ANGELES   SHORTSTOP   34 Years Old

Runs Created: 31   Offensive Winning Percentage: .202
Batting Average: .210   Secondary Average: .119

Most Often Bats: 8th
Hits First Pitch: 22%
Gets Ahead of the Pitcher: 42%
Hits Behind the Pitcher: 58%

1990 On Base Percentage: .258   Career: .286
1990 Slugging Percentage: .254   Career: .324
Batting Avg with Men in Scoring Position: .213

Switch Hitter	AB	R	H	2B	3B	HR	RBI	BB	SO	SB	AVG
Vs. RHP	292	18	62	9	3	0	23	18	35	5	.212
Vs. LHP	169	20	35	2	0	1	12	11	30	1	.207
At Home	68	218	17	48	4	1	0	22	14	36	3	.220
On the Road	73	243	21	49	7	2	1	13	15	29	3	.202
1990 Season	141	461	38	97	11	3	1	35	29	65	6	.210
Life	10.8 Years	575	65	144	21	7	2	45	28	54	17	.250

Kevin GROSS

MONTREAL   STARTING PITCHER   29 Years Old
9-12   4.57 ERA

Opponents Batting Average: .272
Offensive Support: 3.97 Runs Per Nine Innings
Double Play Support: .39 GDP Per Nine Innings

First Pitch is Hit: 15%
Gets Ahead of the Hitter: 44%
Gets Behind the Hitter: 56%
Gets Leadoff Man Out: 63%

1990 On Base Pct Allowed: .340 Slugging Percentage: .368
Stolen Bases Allowed: 31   Caught Stealing: 5

Pitches Right	AB	H	2B	3B	HR	RBI	BB	SO	AVG
Vs. RHB	259	63	8	1	2	21	17	38	.243
Vs. LHB	369	108	21	1	7	52	48	73	.293

	G	IP	W-L	Pct	SO	BB	ERA
At Home	13	69	3-5		40	27	4.43
On the Road	18	94	6-7		71	38	4.67
1990 Season	31	163	9-12	.429	111	65	4.57
Life 6.6 Years	40	224	12-14	.471	152	89	4.02

Kelly GRUBER

TORONTO   THIRD BASE   29 Years Old

Runs Created: 101   Offensive Winning Percentage: .645
Batting Average: .274   Secondary Average: .343

Most Often Bats: 3rd
Hits First Pitch: 20%
Gets Ahead of the Pitcher: 46%
Hits Behind the Pitcher: 54%

1990 On Base Percentage: .330   Career: .313
1990 Slugging Percentage: .512   Career: .445
Batting Avg with Men in Scoring Position: .313

Bats Right-Handed		AB	R	H	2B	3B	HR	RBI	BB	SO	SB	AVG
Vs. RHP		426	61	113	25	2	23	84	32	67	11	.265
Vs. LHP		166	31	49	11	4	8	34	16	27	3	.295
At Home	77	305	48	89	13	4	23	62	17	47	5	.292
On the Road	73	287	44	73	23	2	8	56	31	47	9	.254
1990 Season	150	592	92	162	36	6	31	118	48	94	14	.274
Life 4.2 Years		522	76	139	26	4	20	77	32	83	14	.266

Pedro GUERRERO

ST. LOUIS   FIRST BASE   34 Years Old

Runs Created: 69   Offensive Winning Percentage: .598
Batting Average: .281   Secondary Average: .235

Most Often Bats: 4th
Hits First Pitch: 17%
Gets Ahead of the Pitcher: 43%
Hits Behind the Pitcher: 57%

1990 On Base Percentage: .334   Career: .377
1990 Slugging Percentage: .426   Career: .496
Batting Avg with Men in Scoring Position: .252

Bats Right-Handed		AB	R	H	2B	3B	HR	RBI	BB	SO	SB	AVG
Vs. RHP		330	27	94	14	1	9	50	31	42	1	.285
Vs. LHP		168	15	46	17	0	4	30	13	28	0	.274
At Home	72	261	22	72	18	0	8	50	26	42	0	.276
On the Road	64	237	20	68	13	1	5	30	18	28	1	.287
1990 Season	136	498	42	140	31	1	13	80	44	70	1	.281
Life 8.5 Years		567	80	173	29	3	24	95	66	93	11	.305

Mark GUBICZA

KANSAS CITY   STARTING PITCHER   28 Years Old
4-7   4.50 ERA

Opponents Batting Average: .283
Offensive Support: 3.64 Runs Per Nine Innings
Double Play Support: 1.15 GDP Per Nine Innings

First Pitch is Hit: 14%
Gets Ahead of the Hitter: 54%
Gets Behind the Hitter: 46%
Gets Leadoff Man Out: 58%

1990 On Base Pct Allowed: .355 Slugging Percentage: .389
Stolen Bases Allowed: 11   Caught Stealing: 2

Pitches Right	AB	H	2B	3B	HR	RBI	BB	SO	AVG
Vs. RHB	199	59	12	2	2	30	14	41	.296
Vs. LHB	158	42	7	0	3	11	24	30	.266

	G	IP	W-L	Pct	SO	BB	ERA
At Home	7	38	3-2		28	16	5.45
On the Road	9	56	1-5		43	22	3.86
1990 Season	16	94	4-7	.364	71	38	4.50
Life 5.6 Years	38	249	16-13	.543	163	96	3.57

Lee GUETTERMAN

NEW YORK   RELIEF PITCHER   32 Years Old
11-7   3.39 ERA   2 SAVES

Blown Saves: 5   Holds: 12   Save Efficiency: 74%
Inherited Runners who Scored: 26%
Opponents Batting Average: .236
Double Play Support: 1.06 GDP Per Nine Innings

First Pitch is Hit: 11%
Gets Ahead of the Hitter: 47%
Gets Behind the Hitter: 53%
Gets First Batter Out: 72%

1990 On Base Pct Allowed: .288 Slugging Percentage: .342
Stolen Bases Allowed: 8   Caught Stealing: 2

Pitches Left	AB	H	2B	3B	HR	RBI	BB	SO	AVG
Vs. RHB	240	55	6	2	5	31	17	27	.229
Vs. LHB	99	25	2	3	1	11	9	21	.253

	G	IP	W-L	Pct	SO	BB	ERA
1990 Season	64	93	11-7	.611	48	26	3.39
Life 3.3 Years	67	129	8-7	.560	59	40	4.10

Ozzie GUILLEN

CHICAGO   SHORTSTOP   27 Years Old

Runs Created: 52   Offensive Winning Percentage: .411
Batting Average: .279   Secondary Average: .138

Most Often Bats: 9th
Hits First Pitch: 26%
Gets Ahead of the Pitcher: 45%
Hits Behind the Pitcher: 55%

1990 On Base Percentage: .312   Career: .289
1990 Slugging Percentage: .341   Career: .332
Batting Avg with Men in Scoring Position: .331

Bats Left-Handed	AB	R	H	2B	3B	HR	RBI	BB	SO	SB	AVG
Vs. RHP	310	41	89	13	3	1	30	20	18	9	.287
Vs. LHP	206	20	55	8	1	0	28	6	19	4	.267

		AB	R	H	2B	3B	HR	RBI	BB	SO	SB	AVG
At Home	79	247	29	69	10	3	1	25	14	19	8	.279
On the Road	81	269	32	75	11	1	0	33	12	18	5	.279
1990 Season	160	516	61	144	21	4	1	58	26	37	13	.279
Life 5.7 Years		571	65	152	21	7	1	49	20	46	20	.265

•

Bill GULLICKSON

HOUSTON   STARTING PITCHER   32 Years Old
                 10-14   3.82 ERA

Opponents Batting Average: .287
Offensive Support: 3.68 Runs Per Nine Innings
Double Play Support: .84 GDP Per Nine Innings

First Pitch is Hit: 17%
Gets Ahead of the Hitter: 49%
Gets Behind the Hitter: 51%
Gets Leadoff Man Out: 68%

1990 On Base Pct Allowed: .338 Slugging Percentage: .441
Stolen Bases Allowed: 23   Caught Stealing: 9

Pitches Right	AB	H	2B	3B	HR	RBI	BB	SO	AVG
Vs. RHB	301	73	13	5	9	36	18	43	.243
Vs. LHB	468	148	24	4	12	54	43	30	.316

	G	IP	W-L	Pct	SO	BB	ERA
At Home	19	114	8-7		45	31	3.94
On the Road	13	79	2-7		28	30	3.65
1990 Season	32	193	10-14	.417	73	61	3.82
Life 7.5 Years	37	245	15-13	.526	132	61	3.64

Mark GUTHRIE

MINNESOTA   STARTING PITCHER   25 Years Old
                   7-9   3.79 ERA

Opponents Batting Average: .276
Offensive Support: 3.92 Runs Per Nine Innings
Double Play Support: .75 GDP Per Nine Innings

First Pitch is Hit: 12%
Gets Ahead of the Hitter: 50%
Gets Behind the Hitter: 50%
Gets Leadoff Man Out: 73%

1990 On Base Pct Allowed: .325 Slugging Percentage: .370
Stolen Bases Allowed: 17   Caught Stealing: 12

Pitches Left	AB	H	2B	3B	HR	RBI	BB	SO	AVG
Vs. RHB	458	120	24	0	7	40	36	88	.262
Vs. LHB	99	34	4	0	1	10	3	13	.343

	G	IP	W-L	Pct	SO	BB	ERA
At Home	11	69	2-4		55	16	3.93
On the Road	13	76	5-5		46	23	3.67
1990 Season	24	145	7-9	.438	101	39	3.79
Life 0.9 Years	41	226	10-15	.409	156	67	4.01

•

Tony GWYNN

SAN DIEGO   RIGHT FIELD   30 Years Old

Runs Created: 83   Offensive Winning Percentage: .613
Batting Average: .309   Secondary Average: .213

Most Often Bats: 3rd
Hits First Pitch: 14%
Gets Ahead of the Pitcher: 53%
Hits Behind the Pitcher: 47%

1990 On Base Percentage: .357   Career: .385
1990 Slugging Percentage: .415   Career: .435
Batting Avg with Men in Scoring Position: .305

Bats Left-Handed	AB	R	H	2B	3B	HR	RBI	BB	SO	SB	AVG
Vs. RHP	345	58	113	21	8	1	44	36	13	14	.328
Vs. LHP	228	21	64	8	2	3	28	8	10	3	.281

		AB	R	H	2B	3B	HR	RBI	BB	SO	SB	AVG
At Home	76	306	43	95	16	6	2	42	22	10	10	.310
On the Road	65	267	36	82	13	4	2	30	22	13	7	.307
1990 Season	141	573	79	177	29	10	4	72	44	23	17	.309
Life 7.4 Years		627	94	207	30	8	7	66	57	35	32	.329

•H•

Mel HALL

NEW YORK   DESIGNATED HITTER   30 Years Old

Runs Created: 41   Offensive Winning Percentage: .473
Batting Average: .258   Secondary Average: .192

Most Often Bats: 4th
Hits First Pitch: 18%
Gets Ahead of the Pitcher: 43%
Hits Behind the Pitcher: 57%

1990 On Base Percentage: .272   Career: .320
1990 Slugging Percentage: .433   Career: .438
Batting Avg with Men in Scoring Position: .250

Bats Left-Handed		AB	R	H	2B	3B	HR	RBI	BB	SO	SB	AVG
Vs. RHP		302	36	81	20	2	11	41	6	35	0	.268
Vs. LHP		58	5	12	3	0	1	5	0	11	0	.207
At Home	60	187	16	51	13	2	3	25	3	27	0	.273
On the Road	53	173	25	42	10	0	9	21	3	19	0	.243
1990 Season	113	360	41	93	23	2	12	46	6	46	0	.258
Life 5.9 Years		530	73	146	29	3	17	77	36	81	5	.276

•

Atlee HAMMAKER

SAN DIEGO   RELIEF PITCHER   33 Years Old
4-9   4.36 ERA   0 SAVES

Blown Saves: 0   Holds: 2   Save Efficiency: 100%
Inherited Runners who Scored: 46%
Opponents Batting Average: .259
Double Play Support: .93 GDP Per Nine Innings

First Pitch is Hit: 19%
Gets Ahead of the Hitter: 54%
Gets Behind the Hitter: 46%
Gets First Batter Out: 88%

1990 On Base Pct Allowed: .312 Slugging Percentage: .381
Stolen Bases Allowed: 6   Caught Stealing: 3

Pitches Left	AB	H	2B	3B	HR	RBI	BB	SO	AVG
Vs. RHB	261	72	9	2	6	31	20	32	.276
Vs. LHB	67	13	3	0	2	5	7	12	.194

	G	IP	W-L	Pct	SO	BB	ERA
1990 Season	34	87	4-9	.308	44	27	4.36
Life 5.2 Years	45	205	11-13	.472	118	53	3.60

Erik HANSON

SEATTLE   STARTING PITCHER   25 Years Old
18-9   3.24 ERA

Opponents Batting Average: .232
Offensive Support: 4.54 Runs Per Nine Innings
Double Play Support: .65 GDP Per Nine Innings

First Pitch is Hit: 13%
Gets Ahead of the Hitter: 52%
Gets Behind the Hitter: 48%
Gets Leadoff Man Out: 76%

1990 On Base Pct Allowed: .287 Slugging Percentage: .332
Stolen Bases Allowed: 18   Caught Stealing: 8

Pitches Right	AB	H	2B	3B	HR	RBI	BB	SO	AVG
Vs. RHB	418	102	14	2	10	42	27	97	.244
Vs. LHB	465	103	21	2	5	33	41	114	.222

	G	IP	W-L	Pct	SO	BB	ERA
At Home	16	111	7-6		94	32	3.56
On the Road	17	125	11-3		117	36	2.96
1990 Season	33	236	18-9	.667	211	68	3.24
Life 1.5 Years	37	258	19-11	.630	213	74	3.22

•

Mike HARKEY

CHICAGO   STARTING PITCHER   24 Years Old
12-6   3.26 ERA

Opponents Batting Average: .234
Offensive Support: 4.61 Runs Per Nine Innings
Double Play Support: .52 GDP Per Nine Innings

First Pitch is Hit: 14%
Gets Ahead of the Hitter: 48%
Gets Behind the Hitter: 52%
Gets Leadoff Man Out: 75%

1990 On Base Pct Allowed: .303 Slugging Percentage: .358
Stolen Bases Allowed: 8   Caught Stealing: 6

Pitches Right	AB	H	2B	3B	HR	RBI	BB	SO	AVG
Vs. RHB	249	56	8	3	7	27	22	38	.225
Vs. LHB	404	97	21	2	7	34	37	56	.240

	G	IP	W-L	Pct	SO	BB	ERA
At Home	12	85	5-2		46	28	2.43
On the Road	15	88	7-4		48	31	4.08
1990 Season	27	174	12-6	.667	94	59	3.26
Life 0.9 Years	37	241	14-10	.571	130	86	3.15

Pete HARNISCH

BALTIMORE	STARTING PITCHER	24 Years Old
	11-11 4.34 ERA	

Opponents Batting Average: .261
Offensive Support: 5.77 Runs Per Nine Innings
Double Play Support: .52 GDP Per Nine Innings

First Pitch is Hit: 11%
Gets Ahead of the Hitter: 55%
Gets Behind the Hitter: 45%
Gets Leadoff Man Out: 67%

1990 On Base Pct Allowed: .339 Slugging Percentage: .394
Stolen Bases Allowed: 18   Caught Stealing: 10

Pitches Right	AB	H	2B	3B	HR	RBI	BB	SO	AVG
Vs. RHB	288	64	7	1	7	30	37	63	.222
Vs. LHB	435	125	26	5	10	50	49	59	.287

	G	IP	W-L	Pct	SO	BB	ERA
At Home	15	89	7-6		67	33	4.63
On the Road	16	99	4-5		55	53	4.08
1990 Season	31	189	11-11	.500	122	86	4.34
Life 1.4 Years	37	223	12-16	.421	148	116	4.49

•

Brian HARPER

MINNESOTA	CATCHER	31 Years Old

Runs Created: 62   Offensive Winning Percentage: .532
Batting Average: .294   Secondary Average: .184

Most Often Bats: 6th
Hits First Pitch: 15%
Gets Ahead of the Pitcher: 47%
Hits Behind the Pitcher: 53%

1990 On Base Percentage: .328   Career: .317
1990 Slugging Percentage: .432   Career: .417
Batting Avg with Men in Scoring Position: .303

Bats Right-Handed	AB	R	H	2B	3B	HR	RBI	BB	SO	SB	AVG
Vs. RHP	333	31	95	23	2	2	34	11	17	2	.285
Vs. LHP	146	30	46	19	1	4	20	8	10	1	.315
At Home	66	230	29	65	18	2	1	24	12	15	2	.283
On the Road	68	249	32	76	24	1	5	30	7	12	1	.305
1990 Season 134	479	61	141	42	3	6	54	19	27	3	.294
Life 3.2 Years	438	47	125	28	2	9	56	17	30	2	.286

Greg HARRIS

BOSTON	STARTING PITCHER	35 Years Old
	13-9 4.00 ERA	

Opponents Batting Average: .265
Offensive Support: 4.98 Runs Per Nine Innings
Double Play Support: .83 GDP Per Nine Innings

First Pitch is Hit: 14%
Gets Ahead of the Hitter: 46%
Gets Behind the Hitter: 54%
Gets Leadoff Man Out: 68%

1990 On Base Pct Allowed: .338 Slugging Percentage: .381
Stolen Bases Allowed: 15   Caught Stealing: 7

Pitches Right	AB	H	2B	3B	HR	RBI	BB	SO	AVG
Vs. RHB	351	102	19	2	8	42	40	65	.291
Vs. LHB	352	84	18	1	5	29	37	52	.239

	G	IP	W-L	Pct	SO	BB	ERA
At Home	17	89	8-5		66	37	4.45
On the Road	17	95	5-4		51	40	3.59
1990 Season	34	184	13-9	.591	117	77	4.00
Life 6.6 Years	63	147	7-8	.471	112	63	3.61

•

Greg W. HARRIS

SAN DIEGO	RELIEF PITCHER	27 Years Old
	8-8 2.30 ERA 9 SAVES	

Blown Saves: 7   Holds: 10   Save Efficiency: 73%
Inherited Runners who Scored: 50%
Opponents Batting Average: .220
Double Play Support: .46 GDP Per Nine Innings

First Pitch is Hit: 16%
Gets Ahead of the Hitter: 48%
Gets Behind the Hitter: 52%
Gets First Batter Out: 65%

1990 On Base Pct Allowed: .303 Slugging Percentage: .310
Stolen Bases Allowed: 8   Caught Stealing: 2

Pitches Right	AB	H	2B	3B	HR	RBI	BB	SO	AVG
Vs. RHB	199	32	5	1	4	22	22	61	.161
Vs. LHB	220	60	11	1	2	25	27	36	.273

	G	IP	W-L	Pct	SO	BB	ERA
1990 Season	73	117	8-8	.500	97	49	2.30
Life 1.9 Years	69	142	9-9	.514	114	55	2.40

Lenny HARRIS

LOS ANGELES   THIRD BASE   26 Years Old

Runs Created: 55   Offensive Winning Percentage: .526
Batting Average: .304   Secondary Average: .172

Most Often Bats: 1st
Hits First Pitch: 22%
Gets Ahead of the Pitcher: 50%
Hits Behind the Pitcher: 50%

1990 On Base Percentage: .348   Career: .326
1990 Slugging Percentage: .374   Career: .344
Batting Avg with Men in Scoring Position: .301

Bats Left-Handed	AB	R	H	2B	3B	HR	RBI	BB	SO	SB	AVG
Vs. RHP	389	53	121	16	3	2	23	26	26	15	.311
Vs. LHP	42	8	10	0	1	0	6	3	5	0	.238
At Home	69	217	27	60	8	2	0	9	15	15	10	.276
On the Road	68	214	34	71	8	2	2	20	14	16	5	.332
1990 Season 137	431	61	131	16	4	2	29	29	31	15	.304
Life 1.7 Years	489	63	137	16	3	3	38	33	41	20	.279

●

Mike HARTLEY

LOS ANGELES   RELIEF PITCHER   29 Years Old
6-3   2.95 ERA   1 SAVES

Blown Saves: 1   Holds: 1   Save Efficiency: 67%
Inherited Runners who Scored: 18%
Opponents Batting Average: .200
Double Play Support: .34 GDP Per Nine Innings

First Pitch is Hit: 11%
Gets Ahead of the Hitter: 52%
Gets Behind the Hitter: 48%
Gets First Batter Out: 77%

1990 On Base Pct Allowed: .279 Slugging Percentage: .321
Stolen Bases Allowed: 14   Caught Stealing: 1

Pitches Right	AB	H	2B	3B	HR	RBI	BB	SO	AVG
Vs. RHB	136	25	4	0	5	19	6	36	.184
Vs. LHB	154	33	4	3	2	10	24	40	.214

	G	IP	W-L	Pct	SO	BB	ERA
1990 Season	32	79	6-3	.667	76	30	2.95
Life 0.6 Years	64	147	10-7	.600	138	52	2.85

Bryan HARVEY

CALIFORNIA   RELIEF PITCHER   27 Years Old
4-4   3.22 ERA   25 SAVES

Blown Saves: 6   Holds: 1   Save Efficiency: 81%
Inherited Runners who Scored: 21%
Opponents Batting Average: .201
Double Play Support: .56 GDP Per Nine Innings

First Pitch is Hit: 10%
Gets Ahead of the Hitter: 55%
Gets Behind the Hitter: 45%
Gets First Batter Out: 63%

1990 On Base Pct Allowed: .304 Slugging Percentage: .295
Stolen Bases Allowed: 3   Caught Stealing: 2

Pitches Right	AB	H	2B	3B	HR	RBI	BB	SO	AVG
Vs. RHB	118	23	3	0	3	11	14	40	.195
Vs. LHB	106	22	4	1	1	14	21	42	.208

	G	IP	W-L	Pct	SO	BB	ERA
1990 Season	54	64	4-4	.500	82	35	3.22
Life 2.1 Years	74	94	7-6	.538	108	46	2.79

●

Billy HATCHER

CINCINNATI   CENTER FIELD   30 Years Old

Runs Created: 66   Offensive Winning Percentage: .576
Batting Average: .276   Secondary Average: .230

Most Often Bats: 1st
Hits First Pitch: 18%
Gets Ahead of the Pitcher: 49%
Hits Behind the Pitcher: 51%

1990 On Base Percentage: .327   Career: .315
1990 Slugging Percentage: .381   Career: .367
Batting Avg with Men in Scoring Position: .198

Bats Right-Handed	AB	R	H	2B	3B	HR	RBI	BB	SO	SB	AVG
Vs. RHP	297	47	88	18	4	4	17	17	26	18	.296
Vs. LHP	207	21	51	10	1	1	8	16	16	12	.246
At Home	73	246	32	65	16	3	2	11	16	18	15	.264
On the Road	66	258	36	74	12	2	3	14	17	24	15	.287
1990 Season 139	504	68	139	28	5	5	25	33	42	30	.276
Life 4.6 Years	578	83	153	28	4	8	51	37	64	39	.265

Andy HAWKINS

NEW YORK	STARTING PITCHER	31 Years Old
	5-12 5.37 ERA	

Opponents Batting Average: .260
Offensive Support: 2.97 Runs Per Nine Innings
Double Play Support: .97 GDP Per Nine Innings

First Pitch is Hit: 15%
Gets Ahead of the Hitter: 45%
Gets Behind the Hitter: 55%
Gets Leadoff Man Out: 66%

1990 On Base Pct Allowed: .349 Slugging Percentage: .421
Stolen Bases Allowed: 11   Caught Stealing: 8

Pitches Right	AB	H	2B	3B	HR	RBI	BB	SO	AVG
Vs. RHB	286	64	17	0	12	45	27	43	.224
Vs. LHB	313	92	13	3	8	37	55	31	.294

	G	IP	W-L	Pct	SO	BB	ERA
At Home	15	89	2-8		41	49	5.44
On the Road	13	68	3-4		33	33	5.27
1990 Season	28	158	5-12	.294	74	82	5.37
Life 6.7 Years	39	220	12-13	.485	99	86	4.14

•

Charlie HAYES

PHILADELPHIA	THIRD BASE	25 Years Old

Runs Created: 55   Offensive Winning Percentage: .391
Batting Average: .258   Secondary Average: .146

Most Often Bats: 6th
Hits First Pitch: 20%
Gets Ahead of the Pitcher: 45%
Hits Behind the Pitcher: 55%

1990 On Base Percentage: .293   Career: .286
1990 Slugging Percentage: .348   Career: .360
Batting Avg with Men in Scoring Position: .232

Bats Right-Handed	AB	R	H	2B	3B	HR	RBI	BB	SO	SB	AVG
Vs. RHP		368	28	88	10	0	5	35	20	65	2	.239
Vs. LHP		193	28	57	10	0	5	22	8	26	2	.295
At Home	77	282	29	69	9	0	3	26	12	47	2	.245
On the Road	75	279	27	76	11	0	7	31	16	44	2	.272
1990 Season	152	561	56	145	20	0	10	57	28	91	4	.258
Life 1.5 Years		577	54	148	23	1	12	66	26	95	5	.256

Von HAYES

PHILADELPHIA	RIGHT FIELD	32 Years Old

Runs Created: 78   Offensive Winning Percentage: .640
Batting Average: .261   Secondary Average: .373

Most Often Bats: 3rd
Hits First Pitch: 10%
Gets Ahead of the Pitcher: 53%
Hits Behind the Pitcher: 47%

1990 On Base Percentage: .375   Career: .360
1990 Slugging Percentage: .413   Career: .430
Batting Avg with Men in Scoring Position: .254

Bats Left-Handed	AB	R	H	2B	3B	HR	RBI	BB	SO	SB	AVG
Vs. RHP		288	46	73	8	2	11	45	63	45	14	.253
Vs. LHP		179	24	49	6	1	6	28	24	36	2	.274
At Home	58	203	37	56	5	3	10	36	40	33	8	.276
On the Road	71	264	33	66	9	0	7	37	47	48	8	.250
1990 Season	129	467	70	122	14	3	17	73	87	81	16	.261
Life 8.2 Years	570	84	155	31	4	17	79	79	87	29	.272

•

Mike HEATH

DETROIT	CATCHER	36 Years Old

Runs Created: 41   Offensive Winning Percentage: .399
Batting Average: .270   Secondary Average: .186

Most Often Bats: 9th
Hits First Pitch: 14%
Gets Ahead of the Pitcher: 45%
Hits Behind the Pitcher: 55%

1990 On Base Percentage: .311   Career: .301
1990 Slugging Percentage: .386   Career: .370
Batting Avg with Men in Scoring Position: .210

Bats Right-Handed	AB	R	H	2B	3B	HR	RBI	BB	SO	SB	AVG
Vs. RHP		221	35	66	12	2	4	23	11	43	3	.299
Vs. LHP		149	11	34	6	0	3	15	8	28	4	.228
At Home	58	169	21	46	9	2	3	15	10	35	4	.272
On the Road	64	201	25	54	9	0	4	23	9	36	3	.269
1990 Season	122	370	46	100	18	2	7	38	19	71	7	.270
Life 7.9 Years	517	58	131	22	3	11	58	34	75	7	.253

Neal HEATON

PITTSBURGH	STARTING PITCHER	31 Years Old
	12-9 3.45 ERA	

Opponents Batting Average: .263
Offensive Support: 4.93 Runs Per Nine Innings
Double Play Support: .62 GDP Per Nine Innings

First Pitch is Hit: 19%
Gets Ahead of the Hitter: 47%
Gets Behind the Hitter: 53%
Gets Leadoff Man Out: 66%

1990 On Base Pct Allowed: .311 Slugging Percentage: .413
Stolen Bases Allowed: 15   Caught Stealing: 13

Pitches Left	AB	H	2B	3B	HR	RBI	BB	SO	AVG
Vs. RHB	453	115	19	2	13	48	28	55	.254
Vs. LHB	90	28	7	0	4	9	10	13	.311

	G	IP	W-L	Pct	SO	BB	ERA
At Home	16	80	6-5		40	27	3.02
On the Road	14	66	6-4		28	11	3.97
1990 Season	30	146	12-9	.571	68	38	3.45
Life 6.6 Years	44	206	11-14	.442	93	71	4.35

•

Dave HENDERSON

OAKLAND	CENTER FIELD	32 Years Old

Runs Created: 71   Offensive Winning Percentage: .667
Batting Average: .271   Secondary Average: .291

Most Often Bats: 5th
Hits First Pitch: 11%
Gets Ahead of the Pitcher: 50%
Hits Behind the Pitcher: 50%

1990 On Base Percentage: .331   Career: .324
1990 Slugging Percentage: .467   Career: .438
Batting Avg with Men in Scoring Position: .252

Bats Right-Handed	AB	R	H	2B	3B	HR	RBI	BB	SO	SB	AVG
Vs. RHP	317	34	75	21	0	9	40	30	83	0	.237
Vs. LHP	133	31	47	7	0	11	23	10	22	3	.353
At Home	62	222	34	67	14	0	11	36	18	46	1	.302
On the Road	65	228	31	55	14	0	9	27	22	59	2	.241
1990 Season	127	450	65	122	28	0	20	63	40	105	3	.271
Life 7.4 Years	526	75	138	29	2	20	72	48	112	6	.262

Rickey HENDERSON

OAKLAND	LEFT FIELD	32 Years Old

Runs Created: 137   Offensive Winning Percentage: .868
Batting Average: .325   Secondary Average: .583

Most Often Bats: 1st
Hits First Pitch: 4%
Gets Ahead of the Pitcher: 58%
Hits Behind the Pitcher: 42%

1990 On Base Percentage: .439   Career: .403
1990 Slugging Percentage: .577   Career: .441
Batting Avg with Men in Scoring Position: .271

Bats Right-Handed	AB	R	H	2B	3B	HR	RBI	BB	SO	SB	AVG
Vs. RHP	355	86	117	21	3	19	44	73	38	47	.330
Vs. LHP	134	33	42	12	0	9	17	24	22	18	.313
At Home	64	220	47	67	12	2	8	22	44	26	34	.305
On the Road	72	269	72	92	21	1	20	39	53	34	31	.342
1990 Season	136	489	119	159	33	3	28	61	97	60	65	.325
Life 9.9 Years	606	130	178	30	5	17	63	110	80	94	.293

•

Tom HENKE

TORONTO	RELIEF PITCHER	33 Years Old
	2-4 2.17 ERA 32 SAVES	

Blown Saves: 6   Holds: 2   Save Efficiency: 85%
Inherited Runners who Scored: 19%
Opponents Batting Average: .213
Double Play Support: .48 GDP Per Nine Innings

First Pitch is Hit: 13%
Gets Ahead of the Hitter: 54%
Gets Behind the Hitter: 46%
Gets First Batter Out: 74%

1990 On Base Pct Allowed: .266 Slugging Percentage: .342
Stolen Bases Allowed: 5   Caught Stealing: 0

Pitches Right	AB	H	2B	3B	HR	RBI	BB	SO	AVG
Vs. RHB	134	29	3	0	4	7	8	33	.216
Vs. LHB	138	29	6	1	4	17	11	42	.210

	G	IP	W-L	Pct	SO	BB	ERA
1990 Season	61	75	2-4	.333	75	19	2.17
Life 5.1 Years	74	100	6-5	.527	116	32	2.72

Mike HENNEMAN

DETROIT   RELIEF PITCHER   29 Years Old
            8-6   3.05 ERA   22 SAVES

Blown Saves: 6   Holds: 4   Save Efficiency: 81%
Inherited Runners who Scored: 19%
Opponents Batting Average: .253
Double Play Support: 1.24 GDP Per Nine Innings

First Pitch is Hit: 15%
Gets Ahead of the Hitter: 54%
Gets Behind the Hitter: 46%
Gets First Batter Out: 69%

1990 On Base Pct Allowed: .320 Slugging Percentage: .334
Stolen Bases Allowed: 7   Caught Stealing: 2

Pitches Right	AB	H	2B	3B	HR	RBI	BB	SO	AVG
Vs. RHB	212	50	8	1	4	24	15	36	.236
Vs. LHB	144	40	7	0	0	10	18	14	.278

	G	IP	W-L	Pct	SO	BB	ERA
1990 Season	69	94	8-6	.571	50	33	3.05
Life 3.4 Years	74	111	12-6	.672	75	41	2.90

•

Tommy HERR

NEW YORK   SECOND BASE   35 Years Old

Runs Created: 63   Offensive Winning Percentage: .470
Batting Average: .261   Secondary Average: .190

Most Often Bats: 2nd
Hits First Pitch: 11%
Gets Ahead of the Pitcher: 54%
Hits Behind the Pitcher: 46%

1990 On Base Percentage: .324   Career: .347
1990 Slugging Percentage: .347   Career: .353
Batting Avg with Men in Scoring Position: .235

Switch Hitter	AB	R	H	2B	3B	HR	RBI	BB	SO	SB	AVG
Vs. RHP	339	36	88	18	2	4	40	30	39	4	.260
Vs. LHP	208	12	55	8	1	1	20	20	19	3	.264
At Home	70	265	28	72	15	2	4	38	27	31	2	.272
On the Road	76	282	20	71	11	1	1	22	23	27	5	.252
1990 Season	146	547	48	143	26	3	5	60	50	58	7	.261
Life 8.7 Years	589	75	161	28	5	3	63	67	64	21	.274

Greg HIBBARD

CHICAGO   STARTING PITCHER   26 Years Old
            14-9   3.16 ERA

Opponents Batting Average: .255
Offensive Support: 3.75 Runs Per Nine Innings
Double Play Support: 1.07 GDP Per Nine Innings

First Pitch is Hit: 16%
Gets Ahead of the Hitter: 46%
Gets Behind the Hitter: 54%
Gets Leadoff Man Out: 75%

1990 On Base Pct Allowed: .305 Slugging Percentage: .355
Stolen Bases Allowed: 11   Caught Stealing: 8

Pitches Left	AB	H	2B	3B	HR	RBI	BB	SO	AVG
Vs. RHB	701	183	28	6	11	59	47	82	.261
Vs. LHB	91	19	6	0	0	7	8	10	.209

	G	IP	W-L	Pct	SO	BB	ERA
At Home	19	121	8-5		51	33	2.98
On the Road	14	90	6-4		41	22	3.39
1990 Season	33	211	14-9	.609	92	55	3.16
Life 1.5 Years	37	230	13-11	.556	97	63	3.18

•

Ted HIGUERA

MILWAUKEE   STARTING PITCHER   32 Years Old
            11-10   3.76 ERA

Opponents Batting Average: .256
Offensive Support: 4.66 Runs Per Nine Innings
Double Play Support: .74 GDP Per Nine Innings

First Pitch is Hit: 18%
Gets Ahead of the Hitter: 51%
Gets Behind the Hitter: 49%
Gets Leadoff Man Out: 69%

1990 On Base Pct Allowed: .310 Slugging Percentage: .378
Stolen Bases Allowed: 15   Caught Stealing: 4

Pitches Left	AB	H	2B	3B	HR	RBI	BB	SO	AVG
Vs. RHB	527	136	27	1	15	61	43	106	.258
Vs. LHB	126	31	3	0	1	12	7	23	.246

	G	IP	W-L	Pct	SO	BB	ERA
At Home	15	96	7-4		79	24	3.36
On the Road	12	74	4-6		50	26	4.28
1990 Season	27	170	11-10	.524	129	50	3.76
Life 4.9 Years	37	258	18-11	.622	203	78	3.34

Donnie HILL

CALIFORNIA   SECOND BASE   30 Years Old

Runs Created: 39   Offensive Winning Percentage: .429
Batting Average: .264   Secondary Average: .173

Most Often Bats: 2nd
Hits First Pitch: 11%
Gets Ahead of the Pitcher: 52%
Hits Behind the Pitcher: 48%

1990 On Base Percentage: .319   Career: .304
1990 Slugging Percentage: .352   Career: .347
Batting Avg with Men in Scoring Position: .250

Switch Hitter		AB	R	H	2B	3B	HR	RBI	BB	SO	SB	AVG
Vs. RHP		254	24	70	10	2	2	20	17	17	0	.276
Vs. LHP		98	12	23	8	0	1	12	12	10	1	.235
At Home	52	169	13	42	9	0	0	9	18	11	0	.249
On the Road	50	183	23	51	9	2	3	23	11	16	1	.279
1990 Season	102	352	36	93	18	2	3	32	29	27	1	.264
Life 4.0 Years		508	58	131	20	3	6	51	35	49	5	.258

•

Ken HILL

ST. LOUIS   STARTING PITCHER   25 Years Old
5-6   5.49 ERA

Opponents Batting Average: .264
Offensive Support: 4.81 Runs Per Nine Innings
Double Play Support: .34 GDP Per Nine Innings

First Pitch is Hit: 14%
Gets Ahead of the Hitter: 48%
Gets Behind the Hitter: 52%
Gets Leadoff Man Out: 66%

1990 On Base Pct Allowed: .334 Slugging Percentage: .411
Stolen Bases Allowed: 9   Caught Stealing: 4

Pitches Right	AB	H	2B	3B	HR	RBI	BB	SO	AVG
Vs. RHB	115	31	8	1	3	18	8	27	.270
Vs. LHB	184	48	9	2	4	21	25	31	.261

	G	IP	W-L	Pct	SO	BB	ERA
At Home	7	28	2-2		15	10	6.75
On the Road	10	51	3-4		43	23	4.80
1990 Season	17	79	5-6	.455	58	33	5.49
Life 1.4 Years	39	210	9-16	.353	128	100	4.32

Brian HOLMAN

SEATTLE   STARTING PITCHER   26 Years Old
11-11   4.03 ERA

Opponents Batting Average: .260
Offensive Support: 4.27 Runs Per Nine Innings
Double Play Support: .71 GDP Per Nine Innings

First Pitch is Hit: 14%
Gets Ahead of the Hitter: 48%
Gets Behind the Hitter: 52%
Gets Leadoff Man Out: 68%

1990 On Base Pct Allowed: .324 Slugging Percentage: .383
Stolen Bases Allowed: 8   Caught Stealing: 8

Pitches Right	AB	H	2B	3B	HR	RBI	BB	SO	AVG
Vs. RHB	345	82	14	1	7	42	28	72	.238
Vs. LHB	379	106	20	1	10	37	38	49	.280

	G	IP	W-L	Pct	SO	BB	ERA
At Home	15	105	4-6		59	44	4.04
On the Road	13	85	7-5		62	22	4.02
1990 Season	28	190	11-11	.500	121	66	4.03
Life 2.0 Years	40	241	12-16	.436	142	89	3.72

•

Rick HONEYCUTT

OAKLAND   RELIEF PITCHER   36 Years Old
2-2   2.70 ERA   7 SAVES

Blown Saves: 3   Holds: 27   Save Efficiency: 92%
Inherited Runners who Scored: 26%
Opponents Batting Average: .204
Double Play Support: .57 GDP Per Nine Innings

First Pitch is Hit: 14%
Gets Ahead of the Hitter: 50%
Gets Behind the Hitter: 50%
Gets First Batter Out: 82%

1990 On Base Pct Allowed: .272 Slugging Percentage: .276
Stolen Bases Allowed: 2   Caught Stealing: 3

Pitches Left	AB	H	2B	3B	HR	RBI	BB	SO	AVG
Vs. RHB	139	32	6	1	1	18	17	21	.230
Vs. LHB	86	14	2	0	1	7	5	17	.163

	G	IP	W-L	Pct	SO	BB	ERA
1990 Season	63	63	2-2	.500	38	22	2.70
Life 10.3 Years	48	187	9-12	.433	87	57	3.73

Sam HORN

BALTIMORE   DESIGNATED HITTER   27 Years Old

Runs Created: 38   Offensive Winning Percentage: .607
Batting Average: .248   Secondary Average: .354

Most Often Bats: 4th
Hits First Pitch: 15%
Gets Ahead of the Pitcher: 46%
Hits Behind the Pitcher: 54%

1990 On Base Percentage: .332   Career: .324
1990 Slugging Percentage: .472   Career: .451
Batting Avg with Men in Scoring Position: .265

Bats Left-Handed	AB	R	H	2B	3B	HR	RBI	BB	SO	SB	AVG
Vs. RHP	229	28	60	13	0	14	45	32	55	0	.262
Vs. LHP	17	2	1	0	0	0	0	0	7	0	.059
At Home	40	120	18	30	6	0	8	21	22	38	0	.250
On the Road	39	126	12	31	7	0	6	24	10	24	0	.246
1990 Season	79	246	30	61	13	0	14	45	32	62	0	.248
Life 1.1 Years	462	59	109	20	0	27	81	61	136	0	.235

•

Charlie HOUGH

TEXAS   STARTING PITCHER   43 Years Old
12-12   4.07 ERA

Opponents Batting Average: .235
Offensive Support: 4.65 Runs Per Nine Innings
Double Play Support: .82 GDP Per Nine Innings

First Pitch is Hit: 14%
Gets Ahead of the Hitter: 40%
Gets Behind the Hitter: 60%
Gets Leadoff Man Out: 65%

1990 On Base Pct Allowed: .338 Slugging Percentage: .369
Stolen Bases Allowed: 33   Caught Stealing: 6

Pitches Right	AB	H	2B	3B	HR	RBI	BB	SO	AVG
Vs. RHB	458	106	16	2	17	60	63	66	.231
Vs. LHB	349	84	12	2	7	34	56	48	.241

	G	IP	W-L	Pct	SO	BB	ERA
At Home	14	97	5-8		48	53	4.47
On the Road	18	122	7-4		66	66	3.76
1990 Season	32	219	12-12	.500	114	119	4.07
Life 14.5 Years	51	214	13-12	.524	137	95	3.63

Jack HOWELL

CALIFORNIA   THIRD BASE   29 Years Old

Runs Created: 42   Offensive Winning Percentage: .520
Batting Average: .228   Secondary Average: .297

Most Often Bats: 8th
Hits First Pitch: 14%
Gets Ahead of the Pitcher: 49%
Hits Behind the Pitcher: 51%

1990 On Base Percentage: .326   Career: .321
1990 Slugging Percentage: .370   Career: .418
Batting Avg with Men in Scoring Position: .167

Bats Left-Handed	AB	R	H	2B	3B	HR	RBI	BB	SO	SB	AVG
Vs. RHP	254	29	61	17	1	8	28	37	45	2	.240
Vs. LHP	62	6	11	2	0	0	5	9	16	1	.177
At Home	53	156	16	34	9	0	3	17	20	31	0	.218
On the Road	52	160	19	38	10	1	5	16	26	30	3	.237
1990 Season	105	316	35	72	19	1	8	33	46	61	3	.228
Life 4.0 Years	508	65	121	27	4	19	63	59	124	3	.239

•

Jay HOWELL

LOS ANGELES   RELIEF PITCHER   35 Years Old
5-5   2.18 ERA   16 SAVES

Blown Saves: 8   Holds: 1   Save Efficiency: 68%
Inherited Runners who Scored: 60%
Opponents Batting Average: .242
Double Play Support: .82 GDP Per Nine Innings

First Pitch is Hit: 13%
Gets Ahead of the Hitter: 51%
Gets Behind the Hitter: 49%
Gets First Batter Out: 56%

1990 On Base Pct Allowed: .315 Slugging Percentage: .344
Stolen Bases Allowed: 10   Caught Stealing: 1

Pitches Right	AB	H	2B	3B	HR	RBI	BB	SO	AVG
Vs. RHB	95	23	3	0	2	11	10	18	.242
Vs. LHB	149	36	5	1	3	14	10	41	.242

	G	IP	W-L	Pct	SO	BB	ERA
1990 Season	45	66	5-5	.500	59	20	2.18
Life 5.5 Years	70	116	8-7	.518	96	42	3.43

Ken HOWELL

PHILADELPHIA	STARTING PITCHER	30 Years Old
	8-7 4.64 ERA	

Opponents Batting Average: .260
Offensive Support: 4.47 Runs Per Nine Innings
Double Play Support: .51 GDP Per Nine Innings

First Pitch is Hit: 15%
Gets Ahead of the Hitter: 46%
Gets Behind the Hitter: 54%
Gets Leadoff Man Out: 68%

1990 On Base Pct Allowed: .343 Slugging Percentage: .423
Stolen Bases Allowed: 11   Caught Stealing: 4

Pitches Right	AB	H	2B	3B	HR	RBI	BB	SO	AVG
Vs. RHB	153	31	8	0	5	10	13	37	.203
Vs. LHB	254	75	18	2	7	43	36	33	.295

	G	IP	W-L	Pct	SO	BB	ERA
At Home	11	61	4-4		32	29	5.43
On the Road	7	45	4-3		38	20	3.57
1990 Season	18	107	8-7	.533	70	49	4.64
Life 4.0 Years	61	152	9-12	.442	136	68	3.95

Bruce HURST

SAN DIEGO	STARTING PITCHER	33 Years Old
	11-9 3.14 ERA	

Opponents Batting Average: .228
Offensive Support: 3.62 Runs Per Nine Innings
Double Play Support: .85 GDP Per Nine Innings

First Pitch is Hit: 16%
Gets Ahead of the Hitter: 53%
Gets Behind the Hitter: 47%
Gets Leadoff Man Out: 69%

1990 On Base Pct Allowed: .284 Slugging Percentage: .357
Stolen Bases Allowed: 19   Caught Stealing: 7

Pitches Left	AB	H	2B	3B	HR	RBI	BB	SO	AVG
Vs. RHB	658	150	32	2	14	49	46	119	.228
Vs. LHB	165	38	3	2	7	23	17	43	.230

	G	IP	W-L	Pct	SO	BB	ERA
At Home	17	122	7-3		97	33	2.66
On the Road	16	102	4-6		65	30	3.72
1990 Season	33	224	11-9	.550	162	63	3.14
Life 7.9 Years	38	243	14-12	.551	175	77	3.91

Kent HRBEK

MINNESOTA	FIRST BASE	30 Years Old

Runs Created: 89	Offensive Winning Percentage: .681
Batting Average: .287	Secondary Average: .337

Most Often Bats: 4th
Hits First Pitch: 21%
Gets Ahead of the Pitcher: 51%
Hits Behind the Pitcher: 49%

1990 On Base Percentage: .377	Career: .369
1990 Slugging Percentage: .474	Career: .493

Batting Avg with Men in Scoring Position: .276

Bats Left-Handed	AB	R	H	2B	3B	HR	RBI	BB	SO	SB	AVG
Vs. RHP	363	43	104	23	0	20	62	52	32	4	.287
Vs. LHP	129	18	37	3	0	2	17	17	13	1	.287
At Home	72	247	28	69	15	0	8	43	32	16	2	.279
On the Road	71	245	33	72	11	0	14	36	37	29	3	.294
1990 Season	143	492	61	141	26	0	22	79	69	45	5	.287
Life 8.0 Years	582	85	169	31	2	28	100	74	76	3	.290

Jeff HUSON

TEXAS	SHORTSTOP	26 Years Old

Runs Created: 39	Offensive Winning Percentage: .371
Batting Average: .240	Secondary Average: .187

Most Often Bats: 1st
Hits First Pitch: 12%
Gets Ahead of the Pitcher: 51%
Hits Behind the Pitcher: 49%

1990 On Base Percentage: .320	Career: .311
1990 Slugging Percentage: .280	Career: .279

Batting Avg with Men in Scoring Position: .250

Bats Left-Handed	AB	R	H	2B	3B	HR	RBI	BB	SO	SB	AVG
Vs. RHP	350	48	83	11	2	0	25	42	45	11	.237
Vs. LHP	46	9	12	1	0	0	3	4	9	1	.261
At Home	74	191	28	42	8	1	0	11	18	33	5	.220
On the Road	71	205	29	53	4	1	0	17	28	21	7	.259
1990 Season	145	396	57	95	12	2	0	28	46	54	12	.240
Life 1.2 Years	421	53	99	16	2	0	27	46	52	14	.234

•I•

Pete INCAVIGLIA

TEXAS   LEFT FIELD   27 Years Old

Runs Created: 63   Offensive Winning Percentage: .464
Batting Average: .233   Secondary Average: .278

Most Often Bats: 6th
Hits First Pitch: 16%
Gets Ahead of the Pitcher: 43%
Hits Behind the Pitcher: 57%

1990 On Base Percentage: .302   Career: .314
1990 Slugging Percentage: .420   Career: .459
Batting Avg with Men in Scoring Position: .233

Bats Right-Handed	AB	R	H	2B	3B	HR	RBI	BB	SO	SB	AVG
Vs. RHP	360	38	81	18	0	16	55	24	110	1	.225
Vs. LHP	169	21	42	9	0	8	30	21	36	2	.249

		AB	R	H	2B	3B	HR	RBI	BB	SO	SB	AVG
At Home	76	247	33	61	13	0	15	45	28	73	3	.247
On the Road	77	282	26	62	14	0	9	40	17	73	0	.220
1990 Season	153	529	59	123	27	0	24	85	45	146	3	.233
Life 4.3 Years		572	78	142	28	3	29	91	51	184	6	.248

•J•

Bo JACKSON

KANSAS CITY   CENTER FIELD   28 Years Old

Runs Created: 70   Offensive Winning Percentage: .648
Batting Average: .272   Secondary Average: .398

Most Often Bats: 4th
Hits First Pitch: 14%
Gets Ahead of the Pitcher: 42%
Hits Behind the Pitcher: 58%

1990 On Base Percentage: .342   Career: .308
1990 Slugging Percentage: .523   Career: .480
Batting Avg with Men in Scoring Position: .239

Bats Right-Handed	AB	R	H	2B	3B	HR	RBI	BB	SO	SB	AVG
Vs. RHP	262	46	71	12	1	18	54	28	82	9	.271
Vs. LHP	143	28	39	4	0	10	24	16	46	6	.273

		AB	R	H	2B	3B	HR	RBI	BB	SO	SB	AVG
At Home	52	192	41	59	15	0	12	37	21	58	3	.307
On the Road	59	213	33	51	1	1	16	41	23	70	12	.239
1990 Season	111	405	74	110	16	1	28	78	44	128	15	.272
Life 3.2 Years		582	88	146	21	4	35	99	46	202	26	.250

•

Danny JACKSON

CINCINNATI   STARTING PITCHER   29 Years Old
                         6-6   3.61 ERA

Opponents Batting Average: .266
Offensive Support: 4.45 Runs Per Nine Innings
Double Play Support: .84 GDP Per Nine Innings

First Pitch is Hit: 16%
Gets Ahead of the Hitter: 47%
Gets Behind the Hitter: 53%
Gets Leadoff Man Out: 69%

1990 On Base Pct Allowed: .325 Slugging Percentage: .386
Stolen Bases Allowed: 15   Caught Stealing: 3

Pitches Left	AB	H	2B	3B	HR	RBI	BB	SO	AVG
Vs. RHB	369	100	10	3	9	44	29	63	.271
Vs. LHB	79	19	3	1	2	5	11	13	.241

	G	IP	W-L	Pct	SO	BB	ERA
At Home	11	54	2-3		36	17	3.83
On the Road	11	63	4-3		40	23	3.41
1990 Season	22	117	6-6	.500	76	40	3.61
Life 5.1 Years	38	236	14-14	.493	144	92	3.66

Mike JACKSON

SEATTLE   RELIEF PITCHER   26 Years Old
5-7   4.54 ERA   3 SAVES

Blown Saves: 9   Holds: 13   Save Efficiency: 64%
Inherited Runners who Scored: 40%
Opponents Batting Average: .229
Double Play Support: .58 GDP Per Nine Innings

First Pitch is Hit: 12%
Gets Ahead of the Hitter: 47%
Gets Behind the Hitter: 53%
Gets First Batter Out: 62%

1990 On Base Pct Allowed: .333 Slugging Percentage: .348
Stolen Bases Allowed: 12   Caught Stealing: 2

Pitches Right	AB	H	2B	3B	HR	RBI	BB	SO	AVG
Vs. RHB	174	37	5	0	3	31	23	60	.213
Vs. LHB	105	27	4	0	5	18	21	9	.257

	G	IP	W-L	Pct	SO	BB	ERA
1990 Season	63	77	5-7	.417	69	44	4.54
Life 3.5 Years	72	113	6-8	.391	95	57	3.59

•

Brook JACOBY

CLEVELAND   THIRD BASE   31 Years Old

Runs Created: 83   Offensive Winning Percentage: .579
Batting Average: .293   Secondary Average: .250

Most Often Bats: 6th
Hits First Pitch: 24%
Gets Ahead of the Pitcher: 53%
Hits Behind the Pitcher: 47%

1990 On Base Percentage: .365   Career: .341
1990 Slugging Percentage: .427   Career: .422
Batting Avg with Men in Scoring Position: .293

Bats Right-Handed	AB	R	H	2B	3B	HR	RBI	BB	SO	SB	AVG
Vs. RHP	395	58	112	20	3	11	57	47	45	1	.284
Vs. LHP	158	19	50	4	1	3	18	16	13	0	.316
At Home	78	261	33	75	10	3	10	41	36	21	1	.287
On the Road	77	292	44	87	14	1	4	34	27	37	0	.298
1990 Season	155	553	77	162	24	4	14	75	63	58	1	.293
Life 6.6 Years		577	72	159	27	3	17	70	58	99	2	.276

Chris JAMES

CLEVELAND   DESIGNATED HITTER   28 Years Old

Runs Created: 78   Offensive Winning Percentage: .586
Batting Average: .299   Secondary Average: .210

Most Often Bats: 5th
Hits First Pitch: 13%
Gets Ahead of the Pitcher: 51%
Hits Behind the Pitcher: 49%

1990 On Base Percentage: .341   Career: .309
1990 Slugging Percentage: .443   Career: .423
Batting Avg with Men in Scoring Position: .324

Bats Right-Handed	AB	R	H	2B	3B	HR	RBI	BB	SO	SB	AVG
Vs. RHP	366	42	109	25	3	8	48	16	46	1	.298
Vs. LHP	162	20	49	7	1	4	22	15	25	3	.302
At Home	67	234	27	67	13	1	6	33	15	33	1	.286
On the Road	73	294	35	91	19	3	6	37	16	38	3	.310
1990 Season	140	528	62	158	32	4	12	70	31	71	4	.299
Life 3.4 Years		580	66	155	28	4	18	76	34	86	6	.268

•

Stan JAVIER

LOS ANGELES   CENTER FIELD   25 Years Old

Runs Created: 48   Offensive Winning Percentage: .609
Batting Average: .298   Secondary Average: .275

Most Often Bats: 2nd
Hits First Pitch: 13%
Gets Ahead of the Pitcher: 56%
Hits Behind the Pitcher: 44%

1990 On Base Percentage: .376   Career: .324
1990 Slugging Percentage: .395   Career: .325
Batting Avg with Men in Scoring Position: .294

Switch Hitter	AB	R	H	2B	3B	HR	RBI	BB	SO	SB	AVG
Vs. RHP	185	32	53	7	3	2	17	22	36	10	.286
Vs. LHP	124	28	39	2	3	1	10	18	14	5	.315
At Home	64	161	25	46	3	2	1	16	21	24	6	.286
On the Road	59	148	35	46	6	4	2	11	19	26	9	.311
1990 Season	123	309	60	92	9	6	3	27	40	50	15	.298
Life 3.1 Years		412	60	103	14	4	3	34	44	70	19	.251

Mike JEFFCOAT

TEXAS   RELIEF PITCHER   31 Years Old
              5-6   4.47 ERA   5 SAVES

Blown Saves: 5   Holds: 4   Save Efficiency: 64%
Inherited Runners who Scored: 40%
Opponents Batting Average: .283
Double Play Support: .98 GDP Per Nine Innings

First Pitch is Hit: 14%
Gets Ahead of the Hitter: 48%
Gets Behind the Hitter: 52%
Gets First Batter Out: 69%

1990 On Base Pct Allowed: .328 Slugging Percentage: .427
Stolen Bases Allowed: 0   Caught Stealing: 6

Pitches Left	AB	H	2B	3B	HR	RBI	BB	SO	AVG
Vs. RHB	341	101	21	1	12	44	26	45	.296
Vs. LHB	90	21	3	0	0	10	2	13	.233

	G	IP	W-L	Pct	SO	BB	ERA
1990 Season	44	111	5-6	.455	58	28	4.47
Life 2.9 Years	60	136	7-8	.476	65	41	4.14

•

Gregg JEFFERIES

NEW YORK   SECOND BASE   23 Years Old

Runs Created: 89   Offensive Winning Percentage: .605
Batting Average: .283   Secondary Average: .245

Most Often Bats: 3rd
Hits First Pitch: 10%
Gets Ahead of the Pitcher: 55%
Hits Behind the Pitcher: 45%

1990 On Base Percentage: .337   Career: .331
1990 Slugging Percentage: .434   Career: .432
Batting Avg with Men in Scoring Position: .271

Switch Hitter	AB	R	H	2B	3B	HR	RBI	BB	SO	SB	AVG
Vs. RHP	382	69	112	25	1	10	45	33	23	9	.293
Vs. LHP	222	27	59	15	2	5	23	13	17	2	.266
At Home	80	311	57	99	26	1	9	41	28	17	7	.318
On the Road	73	293	39	72	14	2	6	27	18	23	4	.246
1990 Season	153	604	96	171	40	3	15	68	46	40	11	.283
Life 2.0 Years		604	92	167	38	3	16	70	46	47	18	.277

Dave JOHNSON

BALTIMORE   STARTING PITCHER   31 Years Old
              13-9   4.10 ERA

Opponents Batting Average: .280
Offensive Support: 4.85 Runs Per Nine Innings
Double Play Support: .90 GDP Per Nine Innings

First Pitch is Hit: 17%
Gets Ahead of the Hitter: 46%
Gets Behind the Hitter: 54%
Gets Leadoff Man Out: 69%

1990 On Base Pct Allowed: .321 Slugging Percentage: .476
Stolen Bases Allowed: 1   Caught Stealing: 4

Pitches Right	AB	H	2B	3B	HR	RBI	BB	SO	AVG
Vs. RHB	353	93	14	0	15	36	19	44	.263
Vs. LHB	347	103	29	2	15	37	24	24	.297

	G	IP	W-L	Pct	SO	BB	ERA
At Home	14	87	5-6		30	25	3.72
On the Road	16	93	8-3		38	18	4.45
1990 Season	30	180	13-9	.591	68	43	4.10
Life 1.2 Years	39	222	14-13	.515	79	59	4.28

•

Howard JOHNSON

NEW YORK   THIRD BASE   30 Years Old

Runs Created: 87   Offensive Winning Percentage: .577
Batting Average: .244   Secondary Average: .364

Most Often Bats: 3rd
Hits First Pitch: 16%
Gets Ahead of the Pitcher: 53%
Hits Behind the Pitcher: 47%

1990 On Base Percentage: .319   Career: .341
1990 Slugging Percentage: .434   Career: .454
Batting Avg with Men in Scoring Position: .297

Switch Hitter	AB	R	H	2B	3B	HR	RBI	BB	SO	SB	AVG
Vs. RHP	369	63	98	25	3	17	67	40	50	25	.266
Vs. LHP	221	26	46	12	0	6	23	29	50	9	.208
At Home	77	291	43	68	12	1	13	45	27	49	17	.234
On the Road	77	299	46	76	25	2	10	45	42	51	17	.254
1990 Season	154	590	89	144	37	3	23	90	69	100	34	.244
Life 6.3 Years		538	82	137	27	2	25	81	70	110	25	.256

Lance JOHNSON

| CHICAGO | CENTER FIELD | 27 Years Old |

Runs Created: 59   Offensive Winning Percentage: .455
Batting Average: .285   Secondary Average: .200

Most Often Bats: 1st
Hits First Pitch: 27%
Gets Ahead of the Pitcher: 50%
Hits Behind the Pitcher: 50%

1990 On Base Percentage: .325   Career: .315
1990 Slugging Percentage: .357   Career: .337
Batting Avg with Men in Scoring Position: .345

Bats Left-Handed	AB	R	H	2B	3B	HR	RBI	BB	SO	SB	AVG
Vs. RHP	385	61	104	15	6	1	32	24	27	24	.270
Vs. LHP	156	15	50	3	3	0	19	9	18	12	.321
At Home	75	265	42	80	9	6	0	25	15	20	24	.302
On the Road	76	276	34	74	9	3	1	26	18	25	12	.268
1990 Season	151	541	76	154	18	9	1	51	33	45	36	.285
Life	1.6 Years	548	72	148	19	8	1	49	36	52	39	.270

•

Randy JOHNSON

| SEATTLE | STARTING PITCHER | 27 Years Old |
| | 14-11   3.65 ERA | |

Opponents Batting Average: .216
Offensive Support: 4.59 Runs Per Nine Innings
Double Play Support: .66 GDP Per Nine Innings

First Pitch is Hit: 12%
Gets Ahead of the Hitter: 49%
Gets Behind the Hitter: 51%
Gets Leadoff Man Out: 63%

1990 On Base Pct Allowed: .319 Slugging Percentage: .355
Stolen Bases Allowed: 28   Caught Stealing: 8

Pitches Left	AB	H	2B	3B	HR	RBI	BB	SO	AVG
Vs. RHB	724	158	23	4	26	76	113	171	.218
Vs. LHB	82	16	3	0	0	4	7	23	.195

	G	IP	W-L	Pct	SO	BB	ERA
At Home	15	102	8-4		84	60	2.90
On the Road	18	117	6-7		110	60	4.30
1990 Season	33	220	14-11	.560	194	120	3.65
Life 1.8 Years	37	230	14-14	.500	197	126	4.03

Barry JONES

| CHICAGO | RELIEF PITCHER | 28 Years Old |
| | 11-4   2.31 ERA   1 SAVES | |

Blown Saves: 7   Holds: 30   Save Efficiency: 82%
Inherited Runners who Scored: 34%
Opponents Batting Average: .235
Double Play Support: .85 GDP Per Nine Innings

First Pitch is Hit: 12%
Gets Ahead of the Hitter: 48%
Gets Behind the Hitter: 52%
Gets First Batter Out: 67%

1990 On Base Pct Allowed: .317 Slugging Percentage: .292
Stolen Bases Allowed: 3   Caught Stealing: 2

Pitches Right	AB	H	2B	3B	HR	RBI	BB	SO	AVG
Vs. RHB	152	28	4	0	0	14	20	32	.184
Vs. LHB	112	34	5	0	2	19	13	13	.304

	G	IP	W-L	Pct	SO	BB	ERA
1990 Season	65	74	11-4	.733	45	33	2.31
Life 2.8 Years	74	97	8-6	.564	61	45	3.10

•

Doug JONES

| CLEVELAND | RELIEF PITCHER | 33 Years Old |
| | 5-5   2.56 ERA   43 SAVES | |

Blown Saves: 8   Holds: 0   Save Efficiency: 84%
Inherited Runners who Scored: 27%
Opponents Batting Average: .218
Double Play Support: 1.39 GDP Per Nine Innings

First Pitch is Hit: 12%
Gets Ahead of the Hitter: 53%
Gets Behind the Hitter: 47%
Gets First Batter Out: 70%

1990 On Base Pct Allowed: .274 Slugging Percentage: .323
Stolen Bases Allowed: 3   Caught Stealing: 1

Pitches Right	AB	H	2B	3B	HR	RBI	BB	SO	AVG
Vs. RHB	138	33	5	1	2	16	11	29	.239
Vs. LHB	165	33	8	1	3	18	11	26	.200

	G	IP	W-L	Pct	SO	BB	ERA
1990 Season	66	84	5-5	.500	55	22	2.56
Life 3.2 Years	74	111	7-7	.478	90	25	2.65

Ricky JORDAN

PHILADELPHIA	FIRST BASE	25 Years Old

Runs Created: 30
Batting Average: .241

Offensive Winning Percentage: .356
Secondary Average: .157

Most Often Bats: 4th
Hits First Pitch: 15%
Gets Ahead of the Pitcher: 43%
Hits Behind the Pitcher: 57%

1990 On Base Percentage: .277   Career: .307
1990 Slugging Percentage: .352   Career: .412
Batting Avg with Men in Scoring Position: .221

Bats Right-Handed		AB	R	H	2B	3B	HR	RBI	BB	SO	SB	AVG
Vs. RHP		206	18	49	12	0	3	32	3	30	1	.238
Vs. LHP		118	14	29	9	0	2	12	10	9	1	.246
At Home	44	145	14	34	6	0	2	18	2	26	1	.234
On the Road	48	179	18	44	15	0	3	26	11	13	1	.246
1990 Season	92	324	32	78	21	0	5	44	13	39	2	.241
Life	1.9 Years	595	72	165	31	2	15	86	23	74	4	.278

Wally JOYNER

CALIFORNIA	FIRST BASE	28 Years Old

Runs Created: 43
Batting Average: .268

Offensive Winning Percentage: .553
Secondary Average: .265

Most Often Bats: 3rd
Hits First Pitch: 14%
Gets Ahead of the Pitcher: 57%
Hits Behind the Pitcher: 43%

1990 On Base Percentage: .350   Career: .351
1990 Slugging Percentage: .394   Career: .448
Batting Avg with Men in Scoring Position: .282

Bats Left-Handed		AB	R	H	2B	3B	HR	RBI	BB	SO	SB	AVG
Vs. RHP		204	29	59	13	0	6	24	31	19	2	.289
Vs. LHP		106	6	24	2	0	2	17	10	15	0	.226
At Home	37	135	19	37	5	0	5	21	21	13	0	.274
On the Road	46	175	16	46	10	0	3	20	20	21	2	.263
1990 Season	83	310	35	83	15	0	8	41	41	34	2	.268
Life	4.3 Years	612	87	175	31	2	21	97	62	61	6	.286

Felix JOSE

ST. LOUIS	RIGHT FIELD	25 Years Old

Runs Created: 50
Batting Average: .265

Offensive Winning Percentage: .508
Secondary Average: .204

Most Often Bats: 6th
Hits First Pitch: 19%
Gets Ahead of the Pitcher: 44%
Hits Behind the Pitcher: 56%

1990 On Base Percentage: .311   Career: .304
1990 Slugging Percentage: .385   Career: .368
Batting Avg with Men in Scoring Position: .325

Switch Hitter		AB	R	H	2B	3B	HR	RBI	BB	SO	SB	AVG
Vs. RHP		323	43	82	11	0	9	36	17	60	9	.254
Vs. LHP		103	11	31	5	1	2	16	7	21	3	.301
At Home	65	210	26	49	7	1	5	27	16	44	5	.233
On the Road	61	216	28	64	9	0	6	25	8	37	7	.296
1990 Season	126	426	54	113	16	1	11	52	24	81	12	.265
Life	1.0 Years	514	62	133	20	1	12	61	29	100	14	.258

Dave JUSTICE

ATLANTA	FIRST BASE	25 Years Old

Runs Created: 92
Batting Average: .282

Offensive Winning Percentage: .730
Secondary Average: .424

Most Often Bats: 4th
Hits First Pitch: 11%
Gets Ahead of the Pitcher: 51%
Hits Behind the Pitcher: 49%

1990 On Base Percentage: .373   Career: .365
1990 Slugging Percentage: .535   Career: .516
Batting Avg with Men in Scoring Position: .319

Bats Left-Handed		AB	R	H	2B	3B	HR	RBI	BB	SO	SB	AVG
Vs. RHP		308	47	76	15	2	18	46	46	70	7	.247
Vs. LHP		131	29	48	8	0	10	32	18	22	4	.366
At Home	64	225	42	72	18	1	19	48	32	49	5	.320
On the Road	63	214	34	52	5	1	9	30	32	43	6	.243
1990 Season	127	439	76	124	23	2	28	78	64	92	11	.282
Life	0.9 Years	555	94	154	29	2	33	92	76	114	15	.278

•K•

Roberto KELLY

NEW YORK   CENTER FIELD   26 Years Old

Runs Created: 87   Offensive Winning Percentage: .568
Batting Average: .285   Secondary Average: .250

Most Often Bats: 1st
Hits First Pitch: 14%
Gets Ahead of the Pitcher: 45%
Hits Behind the Pitcher: 55%

1990 On Base Percentage: .323   Career: .337
1990 Slugging Percentage: .418   Career: .413
Batting Avg with Men in Scoring Position: .246

Bats Right-Handed	AB	R	H	2B	3B	HR	RBI	BB	SO	SB	AVG
Vs. RHP	460	56	128	22	4	10	44	21	102	26	.278
Vs. LHP	181	29	55	10	0	5	17	12	46	16	.304
At Home	81	315	44	96	22	2	5	25	14	57	24	.305
On the Road	01	026	41	87	10	2	10	36	19	91	18	.267
1990 Season 162	641	85	183	32	4	15	61	33	148	42	.285
Life 2.2 Years	545	77	157	26	4	12	55	37	120	41	.288

•

Terry KENNEDY

SAN FRANCISCO   CATCHER   34 Years Old

Runs Created: 38   Offensive Winning Percentage: .499
Batting Average: .277   Secondary Average: .198

Most Often Bats: 6th
Hits First Pitch: 21%
Gets Ahead of the Pitcher: 51%
Hits Behind the Pitcher: 49%

1990 On Base Percentage: .342   Career: .315
1990 Slugging Percentage: .370   Career: .387
Batting Avg with Men in Scoring Position: .238

Bats Left-Handed	AB	R	H	2B	3B	HR	RBI	BB	SO	SB	AVG
Vs. RHP	271	21	78	21	0	2	25	28	34	0	.288
Vs. LHP	32	4	6	1	0	0	1	3	4	1	.188
At Home	55	148	15	43	10	0	2	18	19	14	0	.291
On the Road	52	155	10	41	12	0	0	8	12	24	1	.265
1990 Season 107	303	25	84	22	0	2	26	31	38	1	.277
Life 8.8 Years	548	53	145	27	1	13	70	40	94	1	.265

Jimmy KEY

TORONTO   STARTING PITCHER   29 Years Old
13-7   4.25 ERA

Opponents Batting Average: .281
Offensive Support: 5.53 Runs Per Nine Innings
Double Play Support: .99 GDP Per Nine Innings

First Pitch is Hit: 15%
Gets Ahead of the Hitter: 52%
Gets Behind the Hitter: 48%
Gets Leadoff Man Out: 69%

1990 On Base Pct Allowed: .304   Slugging Percentage: .439
Stolen Bases Allowed: 6   Caught Stealing: 4

Pitches Left	AB	H	2B	3B	HR	RBI	BB	SO	AVG
Vs. RHB	514	153	30	2	20	61	18	74	.298
Vs. LHB	88	16	1	0	0	5	4	14	.182

	G	IP	W-L	Pct	SO	BB	ERA
At Home	16	89	7-3		52	13	4.47
On the Road	11	66	6-4		36	9	3.95
1990 Season	27	155	13-7	.650	88	22	4.25
Life 5.9 Years	43	216	15-10	.608	119	51	3.47

•

Dana KIECKER

BOSTON   STARTING PITCHER   30 Years Old
8-9   3.97 ERA

Opponents Batting Average: .253
Offensive Support: 4.80 Runs Per Nine Innings
Double Play Support: .95 GDP Per Nine Innings

First Pitch is Hit: 18%
Gets Ahead of the Hitter: 51%
Gets Behind the Hitter: 49%
Gets Leadoff Man Out: 65%

1990 On Base Pct Allowed: .325   Slugging Percentage: .355
Stolen Bases Allowed: 15   Caught Stealing: 6

Pitches Right	AB	H	2B	3B	HR	RBI	BB	SO	AVG
Vs. RHB	273	50	13	1	3	26	25	72	.183
Vs. LHB	299	95	18	2	4	34	29	21	.318

	G	IP	W-L	Pct	SO	BB	ERA
At Home	17	64	3-5		30	24	6.50
On the Road	15	88	5-4		63	30	2.14
1990 Season	32	152	8-9	.471	93	54	3.97
Life 0.8 Years	42	197	10-12	.471	121	70	3.97

Eric KING

CHICAGO   STARTING PITCHER   27 Years Old
                    12-4   3.28 ERA

Opponents Batting Average: .237
Offensive Support: 4.41 Runs Per Nine Innings
Double Play Support: .72 GDP Per Nine Innings

First Pitch is Hit: 14%
Gets Ahead of the Hitter: 49%
Gets Behind the Hitter: 51%
Gets Leadoff Man Out: 73%

1990 On Base Pct Allowed: .293 Slugging Percentage: .333
Stolen Bases Allowed: 8   Caught Stealing: 5

Pitches Right	AB	H	2B	3B	HR	RBI	BB	SO	AVG
Vs. RHB	302	77	10	1	5	27	15	40	.255
Vs. LHB	268	58	7	3	5	27	25	30	.216

	G	IP	W-L	Pct	SO	BB	ERA
At Home	13	76	5-3		26	18	3.93
On the Road	12	75	7-1		44	22	2.63
1990 Season	25	151	12-4	.750	70	40	3.28
Life 3.2 Years	50	199	13-9	.600	111	82	3.67

•

Jeff KING

PITTSBURGH   THIRD BASE   26 Years Old

Runs Created: 40   Offensive Winning Percentage: .421
Batting Average: .245   Secondary Average: .229

Most Often Bats: 6th
Hits First Pitch: 15%
Gets Ahead of the Pitcher: 50%
Hits Behind the Pitcher: 50%

1990 On Base Percentage: .282   Career: .276
1990 Slugging Percentage: .410   Career: .389
Batting Avg with Men in Scoring Position: .232

Bats Right-Handed	AB	R	H	2B	3B	HR	RBI	BB	SO	SB	AVG
Vs. RHP	140	17	30	4	0	5	17	7	26	0	.214
Vs. LHP	231	29	61	13	1	9	36	14	24	3	.264
At Home	63	179	26	49	9	0	9	30	9	23	1	.274
On the Road	64	192	20	42	8	1	5	23	12	27	2	.219
1990 Season	127	371	46	91	17	1	14	53	21	50	3	.245
Life 1.2 Years		470	62	107	24	3	15	58	33	67	6	.227

Ron KITTLE

BALTIMORE   DESIGNATED HITTER   33 Years Old

Runs Created: 43   Offensive Winning Percentage: .514
Batting Average: .231   Secondary Average: .284

Most Often Bats: 4th
Hits First Pitch: 15%
Gets Ahead of the Pitcher: 46%
Hits Behind the Pitcher: 54%

1990 On Base Percentage: .293   Career: .306
1990 Slugging Percentage: .438   Career: .476
Batting Avg with Men in Scoring Position: .207

Bats Right-Handed	AB	R	H	2B	3B	HR	RBI	BB	SO	SB	AVG
Vs. RHP	187	12	44	10	0	5	21	13	53	0	.235
Vs. LHP	151	21	34	6	0	13	25	13	38	0	.225
At Home	57	185	17	42	13	0	8	20	14	53	0	.227
On the Road	48	153	16	36	3	0	10	26	12	38	0	.235
1990 Season 105	338	33	78	16	0	18	46	26	91	0	.231
Life 5.1 Years	522	68	125	20	1	34	89	45	144	3	.240

•

Mark KNUDSON

MILWAUKEE   STARTING PITCHER   30 Years Old
                    10-9   4.12 ERA

Opponents Batting Average: .282
Offensive Support: 4.33 Runs Per Nine Innings
Double Play Support: .86 GDP Per Nine Innings

First Pitch is Hit: 16%
Gets Ahead of the Hitter: 50%
Gets Behind the Hitter: 50%
Gets Leadoff Man Out: 68%

1990 On Base Pct Allowed: .322 Slugging Percentage: .419
Stolen Bases Allowed: 8   Caught Stealing: 9

Pitches Right	AB	H	2B	3B	HR	RBI	BB	SO	AVG
Vs. RHB	324	92	20	2	8	39	17	27	.284
Vs. LHB	340	95	19	3	6	29	23	29	.279

	G	IP	W-L	Pct	SO	BB	ERA
At Home	13	79	5-3		29	19	3.55
On the Road	17	90	5-6		27	21	4.62
1990 Season	30	168	10-9	.526	56	40	4.12
Life 2.1 Years	49	208	11-12	.469	80	51	4.24

Bill KRUEGER

MILWAUKEE STARTING PITCHER 32 Years Old
6-8 3.98 ERA

Opponents Batting Average: .276
Offensive Support: 4.19 Runs Per Nine Innings
Double Play Support: .98 GDP Per Nine Innings

First Pitch is Hit: 17%
Gets Ahead of the Hitter: 40%
Gets Behind the Hitter: 60%
Gets Leadoff Man Out: 65%

1990 On Base Pct Allowed: .345 Slugging Percentage: .401
Stolen Bases Allowed: 9   Caught Stealing: 6

Pitches Left	AB	H	2B	3B	HR	RBI	BB	SO	AVG
Vs. RHB	403	115	19	4	9	53	50	50	.285
Vs. LHB	93	22	3	1	1	13	4	14	.237

	G	IP	W-L	Pct	SO	BB	ERA
At Home	16	77	4-6		44	28	4.23
On the Road	14	52	2-2		20	26	3.61
1990 Season	30	129	6-8	.429	64	54	3.98
Life 3.4 Years	48	198	11-12	.468	96	94	4.35

John KRUK

PHILADELPHIA LEFT FIELD 30 Years Old

Runs Created: 75   Offensive Winning Percentage: .671
Batting Average: .291   Secondary Average: .318

Most Often Bats: 5th
Hits First Pitch: 14%
Gets Ahead of the Pitcher: 47%
Hits Behind the Pitcher: 53%

1990 On Base Percentage: .386   Career: .388
1990 Slugging Percentage: .431   Career: .431
Batting Avg with Men in Scoring Position: .298

Bats Left-Handed	AB	R	H	2B	3B	HR	RBI	BB	SO	SB	AVG
Vs. RHP	326	41	103	23	6	5	52	55	50	8	.316
Vs. LHP	117	11	26	2	2	2	15	14	20	2	.222
At Home	70	220	22	70	15	4	2	37	31	29	3	.318
On the Road	72	223	30	59	10	4	5	30	38	41	7	.265
1990 Season	142	443	52	129	25	8	7	67	69	70	10	.291
Life 3.9 Years	486	67	141	22	5	12	73	79	87	10	.291

•L•

Mike LaCOSS

SAN FRANCISCO STARTING PITCHER 34 Years Old
6-4 3.94 ERA

Opponents Batting Average: .259
Offensive Support: 5.79 Runs Per Nine Innings
Double Play Support: 1.04 GDP Per Nine Innings

First Pitch is Hit: 14%
Gets Ahead of the Hitter: 48%
Gets Behind the Hitter: 52%
Gets Leadoff Man Out: 69%

1990 On Base Pct Allowed: .342 Slugging Percentage: .352
Stolen Bases Allowed: 11   Caught Stealing: 2

Pitches Right	AB	H	2B	3B	HR	RBI	BB	SO	AVG
Vs. RHB	112	32	5	0	2	16	11	19	.286
Vs. LHB	178	43	7	0	3	16	28	20	.242

	G	IP	W-L	Pct	SO	BB	ERA
At Home	4	27	2-2		18	12	3.67
On the Road	9	51	4-2		21	27	4.09
1990 Season	13	78	6-4	.600	39	39	3.94
Life 8.6 Years	46	197	11-11	.497	88	82	3.93

Dennis LAMP

BOSTON RELIEF PITCHER 30 Years Old
3-5 4.68 ERA 0 SAVES

Blown Saves: 2   Holds: 7   Save Efficiency: 78%
Inherited Runners who Scored: 43%
Opponents Batting Average: .279
Double Play Support: .85 GDP Per Nine Innings

First Pitch is Hit: 13%
Gets Ahead of the Hitter: 52%
Gets Behind the Hitter: 48%
Gets First Batter Out: 64%

1990 On Base Pct Allowed: .330 Slugging Percentage: .422
Stolen Bases Allowed: 12   Caught Stealing: 4

Pitches Right	AB	H	2B	3B	HR	RBI	BB	SO	AVG
Vs. RHB	214	56	12	1	7	47	13	25	.262
Vs. LHB	194	58	10	2	3	26	17	24	.299

	G	IP	W-L	Pct	SO	BB	ERA
1990 Season	47	106	3-5	.375	49	30	4.68
Life 9.9 Years	57	173	9-9	.492	80	52	3.87

Les LANCASTER

CHICAGO   RELIEF PITCHER   28 Years Old
                9-5   4.62 ERA   6 SAVES

Blown Saves: 5   Holds: 5   Save Efficiency: 69%
Inherited Runners who Scored: 41%
Opponents Batting Average: .283
Double Play Support: .58 GDP Per Nine Innings

First Pitch is Hit: 16%
Gets Ahead of the Hitter: 51%
Gets Behind the Hitter: 49%
Gets First Batter Out: 67%

1990 On Base Pct Allowed: .342 Slugging Percentage: .412
Stolen Bases Allowed: 4   Caught Stealing: 3

Pitches Right	AB	H	2B	3B	HR	RBI	BB	SO	AVG
Vs. RHB	201	57	8	1	8	39	11	35	.284
Vs. LHB	226	64	12	0	3	23	29	30	.283

	G	IP	W-L	Pct	SO	BB	ERA
1990 Season	55	109	9-5	.643	65	40	4.62
Life 2.6 Years	64	152	9-6	.610	89	53	3.94

●

Bill LANDRUM

PITTSBURGH   RELIEF PITCHER   33 Years Old
                7-3   2.13 ERA   13 SAVES

Blown Saves: 3   Holds: 1   Save Efficiency: 82%
Inherited Runners who Scored: 32%
Opponents Batting Average: .262
Double Play Support: 1.26 GDP Per Nine Innings

First Pitch is Hit: 14%
Gets Ahead of the Hitter: 46%
Gets Behind the Hitter: 54%
Gets First Batter Out: 57%

1990 On Base Pct Allowed: .314 Slugging Percentage: .342
Stolen Bases Allowed: 8   Caught Stealing: 2

Pitches Right	AB	H	2B	3B	HR	RBI	BB	SO	AVG
Vs. RHB	126	32	2	1	2	13	8	23	.254
Vs. LHB	137	37	1	2	2	16	13	16	.270

	G	IP	W-L	Pct	SO	BB	ERA
1990 Season	54	72	7-3	.700	39	21	2.13
Life 2.3 Years	73	104	6-3	.619	65	38	3.11

Mark LANGSTON

CALIFORNIA   STARTING PITCHER   30 Years Old
                10-17   4.40 ERA

Opponents Batting Average: .259
Offensive Support: 3.91 Runs Per Nine Innings
Double Play Support: .81 GDP Per Nine Innings

First Pitch is Hit: 12%
Gets Ahead of the Hitter: 48%
Gets Behind the Hitter: 52%
Gets Leadoff Man Out: 66%

1990 On Base Pct Allowed: .343 Slugging Percentage: .374
Stolen Bases Allowed: 22   Caught Stealing: 14

Pitches Left	AB	H	2B	3B	HR	RBI	BB	SO	AVG
Vs. RHB	691	181	31	7	12	89	89	168	.262
Vs. LHB	138	34	9	1	1	15	15	27	.246

	G	IP	W-L	Pct	SO	BB	ERA
At Home	17	119	3-11		104	52	4.55
On the Road	16	104	7-6		91	52	4.23
1990 Season	33	223	10-17	.370	195	104	4.40
Life 6.3 Years	37	255	15-15	.508	231	123	3.88

●

Carney LANSFORD

OAKLAND   THIRD BASE   34 Years Old

Runs Created: 54   Offensive Winning Percentage: .447
Batting Average: .268   Secondary Average: .172

Most Often Bats: 2nd
Hits First Pitch: 23%
Gets Ahead of the Pitcher: 51%
Hits Behind the Pitcher: 49%

1990 On Base Percentage: .333   Career: .345
1990 Slugging Percentage: .320   Career: .415
Batting Avg with Men in Scoring Position: .266

Bats Right-Handed		AB	R	H	2B	3B	HR	RBI	BB	SO	SB	AVG
Vs. RHP		388	34	95	10	0	2	39	26	37	8	.245
Vs. LHP		119	24	41	5	1	1	11	19	13	8	.345
At Home	59	215	20	64	5	0	1	19	23	22	10	.298
On the Road	75	292	38	72	10	1	2	31	22	28	6	.247
1990 Season	134	507	58	136	15	1	3	50	45	50	16	.268
Life 10.6 Years	625	89	183	28	4	14	75	48	64	20	.292

Dave LaPOINT

NEW YORK	STARTING PITCHER	31 Years Old
	7-10 4.11 ERA	

Opponents Batting Average: .292
Offensive Support: 4.62 Runs Per Nine Innings
Double Play Support: 1.20 GDP Per Nine Innings

First Pitch is Hit: 18%
Gets Ahead of the Hitter: 44%
Gets Behind the Hitter: 56%
Gets Leadoff Man Out: 65%

1990 On Base Pct Allowed: .347 Slugging Percentage: .417
Stolen Bases Allowed: 10   Caught Stealing: 9

Pitches Left	AB	H	2B	3B	HR	RBI	BB	SO	AVG
Vs. RHB	522	152	31	4	9	61	48	60	.291
Vs. LHB	95	28	1	2	2	9	9	7	.295

	G	IP	W-L	Pct	SO	BB	ERA
At Home	15	95	6-3		38	33	3.13
On the Road	13	63	1-7		29	24	5.60
1990 Season	28	158	7-10	.412	67	57	4.11
Life 7.0 Years	42	212	11-12	.485	114	79	3.98

•

Barry LARKIN

CINCINNATI	SHORTSTOP	26 Years Old

Runs Created: 91   Offensive Winning Percentage: .642
Batting Average: .301   Secondary Average: .223

Most Often Bats: 3rd
Hits First Pitch: 11%
Gets Ahead of the Pitcher: 56%
Hits Behind the Pitcher: 44%

1990 On Base Percentage: .358   Career: .344
1990 Slugging Percentage: .396   Career: .408
Batting Avg with Men in Scoring Position: .311

Bats Right-Handed	AB	R	H	2B	3B	HR	RBI	BB	SO	SB	AVG
Vs. RHP	411	51	131	15	3	3	46	26	39	21	.319
Vs. LHP	203	34	54	10	3	4	21	23	10	9	.266
At Home	78	286	36	78	8	2	4	26	29	21	11	.273
On the Road	80	328	49	107	17	4	3	41	20	28	19	.326
1990 Season	158	614	85	185	25	6	7	67	49	49	30	.301
Life 3.5 Years		602	89	176	26	6	11	63	44	48	31	.293

Gene LARKIN

MINNESOTA	RIGHT FIELD	28 Years Old

Runs Created: 56   Offensive Winning Percentage: .558
Batting Average: .269   Secondary Average: .239

Most Often Bats: 2nd
Hits First Pitch: 15%
Gets Ahead of the Pitcher: 59%
Hits Behind the Pitcher: 41%

1990 On Base Percentage: .343   Career: .353
1990 Slugging Percentage: .392   Career: .380
Batting Avg with Men in Scoring Position: .245

Switch Hitter		AB	R	H	2B	3B	HR	RBI	BB	SO	SB	AVG
Vs. RHP		280	31	78	20	2	5	30	32	41	3	.279
Vs. LHP		121	15	30	6	2	0	12	10	14	2	.248
At Home	58	199	30	57	16	2	5	26	20	25	1	.286
On the Road	61	202	16	51	10	2	0	16	22	30	4	.252
1990 Season	119	401	46	108	26	4	5	42	42	55	5	.269
Life 3.0 Years		525	62	140	30	3	8	62	63	66	5	.268

•

Mike LaVALLIERE

PITTSBURGH	CATCHER	30 Years Old

Runs Created: 36   Offensive Winning Percentage: .524
Batting Average: .258   Secondary Average: .244

Most Often Bats: 7th
Hits First Pitch: 20%
Gets Ahead of the Pitcher: 51%
Hits Behind the Pitcher: 49%

1990 On Base Percentage: .362   Career: .357
1990 Slugging Percentage: .344   Career: .340
Batting Avg with Men in Scoring Position: .303

Bats Left-Handed		AB	R	H	2B	3B	HR	RBI	BB	SO	SB	AVG
Vs. RHP		223	20	51	12	0	1	20	35	14	0	.229
Vs. LHP		56	7	21	3	0	2	11	9	6	0	.375
At Home	46	127	12	35	7	0	2	15	18	6	0	.276
On the Road	50	152	15	37	8	0	1	16	26	14	0	.243
1990 Season	96	279	27	72	15	0	3	31	44	20	0	.258
Life 3.3 Years		457	36	122	22	1	3	53	64	46	1	.267

Tim LAYANA

CINCINNATI   RELIEF PITCHER   27 Years Old
5-3   3.49 ERA   2 SAVES

Blown Saves: 0   Holds: 3   Save Efficiency: 100%
Inherited Runners who Scored: 40%
Opponents Batting Average: .244
Double Play Support: .90 GDP Per Nine Innings

First Pitch is Hit: 16%
Gets Ahead of the Hitter: 47%
Gets Behind the Hitter: 53%
Gets First Batter Out: 56%

1990 On Base Pct Allowed: .344 Slugging Percentage: .381
Stolen Bases Allowed: 9   Caught Stealing: 5

Pitches Right	AB	H	2B	3B	HR	RBI	BB	SO	AVG
Vs. RHB	158	37	7	0	4	17	19	31	.234
Vs. LHB	133	34	12	0	3	17	25	22	.256

	G	IP	W-L	Pct	SO	BB	ERA
1990 Season	55	80	5-3	.625	53	44	3.49
Life 0.7 Years	74	108	7-4	.625	71	59	3.49

•

Terry LEACH

MINNESOTA   RELIEF PITCHER   37 Years Old
2-5   3.20 ERA   2 SAVES

Blown Saves: 4   Holds: 4   Save Efficiency: 60%
Inherited Runners who Scored: 27%
Opponents Batting Average: .268
Double Play Support: .44 GDP Per Nine Innings

First Pitch is Hit: 17%
Gets Ahead of the Hitter: 53%
Gets Behind the Hitter: 47%
Gets First Batter Out: 81%

1990 On Base Pct Allowed: .315 Slugging Percentage: .364
Stolen Bases Allowed: 6   Caught Stealing: 1

Pitches Right	AB	H	2B	3B	HR	RBI	BB	SO	AVG
Vs. RHB	187	50	10	0	2	28	10	37	.267
Vs. LHB	126	34	8	3	0	11	11	9	.270

	G	IP	W-L	Pct	SO	BB	ERA
1990 Season	55	82	2-5	.286	46	21	3.20
Life 3.8 Years	68	142	8-5	.608	72	42	3.27

Tim LEARY

NEW YORK   STARTING PITCHER   32 Years Old
9-19   4.11 ERA

Opponents Batting Average: .257
Offensive Support: 3.07 Runs Per Nine Innings
Double Play Support: .87 GDP Per Nine Innings

First Pitch is Hit: 16%
Gets Ahead of the Hitter: 47%
Gets Behind the Hitter: 53%
Gets Leadoff Man Out: 66%

1990 On Base Pct Allowed: .328 Slugging Percentage: .378
Stolen Bases Allowed: 18   Caught Stealing: 8

Pitches Right	AB	H	2B	3B	HR	RBI	BB	SO	AVG
Vs. RHB	377	96	17	0	8	37	32	77	.255
Vs. LHB	408	106	22	1	10	47	46	61	.260

	G	IP	W-L	Pct	SO	BB	ERA
At Home	13	84	1-9		59	34	4.73
On the Road	18	124	8-10		79	44	3.69
1990 Season	31	208	9-19	.321	138	78	4.11
Life 4.8 Years	42	218	11-16	.419	143	68	3.79

•

Manny LEE

TORONTO   SECOND BASE   25 Years Old

Runs Created: 38   Offensive Winning Percentage: .358
Batting Average: .243   Secondary Average: .171

Most Often Bats: 8th
Hits First Pitch: 10%
Gets Ahead of the Pitcher: 45%
Hits Behind the Pitcher: 55%

1990 On Base Percentage: .288   Career: .301
1990 Slugging Percentage: .340   Career: .338
Batting Avg with Men in Scoring Position: .248

Switch Hitter	AB	R	H	2B	3B	HR	RBI	BB	SO	SB	AVG
Vs. RHP	213	23	52	4	2	0	21	20	49	2	.244
Vs. LHP	178	22	43	8	2	6	20	6	41	1	.242
At Home	58	190	21	50	4	2	2	19	11	45	3	.263
On the Road	59	201	24	45	8	2	4	22	15	45	0	.224
1990 Season	117	391	45	95	12	4	6	41	26	90	3	.243
Life 3.0 Years	436	47	113	13	4	4	44	28	82	4	.259

Craig LEFFERTS

SAN DIEGO   RELIEF PITCHER   33 Years Old

7-5   2.52 ERA   23 SAVES

Blown Saves: 7   Holds: 1   Save Efficiency: 77%
Inherited Runners who Scored: 22%
Opponents Batting Average: .228
Double Play Support: .57 GDP Per Nine Innings

First Pitch is Hit: 13%
Gets Ahead of the Hitter: 58%
Gets Behind the Hitter: 42%
Gets First Batter Out: 73%

1990 On Base Pct Allowed: .283   Slugging Percentage: .352
Stolen Bases Allowed: 3   Caught Stealing: 2

Pitches Left	AB	H	2B	3B	HR	RBI	BB	SO	AVG
Vs. RHB	211	50	7	0	9	28	14	42	.237
Vs. LHB	87	18	0	0	1	5	8	18	.207

	G	IP	W-L	Pct	SO	BB	ERA
1990 Season	56	79	7-5	.583	60	22	2.52
Life 7.2 Years	73	106	5-6	.470	67	32	2.95

•

Charlie LEIBRANDT

ATLANTA   STARTING PITCHER   34 Years Old

9-11   3.16 ERA

Opponents Batting Average: .261
Offensive Support: 4.71 Runs Per Nine Innings
Double Play Support: .55 GDP Per Nine Innings

First Pitch is Hit: 15%
Gets Ahead of the Hitter: 53%
Gets Behind the Hitter: 47%
Gets Leadoff Man Out: 73%

1990 On Base Pct Allowed: .302   Slugging Percentage: .374
Stolen Bases Allowed: 21   Caught Stealing: 3

Pitches Left	AB	H	2B	3B	HR	RBI	BB	SO	AVG
Vs. RHB	529	143	36	3	6	51	29	62	.270
Vs. LHB	99	21	2	0	3	14	6	14	.212

	G	IP	W-L	Pct	SO	BB	ERA
At Home	12	87	6-5		33	17	2.59
On the Road	12	75	3-6		43	18	3.82
1990 Season	24	162	9-11	.450	76	35	3.16
Life 7.5 Years	40	232	14-12	.532	107	69	3.71

Chet LEMON

DETROIT   RIGHT FIELD   36 Years Old

Runs Created: 46   Offensive Winning Percentage: .525
Batting Average: .258   Secondary Average: .280

Most Often Bats: 8th
Hits First Pitch: 12%
Gets Ahead of the Pitcher: 53%
Hits Behind the Pitcher: 47%

1990 On Base Percentage: .359   Career: .355
1990 Slugging Percentage: .379   Career: .442
Batting Avg with Men in Scoring Position: .225

Bats Right-Handed	AB	R	H	2B	3B	HR	RBI	BB	SO	SB	AVG
Vs. RHP	184	22	44	12	1	2	20	27	39	3	.239
Vs. LHP	138	17	39	4	3	3	12	21	22	0	.283
At Home	47	133	17	34	6	1	2	17	25	27	0	.256
On the Road	57	189	22	49	10	3	3	15	23	34	3	.259
1990 Season	104	322	39	83	16	4	5	32	48	61	3	.258
Life 12.3 Years		560	79	153	32	5	18	72	61	83	5	.273

•

Jeff LEONARD

SEATTLE   LEFT FIELD   35 Years Old

Runs Created: 49   Offensive Winning Percentage: .409
Batting Average: .251   Secondary Average: .190

Most Often Bats: 4th
Hits First Pitch: 17%
Gets Ahead of the Pitcher: 48%
Hits Behind the Pitcher: 52%

1990 On Base Percentage: .305   Career: .312
1990 Slugging Percentage: .356   Career: .411
Batting Avg with Men in Scoring Position: .306

Bats Right-Handed	AB	R	H	2B	3B	HR	RBI	BB	SO	SB	AVG
Vs. RHP	303	21	66	11	0	4	35	22	69	3	.218
Vs. LHP	175	18	54	9	0	6	40	15	28	1	.309
At Home	66	234	20	52	12	0	7	37	21	50	1	.222
On the Road	68	244	19	68	8	0	3	38	16	47	3	.279
1990 Season	134	478	39	120	20	0	10	75	37	97	4	.251
Life 8.7 Years		578	70	154	26	4	16	83	39	114	19	.266

Jim LEYRITZ

NEW YORK   THIRD BASE   27 Years Old

Runs Created: 34   Offensive Winning Percentage: .459
Batting Average: .257   Secondary Average: .195

Most Often Bats: 7th
Hits First Pitch: 7%
Gets Ahead of the Pitcher: 50%
Hits Behind the Pitcher: 50%

1990 On Base Percentage: .331   Career: .331
1990 Slugging Percentage: .356   Career: .356
Batting Avg with Men in Scoring Position: .194

Bats Right-Handed	AB	R	H	2B	3B	HR	RBI	BB	SO	SB	AVG
Vs. RHP	200	18	48	6	0	3	18	12	36	0	.240
Vs. LHP	103	10	30	7	1	2	7	15	15	2	.291
At Home	49	166	15	44	11	1	1	13	15	25	1	.265
On the Road	43	137	13	34	2	0	4	12	12	26	1	.248
1990 Season	92	303	28	78	13	1	5	25	27	51	2	.257
Life	0.6 Years	534	49	137	23	2	9	44	48	90	4	.257

Jose LIND

PITTSBURGH   SECOND BASE   26 Years Old

Runs Created: 51   Offensive Winning Percentage: .388
Batting Average: .261   Secondary Average: .163

Most Often Bats: 8th
Hits First Pitch: 10%
Gets Ahead of the Pitcher: 49%
Hits Behind the Pitcher: 51%

1990 On Base Percentage: .305   Career: .302
1990 Slugging Percentage: .340   Career: .326
Batting Avg with Men in Scoring Position: .285

Bats Right-Handed	AB	R	H	2B	3B	HR	RBI	BB	SO	SB	AVG
Vs. RHP	298	30	84	16	2	0	29	17	31	7	.282
Vs. LHP	216	16	50	12	3	1	19	18	21	1	.231
At Home	75	245	17	64	14	2	1	30	13	26	6	.261
On the Road	77	269	29	70	14	3	0	18	22	26	2	.260
1990 Season	152	514	46	134	28	5	1	48	35	52	8	.261
Life	3.0 Years	605	66	155	27	5	2	51	41	67	13	.257

Derek LILLIQUIST

SAN DIEGO   STARTING PITCHER   25 Years Old
                     5-11   5.31 ERA

Opponents Batting Average: .285
Offensive Support: 3.69 Runs Per Nine Innings
Double Play Support: .66 GDP Per Nine Innings

First Pitch is Hit: 15%
Gets Ahead of the Hitter: 51%
Gets Behind the Hitter: 49%
Gets Leadoff Man Out: 65%

1990 On Base Pct Allowed: .343 Slugging Percentage: .437
Stolen Bases Allowed: 12   Caught Stealing: 3

Pitches Left	AB	H	2B	3B	HR	RBI	BB	SO	AVG
Vs. RHB	386	106	20	0	13	51	33	40	.275
Vs. LHB	92	30	5	0	3	8	9	23	.326

	G	IP	W-L	Pct	SO	BB	ERA
At Home	14	57	2-6		38	18	4.71
On the Road	14	65	3-5		25	24	5.85
1990 Season	28	122	5-11	.313	63	42	5.31
Life 1.5 Years	41	197	9-14	.382	97	52	4.54

•M•

Kevin MAAS

NEW YORK	FIRST BASE	26 Years Old

Runs Created: 51   Offensive Winning Percentage: .747
Batting Average: .252   Secondary Average: .457

Most Often Bats: 5th
Hits First Pitch: 12%
Gets Ahead of the Pitcher: 53%
Hits Behind the Pitcher: 47%

1990 On Base Percentage: .367   Career: .367
1990 Slugging Percentage: .535   Career: .535
Batting Avg with Men in Scoring Position: .207

Bats Left-Handed	AB	R	H	2B	3B	HR	RBI	BB	SO	SB	AVG
Vs. RHP	187	38	53	8	0	18	33	33	48	1	.283
Vs. LHP	67	4	11	1	0	3	8	10	28	0	.164
At Home	43 135	26	38	6	0	12	27	23	38	1	.281
On the Road	36 119	16	26	3	0	9	14	20	38	0	.218
1990 Season	79 254	42	64	9	0	21	41	43	76	1	.252
Life 0.5 Years	521	86	131	18	0	43	84	88	156	2	.252

Shane MACK

MINNESOTA	CENTER FIELD	27 Years Old

Runs Created: 57   Offensive Winning Percentage: .714
Batting Average: .326   Secondary Average: .268

Most Often Bats: 8th
Hits First Pitch: 19%
Gets Ahead of the Pitcher: 44%
Hits Behind the Pitcher: 56%

1990 On Base Percentage: .392   Career: .349
1990 Slugging Percentage: .460   Career: .391
Batting Avg with Men in Scoring Position: .352

Bats Right-Handed	AB	R	H	2B	3B	HR	RBI	BB	SO	SB	AVG
Vs. RHP	167	30	48	1	3	3	17	14	43	9	.287
Vs. LHP	146	20	54	9	1	5	27	15	26	4	.370
At Home	59 141	31	52	6	3	5	21	14	33	3	.369
On the Road	66 172	19	50	4	1	3	23	15	36	10	.291
1990 Season	125 313	50	102	10	4	8	44	29	69	13	.326
Life 1.8 Years	380	52	106	14	4	7	46	35	78	12	.281

Mike MACFARLANE

KANSAS CITY	CATCHER	27 Years Old

Runs Created: 47   Offensive Winning Percentage: .455
Batting Average: .255   Secondary Average: .190

Most Often Bats: 8th
Hits First Pitch: 17%
Gets Ahead of the Pitcher: 50%
Hits Behind the Pitcher: 50%

1990 On Base Percentage: .306   Career: .304
1990 Slugging Percentage: .380   Career: .365
Batting Avg with Men in Scoring Position: .256

Bats Right-Handed	AB	R	H	2B	3B	HR	RBI	BB	SO	SB	AVG
Vs. RHP	253	22	66	16	1	4	46	16	43	0	.261
Vs. LHP	147	15	36	8	3	2	12	9	26	1	.245
At Home	61 191	17	49	13	3	1	30	13	32	0	.257
On the Road	63 209	20	53	11	1	5	28	12	37	1	.254
1990 Season	124 400	37	102	24	4	6	58	25	69	1	.255
Life 1.7 Years	470	45	118	27	2	7	63	33	81	1	.250

Greg MADDUX

CHICAGO	STARTING PITCHER	25 Years Old
	15-15 3.46 ERA	

Opponents Batting Average: .265
Offensive Support: 3.91 Runs Per Nine Innings
Double Play Support: 1.03 GDP Per Nine Innings

First Pitch is Hit: 17%
Gets Ahead of the Hitter: 51%
Gets Behind the Hitter: 49%
Gets Leadoff Man Out: 67%

1990 On Base Pct Allowed: .319   Slugging Percentage: .354
Stolen Bases Allowed: 13   Caught Stealing: 4

Pitches Right	AB	H	2B	3B	HR	RBI	BB	SO	AVG
Vs. RHB	351	78	16	1	5	28	18	65	.222
Vs. LHB	562	164	26	2	6	70	53	79	.292

	G	IP	W-L	Pct	SO	BB	ERA
At Home	16	116	8-6		66	40	3.58
On the Road	19	121	7-9		78	31	3.34
1990 Season	35	237	15-15	.500	144	71	3.46
Life 3.7 Years	38	244	16-14	.531	145	86	3.68

Dave MAGADAN

NEW YORK	FIRST BASE	28 Years Old

Runs Created: 92   Offensive Winning Percentage: .756
Batting Average: .328   Secondary Average: .297

Most Often Bats: 2nd
Hits First Pitch: 9%
Gets Ahead of the Pitcher: 54%
Hits Behind the Pitcher: 46%

1990 On Base Percentage: .417		Career: .395
1990 Slugging Percentage: .457		Career: .408

Batting Avg with Men in Scoring Position: .382

Bats Left-Handed	AB	R	H	2B	3B	HR	RBI	BB	SO	SB	AVG
Vs. RHP	283	50	105	22	4	4	45	54	33	1	.371
Vs. LHP	168	24	43	6	2	2	27	20	22	1	.256
At Home	73	212	40	59	10	2	2	34	42	26	1	.278
On the Road	71	239	34	89	18	4	4	38	32	29	1	.372
1990 Season	144	451	74	148	28	6	6	72	74	55	2	.328
Life	3.0 Years	457	62	139	26	3	5	59	70	52	1	.305

●

Joe MAGRANE

ST. LOUIS	STARTING PITCHER	26 Years Old
	10-17 3.59 ERA	

Opponents Batting Average: .264
Offensive Support: 3.01 Runs Per Nine Innings
Double Play Support: .66 GDP Per Nine Innings

First Pitch is Hit: 16%
Gets Ahead of the Hitter: 46%
Gets Behind the Hitter: 54%
Gets Leadoff Man Out: 65%

1990 On Base Pct Allowed: .320 Slugging Percentage: .373
Stolen Bases Allowed: 21   Caught Stealing: 16

Pitches Left	AB	H	2B	3B	HR	RBI	BB	SO	AVG
Vs. RHB	624	161	29	7	9	56	43	75	.258
Vs. LHB	150	43	7	2	1	14	16	25	.287

	G	IP	W-L	Pct	SO	BB	ERA
At Home	18	116	4-10		49	28	4.27
On the Road	13	87	6-7		51	31	2.68
1990 Season	31	203	10-17	.370	100	59	3.59
Life 3.1 Years	37	249	14-14	.500	138	78	3.07

Rick MAHLER

CINCINNATI	RELIEF PITCHER	37 Years Old
	7-6 4.28 ERA 4 SAVES	

Blown Saves: 0   Holds: 1   Save Efficiency: 100%
Inherited Runners who Scored: 0%
Opponents Batting Average: .261
Double Play Support: .74 GDP Per Nine Innings

First Pitch is Hit: 17%
Gets Ahead of the Hitter: 51%
Gets Behind the Hitter: 49%
Gets First Batter Out: 74%

1990 On Base Pct Allowed: .314 Slugging Percentage: .403
Stolen Bases Allowed: 9   Caught Stealing: 4

Pitches Right	AB	H	2B	3B	HR	RBI	BB	SO	AVG
Vs. RHB	219	52	7	1	7	25	17	35	.237
Vs. LHB	295	82	14	1	9	34	22	33	.278

	G	IP	W-L	Pct	SO	BB	ERA
1990 Season	35	135	7-6	.538	68	39	4.28
Life 8.5 Years	43	221	11-13	.468	108	68	3.98

●

Candy MALDONADO

CLEVELAND	LEFT FIELD	30 Years Old

Runs Created: 85   Offensive Winning Percentage: .555
Batting Average: .273   Secondary Average: .261

Most Often Bats: 4th
Hits First Pitch: 13%
Gets Ahead of the Pitcher: 49%
Hits Behind the Pitcher: 51%

1990 On Base Percentage: .330		Career: .312
1990 Slugging Percentage: .446		Career: .418

Batting Avg with Men in Scoring Position: .268

Bats Right-Handed	AB	R	H	2B	3B	HR	RBI	BB	SO	SB	AVG
Vs. RHP	415	49	103	25	2	12	61	33	102	1	.248
Vs. LHP	175	27	58	7	0	10	34	16	32	2	.331
At Home	78	298	35	80	11	0	12	48	19	73	1	.268
On the Road	77	292	41	81	21	2	10	47	30	61	2	.277
1990 Season	155	590	76	161	32	2	22	95	49	134	3	.273
Life	6.0 Years	471	56	120	26	2	15	71	37	89	4	.256

Dave MARTINEZ

MONTREAL   CENTER FIELD   26 Years Old

Runs Created: 49   Offensive Winning Percentage: .557
Batting Average: .279   Secondary Average: .238

Most Often Bats: 2nd
Hits First Pitch: 13%
Gets Ahead of the Pitcher: 57%
Hits Behind the Pitcher: 43%

1990 On Base Percentage: .321   Career: .325
1990 Slugging Percentage: .422   Career: .381
Batting Avg with Men in Scoring Position: .231

Bats Left-Handed	AB	R	H	2B	3B	HR	RBI	BB	SO	SB	AVG
Vs. RHP	317	50	91	13	4	10	28	13	33	10	.287
Vs. LHP	78	10	19	0	1	1	11	11	15	3	.244
At Home	62	204	33	56	7	0	5	18	11	27	10	.275
On the Road	57	191	27	54	6	5	6	21	13	21	3	.283
1990 Season	118	391	60	109	13	5	11	39	24	48	13	.279
Life 3.6 Years	496	66	132	17	8	8	44	43	89	22	.267

Edgar MARTINEZ

SEATTLE   THIRD BASE   28 Years Old

Runs Created: 85   Offensive Winning Percentage: .711
Batting Average: .302   Secondary Average: .285

Most Often Bats: 6th
Hits First Pitch: 6%
Gets Ahead of the Pitcher: 52%
Hits Behind the Pitcher: 48%

1990 On Base Percentage: .397   Career: .377
1990 Slugging Percentage: .433   Career: .411
Batting Avg with Men in Scoring Position: .244

Bats Right-Handed	AB	R	H	2B	3B	HR	RBI	BB	SO	SB	AVG
Vs. RHP	331	42	99	19	1	5	25	47	41	1	.299
Vs. LHP	156	29	48	8	1	6	24	27	21	0	.308
At Home	73	244	33	73	17	1	3	20	42	31	0	.299
On the Road	71	243	38	74	10	1	8	29	32	31	1	.305
1990 Season	144	487	71	147	27	2	11	49	74	62	1	.302
Life 1.5 Years	503	67	146	28	3	9	54	67	69	2	.291

Dennis MARTINEZ

MONTREAL   STARTING PITCHER   35 Years Old
10-11   2.95 ERA

Opponents Batting Average: .228
Offensive Support: 4.02 Runs Per Nine Innings
Double Play Support: .52 GDP Per Nine Innings

First Pitch is Hit: 15%
Gets Ahead of the Hitter: 54%
Gets Behind the Hitter: 46%
Gets Leadoff Man Out: 73%

1990 On Base Pct Allowed: .274 Slugging Percentage: .335
Stolen Bases Allowed: 19   Caught Stealing: 9

Pitches Right	AB	H	2B	3B	HR	RBI	BB	SO	AVG
Vs. RHB	340	78	11	4	7	30	21	65	.229
Vs. LHB	499	113	19	2	9	46	28	91	.226

	G	IP	W-L	Pct	SO	BB	ERA
At Home	18	135	6-10		84	26	3.41
On the Road	14	91	4-1		72	23	2.27
1990 Season	32	226	10-11	.476	156	49	2.95
Life 11.3 Years	41	239	14-12	.549	126	71	3.82

Ramon MARTINEZ

LOS ANGELES   STARTING PITCHER   23 Years Old
20-6   2.92 ERA

Opponents Batting Average: .221
Offensive Support: 5.42 Runs Per Nine Innings
Double Play Support: .42 GDP Per Nine Innings

First Pitch is Hit: 11%
Gets Ahead of the Hitter: 50%
Gets Behind the Hitter: 50%
Gets Leadoff Man Out: 72%

1990 On Base Pct Allowed: .278 Slugging Percentage: .357
Stolen Bases Allowed: 22   Caught Stealing: 13

Pitches Right	AB	H	2B	3B	HR	RBI	BB	SO	AVG
Vs. RHB	356	67	12	3	9	30	14	105	.188
Vs. LHB	509	124	26	4	13	55	53	118	.244

	G	IP	W-L	Pct	SO	BB	ERA
At Home	17	130	12-2		134	39	2.71
On the Road	16	105	8-4		89	28	3.18
1990 Season	33	234	20-6	.769	223	67	2.92
Life 1.5 Years	38	246	18-9	.675	223	87	3.08

Don MATTINGLY

NEW YORK	FIRST BASE	29 Years Old

Runs Created: 39   Offensive Winning Percentage: .395
Batting Average: .256   Secondary Average: .152

Most Often Bats: 3rd
Hits First Pitch: 8%
Gets Ahead of the Pitcher: 52%
Hits Behind the Pitcher: 48%

1990 On Base Percentage: .308   Career: .363
1990 Slugging Percentage: .335   Career: .504
Batting Avg with Men in Scoring Position: .289

Bats Left-Handed	AB	R	H	2B	3B	HR	RBI	BB	SO	SB	AVG
Vs. RHP	268	29	68	10	0	5	25	21	12	1	.254
Vs. LHP	126	11	33	6	0	0	17	7	8	0	.262
At Home	48	183	14	45	4	0	4	20	16	11	1	.246
On the Road	54	211	26	56	12	0	1	22	12	9	0	.265
1990 Season	102	394	40	101	16	0	5	42	28	20	1	.256
Life 6.9 Years	640	95	203	42	2	25	110	50	37	1	.317

•

Kirk McCASKILL

CALIFORNIA	STARTING PITCHER	30 Years Old
	12-11 3.25 ERA	

Opponents Batting Average: .244
Offensive Support: 4.54 Runs Per Nine Innings
Double Play Support: .98 GDP Per Nine Innings

First Pitch is Hit: 16%
Gets Ahead of the Hitter: 48%
Gets Behind the Hitter: 52%
Gets Leadoff Man Out: 69%

1990 On Base Pct Allowed: .320 Slugging Percentage: .332
Stolen Bases Allowed: 6   Caught Stealing: 10

Pitches Right	AB	H	2B	3B	HR	RBI	BB	SO	AVG
Vs. RHB	326	77	8	1	3	32	38	48	.236
Vs. LHB	334	84	11	5	6	35	34	30	.251

	G	IP	W-L	Pct	SO	BB	ERA
At Home	14	81	7-3		37	31	2.77
On the Road	15	93	5-8		41	41	3.68
1990 Season	29	174	12-11	.522	78	72	3.25
Life 4.3 Years	37	241	16-13	.553	148	88	3.80

Ben McDONALD

BALTIMORE	STARTING PITCHER	23 Years Old
	8-5 2.43 ERA	

Opponents Batting Average: .205
Offensive Support: 3.49 Runs Per Nine Innings
Double Play Support: .38 GDP Per Nine Innings

First Pitch is Hit: 15%
Gets Ahead of the Hitter: 50%
Gets Behind the Hitter: 50%
Gets Leadoff Man Out: 72%

1990 On Base Pct Allowed: .262 Slugging Percentage: .301
Stolen Bases Allowed: 10   Caught Stealing: 2

Pitches Right	AB	H	2B	3B	HR	RBI	BB	SO	AVG
Vs. RHB	213	49	8	0	7	23	18	27	.230
Vs. LHB	216	39	6	0	2	8	17	38	.181

	G	IP	W-L	Pct	SO	BB	ERA
At Home	13	75	4-3		43	18	2.41
On the Road	8	44	4-2		22	17	2.45
1990 Season	21	119	8-5	.615	65	35	2.43
Life 0.6 Years	48	222	16-9	.643	120	69	2.79

•

Jack McDOWELL

CHICAGO	STARTING PITCHER	25 Years Old
	14-9 3.82 ERA	

Opponents Batting Average: .244
Offensive Support: 5.22 Runs Per Nine Innings
Double Play Support: .53 GDP Per Nine Innings

First Pitch is Hit: 14%
Gets Ahead of the Hitter: 52%
Gets Behind the Hitter: 48%
Gets Leadoff Man Out: 74%

1990 On Base Pct Allowed: .316 Slugging Percentage: .380
Stolen Bases Allowed: 23   Caught Stealing: 11

Pitches Right	AB	H	2B	3B	HR	RBI	BB	SO	AVG
Vs. RHB	368	90	17	3	9	46	43	89	.245
Vs. LHB	408	99	15	4	11	37	34	76	.243

	G	IP	W-L	Pct	SO	BB	ERA
At Home	20	128	9-4		108	45	3.30
On the Road	13	77	5-5		57	32	4.70
1990 Season	33	205	14-9	.609	165	77	3.82
Life 1.7 Years	37	230	13-11	.537	155	89	3.75

Oddibe McDOWELL

ATLANTA   CENTER FIELD   28 Years Old

Runs Created: 34   Offensive Winning Percentage: .414
Batting Average: .243   Secondary Average: .226

Most Often Bats: 1st
Hits First Pitch: 14%
Gets Ahead of the Pitcher: 53%
Hits Behind the Pitcher: 47%

1990 On Base Percentage: .295   Career: .321
1990 Slugging Percentage: .357   Career: .401
Batting Avg with Men in Scoring Position: .340

Bats Left-Handed	AB	R	H	2B	3B	HR	RBI	BB	SO	SB	AVG
Vs. RHP	266	43	70	14	0	7	24	16	45	13	.263
Vs. LHP	39	4	4	0	0	0	1	5	8	0	.103
At Home	58	150	26	41	7	0	4	14	10	21	10	.273
On the Road	55	155	21	33	7	0	3	11	11	32	3	.213
1990 Season	113	305	47	74	14	0	7	25	21	53	13	.243
Life 4.8 Years	556	89	140	25	6	15	53	56	107	33	.252

•

Roger McDOWELL

PHILADELPHIA   RELIEF PITCHER   30 Years Old
6-8   3.86 ERA   22 SAVES

Blown Saves: 6   Holds: 1   Save Efficiency: 79%
Inherited Runners who Scored: 36%
Opponents Batting Average: .286
Double Play Support: 1.67 GDP Per Nine Innings

First Pitch is Hit: 16%
Gets Ahead of the Hitter: 50%
Gets Behind the Hitter: 50%
Gets First Batter Out: 69%

1990 On Base Pct Allowed: .355 Slugging Percentage: .363
Stolen Bases Allowed: 7   Caught Stealing: 2

Pitches Right	AB	H	2B	3B	HR	RBI	BB	SO	AVG
Vs. RHB	139	32	7	1	0	15	7	23	.230
Vs. LHB	183	60	8	1	2	35	28	16	.328

	G	IP	W-L	Pct	SO	BB	ERA
1990 Season	72	86	6-8	.429	39	35	3.86
Life 5.4 Years	74	114	8-7	.512	56	39	3.05

Andy McGAFFIGAN

KANSAS CITY   RELIEF PITCHER   34 Years Old
4-3   3.89 ERA   1 SAVES

Blown Saves: 0   Holds: 1   Save Efficiency: 100%
Inherited Runners who Scored: 57%
Opponents Batting Average: .262
Double Play Support: 1.08 GDP Per Nine Innings

First Pitch is Hit: 12%
Gets Ahead of the Hitter: 49%
Gets Behind the Hitter: 51%
Gets First Batter Out: 65%

1990 On Base Pct Allowed: .330 Slugging Percentage: .382
Stolen Bases Allowed: 14   Caught Stealing: 0

Pitches Right	AB	H	2B	3B	HR	RBI	BB	SO	AVG
Vs. RHB	156	40	5	1	2	15	14	29	.256
Vs. LHB	169	45	6	1	6	31	18	24	.266

	G	IP	W-L	Pct	SO	BB	ERA
1990 Season	28	83	4-3	.571	53	32	3.89
Life 5.7 Years	63	145	7-6	.535	107	51	3.37

•

Willie McGEE

OAKLAND   CENTER FIELD   32 Years Old

Runs Created: 97   Offensive Winning Percentage: .687
Batting Average: .324   Secondary Average: .223

Most Often Bats: 3rd
Hits First Pitch: 14%
Gets Ahead of the Pitcher: 43%
Hits Behind the Pitcher: 57%

1990 On Base Percentage: .373   Career: .332
1990 Slugging Percentage: .419   Career: .407
Batting Avg with Men in Scoring Position: .309

Switch Hitter	AB	R	H	2B	3B	HR	RBI	BB	SO	SB	AVG
Vs. RHP	389	70	126	24	4	1	50	38	61	24	.324
Vs. LHP	225	29	73	11	3	2	27	10	43	7	.324
At Home	82	328	53	110	18	4	1	47	24	45	20	.335
On the Road	72	286	46	89	17	3	2	30	24	59	11	.311
1990 Season	154	614	99	199	35	7	3	77	48	104	31	.324
Life 7.4 Years	638	88	189	28	11	7	76	34	97	38	.297

Fred McGRIFF

TORONTO   FIRST BASE   27 Years Old

Runs Created: 124   Offensive Winning Percentage: .778
Batting Average: .300   Secondary Average: .408

Most Often Bats: 5th
Hits First Pitch: 13%
Gets Ahead of the Pitcher: 56%
Hits Behind the Pitcher: 44%

1990 On Base Percentage: .400   Career: .389
1990 Slugging Percentage: .530   Career: .530
Batting Avg with Men in Scoring Position: .264

Bats Left-Handed	AB	R	H	2B	3B	HR	RBI	BB	SO	SB	AVG
Vs. RHP	355	65	115	16	0	27	58	73	60	5	.324
Vs. LHP	202	26	52	5	1	8	30	21	48	0	.257
At Home	77	264	42	73	10	0	14	38	55	37	1	.277
On the Road	76	293	49	94	11	1	21	50	39	71	4	.321
1990 Season	153	557	91	167	21	1	35	88	94	108	5	.300
Life 3.6 Years	545	98	151	28	2	35	85	99	139	6	.278

Kevin McREYNOLDS

NEW YORK   LEFT FIELD   31 Years Old

Runs Created: 88   Offensive Winning Percentage: .659
Batting Average: .269   Secondary Average: .340

Most Often Bats: 5th
Hits First Pitch: 10%
Gets Ahead of the Pitcher: 55%
Hits Behind the Pitcher: 45%

1990 On Base Percentage: .353   Career: .327
1990 Slugging Percentage: .455   Career: .458
Batting Avg with Men in Scoring Position: .295

Bats Right-Handed	AB	R	H	2B	3B	HR	RBI	BB	SO	SB	AVG
Vs. RHP	327	52	95	12	1	20	67	33	41	7	.291
Vs. LHP	194	23	45	11	0	4	15	38	20	2	.232
At Home	72	244	37	63	8	0	11	39	31	25	4	.258
On the Road	75	277	38	77	15	1	13	43	40	36	5	.278
1990 Season	147	521	75	140	23	1	24	82	71	61	9	.269
Life 6.7 Years	595	82	161	29	4	25	92	52	78	11	.270

Mark McGWIRE

OAKLAND   FIRST BASE   27 Years Old

Runs Created: 101   Offensive Winning Percentage: .718
Batting Average: .235   Secondary Average: .468

Most Often Bats: 4th
Hits First Pitch: 14%
Gets Ahead of the Pitcher: 50%
Hits Behind the Pitcher: 50%

1990 On Base Percentage: .370   Career: .356
1990 Slugging Percentage: .489   Career: .512
Batting Avg with Men in Scoring Position: .248

Bats Right-Handed	AB	R	H	2B	3B	HR	RBI	BB	SO	SB	AVG
Vs. RHP	391	61	89	13	0	28	70	81	97	2	.228
Vs. LHP	132	26	34	3	0	11	38	29	19	0	.258
At Home	76	245	34	55	8	0	14	37	54	61	1	.224
On the Road	80	278	53	68	8	0	25	71	56	55	1	.245
1990 Season	156	523	87	123	16	0	39	108	110	116	2	.235
Life 3.8 Years	565	92	143	22	1	41	112	89	124	1	.253

Bob MELVIN

BALTIMORE   CATCHER   29 Years Old

Runs Created: 26   Offensive Winning Percentage: .315
Batting Average: .243   Secondary Average: .140

Most Often Bats: 7th
Hits First Pitch: 14%
Gets Ahead of the Pitcher: 48%
Hits Behind the Pitcher: 52%

1990 On Base Percentage: .267   Career: .264
1990 Slugging Percentage: .346   Career: .343
Batting Avg with Men in Scoring Position: .276

Bats Right-Handed	AB	R	H	2B	3B	HR	RBI	BB	SO	SB	AVG
Vs. RHP	149	14	31	3	1	2	21	5	35	0	.208
Vs. LHP	152	16	42	11	0	3	16	6	18	0	.276
At Home	40	121	9	21	3	1	3	13	3	28	0	.174
On the Road	53	180	21	52	11	0	2	24	8	25	0	.289
1990 Season	93	301	30	73	14	1	5	37	11	53	0	.243
Life 3.0 Years	485	47	111	21	2	10	52	25	96	1	.229

Bob MILACKI

BALTIMORE   STARTING PITCHER   26 Years Old
5-8   4.46 ERA

Opponents Batting Average: .273
Offensive Support: 4.26 Runs Per Nine Innings
Double Play Support: .86 GDP Per Nine Innings

First Pitch is Hit: 13%
Gets Ahead of the Hitter: 44%
Gets Behind the Hitter: 56%
Gets Leadoff Man Out: 66%

1990 On Base Pct Allowed: .346 Slugging Percentage: .434
Stolen Bases Allowed: 19   Caught Stealing: 3

Pitches Right	AB	H	2B	3B	HR	RBI	BB	SO	AVG
Vs. RHB	262	71	13	0	12	41	26	29	.271
Vs. LHB	261	72	17	0	6	26	35	31	.276

	G	IP	W-L	Pct	SO	BB	ERA
At Home	12	49	1-3		23	24	5.29
On the Road	15	86	4-5		37	37	3.98
1990 Season	27	135	5-8	.385	60	61	4.46
Life 1.8 Years	38	230	12-11	.512	109	90	3.79

John MITCHELL

BALTIMORE   STARTING PITCHER   25 Years Old
6-6   4.64 ERA

Opponents Batting Average: .300
Offensive Support: 5.27 Runs Per Nine Innings
Double Play Support: 1.18 GDP Per Nine Innings

First Pitch is Hit: 17%
Gets Ahead of the Hitter: 43%
Gets Behind the Hitter: 57%
Gets Leadoff Man Out: 64%

1990 On Base Pct Allowed: .366 Slugging Percentage: .423
Stolen Bases Allowed: 1   Caught Stealing: 2

Pitches Right	AB	H	2B	3B	HR	RBI	BB	SO	AVG
Vs. RHB	242	69	18	0	3	33	19	27	.285
Vs. LHB	202	64	16	0	4	23	29	16	.317

	G	IP	W-L	Pct	SO	BB	ERA
At Home	10	50	2-2		17	26	4.47
On the Road	14	64	4-4		26	22	4.78
1990 Season	24	114	6-6	.500	43	48	4.64
Life 1.2 Years	43	202	8-12	.391	90	78	4.35

•

Randy MILLIGAN

BALTIMORE   FIRST BASE   29 Years Old

Runs Created: 77   Offensive Winning Percentage: .751
Batting Average: .265   Secondary Average: .486

Most Often Bats: 3rd
Hits First Pitch: 8%
Gets Ahead of the Pitcher: 51%
Hits Behind the Pitcher: 49%

1990 On Base Percentage: .408   Career: .399
1990 Slugging Percentage: .492   Career: .465
Batting Avg with Men in Scoring Position: .253

Bats Right-Handed		AB	R	H	2B	3B	HR	RBI	BB	SO	SB	AVG
Vs. RHP		262	45	63	11	0	12	38	60	54	6	.240
Vs. LHP		100	19	33	9	1	8	22	28	14	0	.330
At Home	53	166	32	44	10	1	11	31	45	33	4	.265
On the Road	56	196	32	52	10	0	9	29	43	35	2	.265
1990 Season	109	362	64	96	20	1	20	60	88	68	6	.265
Life 1.7 Years	475	76	124	28	4	21	66	107	99	9	.262

Kevin MITCHELL

SAN FRANCISCO   LEFT FIELD   29 Years Old

Runs Created: 101   Offensive Winning Percentage: .711
Batting Average: .290   Secondary Average: .372

Most Often Bats: 4th
Hits First Pitch: 16%
Gets Ahead of the Pitcher: 47%
Hits Behind the Pitcher: 53%

1990 On Base Percentage: .360   Career: .353
1990 Slugging Percentage: .544   Career: .517
Batting Avg with Men in Scoring Position: .221

Bats Right-Handed		AB	R	H	2B	3B	HR	RBI	BB	SO	SB	AVG
Vs. RHP		354	65	100	13	2	25	64	31	63	3	.282
Vs. LHP		170	25	52	11	0	10	29	27	24	1	.306
At Home	66	241	46	67	10	1	15	39	31	36	2	.278
On the Road	74	283	44	85	14	1	20	54	27	51	2	.300
1990 Season	140	524	90	152	24	2	35	93	58	87	4	.290
Life 4.2 Years	560	87	156	29	4	32	97	65	103	6	.278

Paul MOLITOR

MILWAUKEE	SECOND BASE	34 Years Old

Runs Created: 68   Offensive Winning Percentage: .625
Batting Average: .285   Secondary Average: .311

Most Often Bats: 1st
Hits First Pitch: 16%
Gets Ahead of the Pitcher: 56%
Hits Behind the Pitcher: 44%

1990 On Base Percentage: .343   Career: .361
1990 Slugging Percentage: .464   Career: .437
Batting Avg with Men in Scoring Position: .313

Bats Right-Handed	AB	R	H	2B	3B	HR	RBI	BB	SO	SB	AVG
Vs. RHP	306	44	84	18	4	7	31	28	35	14	.275
Vs. LHP	112	20	35	9	2	5	14	9	16	4	.313
At Home	48	185	27	53	14	1	6	19	17	20	10	.286
On the Road	55	233	37	66	13	5	6	26	20	31	8	.283
1990 Season	103	418	64	119	27	6	12	45	37	51	18	.285
Life 9.5 Years	657	111	197	35	7	14	66	64	79	38	.299

•

Jeff MONTGOMERY

KANSAS CITY	RELIEF PITCHER	29 Years Old
	6-5 2.39 ERA 24 SAVES	

Blown Saves: 10   Holds: 7   Save Efficiency: 76%
Inherited Runners who Scored: 39%
Opponents Batting Average: .228
Double Play Support: .19 GDP Per Nine Innings

First Pitch is Hit: 14%
Gets Ahead of the Hitter: 48%
Gets Behind the Hitter: 52%
Gets First Batter Out: 74%

1990 On Base Pct Allowed: .302 Slugging Percentage: .331
Stolen Bases Allowed: 14   Caught Stealing: 3

Pitches Right	AB	H	2B	3B	HR	RBI	BB	SO	AVG
Vs. RHB	179	32	7	0	2	20	13	67	.179
Vs. LHB	176	49	10	1	4	22	21	27	.278

	G	IP	W-L	Pct	SO	BB	ERA
1990 Season	73	94	6-5	.545	94	34	2.39
Life 2.6 Years	74	101	8-5	.647	94	37	2.58

Mike MOORE

OAKLAND	STARTING PITCHER	31 Years Old
	13-15 4.65 ERA	

Opponents Batting Average: .267
Offensive Support: 4.20 Runs Per Nine Innings
Double Play Support: 1.04 GDP Per Nine Innings

First Pitch is Hit: 15%
Gets Ahead of the Hitter: 43%
Gets Behind the Hitter: 57%
Gets Leadoff Man Out: 67%

1990 On Base Pct Allowed: .339 Slugging Percentage: .397
Stolen Bases Allowed: 17   Caught Stealing: 6

Pitches Right	AB	H	2B	3B	HR	RBI	BB	SO	AVG
Vs. RHB	360	99	18	4	9	43	37	39	.275
Vs. LHB	404	105	23	4	5	53	47	34	.260

	G	IP	W-L	Pct	SO	BB	ERA
At Home	20	120	7-10		43	47	4.66
On the Road	13	80	6-5		30	37	4.63
1990 Season	33	199	13-15	.464	73	84	4.65
Life 7.8 Years	38	242	13-16	.445	151	90	4.18

•

Mike MORGAN

LOS ANGELES	STARTING PITCHER	31 Years Old
	11-15 3.75 ERA	

Opponents Batting Average: .266
Offensive Support: 4.05 Runs Per Nine Innings
Double Play Support: .81 GDP Per Nine Innings

First Pitch is Hit: 18%
Gets Ahead of the Hitter: 47%
Gets Behind the Hitter: 53%
Gets Leadoff Man Out: 70%

1990 On Base Pct Allowed: .319 Slugging Percentage: .392
Stolen Bases Allowed: 16   Caught Stealing: 13

Pitches Right	AB	H	2B	3B	HR	RBI	BB	SO	AVG
Vs. RHB	356	86	8	3	10	40	26	53	.242
Vs. LHB	455	130	29	1	9	46	34	53	.286

	G	IP	W-L	Pct	SO	BB	ERA
At Home	16	105	5-6		56	24	3.77
On the Road	17	106	6-9		50	36	3.74
1990 Season	33	211	11-15	.423	106	60	3.75
Life 5.4 Years	42	212	10-17	.361	96	75	4.37

Hal MORRIS

CINCINNATI   FIRST BASE   26 Years Old

Runs Created: 55   Offensive Winning Percentage: .737
Batting Average: .340   Secondary Average: .256

Most Often Bats: 5th
Hits First Pitch: 18%
Gets Ahead of the Pitcher: 53%
Hits Behind the Pitcher: 47%

1990 On Base Percentage: .381   Career: .363
1990 Slugging Percentage: .498   Career: .464
Batting Avg with Men in Scoring Position: .337

Bats Left-Handed	AB	R	H	2B	3B	HR	RBI	BB	SO	SB	AVG
Vs. RHP	233	40	88	22	3	7	31	15	19	8	.378
Vs. LHP	76	10	17	0	0	0	5	6	13	1	.224

		AB	R	H	2B	3B	HR	RBI	BB	SO	SB	AVG
At Home	57	148	19	50	12	1	3	20	12	13	3	.338
On the Road	50	161	31	55	10	2	4	16	9	19	6	.342
1990 Season	107	309	50	105	22	3	7	36	21	32	9	.340
Life	0.8 Years	410	63	132	26	4	8	47	26	53	11	.323

•

Jack MORRIS

DETROIT   STARTING PITCHER   35 Years Old
15-18   4.51 ERA

Opponents Batting Average: .242
Offensive Support: 5.23 Runs Per Nine Innings
Double Play Support: .83 GDP Per Nine Innings

First Pitch is Hit: 15%
Gets Ahead of the Hitter: 53%
Gets Behind the Hitter: 47%
Gets Leadoff Man Out: 66%

1990 On Base Pct Allowed: .313 Slugging Percentage: .375
Stolen Bases Allowed: 45   Caught Stealing: 6

Pitches Right	AB	H	2B	3B	HR	RBI	BB	SO	AVG
Vs. RHB	487	106	23	2	13	64	39	92	.218
Vs. LHB	466	125	19	1	13	60	58	70	.268

	G	IP	W-L	Pct	SO	BB	ERA
At Home	16	113	8-8		71	30	4.06
On the Road	20	137	7-10		91	67	4.87
1990 Season	36	250	15-18	.455	162	97	4.51
Life 11.3 Years	38	269	17-13	.569	175	96	3.73

Lloyd MOSEBY

DETROIT   CENTER FIELD   31 Years Old

Runs Created: 57   Offensive Winning Percentage: .478
Batting Average: .248   Secondary Average: .309

Most Often Bats: 5th
Hits First Pitch: 11%
Gets Ahead of the Pitcher: 55%
Hits Behind the Pitcher: 45%

1990 On Base Percentage: .329   Career: .332
1990 Slugging Percentage: .406   Career: .415
Batting Avg with Men in Scoring Position: .202

Bats Left-Handed	AB	R	H	2B	3B	HR	RBI	BB	SO	SB	AVG
Vs. RHP	299	52	83	14	5	12	42	38	51	14	.278
Vs. LHP	132	12	24	2	0	2	9	10	26	3	.182

		AB	R	H	2B	3B	HR	RBI	BB	SO	SB	AVG
At Home	65	221	38	53	4	3	8	25	31	39	11	.240
On the Road	57	210	26	54	12	2	6	26	17	38	6	.257
1990 Season	122	431	64	107	16	5	14	51	48	77	17	.248
Life	9.3 Years	594	89	153	28	7	17	75	64	117	29	.257

•

Jamie MOYER

TEXAS   RELIEF PITCHER   28 Years Old
2-6   4.66 ERA   0 SAVES

Blown Saves: 0   Holds: 1   Save Efficiency: 100%
Inherited Runners who Scored: 26%
Opponents Batting Average: .290
Double Play Support: 1.32 GDP Per Nine Innings

First Pitch is Hit: 14%
Gets Ahead of the Hitter: 49%
Gets Behind the Hitter: 51%
Gets First Batter Out: 61%

1990 On Base Pct Allowed: .354 Slugging Percentage: .434
Stolen Bases Allowed: 9   Caught Stealing: 7

Pitches Left	AB	H	2B	3B	HR	RBI	BB	SO	AVG
Vs. RHB	315	97	29	2	5	39	35	49	.308
Vs. LHB	81	18	4	1	1	12	4	9	.222

	G	IP	W-L	Pct	SO	BB	ERA
1990 Season	33	102	2-6	.250	58	39	4.66
Life 3.2 Years	42	209	11-15	.410	130	83	4.51

Terry MULHOLLAND

PHILADELPHIA   STARTING PITCHER   28 Years Old
9-10   3.34 ERA

Opponents Batting Average: .252
Offensive Support: 4.33 Runs Per Nine Innings
Double Play Support: .80 GDP Per Nine Innings

First Pitch is Hit: 19%
Gets Ahead of the Hitter: 49%
Gets Behind the Hitter: 51%
Gets Leadoff Man Out: 65%

1990 On Base Pct Allowed: .292 Slugging Percentage: .388
Stolen Bases Allowed: 3   Caught Stealing: 3

Pitches Left	AB	H	2B	3B	HR	RBI	BB	SO	AVG
Vs. RHB	582	144	37	4	13	61	39	62	.247
Vs. LHB	101	28	3	0	2	12	3	13	.277

	G	IP	W-L	Pct	SO	BB	ERA
At Home	12	71	3-4		33	13	2.66
On the Road	21	110	6-6		42	29	3.78
1990 Season	33	181	9-10	.474	75	42	3.34
Life 1.9 Years	43	207	8-13	.390	97	63	4.06

•

Dale MURPHY

PHILADELPHIA   RIGHT FIELD   35 Years Old

Runs Created: 71   Offensive Winning Percentage: .496
Batting Average: .245   Secondary Average: .297

Most Often Bats: 5th
Hits First Pitch: 16%
Gets Ahead of the Pitcher: 50%
Hits Behind the Pitcher: 50%

1990 On Base Percentage: .318   Career: .351
1990 Slugging Percentage: .417   Career: .476
Batting Avg with Men in Scoring Position: .292

Bats Right-Handed	AB	R	H	2B	3B	HR	RBI	BB	SO	SB	AVG
Vs. RHP	383	34	82	12	0	10	45	30	108	8	.214
Vs. LHP	180	26	56	11	1	14	38	31	22	1	.311
At Home	77	279	28	64	9	1	9	27	31	66	4	.229
On the Road	77	284	32	74	14	0	15	56	30	64	5	.261
1990 Season	154	563	60	138	23	1	24	83	61	130	9	.245
Life 12.2 Years	597	92	160	26	3	31	96	76	133	13	.268

Eddie MURRAY

LOS ANGELES   FIRST BASE   35 Years Old

Runs Created: 117   Offensive Winning Percentage: .766
Batting Average: .330   Secondary Average: .351

Most Often Bats: 4th
Hits First Pitch: 17%
Gets Ahead of the Pitcher: 51%
Hits Behind the Pitcher: 49%

1990 On Base Percentage: .414   Career: .372
1990 Slugging Percentage: .520   Career: .494
Batting Avg with Men in Scoring Position: .327

Switch Hitter	AB	R	H	2B	3B	HR	RBI	BB	SO	SB	AVG
Vs. RHP	352	68	119	15	3	18	59	57	42	3	.338
Vs. LHP	206	28	65	7	0	8	36	25	22	5	.316
At Home	79	271	47	93	11	1	12	43	49	28	7	.343
On the Road	76	287	49	91	11	2	14	52	33	36	1	.317
1990 Season	155	558	96	184	22	3	26	95	82	64	8	.330
Life 13.2 Years	607	92	178	31	2	29	104	78	82	6	.294

•

Randy MYERS

CINCINNATI   RELIEF PITCHER   28 Years Old
4-6   2.08 ERA   31 SAVES

Blown Saves: 6   Holds: 0   Save Efficiency: 84%
Inherited Runners who Scored: 9%
Opponents Batting Average: .193
Double Play Support: .42 GDP Per Nine Innings

First Pitch is Hit: 8%
Gets Ahead of the Hitter: 53%
Gets Behind the Hitter: 47%
Gets First Batter Out: 77%

1990 On Base Pct Allowed: .287 Slugging Percentage: .281
Stolen Bases Allowed: 2   Caught Stealing: 4

Pitches Left	AB	H	2B	3B	HR	RBI	BB	SO	AVG
Vs. RHB	234	46	7	1	4	21	26	66	.197
Vs. LHB	72	13	0	0	2	5	12	32	.181

	G	IP	W-L	Pct	SO	BB	ERA
1990 Season	66	87	4-6	.400	98	38	2.08
Life 3.4 Years	74	96	6-6	.525	107	40	2.56

•N•

Jaime NAVARRO

MILWAUKEE STARTING PITCHER 24 Years Old
8-7 4.46 ERA

Opponents Batting Average: .293
Offensive Support: 5.42 Runs Per Nine Innings
Double Play Support: .84 GDP Per Nine Innings

First Pitch is Hit: 14%
Gets Ahead of the Hitter: 48%
Gets Behind the Hitter: 52%
Gets Leadoff Man Out: 70%

1990 On Base Pct Allowed: .340 Slugging Percentage: .403
Stolen Bases Allowed: 11 Caught Stealing: 4

Pitches Right	AB	H	2B	3B	HR	RBI	BB	SO	AVG
Vs. RHB	279	80	13	4	7	32	16	38	.287
Vs. LHB	321	96	12	0	4	33	25	37	.299

	G	IP	W-L	Pct	SO	BB	ERA
At Home	16	73	4-4		33	26	4.09
On the Road	16	77	4-3		42	15	4.81
1990 Season	32	149	8-7	.533	75	41	4.46
Life 1.2 Years	42	213	12-12	.500	108	60	3.89

•

Jim NEIDLINGER

LOS ANGELES STARTING PITCHER 26 Years Old
5-3 3.28 ERA

Opponents Batting Average: .241
Offensive Support: 5.59 Runs Per Nine Innings
Double Play Support: .85 GDP Per Nine Innings

First Pitch is Hit: 14%
Gets Ahead of the Hitter: 50%
Gets Behind the Hitter: 50%
Gets Leadoff Man Out: 74%

1990 On Base Pct Allowed: .279 Slugging Percentage: .309
Stolen Bases Allowed: 3 Caught Stealing: 2

Pitches Right	AB	H	2B	3B	HR	RBI	BB	SO	AVG
Vs. RHB	112	20	2	0	3	11	4	25	.179
Vs. LHB	166	47	3	1	1	14	11	21	.283

	G	IP	W-L	Pct	SO	BB	ERA
At Home	5	30	2-1		20	5	3.34
On the Road	7	44	3-2		26	10	3.25
1990 Season	12	74	5-3	.625	46	15	3.28
Life 0.3 Years	37	228	15-9	.625	142	46	3.28

Gene NELSON

OAKLAND RELIEF PITCHER 30 Years Old
3-3 1.57 ERA 5 SAVES

Blown Saves: 3 Holds: 18 Save Efficiency: 88%
Inherited Runners who Scored: 25%
Opponents Batting Average: .208
Double Play Support: 1.21 GDP Per Nine Innings

First Pitch is Hit: 18%
Gets Ahead of the Hitter: 50%
Gets Behind the Hitter: 50%
Gets First Batter Out: 74%

1990 On Base Pct Allowed: .259 Slugging Percentage: .306
Stolen Bases Allowed: 1 Caught Stealing: 2

Pitches Right	AB	H	2B	3B	HR	RBI	BB	SO	AVG
Vs. RHB	155	29	7	0	3	11	12	21	.187
Vs. LHB	110	26	4	0	2	8	5	17	.236

	G	IP	W-L	Pct	SO	BB	ERA
1990 Season	51	75	3-3	.500	38	17	1.57
Life 5.9 Years	63	156	8-9	.480	98	59	3.93

•

Al NEWMAN

MINNESOTA SECOND BASE 30 Years Old

Runs Created: 35 Offensive Winning Percentage: .318
Batting Average: .242 Secondary Average: .155

Most Often Bats: 2nd
Hits First Pitch: 23%
Gets Ahead of the Pitcher: 57%
Hits Behind the Pitcher: 43%

1990 On Base Percentage: .304 Career: .309
1990 Slugging Percentage: .278 Career: .279
Batting Avg with Men in Scoring Position: .218

Switch Hitter	AB	R	H	2B	3B	HR	RBI	BB	SO	SB	AVG
Vs. RHP	265	28	63	8	0	0	24	18	20	11	.238
Vs. LHP	123	15	31	6	0	0	6	15	14	2	.252
At Home	72	199	27	52	8	0	0	19	23	13	8	.261
On the Road	72	189	16	42	6	0	0	11	10	21	5	.222
1990 Season 144	388	43	94	14	0	0	30	33	34	13	.242
Life 3.8 Years	422	56	98	15	2	0	33	47	43	20	.232

Matt NOKES

NEW YORK	CATCHER	27 Years Old

Runs Created: 38   Offensive Winning Percentage: .437
Batting Average: .248   Secondary Average: .199

Most Often Bats: 6th
Hits First Pitch: 17%
Gets Ahead of the Pitcher: 56%
Hits Behind the Pitcher: 44%

1990 On Base Percentage: .306   Career: .316
1990 Slugging Percentage: .373   Career: .439
Batting Avg with Men in Scoring Position: .300

Bats Left-Handed	AB	R	H	2B	3B	HR	RBI	BB	SO	SB	AVG
Vs. RHP	337	32	85	9	1	11	38	24	42	2	.252
Vs. LHP	14	1	2	0	0	0	2	0	5	0	.143
At Home	64	157	13	40	3	0	4	20	12	13	1	.255
On the Road	72	194	20	47	6	1	7	20	12	34	1	.242
1990 Season	136	351	33	87	9	1	11	40	24	47	2	.248
Life 3.1 Years	493	56	129	17	1	23	72	36	71	2	.261

•

Edwin NUNEZ

DETROIT	RELIEF PITCHER	27 Years Old
	3-1 2.24 ERA 6 SAVES	

Blown Saves: 1   Holds: 6   Save Efficiency: 92%
Inherited Runners who Scored: 24%
Opponents Batting Average: .218
Double Play Support: .90 GDP Per Nine Innings

First Pitch is Hit: 13%
Gets Ahead of the Hitter: 53%
Gets Behind the Hitter: 47%
Gets First Batter Out: 69%

1990 On Base Pct Allowed: .308 Slugging Percentage: .309
Stolen Bases Allowed: 5   Caught Stealing: 2

Pitches Right	AB	H	2B	3B	HR	RBI	BB	SO	AVG
Vs. RHB	188	42	9	0	2	18	20	37	.223
Vs. LHB	110	23	6	0	2	10	17	29	.209

	G	IP	W-L	Pct	SO	BB	ERA
1990 Season	42	80	3-1	.750	66	37	2.24
Life 4.0 Years	71	118	5-6	.458	90	51	3.83

•O•

Pete O'BRIEN

SEATTLE	FIRST BASE	33 Years Old

Runs Created: 36   Offensive Winning Percentage: .385
Batting Average: .224   Secondary Average: .210

Most Often Bats: 5th
Hits First Pitch: 16%
Gets Ahead of the Pitcher: 56%
Hits Behind the Pitcher: 44%

1990 On Base Percentage: .308   Career: .345
1990 Slugging Percentage: .314   Career: .414
Batting Avg with Men in Scoring Position: .156

Bats Left-Handed	AB	R	H	2B	3B	HR	RBI	BB	SO	SB	AVG
Vs. RHP	236	22	56	16	0	4	15	28	20	0	.237
Vs. LHP	130	10	26	2	0	1	12	16	13	0	.200
At Home	52	172	17	45	10	0	3	14	26	13	0	.262
On the Road	56	194	15	37	8	0	2	13	18	20	0	.191
1990 Season	108	366	32	82	18	0	5	27	44	33	0	.224
Life 7.5 Years	572	70	153	27	2	18	76	71	61	3	.267

•

Bobby OJEDA

NEW YORK	RELIEF PITCHER	33 Years Old
	7-6 3.66 ERA 0 SAVES	

Blown Saves: 2   Holds: 3   Save Efficiency: 60%
Inherited Runners who Scored: 20%
Opponents Batting Average: .272
Double Play Support: .84 GDP Per Nine Innings

First Pitch is Hit: 16%
Gets Ahead of the Hitter: 48%
Gets Behind the Hitter: 52%
Gets First Batter Out: 62%

1990 On Base Pct Allowed: .332 Slugging Percentage: .414
Stolen Bases Allowed: 14   Caught Stealing: 11

Pitches Left	AB	H	2B	3B	HR	RBI	BB	SO	AVG
Vs. RHB	339	104	21	3	9	42	33	42	.307
Vs. LHB	113	19	5	1	1	7	7	20	.168

	G	IP	W-L	Pct	SO	BB	ERA
1990 Season	38	118	7-6	.538	62	40	3.66
Life 6.8 Years	41	219	14-12	.546	130	73	3.65

John OLERUD

TORONTO   DESIGNATED HITTER   22 Years Old

Runs Created: 59   Offensive Winning Percentage: .633
Batting Average: .265   Secondary Average: .324

Most Often Bats: 6th
Hits First Pitch: 10%
Gets Ahead of the Pitcher: 48%
Hits Behind the Pitcher: 52%

1990 On Base Percentage: .364   Career: .364
1990 Slugging Percentage: .430   Career: .429
Batting Avg with Men in Scoring Position: .294

Bats Left-Handed		AB	R	H	2B	3B	HR	RBI	BB	SO	SB	AVG
Vs. RHP		285	33	70	10	1	11	33	42	57	0	.246
Vs. LHP		73	10	25	5	0	3	15	15	18	0	.342
At Home	58	187	25	51	7	1	11	26	29	43	0	.273
On the Road	53	171	18	44	8	0	3	22	28	32	0	.257
1990 Season	111	358	43	95	15	1	14	48	57	75	0	.265
Life 0.7 Years		507	62	136	21	1	19	66	79	105	0	.268

Joe OLIVER

CINCINNATI   CATCHER   25 Years Old

Runs Created: 40   Offensive Winning Percentage: .461
Batting Average: .231   Secondary Average: .234

Most Often Bats: 8th
Hits First Pitch: 22%
Gets Ahead of the Pitcher: 43%
Hits Behind the Pitcher: 57%

1990 On Base Percentage: .304   Career: .303
1990 Slugging Percentage: .360   Career: .367
Batting Avg with Men in Scoring Position: .274

Bats Right-Handed		AB	R	H	2B	3B	HR	RBI	BB	SO	SB	AVG
Vs. RHP		184	16	33	10	0	3	24	19	41	1	.179
Vs. LHP		180	18	51	13	0	5	28	18	34	0	.283
At Home	60	172	18	38	13	0	3	25	20	38	0	.221
On the Road	61	192	16	46	10	0	5	27	17	37	1	.240
1990 Season	121	364	34	84	23	0	8	52	37	75	1	.231
Life 1.0 Years		491	45	119	30	0	10	71	41	98	1	.243

Steve OLIN

CLEVELAND   RELIEF PITCHER   25 Years Old
4-4   3.41 ERA   1 SAVES

Blown Saves: 2   Holds: 4   Save Efficiency: 71%
Inherited Runners who Scored: 37%
Opponents Batting Average: .270
Double Play Support: 1.27 GDP Per Nine Innings

First Pitch is Hit: 14%
Gets Ahead of the Hitter: 48%
Gets Behind the Hitter: 52%
Gets First Batter Out: 71%

1990 On Base Pct Allowed: .329 Slugging Percentage: .338
Stolen Bases Allowed: 9   Caught Stealing: 3

Pitches Right	AB	H	2B	3B	HR	RBI	BB	SO	AVG
Vs. RHB	215	54	6	1	2	36	15	45	.251
Vs. LHB	140	42	7	0	1	15	11	19	.300

	G	IP	W-L	Pct	SO	BB	ERA
1990 Season	50	92	4-4	.500	64	26	3.41
Life 1.0 Years	73	125	5-8	.385	86	39	3.51

Greg OLSON

ATLANTA   CATCHER   30 Years Old

Runs Created: 37   Offensive Winning Percentage: .466
Batting Average: .262   Secondary Average: .221

Most Often Bats: 8th
Hits First Pitch: 14%
Gets Ahead of the Pitcher: 52%
Hits Behind the Pitcher: 48%

1990 On Base Percentage: .332   Career: .333
1990 Slugging Percentage: .379   Career: .380
Batting Avg with Men in Scoring Position: .216

Bats Right-Handed		AB	R	H	2B	3B	HR	RBI	BB	SO	SB	AVG
Vs. RHP		144	15	30	3	0	2	11	15	25	1	.208
Vs. LHP		154	21	48	9	1	5	25	15	26	0	.312
At Home	50	151	17	43	6	1	4	21	12	20	1	.285
On the Road	50	147	19	35	6	0	3	15	18	31	0	.238
1990 Season	100	298	36	78	12	1	7	36	30	51	1	.262
Life 0.6 Years		472	57	124	19	2	11	57	47	80	2	.263

Gregg OLSON

BALTIMORE	RELIEF PITCHER	24 Years Old
	6-5 2.42 ERA 37 SAVES	

Blown Saves: 5   Holds: 0   Save Efficiency: 88%
Inherited Runners who Scored: 27%
Opponents Batting Average: .213
Double Play Support: .73 GDP Per Nine Innings

First Pitch is Hit: 10%
Gets Ahead of the Hitter: 54%
Gets Behind the Hitter: 46%
Gets First Batter Out: 69%

1990 On Base Pct Allowed: .299 Slugging Percentage: .276
Stolen Bases Allowed: 11   Caught Stealing: 2

Pitches Right	AB	H	2B	3B	HR	RBI	BB	SO	AVG
Vs. RHB	123	28	4	0	2	14	12	40	.228
Vs. LHB	145	29	4	0	1	13	19	34	.200

	G	IP	W-L	Pct	SO	BB	ERA
1990 Season	64	74	6-5	.545	74	31	2.42
Life 1.9 Years	74	91	6-4	.600	93	47	2.11

•

Paul O'NEILL

CINCINNATI	RIGHT FIELD	28 Years Old

Runs Created: 69   Offensive Winning Percentage: .586
Batting Average: .270   Secondary Average: .282

Most Often Bats: 5th
Hits First Pitch: 12%
Gets Ahead of the Pitcher: 55%
Hits Behind the Pitcher: 45%

1990 On Base Percentage: .339   Career: .330
1990 Slugging Percentage: .421   Career: .432
Batting Avg with Men in Scoring Position: .292

Bats Left-Handed	AB	R	H	2B	3B	HR	RBI	BB	SO	SB	AVG
Vs. RHP	360	45	99	16	0	13	53	42	58	13	.275
Vs. LHP	143	14	37	12	0	3	25	11	45	0	.259
At Home	70	241	33	70	10	0	10	36	25	48	4	.290
On the Road	75	262	26	66	18	0	6	42	28	55	9	.252
1990 Season	145	503	59	136	28	0	16	78	53	103	13	.270
Life 3.1 Years	516	62	137	30	2	18	82	51	86	14	.265

Jose OQUENDO

ST. LOUIS	SECOND BASE	27 Years Old

Runs Created: 57   Offensive Winning Percentage: .519
Batting Average: .252   Secondary Average: .224

Most Often Bats: 8th
Hits First Pitch: 13%
Gets Ahead of the Pitcher: 54%
Hits Behind the Pitcher: 46%

1990 On Base Percentage: .350   Career: .346
1990 Slugging Percentage: .316   Career: .324
Batting Avg with Men in Scoring Position: .263

Switch Hitter		AB	R	H	2B	3B	HR	RBI	BB	SO	SB	AVG
Vs. RHP		305	29	82	13	3	0	30	50	33	1	.269
Vs. LHP		164	9	36	4	2	1	7	24	13	0	.220
At Home	79	238	20	57	8	1	1	17	33	21	1	.239
On the Road	77	231	18	61	9	4	0	20	41	25	0	.264
1990 Season	156	469	38	118	17	5	1	37	74	46	1	.252
Life 5.3 Years	448	47	118	15	3	2	37	58	53	6	.264

•

Jesse OROSCO

CLEVELAND	RELIEF PITCHER	33 Years Old
	5-4 3.90 ERA 2 SAVES	

Blown Saves: 1   Holds: 2   Save Efficiency: 80%
Inherited Runners who Scored: 26%
Opponents Batting Average: .239
Double Play Support: .70 GDP Per Nine Innings

First Pitch is Hit: 13%
Gets Ahead of the Hitter: 51%
Gets Behind the Hitter: 49%
Gets First Batter Out: 70%

1990 On Base Pct Allowed: .338 Slugging Percentage: .407
Stolen Bases Allowed: 3   Caught Stealing: 1

Pitches Left	AB	H	2B	3B	HR	RBI	BB	SO	AVG
Vs. RHB	176	43	7	2	7	26	26	39	.244
Vs. LHB	67	15	3	0	2	12	12	16	.224

	G	IP	W-L	Pct	SO	BB	ERA
1990 Season	55	65	5-4	.556	55	38	3.90
Life 7.5 Years	73	105	8-8	.504	91	45	2.76

Joe ORSULAK

BALTIMORE RIGHT FIELD 28 Years Old

Runs Created: 55 Offensive Winning Percentage: .544
Batting Average: .269 Secondary Average: .254

Most Often Bats: 2nd
Hits First Pitch: 12%
Gets Ahead of the Pitcher: 49%
Hits Behind the Pitcher: 51%

1990 On Base Percentage: .343 Career: .331
1990 Slugging Percentage: .397 Career: .386
Batting Avg with Men in Scoring Position: .300

Bats Left-Handed	AB	R	H	2B	3B	HR	RBI	BB	SO	SB	AVG
Vs. RHP	341	43	93	14	2	11	50	38	40	6	.273
Vs. LHP	72	6	18	0	1	0	7	8	8	0	.250
At Home	63	202	26	55	5	1	9	34	23	28	3	.272
On the Road	61	211	23	56	9	2	2	23	23	20	3	.265
1990 Season	124	413	49	111	14	3	11	57	46	48	6	.269
Life 4.1 Years	498	68	138	22	6	7	44	40	45	17	.276

Spike OWEN

MONTREAL SHORTSTOP 29 Years Old

Runs Created: 55 Offensive Winning Percentage: .519
Batting Average: .234 Secondary Average: .280

Most Often Bats: 8th
Hits First Pitch: 8%
Gets Ahead of the Pitcher: 56%
Hits Behind the Pitcher: 44%

1990 On Base Percentage: .333 Career: .318
1990 Slugging Percentage: .342 Career: .332
Batting Avg with Men in Scoring Position: .170

Switch Hitter	AB	R	H	2B	3B	HR	RBI	BB	SO	SB	AVG
Vs. RHP	252	29	54	8	3	2	18	47	35	5	.214
Vs. LHP	201	26	52	16	2	3	17	23	25	3	.259
At Home	74	215	24	49	11	3	2	16	34	25	4	.228
On the Road	75	238	31	57	13	2	3	19	36	35	4	.239
1990 Season	149	453	55	106	24	5	5	35	70	60	8	.234
Life 6.3 Years	526	65	126	22	7	5	46	61	57	10	.239

•P•

Mike PAGLIARULO

SAN DIEGO THIRD BASE 31 Years Old

Runs Created: 47 Offensive Winning Percentage: .477
Batting Average: .254 Secondary Average: .221

Most Often Bats: 7th
Hits First Pitch: 19%
Gets Ahead of the Pitcher: 48%
Hits Behind the Pitcher: 52%

1990 On Base Percentage: .322 Career: .302
1990 Slugging Percentage: .374 Career: .413
Batting Avg with Men in Scoring Position: .223

Bats Left-Handed	AB	R	H	2B	3B	HR	RBI	BB	SO	SB	AVG
Vs. RHP	297	19	76	20	2	3	25	24	45	1	.256
Vs. LHP	101	10	25	3	0	4	13	15	21	0	.248
At Home	60	169	13	46	10	1	1	14	19	31	1	.272
On the Road	68	229	16	55	13	1	6	24	20	35	0	.240
1990 Season	128	398	29	101	23	2	7	38	39	66	1	.254
Life 5.4 Years	519	61	120	26	3	21	72	51	113	2	.231

Donn PALL

CHICAGO RELIEF PITCHER 29 Years Old
3-5 3.32 ERA 2 SAVES

Blown Saves: 1 Holds: 13 Save Efficiency: 94%
Inherited Runners who Scored: 32%
Opponents Batting Average: .232
Double Play Support: 1.54 GDP Per Nine Innings

First Pitch is Hit: 16%
Gets Ahead of the Hitter: 48%
Gets Behind the Hitter: 52%
Gets First Batter Out: 69%

1990 On Base Pct Allowed: .301 Slugging Percentage: .379
Stolen Bases Allowed: 7 Caught Stealing: 3

Pitches Right	AB	H	2B	3B	HR	RBI	BB	SO	AVG
Vs. RHB	157	31	5	1	6	19	12	22	.197
Vs. LHB	115	32	6	3	1	17	12	17	.278

	G	IP	W-L	Pct	SO	BB	ERA
1990 Season	56	76	3-5	.375	39	24	3.32
Life 1.7 Years	74	113	4-7	.368	66	30	3.33

Rafael PALMEIRO

TEXAS   FIRST BASE   26 Years Old

Runs Created: 94   Offensive Winning Percentage: .647
Batting Average: .319   Secondary Average: .221

Most Often Bats: 3rd
Hits First Pitch: 14%
Gets Ahead of the Pitcher: 53%
Hits Behind the Pitcher: 47%

1990 On Base Percentage: .361   Career: .351
1990 Slugging Percentage: .468   Career: .440
Batting Avg with Men in Scoring Position: .324

Bats Left-Handed	AB	R	H	2B	3B	HR	RBI	BB	SO	SB	AVG
Vs. RHP	409	46	127	26	5	9	57	32	42	2	.311
Vs. LHP	189	26	64	9	1	5	32	8	17	1	.339

		AB	R	H	2B	3B	HR	RBI	BB	SO	SB	AVG
At Home	78	295	38	85	19	5	9	46	30	31	1	.288
On the Road	76	303	34	106	16	1	5	43	10	28	2	.350

		AB	R	H	2B	3B	HR	RBI	BB	SO	SB	AVG
1990 Season	154	598	72	191	35	6	14	89	40	59	3	.319
Life	3.5 Years	579	75	172	34	5	13	71	47	49	6	.296

•

Dave PARKER

MILWAUKEE   DESIGNATED HITTER   39 Years Old

Runs Created: 86   Offensive Winning Percentage: .532
Batting Average: .289   Secondary Average: .236

Most Often Bats: 4th
Hits First Pitch: 22%
Gets Ahead of the Pitcher: 46%
Hits Behind the Pitcher: 54%

1990 On Base Percentage: .330   Career: .342
1990 Slugging Percentage: .451   Career: .477
Batting Avg with Men in Scoring Position: .261

Bats Left-Handed	AB	R	H	2B	3B	HR	RBI	BB	SO	SB	AVG
Vs. RHP	425	54	128	24	3	15	68	36	67	3	.301
Vs. LHP	185	17	48	6	0	6	24	5	35	1	.259

		AB	R	H	2B	3B	HR	RBI	BB	SO	SB	AVG
At Home	77	293	33	80	16	1	9	46	20	58	1	.273
On the Road	80	317	38	96	14	2	12	46	21	44	3	.303

		AB	R	H	2B	3B	HR	RBI	BB	SO	SB	AVG
1990 Season	157	610	71	176	30	3	21	92	41	102	4	.289
Life	14.4 Years	615	85	180	35	5	23	100	45	100	10	.293

Jeff PARRETT

ATLANTA   RELIEF PITCHER   29 Years Old
5-10   4.64 ERA   2 SAVES

Blown Saves: 6   Holds: 11   Save Efficiency: 68%
Inherited Runners who Scored: 41%
Opponents Batting Average: .290
Double Play Support: .83 GDP Per Nine Innings

First Pitch is Hit: 12%
Gets Ahead of the Hitter: 46%
Gets Behind the Hitter: 54%
Gets First Batter Out: 66%

1990 On Base Pct Allowed: .373 Slugging Percentage: .441
Stolen Bases Allowed: 8   Caught Stealing: 7

Pitches Right	AB	H	2B	3B	HR	RBI	BB	SO	AVG
Vs. RHB	203	62	9	2	4	29	16	50	.305
Vs. LHB	207	57	8	4	7	31	39	36	.275

	G	IP	W-L	Pct	SO	BB	ERA
1990 Season	67	109	5-10	.333	86	55	4.64
Life 3.5 Years	73	110	10-8	.571	91	53	3.66

•

Lance PARRISH

CALIFORNIA   CATCHER   34 Years Old

Runs Created: 70   Offensive Winning Percentage: .597
Batting Average: .268   Secondary Average: .285

Most Often Bats: 7th
Hits First Pitch: 14%
Gets Ahead of the Pitcher: 50%
Hits Behind the Pitcher: 50%

1990 On Base Percentage: .338   Career: .316
1990 Slugging Percentage: .451   Career: .450
Batting Avg with Men in Scoring Position: .252

Bats Right-Handed	AB	R	H	2B	3B	HR	RBI	BB	SO	SB	AVG
Vs. RHP	345	34	88	12	0	17	53	33	80	1	.255
Vs. LHP	125	20	38	2	0	7	17	13	27	1	.304

		AB	R	H	2B	3B	HR	RBI	BB	SO	SB	AVG
At Home	66	235	26	65	7	0	14	39	23	55	0	.277
On the Road	67	235	28	61	7	0	10	31	23	52	2	.260

		AB	R	H	2B	3B	HR	RBI	BB	SO	SB	AVG
1990 Season	133	470	54	126	14	0	24	70	46	107	2	.268
Life	10.2 Years	593	75	152	26	3	28	93	50	123	2	.257

Dan PASQUA

CHICAGO   DESIGNATED HITTER   29 Years Old

Runs Created: 57   Offensive Winning Percentage: .707
Batting Average: .274   Secondary Average: .338

Most Often Bats: 4th
Hits First Pitch: 8%
Gets Ahead of the Pitcher: 54%
Hits Behind the Pitcher: 46%

1990 On Base Percentage: .347   Career: .332
1990 Slugging Percentage: .495   Career: .452
Batting Avg with Men in Scoring Position: .283

Bats Left-Handed	AB	R	H	2B	3B	HR	RBI	BB	SO	SB	AVG
Vs. RHP	294	40	83	24	3	13	54	35	58	1	.282
Vs. LHP	31	3	6	3	0	0	4	2	8	0	.194
At Home	54	157	24	50	15	3	4	29	19	28	1	.318
On the Road	58	168	19	39	12	0	9	29	18	38	0	.232
1990 Season	112	325	43	89	27	3	13	58	37	66	1	.274
Life 3.6 Years	478	61	119	22	2	24	73	58	121	1	.249

•

Bob PATTERSON

PITTSBURGH   RELIEF PITCHER   31 Years Old
8-5   2.95 ERA   5 SAVES

Blown Saves: 3   Holds: 8   Save Efficiency: 81%
Inherited Runners who Scored: 31%
Opponents Batting Average: .249
Double Play Support: .76 GDP Per Nine Innings

First Pitch is Hit: 17%
Gets Ahead of the Hitter: 54%
Gets Behind the Hitter: 46%
Gets First Batter Out: 69%

1990 On Base Pct Allowed: .294 Slugging Percentage: .373
Stolen Bases Allowed: 5   Caught Stealing: 4

Pitches Left	AB	H	2B	3B	HR	RBI	BB	SO	AVG
Vs. RHB	251	67	13	0	8	28	15	41	.267
Vs. LHB	103	21	2	1	1	8	6	29	.204

	G	IP	W-L	Pct	SO	BB	ERA
1990 Season	55	95	8-5	.615	70	21	2.95
Life 1.6 Years	61	131	10-10	.500	88	38	4.66

Alejandro PENA

NEW YORK   RELIEF PITCHER   31 Years Old
3-3   3.20 ERA   5 SAVES

Blown Saves: 0   Holds: 6   Save Efficiency: 100%
Inherited Runners who Scored: 33%
Opponents Batting Average: .245
Double Play Support: .36 GDP Per Nine Innings

First Pitch is Hit: 18%
Gets Ahead of the Hitter: 55%
Gets Behind the Hitter: 45%
Gets First Batter Out: 71%

1990 On Base Pct Allowed: .295 Slugging Percentage: .338
Stolen Bases Allowed: 11   Caught Stealing: 0

Pitches Right	AB	H	2B	3B	HR	RBI	BB	SO	AVG
Vs. RHB	159	38	7	1	3	17	8	37	.239
Vs. LHB	131	33	4	1	1	16	14	39	.252

	G	IP	W-L	Pct	SO	BB	ERA
1990 Season	52	76	3-3	.500	76	22	3.20
Life 5.5 Years	61	154	7-7	.500	118	49	2.95

•

Tony PENA

BOSTON   CATCHER   33 Years Old

Runs Created: 50   Offensive Winning Percentage: .399
Batting Average: .263   Secondary Average: .189

Most Often Bats: 8th
Hits First Pitch: 14%
Gets Ahead of the Pitcher: 53%
Hits Behind the Pitcher: 47%

1990 On Base Percentage: .322   Career: .320
1990 Slugging Percentage: .348   Career: .385
Batting Avg with Men in Scoring Position: .299

Bats Right-Handed	AB	R	H	2B	3B	HR	RBI	BB	SO	SB	AVG
Vs. RHP	336	41	84	15	1	2	34	31	57	6	.250
Vs. LHP	155	21	45	4	0	5	22	12	14	2	.290
At Home	74	247	33	68	9	0	3	30	27	41	5	.275
On the Road	69	244	29	61	10	1	4	26	16	30	3	.250
1990 Season	143	491	62	129	19	1	7	56	43	71	8	.263
Life 8.3 Years	561	60	153	25	3	11	63	39	71	8	.273

Terry PENDLETON

ST. LOUIS   THIRD BASE   30 Years Old

Runs Created: 38   Offensive Winning Percentage: .329
Batting Average: .230   Secondary Average: .177

Most Often Bats: 5th
Hits First Pitch: 16%
Gets Ahead of the Pitcher: 45%
Hits Behind the Pitcher: 55%

1990 On Base Percentage: .277   Career: .308
1990 Slugging Percentage: .324   Career: .356
Batting Avg with Men in Scoring Position: .231

Switch Hitter		AB	R	H	2B	3B	HR	RBI	BB	SO	SB	AVG
Vs. RHP		289	34	70	8	2	2	35	24	43	5	.242
Vs. LHP		158	12	33	12	0	4	23	6	15	2	.209
At Home	67	251	32	61	13	1	6	32	17	31	2	.243
On the Road	54	196	14	42	7	1	0	26	13	27	5	.214
1990 Season	121	447	46	103	20	2	6	58	30	58	7	.230
Life	5.7 Years	600	71	155	27	4	8	77	44	75	17	.259

Gerald PERRY

KANSAS CITY   DESIGNATED HITTER   30 Years Old

Runs Created: 52   Offensive Winning Percentage: .427
Batting Average: .254   Secondary Average: .228

Most Often Bats: 3rd
Hits First Pitch: 12%
Gets Ahead of the Pitcher: 47%
Hits Behind the Pitcher: 53%

1990 On Base Percentage: .313   Career: .333
1990 Slugging Percentage: .361   Career: .374
Batting Avg with Men in Scoring Position: .258

Bats Left-Handed		AB	R	H	2B	3B	HR	RBI	BB	SO	SB	AVG
Vs. RHP		331	45	90	17	2	7	43	32	37	10	.272
Vs. LHP		134	12	28	5	0	1	14	7	19	7	.209
At Home	68	238	29	68	15	1	3	30	17	28	5	.286
On the Road	65	227	28	50	7	1	5	27	22	28	12	.220
1990 Season	133	465	57	118	22	2	8	57	39	56	17	.254
Life	4.8 Years	523	63	140	25	1	9	63	53	56	25	.267

Melido PEREZ

CHICAGO   STARTING PITCHER   25 Years Old
13-14   4.61 ERA

Opponents Batting Average: .241
Offensive Support: 4.75 Runs Per Nine Innings
Double Play Support: .91 GDP Per Nine Innings

First Pitch is Hit: 13%
Gets Ahead of the Hitter: 46%
Gets Behind the Hitter: 54%
Gets Leadoff Man Out: 64%

1990 On Base Pct Allowed: .320 Slugging Percentage: .367
Stolen Bases Allowed: 12   Caught Stealing: 11

Pitches Right	AB	H	2B	3B	HR	RBI	BB	SO	AVG
Vs. RHB	355	82	16	3	8	36	44	80	.231
Vs. LHB	380	95	15	7	6	47	42	81	.250

	G	IP	W-L	Pct	SO	BB	ERA
At Home	15	81	5-6		62	32	5.11
On the Road	20	116	8-8		99	54	4.27
1990 Season	35	197	13-14	.481	161	86	4.61
Life 2.7 Years	37	215	14-14	.487	163	93	4.52

Adam PETERSON

CHICAGO   STARTING PITCHER   25 Years Old
2-5   4.55 ERA

Opponents Batting Average: .278
Offensive Support: 4.87 Runs Per Nine Innings
Double Play Support: .95 GDP Per Nine Innings

First Pitch is Hit: 15%
Gets Ahead of the Hitter: 49%
Gets Behind the Hitter: 51%
Gets Leadoff Man Out: 61%

1990 On Base Pct Allowed: .332 Slugging Percentage: .451
Stolen Bases Allowed: 2   Caught Stealing: 5

Pitches Right	AB	H	2B	3B	HR	RBI	BB	SO	AVG
Vs. RHB	177	38	3	2	6	19	20	24	.215
Vs. LHB	147	52	7	3	6	21	6	5	.354

	G	IP	W-L	Pct	SO	BB	ERA
At Home	8	34	1-0		10	16	3.48
On the Road	12	51	1-5		19	10	5.26
1990 Season	20	85	2-5	.286	29	26	4.55
Life 0.6 Years	46	177	4-12	.222	67	65	6.01

Geno PETRALLI

TEXAS	CATCHER	31 Years Old

Runs Created: 36   Offensive Winning Percentage: .439
Batting Average: .255   Secondary Average: .200

Most Often Bats: 7th
Hits First Pitch: 17%
Gets Ahead of the Pitcher: 51%
Hits Behind the Pitcher: 49%

1990 On Base Percentage: .357   Career: .354
1990 Slugging Percentage: .302   Career: .379
Batting Avg with Men in Scoring Position: .230

Bats Left-Handed		AB	R	H	2B	3B	HR	RBI	BB	SO	SB	AVG
Vs. RHP		305	24	77	13	1	0	18	42	48	0	.252
Vs. LHP		20	4	6	0	0	0	3	8	1	0	.300
At Home	69	170	16	45	7	0	0	11	28	31	0	.265
On the Road	64	155	12	38	6	1	0	10	22	18	0	.245
1990 Season	133	325	28	83	13	1	0	21	50	49	0	.255
Life	3.5 Years	384	39	107	17	2	6	40	44	53	1	.279

●

Dan PETRY

DETROIT	STARTING PITCHER	32 Years Old
	10-9 4.45 ERA	

Opponents Batting Average: .263
Offensive Support: 4.39 Runs Per Nine Innings
Double Play Support: .78 GDP Per Nine Innings

First Pitch is Hit: 15%
Gets Ahead of the Hitter: 46%
Gets Behind the Hitter: 54%
Gets Leadoff Man Out: 63%

1990 On Base Pct Allowed: .349 Slugging Percentage: .403
Stolen Bases Allowed: 13   Caught Stealing: 6

Pitches Right	AB	H	2B	3B	HR	RBI	BB	SO	AVG
Vs. RHB	318	87	15	3	11	41	40	41	.274
Vs. LHB	245	61	16	0	3	24	37	32	.249

	G	IP	W-L	Pct	SO	BB	ERA
At Home	16	62	4-5		28	37	5.49
On the Road	16	87	6-4		45	40	3.71
1990 Season	32	150	10-9	.526	73	77	4.45
Life 8.4 Years	39	235	15-12	.549	121	96	3.89

Gary PETTIS

TEXAS	CENTER FIELD	33 Years Old

Runs Created: 52   Offensive Winning Percentage: .467
Batting Average: .239   Secondary Average: .322

Most Often Bats: 1st
Hits First Pitch: 11%
Gets Ahead of the Pitcher: 48%
Hits Behind the Pitcher: 52%

1990 On Base Percentage: .333   Career: .332
1990 Slugging Percentage: .336   Career: .314
Batting Avg with Men in Scoring Position: .221

Switch Hitter		AB	R	H	2B	3B	HR	RBI	BB	SO	SB	AVG
Vs. RHP		271	41	68	10	5	3	24	34	80	23	.251
Vs. LHP		152	25	33	6	3	0	7	23	38	15	.217
At Home	71	221	34	56	7	4	3	21	30	59	19	.253
On the Road	65	202	32	45	9	4	0	10	27	59	19	.223
1990 Season	136	423	66	101	16	8	3	31	57	118	38	.239
Life	6.0 Years	534	84	128	16	7	3	38	73	138	52	.239

●

Tony PHILLIPS

DETROIT	THIRD BASE	32 Years Old

Runs Created: 81   Offensive Winning Percentage: .512
Batting Average: .251   Secondary Average: .305

Most Often Bats: 1st
Hits First Pitch: 13%
Gets Ahead of the Pitcher: 52%
Hits Behind the Pitcher: 48%

1990 On Base Percentage: .364   Career: .343
1990 Slugging Percentage: .351   Career: .350
Batting Avg with Men in Scoring Position: .283

Switch Hitter		AB	R	H	2B	3B	HR	RBI	BB	SO	SB	AVG
Vs. RHP		371	69	94	12	3	6	36	72	63	16	.253
Vs. LHP		202	28	50	11	2	2	19	27	22	3	.248
At Home	79	286	46	69	7	2	4	23	50	53	7	.241
On the Road	73	287	51	75	16	3	4	32	49	32	12	.261
1990 Season	152	573	97	144	23	5	8	55	99	85	19	.251
Life	6.1 Years	519	74	130	21	5	7	52	72	94	12	.251

Jeff PICO

CHICAGO   RELIEF PITCHER   25 Years Old
              4-4   4.79 ERA   2 SAVES

Blown Saves: 1   Holds: 0   Save Efficiency: 67%
Inherited Runners who Scored: 48%
Opponents Batting Average: .321
Double Play Support: 1.08 GDP Per Nine Innings

First Pitch is Hit: 13%
Gets Ahead of the Hitter: 43%
Gets Behind the Hitter: 57%
Gets First Batter Out: 57%

1990 On Base Pct Allowed: .382 Slugging Percentage: .455
Stolen Bases Allowed: 0   Caught Stealing: 4

Pitches Right	AB	H	2B	3B	HR	RBI	BB	SO	AVG
Vs. RHB	176	46	8	3	4	30	12	24	.261
Vs. LHB	198	74	11	2	3	28	25	13	.374

	G	IP	W-L	Pct	SO	BB	ERA
1990 Season	31	92	4-4	.500	37	37	4.79
Life 1.9 Years	60	157	7-6	.520	70	56	4.24

•

Dan PLESAC

MILWAUKEE   RELIEF PITCHER   29 Years Old
              3-7   4.43 ERA   24 SAVES

Blown Saves: 10   Holds: 2   Save Efficiency: 72%
Inherited Runners who Scored: 31%
Opponents Batting Average: .257
Double Play Support: 1.04 GDP Per Nine Innings

First Pitch is Hit: 14%
Gets Ahead of the Hitter: 53%
Gets Behind the Hitter: 47%
Gets First Batter Out: 67%

1990 On Base Pct Allowed: .340 Slugging Percentage: .372
Stolen Bases Allowed: 8   Caught Stealing: 1

Pitches Left	AB	H	2B	3B	HR	RBI	BB	SO	AVG
Vs. RHB	199	57	11	0	5	34	25	47	.286
Vs. LHB	62	10	2	1	0	13	6	18	.161

	G	IP	W-L	Pct	SO	BB	ERA
1990 Season	66	69	3-7	.300	65	31	4.43
Life 3.7 Years	74	95	6-7	.458	89	30	2.98

Eric PLUNK

NEW YORK   RELIEF PITCHER   27 Years Old
              6-3   2.72 ERA   0 SAVES

Blown Saves: 1   Holds: 3   Save Efficiency: 75%
Inherited Runners who Scored: 38%
Opponents Batting Average: .225
Double Play Support: .50 GDP Per Nine Innings

First Pitch is Hit: 12%
Gets Ahead of the Hitter: 47%
Gets Behind the Hitter: 53%
Gets First Batter Out: 61%

1990 On Base Pct Allowed: .340 Slugging Percentage: .341
Stolen Bases Allowed: 4   Caught Stealing: 8

Pitches Right	AB	H	2B	3B	HR	RBI	BB	SO	AVG
Vs. RHB	167	32	6	0	5	27	26	42	.192
Vs. LHB	91	26	0	3	1	9	17	25	.286

	G	IP	W-L	Pct	SO	BB	ERA
1990 Season	47	73	6-3	.667	67	43	2.72
Life 3.2 Years	64	147	9-7	.547	131	97	3.96

•

Luis POLONIA

CALIFORNIA   LEFT FIELD   26 Years Old

Runs Created: 59   Offensive Winning Percentage: .608
Batting Average: .335   Secondary Average: .191

Most Often Bats: 1st
Hits First Pitch: 13%
Gets Ahead of the Pitcher: 48%
Hits Behind the Pitcher: 52%

1990 On Base Percentage: .372   Career: .346
1990 Slugging Percentage: .412   Career: .395
Batting Avg with Men in Scoring Position: .325

Bats Left-Handed		AB	R	H	2B	3B	HR	RBI	BB	SO	SB	AVG
Vs. RHP		352	41	120	7	7	2	32	21	32	18	.341
Vs. LHP		51	11	15	0	2	0	3	4	11	3	.294
At Home	60	207	23	73	2	4	2	23	8	23	5	.353
On the Road	60	196	29	62	5	5	0	12	17	20	16	.316
1990 Season	120	403	52	135	7	9	2	35	25	43	21	.335
Life 2.8 Years		556	90	169	18	10	4	56	37	68	34	.304

Mark PORTUGAL

HOUSTON	STARTING PITCHER	28 Years Old
	11-10 3.62 ERA	

Opponents Batting Average: .250
Offensive Support: 3.48 Runs Per Nine Innings
Double Play Support: .73 GDP Per Nine Innings

First Pitch is Hit: 13%
Gets Ahead of the Hitter: 49%
Gets Behind the Hitter: 51%
Gets Leadoff Man Out: 65%

1990 On Base Pct Allowed: .313 Slugging Percentage: .375
Stolen Bases Allowed: 23   Caught Stealing: 9

Pitches Right	AB	H	2B	3B	HR	RBI	BB	SO	AVG
Vs. RHB	322	92	16	0	11	39	23	48	.286
Vs. LHB	425	95	12	1	10	41	44	88	.224

	G	IP	W-L	Pct	SO	BB	ERA
At Home	15	101	8-2		74	31	1.78
On the Road	17	95	3-8		62	36	5.57
1990 Season	32	197	11-10	.524	136	67	3.62
Life 2.7 Years	47	204	11-11	.492	135	79	4.11

•

Jim PRESLEY

ATLANTA	THIRD BASE	29 Years Old

Runs Created: 62   Offensive Winning Percentage: .419
Batting Average: .242   Secondary Average: .227

Most Often Bats: 4th
Hits First Pitch: 15%
Gets Ahead of the Pitcher: 45%
Hits Behind the Pitcher: 55%

1990 On Base Percentage: .282   Career: .292
1990 Slugging Percentage: .414   Career: .424
Batting Avg with Men in Scoring Position: .215

Bats Right-Handed	AB	R	H	2B	3B	HR	RBI	BB	SO	SB	AVG
Vs. RHP	361	39	83	19	1	13	44	13	92	1	.230
Vs. LHP	180	20	48	15	0	6	28	16	38	0	.267
At Home	75	288	33	75	18	0	10	38	16	64	1	.260
On the Road	65	253	26	56	16	1	9	34	13	66	0	.221
1990 Season 140	541	59	131	34	1	19	72	29	130	1	.242
Life 5.8 Years	602	71	150	31	2	23	85	36	145	2	.249

Kirby PUCKETT

MINNESOTA	CENTER FIELD	30 Years Old

Runs Created: 88   Offensive Winning Percentage: .643
Batting Average: .298   Secondary Average: .261

Most Often Bats: 3rd
Hits First Pitch: 23%
Gets Ahead of the Pitcher: 50%
Hits Behind the Pitcher: 50%

1990 On Base Percentage: .365   Career: .358
1990 Slugging Percentage: .446   Career: .466
Batting Avg with Men in Scoring Position: .341

Bats Right-Handed	AB	R	H	2B	3B	HR	RBI	BB	SO	SB	AVG
Vs. RHP	387	63	115	29	2	8	58	35	52	3	.297
Vs. LHP	164	19	49	11	1	4	22	22	21	2	.299
At Home	73	273	44	94	24	1	6	47	27	40	2	.344
On the Road	73	278	38	70	16	2	6	33	30	33	3	.252
1990 Season 146	551	82	164	40	3	12	80	57	73	5	.298
Life 6.6 Years	665	94	213	36	6	16	89	37	85	13	.320

•Q•

Carlos QUINTANA

BOSTON	FIRST BASE	25 Years Old

Runs Created: 67   Offensive Winning Percentage: .548
Batting Average: .287   Secondary Average: .199

Most Often Bats: 2nd
Hits First Pitch: 17%
Gets Ahead of the Pitcher: 49%
Hits Behind the Pitcher: 51%

1990 On Base Percentage: .354   Career: .345
1990 Slugging Percentage: .383   Career: .368
Batting Avg with Men in Scoring Position: .310

Bats Right-Handed		AB	R	H	2B	3B	HR	RBI	BB	SO	SB	AVG
Vs. RHP		330	31	83	16	0	4	40	36	50	1	.252
Vs. LHP		182	25	64	12	0	3	27	16	24	0	.352
At Home	74	251	30	75	11	0	3	31	26	36	0	.299
On the Road	75	261	26	72	17	0	4	36	26	38	1	.276
1990 Season	149	512	56	147	28	0	7	67	52	74	1	.287
Life	1.2 Years	513	54	142	28	0	6	65	53	77	1	.277

•R•

Tim RAINES

MONTREAL	LEFT FIELD	31 Years Old

Runs Created: 75   Offensive Winning Percentage: .678
Batting Average: .287   Secondary Average: .365

Most Often Bats: 3rd
Hits First Pitch: 16%
Gets Ahead of the Pitcher: 59%
Hits Behind the Pitcher: 41%

1990 On Base Percentage: .379   Career: .390
1990 Slugging Percentage: .392   Career: .438
Batting Avg with Men in Scoring Position: .312

Switch Hitter		AB	R	H	2B	3B	HR	RBI	BB	SO	SB	AVG
Vs. RHP		277	41	79	11	3	6	35	49	30	31	.285
Vs. LHP		180	24	52	0	2	3	27	21	13	18	.289
At Home	59	202	32	62	6	2	6	28	28	18	30	.307
On the Road	71	255	33	69	5	3	3	34	42	25	19	.271
1990 Season	130	457	65	131	11	5	9	62	70	43	49	.287
Life	8.7 Years	612	108	184	31	9	11	64	89	65	73	.301

•

Rafael RAMIREZ

HOUSTON	SHORTSTOP	32 Years Old

Runs Created: 43   Offensive Winning Percentage: .426
Batting Average: .261   Secondary Average: .146

Most Often Bats: 8th
Hits First Pitch: 11%
Gets Ahead of the Pitcher: 46%
Hits Behind the Pitcher: 54%

1990 On Base Percentage: .299   Career: .297
1990 Slugging Percentage: .330   Career: .345
Batting Avg with Men in Scoring Position: .311

Bats Right-Handed		AB	R	H	2B	3B	HR	RBI	BB	SO	SB	AVG
Vs. RHP		253	22	66	10	2	1	22	11	29	6	.261
Vs. LHP		192	22	50	9	1	1	15	13	17	4	.260
At Home	64	206	19	55	8	3	1	20	16	21	7	.267
On the Road	68	239	25	61	11	0	1	17	8	25	3	.255
1990 Season	132	445	44	116	19	3	2	37	24	46	10	.261
Life	8.4 Years	603	63	158	25	4	6	54	29	66	13	.262

Willie RANDOLPH

OAKLAND   SECOND BASE   36 Years Old

Runs Created: 44   Offensive Winning Percentage: .470
Batting Average: .260   Secondary Average: .198

Most Often Bats: 2nd
Hits First Pitch: 16%
Gets Ahead of the Pitcher: 59%
Hits Behind the Pitcher: 41%

1990 On Base Percentage: .339   Career: .371
1990 Slugging Percentage: .325   Career: .351
Batting Avg with Men in Scoring Position: .252

Bats Right-Handed		AB	R	H	2B	3B	HR	RBI	BB	SO	SB	AVG
Vs. RHP		272	31	60	5	2	2	18	35	29	6	.221
Vs. LHP		116	21	41	8	1	0	12	10	5	1	.353
At Home	54	164	23	41	5	1	1	11	18	12	6	.250
On the Road	65	224	29	60	8	2	1	19	27	22	1	.268
1990 Season	119	388	52	101	13	3	2	30	45	34	7	.260
Life 12.3 Years		595	94	163	24	5	4	50	92	49	22	.274

Johnny RAY

CALIFORNIA   SECOND BASE   34 Years Old

Runs Created: 44   Offensive Winning Percentage: .436
Batting Average: .277   Secondary Average: .146

Most Often Bats: 2nd
Hits First Pitch: 14%
Gets Ahead of the Pitcher: 51%
Hits Behind the Pitcher: 49%

1990 On Base Percentage: .308   Career: .333
1990 Slugging Percentage: .371   Career: .391
Batting Avg with Men in Scoring Position: .287

Switch Hitter		AB	R	H	2B	3B	HR	RBI	BB	SO	SB	AVG
Vs. RHP		284	38	76	18	0	5	28	16	30	2	.268
Vs. LHP		120	9	36	5	0	0	15	3	14	0	.300
At Home	57	210	27	57	9	0	5	21	10	19	0	.271
On the Road	48	194	20	55	14	0	0	22	9	25	2	.284
1990 Season	105	404	47	112	23	0	5	43	19	44	2	.277
Life 8.4 Years		621	72	180	35	4	6	71	42	39	10	.290

Dennis RASMUSSEN

SAN DIEGO   STARTING PITCHER   31 Years Old
                   11-15   4.51 ERA

Opponents Batting Average: .292
Offensive Support: 5.66 Runs Per Nine Innings
Double Play Support: .62 GDP Per Nine Innings

First Pitch is Hit: 16%
Gets Ahead of the Hitter: 47%
Gets Behind the Hitter: 53%
Gets Leadoff Man Out: 65%

1990 On Base Pct Allowed: .348 Slugging Percentage: .451
Stolen Bases Allowed: 21   Caught Stealing: 16

Pitches Left	AB	H	2B	3B	HR	RBI	BB	SO	AVG
Vs. RHB	634	181	25	1	23	77	55	74	.285
Vs. LHB	108	36	5	1	5	17	7	12	.333

	G	IP	W-L	Pct	SO	BB	ERA
At Home	17	101	5-9		45	31	4.37
On the Road	15	87	6-6		41	31	4.67
1990 Season	32	188	11-15	.423	86	62	4.51
Life 5.5 Years	38	222	14-11	.571	132	80	4.13

Gary REDUS

PITTSBURGH   FIRST BASE   34 Years Old

Runs Created: 36   Offensive Winning Percentage: .616
Batting Average: .247   Secondary Average: .366

Most Often Bats: 1st
Hits First Pitch: 13%
Gets Ahead of the Pitcher: 59%
Hits Behind the Pitcher: 41%

1990 On Base Percentage: .341   Career: .344
1990 Slugging Percentage: .419   Career: .411
Batting Avg with Men in Scoring Position: .235

Bats Right-Handed		AB	R	H	2B	3B	HR	RBI	BB	SO	SB	AVG
Vs. RHP		25	6	3	0	0	0	0	6	9	2	.120
Vs. LHP		202	26	53	15	3	6	23	27	29	9	.262
At Home	54	108	20	22	7	1	2	12	21	15	6	.204
On the Road	42	119	12	34	8	2	4	11	12	23	5	.286
1990 Season	96	227	32	56	15	3	6	23	33	38	11	.247
Life 5.5 Years		515	89	129	27	8	13	52	74	106	53	.249

Jody REED

BOSTON   SECOND BASE   28 Years Old

Runs Created: 87   Offensive Winning Percentage: .592
Batting Average: .289   Secondary Average: .232

Most Often Bats: 2nd
Hits First Pitch: 8%
Gets Ahead of the Pitcher: 52%
Hits Behind the Pitcher: 48%

1990 On Base Percentage: .371   Career: .375
1990 Slugging Percentage: .390   Career: .388
Batting Avg with Men in Scoring Position: .277

Bats Right-Handed		AB	R	H	2B	3B	HR	RBI	BB	SO	SB	AVG
Vs. RHP		414	41	118	29	0	5	37	52	48	3	.285
Vs. LHP		184	29	55	16	0	0	14	23	17	1	.299
At Home	80	311	40	91	26	0	3	31	34	39	1	.293
On the Road	75	287	30	82	19	0	2	20	41	26	3	.286
1990 Season	155	598	70	173	45	0	5	51	75	65	4	.289
Life	2.6 Years	576	81	167	43	2	3	49	76	50	4	.290

Harold REYNOLDS

SEATTLE   SECOND BASE   30 Years Old

Runs Created: 80   Offensive Winning Percentage: .512
Batting Average: .252   Secondary Average: .269

Most Often Bats: 1st
Hits First Pitch: 11%
Gets Ahead of the Pitcher: 56%
Hits Behind the Pitcher: 44%

1990 On Base Percentage: .336   Career: .326
1990 Slugging Percentage: .347   Career: .348
Batting Avg with Men in Scoring Position: .301

Switch Hitter		AB	R	H	2B	3B	HR	RBI	BB	SO	SB	AVG
Vs. RHP		435	55	103	21	3	4	33	64	45	21	.237
Vs. LHP		207	45	59	15	2	1	22	17	7	10	.285
At Home	79	297	42	75	15	1	0	21	46	18	19	.253
On the Road	81	345	58	87	21	4	5	34	35	34	12	.252
1990 Season	160	642	100	162	36	5	5	55	81	52	31	.252
Life	5.3 Years	569	75	150	27	7	2	39	52	47	35	.263

Rick REUSCHEL

SAN FRANCISCO   STARTING PITCHER   41 Years Old
                3-6   3.93 ERA

Opponents Batting Average: .297
Offensive Support: 4.34 Runs Per Nine Innings
Double Play Support: .62 GDP Per Nine Innings

First Pitch is Hit: 21%
Gets Ahead of the Hitter: 44%
Gets Behind the Hitter: 56%
Gets Leadoff Man Out: 70%

1990 On Base Pct Allowed: .353 Slugging Percentage: .440
Stolen Bases Allowed: 4   Caught Stealing: 4

Pitches Right	AB	H	2B	3B	HR	RBI	BB	SO	AVG
Vs. RHB	137	35	6	0	2	15	9	28	.255
Vs. LHB	206	67	17	1	6	23	22	21	.325

	G	IP	W-L	Pct	SO	BB	ERA
At Home	7	43	2-1		27	10	3.14
On the Road	8	44	1-5		22	21	4.70
1990 Season	15	87	3-6	.333	49	31	3.93
Life 14.6 Years	38	242	15-13	.531	138	64	3.37

Jose RIJO

CINCINNATI   STARTING PITCHER   25 Years Old
                14-8   2.70 ERA

Opponents Batting Average: .212
Offensive Support: 4.25 Runs Per Nine Innings
Double Play Support: .46 GDP Per Nine Innings

First Pitch is Hit: 14%
Gets Ahead of the Hitter: 51%
Gets Behind the Hitter: 49%
Gets Leadoff Man Out: 74%

1990 On Base Pct Allowed: .291 Slugging Percentage: .313
Stolen Bases Allowed: 19   Caught Stealing: 4

Pitches Right	AB	H	2B	3B	HR	RBI	BB	SO	AVG
Vs. RHB	303	62	18	2	3	21	20	69	.205
Vs. LHB	409	89	16	2	7	32	58	83	.218

	G	IP	W-L	Pct	SO	BB	ERA
At Home	15	108	8-4		93	45	2.24
On the Road	14	89	6-4		59	33	3.25
1990 Season	29	197	14-8	.636	152	78	2.70
Life 4.2 Years	45	206	12-12	.505	177	94	3.60

Billy RIPKEN

BALTIMORE   SECOND BASE   26 Years Old

Runs Created: 55   Offensive Winning Percentage: .549
Batting Average: .291   Secondary Average: .177

Most Often Bats: 9th
Hits First Pitch: 17%
Gets Ahead of the Pitcher: 52%
Hits Behind the Pitcher: 48%

1990 On Base Percentage: .342   Career: .304
1990 Slugging Percentage: .387   Career: .322
Batting Avg with Men in Scoring Position: .310

Bats Right-Handed	AB	R	H	2B	3B	HR	RBI	BB	SO	SB	AVG
Vs. RHP	266	35	74	19	1	1	27	16	27	4	.278
Vs. LHP	140	13	44	9	0	2	11	12	16	1	.314
At Home	65	198	25	55	17	0	2	20	13	16	2	.278
On the Road	64	208	23	63	11	1	1	18	15	27	3	.303
1990 Season	129	406	48	118	28	1	3	38	28	43	5	.291
Life	2.8 Years	527	57	133	24	1	3	42	37	65	6	.253

Luis RIVERA

BOSTON   SHORTSTOP   27 Years Old

Runs Created: 32   Offensive Winning Percentage: .326
Batting Average: .225   Secondary Average: .202

Most Often Bats: 9th
Hits First Pitch: 19%
Gets Ahead of the Pitcher: 49%
Hits Behind the Pitcher: 51%

1990 On Base Percentage: .279   Career: .281
1990 Slugging Percentage: .344   Career: .330
Batting Avg with Men in Scoring Position: .248

Bats Right-Handed	AB	R	H	2B	3B	HR	RBI	BB	SO	SB	AVG
Vs. RHP	230	28	58	15	0	5	30	17	34	4	.252
Vs. LHP	116	10	20	5	0	2	15	8	24	0	.172
At Home	64	177	21	41	12	0	4	32	14	24	2	.232
On the Road	54	169	17	37	8	0	3	13	11	34	2	.219
1990 Season	118	346	38	78	20	0	7	45	25	58	4	.225
Life	2.5 Years	493	51	113	27	2	6	47	35	91	4	.229

Cal RIPKEN

BALTIMORE   SHORTSTOP   30 Years Old

Runs Created: 88   Offensive Winning Percentage: .585
Batting Average: .250   Secondary Average: .307

Most Often Bats: 3rd
Hits First Pitch: 11%
Gets Ahead of the Pitcher: 55%
Hits Behind the Pitcher: 45%

1990 On Base Percentage: .341   Career: .347
1990 Slugging Percentage: .415   Career: .456
Batting Avg with Men in Scoring Position: .204

Bats Right-Handed	AB	R	H	2B	3B	HR	RBI	BB	SO	SB	AVG
Vs. RHP	418	53	102	19	3	12	60	52	49	2	.244
Vs. LHP	182	25	48	9	1	9	24	30	17	1	.264
At Home	80	300	30	64	13	2	8	42	35	33	0	.213
On the Road	81	300	48	86	15	2	13	42	47	33	3	.287
1990 Season	161	600	78	150	28	4	21	84	82	66	3	.250
Life	9.1 Years	621	96	170	32	3	25	91	70	77	2	.274

Bip ROBERTS

SAN DIEGO   LEFT FIELD   27 Years Old

Runs Created: 97   Offensive Winning Percentage: .697
Batting Average: .309   Secondary Average: .306

Most Often Bats: 1st
Hits First Pitch: 14%
Gets Ahead of the Pitcher: 52%
Hits Behind the Pitcher: 48%

1990 On Base Percentage: .375   Career: .364
1990 Slugging Percentage: .433   Career: .402
Batting Avg with Men in Scoring Position: .280

Switch Hitter	AB	R	H	2B	3B	HR	RBI	BB	SO	SB	AVG
Vs. RHP	335	65	107	19	3	5	28	39	39	31	.319
Vs. LHP	221	39	65	17	0	4	16	16	26	15	.294
At Home	74	287	53	81	14	2	4	17	19	31	19	.282
On the Road	75	269	51	91	22	1	5	27	36	34	27	.338
1990 Season	149	556	104	172	36	3	9	44	55	65	46	.309
Life	2.3 Years	494	96	146	24	6	6	35	52	61	35	.295

Don ROBINSON

SAN FRANCISCO   STARTING PITCHER   33 Years Old
10-7   4.57 ERA

Opponents Batting Average: .280
Offensive Support: 4.00 Runs Per Nine Innings
Double Play Support: .34 GDP Per Nine Innings

First Pitch is Hit: 19%
Gets Ahead of the Hitter: 48%
Gets Behind the Hitter: 52%
Gets Leadoff Man Out: 70%

1990 On Base Pct Allowed: .324 Slugging Percentage: .432
Stolen Bases Allowed: 19   Caught Stealing: 8

Pitches Right	AB	H	2B	3B	HR	RBI	BB	SO	AVG
Vs. RHB	253	68	12	1	6	35	9	39	.269
Vs. LHB	365	105	24	1	12	43	32	39	.288

	G	IP	W-L	Pct	SO	BB	ERA
At Home	11	61	4-1		37	10	5.04
On the Road	15	97	6-6		41	31	4.27
1990 Season	26	158	10-7	.588	78	41	4.57
Life 9.2 Years	52	193	11-10	.523	125	64	3.70

●

Jeff ROBINSON

NEW YORK   RELIEF PITCHER   30 Years Old
3-6   3.45 ERA   0 SAVES

Blown Saves: 2   Holds: 11   Save Efficiency: 85%
Inherited Runners who Scored: 26%
Opponents Batting Average: .248
Double Play Support: 1.22 GDP Per Nine Innings

First Pitch is Hit: 16%
Gets Ahead of the Hitter: 47%
Gets Behind the Hitter: 53%
Gets First Batter Out: 66%

1990 On Base Pct Allowed: .319 Slugging Percentage: .378
Stolen Bases Allowed: 6   Caught Stealing: 5

Pitches Right	AB	H	2B	3B	HR	RBI	BB	SO	AVG
Vs. RHB	191	51	11	2	5	26	24	29	.267
Vs. LHB	140	31	4	0	3	13	10	14	.221

	G	IP	W-L	Pct	SO	BB	ERA
1990 Season	54	89	3-6	.333	43	34	3.45
Life 5.7 Years	64	134	7-9	.452	92	49	3.76

Jeff M. ROBINSON

DETROIT   STARTING PITCHER   29 Years Old
10-9   5.96 ERA

Opponents Batting Average: .256
Offensive Support: 7.08 Runs Per Nine Innings
Double Play Support: .81 GDP Per Nine Innings

First Pitch is Hit: 11%
Gets Ahead of the Hitter: 41%
Gets Behind the Hitter: 59%
Gets Leadoff Man Out: 70%

1990 On Base Pct Allowed: .362 Slugging Percentage: .457
Stolen Bases Allowed: 10   Caught Stealing: 9

Pitches Right	AB	H	2B	3B	HR	RBI	BB	SO	AVG
Vs. RHB	298	79	21	1	13	54	49	41	.265
Vs. LHB	254	62	13	3	10	32	39	35	.244

	G	IP	W-L	Pct	SO	BB	ERA
At Home	15	86	6-4		45	54	5.63
On the Road	12	59	4-5		31	34	6.44
1990 Season	27	145	10-9	.526	76	88	5.96
Life 2.5 Years	39	211	15-11	.581	133	105	4.65

●

Ron ROBINSON

MILWAUKEE   STARTING PITCHER   29 Years Old
14-7   3.26 ERA

Opponents Batting Average: .279
Offensive Support: 5.76 Runs Per Nine Innings
Double Play Support: .70 GDP Per Nine Innings

First Pitch is Hit: 14%
Gets Ahead of the Hitter: 51%
Gets Behind the Hitter: 49%
Gets Leadoff Man Out: 67%

1990 On Base Pct Allowed: .330 Slugging Percentage: .364
Stolen Bases Allowed: 15   Caught Stealing: 11

Pitches Right	AB	H	2B	3B	HR	RBI	BB	SO	AVG
Vs. RHB	326	96	18	1	3	37	21	39	.294
Vs. LHB	370	98	18	0	4	31	30	32	.265

	G	IP	W-L	Pct	SO	BB	ERA
At Home	12	86	6-3		33	21	2.40
On the Road	16	93	8-4		38	30	4.05
1990 Season	28	180	14-7	.667	71	51	3.26
Life 4.3 Years	52	178	11-8	.580	108	55	3.52

Kenny ROGERS

TEXAS	RELIEF PITCHER	26 Years Old
	10-6 3.13 ERA 15 SAVES	

Blown Saves: 8   Holds: 6   Save Efficiency: 72%
Inherited Runners who Scored: 33%
Opponents Batting Average: .249
Double Play Support: .46 GDP Per Nine Innings

First Pitch is Hit: 11%
Gets Ahead of the Hitter: 50%
Gets Behind the Hitter: 50%
Gets First Batter Out: 63%

1990 On Base Pct Allowed: .323 Slugging Percentage: .372
Stolen Bases Allowed: 6   Caught Stealing: 1

Pitches Left	AB	H	2B	3B	HR	RBI	BB	SO	AVG
Vs. RHB	278	72	16	2	5	36	36	55	.259
Vs. LHB	96	21	6	1	1	10	6	19	.219

	G	IP	W-L	Pct	SO	BB	ERA
1990 Season	69	98	10-6	.625	74	42	3.13
Life 2.0 Years	72	87	7-5	.565	70	43	3.05

•

Bruce RUFFIN

PHILADELPHIA	STARTING PITCHER	27 Years Old
	6-13 5.38 ERA	

Opponents Batting Average: .297
Offensive Support: 3.99 Runs Per Nine Innings
Double Play Support: .60 GDP Per Nine Innings

First Pitch is Hit: 15%
Gets Ahead of the Hitter: 42%
Gets Behind the Hitter: 58%
Gets Leadoff Man Out: 66%

1990 On Base Pct Allowed: .361 Slugging Percentage: .456
Stolen Bases Allowed: 3   Caught Stealing: 4

Pitches Left	AB	H	2B	3B	HR	RBI	BB	SO	AVG
Vs. RHB	479	143	37	4	14	61	50	60	.299
Vs. LHB	120	35	8	0	0	29	12	19	.292

	G	IP	W-L	Pct	SO	BB	ERA
At Home	16	78	5-7		41	40	5.40
On the Road	16	71	1-6		38	22	5.35
1990 Season	32	149	6-13	.316	79	62	5.38
Life 3.9 Years	43	199	10-13	.427	102	83	4.22

Nolan RYAN

TEXAS	STARTING PITCHER	44 Years Old
	13-9 3.44 ERA	

Opponents Batting Average: .188
Offensive Support: 4.46 Runs Per Nine Innings
Double Play Support: .22 GDP Per Nine Innings

First Pitch is Hit: 11%
Gets Ahead of the Hitter: 50%
Gets Behind the Hitter: 50%
Gets Leadoff Man Out: 77%

1990 On Base Pct Allowed: .267 Slugging Percentage: .322
Stolen Bases Allowed: 25   Caught Stealing: 9

Pitches Right	AB	H	2B	3B	HR	RBI	BB	SO	AVG
Vs. RHB	367	58	10	4	10	41	31	140	.158
Vs. LHB	362	79	10	8	8	31	43	92	.218

	G	IP	W-L	Pct	SO	BB	ERA
At Home	19	130	8-5		158	43	3.32
On the Road	11	74	5-4		74	31	3.65
1990 Season	30	204	13-9	.591	232	74	3.44
Life 19.5 Years	38	255	15-14	.526	272	134	3.16

•S•

Bret SABERHAGEN

KANSAS CITY	STARTING PITCHER	27 Years Old
	5-9 3.27 ERA	

Opponents Batting Average: .279
Offensive Support: 3.67 Runs Per Nine Innings
Double Play Support: .67 GDP Per Nine Innings

First Pitch is Hit: 16%
Gets Ahead of the Hitter: 56%
Gets Behind the Hitter: 44%
Gets Leadoff Man Out: 67%

1990 On Base Pct Allowed: .314 Slugging Percentage: .387
Stolen Bases Allowed: 2   Caught Stealing: 5

Pitches Right	AB	H	2B	3B	HR	RBI	BB	SO	AVG
Vs. RHB	302	85	14	1	4	23	12	45	.281
Vs. LHB	222	61	6	4	5	25	16	42	.275

	G	IP	W-L	Pct	SO	BB	ERA
At Home	11	74	3-5		52	14	3.42
On the Road	9	61	2-4		35	14	3.08
1990 Season	20	135	5-9	.357	87	28	3.27
Life 5.7 Years	39	257	17-12	.581	168	50	3.23

Chris SABO

CINCINNATI	THIRD BASE	29 Years Old

Runs Created: 94   Offensive Winning Percentage: .683
Batting Average: .270   Secondary Average: .358

Most Often Bats: 1st
Hits First Pitch: 12%
Gets Ahead of the Pitcher: 49%
Hits Behind the Pitcher: 51%

1990 On Base Percentage: .343   Career: .326
1990 Slugging Percentage: .476   Career: .435
Batting Avg with Men in Scoring Position: .243

Bats Right-Handed	AB	R	H	2B	3B	HR	RBI	BB	SO	SB	AVG
Vs. RHP	353	49	83	26	1	11	38	34	46	11	.235
Vs. LHP	214	46	70	12	1	14	33	27	12	14	.327
At Home	76	275	49	77	18	0	15	45	33	28	15	.280
On the Road	72	292	46	76	20	2	10	26	28	30	10	.260
1990 Season	148	567	95	153	38	2	25	71	61	58	25	.270
Life	2.3 Years	622	92	167	44	2	19	64	51	63	38	.268

Luis SALAZAR

CHICAGO	THIRD BASE	34 Years Old

Runs Created: 47   Offensive Winning Percentage: .446
Batting Average: .254   Secondary Average: .188

Most Often Bats: 6th
Hits First Pitch: 8%
Gets Ahead of the Pitcher: 54%
Hits Behind the Pitcher: 46%

1990 On Base Percentage: .293   Career: .297
1990 Slugging Percentage: .388   Career: .381
Batting Avg with Men in Scoring Position: .243

Bats Right-Handed	AB	R	H	2B	3B	HR	RBI	BB	SO	SB	AVG
Vs. RHP	253	25	58	6	2	6	25	13	41	2	.229
Vs. LHP	157	19	46	7	1	6	22	6	18	1	.293
At Home	61	218	26	64	7	2	7	20	11	29	2	.294
On the Road	54	192	18	40	6	1	5	27	8	30	1	.208
1990 Season	115	410	44	104	13	3	12	47	19	59	3	.254
Life	6.8 Years	517	57	137	18	4	11	58	23	84	17	.265

Bill SAMPEN

MONTREAL	RELIEF PITCHER	28 Years Old
	12-7 2.99 ERA 2 SAVES	

Blown Saves: 1   Holds: 1   Save Efficiency: 75%
Inherited Runners who Scored: 36%
Opponents Batting Average: .268
Double Play Support: .40 GDP Per Nine Innings

First Pitch is Hit: 15%
Gets Ahead of the Hitter: 49%
Gets Behind the Hitter: 51%
Gets First Batter Out: 62%

1990 On Base Pct Allowed: .332 Slugging Percentage: .362
Stolen Bases Allowed: 15   Caught Stealing: 3

Pitches Right	AB	H	2B	3B	HR	RBI	BB	SO	AVG
Vs. RHB	176	49	6	0	6	20	15	43	.278
Vs. LHB	175	45	6	0	1	19	18	26	.257

	G	IP	W-L	Pct	SO	BB	ERA
1990 Season	59	90	12-7	.632	69	33	2.99
Life 0.9 Years	69	106	14-8	.632	81	39	2.99

Juan SAMUEL

LOS ANGELES　　SECOND BASE　　30 Years Old

Runs Created: 60　　Offensive Winning Percentage: .447
Batting Average: .242　　Secondary Average: .321

Most Often Bats: 7th
Hits First Pitch: 9%
Gets Ahead of the Pitcher: 50%
Hits Behind the Pitcher: 50%

1990 On Base Percentage: .316　　Career: .309
1990 Slugging Percentage: .382　　Career: .422
Batting Avg with Men in Scoring Position: .206

Bats Right-Handed		AB	R	H	2B	3B	HR	RBI	BB	SO	SB	AVG
Vs. RHP		305	34	65	14	1	3	27	34	83	28	.213
Vs. LHP		187	28	54	10	2	10	25	17	43	10	.289
At Home	69	224	31	55	8	3	6	26	25	60	14	.246
On the Road	74	268	31	64	16	0	7	26	26	66	24	.239
1990 Season	143	492	62	119	24	3	13	52	51	126	38	.242
Life	6.7 Years	649	93	167	32	11	17	74	42	164	48	.258

•

Ryne SANDBERG

CHICAGO　　SECOND BASE　　31 Years Old

Runs Created: 124　　Offensive Winning Percentage: .729
Batting Average: .306　　Secondary Average: .376

Most Often Bats: 2nd
Hits First Pitch: 11%
Gets Ahead of the Pitcher: 53%
Hits Behind the Pitcher: 47%

1990 On Base Percentage: .354　　Career: .342
1990 Slugging Percentage: .559　　Career: .452
Batting Avg with Men in Scoring Position: .298

Bats Right-Handed		AB	R	H	2B	3B	HR	RBI	BB	SO	SB	AVG
Vs. RHP		401	78	134	17	3	30	77	29	50	18	.334
Vs. LHP		214	38	54	13	0	10	23	21	34	7	.252
At Home	78	305	67	109	21	1	25	62	27	44	12	.357
On the Road	77	310	49	79	9	2	15	38	23	40	13	.255
1990 Season	155	615	116	188	30	3	40	100	50	84	25	.306
Life	8.6 Years	642	102	185	30	7	21	76	54	92	32	.287

Scott SANDERSON

OAKLAND　　STARTING PITCHER　　34 Years Old
17-11　　3.88 ERA

Opponents Batting Average: .255
Offensive Support: 4.62 Runs Per Nine Innings
Double Play Support: .26 GDP Per Nine Innings

First Pitch is Hit: 15%
Gets Ahead of the Hitter: 53%
Gets Behind the Hitter: 47%
Gets Leadoff Man Out: 73%

1990 On Base Pct Allowed: .312　Slugging Percentage: .422
Stolen Bases Allowed: 13　　Caught Stealing: 5

Pitches Right		AB	H	2B	3B	HR	RBI	BB	SO	AVG
Vs. RHB		401	111	25	2	14	45	27	74	.277
Vs. LHB		402	94	14	5	13	46	39	54	.234

	G	IP	W-L	Pct	SO	BB	ERA
At Home	15	97	6-7		60	30	3.17
On the Road	19	110	11-4		68	36	4.51
1990 Season	34	206	17-11	.607	128	66	3.88
Life 8.5 Years	40	215	14-12	.535	142	56	3.59

•

Benito SANTIAGO

SAN DIEGO　　CATCHER　　26 Years Old

Runs Created: 47　　Offensive Winning Percentage: .568
Batting Average: .270　　Secondary Average: .241

Most Often Bats: 6th
Hits First Pitch: 20%
Gets Ahead of the Pitcher: 48%
Hits Behind the Pitcher: 52%

1990 On Base Percentage: .323　　Career: .301
1990 Slugging Percentage: .419　　Career: .412
Batting Avg with Men in Scoring Position: .244

Bats Right-Handed		AB	R	H	2B	3B	HR	RBI	BB	SO	SB	AVG
Vs. RHP		228	32	61	5	5	10	41	18	34	4	.268
Vs. LHP		116	10	32	3	0	1	12	9	21	1	.276
At Home	59	189	30	54	4	4	5	26	19	31	5	.286
On the Road	41	155	12	39	4	1	6	27	8	24	0	.252
1990 Season	100	344	42	93	8	5	11	53	27	55	5	.270
Life	3.3 Years	581	66	154	25	4	18	75	29	107	16	.265

Mackey SASSER

NEW YORK   CATCHER   28 Years Old

Runs Created: 38   Offensive Winning Percentage: .595
Batting Average: .307   Secondary Average: .174

Most Often Bats: 7th
Hits First Pitch: 31%
Gets Ahead of the Pitcher: 49%
Hits Behind the Pitcher: 51%

1990 On Base Percentage: .344   Career: .322
1990 Slugging Percentage: .426   Career: .405
Batting Avg with Men in Scoring Position: .300

Bats Left-Handed	AB	R	H	2B	3B	HR	RBI	BB	SO	SB	AVG
Vs. RHP	217	26	72	11	0	5	34	12	9	0	.332
Vs. LHP	53	5	11	3	0	1	7	3	10	0	.208
At Home	55	143	19	35	9	0	3	21	10	10	0	.245
On the Road	45	127	12	48	5	0	3	20	5	9	0	.378
1990 Season 100	270	31	83	14	0	6	41	15	19	0	.307
Life 1.5 Years	396	39	116	25	2	5	54	18	30	0	.292

●

Steve SAX

NEW YORK   SECOND BASE   31 Years Old

Runs Created: 68   Offensive Winning Percentage: .447
Batting Average: .260   Secondary Average: .215

Most Often Bats: 2nd
Hits First Pitch: 10%
Gets Ahead of the Pitcher: 52%
Hits Behind the Pitcher: 48%

1990 On Base Percentage: .316   Career: .339
1990 Slugging Percentage: .325   Career: .357
Batting Avg with Men in Scoring Position: .239

Bats Right-Handed	AB	R	H	2B	3B	HR	RBI	BB	SO	SB	AVG
Vs. RHP	438	51	116	17	1	4	31	29	36	26	.265
Vs. LHP	177	19	44	7	1	0	11	20	10	17	.249
At Home	77	294	36	76	13	2	3	27	30	22	23	.259
On the Road	78	321	34	84	11	0	1	15	19	24	20	.262
1990 Season 155	615	70	160	24	2	4	42	49	46	43	.260
Life 8.7 Years	644	84	183	24	5	4	51	54	57	43	.284

Calvin SCHIRALDI

SAN DIEGO   RELIEF PITCHER   28 Years Old
3-8   4.41 ERA   1 SAVES

Blown Saves: 1   Holds: 1   Save Efficiency: 67%
Inherited Runners who Scored: 100%
Opponents Batting Average: .264
Double Play Support: .52 GDP Per Nine Innings

First Pitch is Hit: 16%
Gets Ahead of the Hitter: 52%
Gets Behind the Hitter: 48%
Gets First Batter Out: 65%

1990 On Base Pct Allowed: .360 Slugging Percentage: .423
Stolen Bases Allowed: 15   Caught Stealing: 7

Pitches Right	AB	H	2B	3B	HR	RBI	BB	SO	AVG
Vs. RHB	197	55	11	3	4	31	20	43	.279
Vs. LHB	200	50	7	3	7	32	40	31	.250

	G	IP	W-L	Pct	SO	BB	ERA
1990 Season	42	104	3-8	.273	74	60	4.41
Life 3.8 Years	62	146	8-10	.457	125	69	4.22

●

Dick SCHOFIELD

CALIFORNIA   SHORTSTOP   28 Years Old

Runs Created: 38   Offensive Winning Percentage: .471
Batting Average: .255   Secondary Average: .219

Most Often Bats: 9th
Hits First Pitch: 10%
Gets Ahead of the Pitcher: 49%
Hits Behind the Pitcher: 51%

1990 On Base Percentage: .363   Career: .305
1990 Slugging Percentage: .297   Career: .330
Batting Avg with Men in Scoring Position: .296

Bats Right-Handed	AB	R	H	2B	3B	HR	RBI	BB	SO	SB	AVG
Vs. RHP	221	23	54	6	1	0	12	34	47	2	.244
Vs. LHP	89	18	25	2	0	1	6	18	14	1	.281
At Home	54	158	24	43	4	1	1	12	30	26	2	.272
On the Road	45	152	17	36	4	0	0	6	22	35	1	.237
1990 Season 99	310	41	79	8	1	1	18	52	61	3	.255
Life 5.7 Years	519	62	121	17	4	8	43	49	77	16	.233

Mike SCIOSCIA

LOS ANGELES   CATCHER   32 Years Old

Runs Created: 62	Offensive Winning Percentage: .566
Batting Average: .264	Secondary Average: .276

Most Often Bats: 6th
Hits First Pitch: 10%
Gets Ahead of the Pitcher: 57%
Hits Behind the Pitcher: 43%

1990 On Base Percentage: .348	Career: .348
1990 Slugging Percentage: .405	Career: .360

Batting Avg with Men in Scoring Position: .311

Bats Left-Handed	AB	R	H	2B	3B	HR	RBI	BB	SO	SB	AVG
Vs. RHP	316	33	87	20	0	10	48	45	20	2	.275
Vs. LHP	119	13	28	5	0	2	18	10	11	2	.235
At Home	67	208	26	58	12	0	5	32	29	12	3	.279
On the Road	68	227	20	57	13	0	7	34	26	19	1	.251
1990 Season 135	435	46	115	25	0	12	66	55	31	4	.264
Life 7.4 Years	495	46	129	24	1	8	51	66	33	3	.262

•

Mike SCOTT

HOUSTON   STARTING PITCHER   35 Years Old
9-13   3.81 ERA

Opponents Batting Average: .246
Offensive Support: 3.11 Runs Per Nine Innings
Double Play Support: .39 GDP Per Nine Innings

First Pitch is Hit: 18%
Gets Ahead of the Hitter: 52%
Gets Behind the Hitter: 48%
Gets Leadoff Man Out: 74%

1990 On Base Pct Allowed: .302 Slugging Percentage: .403
Stolen Bases Allowed: 53   Caught Stealing: 7

Pitches Right	AB	H	2B	3B	HR	RBI	BB	SO	AVG
Vs. RHB	346	88	12	2	16	44	23	67	.254
Vs. LHB	443	106	21	3	11	49	43	54	.239

	G	IP	W-L	Pct	SO	BB	ERA
At Home	19	130	5-4		81	38	2.42
On the Road	13	76	4-9		40	28	6.19
1990 Season	32	206	9-13	.409	121	66	3.81
Life 8.9 Years	39	230	14-12	.539	164	70	3.51

Scott SCUDDER

CINCINNATI   RELIEF PITCHER   23 Years Old
5-5   4.90 ERA   0 SAVES

Blown Saves: 0   Holds: 0   Save Efficiency: 0%
Inherited Runners who Scored: 13%
Opponents Batting Average: .265
Double Play Support: .50 GDP Per Nine Innings

First Pitch is Hit: 14%
Gets Ahead of the Hitter: 43%
Gets Behind the Hitter: 57%
Gets First Batter Out: 55%

1990 On Base Pct Allowed: .342 Slugging Percentage: .466
Stolen Bases Allowed: 10   Caught Stealing: 4

Pitches Right	AB	H	2B	3B	HR	RBI	BB	SO	AVG
Vs. RHB	121	27	5	0	8	18	13	25	.223
Vs. LHB	158	47	9	3	4	20	17	17	.297

	G	IP	W-L	Pct	SO	BB	ERA
1990 Season	21	72	5-5	.500	42	30	4.90
Life 1.0 Years	46	179	9-15	.391	113	95	4.66

•

Steve SEARCY

DETROIT   STARTING PITCHER   26 Years Old
2-7   4.66 ERA

Opponents Batting Average: .270
Offensive Support: 2.75 Runs Per Nine Innings
Double Play Support: 1.08 GDP Per Nine Innings

First Pitch is Hit: 12%
Gets Ahead of the Hitter: 46%
Gets Behind the Hitter: 54%
Gets Leadoff Man Out: 69%

1990 On Base Pct Allowed: .375 Slugging Percentage: .418
Stolen Bases Allowed: 9   Caught Stealing: 5

Pitches Left	AB	H	2B	3B	HR	RBI	BB	SO	AVG
Vs. RHB	236	61	10	1	8	32	44	63	.258
Vs. LHB	46	15	3	0	1	9	7	3	.326

	G	IP	W-L	Pct	SO	BB	ERA
At Home	9	41	2-2		28	23	4.65
On the Road	7	35	0-5		38	28	4.67
1990 Season	16	75	2-7	.222	66	51	4.66
Life 0.6 Years	46	186	5-18	.231	144	118	5.03

Kevin SEITZER

KANSAS CITY   THIRD BASE   29 Years Old

Runs Created: 82   Offensive Winning Percentage: .529
Batting Average: .275   Secondary Average: .214

Most Often Bats: 1st
Hits First Pitch: 15%
Gets Ahead of the Pitcher: 57%
Hits Behind the Pitcher: 43%

1990 On Base Percentage: .346   Career: .382
1990 Slugging Percentage: .370   Career: .398
Batting Avg with Men in Scoring Position: .268

Bats Right-Handed		AB	R	H	2B	3B	HR	RBI	BB	SO	SB	AVG
Vs. RHP		413	62	113	14	1	2	15	45	44	7	.274
Vs. LHP		209	29	58	17	4	4	23	22	22	0	.278
At Home	80	308	56	96	22	3	5	26	35	32	4	.312
On the Road	78	314	35	75	9	2	1	12	32	34	3	.239
1990 Season	158	622	91	171	31	5	6	38	67	66	7	.275
Life	4.0 Years	621	94	184	29	5	8	59	84	75	11	.297

Larry SHEETS

DETROIT   LEFT FIELD   31 Years Old

Runs Created: 42   Offensive Winning Percentage: .418
Batting Average: .261   Secondary Average: .211

Most Often Bats: 5th
Hits First Pitch: 19%
Gets Ahead of the Pitcher: 52%
Hits Behind the Pitcher: 48%

1990 On Base Percentage: .308   Career: .321
1990 Slugging Percentage: .403   Career: .438
Batting Avg with Men in Scoring Position: .277

Bats Left-Handed		AB	R	H	2B	3B	HR	RBI	BB	SO	SB	AVG
Vs. RHP		343	37	90	17	2	10	51	23	39	1	.262
Vs. LHP		17	3	4	0	0	0	1	1	3	0	.235
At Home	67	179	17	44	8	1	7	30	11	27	1	.246
On the Road	64	181	23	50	9	1	3	22	13	15	0	.276
1990 Season	131	360	40	94	17	2	10	52	24	42	1	.261
Life	4.5 Years	498	60	133	21	1	21	74	38	77	1	.267

Mike SHARPERSON

LOS ANGELES   THIRD BASE   29 Years Old

Runs Created: 54   Offensive Winning Percentage: .598
Batting Average: .297   Secondary Average: .246

Most Often Bats: 2nd
Hits First Pitch: 16%
Gets Ahead of the Pitcher: 53%
Hits Behind the Pitcher: 47%

1990 On Base Percentage: .376   Career: .347
1990 Slugging Percentage: .373   Career: .344
Batting Avg with Men in Scoring Position: .273

Bats Right-Handed		AB	R	H	2B	3B	HR	RBI	BB	SO	SB	AVG
Vs. RHP		149	13	39	6	1	2	19	21	16	5	.262
Vs. LHP		208	29	67	8	1	1	17	25	23	10	.322
At Home	69	195	22	60	7	1	1	19	21	18	7	.308
On the Road	60	162	20	46	7	1	2	17	25	21	8	.284
1990 Season	129	357	42	106	14	2	3	36	46	39	15	.297
Life	1.5 Years	380	42	105	16	2	2	37	41	52	11	.276

Gary SHEFFIELD

MILWAUKEE   THIRD BASE   22 Years Old

Runs Created: 73   Offensive Winning Percentage: .563
Batting Average: .294   Secondary Average: .269

Most Often Bats: 3rd
Hits First Pitch: 18%
Gets Ahead of the Pitcher: 52%
Hits Behind the Pitcher: 48%

1990 On Base Percentage: .350   Career: .327
1990 Slugging Percentage: .421   Career: .386
Batting Avg with Men in Scoring Position: .336

Bats Right-Handed		AB	R	H	2B	3B	HR	RBI	BB	SO	SB	AVG
Vs. RHP		352	45	106	18	0	7	49	30	26	17	.301
Vs. LHP		135	22	37	12	1	3	18	14	15	8	.274
At Home	63	239	32	65	15	1	3	28	24	22	13	.272
On the Road	62	248	35	78	15	0	7	39	20	19	12	.315
1990 Season	125	487	67	143	30	1	10	67	44	41	25	.294
Life	1.5 Years	621	75	168	33	1	13	74	52	54	25	.271

Eric SHOW

SAN DIEGO	RELIEF PITCHER	34 Years Old
	6-8 5.76 ERA 1 SAVES	

Blown Saves: 0   Holds: 0   Save Efficiency: 100%
Inherited Runners who Scored: 46%
Opponents Batting Average: .306
Double Play Support: .59 GDP Per Nine Innings

First Pitch is Hit: 18%
Gets Ahead of the Hitter: 48%
Gets Behind the Hitter: 52%
Gets First Batter Out: 67%

1990 On Base Pct Allowed: .369 Slugging Percentage: .472
Stolen Bases Allowed: 15   Caught Stealing: 8

Pitches Right	AB	H	2B	3B	HR	RBI	BB	SO	AVG
Vs. RHB	196	60	9	0	8	41	10	30	.306
Vs. LHB	232	71	6	4	8	31	31	25	.306

	G	IP	W-L	Pct	SO	BB	ERA
1990 Season	39	106	6-8	.429	55	41	5.76
Life 7.3 Years	42	220	14-12	.535	131	81	3.59

●

Ruben SIERRA

TEXAS	RIGHT FIELD	25 Years Old

Runs Created: 85   Offensive Winning Percentage: .583
Batting Average: .280   Secondary Average: .242

Most Often Bats: 4th
Hits First Pitch: 12%
Gets Ahead of the Pitcher: 55%
Hits Behind the Pitcher: 45%

1990 On Base Percentage: .330   Career: .318
1990 Slugging Percentage: .426   Career: .468
Batting Avg with Men in Scoring Position: .320

Switch Hitter	AB	R	H	2B	3B	HR	RBI	BB	SO	SB	AVG
Vs. RHP	392	46	100	21	2	13	65	35	61	3	.255
Vs. LHP	216	24	70	16	0	3	31	14	25	6	.324
At Home	80	301	38	80	17	1	10	46	23	51	5	.266
On the Road	79	307	32	90	20	1	6	50	26	35	4	.293
1990 Season	159	608	70	170	37	2	16	96	49	86	9	.280
Life 4.6 Years	624	86	171	33	7	25	102	43	95	13	.274

John SMILEY

PITTSBURGH	STARTING PITCHER	26 Years Old
	9-10 4.64 ERA	

Opponents Batting Average: .275
Offensive Support: 4.28 Runs Per Nine Innings
Double Play Support: .54 GDP Per Nine Innings

First Pitch is Hit: 20%
Gets Ahead of the Hitter: 57%
Gets Behind the Hitter: 43%
Gets Leadoff Man Out: 66%

1990 On Base Pct Allowed: .317 Slugging Percentage: .426
Stolen Bases Allowed: 13   Caught Stealing: 6

Pitches Left	AB	H	2B	3B	HR	RBI	BB	SO	AVG
Vs. RHB	492	133	25	5	12	55	29	77	.270
Vs. LHB	93	28	4	2	3	14	7	9	.301

	G	IP	W-L	Pct	SO	BB	ERA
At Home	11	64	3-4		43	20	3.80
On the Road	15	85	6-6		43	16	5.27
1990 Season	26	149	9-10	.474	86	36	4.64
Life 3.4 Years	49	193	12-10	.541	121	55	3.73

●

Bryn SMITH

ST. LOUIS	STARTING PITCHER	35 Years Old
	9-8 4.27 ERA	

Opponents Batting Average: .286
Offensive Support: 4.84 Runs Per Nine Innings
Double Play Support: .83 GDP Per Nine Innings

First Pitch is Hit: 19%
Gets Ahead of the Hitter: 54%
Gets Behind the Hitter: 46%
Gets Leadoff Man Out: 71%

1990 On Base Pct Allowed: .324 Slugging Percentage: .401
Stolen Bases Allowed: 21   Caught Stealing: 4

Pitches Right	AB	H	2B	3B	HR	RBI	BB	SO	AVG
Vs. RHB	220	58	9	0	8	32	12	43	.264
Vs. LHB	339	102	14	4	3	41	18	35	.301

	G	IP	W-L	Pct	SO	BB	ERA
At Home	14	84	6-4		50	21	3.84
On the Road	12	57	3-4		28	9	4.89
1990 Season	26	141	9-8	.529	78	30	4.27
Life 7.1 Years	43	216	13-11	.533	128	52	3.37

Dwight SMITH

CHICAGO   LEFT FIELD   27 Years Old

Runs Created: 36   Offensive Winning Percentage: .463
Batting Average: .262   Secondary Average: .248

Most Often Bats: 5th
Hits First Pitch: 16%
Gets Ahead of the Pitcher: 51%
Hits Behind the Pitcher: 49%

1990 On Base Percentage: .329   Career: .358
1990 Slugging Percentage: .376   Career: .439
Batting Avg with Men in Scoring Position: .263

Bats Left-Handed		AB	R	H	2B	3B	HR	RBI	BB	SO	SB	AVG
Vs. RHP		254	30	68	13	0	5	24	27	35	11	.268
Vs. LHP		36	4	8	2	0	1	3	1	11	0	.222
At Home	58	131	16	33	8	0	3	12	13	25	2	.252
On the Road	59	159	18	43	7	0	3	15	15	21	9	.270
1990 Season	117	290	34	76	15	0	6	27	28	46	11	.262
Life	1.4 Years	454	62	134	24	4	11	57	42	70	14	.295

●

Lee SMITH

ST. LOUIS   RELIEF PITCHER   33 Years Old
        5-5   2.06 ERA   31 SAVES

Blown Saves: 6   Holds: 1   Save Efficiency: 84%
Inherited Runners who Scored: 18%
Opponents Batting Average: .229
Double Play Support: .22 GDP Per Nine Innings

First Pitch is Hit: 11%
Gets Ahead of the Hitter: 50%
Gets Behind the Hitter: 50%
Gets First Batter Out: 66%

1990 On Base Pct Allowed: .292 Slugging Percentage: .316
Stolen Bases Allowed: 14   Caught Stealing: 5

Pitches Right	AB	H	2B	3B	HR	RBI	BB	SO	AVG
Vs. RHB	132	31	6	1	0	7	5	33	.235
Vs. LHB	178	40	10	0	3	19	24	54	.225

	G	IP	W-L	Pct	SO	BB	ERA
1990 Season	64	83	5-5	.500	87	29	2.06
Life 8.9 Years	73	104	6-7	.470	104	41	2.88

Lonnie SMITH

ATLANTA   LEFT FIELD   35 Years Old

Runs Created: 86   Offensive Winning Percentage: .681
Batting Average: .305   Secondary Average: .300

Most Often Bats: 1st
Hits First Pitch: 20%
Gets Ahead of the Pitcher: 49%
Hits Behind the Pitcher: 51%

1990 On Base Percentage: .384   Career: .371
1990 Slugging Percentage: .459   Career: .422
Batting Avg with Men in Scoring Position: .233

Bats Right-Handed		AB	R	H	2B	3B	HR	RBI	BB	SO	SB	AVG
Vs. RHP		269	39	84	13	6	3	24	37	47	8	.312
Vs. LHP		197	33	58	14	3	6	18	21	22	2	.294
At Home	67	231	35	72	16	4	2	16	27	34	9	.312
On the Road	68	235	37	70	11	5	7	26	31	35	1	.298
1990 Season	135	466	72	142	27	9	9	42	58	69	10	.305
Life	7.8 Years	559	99	163	30	7	10	55	63	87	44	.292

●

Ozzie SMITH

ST. LOUIS   SHORTSTOP   36 Years Old

Runs Created: 60   Offensive Winning Percentage: .486
Batting Average: .254   Secondary Average: .232

Most Often Bats: 2nd
Hits First Pitch: 13%
Gets Ahead of the Pitcher: 56%
Hits Behind the Pitcher: 44%

1990 On Base Percentage: .330   Career: .333
1990 Slugging Percentage: .305   Career: .321
Batting Avg with Men in Scoring Position: .240

Switch Hitter		AB	R	H	2B	3B	HR	RBI	BB	SO	SB	AVG
Vs. RHP		311	34	72	9	0	0	27	40	22	20	.232
Vs. LHP		201	27	58	12	1	1	23	21	11	12	.289
At Home	73	256	35	68	15	1	0	25	35	17	21	.266
On the Road	70	256	26	62	6	0	1	25	26	16	11	.242
1990 Season	143	512	61	130	21	1	1	50	61	33	32	.254
Life	11.9 Years	590	77	151	25	4	2	50	68	38	39	.256

Pete SMITH

ATLANTA	STARTING PITCHER	25 Years Old
	5-6 4.79 ERA	

Opponents Batting Average: .260
Offensive Support: 5.38 Runs Per Nine Innings
Double Play Support: .82 GDP Per Nine Innings

First Pitch is Hit: 16%
Gets Ahead of the Hitter: 49%
Gets Behind the Hitter: 51%
Gets Leadoff Man Out: 67%

1990 On Base Pct Allowed: .313 Slugging Percentage: .405
Stolen Bases Allowed: 9   Caught Stealing: 3

Pitches Right	AB	H	2B	3B	HR	RBI	BB	SO	AVG
Vs. RHB	130	28	2	0	8	19	7	37	.215
Vs. LHB	166	49	8	0	3	18	17	19	.295

	G	IP	W-L	Pct	SO	BB	ERA
At Home	7	40	3-3		33	14	6.35
On the Road	6	37	2-3		23	10	3.13
1990 Season	13	77	5-6	.455	56	24	4.79
Life 2.1 Years	37	210	8-17	.327	144	86	4.30

Zane SMITH

PITTSBURGH	STARTING PITCHER	30 Years Old
	12-9 2.55 ERA	

Opponents Batting Average: .245
Offensive Support: 3.13 Runs Per Nine Innings
Double Play Support: 1.42 GDP Per Nine Innings

First Pitch is Hit: 14%
Gets Ahead of the Hitter: 53%
Gets Behind the Hitter: 47%
Gets Leadoff Man Out: 72%

1990 On Base Pct Allowed: .291 Slugging Percentage: .350
Stolen Bases Allowed: 27   Caught Stealing: 4

Pitches Left	AB	H	2B	3B	HR	RBI	BB	SO	AVG
Vs. RHB	685	177	20	7	14	60	40	102	.258
Vs. LHB	116	19	5	0	1	8	10	28	.164

	G	IP	W-L	Pct	SO	BB	ERA
At Home	18	118	9-3		83	27	2.05
On the Road	15	97	3-6		47	23	3.15
1990 Season	33	215	12-9	.571	130	50	2.55
Life 5.2 Years	43	216	10-13	.429	126	84	3.66

Roy SMITH

MINNESOTA	STARTING PITCHER	29 Years Old
	5-10 4.81 ERA	

Opponents Batting Average: .313
Offensive Support: 5.40 Runs Per Nine Innings
Double Play Support: .65 GDP Per Nine Innings

First Pitch is Hit: 11%
Gets Ahead of the Hitter: 52%
Gets Behind the Hitter: 48%
Gets Leadoff Man Out: 65%

1990 On Base Pct Allowed: .356 Slugging Percentage: .480
Stolen Bases Allowed: 15   Caught Stealing: 13

Pitches Right	AB	H	2B	3B	HR	RBI	BB	SO	AVG
Vs. RHB	324	85	16	0	11	38	16	51	.262
Vs. LHB	287	106	18	4	9	47	31	36	.369

	G	IP	W-L	Pct	SO	BB	ERA
At Home	14	73	4-5		44	17	4.30
On the Road	18	80	1-5		43	30	5.29
1990 Season	32	153	5-10	.333	87	47	4.81
Life 2.7 Years	44	201	9-10	.481	110	67	4.45

John SMOLTZ

ATLANTA	STARTING PITCHER	23 Years Old
	14-11 3.85 ERA	

Opponents Batting Average: .240
Offensive Support: 5.14 Runs Per Nine Innings
Double Play Support: .62 GDP Per Nine Innings

First Pitch is Hit: 13%
Gets Ahead of the Hitter: 44%
Gets Behind the Hitter: 56%
Gets Leadoff Man Out: 73%

1990 On Base Pct Allowed: .310 Slugging Percentage: .358
Stolen Bases Allowed: 31   Caught Stealing: 10

Pitches Right	AB	H	2B	3B	HR	RBI	BB	SO	AVG
Vs. RHB	352	71	11	1	10	44	27	94	.202
Vs. LHB	506	135	20	4	10	51	63	76	.267

	G	IP	W-L	Pct	SO	BB	ERA
At Home	17	124	9-4		104	48	2.76
On the Road	17	107	5-7		66	42	5.11
1990 Season	34	231	14-11	.560	170	90	3.85
Life 2.0 Years	37	248	14-14	.491	185	96	3.68

Cory SNYDER

CLEVELAND   RIGHT FIELD   28 Years Old

Runs Created: 44   Offensive Winning Percentage: .349
Batting Average: .233   Secondary Average: .221

Most Often Bats: 7th
Hits First Pitch: 18%
Gets Ahead of the Pitcher: 41%
Hits Behind the Pitcher: 59%

1990 On Base Percentage: .268   Career: .283
1990 Slugging Percentage: .404   Career: .441
Batting Avg with Men in Scoring Position: .229

Bats Right-Handed		AB	R	H	2B	3B	HR	RBI	BB	SO	SB	AVG
Vs. RHP		303	30	72	21	2	10	41	9	82	0	.238
Vs. LHP		135	16	30	6	1	4	14	12	36	1	.222
At Home	59	196	18	46	13	1	3	17	14	55	0	.235
On the Road	64	242	28	56	14	2	11	38	7	63	1	.231
1990 Season	123	438	46	102	27	3	14	55	21	118	1	.233
Life	4.1 Years	599	73	147	28	2	28	84	33	158	5	.245

Bill SPIERS

MILWAUKEE   SHORTSTOP   24 Years Old

Runs Created: 29   Offensive Winning Percentage: .241
Batting Average: .242   Secondary Average: .149

Most Often Bats: 9th
Hits First Pitch: 20%
Gets Ahead of the Pitcher: 44%
Hits Behind the Pitcher: 56%

1990 On Base Percentage: .274   Career: .286
1990 Slugging Percentage: .317   Career: .325
Batting Avg with Men in Scoring Position: .253

Bats Left-Handed		AB	R	H	2B	3B	HR	RBI	BB	SO	SB	AVG
Vs. RHP		282	37	69	12	2	2	29	11	32	11	.245
Vs. LHP		81	7	19	3	1	0	7	5	13	0	.235
At Home	56	176	22	47	7	3	2	22	9	19	5	.267
On the Road	56	187	22	41	8	0	0	14	7	26	6	.219
1990 Season	112	363	44	88	15	3	2	36	16	45	11	.242
Life	1.4 Years	508	63	126	17	4	4	49	27	77	15	.249

Sammy SOSA

CHICAGO   RIGHT FIELD   22 Years Old

Runs Created: 58   Offensive Winning Percentage: .434
Batting Average: .233   Secondary Average: .293

Most Often Bats: 1st
Hits First Pitch: 15%
Gets Ahead of the Pitcher: 42%
Hits Behind the Pitcher: 58%

1990 On Base Percentage: .282   Career: .288
1990 Slugging Percentage: .404   Career: .394
Batting Avg with Men in Scoring Position: .243

Bats Right-Handed		AB	R	H	2B	3B	HR	RBI	BB	SO	SB	AVG
Vs. RHP		299	36	63	12	7	3	33	13	91	15	.211
Vs. LHP		233	36	61	14	3	12	37	20	59	17	.262
At Home	77	266	40	68	15	7	10	36	19	72	17	.256
On the Road	76	266	32	56	11	3	5	34	14	78	15	.211
1990 Season	153	532	72	124	26	10	15	70	33	150	32	.233
Life	1.3 Years	549	76	131	26	8	15	64	34	151	30	.239

Terry STEINBACH

OAKLAND   CATCHER   29 Years Old

Runs Created: 39   Offensive Winning Percentage: .427
Batting Average: .251   Secondary Average: .172

Most Often Bats: 7th
Hits First Pitch: 16%
Gets Ahead of the Pitcher: 52%
Hits Behind the Pitcher: 48%

1990 On Base Percentage: .291   Career: .324
1990 Slugging Percentage: .372   Career: .399
Batting Avg with Men in Scoring Position: .297

Bats Right-Handed		AB	R	H	2B	3B	HR	RBI	BB	SO	SB	AVG
Vs. RHP		270	18	64	9	1	6	41	11	51	0	.237
Vs. LHP		109	14	31	6	1	3	16	8	15	0	.284
At Home	57	185	18	46	5	0	3	28	12	33	0	.249
On the Road	57	194	14	49	10	2	6	29	7	33	0	.253
1990 Season	114	379	32	95	15	2	9	57	19	66	0	.251
Life	2.9 Years	541	61	146	21	2	15	71	39	83	2	.269

Dave STEWART

OAKLAND STARTING PITCHER 34 Years Old
22-11 2.56 ERA

Opponents Batting Average: .231
Offensive Support: 5.02 Runs Per Nine Innings
Double Play Support: .78 GDP Per Nine Innings

First Pitch is Hit: 15%
Gets Ahead of the Hitter: 53%
Gets Behind the Hitter: 47%
Gets Leadoff Man Out: 69%

1990 On Base Pct Allowed: .291 Slugging Percentage: .326
Stolen Bases Allowed: 13   Caught Stealing: 6

Pitches Right	AB	H	2B	3B	HR	RBI	BB	SO	AVG
Vs. RHB	502	127	20	1	8	43	35	86	.253
Vs. LHB	478	99	19	2	8	39	48	80	.207

	G	IP	W-L	Pct	SO	BB	ERA
At Home	18	145	11-4		86	39	1.74
On the Road	18	122	11-7		80	44	3.54
1990 Season	36	267	22-11	.667	166	83	2.56
Life 8.3 Years	48	221	15-10	.591	146	82	3.52

Dave STIEB

TORONTO STARTING PITCHER 33 Years Old
18-6 2.93 ERA

Opponents Batting Average: .230
Offensive Support: 4.36 Runs Per Nine Innings
Double Play Support: .30 GDP Per Nine Innings

First Pitch is Hit: 14%
Gets Ahead of the Hitter: 50%
Gets Behind the Hitter: 50%
Gets Leadoff Man Out: 75%

1990 On Base Pct Allowed: .296 Slugging Percentage: .320
Stolen Bases Allowed: 6   Caught Stealing: 8

Pitches Right	AB	H	2B	3B	HR	RBI	BB	SO	AVG
Vs. RHB	375	77	17	1	3	29	24	78	.205
Vs. LHB	403	102	14	2	8	39	40	47	.253

	G	IP	W-L	Pct	SO	BB	ERA
At Home	17	103	9-5		64	35	3.15
On the Road	16	106	9-1		61	29	2.73
1990 Season	33	209	18-6	.750	125	64	2.93
Life 10.4 Years	37	256	16-12	.574	149	90	3.34

Kurt STILLWELL

KANSAS CITY SHORTSTOP 25 Years Old

Runs Created: 54   Offensive Winning Percentage: .405
Batting Average: .249   Secondary Average: .180

Most Often Bats: 2nd
Hits First Pitch: 13%
Gets Ahead of the Pitcher: 52%
Hits Behind the Pitcher: 48%

1990 On Base Percentage: .304   Career: .315
1990 Slugging Percentage: .352   Career: .360
Batting Avg with Men in Scoring Position: .244

Switch Hitter	AB	R	H	2B	3B	HR	RBI	BB	SO	SB	AVG
Vs. RHP	378	39	99	26	2	3	31	22	45	0	.262
Vs. LHP	128	21	27	9	2	0	20	17	15	0	.211
At Home	73	254	37	68	20	4	3	34	20	32	0	.268
On the Road	71	252	23	58	15	0	0	17	19	28	0	.230
1990 Season 144	506	60	126	35	4	3	51	39	60	0	.249
Life 3.9 Years	535	66	134	28	6	6	55	48	76	6	.251

Todd STOTTLEMYRE

TORONTO STARTING PITCHER 25 Years Old
13-17 4.34 ERA

Opponents Batting Average: .274
Offensive Support: 5.81 Runs Per Nine Innings
Double Play Support: .58 GDP Per Nine Innings

First Pitch is Hit: 14%
Gets Ahead of the Hitter: 49%
Gets Behind the Hitter: 51%
Gets Leadoff Man Out: 67%

1990 On Base Pct Allowed: .337 Slugging Percentage: .410
Stolen Bases Allowed: 23   Caught Stealing: 13

Pitches Right	AB	H	2B	3B	HR	RBI	BB	SO	AVG
Vs. RHB	388	96	14	3	10	44	32	73	.247
Vs. LHB	393	118	22	5	8	52	37	42	.300

	G	IP	W-L	Pct	SO	BB	ERA
At Home	16	103	7-8		62	35	4.28
On the Road	17	100	6-9		53	34	4.41
1990 Season	33	203	13-17	.433	115	69	4.34
Life 2.1 Years	42	205	11-15	.429	117	76	4.51

Darryl STRAWBERRY

NEW YORK   RIGHT FIELD   29 Years Old

Runs Created: 104   Offensive Winning Percentage: .720
Batting Average: .277   Secondary Average: .399

Most Often Bats: 4th
Hits First Pitch: 11%
Gets Ahead of the Pitcher: 51%
Hits Behind the Pitcher: 49%

1990 On Base Percentage: .361   Career: .359
1990 Slugging Percentage: .518   Career: .520
Batting Avg with Men in Scoring Position: .304

Bats Left-Handed	AB	R	H	2B	3B	HR	RBI	BB	SO	SB	AVG
Vs. RHP	325	69	97	10	1	28	79	53	59	10	.298
Vs. LHP	217	23	53	8	0	9	29	17	51	5	.244
At Home	77	268	49	68	5	1	24	67	31	52	5	.254
On the Road	75	274	43	82	13	0	13	41	39	58	10	.299
1990 Season	152	542	92	150	18	1	37	108	70	110	15	.277
Life	6.8 Years	570	97	150	27	4	37	107	85	140	28	.263

B.J. SURHOFF

MILWAUKEE   CATCHER   26 Years Old

Runs Created: 61   Offensive Winning Percentage: .480
Batting Average: .276   Secondary Average: .224

Most Often Bats: 7th
Hits First Pitch: 13%
Gets Ahead of the Pitcher: 52%
Hits Behind the Pitcher: 48%

1990 On Base Percentage: .331   Career: .314
1990 Slugging Percentage: .376   Career: .362
Batting Avg with Men in Scoring Position: .275

Bats Left-Handed	AB	R	H	2B	3B	HR	RBI	BB	SO	SB	AVG
Vs. RHP	370	47	98	17	3	4	42	33	28	13	.265
Vs. LHP	104	8	33	4	1	2	17	8	9	5	.317
At Home	69	235	32	72	10	2	4	35	22	18	10	.306
On the Road	66	239	23	59	11	2	2	24	19	19	8	.247
1990 Season	135	474	55	131	21	4	6	59	41	37	18	.276
Life	3.2 Years	566	61	150	25	3	7	69	42	46	20	.266

Franklin STUBBS

HOUSTON   FIRST BASE   30 Years Old

Runs Created: 74   Offensive Winning Percentage: .702
Batting Average: .261   Secondary Average: .364

Most Often Bats: 4th
Hits First Pitch: 16%
Gets Ahead of the Pitcher: 53%
Hits Behind the Pitcher: 47%

1990 On Base Percentage: .334   Career: .304
1990 Slugging Percentage: .475   Career: .419
Batting Avg with Men in Scoring Position: .220

Bats Left-Handed	AB	R	H	2B	3B	HR	RBI	BB	SO	SB	AVG
Vs. RHP	289	40	76	13	1	16	48	38	73	15	.263
Vs. LHP	159	19	41	10	1	7	23	10	41	4	.258
At Home	74	229	27	58	15	1	9	39	25	57	12	.253
On the Road	72	219	32	59	8	1	14	32	23	57	7	.269
1990 Season	146	448	59	117	23	2	23	71	48	114	19	.261
Life	4.2 Years	430	53	101	17	2	19	59	42	108	12	.236

Bill SWIFT

SEATTLE   RELIEF PITCHER   29 Years Old
6-4   2.39 ERA   6 SAVES

Blown Saves: 1   Holds: 7   Save Efficiency: 93%
Inherited Runners who Scored: 37%
Opponents Batting Average: .272
Double Play Support: 1.20 GDP Per Nine Innings

First Pitch is Hit: 19%
Gets Ahead of the Hitter: 49%
Gets Behind the Hitter: 51%
Gets First Batter Out: 73%

1990 On Base Pct Allowed: .309 Slugging Percentage: .351
Stolen Bases Allowed: 0   Caught Stealing: 2

Pitches Right	AB	H	2B	3B	HR	RBI	BB	SO	AVG
Vs. RHB	280	73	15	0	0	27	13	27	.261
Vs. LHB	216	62	12	0	4	27	8	15	.287

	G	IP	W-L	Pct	SO	BB	ERA
1990 Season	55	128	6-4	.600	42	21	2.39
Life 3.6 Years	50	185	8-10	.433	67	63	4.32

Greg SWINDELL

CLEVELAND	STARTING PITCHER	26 Years Old
	12-9 4.40 ERA	

Opponents Batting Average: .288
Offensive Support: 4.40 Runs Per Nine Innings
Double Play Support: .59 GDP Per Nine Innings

First Pitch is Hit: 17%
Gets Ahead of the Hitter: 52%
Gets Behind the Hitter: 48%
Gets Leadoff Man Out: 67%

1990 On Base Pct Allowed: .324 Slugging Percentage: .451
Stolen Bases Allowed: 3   Caught Stealing: 12

Pitches Left	AB	H	2B	3B	HR	RBI	BB	SO	AVG
Vs. RHB	724	208	36	8	23	84	41	117	.287
Vs. LHB	126	37	5	0	4	15	6	18	.294

	G	IP	W-L	Pct	SO	BB	ERA
At Home	18	114	7-4		63	23	4.67
On the Road	16	101	5-5		72	24	4.10
1990 Season	34	215	12-9	.571	135	47	4.40
Life 3.2 Years	37	249	16-12	.567	182	60	3.88

•T•

Frank TANANA

DETROIT	STARTING PITCHER	37 Years Old
	9-8 5.31 ERA	

Opponents Batting Average: .280
Offensive Support: 5.00 Runs Per Nine Innings
Double Play Support: .71 GDP Per Nine Innings

First Pitch is Hit: 11%
Gets Ahead of the Hitter: 49%
Gets Behind the Hitter: 51%
Gets Leadoff Man Out: 67%

1990 On Base Pct Allowed: .349 Slugging Percentage: .453
Stolen Bases Allowed: 9   Caught Stealing: 15

Pitches Left	AB	H	2B	3B	HR	RBI	BB	SO	AVG
Vs. RHB	565	164	36	1	24	89	59	99	.290
Vs. LHB	113	26	4	0	1	10	7	15	.230

	G	IP	W-L	Pct	SO	BB	ERA
At Home	19	99	4-6		70	37	6.00
On the Road	15	77	5-2		44	29	4.42
1990 Season	34	176	9-8	.529	114	66	5.31
Life 14.3 Years	38	250	14-14	.514	172	72	3.58

•

Kevin TAPANI

MINNESOTA	STARTING PITCHER	27 Years Old
	12-8 4.07 ERA	

Opponents Batting Average: .264
Offensive Support: 4.80 Runs Per Nine Innings
Double Play Support: .51 GDP Per Nine Innings

First Pitch is Hit: 17%
Gets Ahead of the Hitter: 54%
Gets Behind the Hitter: 46%
Gets Leadoff Man Out: 76%

1990 On Base Pct Allowed: .297 Slugging Percentage: .393
Stolen Bases Allowed: 9   Caught Stealing: 9

Pitches Right	AB	H	2B	3B	HR	RBI	BB	SO	AVG
Vs. RHB	304	74	12	1	6	32	8	48	.243
Vs. LHB	317	90	16	7	6	30	21	53	.284

	G	IP	W-L	Pct	SO	BB	ERA
At Home	12	75	8-2		44	16	3.38
On the Road	16	85	4-6		57	13	4.68
1990 Season	28	159	12-8	.600	101	29	4.07
Life 0.9 Years	39	214	15-11	.583	133	44	4.02

Danny TARTABULL

KANSAS CITY   RIGHT FIELD   28 Years Old

Runs Created: 50   Offensive Winning Percentage: .616
Batting Average: .268   Secondary Average: .323

Most Often Bats: 4th
Hits First Pitch: 12%
Gets Ahead of the Pitcher: 49%
Hits Behind the Pitcher: 51%

1990 On Base Percentage: .341   Career: .367
1990 Slugging Percentage: .473   Career: .498
Batting Avg with Men in Scoring Position: .260

Bats Right-Handed	AB	R	H	2B	3B	HR	RBI	BB	SO	SB	AVG
Vs. RHP	207	26	50	14	0	10	43	15	65	1	.242
Vs. LHP	106	15	34	5	0	5	17	21	28	0	.321
At Home	41	142	15	33	4	0	5	25	13	40	1	.232
On the Road	47	171	26	51	15	0	10	35	23	53	0	.298
1990 Season	88	313	41	84	19	0	15	60	36	93	1	.268
Life	4.3 Years	571	84	161	33	3	28	102	78	151	6	.281

●

Garry TEMPLETON

SAN DIEGO   SHORTSTOP   35 Years Old

Runs Created: 46   Offensive Winning Percentage: .344
Batting Average: .248   Secondary Average: .164

Most Often Bats: 8th
Hits First Pitch: 20%
Gets Ahead of the Pitcher: 44%
Hits Behind the Pitcher: 56%

1990 On Base Percentage: .280   Career: .306
1990 Slugging Percentage: .362   Career: .371
Batting Avg with Men in Scoring Position: .287

Switch Hitter	AB	R	H	2B	3B	HR	RBI	BB	SO	SB	AVG
Vs. RHP	316	22	77	17	2	5	30	15	38	1	.244
Vs. LHP	189	23	48	8	1	4	29	9	21	0	.254
At Home	75	255	26	63	12	2	6	36	12	36	1	.247
On the Road	69	250	19	62	13	1	3	23	12	23	0	.248
1990 Season	144	505	45	125	25	3	9	59	24	59	1	.248
Life	12.1 Years	613	71	168	26	9	6	58	30	87	20	.273

Walt TERRELL

DETROIT   STARTING PITCHER   32 Years Old
8-11   5.24 ERA

Opponents Batting Average: .293
Offensive Support: 4.84 Runs Per Nine Innings
Double Play Support: 1.20 GDP Per Nine Innings

First Pitch is Hit: 16%
Gets Ahead of the Hitter: 45%
Gets Behind the Hitter: 55%
Gets Leadoff Man Out: 64%

1990 On Base Pct Allowed: .361 Slugging Percentage: .458
Stolen Bases Allowed: 10   Caught Stealing: 6

Pitches Right	AB	H	2B	3B	HR	RBI	BB	SO	AVG
Vs. RHB	288	74	14	3	4	26	20	30	.257
Vs. LHB	341	110	22	1	16	53	37	34	.323

	G	IP	W-L	Pct	SO	BB	ERA
At Home	14	79	5-4		31	25	4.58
On the Road	15	79	3-7		33	32	5.90
1990 Season	29	158	8-11	.421	64	57	5.24
Life 6.7 Years	37	243	14-15	.479	117	92	4.13

●

Scott TERRY

ST. LOUIS   RELIEF PITCHER   31 Years Old
2-6   4.75 ERA   2 SAVES

Blown Saves: 1   Holds: 0   Save Efficiency: 67%
Inherited Runners who Scored: 36%
Opponents Batting Average: .264
Double Play Support: .13 GDP Per Nine Innings

First Pitch is Hit: 18%
Gets Ahead of the Hitter: 49%
Gets Behind the Hitter: 51%
Gets First Batter Out: 60%

1990 On Base Pct Allowed: .331 Slugging Percentage: .415
Stolen Bases Allowed: 7   Caught Stealing: 3

Pitches Right	AB	H	2B	3B	HR	RBI	BB	SO	AVG
Vs. RHB	158	43	12	0	3	23	12	15	.272
Vs. LHB	126	32	8	1	4	26	15	20	.254

	G	IP	W-L	Pct	SO	BB	ERA
1990 Season	50	72	2-6	.250	35	27	4.75
Life 2.9 Years	60	147	7-8	.455	74	51	3.91

Mickey TETTLETON

BALTIMORE   CATCHER   30 Years Old

Runs Created: 71   Offensive Winning Percentage: .613
Batting Average: .223   Secondary Average: .401

Most Often Bats: 4th
Hits First Pitch: 6%
Gets Ahead of the Pitcher: 57%
Hits Behind the Pitcher: 43%

1990 On Base Percentage: .376   Career: .348
1990 Slugging Percentage: .381   Career: .406
Batting Avg with Men in Scoring Position: .155

Switch Hitter	AB	R	H	2B	3B	HR	RBI	BB	SO	SB	AVG
Vs. RHP	316	52	69	13	2	10	33	82	110	1	.218
Vs. LHP	128	16	30	8	0	5	18	24	50	1	.234
At Home	66	215	31	51	11	2	8	27	56	79	2	.237
On the Road	69	229	37	48	10	0	7	24	50	81	0	.210
1990 Season 135	444	68	99	21	2	15	51	106	160	2	.223
Life 3.8 Years	482	65	114	21	2	19	61	82	142	4	.236

Bob TEWKSBURY

ST. LOUIS   STARTING PITCHER   30 Years Old
10-9   3.47 ERA

Opponents Batting Average: .267
Offensive Support: 4.95 Runs Per Nine Innings
Double Play Support: .56 GDP Per Nine Innings

First Pitch is Hit: 19%
Gets Ahead of the Hitter: 57%
Gets Behind the Hitter: 43%
Gets Leadoff Man Out: 75%

1990 On Base Pct Allowed: .286 Slugging Percentage: .379
Stolen Bases Allowed: 8   Caught Stealing: 5

Pitches Right	AB	H	2B	3B	HR	RBI	BB	SO	AVG
Vs. RHB	231	58	15	2	3	22	2	28	.251
Vs. LHB	334	93	21	1	4	37	13	22	.278

	G	IP	W-L	Pct	SO	BB	ERA
At Home	13	66	4-5		22	5	3.66
On the Road	15	79	6-4		28	10	3.30
1990 Season	28	145	10-9	.526	50	15	3.47
Life 1.7 Years	43	208	12-13	.488	80	45	3.90

Bobby THIGPEN

CHICAGO   RELIEF PITCHER   27 Years Old
4-6   1.83 ERA   57 SAVES

Blown Saves: 8   Holds: 0   Save Efficiency: 88%
Inherited Runners who Scored: 18%
Opponents Batting Average: .195
Double Play Support: 1.22 GDP Per Nine Innings

First Pitch is Hit: 13%
Gets Ahead of the Hitter: 49%
Gets Behind the Hitter: 51%
Gets First Batter Out: 76%

1990 On Base Pct Allowed: .271 Slugging Percentage: .283
Stolen Bases Allowed: 3   Caught Stealing: 0

Pitches Right	AB	H	2B	3B	HR	RBI	BB	SO	AVG
Vs. RHB	149	26	4	1	2	13	14	35	.174
Vs. LHB	158	34	4	1	3	12	18	35	.215

	G	IP	W-L	Pct	SO	BB	ERA
1990 Season	77	89	4-6	.400	70	32	1.83
Life 3.7 Years	74	102	5-7	.444	67	38	2.78

Andres THOMAS

ATLANTA   SHORTSTOP   27 Years Old

Runs Created: 18   Offensive Winning Percentage: .179
Batting Average: .219   Secondary Average: .129

Most Often Bats: 7th
Hits First Pitch: 20%
Gets Ahead of the Pitcher: 45%
Hits Behind the Pitcher: 55%

1990 On Base Percentage: .248   Career: .255
1990 Slugging Percentage: .302   Career: .334
Batting Avg with Men in Scoring Position: .260

Bats Right-Handed	AB	R	H	2B	3B	HR	RBI	BB	SO	SB	AVG
Vs. RHP	176	12	38	6	0	1	15	6	28	2	.216
Vs. LHP	102	14	23	2	0	4	15	5	15	0	.225
At Home	46	157	13	36	4	0	1	12	7	24	1	.229
On the Road	38	121	13	25	4	0	4	18	4	19	1	.207
1990 Season 84	278	26	61	8	0	5	30	11	43	2	.219
Life 3.6 Years	590	51	138	21	1	12	64	17	85	6	.234

Milt THOMPSON

ST. LOUIS   RIGHT FIELD   32 Years Old

Runs Created: 44   Offensive Winning Percentage: .434
Batting Average: .218   Secondary Average: .263

Most Often Bats: 6th
Hits First Pitch: 13%
Gets Ahead of the Pitcher: 53%
Hits Behind the Pitcher: 47%

1990 On Base Percentage: .292   Career: .334
1990 Slugging Percentage: .328   Career: .374
Batting Avg with Men in Scoring Position: .211

Bats Left-Handed	AB	R	H	2B	3B	HR	RBI	BB	SO	SB	AVG
Vs. RHP	298	31	70	11	5	6	26	34	34	22	.235
Vs. LHP	120	11	21	3	2	0	4	5	26	3	.175
At Home	73	221	23	47	5	4	3	20	21	27	17	.213
On the Road	62	197	19	44	9	3	3	10	18	33	8	.223
1990 Season 135	418	42	91	14	7	6	30	39	60	25	.218
Life 4.7 Years	525	67	145	21	6	6	44	44	87	34	.277

Dickie THON

PHILADELPHIA   SHORTSTOP   32 Years Old

Runs Created: 57   Offensive Winning Percentage: .411
Batting Average: .255   Secondary Average: .183

Most Often Bats: 7th
Hits First Pitch: 20%
Gets Ahead of the Pitcher: 47%
Hits Behind the Pitcher: 53%

1990 On Base Percentage: .305   Career: .323
1990 Slugging Percentage: .350   Career: .382
Batting Avg with Men in Scoring Position: .240

Bats Right-Handed	AB	R	H	2B	3B	HR	RBI	BB	SO	SB	AVG
Vs. RHP	350	33	88	11	3	3	27	23	52	10	.251
Vs. LHP	202	21	53	9	1	5	21	14	25	2	.262
At Home	73	254	22	63	7	0	3	28	25	37	8	.248
On the Road	76	298	32	78	13	4	5	20	12	40	4	.262
1990 Season 149	552	54	141	20	4	8	48	37	77	12	.255
Life 6.5 Years	518	61	138	23	5	9	49	43	76	21	.267

Robby THOMPSON

SAN FRANCISCO   SECOND BASE   28 Years Old

Runs Created: 59   Offensive Winning Percentage: .452
Batting Average: .245   Secondary Average: .243

Most Often Bats: 7th
Hits First Pitch: 12%
Gets Ahead of the Pitcher: 47%
Hits Behind the Pitcher: 53%

1990 On Base Percentage: .299   Career: .322
1990 Slugging Percentage: .392   Career: .392
Batting Avg with Men in Scoring Position: .248

Bats Right-Handed	AB	R	H	2B	3B	HR	RBI	BB	SO	SB	AVG
Vs. RHP	315	34	72	11	2	7	29	21	62	9	.229
Vs. LHP	183	33	50	11	1	8	27	13	34	5	.273
At Home	76	248	35	66	14	2	8	37	24	47	7	.266
On the Road	68	250	32	56	8	1	7	19	10	49	7	.224
1990 Season 144	498	67	122	22	3	15	56	34	96	14	.245
Life 4.4 Years	568	82	146	28	6	12	56	47	124	15	.257

Randy TOMLIN

PITTSBURGH   STARTING PITCHER   24 Years Old
4-4   2.55 ERA

Opponents Batting Average: .221
Offensive Support: 3.94 Runs Per Nine Innings
Double Play Support: .58 GDP Per Nine Innings

First Pitch is Hit: 11%
Gets Ahead of the Hitter: 47%
Gets Behind the Hitter: 53%
Gets Leadoff Man Out: 78%

1990 On Base Pct Allowed: .254 Slugging Percentage: .343
Stolen Bases Allowed: 2   Caught Stealing: 6

Pitches Left	AB	H	2B	3B	HR	RBI	BB	SO	AVG
Vs. RHB	235	50	15	1	3	15	11	31	.213
Vs. LHB	45	12	2	0	2	5	1	11	.267

	G	IP	W-L	Pct	SO	BB	ERA
At Home	8	51	2-3		26	4	3.02
On the Road	4	27	2-1		16	8	1.67
1990 Season	12	78	4-4	.500	42	12	2.55
Life 0.3 Years	37	239	12-12	.500	130	37	2.55

Alan TRAMMELL

DETROIT	SHORTSTOP	33 Years Old

Runs Created: 95   Offensive Winning Percentage: .636
Batting Average: .304   Secondary Average: .288

Most Often Bats: 3rd
Hits First Pitch: 12%
Gets Ahead of the Pitcher: 55%
Hits Behind the Pitcher: 45%

1990 On Base Percentage: .377   Career: .355
1990 Slugging Percentage: .449   Career: .420
Batting Avg with Men in Scoring Position: .379

Bats Right-Handed		AB	R	H	2B	3B	HR	RBI	BB	SO	SB	AVG
Vs. RHP		386	48	120	26	0	7	62	45	41	10	.311
Vs. LHP		173	23	50	11	1	7	27	23	14	2	.289
At Home	74	271	41	92	18	1	9	59	36	24	6	.339
On the Road	72	288	30	78	19	0	5	30	32	31	6	.271
1990 Season	146	559	71	170	37	1	14	89	68	55	12	.304
Life 11.3 Years		592	89	170	29	4	13	72	62	63	18	.288

•

Jeff TREADWAY

ATLANTA	SECOND BASE	28 Years Old

Runs Created: 59   Offensive Winning Percentage: .474
Batting Average: .283   Secondary Average: .179

Most Often Bats: 2nd
Hits First Pitch: 22%
Gets Ahead of the Pitcher: 51%
Hits Behind the Pitcher: 49%

1990 On Base Percentage: .320   Career: .320
1990 Slugging Percentage: .403   Career: .388
Batting Avg with Men in Scoring Position: .341

Bats Left-Handed		AB	R	H	2B	3B	HR	RBI	BB	SO	SB	AVG
Vs. RHP		355	42	98	15	2	7	39	15	32	2	.276
Vs. LHP		119	14	36	5	0	4	20	10	10	1	.303
At Home	58	219	24	66	10	0	5	27	9	20	1	.301
On the Road	70	255	32	68	10	2	6	32	16	22	2	.267
1990 Season	128	474	56	134	20	2	11	59	25	42	3	.283
Life 2.4 Years		556	64	154	25	4	10	53	35	48	4	.277

John TUDOR

ST. LOUIS	STARTING PITCHER	37 Years Old
	12-4 2.40 ERA	

Opponents Batting Average: .225
Offensive Support: 4.80 Runs Per Nine Innings
Double Play Support: .43 GDP Per Nine Innings

First Pitch is Hit: 18%
Gets Ahead of the Hitter: 47%
Gets Behind the Hitter: 53%
Gets Leadoff Man Out: 73%

1990 On Base Pct Allowed: .268 Slugging Percentage: .331
Stolen Bases Allowed: 8   Caught Stealing: 9

Pitches Left	AB	H	2B	3B	HR	RBI	BB	SO	AVG
Vs. RHB	408	93	20	1	9	32	25	40	.228
Vs. LHB	126	27	5	0	1	7	5	23	.214

	G	IP	W-L	Pct	SO	BB	ERA
At Home	12	75	4-1		32	17	2.52
On the Road	13	71	8-3		31	13	2.27
1990 Season	25	146	12-4	.750	63	30	2.40
Life 7.4 Years	38	244	16-10	.619	134	65	3.12

•U•

Jose URIBE

SAN FRANCISCO   SHORTSTOP   31 Years Old

Runs Created: 35   Offensive Winning Percentage: .287
Batting Average: .248   Secondary Average: .137

Most Often Bats: 8th
Hits First Pitch: 19%
Gets Ahead of the Pitcher: 52%
Hits Behind the Pitcher: 48%

1990 On Base Percentage: .297   Career: .300
1990 Slugging Percentage: .304   Career: .314
Batting Avg with Men in Scoring Position: .216

Switch Hitter		AB	R	H	2B	3B	HR	RBI	BB	SO	SB	AVG
Vs. RHP		273	22	63	4	5	1	17	20	36	5	.231
Vs. LHP		142	13	40	4	1	0	7	9	13	0	.282
At Home	68	197	12	44	4	2	0	8	17	27	2	.223
On the Road	70	218	23	59	4	4	1	16	12	22	3	.271
1990 Season	138	415	35	103	8	6	1	24	29	49	5	.248
Life	5.2 Years	507	50	123	16	6	3	37	41	70	13	.243

•V•

Sergio VALDEZ

CLEVELAND   RELIEF PITCHER   25 Years Old
6-6   4.85 ERA   0 SAVES

Blown Saves: 0   Holds: 1   Save Efficiency: 100%
Inherited Runners who Scored: 25%
Opponents Batting Average: .276
Double Play Support: .84 GDP Per Nine Innings

First Pitch is Hit: 21%
Gets Ahead of the Hitter: 48%
Gets Behind the Hitter: 52%
Gets First Batter Out: 76%

1990 On Base Pct Allowed: .334 Slugging Percentage: .468
Stolen Bases Allowed: 6   Caught Stealing: 4

Pitches Right	AB	H	2B	3B	HR	RBI	BB	SO	AVG
Vs. RHB	225	75	17	0	11	40	17	37	.333
Vs. LHB	192	40	10	1	6	19	21	29	.208

	G	IP	W-L	Pct	SO	BB	ERA
1990 Season	30	108	6-6	.500	66	38	4.85
Life 1.0 Years	55	168	7-12	.368	114	67	5.39

•

Fernando VALENZUELA

LOS ANGELES   STARTING PITCHER   30 Years Old
13-13   4.59 ERA

Opponents Batting Average: .276
Offensive Support: 5.65 Runs Per Nine Innings
Double Play Support: .40 GDP Per Nine Innings

First Pitch is Hit: 15%
Gets Ahead of the Hitter: 47%
Gets Behind the Hitter: 53%
Gets Leadoff Man Out: 67%

1990 On Base Pct Allowed: .337 Slugging Percentage: .412
Stolen Bases Allowed: 19   Caught Stealing: 7

Pitches Left	AB	H	2B	3B	HR	RBI	BB	SO	AVG
Vs. RHB	678	182	45	1	15	86	62	96	.268
Vs. LHB	130	41	6	0	4	18	15	19	.315

	G	IP	W-L	Pct	SO	BB	ERA
At Home	18	118	8-5		61	44	3.75
On the Road	15	86	5-8		54	33	5.73
1990 Season	33	204	13-13	.500	115	77	4.59
Life 8.8 Years	38	267	16-13	.549	200	104	3.31

Dave VALLE

SEATTLE	CATCHER	30 Years Old

Runs Created: 34   Offensive Winning Percentage: .432
Batting Average: .214   Secondary Average: .266

Most Often Bats: 8th
Hits First Pitch: 9%
Gets Ahead of the Pitcher: 53%
Hits Behind the Pitcher: 47%

1990 On Base Percentage: .328   Career: .305
1990 Slugging Percentage: .331   Career: .383
Batting Avg with Men in Scoring Position: .233

Bats Right-Handed		AB	R	H	2B	3B	HR	RBI	BB	SO	SB	AVG
Vs. RHP		204	22	45	11	0	5	23	31	31	0	.221
Vs. LHP		104	15	21	4	0	2	10	14	17	1	.202
At Home	50	131	18	26	9	0	1	13	23	21	1	.198
On the Road	57	177	19	40	6	0	6	20	22	27	0	.226
1990 Season	107	308	37	66	15	0	7	33	45	48	1	.214
Life	2.8 Years	495	55	117	22	3	15	69	41	69	1	.236

Greg VAUGHN

MILWAUKEE	LEFT FIELD	25 Years Old

Runs Created: 44   Offensive Winning Percentage: .390
Batting Average: .220   Secondary Average: .317

Most Often Bats: 6th
Hits First Pitch: 15%
Gets Ahead of the Pitcher: 48%
Hits Behind the Pitcher: 52%

1990 On Base Percentage: .280   Career: .293
1990 Slugging Percentage: .432   Career: .430
Batting Avg with Men in Scoring Position: .283

Bats Right-Handed		AB	R	H	2B	3B	HR	RBI	BB	SO	SB	AVG
Vs. RHP		255	37	59	16	1	13	49	23	62	6	.231
Vs. LHP		127	14	25	10	1	4	12	10	29	1	.197
At Home	61	193	31	42	13	1	9	32	17	42	3	.218
On the Road	59	189	20	42	13	1	8	29	16	49	4	.222
1990 Season	120	382	51	84	26	2	17	61	33	91	7	.220
Life	1.0 Years	508	71	117	30	2	23	86	47	117	11	.230

Andy VAN SLYKE

PITTSBURGH	CENTER FIELD	30 Years Old

Runs Created: 89   Offensive Winning Percentage: .709
Batting Average: .284   Secondary Average: .343

Most Often Bats: 3rd
Hits First Pitch: 15%
Gets Ahead of the Pitcher: 55%
Hits Behind the Pitcher: 45%

1990 On Base Percentage: .367   Career: .346
1990 Slugging Percentage: .465   Career: .448
Batting Avg with Men in Scoring Position: .293

Bats Left-Handed		AB	R	H	2B	3B	HR	RBI	BB	SO	SB	AVG
Vs. RHP		305	46	91	23	4	12	49	40	54	12	.298
Vs. LHP		188	21	49	3	2	5	28	26	35	2	.261
At Home	64	219	27	63	15	1	6	35	31	40	5	.288
On the Road	72	274	40	77	11	5	11	42	35	49	9	.281
1990 Season	136	493	67	140	26	6	17	77	66	89	14	.284
Life	6.8 Years	536	78	144	27	9	17	76	63	105	29	.270

Robin VENTURA

CHICAGO	THIRD BASE	23 Years Old

Runs Created: 54   Offensive Winning Percentage: .454
Batting Average: .249   Secondary Average: .183

Most Often Bats: 2nd
Hits First Pitch: 12%
Gets Ahead of the Pitcher: 55%
Hits Behind the Pitcher: 45%

1990 On Base Percentage: .324   Career: .322
1990 Slugging Percentage: .318   Career: .312
Batting Avg with Men in Scoring Position: .300

Bats Left-Handed		AB	R	H	2B	3B	HR	RBI	BB	SO	SB	AVG
Vs. RHP		339	34	89	15	0	5	42	33	27	1	.263
Vs. LHP		154	14	34	2	1	0	12	22	26	0	.221
At Home	75	238	21	65	4	1	2	25	27	24	0	.273
On the Road	75	255	27	58	13	0	3	29	28	29	1	.227
1990 Season	150	493	48	123	17	1	5	54	55	53	1	.249
Life	1.0 Years	525	52	128	20	1	5	60	61	58	1	.243

Frank VIOLA

NEW YORK   STARTING PITCHER   30 Years Old
                     20-12   2.67 ERA

Opponents Batting Average: .242
Offensive Support: 4.94 Runs Per Nine Innings
Double Play Support: .61 GDP Per Nine Innings

First Pitch is Hit: 16%
Gets Ahead of the Hitter: 53%
Gets Behind the Hitter: 47%
Gets Leadoff Man Out: 71%

1990 On Base Pct Allowed: .288 Slugging Percentage: .333
Stolen Bases Allowed: 25   Caught Stealing: 15

Pitches Left	AB	H	2B	3B	HR	RBI	BB	SO	AVG
Vs. RHB	755	180	26	2	14	60	46	135	.238
Vs. LHB	183	47	10	0	1	12	14	47	.257

	G	IP	W-L	Pct	SO	BB	ERA
At Home	17	126	12-5		104	22	2.44
On the Road	18	124	8-7		78	38	2.90
1990 Season	35	250	20-12	.625	182	60	2.67
Life 8.3 Years	37	254	17-13	.555	177	73	3.70

Omar VIZQUEL

SEATTLE   SHORTSTOP   23 Years Old

Runs Created: 23   Offensive Winning Percentage: .336
Batting Average: .247   Secondary Average: .137

Most Often Bats: 9th
Hits First Pitch: 12%
Gets Ahead of the Pitcher: 46%
Hits Behind the Pitcher: 54%

1990 On Base Percentage: .295   Career: .281
1990 Slugging Percentage: .298   Career: .276
Batting Avg with Men in Scoring Position: .171

Switch Hitter	AB	R	H	2B	3B	HR	RBI	BB	SO	SB	AVG
Vs. RHP	174	13	44	1	2	1	10	13	14	4	.253
Vs. LHP	81	6	19	2	0	1	8	5	8	0	.235
At Home	39	114	7	27	2	0	0	6	11	14	1	.237
On the Road	42	141	12	36	1	2	2	12	7	8	3	.255
1990 Season	81	255	19	63	3	2	2	18	18	22	4	.247
Life 1.4 Years		464	46	107	7	4	2	27	33	45	4	.231

Bob WALK

PITTSBURGH   STARTING PITCHER   34 Years Old
                   7-5   3.75 ERA

Opponents Batting Average: .270
Offensive Support: 4.65 Runs Per Nine Innings
Double Play Support: .42 GDP Per Nine Innings

First Pitch is Hit: 13%
Gets Ahead of the Hitter: 47%
Gets Behind the Hitter: 53%
Gets Leadoff Man Out: 67%

1990 On Base Pct Allowed: .322 Slugging Percentage: .419
Stolen Bases Allowed: 13   Caught Stealing: 9

Pitches Right	AB	H	2B	3B	HR	RBI	BB	SO	AVG
Vs. RHB	206	58	12	0	8	19	10	37	.282
Vs. LHB	297	78	10	1	9	32	26	36	.263

	G	IP	W-L	Pct	SO	BB	ERA
At Home	11	60	3-3		31	17	3.90
On the Road	15	70	4-2		42	19	3.62
1990 Season	26	130	7-5	.583	73	36	3.75
Life 6.0 Years	43	204	12-10	.553	107	76	3.91

Larry WALKER

MONTREAL   RIGHT FIELD   24 Years Old

Runs Created: 61   Offensive Winning Percentage: .612
Batting Average: .241   Secondary Average: .360

Most Often Bats: 6th
Hits First Pitch: 17%
Gets Ahead of the Pitcher: 49%
Hits Behind the Pitcher: 51%

1990 On Base Percentage: .326   Career: .320
1990 Slugging Percentage: .434   Career: .408
Batting Avg with Men in Scoring Position: .194

Bats Left-Handed	AB	R	H	2B	3B	HR	RBI	BB	SO	SB	AVG
Vs. RHP	303	43	77	12	3	13	33	41	82	16	.254
Vs. LHP	116	16	24	6	0	6	18	8	30	5	.207
At Home	64	196	32	50	8	2	9	27	22	50	9	.255
On the Road	69	223	27	51	10	1	10	24	27	62	12	.229
1990 Season	133	419	59	101	18	3	19	51	49	112	21	.241
Life 0.9 Years		493	67	115	19	3	20	58	57	132	23	.234

Mike WALKER

CLEVELAND STARTING PITCHER 24 Years Old
2-6 4.88 ERA

Opponents Batting Average: .277
Offensive Support: 3.81 Runs Per Nine Innings
Double Play Support: 1.31 GDP Per Nine Innings

First Pitch is Hit: 18%
Gets Ahead of the Hitter: 43%
Gets Behind the Hitter: 57%
Gets Leadoff Man Out: 70%

1990 On Base Pct Allowed: .376 Slugging Percentage: .402
Stolen Bases Allowed: 9 Caught Stealing: 1

Pitches Right	AB	H	2B	3B	HR	RBI	BB	SO	AVG
Vs. RHB	156	47	9	1	3	21	22	14	.301
Vs. LHB	140	35	6	1	3	16	20	20	.250

	G	IP	W-L	Pct	SO	BB	ERA
At Home	9	34	1-3		14	17	4.54
On the Road	9	42	1-3		20	25	5.14
1990 Season	18	76	2-6	.250	34	42	4.88
Life 0.4 Years	47	189	4-16	.222	92	117	5.12

•

Tim WALLACH

MONTREAL THIRD BASE 33 Years Old

Runs Created: 96 Offensive Winning Percentage: .668
Batting Average: .296 Secondary Average: .252

Most Often Bats: 4th
Hits First Pitch: 14%
Gets Ahead of the Pitcher: 48%
Hits Behind the Pitcher: 52%

1990 On Base Percentage: .339 Career: .322
1990 Slugging Percentage: .471 Career: .435
Batting Avg with Men in Scoring Position: .280

Bats Right-Handed	AB	R	H	2B	3B	HR	RBI	BB	SO	SB	AVG
Vs. RHP	422	47	126	25	3	15	69	21	57	4	.299
Vs. LHP	204	22	59	12	2	6	29	21	23	2	.289
At Home	81	301	34	83	16	5	9	46	24	43	4	.276
On the Road	80	325	35	102	21	0	12	52	18	37	2	.314
1990 Season 161	626	69	185	37	5	21	98	42	80	6	.296
Life 9.0 Years	598	69	160	34	3	20	85	46	91	5	.267

Jerome WALTON

CHICAGO CENTER FIELD 25 Years Old

Runs Created: 49 Offensive Winning Percentage: .486
Batting Average: .263 Secondary Average: .230

Most Often Bats: 1st
Hits First Pitch: 14%
Gets Ahead of the Pitcher: 51%
Hits Behind the Pitcher: 49%

1990 On Base Percentage: .350 Career: .342
1990 Slugging Percentage: .329 Career: .360
Batting Avg with Men in Scoring Position: .233

Bats Right-Handed	AB	R	H	2B	3B	HR	RBI	BB	SO	SB	AVG
Vs. RHP	246	43	61	9	1	1	9	31	50	8	.248
Vs. LHP	146	20	42	7	1	1	12	19	20	6	.288
At Home	52	200	43	58	5	2	2	8	24	32	7	.290
On the Road	49	192	20	45	11	0	0	13	26	38	7	.234
1990 Season 101	392	63	103	16	2	2	21	50	70	14	.263
Life 1.3 Years	647	95	181	29	4	5	50	57	110	28	.279

•

Duane WARD

TORONTO RELIEF PITCHER 26 Years Old
2-8 3.45 ERA 11 SAVES

Blown Saves: 7 Holds: 11 Save Efficiency: 76%
Inherited Runners who Scored: 39%
Opponents Batting Average: .221
Double Play Support: .99 GDP Per Nine Innings

First Pitch is Hit: 13%
Gets Ahead of the Hitter: 56%
Gets Behind the Hitter: 44%
Gets First Batter Out: 84%

1990 On Base Pct Allowed: .287 Slugging Percentage: .322
Stolen Bases Allowed: 12 Caught Stealing: 6

Pitches Right	AB	H	2B	3B	HR	RBI	BB	SO	AVG
Vs. RHB	268	52	6	2	4	27	9	63	.194
Vs. LHB	189	49	7	1	5	26	33	49	.259

	G	IP	W-L	Pct	SO	BB	ERA
1990 Season	73	128	2-8	.200	112	42	3.45
Life 3.1 Years	73	124	5-7	.410	111	59	3.82

Gary WARD

DETROIT   LEFT FIELD   37 Years Old

Runs Created: 38   Offensive Winning Percentage: .443
Batting Average: .256   Secondary Average: .239

Most Often Bats: 5th
Hits First Pitch: 14%
Gets Ahead of the Pitcher: 50%
Hits Behind the Pitcher: 50%

1990 On Base Percentage: .322   Career: .328
1990 Slugging Percentage: .392   Career: .425
Batting Avg with Men in Scoring Position: .286

Bats Right-Handed		AB	R	H	2B	3B	HR	RBI	BB	SO	SB	AVG
Vs. RHP		157	16	40	5	0	4	26	16	28	1	.255
Vs. LHP		152	16	39	6	2	5	20	14	22	1	.257
At Home	47	131	14	34	7	2	2	17	14	24	0	.260
On the Road	59	178	18	45	4	0	7	29	16	26	2	.253
1990 Season	106	309	32	79	11	2	9	46	30	50	2	.256
Life	7.9 Years	564	75	156	25	5	16	75	44	98	10	.276

Walt WEISS

OAKLAND   SHORTSTOP   27 Years Old

Runs Created: 51   Offensive Winning Percentage: .493
Batting Average: .265   Secondary Average: .180

Most Often Bats: 8th
Hits First Pitch: 16%
Gets Ahead of the Pitcher: 54%
Hits Behind the Pitcher: 46%

1990 On Base Percentage: .337   Career: .323
1990 Slugging Percentage: .321   Career: .327
Batting Avg with Men in Scoring Position: .224

Switch Hitter		AB	R	H	2B	3B	HR	RBI	BB	SO	SB	AVG
Vs. RHP		330	39	88	12	1	2	23	38	43	7	.267
Vs. LHP		115	11	30	5	0	0	12	8	10	2	.261
At Home	74	235	24	58	5	0	1	16	22	33	4	.247
On the Road	64	210	26	60	12	1	1	19	24	20	5	.286
1990 Season	138	445	50	118	17	1	2	35	46	53	9	.265
Life	2.4 Years	488	53	125	21	2	3	40	44	63	8	.257

Mitch WEBSTER

CLEVELAND   CENTER FIELD   31 Years Old

Runs Created: 52   Offensive Winning Percentage: .436
Batting Average: .252   Secondary Average: .252

Most Often Bats: 2nd
Hits First Pitch: 20%
Gets Ahead of the Pitcher: 51%
Hits Behind the Pitcher: 49%

1990 On Base Percentage: .285   Career: .336
1990 Slugging Percentage: .407   Career: .409
Batting Avg with Men in Scoring Position: .266

Switch Hitter		AB	R	H	2B	3B	HR	RBI	BB	SO	SB	AVG
Vs. RHP		245	32	54	9	4	4	22	13	47	14	.220
Vs. LHP		192	26	56	11	2	8	33	7	14	8	.292
At Home	66	231	29	57	7	2	6	35	12	32	12	.247
On the Road	62	206	29	53	13	4	6	20	8	29	10	.257
1990 Season	128	437	58	110	20	6	12	55	20	61	22	.252
Life	4.9 Years	536	81	145	24	9	11	53	51	85	29	.270

Bob WELCH

OAKLAND   STARTING PITCHER   34 Years Old
                          27-6   2.95 ERA

Opponents Batting Average: .242
Offensive Support: 5.90 Runs Per Nine Innings
Double Play Support: .95 GDP Per Nine Innings

First Pitch is Hit: 15%
Gets Ahead of the Hitter: 51%
Gets Behind the Hitter: 49%
Gets Leadoff Man Out: 72%

1990 On Base Pct Allowed: .304 Slugging Percentage: .391
Stolen Bases Allowed: 10   Caught Stealing: 7

Pitches Right	AB	H	2B	3B	HR	RBI	BB	SO	AVG
Vs. RHB	421	94	22	0	14	42	34	72	.223
Vs. LHB	465	120	20	6	12	39	43	55	.258

	G	IP	W-L	Pct	SO	BB	ERA
At Home	16	117	14-2		69	39	1.92
On the Road	19	121	13-4		58	38	3.94
1990 Season	35	238	27-6	.818	127	77	2.95
Life 10.4 Years	38	242	17-11	.618	165	77	3.16

David WELLS

TORONTO   STARTING PITCHER   27 Years Old
11-6   3.14 ERA

Opponents Batting Average: .235
Offensive Support: 4.86 Runs Per Nine Innings
Double Play Support: .43 GDP Per Nine Innings

First Pitch is Hit: 13%
Gets Ahead of the Hitter: 48%
Gets Behind the Hitter: 52%
Gets Leadoff Man Out: 72%

1990 On Base Pct Allowed: .283 Slugging Percentage: .371
Stolen Bases Allowed: 11   Caught Stealing: 11

Pitches Left	AB	H	2B	3B	HR	RBI	BB	SO	AVG
Vs. RHB	591	136	28	6	12	50	37	103	.230
Vs. LHB	110	29	11	1	2	15	8	12	.264

	G	IP	W-L	Pct	SO	BB	ERA
At Home	21	83	3-2		48	20	2.61
On the Road	22	106	8-4		67	25	3.55
1990 Season	43	189	11-6	.647	115	45	3.14
Life 2.5 Years	63	149	10-7	.581	114	47	3.29

David WEST

MINNESOTA   STARTING PITCHER   26 Years Old
7-9   5.10 ERA

Opponents Batting Average: .256
Offensive Support: 5.35 Runs Per Nine Innings
Double Play Support: .98 GDP Per Nine Innings

First Pitch is Hit: 12%
Gets Ahead of the Hitter: 45%
Gets Behind the Hitter: 55%
Gets Leadoff Man Out: 73%

1990 On Base Pct Allowed: .350 Slugging Percentage: .451
Stolen Bases Allowed: 5   Caught Stealing: 5

Pitches Left	AB	H	2B	3B	HR	RBI	BB	SO	AVG
Vs. RHB	464	120	32	3	20	70	66	78	.259
Vs. LHB	90	22	3	2	1	13	12	14	.244

	G	IP	W-L	Pct	SO	BB	ERA
At Home	13	63	2-4		46	33	6.03
On the Road	16	84	5-5		46	45	4.41
1990 Season	29	146	7-9	.438	92	78	5.10
Life 1.2 Years	44	184	9-11	.458	123	97	5.54

Lou WHITAKER

DETROIT   SECOND BASE   33 Years Old

Runs Created: 68   Offensive Winning Percentage: .525
Batting Average: .237   Secondary Average: .343

Most Often Bats: 1st
Hits First Pitch: 13%
Gets Ahead of the Pitcher: 52%
Hits Behind the Pitcher: 48%

1990 On Base Percentage: .338   Career: .355
1990 Slugging Percentage: .407   Career: .411
Batting Avg with Men in Scoring Position: .223

Bats Left-Handed	AB	R	H	2B	3B	HR	RBI	BB	SO	SB	AVG
Vs. RHP	373	65	96	21	1	16	53	58	52	8	.257
Vs. LHP	99	10	16	1	1	2	7	16	19	0	.162
At Home	64	219	34	47	10	0	8	27	34	36	6	.215
On the Road	68	253	41	65	12	2	10	33	40	35	2	.257
1990 Season 132	472	75	112	22	2	18	60	74	71	8	.237
Life 11.3 Years	593	92	162	27	5	15	69	78	77	11	.274

Devon WHITE

CALIFORNIA   CENTER FIELD   28 Years Old

Runs Created: 47   Offensive Winning Percentage: .386
Batting Average: .217   Secondary Average: .273

Most Often Bats: 3rd
Hits First Pitch: 8%
Gets Ahead of the Pitcher: 48%
Hits Behind the Pitcher: 52%

1990 On Base Percentage: .290   Career: .295
1990 Slugging Percentage: .343   Career: .389
Batting Avg with Men in Scoring Position: .196

Switch Hitter	AB	R	H	2B	3B	HR	RBI	BB	SO	SB	AVG
Vs. RHP	313	39	64	12	3	8	34	32	94	18	.204
Vs. LHP	130	18	32	5	0	3	10	12	22	3	.246
At Home	61	219	26	47	9	3	5	20	19	55	8	.215
On the Road	64	224	31	49	8	0	6	24	25	61	13	.219
1990 Season 125	443	57	96	17	3	11	44	44	116	21	.217
Life 3.8 Years	591	89	146	24	6	16	64	38	126	33	.247

Ed WHITSON

SAN DIEGO   STARTING PITCHER   35 Years Old
                   14-9   2.60 ERA

Opponents Batting Average: .251
Offensive Support: 4.41 Runs Per Nine Innings
Double Play Support: .59 GDP Per Nine Innings

First Pitch is Hit: 23%
Gets Ahead of the Hitter: 57%
Gets Behind the Hitter: 43%
Gets Leadoff Man Out: 74%

1990 On Base Pct Allowed: .289 Slugging Percentage: .347
Stolen Bases Allowed: 12   Caught Stealing: 7

Pitches Right	AB	H	2B	3B	HR	RBI	BB	SO	AVG
Vs. RHB	333	74	15	0	7	29	17	55	.222
Vs. LHB	522	141	26	1	6	37	30	72	.270

	G	IP	W-L	Pct	SO	BB	ERA
At Home	17	126	5-6		77	21	2.65
On the Road	15	103	9-3		50	26	2.53
1990 Season	32	229	14-9	.609	127	47	2.60
Life 10.3 Years	43	211	12-11	.510	119	66	3.75

Matt D. WILLIAMS

SAN FRANCISCO   THIRD BASE   25 Years Old

Runs Created: 93   Offensive Winning Percentage: .593
Batting Average: .277   Secondary Average: .276

Most Often Bats: 5th
Hits First Pitch: 19%
Gets Ahead of the Pitcher: 46%
Hits Behind the Pitcher: 54%

1990 On Base Percentage: .319   Career: .279
1990 Slugging Percentage: .488   Career: .444
Batting Avg with Men in Scoring Position: .331

Bats Right-Handed	AB	R	H	2B	3B	HR	RBI	BB	SO	SB	AVG
Vs. RHP	409	58	112	18	2	21	74	20	98	1	.274
Vs. LHP	208	29	59	9	0	12	48	13	40	6	.284

		AB	R	H	2B	3B	HR	RBI	BB	SO	SB	AVG
At Home	79	303	51	82	14	1	20	63	15	66	3	.271
On the Road	80	314	36	89	13	1	13	59	18	72	4	.283
1990 Season	159	617	87	171	27	2	33	122	33	138	7	.277
Life	2.3 Years	560	70	132	26	3	29	91	30	136	5	.235

Mitch WILLIAMS

CHICAGO   RELIEF PITCHER   26 Years Old
                 1-8   3.93 ERA   16 SAVES

Blown Saves: 4   Holds: 1   Save Efficiency: 81%
Inherited Runners who Scored: 39%
Opponents Batting Average: .239
Double Play Support: .41 GDP Per Nine Innings

First Pitch is Hit: 7%
Gets Ahead of the Hitter: 42%
Gets Behind the Hitter: 58%
Gets First Batter Out: 64%

1990 On Base Pct Allowed: .364 Slugging Percentage: .390
Stolen Bases Allowed: 6   Caught Stealing: 0

Pitches Left	AB	H	2B	3B	HR	RBI	BB	SO	AVG
Vs. RHB	185	45	15	2	2	30	34	37	.243
Vs. LHB	66	15	5	1	2	14	16	18	.227

	G	IP	W-L	Pct	SO	BB	ERA
1990 Season	59	66	1-8	.111	55	50	3.93
Life 5.0 Years	73	85	5-6	.426	80	64	3.53

Mark WILLIAMSON

BALTIMORE   RELIEF PITCHER   31 Years Old
                   8-2   2.21 ERA   1 SAVES

Blown Saves: 4   Holds: 8   Save Efficiency: 69%
Inherited Runners who Scored: 29%
Opponents Batting Average: .215
Double Play Support: .95 GDP Per Nine Innings

First Pitch is Hit: 14%
Gets Ahead of the Hitter: 53%
Gets Behind the Hitter: 47%
Gets First Batter Out: 73%

1990 On Base Pct Allowed: .276 Slugging Percentage: .351
Stolen Bases Allowed: 5   Caught Stealing: 2

Pitches Right	AB	H	2B	3B	HR	RBI	BB	SO	AVG
Vs. RHB	163	34	9	0	2	18	21	35	.209
Vs. LHB	139	31	4	2	6	19	7	25	.223

	G	IP	W-L	Pct	SO	BB	ERA
1990 Season	49	85	8-2	.800	60	28	2.21
Life 3.0 Years	70	144	10-8	.564	85	46	3.64

Frank WILLS

TORONTO   RELIEF PITCHER   32 Years Old
6-4   4.73 ERA   0 SAVES

Blown Saves: 0   Holds: 3   Save Efficiency: 100%
Inherited Runners who Scored: 21%
Opponents Batting Average: .266
Double Play Support: 1.27 GDP Per Nine Innings

First Pitch is Hit: 18%
Gets Ahead of the Hitter: 46%
Gets Behind the Hitter: 54%
Gets First Batter Out: 65%

1990 On Base Pct Allowed: .333 Slugging Percentage: .424
Stolen Bases Allowed: 8   Caught Stealing: 4

Pitches Right	AB	H	2B	3B	HR	RBI	BB	SO	AVG
Vs. RHB	208	58	9	1	9	39	21	54	.279
Vs. LHB	172	43	10	0	4	14	17	18	.250

	G	IP	W-L	Pct	SO	BB	ERA
1990 Season	44	99	6-4	.600	72	38	4.73
Life 2.5 Years	60	173	9-10	.468	112	77	4.95

•

Glenn WILSON

HOUSTON   RIGHT FIELD   32 Years Old

Runs Created: 35   Offensive Winning Percentage: .409
Batting Average: .245   Secondary Average: .190

Most Often Bats: 6th
Hits First Pitch: 14%
Gets Ahead of the Pitcher: 51%
Hits Behind the Pitcher: 49%

1990 On Base Percentage: .293   Career: .306
1990 Slugging Percentage: .364   Career: .399
Batting Avg with Men in Scoring Position: .286

Bats Right-Handed	AB	R	H	2B	3B	HR	RBI	BB	SO	SB	AVG
Vs. RHP	204	25	47	4	0	8	30	13	37	0	.230
Vs. LHP	164	17	43	10	0	2	25	13	27	0	.262
At Home	58	174	23	45	10	0	5	33	13	28	0	.259
On the Road	60	194	19	45	4	0	5	22	13	36	0	.232
1990 Season 118	368	42	90	14	0	10	55	26	64	0	.245
Life 7.4 Years	563	61	149	28	4	13	71	34	90	4	.265

Mookie WILSON

TORONTO   CENTER FIELD   35 Years Old

Runs Created: 64   Offensive Winning Percentage: .429
Batting Average: .265   Secondary Average: .182

Most Often Bats: 1st
Hits First Pitch: 17%
Gets Ahead of the Pitcher: 44%
Hits Behind the Pitcher: 56%

1990 On Base Percentage: .300   Career: .316
1990 Slugging Percentage: .355   Career: .388
Batting Avg with Men in Scoring Position: .257

Switch Hitter	AB	R	H	2B	3B	HR	RBI	BB	SO	SB	AVG
Vs. RHP	400	59	110	26	2	1	30	17	66	20	.275
Vs. LHP	188	22	46	10	2	2	21	14	36	3	.245
At Home	69	271	31	67	16	2	0	20	12	50	10	.247
On the Road	78	317	50	89	20	2	3	31	19	52	13	.281
1990 Season 147	588	81	156	36	4	3	51	31	102	23	.265
Life 8.1 Years	597	87	165	26	8	8	50	34	102	39	.276

•

Steve WILSON

CHICAGO   RELIEF PITCHER   26 Years Old
4-9   4.79 ERA   1 SAVES

Blown Saves: 1   Holds: 3   Save Efficiency: 80%
Inherited Runners who Scored: 23%
Opponents Batting Average: .259
Double Play Support: .32 GDP Per Nine Innings

First Pitch is Hit: 12%
Gets Ahead of the Hitter: 54%
Gets Behind the Hitter: 46%
Gets First Batter Out: 80%

1990 On Base Pct Allowed: .315 Slugging Percentage: .419
Stolen Bases Allowed: 6   Caught Stealing: 8

Pitches Left	AB	H	2B	3B	HR	RBI	BB	SO	AVG
Vs. RHB	403	110	17	5	14	52	35	61	.273
Vs. LHB	137	30	6	1	3	20	8	34	.219

	G	IP	W-L	Pct	SO	BB	ERA
1990 Season	45	139	4-9	.308	95	43	4.79
Life 1.7 Years	60	139	6-8	.435	96	47	4.61

Trevor WILSON

SAN FRANCISCO   STARTING PITCHER   24 Years Old
                       8-7   4.00 ERA

Opponents Batting Average: .218
Offensive Support: 4.24 Runs Per Nine Innings
Double Play Support: .82 GDP Per Nine Innings

First Pitch is Hit: 16%
Gets Ahead of the Hitter: 48%
Gets Behind the Hitter: 52%
Gets Leadoff Man Out: 70%

1990 On Base Pct Allowed: .304 Slugging Percentage: .333
Stolen Bases Allowed: 3   Caught Stealing: 8

Pitches Left	AB	H	2B	3B	HR	RBI	BB	SO	AVG
Vs. RHB	335	73	10	0	10	36	44	54	.218
Vs. LHB	64	14	3	0	1	8	5	12	.219

	G	IP	W-L	Pct	SO	BB	ERA
At Home	15	69	5-3		37	33	2.88
On the Road	12	42	3-4		29	16	5.83
1990 Season	27	110	8-7	.533	66	49	4.00
Life 0.9 Years	48	181	11-13	.455	109	86	4.09

•

Willie WILSON

KANSAS CITY   CENTER FIELD   35 Years Old

Runs Created: 44   Offensive Winning Percentage: .575
Batting Average: .290   Secondary Average: .257

Most Often Bats: 7th
Hits First Pitch: 14%
Gets Ahead of the Pitcher: 46%
Hits Behind the Pitcher: 54%

1990 On Base Percentage: .354   Career: .329
1990 Slugging Percentage: .371   Career: .382
Batting Avg with Men in Scoring Position: .297

Switch Hitter	AB	R	H	2B	3B	HR	RBI	BB	SO	SB	AVG
Vs. RHP	204	36	61	7	2	2	25	25	38	14	.299
Vs. LHP	103	13	28	6	1	0	17	5	19	10	.272
At Home	59	166	26	55	8	2	1	22	13	27	14	.331
On the Road	56	141	23	34	5	1	1	20	17	30	10	.241
1990 Season 115	307	49	89	13	3	2	42	30	57	24	.290
Life 11.0 Years	616	96	178	22	12	4	46	33	90	55	.289

Dave WINFIELD

CALIFORNIA   RIGHT FIELD   39 Years Old

Runs Created: 70   Offensive Winning Percentage: .579
Batting Average: .267   Secondary Average: .295

Most Often Bats: 4th
Hits First Pitch: 10%
Gets Ahead of the Pitcher: 57%
Hits Behind the Pitcher: 43%

1990 On Base Percentage: .338   Career: .356
1990 Slugging Percentage: .453   Career: .480
Batting Avg with Men in Scoring Position: .248

Bats Right-Handed	AB	R	H	2B	3B	HR	RBI	BB	SO	SB	AVG
Vs. RHP	319	44	82	12	0	16	46	32	59	0	.257
Vs. LHP	156	26	45	9	2	5	32	20	22	0	.288
At Home	69	238	40	62	12	1	13	41	27	44	0	.261
On the Road	63	237	30	65	9	1	8	37	25	37	0	.274
1990 Season 132	475	70	127	21	2	21	78	52	81	0	.267
Life 14.8 Years	600	93	172	29	5	26	102	67	88	14	.286

•

Bobby WITT

TEXAS   STARTING PITCHER   26 Years Old
               17-10   3.36 ERA

Opponents Batting Average: .238
Offensive Support: 4.62 Runs Per Nine Innings
Double Play Support: .73 GDP Per Nine Innings

First Pitch is Hit: 12%
Gets Ahead of the Hitter: 49%
Gets Behind the Hitter: 51%
Gets Leadoff Man Out: 72%

1990 On Base Pct Allowed: .328 Slugging Percentage: .326
Stolen Bases Allowed: 36   Caught Stealing: 7

Pitches Right	AB	H	2B	3B	HR	RBI	BB	SO	AVG
Vs. RHB	433	105	15	1	7	41	56	123	.242
Vs. LHB	396	92	16	2	5	42	54	98	.232

	G	IP	W-L	Pct	SO	BB	ERA
At Home	15	101	7-5		93	46	3.40
On the Road	18	121	10-5		128	64	3.34
1990 Season	33	222	17-10	.630	221	110	3.36
Life 3.8 Years	37	232	15-14	.519	226	158	4.48

Mike WITT

NEW YORK   STARTING PITCHER   30 Years Old
5-9   4.00 ERA

Opponents Batting Average: .241
Offensive Support: 4.15 Runs Per Nine Innings
Double Play Support: .92 GDP Per Nine Innings

First Pitch is Hit: 12%
Gets Ahead of the Hitter: 46%
Gets Behind the Hitter: 54%
Gets Leadoff Man Out: 69%

1990 On Base Pct Allowed: .318 Slugging Percentage: .360
Stolen Bases Allowed: 7   Caught Stealing: 4

Pitches Right	AB	H	2B	3B	HR	RBI	BB	SO	AVG
Vs. RHB	222	48	9	2	6	25	24	45	.216
Vs. LHB	217	58	10	1	3	28	23	29	.267

	G	IP	W-L	Pct	SO	BB	ERA
At Home	11	52	2-5		34	15	3.29
On the Road	15	65	3-4		40	32	4.57
1990 Season	26	117	5-9	.357	74	47	4.00
Life 8.4 Years	40	247	14-14	.502	161	83	3.79

•

Craig WORTHINGTON

BALTIMORE   THIRD BASE   25 Years Old

Runs Created: 47   Offensive Winning Percentage: .414
Batting Average: .226   Secondary Average: .247

Most Often Bats: 7th
Hits First Pitch: 8%
Gets Ahead of the Pitcher: 54%
Hits Behind the Pitcher: 46%

1990 On Base Percentage: .328   Career: .326
1990 Slugging Percentage: .322   Career: .350
Batting Avg with Men in Scoring Position: .196

Bats Right-Handed	AB	R	H	2B	3B	HR	RBI	BB	SO	SB	AVG
Vs. RHP	299	28	64	10	0	6	32	36	75	1	.214
Vs. LHP	126	18	32	7	0	2	12	27	21	0	.254
At Home	67	209	19	49	10	0	3	20	29	49	0	.234
On the Road	66	216	27	47	7	0	5	24	34	47	1	.218
1990 Season	133	425	46	96	17	0	8	44	63	96	1	.226
Life	1.9 Years	534	58	125	22	0	13	63	71	125	2	.233

Eric YELDING

HOUSTON   CENTER FIELD   26 Years Old

Runs Created: 47   Offensive Winning Percentage: .383
Batting Average: .254   Secondary Average: .245

Most Often Bats: 1st
Hits First Pitch: 16%
Gets Ahead of the Pitcher: 44%
Hits Behind the Pitcher: 56%

1990 On Base Percentage: .305   Career: .302
1990 Slugging Percentage: .297   Career: .291
Batting Avg with Men in Scoring Position: .228

Bats Right-Handed	AB	R	H	2B	3B	HR	RBI	BB	SO	SB	AVG
Vs. RHP	276	42	64	3	2	1	12	23	56	35	.232
Vs. LHP	235	27	66	6	3	0	16	16	31	29	.281
At Home	69	245	35	62	1	4	0	13	23	38	41	.253
On the Road	73	266	34	68	8	1	1	15	16	49	23	.256
1990 Season	142	511	69	130	9	5	1	28	39	87	64	.254
Life	1.3 Years	459	67	115	8	4	1	28	35	81	57	.251

•

Curt YOUNG

OAKLAND   STARTING PITCHER   30 Years Old
9-6   4.85 ERA

Opponents Batting Average: .266
Offensive Support: 4.63 Runs Per Nine Innings
Double Play Support: .87 GDP Per Nine Innings

First Pitch is Hit: 11%
Gets Ahead of the Hitter: 45%
Gets Behind the Hitter: 55%
Gets Leadoff Man Out: 66%

1990 On Base Pct Allowed: .342 Slugging Percentage: .418
Stolen Bases Allowed: 9   Caught Stealing: 11

Pitches Left	AB	H	2B	3B	HR	RBI	BB	SO	AVG
Vs. RHB	370	99	16	0	16	45	47	43	.268
Vs. LHB	96	25	4	0	1	12	6	13	.260

	G	IP	W-L	Pct	SO	BB	ERA
At Home	14	71	5-2		40	36	3.18
On the Road	12	54	4-4		16	17	7.04
1990 Season	26	124	9-6	.600	56	53	4.85
Life 4.5 Years	41	211	13-11	.556	107	68	4.28

Matt YOUNG

SEATTLE	STARTING PITCHER	32 Years Old
	8-18 3.51 ERA	

Opponents Batting Average: .237
Offensive Support: 3.75 Runs Per Nine Innings
Double Play Support: 1.08 GDP Per Nine Innings

First Pitch is Hit: 14%
Gets Ahead of the Hitter: 45%
Gets Behind the Hitter: 55%
Gets Leadoff Man Out: 70%

1990 On Base Pct Allowed: .325 Slugging Percentage: .328
Stolen Bases Allowed: 20   Caught Stealing: 14

Pitches Left	AB	H	2B	3B	HR	RBI	BB	SO	AVG
Vs. RHB	735	182	24	3	15	79	100	149	.248
Vs. LHB	101	16	1	0	0	7	7	27	.158

	G	IP	W-L	Pct	SO	BB	ERA
At Home	20	134	4-10		101	62	2.69
On the Road	14	91	4-8		75	45	4.73
1990 Season	34	225	8-18	.308	176	107	3.51
Life 5.3 Years	49	179	10-15	.395	125	77	4.26

•

Robin YOUNT

MILWAUKEE	CENTER FIELD	35 Years Old

Runs Created: 81   Offensive Winning Percentage: .504
Batting Average: .247   Secondary Average: .291

Most Often Bats: 3rd
Hits First Pitch: 13%
Gets Ahead of the Pitcher: 56%
Hits Behind the Pitcher: 44%

1990 On Base Percentage: .337   Career: .345
1990 Slugging Percentage: .380   Career: .437
Batting Avg with Men in Scoring Position: .228

Bats Right-Handed		AB	R	H	2B	3B	HR	RBI	BB	SO	SB	AVG
Vs. RHP		431	71	103	12	4	12	57	55	62	11	.239
Vs. LHP		156	27	42	5	1	5	20	23	27	4	.269
At Home	80	293	42	65	10	4	8	35	36	42	8	.222
On the Road	78	294	56	80	7	1	9	42	42	47	7	.272
1990 Season	158	587	98	145	17	5	17	77	78	89	15	.247
Life 15.1 Years		628	95	182	33	8	15	79	54	73	16	.289

•Z•

Todd ZEILE

ST. LOUIS	CATCHER	25 Years Old

Runs Created: 67   Offensive Winning Percentage: .567
Batting Average: .244   Secondary Average: .293

Most Often Bats: 5th
Hits First Pitch: 8%
Gets Ahead of the Pitcher: 55%
Hits Behind the Pitcher: 45%

1990 On Base Percentage: .333   Career: .332
1990 Slugging Percentage: .398   Career: .392
Batting Avg with Men in Scoring Position: .163

Bats Right-Handed		AB	R	H	2B	3B	HR	RBI	BB	SO	SB	AVG
Vs. RHP		322	41	75	13	2	9	35	46	56	1	.233
Vs. LHP		173	21	46	12	1	6	22	21	21	1	.266
At Home	70	233	33	61	11	2	8	26	34	31	1	.262
On the Road	74	262	29	60	14	1	7	31	33	46	1	.229
1990 Season 144		495	62	121	25	3	15	57	67	77	2	.244
Life 1.1 Years		543	65	134	26	4	15	61	72	86	2	.246

FUN STUFF

BRIAN MURPHY

JACK ETKIN

Muhammad Ali was starting to get the better of Joe Frazier in Rock River, Wyo. Their third and final fight, the 1975 Thrilla in Manila, had moved into the middle rounds on the television set in the corner of the Double Shot Drive-In Bar.

It was a slow Saturday afternoon in May. Maybe no slower than any other day, though, since outside of the Longhorn Lodge across the street and the Rock River Town Hall and the Double Shot, there isn't much to Rock River. Copper cups adorn the bar, along with rifles, model cars and jackalopes, the wonders of taxidermy that result from putting antlers on a jack rabbit.

Two patrons were at the bar besides Brian Murphy. Both were fight fans, particularly the bearded fortysomething fellow. He looked like he was passing through years ago when his car broke down in this middle-of-nowhere spot between Medicine Bow and Bosler, gave up waiting for the vital part that never found its way to Rock River and just stayed. Fortysomething had some boxing insight and some recall of this fifteen-year-old fight but not as much as Murphy, who has the sharp recollection for detail expected of a baseball scout.

Ali began unloading hard rights that ultimately would do in Frazier when a young man, who by his clean-cut, collegiate appearance looked totally misplaced, walked into the Double Shot. "Do you sell beer to go?" he asked the bartender. When told yes, he ordered one can of Busch. "Thirsty, huh?" Fortysomething said softly.

The commentary between rounds by NBC's Marv Albert and Ferdie Pacheco wasn't as skeletal. When Frazier didn't come out for the 15th round, Ali was still champion. Murphy had to continue driving to Casper where another player was to be cross-checked the next morning. He took a last look around the Double Shot, gazing at the empty pool table, the jackalopes and Ali being hugged by Bundini Brown.

"The place that time forgot," Murphy said. "Rod Serling," and he began humming "The Twilight Zone" theme "Do-do-do-do-do-do-do-do. We'll know for sure if we go outside and the car's a '74 Nova."

The interlude at the Double Shot was in keeping with the unpredictability of Murphy's schedule, which two months before the free agent draft took on a helter-skelter bent. True, Murphy did spend nearly two weeks in the Los Angeles area where prospects abound, fanning out from a hotel in Anaheim, Ca., to whatever game he needed to see that day and returning in the evening to this beachhead. More common, though, was the sprint that took Murphy to Castlewood, Va.; the Tennessee meccas of Kingsport (where it rained and the day was lost), Murfreesboro and Gallatin; Cincinnati, not to reacquaint him-self with urban America but to see outfielder Adam Hyzdu of Moeller High, whom the San Francisco Giants would take with their first pick; Bainbridge, Ga.; and Columbus, S. C. Eight cities in eight days. Not surprisingly Murphy calls his atlas and pocket flight guide "the two most important pieces of literature I own."

Charles Kuralt would envy Murphy's travels through the backwaters. But unlike Kuralt, who can plan his trips in advance, Murphy's itinerary in the weeks before the June free agent draft is in constant flux. It would be nice to relay a plan to a travel agent and receive a sheaf of tickets and reservations for flights, rental cars and hotels that would take care of the next couple weeks. It doesn't work that way. "It's an endless stream of reservations you're making," Murphy said, "but never more than two days in advance."

Murphy and Chuck McMichael are the Kansas City Royals' two national cross-checkers. Along with Art Stewart, the Royals' scouting director, they try to see the players whom the Royals could draft in the top fifteen rounds. That's a potentially large list and makes for a lot of travel. In the case of Murphy, who is single and lives, nominally at least, in Fairfield, Conn., the travel becomes endless.

"I'm basically gone from the latter part of February until after the draft," Murphy said. "There's a lot of cross-checkers, they'll be out on the road for ten days, home for two or three. Maybe out for two weeks, home for three or four (days). I suppose I could do that too if I requested it, but I stay out on the road once I get out there and let the other guys go home. That might make me more stupid than the other guys.

"I don't feel a sense of being uneasy, or to me it's not a great burden to be out here, except when my suitcase breaks or something like that."

In the scouting pecking order, the ascension is from area scout to regional supervisor to cross-checker. Before the draft, an area scout combs a fixed territory, which can be vast depending on the part of the country. Some area scouts may go days without seeing a professional prospect and start wondering—like Willy Loman when the selling had dried up—how long those college and high school fields will stay barren.

Nonetheless, the area scout, in his wandering, does put down roots. He knows the off-the-highway places where there is, say, a smorgasbord that shouldn't be missed. Roaming a familiar stretch enables him to develop a network of friends in and out of baseball, and he is rarely a stranger in his travels. As adrift as the area scout might be, he has a settled existence compared with the cross-checker, who isn't frequenting the same hotels and restaurants and being greeted by the same cast of faces season after season.

The cross-checker's purpose is to offer another opinion. He arrives when an area scout has given a player a grade above a certain level for his overall future potential, or OFP. Last year, when they didn't have a No. 1 or No. 2 pick after the free-agent signings of Mark Davis and Storm Davis, the Royals sent a cross-checker to see players with an OFP of 53 or above. "Prior to last year it was 55 and above," Stewart said. "That's what we call a middle-chance major league player. We went to 53 because we felt we were going to be able to cross-check more players."

The cross-checker parachutes in, typically meets the area scout, sees a game and leaves. A different day might bring the company of a different area scout. The cross-checker doesn't cultivate old ground. He is an outsider, albeit with one comforting assurance: there is a player graded high enough to warrant his evaluation. The cross-checker isn't a Willy Loman in the bleachers staring at a diamond wasteland.

"I did area scouting for three years," Murphy said. "I enjoy the cross-checking much more than the area scouting. The area scout has to put up with really a lot of nuts-and-bolts type of situations. Mailing out letters to all the schools in his area in the winter to get the schedules. A lot more paperwork than I have to do. In the free-agent scouting, I just have to turn in reports on the guys I see.

"I don't have to worry about their signability. The area scouts send out player profile forms. They have to go in and give them eye tests, give them psychological tests. I don't have to do that stuff. If I had to go back to being an area scout, I don't think I would. I don't think I would like it. I respect what they do. But you go to too many games where nothing's happening. You might go three or four years without getting a player in the draft."

Murphy, McMichael and Stewart put together the Royals' draft list, a composite rating of players that can only result from having an overview. An area scout will be understandably parochial and loves nothing more than for one of his players to be drafted. The big-picture perspective is critical. To get such an outlook requires a national scope.

"If you didn't have cross-checkers, who are a necessary evil, you'd have your scout in San Francisco ranting and raving about his shortstop, and how he was the best player and all that," Murphy said. "Some scout in Georgia has got a kid who he's claiming is the best. It's just a rhetoric contest. Who can sell the player the most? And some guys are better at that than other guys. Just because you're better at salesmanship doesn't mean you have better judgment. You have to have people that see all those top kids to put them in some sort of order. Or else it's chaos.

"There are some area scouts, longtime guys who've built up recognition. A scouting director might go with an area scout because he's had a good record. A cross-checker comes in and doesn't like (a player) so much; the cross-checker understands, too, this guy's a good scout. He really likes him. We're going to take him anyhow even though you didn't see him (play) that good. We're probably not going to take him first or second, but we'll take him. Guys that have built up a good reputation tend to get more of those guys who are on the fence than a first-time scout."

The plan was to fly from the Orange County airport to Oakland. There Murphy would be met by Dave Herrera, the Royals' scout in northern California. They would make the 20-minute drive to Chabot Junior College in Hayward and arrive in plenty of time for the junior college tournament game between Chabot and Taft College.

"The way my day's going my bag will have split apart," Murphy said, waiting at the luggage carousel in the Oakland Airport.

His original 11:10 A.M. flight from Orange County was canceled because of mechanical problems. The next flight was late departing. Murphy was due in Oakland at 1:30 P.M. Twenty-five minutes later he finally arrived. The game started at two o'clock. When a large suitcase came spinning toward Murphy, his scouting insight was correct; the bag was torn. It was 2:08 when Murphy and Herrera left the airport.

Aaron Ledesma, the Chabot shortstop, is why Murphy has made the trip up the California coast that will launch a journey. Fly to Denver that night. Drive to Laramie, Wyo. Go to Casper the next day. And then? Back to Denver for a flight . . . maybe to Oklahoma City . . . maybe to Birmingham. That leg of the trip is beyond the normal two-day lead time. It might as well be a month away.

It costs 75 cents each half hour in the airport parking lot. Herrera's tab amounted to $5.25. "You have been here a while," Murphy said. His expense account notwithstanding, Herrera would be willing to pay huge sums to park. A visit from a cross-checker is a heralded event for an area scout. One of *his* players will be scrutinized. On the drive to Hayward on Interstate 880, Herrera, upbeat and hopeful, briefed Murphy about Ledesma, at times sounding paternal.

"He's 6-2 and 190," Herrera said, "and can definitely play third base. He's consistently 4.2 down the (first base) line, which makes you think his range is OK."

"Enough bat for third base?" Murphy asked.

"I think so," Herrera said. "Eventually somebody will have to get ahold of him."

Herrera explained he had given Ledesma an OFP of 54, that Ledesma, with one more year at Chabot, appears ready to turn pro, that he has an average arm and that seven or eight teams seem interested in Ledesma.

"How many times have you seen him?" Murphy asked.

"I've seen him four times," Herrera said.

"Performance-wise?" Murphy wondered.

"He never had a five-for-five day," Herrera said. "But he's consistent and makes all the plays. He's big and strong. This kid can throw on the run."

"Art liked him," Murphy said, referring to Stewart, "and said I should see him."

That wasn't just a throwaway line. The area scout welcomes such reinforcement. He is a branch manager working far from corporate headquarters, connected mostly by telephone. Kansas City is somewhere Herrera and most of the other area scouts will see once a year at meetings the week before the draft. Murphy spent three years traveling the northeast for the Royals as an area scout. He knows what it's like to scour the outback and how welcome it is to hear a few kind words filter down from above that support your opinion.

Chabot was leading 2–0 in the top of the third when Herrera and Murphy finally approached the ballpark, made their way down the left field line and sat on a grassy hill behind third base. "Where's our hero; is he out there?" Murphy asked. "Probably got hit with a line drive in the first inning."

Ledesma was at shortstop and within minutes went deep into the hole but couldn't get to a ball. "It would've been great if you could see him make a play like that," Herrera said. Murphy noted that Ledesma is kind of heavy legged.

"Yeah, he's big," Herrera said. "I made sure a couple games of the speed he had. I got him in 4.15, but gave him 4.2 in my report."

Murphy had moved closer to the field. He was behind the fence near the Chabot dugout for a close-up when Ledesma came to bat in the bottom of the third with runners on first and third and no outs. Herrera, still seated on the hill, knew the audition had moved into the harder stages.

The righthanded hitting Ledesma fouled a ball over the first base dugout. "That was a bad cut," Herrera said. "Not the cut I wanted Murphy to see." Another foul tailed down the right field line. Ledesma finally grounded to shortstop and into a double play. Murphy timed him in "a little over 4.2" with one of many stopwatches at work. In addition to other area scouts, the New York Mets, Philadelphia Phillies and Milwaukee Brewers have sent cross-checkers to see Ledesma. There was no timing him on his first at bat when Ledesma drove a pitch over the center field wall.

"That's typical," Murphy said. "Have to blame that on United Airlines."

Just over three weeks remained until the draft. Ninety-seven players will have been selected when the Royals make their first pick in the third round. Ledesma doesn't last that long. The Mets take him in the second round and give him a signing bonus of $82,500.

"He's the one guy in my area I hope to hell we somehow could get," Herrera said, sticking a dip of Copenhagen snuff inside his lower lip. "This one bad habit you've avoided?"

"I've missed a few," Murphy answered. "Not many." He is 47 and played an eon of minor league baseball. Murphy's professional career began in 1962. The flame finally went out in 1978. When the end came, Murphy, a middle infielder, was early in his seventeenth season and in Triple-A. He never took a swing in the majors, never even got to sit on a big league bench during a season and just experience the thrill of being in uniform. Managing in the minor leagues followed and then scouting. It is a resume filled with baseball, no gaps or sidetrips away from the game while sorting out directions and pondering career alternatives. It is an ideal background for scouting.

"I'm not carried away with his hitting approach," Murphy said after Ledesma flied out to center on the first pitch of the seventh. "But it's not something that couldn't be helped. He makes two distinct moves with his hands. This kid's strong enough to hit; he's got good enough bat speed. If this kid plays third, he's going to have to hit a lot.

"Nothing physically is going to hold him back. But he's probably going to lose some of that speed. He's got a good frame, but I don't think he'll carry that weight (as well) at 25–26 years old."

In the field, Ledesma caught everything hit to him. All the plays were routine. Murphy was concerned about the quickness of his feet and his speed in getting into the fielding position. Ledesma wasn't particularly fluid. "But there are guys like that who get the job done," Murphy said, as the game ended and he and Herrera left the field.

At 4:35 P.M., when Hank Greenwald, the Giants' play-by-play voice on KNBR, started his broadcast from Philadelphia, traffic was clotting northbound I-880. "Howell's first pitch to Butler is low for a ball. And we're under way here at the Vet. Giants with three games at Philadelphia." The Chabot Gladiators and Taft Cougars seem to be a fathomless distance from the action wafting over the airwaves. Herrera asked whether it would be worth having Al Kubski, the Royals' West Coast scouting supervisor, come see Ledesma. "Kubski's not going to wonder why he's up here," Murphy said. "It never hurts to have another opinion. He might show something extra for Al."

The Los Angeles Dodgers took Ken Howell in the third round out of Tuskegee Institute in 1982. Brett Butler was a 23rd round pick of the Atlanta Braves in 1979 out of Southeastern Oklahoma State University. Players can come from anywhere. Why not Chabot Junior College?

Murphy's impressions of Ledesma will be written up on a free agent report form. First he will make jottings in a small, battered notebook that he keeps in his back pocket and that looks to be one good windstorm away from being scattered into history. On the page reserved for Ledesma, Murphy made the following notations:

Tense hands restricts swing. Top hand? Loop? Good fastball? (meaning can he handle such a pitch)? First step. Bat speed OK.

5+ arm (which is a little above average on the scale that ascends from two to eight). Steady hands. Feet?

"His natural skills don't lend themselves to major league shortstop," Murphy said. "You have to be able to set up and throw the ball quicker than he showed. If we get the guy, what I'd do is put him at third base and try to get more fluid hitting.

"What I try to do is look at what the player's going to be at 23 or 24, about the age they break in (to the majors) and try to figure out how long they last."

Murphy was back in the Oakland airport, just five hours after arriving there, and about to board a 7 P.M. flight to Denver. Scheduled arrival time in Denver was 10:20 P.M., followed by a drive of nearly three hours to Laramie, Wyo. A day that was endless enough became longer. The plane took off a half hour late. So much time seemed to have passed that Aaron Ledesma must have married and started a family. At cruising altitude, a tray table fell open. "Poltergeist," Murphy said.

It was after 11 P.M. when Murphy stepped into the darkness of a Budget Car Rental bus and headed to the rear seat. Usually Barry Manilow or some easy listening sound can be counted on to be coming softly over the radio of these buses. During the day, anyway. A commendable remake of Al Green's "Love and Happiness," was filling the bus. The driver was black and no doubt has decided the risk of anyone from Budget's top management boarding at this hour was minimal. A little volume is one of his few job perks.

Two businessmen sat down near Murphy. One did most of the talking. It was a conversation laced with talk of market penetration and opportunities with technical terms thrown in about selling something. Just what wasn't clear, but a monstrous flow of corporate memos and a series of meetings could be detected lurking beneath the surface of this informal discussion. Laramie was a long way off. All that awaited Murphy was a 2 A.M. arrival at a Holiday Inn and another baseball game in the afternoon, this one at the University of Wyoming. Love and happiness.

"Murph loves being on the road and seeing baseball games, and time is not an issue," said Chicago Cubs scouting director Dick Balderson, who fired Murphy when he was managing in the minors for the Royals but then hired him to be a scout. "It's surprising how many scouts really don't enjoy seeing baseball games. When you get a guy like a Murphy who really enjoys going to games, then you've got a foot in the door. Then if he's got judgment and has the background that he has, you've got a pretty good guy."

At Fairfield Prep, Murphy was a star basketball player, who received scholarship offers from Providence, Niagara and St. Bonaventure. "Even had a friend of mine that was a year ahead of me who went to Marquette," Murphy said. "He told the coaches out there about me. They were going to take me sight unseen, which, I guess, doesn't happen too much anymore these days."

Murphy graduated in 1961, four years before the inception of the free agent draft. Clubs were then engaged in open bidding for prospects. But scouts saw little of Murphy in his senior year because he only played two games. "I went to a very strict Catholic high school, and the principle of the school didn't think my grades were up to snuff," Murphy said. "I wasn't flunking anything, but they were really strict about the grades."

The coach of Murphy's American Legion team was a Pittsburgh Pirates bird dog, who assisted Pirates scout Bob Whelan. Pittsburgh was then reigning as world champions, having beaten the New York Yankees in the 1960 World Series on Bill Mazeroski's home run over the left field wall in the bottom of the ninth of Game Seven. Murphy brushed these heights when he passed the Pirates' close inspection.

"They brought me out to Forbes Field to work me out in August of '61," Murphy said. "I was seventeen years old. I can remember Dick Groat and (Roberto) Clemente and Elroy Face. I met them all. I knew who they were, but I was a Yankee fan in those days.

"They worked me out extensively. It was about a hundred degrees—it seemed like. It was one of the hottest days they had in Pittsburgh that year. They ran me and didn't like my time in the 60 the first time, so they ran me again. Did a little better. They said, 'You can do better than that. Why don't you run it again?' Third time I almost collapsed.

"I remember I hit a couple off the famous Bill Mazeroski wall. Thought I hit pretty well. And it seemed like (I took) a thousand ground balls. They didn't sign me right on the spot. I went back home and a couple days later, Bob Wehlan came into the house with another scout and signed me for the following year."

Murphy received a signing bonus of $6,500 to play in 1962 and the promise of an additional $4,000 if he made it to Double-A. The Pirates were going to send Murphy to Kingsport, Tenn., in the Appalachian League, which didn't start play until June. He went to spring training in Daytona Beach, Fla., and instead made the farm team in Batavia, N.Y., in what then was the full-season Class D New York-Pennsylvania League. Murphy was beaned in early August ("My left temple area swelled up like a golf ball") and faded in the final weeks to finish at .267. He was named to the second team all-star team. It was a good season for an 18-year-old beginning his professional career.

In the ensuing sixteen seasons, Murphy hit .267 once more—in 50 games with Triple-A Winnipeg in 1970—and topped that average once. His peak of .272, along with a career-high 59 RBIs, came in 105 games with Gastonia in the Western Carolinas League in 1968.

Murphy had first-step quickness, soft hands and good range

at shortstop and second base. His forte was turning the double play. He was so good at taking the shortstop's relay and unloading the ball while evading the runner that Tom Saffell, his manager at Batavia and Reno and now the president of the Gulf Coast League, compared Murphy to Mazeroski. "Brian was one of the best young kids I'd ever seen at getting rid of the ball at second base," Saffell said, "He was agile and had good hands and he never got hurt on the double play."

Murphy wasn't particularly fast, but his real problem was at the plate. A righthanded hitter, Murphy even tried to switch-hit early in his career. "I always had trouble with the breaking ball," he said. "It was my downfall, really. I never learned to handle that."

Murphy spent seven years in the Pirates' system before Boston drafted him after the 1968 season. He rose to their Triple-A club in Louisville in 1970 and was traded that year to Winnipeg, a farm team of the expansion Montreal Expos, who had begun play in 1969. After finishing up at .267 in Winnipeg, Murphy returned there and hit .247 in 1971. The Expos didn't seem that far away.

"I thought I had a decent chance to come up," Murphy said. "But it didn't work out. I played pretty well for them in Triple-A. My average was only like .245 or so, but I thought I could be a valuable utility infielder for them. Gene Mauch was the manager then. He went with Pepe Frias instead of me, and that was probably as close as I came to the big leagues.

"After that, I still loved to play and I wanted to learn as much about the game as I could. But the last five years I played I knew I was biding time until I got into the managerial end of it."

Murphy had a Rand McNally career, playing for teams in ten states and two Canadian provinces. Winnipeg exposed him to Manitoba. Sherbrooke, his stop in the Eastern League in 1972, gave Murphy a chance to see Quebec and a more exciting slice of Canadian life. A season's end would typically bring Murphy uncertainty. Roster moves would be made to give space to younger players. If there was a prospect at shortstop, Murphy played second base. If the player with the bright future was a second baseman, Murphy played shortstop. He was a survivor and found his way into the Royals' organization in 1973.

That season began with Murphy, then 29, riding buses in the Southern League with Orlando, the Minnesota Twins' Double-A team. They released him after the June draft to make way for youth. Billy Gardner, who was managing Jacksonville, the Royals' farm club in that league, recommended Murphy be signed. He finished that 1973 season at Jacksonville and played there the following two years. In 1975, the 31-year-old Murphy was voted Jacksonville's most popular player by the local fans.

Murphy moved up to Omaha and the American Association in 1976, played sparingly there the following season and hurt his knee in spring training 'til 1978. While on the disabled list and recuperating, he returned to Jacksonville and coached for manager Gordy MacKenzie. By May, Murphy's knee had improved, and he was back in Omaha. On June 22, after five games in which he could tell his knee wasn't right, Murphy was released and sent to Class A Fort Myers as a coach for manager Gene Lamont. The career that had started in Batavia had run its course after 1,561 games and not even a one-line entry in *The Baseball Encyclopedia.*

Murphy batted 4,907 times and had a lifetime average of .234. With just 26 home runs, Murphy wasn't a slugger like Crash Davis, the catcher and career minor leaguer in the movie "Bull Durham." Davis fondly recalled the 21 days he spent in The Show as the best 21 days of his life. That's three weeks more than Murphy spent in the majors.

"To me, Murph makes Crash Davis look like a rookie," said McMichael, 33, the Royals' other national cross-checker and a pitcher in their system in 1980 and 1981. "Murph's got such a vast amount of experience in terms of the game itself, in terms of places he's been, things he's seen. You have to know him well to be able to drag it out of him or to have him open up, but, God, he's been around the game. And if you love the game and you're pure in the game, he's gorgeous to be around."

Murphy's managing career began in June 1979 with one of the Royals' two Sarasota teams in the short-season Gulf Coast Rookie League. By 1982, he had experienced some on-field heights but was through as a manager. Two organizations had reached that decision.

In 1980 and 1981, Murphy managed Fort Myers. That second season, his team had an overall record of 72-58. They won a first-half division title as well as a first-round playoff series before losing in the finals. When the Florida State manager of the year award was handed out, it went to Murphy. He was finding a coveted niche in the game. Or so he thought. The problem was Murphy didn't agree with some of the rigid policies drawn up by Balderson, the Royals' scouting and farm director, and implemented by Howie Bedell, their coordinator of instruction.

"Some people aren't cut out to be managers," Murphy said. "I thought I was. I thought I played in the minors long enough to get the most out of minor leaguers. I know you need rules and regulations anywhere, but to me we had become so technical on the stuff we had to do. We had to have 'X' amount of players out every day. We had to be out at a particular time every day.

"He wanted morning workouts every day at Fort Myers. You can imagine how hot it is on the turf. A lot of the guys were living over in Cape Coral (across the Caloosahatchee River from Fort Myers) and the traffic was awful; it took them an hour to get in. You have a morning workout at 10 o'clock; they're leaving at 8:30 or so. You work out even an hour, hour and a half, they leave at 12 and don't get home 'til 1:30.

Then they have to turn around and be at the park at 4 o'clock again."

Balderson thought all the Royals' minor league managers should be managerial timber in the majors. He didn't think Murphy was. And if Murphy wasn't going to follow instructions in the Florida State League, Balderson wondered what would happen if Murphy were to manage at Double- or Triple-A. By firing Murphy, Balderson avoided having to find out.

Murphy moved on to Midland, Texas, where he managed the Cubs' Double-A farm club in 1982. Joe Carter was on that team, along with Carmelo Martinez, Henry Cotto and Mike Diaz, who played briefly with the Cubs, Pirates and White Sox. "We had nice players," Murphy said. "We didn't have much pitching. We won the pennant but lost in the playoffs. That was in Dallas Green's regime, and Dallas was a real disciplinarian. I guess I didn't throw enough chairs or was that animated. Whatever. I have no gripes against Dallas. He wanted his teams run one way, and I was a little more a players manager, a low-key type of guy. So that was the parting of the ways there."

Because of Balderson, Murphy returned to the Royals in November 1982. Balderson had fired Earl Rapp, the Royals' scout in the northeast and needed someone to cover that territory. Murphy had the perfect background for the job, if he wanted it, Balderson thought. "It certainly wasn't a lifelong ambition," Murphy said. "I'd never really considered what scouts did. I was a little disenchanted with managing. I still wanted to manage and personally, I could look myself in the eye and say I did a good job; that's subjective, I guess. I went into scouting with an open mind, just figuring it would expose me to a different area of baseball. And I liked it."

For three years, Murphy roamed a territory that included Washington D.C., Delaware, Maryland, New Jersey, New York and all of New England. Philadelphia was also part of Murphy's domain but not the rest of Pennsylvania. In 1986, Murphy became the Royals' east coast scouting supervisor. "That's when I started to get into a little higher level of scouting, and I really enjoyed it," he said. "You're seeing pretty good kids every day. And you can compare a good kid in Alabama with a good kid in New Jersey or somewhere. It got to be kind of interesting at that point." It became even more intriguing in 1987 when Murphy rose to national cross-checker.

In that role, Murphy can put an imprint on the June draft and hence affect the future composition of the Royals. Such decision-making at the highest scouting levels was why Murphy was driving along I-80 in Wyoming west of Cheyenne at 1:30 in the morning. He was still about 20 miles from Laramie, where a workday that had started in southern California would conclude, and was craving a Pepsi.

Casper and Cheyenne are the only two cities in Wyoming with more than one zip code. It's not a good state to be trying to satisfy a late-night thirst. The exit sign for Buford appeared.

One light was on at the Conoco station that came into view on the left. Murphy slowed down just long enough to see the station was closed. "Buford, Wyo., at two in the morning," Murphy said, laughing. "You got to love it."

At 75, Tom Ferrick was still scouting for the Royals last season. His focus is the National League East, which Ferrick can easily see by making the drive from his home in Havertown, Pa., to Veterans Stadium. Ferrick is not simply an elderly scout grazing in the baseball pasture, a reward for past service. The Royals brought Ferrick to Kansas City for their September organizational meetings and value his knowledge and experience.

"I can tell you from fifteen years of doing it, cross-checking's not a cup of tea," Ferrick said. "You're a one-man gang and all over the country. It's a monastic kind of living, and it can be tiring. It's a young man's job. Once you get 55 or so, you get jet lag and fatigue and you wake up in a different town every day. Sometimes you wake up and say, 'Where the hell am I?' "

That question was the perfect mantra for a morning in Laramie. Drive in at night. Wake up. Where did these mountains come from? Where's the water tower, usually a landmark for the vicinity of the ballpark?

One job can be a steppingstone to another. Cross-checking is no different. The natural progression would be go to the front office as a scouting director. It's a position that would involve some major lifestyle changes for Murphy.

"I don't think I'd function well in an office environment with day in and day out nine to five," he said. "I've never done it. That would be just a big change obviously from my pattern for one thing. Not that it wouldn't be interesting, but I think after a while I'd get that urge either to be out on the field or be out looking at players.

"I think working in the office as a scouting director or minor league director, you'd be dealing with a lot of trivial stuff. I see what Art has to go through working with the budgets and the Latin American program and hiring and firing and constantly having meetings with the other staff in the office. I'd just rather be out there."

Murphy was in Laramie to see Scott Freeman, a righthanded pitcher at the University of Wyoming, start against Colorado State. Freeman is 6-1 and 195 pounds. In 11 previous starts, Freeman was 6-3 with a 4.73 ERA. He had allowed 87 hits in 78 innings, statistics caused by what Murphy called "metal bat syndrome." Freeman had a compact, overhand motion that put no strain on his arm. He had thrown 87–88 miles an hour but was about 5 miles below that on this cloudy, chilly afternoon. His curveball wasn't consistent but occasionally showed some bite. "That curveball's got a chance to be a good major-league pitch for him," said Murphy, adding that Freeman needed to develop a third usable pitch.

In five innings, Freeman allowed five hits and had a 5–2 lead when rain delayed the game. The one-look peril of the cross-checker had come to pass. Murphy wasn't as impressed with Freeman as Jeff McKay, the Royals' scout for this area who was not at the game. "Pitchers are funny, though," Murphy said. "Then again, I don't have the luxury of going back and seeing the kid again."

That point was academic. Freeman was gone by the time the Royals finally had a draft pick. The Los Angeles Dodgers took him as a sandwich pick between the second and third rounds and gave Freeman a $65,000 signing bonus.

By the time the rain ended and Wyoming's game with Colorado State resumed, Freeman had become a dot on Murphy's horizon. He had left rainy Laramie, heading north on the route that would take him to the Double Shot in Rock River. The destination was Casper where Eric Mapp, a Natrona High School outfielder was working out the next morning with an American Legion team.

"I don't like it being on the road, but I can cope with it," Murphy said. "It doesn't fight me. I'd rather be sitting on the beach or playing golf; that's for sure. It's not a question of enjoying it more than other guys; it's disliking it less."

After the June draft, Murphy's pace becomes less frenetic. He turns to his professional scouting, drops in on the Royals' farm clubs, sees their team in the Florida Instructional League, visits their Dominican Republic program and scouts in Puerto Rico. In addition, Murphy goes to the World Series, where trade talks brew, and the winter meetings, where deals and free-agent signings are often consummated. Quite often, he will have evaluated players the Royals acquire through these channels.

The Royals' signing of free agent Mike Boddicker had Murphy's stamp of approval. His professional coverage includes six teams in the International League and the entire American League East. Murphy had scouted Boddicker, 33, first with the Baltimore Orioles and then with the Red Sox. In his report on Boddicker, Murphy wrote: "He's been a No. 2 starter and has pitched well. Hasn't changed much over the years. Deceptive and competitive. Changes speeds and angles on his curveball and change. Is as good as ever. Think he'd be a winner for five more years."

Opinions are, of course, inherent to scouting. Having unwavering belief, going out on a limb and staying there after seeing something in a player—not because of blind faith—can set a scout apart from his peers. When he was the Royals' east coast supervisor in 1986, Murphy did much of the early scouting of pitcher Tom Gordon, whom the Royals ended up drafting in the sixth round and signing for a $17,000 bonus out of Avon Park (Fla.) High School. The problem was at 5-9 and 160 pounds Gordon went against the conventional scouting wisdom that said don't draft small righthanded pitchers.

"A couple years ago at the winter meetings," Ferrick recalled,

"I said, 'Murph, I know you were very much involved with Gordon. How come you liked him?' He said, 'I knew he was 5-9 and strong. Every time I saw him, he got bigger.' I thought it was a perfect description.

"Sometimes as soon as the general manager gives an indication he likes a certain thing, than the other guys hop on the band wagon. Murph's his own man. He'll stick to what he thinks. When you get his judgment, it's his judgment. He's not a yes man."

No conclusion was ever drawn about Mapp, who ended up being drafted by the Dodgers in the 11th round but didn't sign. The workout was rained out. Murphy likes to stay at a La Quinta Inn, since a Denny's Restaurant is guaranteed to be next door. The choice in Casper was another Holiday Inn. After checking out, Murphy pulled into McDonald's for breakfast. Two hash browns, two orange juices and one cinnamon roll came to $3.78. The meal was consumed on I-25, heading south at the start of a 250-mile trip to Denver that was uneventful for about 90 minutes or until a highway patrolman pulled Murphy over.

The officer clocked Murphy going 76 miles an hour and gave him a $60 ticket. Murphy's choices were to make a court appearance in 10 days in Wheatland, Wyo., or pay by mail. The officer explained these options after returning from his car. When he had stepped away, Murphy said, "I tried to flash that World Series ring," referring to his keepsake from the Royals' 1985 championship season. "I had the cruise control set on 74. Must've been going downhill. I don't think that'll appease him."

Murphy had not been in Wyoming since 1963 when he was 19. While playing for Reno in the California League, he broke his leg in Salinas, Calif., near the end of his second professional season. He returned to Reno to pick up his car and, with his foot in a cast, was planning to drive back to Connecticut. Murphy's father thought better of that plan and flew West. Their route home took them across I-80 and along the southern portion of Wyoming.

Now Murphy was again passing through the state, taking a Sunday trip that seemed like the final stages of a rally. Find the Conoco station in Buford. Stop at the Double Shot Drive-In Bar. Make a phone call in Medicine Bow. Don't bypass the general store in Douglas.

Missing the workout in Casper actually was a break. Murphy would be able to get an earlier flight to Birmingham from Denver. There would be the small bonus of a stopover in Memphis. "I'll be able to pick up a Memphis paper in the airport," he said, "and see how the boys are doing. They've won about eight in a row." The boys are the Memphis Chicks, the Royals' Double-A farm club. From Birmingham, it's a two-hour drive to Auburn University. Murphy will see outfielder Chris Hart, ultimately a fifth-round pick of the Oakland Athletics.

Murphy had described this sojourn to Wyoming as "a bit out of the ordinary, but it's by no means a precedent." The Laramie Mountains were off to the west. There wasn't a tree in sight, just sunny sky in all directions and antelope occasionally rambling not far from the highway. Another day in the game was passing for Murphy.

Most people would start their work week the next morning. They would go to an office or a factory, some set location, and have a Monday-to-Friday framework. They wouldn't be a pin in a map, skittering about the country. Live arms? Quick bats? Fast legs? How long can the wandering for these attributes last? How long before an inner voice says enough already, the existence is crazy, unreal, close to living on the lam, and it's finally time to stop being a nomad and do something in the real world. How long?

"This is the real world," Brian Murphy said. "It's the only thing I know. Unless I've been dreaming for 29 years, it's real."

TRACERS

One promise on which Dizzy [Dean] made good concerns Bill Terry, former manager of the Giants. Dizzy visited a children's hospital in St. Louis one day. He wrote his name in autograph books, told the youngsters how he threw his curve and how he wound up to put the batter in the proper mental state. He told them much of his prowess, and when it was time to depart for the ball park, to do on the field the great things he had been doing for them in story, he asked the children if there was any little thing he could do for them to make them happier.

"Anything at all," he volunteered. "I don't bar nuthin' for you kids."

One little fellow had a bright idea: "Strike out Bill Terry for us this afternoon," and soon it was a chorus: "Strike out Terry. Strike out Terry. We'll be listening over the radio. Do that for us."

"I'll do it," he reassured the youngsters. "And if I get a chance, I'll do it with the bases filled. I'll pitch this game for you."

"They would have to pick a guy like that," said Dizzy, as he told me about it in the dugout before the game. "Why didn't they say Vergez or Critz? That Terry is a tough bird."

In the ninth inning, with two out and the Cardinals leading, 2 to 1, a pinch hitter singled, Joe Moore hit safely, and Hughie Critz walked. Up came Terry. Dizzy edged toward the plate.

"I hate to do this, Bill," Dizzy grinned. "But I promised some kids in a hospital today that I'd strike you out with the bases loaded. That's why I walked little Hughie."

Terry struck out on three pitched balls.

—J. Roy Stockton, *The Gashouse Gang,* Page 50.

Assuming all the characters are correctly named, the time frame in which this could have occurred begins in 1932, when Diz joined the Cardinals, and ends in 1934, when Vergez left the Giants. That gives us a field of 66 games, but 33 of them would be on the road, and the story specifies St. Louis.

On July 10, 1933, events very closely resembling this story did occur. With Giants owner Horace Stoneham in attendance at Sportsmen's Park in St. Louis, Dizzy Dean pitched the Cardinals to a 2–0 lead after eight innings. But in the top of the ninth with one out, Gus Mancuso, pinch-hitter Bernie James, and Jo-Jo Moore singled consecutively to score a run. Hughie Critz walked to load the bases, bringing player-manager Terry to the plate with just one out, and Mel Ott on deck. Dean struck out Terry (the number of pitches was not recorded), and then retired Ott on a pop foul.

Did Dean really promise the little kiddies that he'd strike out Bill Terry with the bases loaded? Did he even visit a hospital that day? And would he dare to purposefully walk the bases loaded with two of the game's most feared hitters about to come to the plate?

Heckuva story, ain't it?

—Rob Neyer

JOE OVERFIELD

JACK ETKIN

The writing has never been easy for Joe Overfield. It's always been an avocation, something he *wanted* rather than *had* to do. Overfield spent more than half a century in the real estate title insurance business before retiring June 1, 1990. Research in that field never culminated in prose that might be widely read and where style was of particular consequence in holding an audience.

Overfield sprinkles his conversation with words like *bete noire,* nadir, exigencies, inveterate and salubrious. Four years of Latin at Buffalo's Lafayette High School nearly 60 years ago have given him a lasting curiosity into the origin and usage of words. But writing them, as he has done in *The 100 Seasons of Buffalo Baseball,* published in 1985, and, by his count, "hundreds and hundreds of articles," most on Buffalo baseball, involves grind and tedium rather than stride and rhythm.

"I do my research and make a lot of notes on yellow legal pads," Overfield said. "Then I sit down and write kind of willy-nilly because I'm not under deadline pressure generally. Then it'll be a rough thing. I may rewrite it four or five times, even to change one word.

"I love the research part. The writing becomes arduous at times, but once it's finished, if I feel I've done a good job, there is a great deal of satisfaction. But it's not easy work for me. I have to do a lot of revising and rewriting, but that's the way I've always been."

His articles inevitably are seamless and thorough, accurate and enlightening. Some have appeared in publications of the Society for American Baseball Research such as *The Baseball Research Journal.* Jim Kaplan, editor of the journal, said Overfield "really seems to come up with stuff that nobody seems to find."

The Buffalo Bisons of the Class AAA American Association list Overfield as their historian in the directory on the inside cover of their media guide. Fittingly, it's an unpaid title. Overfield didn't write his book to make money. Publication is the sole reward for most of the articles he has written.

Some 20 years ago, Overfield was given a shoebox filled with baseball letters, the correspondence file of the 1878 Bisons written by some obscure types as well as subsequent Hall of Famers Candy Cummings and Jim Galvin. The letters have been "an absolute bonanza" in his digging, but Overfield is not on the prowl for artifacts and never thinks of their monetary value because "I'm not a wheeler-dealer in memorabilia."

The research is paramount and has its own inherent value to Overfield. His specialties are Buffalo and minor league baseball, and these spheres have given Overfield a notable reputation. "I don't think you can rank researchers any more than you can rank ballplayers," said Tom Heitz, librarian at the Baseball Hall of Fame. "But I think Overfield is certainly one of the top 10 baseball historians in this country at the present time. And probably, he's like the underrated player on the team, so to speak."

Much of Overfield's recent work has been 2,000-word articles for BisonGram, the Buffalo Bisons' publication that comes out eight times a year. Overfield's trips into the past are a regular feature known as Bison tales. "I originally wrote it up t-a-i-l-s," he said, "but the editor made it the other way and that's the way it's come out."

Overfield works at a long table that nearly takes up the entire width of a room in his Tonawanda, N.Y., house. Files are spread over the table. Pictures of Buffalo baseball figures cover the pale blue walls. There is no overhead light, only a lamp next to Overfield's weathered wooden chair. The writing might be somewhat easier if Overfield were staring at a computer screen. He could move paragraphs by touching a few keys and edit with ease. He wouldn't need his array of erasers and pencils, tools of the trade as long as Overfield uses an Olympia typewriter. A manual one, no less.

"I'm too old to change," he said. "I started with a manual typewriter. I'm going to finish with one."

There's another reason Overfield is content to crank the carriage return by hand when hearing the bell and reaching the end of the margin. It has to do with his wife, Clara, bedridden with multiple sclerosis at nearby Kenmore Mercy Hospital.

"I've thought about a word processor," Overfield said. "And you know I thought about modernizing the kitchen and bathroom. But this is the house we lived in a good part of our lives and to go spend six or seven thousand dollars . . . I would have a twinge. I feel she'd lie there and say, 'I wish I could be there.' "

Overfield called his wife "my support and the motivation for everything I have tried to do," on Sept. 28, 1983, when his fellow employees honored him at a testimonial dinner. The occasion was his semi-retirement from Monroe Abstract & Title Co., where he went to work Sept. 20, 1937, for $70 a month. That night Overfield indicated his comfort with parts of the past. He said he was a victim of C.P.S., computer phobia syndrome, that had given him one number for payroll purposes and another to track his type of work. Overfield also gave a poignant example of his divergence from progress and technology.

How outdated I really am was demonstrated earlier in the year, when I picked up an implement from my desk, inserted it in a dark blue bottle and squeezed the plunger. One of the young men who works in the office stood at my desk and stared at me in AWE and wonderment. I really believe he thought I was about to give myself a fix. The truth is he had never seen an old-fashioned fountain pen, let alone the

319

act of filling one. Yes, there are many people around today who think the ball-point pen is the first of its breed. How sad.

Overfield was born in Buffalo on April 7, 1916. John McGraw had that birthday in 1873 and Bobby Doerr in 1918. "Not a bad pair," Overfield said, proud of this link to two Hall of Famers.

For all his burrowing in and love for the past, Overfield has no good-old-days longing. He doesn't believe it is unspeakably venal to compare modern baseball to earlier eras.

Overfield is a Pilot Field regular for the Bisons' home games and can typically be found in the seats behind home plate with Cy Williams. The 76-year-old Williams scouted for 42 years, 29 with the Detroit Tigers followed by 13 with the Major League Scouting Bureau, and retired after the 1987 season. He has become a fan again, free of the need to professionally evaluate players and document his opinions in reports. "I'm enjoying baseball more now than I did since I've been a young kid," Williams said. Overfield hasn't had to rediscover the magnetic pull baseball once exerted in his boyhood; that attraction has never waned. What has grown for him and Williams is the game's aesthetic appeal.

"Cy Williams and I often talk about this subject and agree," Overfield said. "Baseball, even though I don't like the periphery of it, the commercialism of it, the avarice that's on both sides (owners and players), the game itself is played better than it ever was.

"We see plays at Pilot Field, which is Triple-A, routinely made that would've been headline stories. (Al) Gionfriddo's catch in '47 and Willie Mays' in '54—I saw (Andy) Van Slyke the other night on television in Atlanta. (Dale) Murphy was the hitter, two men on, ninth inning. The score was 7–3 Pittsburgh. Murphy hit a ball to dead center field. Van Slyke took one look at it. He went back and caught the ball over his head, crashing face-first into the wall; that play, they don't even mention it in the next day's paper. I've seen Willie Mays' catch recreated, and Van Slyke's catch was even tougher because of the fact that he had the fence to contend with. In the Polo Grounds, there was still plenty of room.

"The pitching is better. Every pitcher today has some kind of a sinkerball, which they didn't have years ago. The batter years ago had to think of a curve, fastball, changeup."

Overfield saw his first baseball game in 1925. He and his brother, Arthur, walked the fifteen blocks from their home on Breckenridge Street to the bleacher entrance of what then was called Bison Stadium. They used coupons clipped from the *Buffalo Evening News* and saw an International League game between Buffalo and Providence. At the time, Overfield knew so little about baseball he thought all the Buffalo players came from Buffalo.

"I was utterly fascinated by it," Overfield said. "My brother, who was only a year older than I, was completely disinterested, and all his life he's never had any interest in baseball at all. Whereas in my case, it became at first a hobby. I tried to play. I wasn't very good."

Overfield was always the "smallest and skinniest kid" in his neighborhood on Buffalo's west side. When he went into the Army Air Corps in 1943, he weighed 123 pounds. Three years later after a tour of duty that included fourteen months in India as a weather observer, he came home and still weighed 123. Overfield is 5 feet 8 and 140 pounds. Glasses that are forever slipping down his nose give him a scholarly appearance.

Baseball research became a pursuit because of a chance discovery Overfield made in 1948. While checking real estate titles in the office of the Erie County clerk, Overfield came across a document entitled: Annual Statement of the Financial Condition of the Buffalo Baseball Association at the Close of the Season, November 1, 1878.

"I ordered a photocopy of that," Overfield said. "I was fascinated by it. I wanted to know where did that team play and who were the players and what was the history. Really, that's what started me on delving into the history of baseball, particularly in Buffalo. It was a completely untapped mine because no one had ever done it locally, and of course the tradition was long and filled with important events in baseball history as I subsequently found out. I had no realization of that when I started out."

The late Lee Allen, a former Cincinnati newspaperman and, from 1959–69, the final 10 years of his life, the historian at the Hall of Fame's baseball library, encouraged Overfield in his research. Indeed, Overfield considers his profile of Allen that appeared in *The National Pastime* in 1987 the best piece he has ever written.

Their fifteen-year relationship began in 1955 after Overfield read Allen's book, *100 Years of Baseball.* Overfield wrote to tell Allen how much he enjoyed the book and pointed out a slight inaccuracy in the death of Will White, a former Buffalo pitcher who was a non-swimmer who died in 1911 at his summer home in Port Carling, Ontario, while teaching his niece to swim.

"Within a few days," Overfield wrote in his profile of Allen, "a long letter arrived from #5 Belsaw Place, Cincinnati. The letterhead read, LEE ALLEN, *Baseball Historian.* Rather pretentious, I thought at the time. I was soon to learn that this self-bestowed appellation was entirely justified. Allen wrote: I am flabbergasted and pleased to learn there is someone out there who remembers Will White, let alone the facts of his death."

Overfield's curiosity with the 1878 Bisons, Buffalo's first professional baseball team, brought a stroke of good luck in 1953. He was visiting the team's offices in Offermann Stadium—as Bison Stadium was renamed in 1935 following the death of team president Frank Offermann—when Joe Ziegler, general manager of the Bisons, brought out an old team picture he had found in a closet. None of the players was identified. In pencil, on the brown wrapper on the back of the picture, was the notation: Buffalo champions 1878. Overfield had happened upon the financial statement of that same team and was then researching those Bisons. What resulted was his first published article. It appeared in the *Buffalo Evening News* in 1953. Within two years, Overfield and Allen began corresponding. It was Allen who urged Overfield to write stories for *Baseball Digest* and pursue the history of Buffalo baseball that culminated in his 1985 book.

While at the Hall of Fame, Allen also enlisted Overfield in his attempts to uncover biographical data on everyone who had ever played a game in the majors. In those days, Clara Overfield was able to travel, and she and Overfield and their son, Jim, born in 1942, would make an annual visit to Allen and his wife, Adele, in Cooperstown.

Allen wondered why Elmer White never appeared in a box score after 1871 when he played 16 games for Cleveland. Elmer White was also believed to be the brother of Will White—that same Will White who had sparked the friendship between Allen and Overfield—and James "Deacon" White, who also played for Buffalo. The White family came from Caton, N.Y., a village in the south-central part of the state near the Pennsylvania line, which Allen suggested the Overfields visit on their way back to Buffalo. What resulted was a discovery and a vivid passage in Overfield's profile on Allen.

He strongly suggested that we swing south on our way home and visit Caton, which is about ten miles south of Corning. 'Look for the Methodist church,' he said, 'and then for the cemetery that no doubt will be behind it. I feel confident you will find there what happened to Elmer White.' We reached Caton at dusk, with ominous thunder clouds forming to the south. We found the church and it did have a cemetery behind it. In the deepening gloom, my teenage son and I hurriedly scanned the tombstones, almost furtively, as though we were infringing on some private world. Then suddenly, Eureka! There it was just as Lee had predicted. The stone was scarred by the elements and the inscription was almost illegible, but it could be made out:

ELMER WHITE
BORN DECEMBER 7, 1850
DIED MARCH 28, 1872
PARENTS
BENJAMIN AND MINERVA WHITE

These few words told with exquisite brevity the story of a short life and a short baseball career.

The names of the parents proved Elmer was a cousin not a brother of James and Will, and Overfield dutifully passed this along. "When the information was mailed to Allen," Overfield wrote, "one would have thought the Kohinoor Diamond had been discovered in a rural graveyard, rather than a few facts about an obscure ballplayer."

Overfield specializes in these slices of life. Insights into his subjects don't result from their quoted remarks, which are few. Instead, Overfield relies on memory, if he knew the individual, and details culled from his research to paint his portraits. In his piece on Kerby Farrell, a longtime minor league manager who guided the Bisons from 1959–63 and part of the 1965 season and won the Junior World Series in 1961, Overfield recalled their late post-game dinners where conversation never veered from baseball. "A favorite pastime of his at these meals," Overfield wrote, "was to tinker with batting orders, which he would write down on the tablecloths with a ballpoint pen, much to the despair and mystification of those who cleaned up after he left."

The quirky and unusual are favorite topics for Overfield. He wrote about Jerry Sullivan, an actor and the first midget ever to appear in a game. While researching his book, Overfield plowed through every Buffalo boxscore on microfilm at the Buffalo Historical Society. In a game in September 1905, he came across someone named Sullivan. "Pinch hitter," Overfield said. "One hit. Batted 1,000. Meant nothing to me. The Bisons were on the road that day in Baltimore."

In some scrapbooks that once belonged to a *Buffalo News* sports editor, Overfield found a squib of information about Jerry Sullivan. The search was on. Overfield asked Bob Davids, a friend and founder of SABR who lives in Washington, D.C., to see what might be on file in the Baltimore library. The game was covered extensively. Instead of simply writing about Sullivan, then in Baltimore with a role in "Simple, Simon, Simple," a musical the *Baltimore Sun* described as "a newspaper cartoon play of major importance with a large cast that included 50 lively chorus girls," Overfield expanded his horizon. He ended up writing an amusing story on the three midgets involved in baseball: Pearl du Monville, a fictional creation who appeared in James Thurber's story, "You Could Look It Up"; Eddie Gaedel, who went to bat in 1951 for Bill Veeck's St. Louis Browns; and Sullivan.

"I gave that story to the *Buffalo News* for a magazine piece," Overfield said. "The editor wrote back saying we're not interested in any nostalgic articles; we're only interested in modern lifestyle. The magazine is called 'Buffalo,' but there is very little in it about Buffalo."

Overfield sent the story to SABR. After some delay, it appeared last summer in *The National Pastime.* Another Overfield piece was published last year in *The Baseball Research Journal.* about "the other George Davis."

Not George Stacey Davis, a turn-of-the-century shortstop who had 2,660 hits and a .297 lifetime average, or George "Kiddo" Davis, a centerfielder who played for five clubs in eight seasons between 1926–38. But George Allen Davis, Jr., whose no-hitter for the 1914 Miracle Braves was the highlight of a 36-game big league career between 1912–15 that ended with a 7-10 record.

This Davis was born in a Buffalo suburb. Overfield traced his career at Williams College and Harvard Law School, which he attended while playing in the majors. In the early 1920s, Davis began taking graduate courses in philosophy and comparative religion at the University of Buffalo and became interested in astronomy. While accumulating what was to become a 1,500-volume library in astronomy, Davis found books written in various languages. Overfield once encountered Davis at Erie County Hall, waiting to close a real estate transaction and reading a book in Arabic. Indeed, Davis taught himself enough Sanskrit, Greek, Latin, Arabic, Persian, German and French to understand his astronomy texts.

This learned man was also a suicide victim. He hanged himself in the basement of his Buffalo home in 1961, six months after retiring from a prestigious Buffalo law firm. He had lost an inherited sum in the 1929 stock market crash and was not a partner in the law firm. Hence, when he retired, Davis apparently had only his Social Security income.

No public explanation was ever given for Davis' death. Overfield was able to speak with one member of Davis' family, a son-in-law, and learned from him of the lost inheritance. Overfield examined the appraisal of Davis' estate and saw listings for two bank accounts, with balances in the hundreds of dollars, three small insurance policies and no real estate. Closing his story, Overfield wrote, "It is the guess here that George Davis could not face a future of impecunity and found escape through suicide."

The piece is vintage Overfield. Enough records are included to touch the highs and lows from Davis' baseball career without the numerical overload that would bog down the reader. The emphasis, instead, is on choices and directions and the avenues lives take. "I'm not a statistical buff or a trivia buff," Overfield said. "I'm more interested in the people."

John Thorn, a Saugerties, N.Y., baseball historian and publisher, called Overfield's prose "as clean as anybody's, certainly cleaner than most of the pros I work with." Something more virtuous than correct grammar and proper punctuation comes when Overfield toils at his manual Olympia.

"What makes Joe's writing different from the average researcher's," Thorn said, "is that while he may labor over it, there is a flavor of wryness and irony to his writing that conveys the pleasure that he has in the subject. He has an attitude toward the subject; he has a stance toward it, as opposed to being a mere data-gatherer.

"I mean there are people in SABR, for example, who win the trivia contest every year who haven't an attitude toward baseball

history. All they do is crunch up facts and spit them out. They're people doing an imitation of a computer."

Thorn co-edited *Total Baseball*, a 2,294-page tome which was published in 1989, and enlisted Overfield to write a chapter entitled "Tragedies and Shortened Careers." He had read a piece by Overfield on the bizarre death of Len Koenecke, an outfielder who had gone from Buffalo to the Brooklyn Dodgers in 1934. In a drunken rage, Koenecke had attempted to take over the controls of a chartered plane in 1935. The pilot bludgeoned him to death with a fire extinguisher. Naturally, Koenecke's violent end was included in Overfield's contribution to *Total Baseball*.

"They paid me a thousand dollars," Overfield said. "He sent me a list of names he thought I should deal with. It was kind of a rough list. I had to do a lot of my own research. I got all these names and wrote to Cooperstown and asked them to send me what they had on these players. I spent a lot of my own money in doing the thing.

"The hardest part of the article was he told me to do twenty typewritten pages. I wound up doing 42. But I called him. I said, 'John, this isn't going to work in twenty pages.' He said, 'Well, go ahead. Do the whole thing.'

"They hardly edited it at all, which was quite complimentary. The thing was, I had to organize it. So I had to do it by suicides, murders, accidents, drugs, alcohol, beanballs. It was time consuming, yet I found it valuable. It was trying to get a lot of stuff together and organizing it in some logical form. It is flattering to be asked to do something like that."

Overfield and Thorn live on opposite sides of New York State and met for the first time last summer. Thorn was returning from Cleveland where the annual SABR convention had been held and drove through Buffalo. After a visit at Overfield's house, Overfield, like some ambassador for the Buffalo Chamber of Commerce, made certain to take Thorn to the Broderick Park Inn, at Niagara and West Ferry Streets near the headquarters of Rich Products Corp.

Robert E. Rich, Jr., president of that firm is also president of the Bisons. The restaurant, in addition to its Buffalo baseball memorabilia, has a set of plaques for the honorees in the Buffalo Baseball Hall of Fame (The other set is in Pilot Field). Overfield is on the nine-member hall of fame committee and is responsible for researching the former players and contributors eligible for consideration by the full committee.

"Joe is my definition of an intelligent person," Thorn said. "And that is someone who is not content to spew out what he knows but is always curious to find out more. He blends the wisdom of an adult with the curiosity of childhood."

Thorn and Overfield share something far more consequential than baseball. Their lives have been affected by multiple sclerosis. Thorn, who turns 44 in April, said he is in "spookily outstanding health." His MS has been in remission for seven years.

That disease was diagnosed when he had a stroke at 19. For 14 years, Thorn walked with the aid of a cane. When he and Overfield began corresponding, Thorn was lame and spastically locked on one side. "Here I am," he said. "I'm not in a wheelchair. I'm not noticeably impaired right now. I can take steps without holding the guard rail. I've had extraordinary luck. And in my correspondence with Joe, MS is certainly a subject. Joe's wife did not have the kind of luck I had."

With his precise memory for dates, Overfield recalled that Sept. 20, 1937, was the day he began working at what then was Monroe Abstract Corp., and his first date with Clara Schurr. They were co-workers at the Goode Cake Shop, an Elmwood Avenue bakery and tea room that Overfield said "kind of catered to Buffalo's silk-stocking clientele." While going to college for two years, Overfield worked there from six P.M. to midnight for 25 cents an hour.

On May 24, 1941, the couple married, and their son, Jim, was born Nov. 13, 1942. Overfield had resumed his career in the title insurance business when he was discharged from the service in 1946. Two years later the trouble started. "We were at a picnic," Overfield said. "My wife was walking and suddenly pitched forward. We didn't think anything of it; we thought she'd tripped over a root or something. She was at the 5-and-10 (store) on Grant Street, and she fell again."

The Overfields' family doctor recommended Clara see Henry Goldstein, a neurologist whom Overfield remembers as "a wonderful man." He made the diagnosis of multiple sclerosis and offered a prognosis.

"He said, 'You can remain stable for many years,'" Overfield recalled. "'You're going to have some bad spells, but you're going to recover.' He called it perfectly. We went on and lived a normal life over quite a number of years. But gradually it went to a cane and then to a walker and then to a wheel chair. We had a nice little house on Argonne Drive, and Henry said, 'Joe, your wife can't go up and down those stairs. Get a house on one floor.'"

They built a one-story house. When they wanted a larger home, the Overfields moved to 21 Pinewoods Avenue in Tonawanda. In their first year there, they celebrated their 25th anniversary. Overfield had to hire a nurse to stay with Clara during the day while he worked. Life was more or less normal, albeit with some bad spells when Clara was in and out of the hospital.

One of those stretches in the hospital came in 1964 when Jim Overfield, now the head of the history department at the University of Vermont, graduated Summa Cum Laude and a member of Phi Beta Kappa from Denison University in Granville, Ohio. "She was in a period when she was completely helpless," Overfield said. "It was very sad. I had to go to the graduation alone. Then as Henry Goldstein predicted, that passed and got back to what was normal for her."

A memorable blizzard buried Buffalo in February 1977. Not long afterward, Clara fell ill and had to return to Kenmore Mercy Hospital. There was no trip home this time. Overfield has since visited her nightly in the skilled nursing facility, arriving in time to feed his wife dinner. He annually takes her the first rose that blooms in his garden and regularly brightens her day with fresh flowers.

"People say to me, 'Gee, that must be rough going to that hospital,'" Overfield said. "It's not. When I go in and see her smile, that's sufficient for me. It's something we have to live with. And I don't consider it a burden, because I look at her and see what a burden she's had to carry. So it makes mine very light.

"She has to be fed. She's diapered. She has trouble communicating. Her voice is very weak. In all the years she's had this illness, never once did she say, 'Why me?' or anything like that. She's always adjusted. I always used to say she had these small victories. When I would come home, she would tell me, 'I was able to do the dishes today,' or some little thing which we would consider minor, but to her it was a small victory. Even now, she can't even move a little finger, she'll be telling me about some of the little things she was able to do.

"And she's been an inspiration to so many different people. We happen to be of the Protestant faith, but the Catholic chaplain who comes in to see her always tells me, 'Joe, she doesn't need us. We need her.'

"I had one motivation in my life. It wasn't to make money. It was to make sure if anything happened to me, my wife would be provided for."

The photographic scroll is eight feet long. Books have to be put on both ends to keep this panorama of Buffalo's Olympic Park from curling up on Overfield's living room carpet. When Bob Rich, Sr., board chairman of both Rich Products and the Bisons, became involved with baseball in 1983, a friend who had moved to Michigan sent him this sweeping view . . . of what?

"I got down on my hands and knees with a magnifying glass and looked at everything I could," Overfield said. "The first thing I noticed was some of the houses had flags on them. It was some kind of holiday."

It wasn't Opening Day because the trees all had leaves. The scoreboard indicated Montreal was playing at Buffalo. The names of the batteries, barely discernible on the scoreboard with the aid of a magnifying glass, indicated Kisinger and Ryan for Buffalo. In his book on Buffalo baseball, Overfield had compiled the team's yearly rosters. Rube Kisinger pitched for Buffalo from 1904–10 and Jack Ryan caught in 1907, 1908 and 1909.

The Montreal pitcher, again from what could barely be detected on the scoreboard, was Burchell. Checking his baseball guides, Overfield learned that Fred Burchell only pitched for Montreal in 1907. All the possible trails had narrowed into one. If the flags meant anything, the game was on a holiday in 1907. Overfield went to the microfilm to consult box scores. On the Fourth of July, Buffalo didn't play Montreal. Memorial Day brought the same result, leaving Labor Day. There it was: Sept. 2, 1907. Montreal 1, Buffalo 0.

"It's like detective work," Overfield said. "If you get some little scrap of evidence, with what I have in my library here, that's all I need."

When he began rummaging around in Buffalo's baseball past in the 1950s, collecting wasn't a craze, and there wasn't a market for memorabilia. Overfield was a lone wolf. Records and artifacts started flowing his way, items that proved vital in his subsequent research. He didn't have to bid for merchandise. People knew that Overfield, for whatever reason, was interested in Buffalo baseball history and often stepped forward to help him on his archaeological dig. Max Felerski was one of those people.

The Detroit Tigers operated the Bisons as a farm club from 1952 through 1955 before abandoning the franchise. After the sale, Overfield received a telephone call from Felerski, who after retiring from his job as an International League umpire became a groundskeeper at Offermann Stadium.

"In the office at Offermann Stadium were the records of the Buffalo baseball club, financial and otherwise," Overfield said. "He said, 'Joe, you better get down here. Most of the stuff has already been hauled away, but there are some things that you should come down for if you want to get them.'

"So I went. I took a few pictures and a daily diary of the box scores of the Bison games from 1926 to 1950, which have proved quite valuable over the years. But all the rest of the stuff was just hauled away and destroyed. Absolutely tragic. I'm sure there were letters that would have been of historical importance. That was a tremendous disappointment to me."

Overfield's baseball research, while always a sideline, had a natural connection to title insurance. In that field, the history being traced is that of the land. Overfield rose at Monroe Abstract & Title, which operates in New York State, to become a director of the firm. For thirteen years until he semi-retired, Overfield ran their Buffalo office of about 60 people. He regularly brought work home evenings and devoted time to his job on weekends.

"Everybody used to say I was a workaholic," Overfield said. "A workaholic is one who is married strictly to one thing. I've always had all these other interests. And I always found time because I didn't waste time.

"Even when I was working all those hours, I still played golf.

I still had the garden. I found time to do those things. Go to the hospital every day."

And plow through bygone eras and become the savant of Buffalo baseball. Overfield originally wanted to be a sportswriter. Through the years he met many of them and realized "where baseball was their main job, they stopped becoming fans of the game. With me, I've never lost that fascination." As a sportswriter wrestling with deadlines, Overfield might have had his fill of the game—today's account inexorably followed by tomorrow's, rain delays complicating matters and doubleheaders the worst of all worlds—so that he never would have started to seek out what once was. Instead, Overfield became a pillar for a colorful past that without him would have disintegrated into rubble.

"If it wasn't for Joe," said Cy Williams, the retired scout, "all that history of Buffalo baseball would've been lost. All of it. Because there's no one who would be that close to it. We have a lot of writers here, a lot of sportscasters, but they weren't here from the time of old Bison Stadium or Offermann Stadium up to the present time.

"I don't think anybody (else) could ever have dug that information up. I really mean that in all sincerity. I don't think there would be a writer who would have the patience or the time to do it and have the love of the game like he has. He's a wonderful fellow, and Buffalo owes an awful lot to him."

Overfield's output hasn't been limited to baseball. He wrote a 30,000-word history of the Baptist denomination of Western New York that he called, "Years of Trial and Triumph," and a history of the now-defunct Lafayette Avenue Baptist Church where he and his family worshiped.

Overfield also chronicled the death of his maternal grandfather, Angus MacDonald. MacDonald was 44 and captain of the Hudson in 1901 when that ship went down with all hands aboard in Lake Superior. Two pictures of the Hudson and one of MacDonald hang near Overfield's front door.

"When I was a little boy, my mother took an old clipping out of the drawer," he said. "I can remember it as though it were yesterday. She said, 'This is a report of your grandfather's drowning.' That's my only memory of that. Some years ago, I said that memory and tradition has got to be kept alive in the family.

"So I went to the Buffalo Historical Society, and it was voluminously covered in the press. I corresponded with historians; a fellow named Dr. Julius Wolfe in Duluth was very helpful. I put together that little monograph about my grandfather, 'The Last Voyage of the Hudson.' I printed maybe a hundred copies and just gave it away to members of the family."

All this writing was done at the manual Olympia in what Overfield calls "the baseball room." A few mementoes not having to do with the national pastime can be found there, such as the scorecard from Aug. 31, 1962, when Overfield, once a low-80s golfer, made a hole-in-one. He plays with a regular group that calls itself the Ecumenical Foursome and includes Overfield, a WASP; Eddie Bylina, who is Polish; Al Reis, a Jew; and Ettore Porreca, an Italian who shares Overfield's interest in words.

A ball that skips off the fairway and nestles near some trees has been known to cause Overfield or Porreca to remark, "It's in the umbra," the Latin word for shade. Words like umbrella, umbrage and penumbra will pass between the two friends as they approach the next shot and try to think of words derived from umbra.

On threatening days, the other three members of the foursome have come to rely on Overfield's knowledge of the clouds for weather predictions. His interest in cloud formations began when Eliza Jane Overfield, his paternal grandmother, used to gather her four grandchildren at family picnics in the country. "She would tell us to look in the sky and see what we could imagine out of the different cloud formations," Overfield said. "It might be a sheep or a man's head or a horse as the clouds changed. And I always remembered that. I still, playing golf with my friends, will say, 'Look. Doesn't that look like the head of an elephant?' as the clouds change."

Being on Lake Erie, Buffalo has few totally blue-sky days. Overfield can gaze toward the heavens and use knowledge from his service during World War II. The white, fluffy cumulus clouds in the lower levels of the sky, the fleecy cirrus ones at about 20,000 feet and the foreboding cumulonimbus clouds at higher levels all come in varieties which, beyond their aesthetics, carry a meterological meaning to which Overfield is attuned daily.

"First thing I do is go to the back window and look out," he said. "That's east. For a couple reasons. I'm very concerned if the Bisons are playing that night. If it's a golf day, I'm concerned. And I'm also concerned about it maybe from the point of view of the garden."

With the authority of a horticulturist, Overfield can walk around his backyard and along his driveway, reciting species and characteristics. Phlox. Impatiens. Salvia. Ageratum. Astilbe. Gaillardia. Nothing is planted haphazardly. Mindful of the variety of colors, Overfield ends up with a dazzling outdoor palette.

"Most people are very ambitious in the spring," he said, "and by late in the summer, their gardens become a disaster area. And it's really not necessary. Not all varieties of plants reflower, but most of them do, roses especially. Once a rose fades, and you cut it off at a certain point in the stem, a new rose will grow from that."

Overfield uses that slow-and-steady approach on twenty-five varieties of rose bushes. When he picks the first rose of the year to take to Clara, Overfield makes a notation in the meterological journal he keeps. Last year that entry was made on June 7. "I can look back," Overfield said, "and see, '1986, June 2, first rose blooms.' That's very early. See how close these things fall. Nature's patterns are almost irrevocable in spite of the weather. Last May we had 7.22 inches of rain, which was a record. This year we had 6.08. Here's a May in 1982, when we only had 1.35 inches. I've done this for years. I've got four books. Just sit down and write a line in. I do it all year."

The entries are made at the long table in "the baseball room." Faces from the past surround Overfield as he makes jottings about the present. The 1882 Bisons are there with their three Hall of Farmers, Jim Galvin, Jim O'Rourke and Dan Brouthers. "And there's one that should be, Jim 'Deacon' White," Overfield said, warming to the subject. "He's never going to make it because nobody remembers him except me."

Buffalo has had baseball since 1877, with a gap between 1971–78, and major league representation in the National League, 1879–85; the Players League, 1890; and Federal League. Those two Federal League teams from 1914–15 are on display, along with the 1878 team, the first one Overfield researched, and the 1961 Junior World Series champions. There is a large 1933 aerial shot of Offermann Stadium and next to it a crowd milling outside the portals of the ballpark beneath a sign: Buffalo Bisons Community Owned. That would have been between 1956 and 1960, the last season before Offermann Stadium was razed to make way for a school, and had to be opening day because the trees have only buds. Overfield is on an explanatory roll.

The scoresheet from the Buffalo Evening News shows Bob Veale of the Columbus Jets striking out 22 Bisons on Aug. 10, 1962, an International League record. Overfield, gathering steam, notes that Veale was taken out in the 10th inning for a pinch hitter and wasn't the winning pitcher.

Bill Dickey and Joe McCarthy are on the wall, the pictures taken in 1946. Howard Ehmke, from nearby Silver Creek, N.Y., is sidearming a pitch for the Federal League Bisons in 1915. Overfield is planning a story on him for a future BisonGram. "Struck out 13 in that famous World Series game in '29," Overfield says. "A lot of people don't realize he was within one pitch of doing what (Johnny) Vandeer Meer did. He had one no-hitter and pitched a one-hitter in the next game."

Luke Easter hangs next to Ollie Carnegie. "The outstanding figures of Buffalo baseball history," Overfield says of those renowned sluggers, two of his favorite players. Al Moore, a handsome outfielder who had three big seasons with the Bisons from 1928–30, is framed beside pitcher Warren "Curley" Ogden. "It's a ballplayer's face isn't it?" Overfield says of Ogden, who was 21-11 with the 1928 Bisons. "Look at the cap." It's tilted toward the left side of Ogden's head. His right eye is little more than a slit, the left one has a demonic stare and Ogden, no hint of a smile on his round face, has a mow-'em-down look.

Twenty-five shares in the Buffalo Bisons Baseball Club, issued on Dec. 15, 1955, can be found. There's a 1938 picture of Carnegie and Babe Ruth, who was a Brooklyn Dodgers coach when he played in Buffalo in an exhibition game Overfield saw. It was Ruth's last professional game. "He was playing first base with Brooklyn," Overfield says. "The funny thing is Carnegie didn't play. He was hurt."

There are pictures of Bisons managers on one wall, including Ray Schalk; George "Specs" Toporcer, whom Overfield notes took over the team in '51 but had to step down that season because of vision problems; Phil Cavarretta; Farrell and John Boles. John Thorn said Overfield has the archetype research personality, someone for whom "the past is every bit as vital as the present." Then leads to now. A tapestry of events unfolds, not disjointed happenings. Overfield has picked the first rose and taken it to Clara, duly made his journal notation, and the garden will soon be in full bloom. Clouds are scudding across the Buffalo sky. Here. There. Gone.

A keepsake newspaper dated Sept. 12, 1982, is on a bookshelf near the manual Olympia. The headline reads: Courier Prints Its Last Edition. It is the final copy of the *Buffalo Courier-Express,* the morning paper that used to be hawked with the cry: COUR-ee-er! COUR-ee-er!

Overfield is rhapsodizing about Jimmy Walsh, who was inducted into the Buffalo Baseball Hall of Fame last year. "He had a glove," Overfield says. "It was like a rag it was so supple. He used to stuff it in his back pocket after he came in from the outfield. I can picture it almost as though it was yesterday." Walsh was 40 when he won his second consecutive International League batting title with Buffalo in 1926. Overfield was just coming to baseball then, beholding something magical from the bleachers of Bison Stadium and beginning a fascination, a love and a commitment that never waned.

"If you get Joe talking about Jack Rowe and Dan Brouthers and Deacon White," Thorn said, "he speaks about these people with an animation that would make you think these people are guys who stopped over at the house last week."

TRACERS

In the early 1900s, a Chicago clothier offered an expensive suit of clothes to the player who led the Chicago Cubs in home runs. This was an era when home runs were rare and there were no regular coaches. The players took turns coaching at first and and third.

Catcher Johnny Kling was one home run ahead of Joe Tinker . . . and had drawn the third-base coaching duties. Tinker was at the plate and slammed a drive that caromed off the fence and ricocheted about the outfield. There was little doubt that it would be an inside-the-park home run. But as Tinker approached third, Kling held up his arms for him to stop—and later collected a fancy new suit.

—Michael G. Bryson, *The Twenty-Four-Inch Home:*
And Other Outlandish, Incredible But True
Events in Baseball History, 1990.
Page 11

We have, incidentally, no clue what the source of this story is. Obviously, an anecdote like this doesn't surface eighty years after the fact without a paper trail, but we don't where it is.

Kling and Tinker were teammates from 1902 through 1911. During that ten-year span, Kling led the Cubs in home runs just once, in 1903. He hit three homers to beat out Tinker and Frank Chance by one for the team lead. (We should also note that Ling was a Cub for two seasons before Tinker's arrival in 1902, but didn't hit any home runs.) So it seems that if Kling really did sabotage Tinker's home run total for the sake of his wardrobe, it must have been in 1903.

I decided to start looking at the *Chicago Tribune* in September, 1903. Specifically, I was keeping an eye out for triples struck by Tinker.

As the month began, Kling had already hit all three of his home runs. On September 5, Joe Tinker hit his second home run of the season, so it was 3–2. Two days later, Tinker tripled. There was no mention in the newspaper regarding the direction or distance of the hit. But in the Cubs lineup, Tinker batted fifth and Kling sixth, making it highly unlikely that Kling would have been in the coaches' box while Tinker was tearing around second base. The next day, September 8, Tinker hit another triple. Again, the newspaper account didn't describe the hit, but again, Tinker batted fifth and Kling sixth in the lineup. **How-**

ever, the *Tribune* noted that Kling "was out of form and retired at the end of the second inning." Thus it seems quite possible that, after leaving the game, Kling could have taken up a position as the third base coach, and flashed an unnecessary stop sign to Tinker.

A couple of other thoughts. If a clothing store was giving a suit as a gift, they would probably have taken out an ad somewhere bragging about it, so that part of the record should still exist. Second, teams began employing full-time coaches about 1908, so that also would suggest that this event, if it happened, would have happened before 1908.

I was not able to tell from the game account when Tinker tripled and what the score was at the time, but the game was certainly not a blowout—the Cubs beat the Pirates in the ninth on a Tinker double. Would Kling have traded a run for a suit?

Hey, the pennant race was over.

—Rob Neyer

CHARLEY LAU, JR.

JACK ETKIN

The bus was rolling from Erie, Pa., taking the Utica Blue Sox on a 56-mile trip, most of it along Route 17. That road slices through southwestern New York and makes a picturesque crossing of Chautauqua Lake before looping south to Jamestown, N.Y. Charley Lau, Jr. wasn't concentrating on the landscape. To him, the outside world was a blur.

Sometimes he'll visualize swings on these bus rides, seeing the flaws of the youthful Blue Sox, a Class A farm club of the Chicago White Sox in the short-season New York-Pennsylvania League, and wonder how as their hitting coach he can bring about improvements. On this morning in late July, Charley was thinking only of Jamestown.

He had never been there, but his father had. Charley Lau launched his professional baseball career catching for the Class D Jamestown Falcons in 1952. His days as a journeyman in the big leagues ended in 1967. Celebrity for Lau came as a hitting coach, primarily with the Royals, New York Yankees and finally the White Sox. He refined the raw hitting techniques of George Brett and Hal McRae, both groping when they came under Lau's tutelage with the Royals. The one season Reggie Jackson hit .300 in his 21-year career came in 1980 when the Yankees' slugger also led the American League with 41 home runs and Lau was scrutinizing his every swing.

He explained his approach in *The Art of Hitting .300*, published in 1980. Two years later, Lau signed a six-year, $600,000 contract with the White Sox, an unprecedented deal for a coach. He wore a White Sox windbreaker when he played himself in the Neil Simon movie "Max Dugan Returns," good-naturedly telling a young character played by Matthew Broderick, "Hey, Dummy. You can't hit what you can't see."

The film came out in 1983. That summer Lau underwent surgery for colon cancer. He was 50 when he died March 18, 1984. Charley, Jr. was within a week of his 19th birthday and had arrived at his father's home in Key Colony Beach, Fla., the day before his death.

"I walked into the room," Charley recalls. "He was all excited and got this glow on his face. He said, 'Son, we've got a lot to talk about.' I was right in front of him, and he said, 'Go get Charley.'

"He went into a coma. I slept on the floor next to him. The next day, I laid on the bed with him. I hugged him, and I talked to him. I didn't want him to go. I was holding his hand. He quit breathing. I said, 'Dad, don't give up,' and he passed away." On the bus to Jamestown, Charley was wondering about his father's earlier days there. How did he hit in 1952? What kind of a guy was he that summer when he was 19? He was so quiet as an adult; was he shy then? Where did he live, in a house or an apartment? Where did he pass his time there?

"You want to go back in time and watch him," Charley says, "and just be an observer without him watching."

Charley found the next best thing: Flo Wick. Or rather, the 58-year-old Wick noticed Charley's name in the program, introduced herself after a game and asked if he was related to the player she had seen 38 summers ago. "He said, 'You knew my father?'" Wick says. "'You didn't know him from down here did you?' I told him he played in this ballpark."

Lau was in a hurry to catch the Utica bus but arranged to meet Wick the following night. They sat in the College Stadium stands behind home plate where Lau once squatted, visiting for 30 minutes during a downpour that eventually would postpone the game.

"Was he a happy guy? That was one thing he wanted to know," Wick says, "and he was. A real fun guy, not a big jokester but just a very friendly person."

Wick is a regular at the Jamestown Expos' games, always bringing her brass goat bell, something of an heirloom. When she was a girl, two farmers gave that bell to her mother, also a devoted baseball fan. They suggested she use it to conserve her voice instead of hollering for the home team. Wick explained this history to Charley.

"I told him, 'This bell rang for your father,'" Wick says. "He said, 'No kidding.' He held it for a minute in his hands, and I think he felt good about it. I was interested for myself, but I suddenly felt I was doing more for him than myself. I felt like maybe I had done somebody a favor without realizing it."

Two nights later, Lau returned to Utica. He fell asleep and dreamt of shortstop Todd Martin, the White Sox's No. 3 pick in June 1989 and one of the rare prospects on a Utica team of little talent. A healthy Charley Lau appeared in the dream, much to the delight of his son.

"We could be buddies," Charley says. "I asked him about Todd Martin. 'Dad, what do I need to get this kid to do?' He told me. He said, 'You need a little more rhythm and need to have him move back a little better.' I told that to Todd the next day when I was working with him. It was so real that when I woke up, I still thought my dad was alive. It was so secure because here he is; all the questions that I've got, he's going to answer. It was really powerful."

Real life had less of the easy give-and-take of this dream and more strain. Charley was about five when his parents were divorced after four children and sixteen years of marriage. He and his three sisters stayed with their mother, Barbara, in Key Biscayne, Fla. Lau and his second wife, Evelyn, were married in

1971. Their meeting in 1969 contributed to the decline of Lau's first marriage.

"I remember one night we were all sitting around the dinner table, and my dad was late for dinner," Charley says. "My mom and dad had their own table off to the side. My dad wasn't home yet. Finally he came home. My mom had made everybody else's dinner. She left a raw plate of hamburger for my dad. She said, 'There's your dinner.' I remember my dad throwing the whole plate against the wall. Everybody was scared."

That was a child's recollection of the event. Barbara Lau said her husband had been drinking, and when he finally came home on that night, she said, "Charley, do you want one hamburger or two? He said, 'I only want one.' I put two on the plate. When he sat down, because he was so terribly intoxicated, he looked at it and threw it against the wall."

There was tension between father and son until the last summer of Lau's life. Then they drank beer together in Lau's Jacuzzi and listened to the Jimmy Buffett music that Lau loved. They reconciled their differences in those final months, making up, as best they could, for all the years of separation, all the seasons when Lau was traveling and ministering more to his players than his son.

"I knew he wanted a relationship," Charley says. "To get it with the little amount of time he had to live, it wasn't much. But at least I got that."

If Lau were alive, Charley believes they would be enjoying exchanges, like the dream sequence dealing with Todd Martin, marked with harmony rather than strain. "My relationship would be more like his relationship with his players and close friends," Charley says. "I think it would be the ideal friendship. He was the most important thing in my life. He still is."

Later With Bob Costas gave George Brett the incentive. While watching the program early one morning, Brett heard Costas reveal he carries a Mickey Mantle baseball card in his wallet. The card is like Costas' driver's license or Social Security card; Mickey Mantle goes everywhere with Costas.

This recollection came as Brett was sitting at his locker at Royals Stadium. He stood up, continuing to speak while reaching for something high in his locker. "So I said to myself, 'Is there anybody that has been such an influence on my life that I should do the same thing?' " Brett says. "There was no doubt who came to mind first."

He had found his wallet and flipped it open. There was a Charley Lau card, taken when he was with the Milwaukee Braves. And tacked to the side of Brett's locker are Lau cards when he was with the Detroit Tigers and Baltimore Orioles.

McRae has his own tribute to Lau, a picture that hangs near the bar in the game room of the home he built in Bradenton, Fla. The photograph was taken at Royals Stadium. A sullen

McRae is sitting against the stands, staring straight ahead, cap pulled low. He looks like he hasn't had a hit in a week and, worse, realizes it may be that long before he even makes hard contact. Lau, seated on McRae's right, has turned toward him.

"He had watched me play," says McRae, the hitting coach for the Montreal Expos. "I had explained to him what I thought was wrong. He listened, and then he told me to go play like hell for 10 days and everything'll change, everything'll get better. And that's what I did, and it did.

"He was like a coach and a friend and a father-type figure to me because you knew he was always in your corner, right or wrong. He would tell you if you were wrong, but you were still his guy. He was still pulling for you and would help you face the problem."

Only when a player was willing would Lau approach, offering his assistance. He was not a chatty sort. Brett recalls, "It was hard to get words out of Charley sometimes unless he was talking about hitting." To outsiders, Lau could seem standoffish, if not downright gruff, chain-smoking Marlboro 100s and uttering monosyllables.

Lau went from dark-haired and dashing as a young man to silver-haired and disintinguished in middle age. He could have passed for a banking executive, albeit one who long ago gave up sitting at a desk. Fishing in the Florida Keys, particularly in the shallow water known as the flats, was a passion of Lau's. To catch pilchard, a bait fish, he would squirt some menhaden oil on the water, maybe toss some bread crumbs or oatmeal overboard and stand in the front of his small boat. Part of the net would be on his shoulder, part in his mouth. With an artful sweep, Lau would cast the net. After it fanned out, weights carried the net downward. A tug of the drawstring and Lau would tighten the net and pull up a school of pilchard.

"He was a Hemingway type of guy," Charley says, "the old rough and rugged fisherman who found his peace and serenity by the sea."

The rough and rugged fisherman actually was moved easily to tears.

Charley remembers visiting his father in the early 1970s. It was a summer when Lau was a roving minor league hitting coach with the Royals. They had returned to Lau's apartment from a long drive and were lying on his bed.

"We were watching TV, eating some fruit," Charley recalls. "He was trying to explain the divorce to me. I asked him, 'Are you still my father?' and he started crying, 'Yes, I'm still your father. I'm just not married to your mother anymore.' "

Lau and Evelyn met in Baltimore where Lau, in seven seasons, played in 286 of his 527 major league games and, in 1969, first worked as a hitting coach. When he introduced her to Bob Watson, owner of a landscaping business in the Baltimore suburb of Lutherville, Md., Lau said, "Come here, Friendly," using the nickname he had for Watson, "I want you to meet somebody, because you're going to know her for a long time."

The couple moved to Key Colony Beach in 1974, so Evelyn could operate a clothing boutique called Key Bana. Mornings in the offseason, Lau would clean the windows and vacuum the floor before Evelyn arrived to open the store.

"He also had a habit," Evelyn says. "I could break his neck. People would come, and he'd let them in and tell them to take what they want and come back later and pay.

"I said, 'Charley, you can't do that.' But everyone always came back."

Handling money wasn't Lau's specialty. Barbara Lau kept the checkbook when they were married. Evelyn sent her husband spending money on the road, basically so he wouldn't always be helping out friends. Bill Fischer, the pitching coach of the Boston Red Sox and a teammate of Lau's in 1963 with the Kansas City A's, says, "If he had five dollars in his pocket, he'd give it to you."

Lau had the same unselfish approach when it came to helping hitters. He would come into the clubhouse, invariably wearing boat shoes, khaki pants, a white T-shirt or white polo shirt and white terrycloth hat. The hats came from Eddie Bauer in Seattle. Lau bought them by the dozen on visits there and handed them out to friends.

"He'd get a cup of coffee," Brett says. "He'd be walking, holding it with both hands, and he'd be shaking and it would be overflowing. He'd have a cigarette in his mouth, and every day his back was out of whack."

Lau's face would be wracked with pain as he dressed for early batting practice. Finally, he would grab a bag of baseballs, and start hobbling out of the clubhouse and down the runway to the dugout. Lau would pour the balls into a basket at the mound, put a dip of Skoal into his mouth and throw his hat down. Then would come about five halting, agonizing throws. With the players wondering just how he was going to manage to get up to speed, Lau would suddenly yell, "OK, get in there."

"And he would throw as long as it took to get your swing down that day," Brett says. "As long as it took."

Lau emphasized hitting the ball to all fields rather than trying to pull everything. "To pull the ball you have to react quicker," Lau said, "and that's why very few pull hitters are consistent. With a pull hitter, tension comes into their swing because they're forcing it to one area of the field. Their reaction time is less."

Any movement of the eyes and head cuts reaction time, a crucial hitting variable. Lau explained this one day in 1981, inviting a reporter to kneel beside him at the batting cage. Aurelio Rodriguez, a third baseman whose .237 lifetime average over seventeen seasons was proof he lasted in the big leagues because of his fielding prowess, was hitting for the Yankees. He lined a ball into left field. Only Lau detected the infinitesimal movement of Rodriguez's head. "That's not good enough, not for the breaking ball," Lau said. "For the fastball, it's OK."

Lau stressed releasing the top hand after contact to get arm extension; otherwise the swing became shortened and weakened. A movement back before beginning the swing was one of Lau's tenets, along with a weight shift from a firm back side to a firm front side. Striding with the front toe closed kept the hips from opening prematurely, and a tension-free swing followed by a high follow-through allowed the hips to open and ensured a proper weight shift.

Doubters said the system produced opposite-field singles hitters who sacrificed power. Lau could point to the eight seasons between 1976–83 when the teams he was with won five division titles and one pennant. To him, fault-finding simply came with the territory. "Charley used to have a saying," Evelyn Lau says. "The higher you shinny up the flagpole, the more you expose of your ass."

Criticism was of less concern to Lau than the fundamentals of any swing. These elements produced what Lau called a domino effect when they fell into place. If they didn't, he could tell why, with a dissection Lau carried to humorous lengths in 1976. The Royals got into a brawl that season in Oakland after Dennis Leonard hit Don Baylor, who charged the mound.

"When the guys got back to the bullpen, all of a sudden there was a commotion going on," says Royals broadcaster Fred White, a close friend of Lau's who shared an apartment with him during the 1978 season. "There was a fight going on between some of the fans and the Royals players. One of the fans had an umbrella. McRae took the umbrella away from the guy, and he's trying to hit him.

"But the umbrella's not rolled up and snapped. Every time he swings it, the umbrella starts to open, and he can't get anything on it. The next morning we're in the coffee shop, and there's a picture of it in the paper. Charley walked in, picked up the paper and sat there very quietly and said, 'Still too much top hand, Mac.' "

After ending his career in the majors with a .255 average, Lau spent one season managing. In 1968, at Class AA Shreveport, La., in the Texas League, one of Lau's players on a second-place team was Walt Hriniak, now the hitting coach for the White Sox.

Like Lau, Hriniak was a left-handed hitting catcher. He was then 25 and in his eighth season in the minors. At the outset of his professional career, Hriniak had batted .311 and .300. Then came the advice to pull the ball and try for home runs, and Hriniak never again topped .275. When Hriniak did reach that level, it was in a stay of just 40 at-bats at Class AAA Richmond, Va., in 1967.

That season at Shreveport, Hriniak hit .313, thanks to Lau, who seized an instructional opening and again got Hriniak to use the whole field.

"I was down in the batting cage, hitting off a pitching machine," Hriniak says. "He was watching me hit. I was hitting real good, but I was pulling everything. My five minutes were over. I turned to him and said, 'What do you think?' I thought his response was going to be, 'Real good,' because I thought I was hitting well. He said, 'Well, one thing about it. They'll know where to play you.' "

The Atlanta Braves called Hriniak up at the end of the 1968 season. He made his debut in the majors on Sept. 10, going hitless in three at-bats, and the following day, Hriniak found himself facing San Francisco's Juan Marichal, whose gaudy record was then 25-7.

"First two times up," Hriniak remembers, "I hit two singles to left-center right in front of Willie Mays. I had a father, who died in '81 and who I loved with all my heart. But the first person I called after the game after those two hits was Charley and my father second."

Hriniak had 23 more hits in a big-league career that spanned 99 at-bats and ended in 1969. Lau would go on to refine his knowledge, using videotape and film to study hitters, including some of the best in history, and analyze their styles. Nonetheless, in that 1968 season, Lau left a lasting impression on Hriniak.

"He had something I'd never seen before in anybody in professional baseball," Hriniak says. "He had a tremendous want and need to help people. He was a natural teacher.

"He was one of the most unique people that I ever met in my life. I think what Charley was able to do was help a .220 hitter hit .250. He had the caring to help the superstar; that's one thing. But he also had the ability and caring to help anybody, not just the stars. Nobody gave a fuck about a .250 hitter. But Charley did."

Because of what Lau did for him in 1968, Hriniak went into coaching. He spent twelve seasons as the hitting coach for the Boston Red Sox before a five-year deal worth $500,000 lured Hriniak to the White Sox after the 1988 season. They wanted someone to teach Lau's system. Who better than Hriniak, forever entwined with Lau. Every time he rises for the National Anthem before the start of another game, Hriniak remembers Lau in prayer.

"Bless my father. Bless my mother. Bless my friend Charley. Let his two wives and son and his three daughters deal with his loss."

Hriniak last saw Lau on a visit to Key Colony Beach in December 1983. Lau was very sick but determined to take Hriniak fishing. This was not the same as making a winter call to Bill Fisher in Sarasota, with the invitation, "The mackerel are wall-to-wall twelve feet down in the water." Hriniak didn't fish. And at the time, Lau couldn't.

They left Lau's house on Coral Lane, walked across the street to the marina and loaded the gear into Lau's 19-foot boat. "We're getting ready to go," Hriniak says, "and he says, 'I can't make it. Walter, I'm sorry.' " After Lau rested, the fishing party set out, this time with the help of Will John, a friend of Lau's. They were going to catch pilchard, which flash in the water like silver dollars when the sunlight hits them. On this overcast day, it was impossible to even see in the water.

"I ran the boat," John says. "Charley stood up in the bow of the boat with the net and was going to attempt to throw it. I kind of signaled to his buddy to be ready to grab him in case he lost his balance. It was so hazy and cloudy we cruised around for half an hour, and I said, 'Charley, we're just wasting our time.'

"He said, 'I'll take the boat in.' We went in the channel and went right for the bank. We weren't going very fast, of course. There were some mangrove bushes there. Out of instinct, he kind of reacted and reached for the pole they use to push off when fishing the flats for bonefish. I said, 'Charley, it's not necessary. Let me take it.' I backed it up and turned it around and took it into the dock. That was the last time he was in the boat."

Lau had made good on his vow to take Hriniak out on the water. Before he left for his home in North Andover, Mass., never again to see Lau alive, Hriniak made a pledge to him. "I just promised him as long as I was in baseball that I would carry on the things that he had taught me," Hriniak says. "Not because you're my friend, but I believe them as much as you do. I promised him that."

The White Sox gave Hriniak the authority to hire batting coaches to teach Lau's method from top to bottom in their farm system. The opening at the bottom rung in Sarasota, Fla., with the Gulf Coast White Sox was something Hriniak had in mind for Charley.

He spent a week at Hriniak's house and worked at his hitting school near Boston in the winter of 1988–89. They talked about how Charley could join in the mission of carrying on his father's beliefs. They discussed the down side, doubters who thought releasing the top hand was bunk. Being a native New Englander, Hriniak drew upon some Calvinist bleakness just before Charley left.

"He tried to give me the other end of the coin, telling me how hard it was going to be," Charley says. " 'People are going to be hard on you. They're going to expect more from you, and you're not going to like it. I wouldn't take the job if I were you, but it's up to you.'

"I took the job. I was 24 years old. I didn't have a solid foundation with my life. I didn't have a plan."

Charley became the hitting coach in 1989 with the White

Sox team in the Rookie Gulf Coast League. Games are played at noon in high heat before crowds so scant that attendance figures aren't kept. Records are. The White Sox were 40-23, second in the southern division. Their .250 average was fourth in the 14-team league, although the hitters' success had little to do with Charley.

"The first year he was pathetic," Hriniak says. "He didn't know how to conduct himself. He was showing up late and leaving early. He just didn't know how to coach.

"I told him, 'I'll fire you because that's what your father would want. You don't have this job because you're Charley Lau's son; you have to earn it. And if you don't, I'll fire you. Your father would be sick over this.' "

Charley received a second chance, a $19,000 salary and a move up a notch to Utica. He also got help. Mike Lum, hired after the 1989 season to be the roving minor league hitting coach for the White Sox, spent a lot of time with Charley in spring training. Having knowledge about hitting is one thing, Lum told Charley. Teaching, though, is more a matter of learning to communicate.

"He said you got to be subtle," Charley says. "You can't make wise-ass remarks to people. You got to respect people. I started thinking about it. How many times do I say things without thinking about what I'm actually saying? This spring I made the biggest change, I guess, in myself. I guess you can call it maturity. I can see myself more aware of what I say and how I say it and who it affects.

"I care about what I do. I'm more responsible. I guess I've just made a 180-degree turn. My heart's in it, whereas last year, I was just here."

Charley was given a choice for the 1991 season. He could return to Utica or again work with the Gulf Coast White Sox. Charley opted for Florida, the familiar and another summer in Sarasota.

Cups, napkins, programs and peanut shells from the night before litter the ground beneath the bleachers at Murnane Field. A worker is loading empty kegs of Matt's Premium onto a truck. It is 10 A.M. Gametime is 9½ hours away. Several Blue Sox have gathered at the batting cage behind the first base grandstand for extra work with Charley.

"Bottom hand to the location and through the location," he tells Brandon Wilson. "You got to be patient. Let the swing do it. The swing takes the weight shift forward against the front side."

"Rhythm is going to maintain balance," Charley says to Kerry Valrie. "Movement will not let tension set in. If we're tense, the muscles are not going to fire properly."

Charley's voice never rises. he remains positive and avoids any sarcasm. The 31-47 Blue Sox, who hit .226, 12th in a 14-team league, present few quick studies. Most will soon be looking for work outside of baseball. Charley imparts a system that can improve their chances to hit, "but it's not like I'm a magic potion." So he simply concentrates on teaching. Worrying about which students will graduate *cum laude* is a needless complication.

"He doesn't get frustrated with you," says Blue Sox outfielder Kevin Coughlin. "He'll work with you anytime you need it. He's got a lot of patience. He's learning just like we are. He's serving his time just like we are."

Lau once told his son he had the ability to be a professional baseball player. Then he added a warning: "But I don't think you realize how hard you have to work." Charley ended up using his father's hitting techniques for a 12-game professional career in 1987. That cameo came when he signed in August with the Miami Marlins, an independent team in the Class A Florida State League. Charley had four hits in 32 at-bats and returned to St. Thomas University in Miami that fall.

He tore the anterior cruciate ligament in his left knee playing intramural football. The doctor told Charley a year and a half of rehabilitation would be necessary. He finished his degree in sports administration and had vague thoughts about getting back into baseball as a hitting instructor when Hriniak called.

Baseball was a familiar world for Charley. Visiting his father in the summer had brought him around big leaguers. "When you're in that atmosphere," Charley says, "you don't really appreciate how lucky you are. You just think, 'Well, this is the lifestyle I'm in.' "

To the Royals players, Charley was "Buckwheat," a nickname they hung on him when he was eight and accompanying his father on a trip to Minnesota. Charley had seen a television commercial for Buckwheat cereal that suggested the cereal makes you feel like a million bucks. While watching his father, McRae, Amos Otis and John Mayberry play poker in the Metropolitan Stadium clubhouse, an urge struck.

"Otis was winning all the money," Charley says. "I said, 'Give me the buckwheats,' and ran off with the money for a while. The next day I was in the paper. I was the batboy and was shaking hands with Mayberry after he hit a home run. They all started calling me 'Buckwheat.' "

Charley did the natural thing for someone looking to fit in. He tried to act like the players. He was loud, cocky, even arrogant, but he was also watching his father and searching for something.

"I saw the way he was with the players," Charley says. "I saw his friendships and how great they were and how much fun they seemed like, and I was always very envious of that. I always wanted to have a relationship that way. I craved that."

"Alright, Charley, where in the hell are you?" Bob Watson is asking. "Maybe he's up farther." Watson knows where to look. He is walking among the tombstones in the Moreland Memorial Cemetery, something he has done many times. A landscaping job might take him from his business, Watson's Garden Center in Lutherville, and Watson will find himself driving down Perring Parkway. Almost by instinct, he exists on Taylor Avenue for the cemetery in Baltimore County, just over the Baltimore city limits.

"I'll pull in," Watson says, "go kick the dirt and just reminisce and say a little prayer."

In Watson's case, it's one his grandmother taught him, one she said would cover everything.

Angel of God
My guardian dear,
To whom his love commits me here.
Ever this day,
Be at my side.
To light and guard and rule and guide.

Watson has found what he was seeking. The marker at his feet reads:

LAU
Charles R. 1933–1984
Evelyn S. 1941–

"April 12, 1933. March the 18th, 1984," Watson says, reciting the dates of Lau's birth and death from memory. Watson lifts the flower holder from the marker, turns it upright and shakes out the water. "Charley," Watson says, "there's no fish in there."

It's 1,234 miles from Watson's front door to Lau's in Key Colony Beach. Watson and his wife, Connie, still make the trip every winter after his busy Christmas season. But there's no pulling up to Lau's after a non-stop drive for the sight that once greeted Watson.

"I got there at 9 A.M.," Watson says. "He said, 'Hurry up, Friendly. You're late.' He was sitting on the boat."

"I still wait to go to Florida. I still wait to see Evelyn. I still look at that little boat parked in front of her house getting dry-rotted."

One winter, the Watsons and Laus drove to Key West Junior College for a Jimmy Buffett concert. Buffett sings about the Florida Keys, bouncing back from past mistakes, the lure of the sun and water, the joy of a cocktail or two and a way of life that Lau loved.

"The lyrics meant so much to him," Charley says. "They symbolized a lot of the lyrics that were embedded deep inside his soul. The Buffett songs seemed to start off with a struggle and end up with a victory. But even though it's a struggle, Buffett makes it sound like it's a fun struggle."

Two of Lau's favorite Buffet songs were "A Pirate Looks at Forty" and "Son of a Son of a Sailor." The former had a financial lament that Lau, not particularly good with money, appreciated: "I made enough money to buy Miami/but I pissed it away so fast./It's never meant to last/Never meant to last." The latter song extolled something more enduring: "I'm just a son of a son/ son of a son/ son of a son of a sailor./ The sea's in my veins/ The tradition remains/ I'm just glad I don't live in a trailer."

Lau was buried in one of his white terrycloth hats, khaki pants, deck shoes and a white shirt. The funeral was held at the Duda-Ruck Funeral Home in the Baltimore suburb of Dundalk. Watson was a pallbearer, along with Brett, McRae, Fred White and White Sox players Carlton Fisk and Greg Luzinski. They carried the casket down six steps, out the door and to the hearse. White, McRae and Brett were in the front. While lifting the casket, they bumped it into the hearse.

"Uh-oh," Brett said. "Charley's going to be mad. Too much top hand."

"Hey, Dummy," Lau might have said. "Keep the head down."

Dummy was a term of affection for Lau. The screenwriters hadn't included it, but Lau insisted on saying "Dummy" when he appeared in "Max Dugan Returns." The camera first finds Lau standing behind a fence. He watches Michael McPhee, played by Matthew Broderick, swing and miss—by wide margins—and throw his bat in disgust. Lau has been hired by Dugan, McPhee's grandfather played by Jason Robards, to teach the boy to hit.

"Are you Michael McPhee?" Lau says, approaching McPhee. "I'm Charley Lau. Ever heard of me? I'm the batting coach for the White Sox."

"What White Sox?" McPhee asks.

"The Chicago White Sox. I've been watching you swing, and you stink. It's not your fault. No one taught you the basics. I want you to be aware of the discipline of your head and the transfer of weight to a firm front side."

Nearly a decade later in Utica, life is imitating art. Charley is having Chris Sparrow do a two-part drill. Sparrow strides, pauses and then takes his swing as Charley flips a ball underhand. Then Charley demonstrates. "Once I stride," he says, moving toward an imaginary pitch, "I'm in the launch position and against a firm front side."

The son is 26 and carrying on the family business. It could be a clothing store or a restaurant, a construction company or an insurance agency. The business just happens to be teaching others to hit a baseball.

"Hopefully just with maturity, I'll be able to be respected somewhat the same way my father was," Charley says. "I think just through time and hard work that'll happen naturally. I got a lot of work in front of me, and I'm not afraid of that. And I know my father's proud of what I'm doing right now."

TRACERS

A debut of another kind was made by Hoyt Wilhelm, the brilliant knuckleball relief pitcher who started his career with the New York Giants in 1952. Wilhelm's knuckler kept him in the majors until 1972 . . .

But it was his debut at the plate that must have made the Giants wonder if Wilhelm was actually a slugging outfielder disguised as a pitcher. His first time up as a major league batter, Wilhelm took a big cut, and he belted one over the left field fence for a home run! A couple of innings later he was up again and showed everyone it was no fluke. This time he shot into the gap between the outfielders and legged it into a triple. You can't start much better than that.

Perhaps the Giants were already thinking they had another Babe Ruth on their hands (the Babe started out as a pitcher before his great bat forced his conversion to the outfield). Luckily, the Giants didn't make any hasty decisions. Before long, Wilhelm settled into a groove as a typical light-hitting pitcher. In fact, during the course of his long career, which saw him pitch for nine teams in both leagues over twenty-one seasons, Hoyt Wilhelm never hit another home run. Nor did he ever hit another triple! He got it all out of his system his first two at bats and then concentrated on being one of the great relief pitchers of all time.

—*Strange and Amazing Baseball Stories,*
Bill Gutman, Page 2.

According to the 1969 edition of *The Baseball Encyclopedia,* which has complete batting stats for pitchers, Hoyt Wilhelm did not hit a triple in 1952.

On April 23, 1952, Wilhelm picked up the first win of his career with 5 and ⅓ innings of relief, as the Giants beat the Braves, 9 to 5. It is well known that he **did** hit a home run his first major league at bat. According to the *New York Times:* "Against Dick Hoover, a rookie southpaw, Hoyt Wilhelm, at bat for the first time in the major leagues, socked a homer into the *lower right-field stands*" (italics mine). The "Times" doesn't mention what happened Wilhelm's next time up, but the box score shows him at one for two.

According to the '69 Macmillan, Wilhelm struck his lone career triple in 1953. Wilhelm hit, for his career, one home run and one triple. In different games. In different seasons. Of course, it's pretty incredible that Wilhelm hit just one home run over the course of a twenty-year career, and that in his very first trip to the plate. But apparently not *strange and amazing.*

—Rob Neyer

CLINT HURDLE

JACK ETKIN

The question was strange for batting practice where coaching inquiries run more along the lines of "Your hands feel better that time?" Howie Freiling was searching for answers, something more really. He craved a cure.

A three-for-34 slump had dropped Freiling's average to .215. A night earlier, the first quarter of the season had ended miserably for Freiling and the Jackson Mets. He struck out and hit three ground balls to second base. The last two were turned into double plays as the Mets fell 8–7 to the Wichita Wranglers, dropping their record to 13-22.

Jackson manager Clint Hurdle stood by the batting cage. Freiling, a lefthanded hitting first baseman, began hitting ground balls and weak flies. His offensive woes seemingly had carried over to another day.

"Did the gamblers get you last night?" Hurdle asked.

"Huh?" Freiling said, dumbfounded.

"Couple double plays," Hurdle said. "Maybe you made some extra money."

"I guess they should've," Freiling admitted, awaiting the next pitch.

He took two more swings. A line drive, which might have signaled an upturn, remained elusive. "You're stroke's real long lately," Hurdle said, "and you're getting jammed. For the next couple days, think about breaking the pane of glass with the bat head."

The pane of glass in front of the hitter is imaginary, of course, a teaching tool Hurdle uses. Freiling had been dragging his hands during his swing, limiting his bat speed. A slow bat isn't going to break that pane of glass or drive the ball.

Freiling's first chance to use these pointers came that night as a pinch hitter in the ninth inning. With three extra-base hits in 79 at bats, Freiling launched a two-run triple to deep center field. The hit capped a four-run rally in Jackson's 6–2 victory. Hurdle's teaching method had worked.

"When you're going good," Freiling said, "he doesn't really say anything to you. If you're struggling, he tends to joke with you more. I like it. It makes you feel you're not killing the team."

The quip about the bribe seemed to be vintage Hurdle. If there is something to say, count on Hurdle to say it. He is irrepressible, energetic, outspoken and self-assured to the point of cocky. That's about how Hurdle was in his younger days when his playing career was on the rise save for one vital difference.

"The game of life to me is how you treat other people," Hurdle said. "I was probably one who if I had something too funny to say at times, I would probably say it at somebody else's expense. And not really mean to hurt him but to make everybody else laugh. Twenty guys laugh and one guy felt bad, that was a pretty good tradeoff. Where now just about with anybody I'm around I'm going to make sure nobody's going to get hurt."

Hurdle had put in two successful years as a manager in the New York Mets' system, spending 1988 and 1989 at St. Lucie in the Class A Florida State League before moving up last season to Jackson, Miss., in the Class AA Texas League. His 1988 team won the Florida State League title. The following year, St. Lucie won the East Division in both halves of the season and had a 79-55 overall record that led the league. In two seasons, Hurdle's teams had won three of four division titles.

That Hurdle would become a leader of men was a preposterous notion in the days when he was a brash, can't-miss kid with the Kansas City Royals. To his players, the heights Hurdle was supposed to reach with the Royals and the depths he eventually touched are vague happenings. Even outfielder Terry McDaniel, a 24-year-old Kansas City native who was a teenager there when Hurdle was having his best season with the Royals and who played for Hurdle in 1989 and 1990, has only the fuzziest, most skeletal details of Hurdle's past.

"All I know is he played in the big leagues with the Royals, the Cardinals and the Mets," McDaniel said. "But that's about all I know. I don't know how many years he spent there. I guess he was a utility man; he played a lot of positions."

Before becoming a first baseman, third baseman and catcher, Hurdle was an outfielder. He was such a promising lefthanded hitter that in March 1978, *Sports Illustrated* put him on the cover, hailing him as "This Year's Phenom."

"I heard that rumor," McDaniel said. "He was supposed to be the next whoever."

Instead, Hurdle's fate was to be released twice within five months after the 1982 season. What followed were four years in the twilight. From 1983–1987, Hurdle had 1,177 at bats with the Tidewater Tides, the Mets' Triple-A farm club and just 272 in the majors while averaging .195.

In his quest to increase his versatility and return to the big leagues, Hurdle even went to the Florida Instructional League in 1984 to learn to catch at age 27. "I just took a physical beating because I had to be built from square one," he said. "I spent more time going to the backstop than to the pitcher's mound. I was a retriever; I wasn't a receiver."

It was Davey Johnson who suggested Hurdle try catching. He had played for Johnson in Tidewater in 1983 and was reunited with him in New York in 1985. The St. Louis Cardinals drafted Hurdle after that season, and he played under Whitey Herzog in 1986. Catching allowed Hurdle to work with pitchers and run a ballgame, invaluable experience when it came to managing. In Johnson and Herzog, Hurdle could observe two highly successful managers with varied approaches. His own big-splash beginning had by then become a threadbare tale, and when the 1987 season was done, Hurdle's playing days were finally history.

During those final four years of his career, Hurdle began looking ahead, wondering where his days as a player were leading him and whether baseball would be in his future. The worst was behind him, on and off the field. But what direction would he go? In Tidewater and on the Mets' and Cardinals' benches, there was plenty of time to observe and reflect.

"I saw the canoe tipping over," Hurdle said. "It was done. The illusions of being in the Hall of Fame and hitting 500 home runs, you can pack that up and send it home; that's not going to happen in this lifetime. And that's when everything started to evolve a little bit.

"I didn't break any records, but from '83 to '87 was the most satisfying time of my career where I split some time in the minor leagues and got two more seasons in the big leagues. I knew every day I showed up nobody was happier to hear the National Anthem. I tried to pick other guys up, keep guys loose and relearn the game from a different aspect. Not from the guy who's going to play everyday because when you're playing every day you worry about your game. When you're not playing, you see the whole picture."

Darrell Johnson, one of the Mets' special assignment scouts, informally operates what Hurdle calls a "MIT Program," meaning manager in training. Previous pupils, all of whom managed in the Mets' system, have included Mike Cubbage, now a coach with the Mets; Cincinnati Reds coach Sam Perlozzo; and Royals coach Bob Schaefer. A former catcher, Johnson, 62, had a big-league career of 134 games that covered minute parts of six seasons with the Browns, White Sox, Yankees, Cardinals, Phillies, Reds and Orioles.

Johnson also managed in the majors from 1974–80 and in 1982. He guided the Red Sox, Mariners and Rangers, winning the American League pennant with the Red Sox in 1975 before losing a memorable World Series to the Reds in seven games. He has little doubt about Hurdle's managing abilities.

"Clint only lacks the experience of different levels," Johnson said. "I can't think of one reason why Clint someday should not be a good big-league manager. He has all of my qualifications, and we (in the Mets' hierarchy) all feel pretty much the same way."

To Johnson, managing comes down to several areas, none of which pose a problem for Hurdle. "Handling the troops is No. 1," Johnson said, "which he can do. Not so much here but managing in the majors, the press is no picnic. Clint's got a good personality. He's an outgoing guy; he's an honest person. I've never seen anybody get in trouble with the press with those qualifications.

"And there's handling adversity, which comes down to handling yourself. Being able to handle adversity and not change character to me was very important. You have to find a line of concentration to relax and do your best. Finding that line and staying on it takes time. I think Clint will handle that very well."

Johnson made one other observation, something that pertained strictly to the short-term. He was spending two days watching Jackson, visiting with Hurdle and pitching coach Bob Apodaca and sizing up the players. The Mets' 13-22 record was of minimal concern to Johnson.

"Watch about the middle of July," Johnson said, "and see what these guys do to the end of the season. They're all kids and overmatched a little bit. Generally speaking when you elevate a ballplayer from level to level, they get stung for six weeks."

Johnson miscalculated. In the season's first half, Shreveport barely won the East Division, going 34-31 (.523) and just edging out Jackson. Despite their sluggish start, that included a nine-game losing streak, the Mets finished the first half 35-32 for a .522 percentage.

"I really was concerned if they were ever going to get angry," Hurdle said. "I knew the talent was there, and I'd seen the talent playing hungry before. When you're in A ball, some guys are hungrier. I thought that maybe they were a little complacent. Some went to big league camp. Some were in Double-A for the first time. Now it's 'Hey, let me spread my chest a little bit. Things'll happen for me; they happened last year.'

"I was just concerned about how long they were going to spin their wheels because you can do all the ranting, the raving you want, but until they take it personally, it's tough to get them headed in the right direction."

After losing the division by .001, Hurdle issued a challenge to his team. He told them: "I'll promise you this. If you can go out and stay hungry and angry the entire second half, we'll blow people away. We'll run away with the second half. But it's up to you."

Hurdle was right. Jackson's 38-30 record in the second half was enough to win the East Division by five games. The Mets' overall record of 73-62 was third best in the league and gave Hurdle a three-season managing record of 226-182 (.554).

After the season, the Mets announced they were leaving Jackson. They had been there since 1975 but moved their Double-A team to Binghamton, N.Y., of the Eastern League. Hurdle will manage Binghamton this year and find himself much closer to Shea Stadium.

"I wanted to manage in New York," Hurdle said. "Within the structure of things, this'll be good for me. I'm only three hours from the city. If we do well, I should get some exposure in the city. And if not, I might even get the opportunity to get ripped again in the New York papers."

From his laugh, it was obvious Hurdle wasn't worried.

Hurdle was born in Big Rapids, Mich., and was about five when he moved to Merritt Island, Fla. Baseball was in Hurdle's genes. His grandfather, Edward Clinton Hurdle, was a left-handed pitcher, who was offered a minor league contract. "I think it was by the Reds," Hurdle said. "Then his father died two days later. He was the only boy in a family of seven, so he couldn't go."

Clinton Edward Hurdle, Hurdle's father, was a shortstop, whom the Cubs offered a contract. His professional career never started because the Army soon drafted him. Hurdle, named Clinton Merrick, his middle name being the first name of his maternal grandfather, was an all-state football quarterback. He signed a letter of intent to go to the University of Miami before opting for baseball.

The Royals made Hurdle the ninth pick in the country in June 1975. Two years later, after bypassing Double-A and hitting .328 with 16 home runs and 66 RBIs at Triple-A Omaha, Hurdle was in the big leagues. In his Royals debut Sept. 18, 1977, Hurdle came up in the fifth inning of a scoreless game with Seattle and hit a 425-foot two-run homer against Glenn Abbott.

That September stay amounted to nine games and a .308 average (eight for 26). It was enough for *Sports Illustrated* to anoint Hurdle the following spring.

Hurdle's best season with the Royals came in 1980. They won their first pennant that year, and Hurdle contributed with a .294 average, 10 home runs and 60 RBIs in 130 games and some fun-loving moments. By the time the Royals came to Metropolitan Stadium in Bloomington, Minn., in September, they had clinched the American League West but were playing poorly.

That didn't stop Hurdle from singing the Southern California fight song in the dugout. The big attraction in the Twin Cities that particular Saturday wasn't the Royals and Twins but the football game between Minnesota and visiting USC. Royals manager Jim Frey, his team going down to another defeat, reached the boiling point when Hurdle, moved by some collegiate spirit, began his dugout serenade.

At the time Hurdle was 23 and finishing a promising season. In Kansas City, Hurdle drew comparisons to George Brett, who is four years older. The analogy was most apt off the field. When he managed the Royals, Herzog had once warned Brett he would be 40 before he was 30. Hurdle was following the same path of revelry with one vital difference. Brett could carouse and still perform well. Hurdle couldn't. He appeared to have no brakes. "It could've gone downhill and out of control," Hurdle said, "and you could've read about me like a Len Bias or something

along those lines. I'm serious because you get those feelings, 'Hey, I'm trying to do the right thing and nothing's working.' " To his teammates, Hurdle was witty and charming, going headlong toward the downside of his career and in no way a candidate to someday manage.

"I think as we go through our life, we mature in stages," Hurdle said. "I think it's important to have a zest for life, an energy to live it to the fullest. I think there's a need in that maturity to also pick up knowledge about life. What's good for you. What's bad for you. What's right for you. What's wrong for you.

"I think there's also a need to understand what are your own personal strengths, what are your own personal weaknesses, what can I do to better myself and where do I want this thing to take me. Am I just going to fly by the seat of my pants? Do I have direction? Do I have priorities? I don't know the order those need to go in, but I know the zest and the zeal was number one for me back when I was playing."

In 1981, Hurdle injured his back while sliding April 14 and played just 28 games with the Royals, averaging .329 in his 76 at bats. Hurdle's troubles went beyond his injury and the 50-day strike by the players. He and his wife, Janice, separated and were later divorced.

Moreover, there was what Hurdle called "the innuendo going around about me," that summer, referring to "the time in my life I became a faggot for a year." The rumors of homosexuality that dogged Hurdle were unsubstantiated. They resulted from a late-night escapade when Hurdle was found passed out in a car in an area in Kansas City known to be frequented by gays.

Regardless, the Royals wearied of Hurdle and traded him to the Reds for minor league pitcher Scott Brown on Dec. 11, 1981. Hurdle was with Cincinnati briefly in 1982 but spent most of the season at Triple-A Indianapolis where he and manager George Scherger didn't get along. There was one bright spot in a season that culminated with Hurdle being released Nov. 15, 1982, by the last-place Reds. He and his wife, Julie, were married that year.

For the second time, Hurdle's father was his best man. The elder Hurdle was initially sensitive to his son's troubles in 1981 and 1982 but then used a sterner motivational technique to keep Hurdle from leaving the game he still loved.

"Why do you deserve so good?," Clinton Edward asked his son. "Why do you deserve every break? Who do you think you are? You've got a life like everybody else has got a life, and breaks come and breaks go. Who do you think you are? You're getting some bad breaks right now. What're you going to do about it? How're you going to handle it?"

"If this is what you really want to do, and you're really going to be fair to yourself and you've gotten some bad breaks, just keep working hard and it'll turn around. If you haven't been fair to yourself and a lot of this is your own fault, who knows what's going to happen."

Getting released by the Reds was expected, even welcome. Getting released by the perpetually floundering Mariners the following spring was a shock. "I had a good rapport with the manager Rene Lachemann," Hurdle said, "and was basically told after we went from Tempe to Las Vegas for a couple exhibition games I'd made the club the day before opening day."

When he was called in to general manager Dan O'Brien's office, Hurdle assumed it was to sign his Mariners contract. Instead, O'Brien told Hurdle that he was being released. The Mariners decided to keep first baseman–designated hitter Ken Phelps instead.

Hurdle's job search led him to the Mets and Lou Gorman, a member of the Royals' front office while Hurdle was in Kansas City. Steve Schryver, formerly the Mets' director of minor league operations, signed Hurdle to a Tidewater contract for 1983 where Johnson was managing and the pitching coach was Al Jackson, a former Mets pitcher and now the Baltimore Orioles' pitching coach. While hitting .285 with 22 homers and 105 RBIs and learning to play third base, Hurdle was doing more than beginning the comeback that would return him to the majors.

"I got to work with two good people, Davey and Al Jackson," Hurdle said. "At the time I was probably more absorbent of coaching and instruction and nuances of the game than ever before. I was too preoccupied as a major-league player to be thinking about what other people were doing; I was concerned with what I had to do within the structure of the team."

In Johnson and Herzog, Hurdle had the opportunity to play for successful managers with varied approaches. Herzog was folksy and outgoing and mingled with his players. Johnson, while more detached, stressed positive thinking even if his team seemed to be hunkered down and under attack from all sides. Hurdle gained some vital insights into managing from being around both.

"Davey has a burning desire to be the best he can be and for his team to be the best they can be," Hurdle said. "He just exudes confidence, no matter what he does. When he's reading the newspaper, I believe he thinks he can read it better than anybody else.

"He has an intense desire to wade through the adversity because that's going to enhance the victory so much more. I can remember going through some tough times early in different parts of seasons. In the minor leagues we lost 13 games in a row. He said, 'You know what, when we drink the champagne at the end, it's just going to taste that much sweeter.' He's always focused and always moving forward regardless of whatever happens to set you back."

Hurdle spent the entire 1986 season with the Cardinals where he was reunited with Herzog, the Royals' manager when Hurdle first arrived in the majors in 1977 as well as 1978 and 1979. In St. Louis, Hurdle played first base, the outfield, third base and catcher, but mostly he sat. He got into just 78 games, batted only 154 times but because of Herzog never felt he was on the Cardinal fringe.

"He just has the innate ability to make the 24th guy on the roster feel as good as number one when you know good and well you're not," Hurdle said. "He just has that characteristic; he knows your wife's name, your kid's name, knows what you do in the offseason. He would always seem to go out of his way and talk to you about something other than baseball, to make contact with each and every one of his players on just about a daily basis.

"His interpersonal skills are unparalleled from what I've seen from people I've worked with. I was just so thankful to get the opportunity to play for him again after I had matured in different areas and grown up. It was just a pleasure."

The fines can run from $1 for a balk or failing to sacrifice or missing a cutoff man or taking a third strike with runners in scoring position up to $50 for missing the team bus a second time. Hurdle jokes the money goes into The Ashley Hurdle Scholarship Fund, named for his daughter, who will be six in July.

Hurdle collected $2 from catcher Todd Hundley, the son of former big league catcher Randy Hundley, for not driving in a runner from third base with less than two outs. That monetary exchange came in mid-May after Hurdle gave Hundley the breathtaking news he was going to join the Mets in San Diego.

"Remember to zone down," Hurdle called out, as the giddy Hundley was leaving the clubhouse. From the coaching box at third base, Hurdle has flashed that same message many times to Hundley, pressing his hands toward the ground. If the count is 2-0 or 3-1, look for a pitch in a certain area. If it's not there, don't swing. In other words, zone down.

"Don't worry," Hundley replied, nearly out the door. "I will."

"You didn't here," Hurdle said, laughing.

To Hundley, drafted second by the Mets in June 1987, the parting shot from Hurdle was expected, one last I'm-pulling-for-you-kid farewell. "He's a great motivator," Hundley said. "He keeps you going in the game. He's got energy every day. You say, 'If he can have this energy every day, I can have it.'

"He's a good manager, period. As a catcher, you're kind of managing along with him. There's things I think I'd do different. He's done them and come out winning."

There's a converse to Hundley's promotion, a day-to-day gnawing that comes with being a manager in the minors. "The hardest part," Hurdle said, "is seeing kids who are having trouble. And you know you can isolate the weakness, and they have trouble making the adjustment and continue throwing away at bats or innings as a pitcher. Not to be the Wizard of Oz, but there are some things I know a little bit about in the game."

In truth, Hurdle has had peaks-to-valleys experiences. His players are about ten years younger and know plenty about M.C. Hammer and little of Granny Hamner. Still, Hurdle has the savvy to deal with his minor leaguers, players he says have to be alternately buffed and burped. "I tell them there's not a whole lot this game has to offer good or bad I haven't experienced," he said. "I'm not proud of that, but it's one of my biggest assets now. I've been in a World Series. I've been released twice."

Hurdle wears his 1988 Florida State League championship ring. His other piece of championship jewelry, a ring from the Royals' 1980 pennant, went to his father. "He worked harder for that one than I did," Hurdle said. "He put up with me."

On July 30, Hurdle will turn 34. Had things worked out, he could be making megabucks and still be hitting line drives in the majors not ground balls with a fungo bat. Hurdle's bottom line as a player was 515 games spread over ten big league seasons, 360 hits and a .259 lifetime average, not much considering the big build-up. More of a mark might come from managing.

"Obviously I was blessed with the talent to play the game," Hurdle said, "and I enjoyed that. But then in learning the game, I think I have a talent for teaching it. And I feel better about my talent for teaching it than I ever did about my talent for playing it. I don't know why. It's just a gut feeling I have.

"I think I'm more confident in myself as an instructor than as a player. Not that I was nervous or ever second-guessed myself as a player. I want to see where I can take this thing. And if it's this level and I top out with it, fine. If it's not and it's Triple-A and you top out there, fine. But I have a good feeling, a very comfortable, peaceful feeling."

TRACERS

Without ceremony, the Yankees unveiled a new left-handed pitcher at Detroit one afternoon in 1931. His name was Vernon Gomez. Just before the contest Bob Shawkey, the New York manager . . . studied the list of Detroit batsmen and outlined the strategy to be used against each of them. "Now this one," he said, "this Gehringer—I want you to be extra careful with him. Don't ever give him a fat one or he'll bust up the game for you."

The Yankees went down in their half of the first and then Gomez went to the mound. He retired the first two Detroiters; then the third man up powdered the ball out of the park. Gomez got the next batter to foul out and returned to the Yankee bench. He was feeling that he hadn't done too bad, all things considered, yet here was Manager Shawkey glaring at him as if he had just walked nine straight batters.

"Skipper," said Gomez, "it was this way. I kinda slipped and stumbled on a bad piece of ground the crazy groundskeepers hadn't smoothed down, and just about then some jerk in the stands shone a mirror in my eyes, and they musta put starch in my uniform because the shirt gave a yank across the back and held my arm back, and that ball has got something wrong with it—they musta brought it up from the minors, it's so lopsided, and— But listen, Skipper. I know how to get that Gehringer guy. I'll fix him when he comes up."

"He's already come up," growled Shawkey. "He hit that homer."

—Ira L. Smith and H. Allen Smith,
Three Men on Third, 1951
(page 128)

Smith and Smith place this story in 1931, although Gomez debuted for the Yankees in early 1930, pitching in fifteen games, so one would assume that by 1931 he had a pretty good idea as to Charlie Gehringer's identity.

It seems logical to begin the search for this event in 1930, and

lo and behold, there she is. The first time Lefty Gomez caught sight of the Detroit team was on May 9, 1930, when the Tigers came into New York for a four game series. Gehringer homered that day, but not off Gomez, who didn't pitch; Ed Wells gave up the blow.

Gomez started the next day, May 10, and after retiring the lead-off man, Liz Funk, up came Gehringer, who promptly hit his second home run in as many days. Gomez escaped the first without further damage, eventually coasting to a 14-5 victory.

The year is wrong, the stadium is wrong, the batting order is wrong—yet the essence of the story is still intact. It may be difficult to believe that Gomez spent the entire afternoon of May 9 holed up in the bullpen, and that before (or after) the game a teammate didn't point out Gehringer, already a star, to the rookie pitcher.

You can believe what you want, but I'll only go so far as to say that yes, Lefty Gomez did allow a home run to Charlie Gehringer, in the first inning, the first time he faced him.

—Rob Neyer

BIOGRAPHICAL ENCYCLOPEDIA

continues

Tony Antanassio, player agent.

Merle Anthony, American League umpire, 1969–1975.

Joe Antolick, manager of the Wilson team in the Coastal Plain League on June 2, 1951, when the Tarboro Athletics scored 24 runs against Wilson in one inning, 21 before the first out was recorded. Antolick became so desperate in the middle of this that he finally put himself in to pitch.

The Tarboro team, which Antolick had managed himself several years earlier, went out of business just four days later—but you've got to admit, they didn't go out with a whimper.

John Antonelli, infielder for the 1945 Phillies.

Antonelli has managed a number of minor league teams since he stopped playing, and was a roving instructor in the Mets system until 1989.

Johnny Antonelli, Boston Braves bonus baby and co-star with Willie Mays of the 1954 World Champion New York Giants.

Antonelli's father, August, emigrated from Italy as a teenager in 1913, and became a baseball fan as well as a successful contractor in Rochester, New York. His mother, Josephine, taught badminton and recreation in the city's adult-education program. The family was close-knit, athletic and comfortable. An older brother, Anthony, was a star fullback at Jefferson High School and played for Bowling Green University in Ohio.

Johnny entered Jefferson High in 1944, and as a sophomore quarterback helped Jefferson to the city championship by completing a sixty-yard pass to a boy with the improbable name of Cosmo Trotto. Antonelli was a basketball star as well, but it was as a baseball player that he made the most impact. He tried out for the team as a first baseman, but his coach, Charley O'Brien, immediately converted him to a pitcher—over Johnny's objections—and Antonelli again led the team to the city championship. Like Richie Ashburn's father (see Ashburn) August Antonelli insisted that his son quit football, rather than risk an injury which might ruin his baseball career.

Antonelli Sr. made up a scrap book of Johnny's heroics, and in March, 1947, took it to Florida on his annual vacation. He made the rounds of the major league spring training offices, talking up his son's accomplishments. No one was interested. In the summer of '47 Antonelli pitched for Rutland in the Vermont Hotel League, a semi-pro league full of good school and college players. His manager at Rutland was Ebba St. Claire, later a teammate with the Braves and Giants. St. Claire taught him to set up the hitters, sharpened his curve and worked on a change of pace. Back in high school that fall Antonelli blistered the competition, pitching five no-hitters. Jeff Jones, a scout for the Braves, saw one of them and reported that "This boy is by far the best big-league prospect I've ever seen. He has the poise of a major-league pitcher right now and has a curve and fast ball to back it up." Carl Hubbell, scouting for the Giants, reported that "I've never seen a kid with so much equipment. The most unusual thing is that he knows how to use it."

August Antonelli, no longer getting the brushoff from major league teams, announced that he would entertain offers as soon as Johnny graduated. Other phenoms were being promoted around the country, however, and August hit upon a unique scheme to set his son apart from the crowd. The senior Antonelli rented the Rochester Red Wings' ballpark, hired the two best semi-pro teams in the area to play each other, and showcased his son as one of the starting pitchers, inviting the press and scouts from every major league team. With 7,000 people in the stands including many of the game's most prominent ivory hunters, Antonelli pitched a no-hit, seventeen-strikeout game, triggering a bidding war.

"That was the damedest rat race I ever saw after the game," said Tom Sheehan, scouting for the Giants. "The Antonellis and all their relatives held court in an Italian restaurant downtown, and the jockeying for pop's ear was like the Oklahoma land rush."

Lou Perini of the Boston Braves won the war, signing Antonelli for a reported $65,000 on June 29, 1948. It was the largest bonus ever given at that time. According to Sheehan, the amount might have been higher, except that the scouts knew that Perini had the edge with the father, being Italian and also a contractor.

John Quinn was the Braves' general manager at the time. Quinn remembered the fight to sign Antonelli as the wildest battle of his career, finally ending when he and Perini flew to Rochester to sign Antonelli for—as he remembered it—$60,000. "Well, after all the signatures were on the contract," Quinn recalled, "the whole Antonelli family started to cry—his mother, his father and some uncles. Perini stood there for a moment and then said, 'They just got $60,000 of my money. I'm the guy who should be crying.' "

Under the rules of the time a "bonus baby" was allowed one year of minor league seasoning, but then was required to spend two full seasons on the major league roster. The deal arranged by Antonelli's father, however, required Antonelli to go straight to the major leagues—a terrible mistake, as it turned out. Johnny, who confessed later that he lived through the entire period in a fog and didn't remember much of what happened, flew to Boston in Perini's private plane, going direct to a midnight press conference at the Kenmore Hotel. The Boston press treated his arrival as the second coming of Walter Johnson, and for two weeks everything he said was recorded for posterity with great seriousness. An article about him in *The Sporting News* began with this:

> "I'm glad to be an American," was the reverent statement, almost whispered, by Johnny Antonelli as he walked through Independence Hall, in Philadelphia.

Antonelli joined a team, the 1948 Boston Braves, which was short of pitchers and fighting for a pennant. His manager, Billy Southworth, resented Antonelli's presence from the day he arrived, and made slight secret of it. As far as Southworth was concerned Antonelli was dead wood, a wasted roster spot. This was the team of the famous rotation of "Spahn and Sain and pray for rain." (As I have pointed out several times, in fact the 1948 Braves' winning percentage with Spahn and Sain on the mound was worse than their overall percentage, this being the first time in National League history that a team had won the pennant with a lower winning percentage from their top two starters than from the team as a whole. Nonetheless, the perception was that Spahn and Sain were the only pitchers the Braves had.) The resentment of Antonelli and the $65,000 he had been paid spread from Southworth to the players. Johnny Sain, fired many times as a pitching coach later for, among other things, advising his pitchers not to be afraid to "climb those golden stairs", marched into Perini's office a few days later, demanding to re-negotiate. "Antonelli may be worth every cent you gave him," Sain told Perini. "But the games he is going to win for the team are in the future. I'm winning them right now and they may mean a pennant this year. If he's worth that kind of money for tomorrow, I guess I'm worth a lot more today." Sain got his new contract, and went on to win 24 games.

Antonelli pitched only four innings in 1948 and, by consent of the A.L. champion Indians, was bumped from the World Series roster to make way for Eddie Stanky, freshly healed from a broken ankle. Led by Southworth, the Braves voted not to allow Antonelli to sit on the bench in the World Series, and also voted him no share of the first-place money. This was an unprecedented thing, widely publicized and viewed as a rejection of Antonelli by his teammates—indeed, as the defining incident forever used to illustrate the uncomfortable relationship between bonus babies and their veteran teammates. One of his teammates was quoted as saying that Antonelli didn't belong in the World Series, he belonged in the Little League.

The resentment grew during the winter, when the National League champion Braves filed into John Quinn's office one at a time to demand their reward. "They shell out sixty-five grand for a kid who doesn't pull his weight," another unnamed teammate told Stanley Frank, "but they won't give me a few thousand more bucks." Resentment of the front office focused on Antonelli.

In his time Southworth had been a fine manager. Near the end of World War II Southworth's son was killed in a training flight. Consumed by grief, Southworth became bitter and difficult to play for. The team divided into warring factions, and dropped out of contention. Southworth blamed Antonelli for the dissension on his team, and continued to use him sparingly even though Antonelli, in 96 innings, had the third-best ERA on the team in 1949.

"I can sympathize with the way Southworth must have felt when he looked at us and thought of his son," Antonelli told Stanley Frank, writing an article for *The Saturday Evening Post* in 1954. "But it was a bum rap to blame me for his trouble with the team. The players always were friendly to me. Practically all of them told me they were glad I got

the bonus. Sain, who was supposed to be one of the ringleaders of the feud, went out of his way to help me. So did Spahn, who worked a lot with me because he's a left-hander too.

"I didn't know there was friction on the ball club until I read about it in the papers. I was a kid trying to keep out of the way while the old pros were battling for the pennant. I dressed in a corner of the clubhouse and kept my mouth shut."

Ironically, Antonelli had signed with the Braves, rejecting a better offer from the Red Sox, because he wanted to pitch for Southworth. Southworth had managed in Rochester, Johnny's home town, for several years, and the Antonelli family were fans of the Red Wings. Antonelli had heard that Southworth was a good man with young players.

In the spring of 1949 the Braves offered a free trip to Florida as a prize in a drawing. The winning ticket was held by Mr. and Mrs. John Carbone, of Medford, Massachusetts. On the train south they met Antonelli and became friendly with him and then with his father, who showed them around in Florida. The Carbones invited Johnny to have dinner with them in Massachusetts. He went, and was amazed to discover that the Carbones had a daughter, Rosemarie.

Antonelli continued to pitch very little through 1949 and 1950. As Johnny remembered it, in 1949 Southworth "finally started me against the Giants, and although I had to be relieved in the ninth, I won the game 4-2. I thought I'd earned another shot, but I didn't touch a ball for six weeks except in batting practice. The next time out, I blanked the Reds, 3-0. Another six weeks went by before I started again." In 1950 he pitched even less, only 58 innings. In essence, Southworth treated Antonelli exactly the same way that the old, bitter Dick Williams treated Mark Langston, setting him up to fail just to prove that the manager was right about him all along.

In March, 1951, with the Korean War heating up, Antonelli—still only twenty years old—was drafted. In the early fifties the commanders of several Army bases maintained quality baseball teams as a source of competitive pride among the bases. Antonelli pitched for the Fort Myer team, in Virginia. He started 44 games in his two years in the Army, completed all 44 and won 42 of them, one of the two losses being to a team from Fort Eustice led by Willie Mays. Capping his military career, Antonelli led the Washington Military District team to the National Baseball Congress Championship in Wichita in 1952, and

was included on an All-Star team which toured Japan. It was the tonic he needed after three years of little activity. While on a furlough from the Army in October, 1951, Antonelli married Rosemarie Carbone.

By the time Antonelli returned to the Braves in 1953 they had changed managers, and cities. Charley Grimm made Antonelli a starter. Antonelli missed several weeks with pneumonia and a few more starts after being hit by a pitch by Dave Koslo, but finished 12-12 with a 3.18 ERA, fifth best in the National League. The Braves, with a rotation of Spahn, Burdette, Buhl, Antonelli and Max Surkont, led the NL in ERA by a huge margin (half a run a game), but finished second, behind the Boys of Summer in their greatest season.

Trading pitching for power, the Braves sent Antonelli to the New York Giants in exchange for Bobby Thomson, who drove in a consistent 100 runs a year. The consensus of sportswriters was that the Braves had suckered the Giants, unloading a five-year disappointment after one so-so season.

Antonelli exploded on the league in 1954, beginning with a shutout over the Phillies. Leo Durocher named Antonelli his top starter before he had pitched a game for the Giants, and pitching coach Frank Shellenback pushed him to throw the change-up he had learned in the Vermont Hotel League in 1947, but never had the confidence to throw before. By the All-Star game he was 11-2, and three weeks later had stretched it to 16-2. With Willie Mays back from the service and playing perhaps the best ball of his career, the Giants seized first place in early June, posted a 24-4 record in the month of June and never surrendered their place on the rail. In late July the Giants lost six straight games and seemed in danger of toppling, a danger made tangible when Durocher benched and berated Whitey Lockman in the middle of a game and in view of the fans. Antonelli stopped the streak with a ten-hit shutout of the Cardinals, triggering a winning streak.

In a stretch in August the Giants lost seven of nine games. Antonelli provided both of the wins, again preventing a disastrous losing streak.

Antonelli finished 21-7, leading the National League in winning percentage, ERA (2.29) and with six shutouts. Had there been a Cy Young Award at the time Antonelli would unquestionably have won it, and would probably have been a unanimous selection. He was named by *The Sporting News* as the Outstanding National League Pitcher of

1954. He finished third in the voting for the National League MVP Award, pitched in the All-Star game, and started the second game of the World Series. Al (Fuzzy) Smith hit his first World Series pitch into the upper deck, but he completed the game and allowed no more runs, winning 3-1, and then came in to save the fourth and final game against the Indians.

Catcher Wes Westrum said that Antonelli "can get you out on any one of three pitches ... Depending on the batter and the situation he can go with a fast ball, a curve, or a change of pace." From 1955 through 1959, although never again as dominant as in 1954, Antonelli remained one of the best pitchers in the National League, posting records of 20-13 in 1956, 16-13 in 1958 and 19-10 in 1959, with more than 200 innings every year and consistently good earned run averages. He was also a good hitter, hitting three or four home runs a year. In 1957 Antonelli pitched the final game for the Giants in the Polo Grounds, a loss to the Pirates.

In 1960 the Giants moved in to Candlestick Park. Antonelli had been the Giants' best pitcher their first two years in San Francisco, winning 35 games for them, but he hated the new park, as players would for the next thirty years, and said so. He couldn't get loose in the cold weather, and developed a sore arm. He complained bitterly about the gusty winds of Candlestick Park, and the Bay Area media began to get down on him. He lost his place in the rotation. Charles Einstein, in A Flag for San Francisco, reported that he was eventually booed out of town. A trade to Cleveland for the 1961 season did nothing to revive his career, and the Indians passed him to Milwaukee, where he posted his last major league victory in 1961. He was 31 years old.

Upon leaving baseball, Antonelli became the owner of a chain of Firestone tire stores in the Rochester area. Now 61, he remains a prosperous businessman.

(B.J. and M.K. Primary sources for this article include "Baseball's Biggest Surprise", by Stanley Frank, Saturday Evening Post, September 18, 1954, "Johnny Antonelli: From Bonus Baby to Big-Leaguer", by Al Hirshberg, Sport Magazine, June, 1955, and Baseball Stars of 1955, edited by Bruce Jacobs and the article by the same author.)

Luis Aparicio, Hall of Fame shortstop of the fifties and sixties.

Aparicio was born on Apr. 29, 1934 in Maracaibo, Venezuela. Maracaibo is the second-largest city in Venezuela. His father, Luis Aparicio, Sr., was the greatest Venezuelan shortstop of the late thirties and forties, and turned down an opportunity to play for the Washington Senators in 1939. He was the shortstop for the Maracaibo Gavilanes as late as 1953 (and co-owner of the team along with his brother Ernesto), but his legs were giving way and it was time to step aside. His son Luis Jr. had played for Venezuela in the Latin American World Series and was presently the shortstop for the Barquisimiento Cardenales.

"My father did everything for me in baseball," the younger Aparicio later recalled. "From the time I was a little boy he played with me. He brought home baseballs and bats and gloves. I was throwing and catching as soon as I could walk." Luis Jr. began his professional career at age sixteen as a shortstop for Caracas, for whom he played for three years before the Aparicios decided to keep Luis Sr.'s job in the family. The changing of the guard took place on Nov. 18, 1953, with pomp and circumstance. According to Dave Condon in The Go-Go Chicago White Sox:

> The elder Aparicio and his talented young son went to the shortstop position. There Aparicio Sr. handed his glove to Little Looey. Then the father embraced his son, gave him a blessing, and forsook the position.

The son would soon forsake the position himself, but for a different reason. Red Kress, a coach with Maracaibo, got in touch with Cleveland General Manager Hank Greenberg, alerting him that Aparicio Jr. was an outstanding prospect. Greenberg dispatched super-scout Cy Slapnicka for a first-hand ap-

Susan McCarthy

Luis Aparicio

praisal. Slapnicka was impressed enough to ask the Aparicio clan "how much?" The Aparicios asked for a $10,000 bonus plus $500 for taxes, and a handshake agreement was reached.

When Slapnicka reported the agreement to Greenberg, however, Greenberg balked. The Indians wanted to cut the bonus in half, and also make it contingent on Aparicio passing muster at a tryout camp in the States. Hard feelings developed between the Aparicios and the Indians. "Greenberg said I was too small to be a big league player," Aparicio later recalled. "He said it to some people, and I heard about it. It bothered me. So I signed the White Sox contract."

White Sox General Manager Frank Lane had been alerted to Aparicio's potential by, among others, the White Sox incumbent shortstop, Venezuelan Chico Carrasquel. Lane was told that the Indians had him in their pocket, but called Pablo Morales, owner of the Caracas club in the Venezuelan League, and learned that no agreement had been signed. Carrasquel played for Caracas in the winter league, which required permission from the White Sox. "If the White Sox don't get Aparicio," he told Morales, "you don't get Carrasquel for next season. We'll buy Aparicio's contract for $6,000 and give him $4,000 to play for one of our farm clubs this season." The Aparicios, angry with the Indians and needing the money to pay off a mortgage, accepted Lane's offer.

Aparicio spent just two years in the minor leagues, one in the Three-I League and one in the Southern Association, hitting .282 and .273. In September 1955 Frank Lane resigned as White Sox General Manager, leaving day-to-day operations in the hands of Vice-Presidents Chuck Comiskey and John Rigney. These two men would eventually engage in almost open warfare, but in October of '55 they agreed on this much: Aparicio was ready. The White Sox traded Carrasquel, an All-Star in four of the five previous years, to Cleveland. The public was stunned, and second baseman Nellie Fox undoubtedly spoke for many when he observed that "Aparicio must be quite a ballplayer, but have people forgotten about Jim Brideweser? I thought he did a great job last season when he filled in for Chico."

White Sox manager Marty Marion, himself the premier defensive shortstop of the 1940s, also had doubts about Aparicio. At spring training in 1956 he noted that "Aparicio has a floppy glove, a lot like a first baseman's. He can dive for spectacular plays, but the glove dangles off his fingers. On the slow grounder I don't see how he can get solid contact with the ball.''

Aparicio was tiny, listed at 5'9", but measured by reporters that spring at five-seven. Marion expressed the concern that he was shying away from baserunners on the double play pivot, and toyed with the idea of starting Brideweser or Buddy Peterson at shortstop.

Once the exhibition season began, however, it quickly became apparent that Aparicio was a superior fielder. Marion got him to use a smaller glove and taught him to throw to first on a line through a baserunner's skull. In the first exhibition game of his first camp, Aparicio won the game by scoring from second on an infield out, prompting Marion to declare that "that kid runs like a scalded dog." Casey Stengel observed that "That little fellah gets balls that other fellah [Carrasquel] never coulda reached.''

The Sox wondered if he would hit. Marion pinch hit for him early in the season, triggering Aparicio's temper, and once batted Aparicio ninth and pitcher Dick Donovan eighth. Aparicio hit .266 as a rookie, however, and led the league in stolen bases (21). At shortstop he led the league in both putouts and assists, although he also led in errors. He was a landslide choice as the American League Rookie of the Year, winning 22 of the 24 votes. At the end of his rookie season Aparicio was married to Sonia Llorente, a cousin of White Sox teammate Jim Rivera. Sonia was born in Puerto Rico but grew up in New York.

Aparicio's glory years were in Chicago from 1956 through 1961. He led the league in stolen bases every year, with totals rising into the fifties, making him the first major league player since Max Carey almost forty years earlier to steal fifty bases a year consistently. His stolen base percentages were extremely good, even by today's standards. He should never have been a leadoff hitter, because his on-base percentages were too low for a leadoff man, but all the same, he was the leadoff hitter, and the White Sox were always in contention.

It was as a defensive player, however, that Aparicio put himself in the Hall of Fame. In 1958 Paul Richards said that "I think maybe he is—or will be—the best shortstop I've ever seen. He's so quick getting the ball to second base that he often saves Fox from being locked out on double plays, and some of his stops make you blink." (In fact, Nellie Fox, who often led the American League in double plays before Aparicio came along, did turn even more double plays after Luis replaced

Carrasquel.) In early 1959 Nick Altrock, who had been around the majors since the 1890s, offered the opinion that Aparicio was the best shortstop he had ever seen. This is not a book about statistical analysis, but I will tell you this as a former statistical analyst, that Aparicio's defensive statistics are probably the best of any shortstop in history before Ozzie Smith.

I am just old enough to have seen both Aparicio and Ozzie Smith in their prime, and perhaps those of you who are not would benefit from a comparison. In general, I would say that Luis was quicker but Ozzie is more acrobatic. Smith has the advantage of playing on artificial turf, where he gets the "true hop" most of the time, which makes him bold enough to try things which one would probably not try on a grass field. Luis broke backward and caught the short fly in shallow left, as Tony Fernandez does, more often than Ozzie. Ozzie makes the spectacular diving play behind second, the back-flip to his partner, which I don't remember Aparicio making. Ozzie *dances*; Luis *scooted*. In my own opinion Ozzie is a slightly greater defensive shortstop, but the two men are comparable, and are the two best I have ever seen.

Al Lopez replaced Marion as the White Sox manager in 1957. From 1956 to 1958 the Sox contended, but the Yankees continued to win the American League annually, as they had for many years. The White Sox, led by Aparicio and Nellie Fox, finished second in 1957 and 1958. In 1959 the Yankees fell out of contention, leaving the White Sox and Indians, the two teams which had fought for Aparicio, to wrestle for the American League. Walter Bingham, writing in *Sports Illustrated* (July 13, 1959):

> The White Sox do not have a great deal to recommend them in this race. Most of what is good about the team can be found several steps to either side of second base. To the left, at shortstop, is Luis Aparicio, a slim, 25-year-old boy from Venezuela. He has dark hair and tan skin. He speaks faltering English. He is married and has two children, a son and a daughter. During the winter he plays baseball in Venezuela and he never gets tired of it.
> Men who have watched shortstops for 30 years say they have never seen a better one than little Luis. Minnie Minoso hits the ball hard just to the left of the third baseman. Aparicio darts over, backhands the ball in his glove and throws it. Minoso is out by three steps. Harvey Kuenn bounces one over the pitcher's head for a single. As the ball takes a big hop past second base, Aparicio appears, racing toward right field. He spears the ball in the webbing of his glove,

> twists and throws to first. Suddenly Kuenn does not have a single. He is out and he shakes his head in disbelief.

A hot streak in late July put the Go-Go Sox in first place, and they held the lead throughout August and September, winning the race by five games. "If they keep up the way they've been going," Bill Veeck told *Sports Illustrated* in August, "they're going to change the entire concept of baseball. Who ever thought a team could win the pennant without a big RBI man, the No. 3 or No. 4 hitter who drives in runs?" Nellie Fox won the MVP Award, with Aparicio finishing second in the voting and receiving six first-place votes.

Although Aparicio's stats remained almost exactly the same, the White Sox dropped to third in 1960 and fourth in 1961. In 1962 Aparicio reported to camp overweight, and wasn't able to play himself into shape until mid-season. His average dropped to .241, his stolen base total to 31, although this still led the American League. Manager Al Lopez felt that his effort was not the same as it had been. The White Sox finished fifth.

Bill Veeck sold the White Sox shortly after the championship year, and General Manager Ed Short tried to cut Aparicio's salary. A rift developed between Aparicio and the White Sox, and by the end of 1962 it appeared beyond repair. The White Sox traded Aparicio to the Baltimore Orioles for a package of players including another Hall of Famer, Hoyt Wilhelm, and another Rookie of the Year, Ron Hansen.

Aparicio spent five years with the Orioles, helping them to a World Championship in 1966. In 1963 and '64 he again led the league in stolen bases, stretching his streak to nine straight years leading the league in steals, which remains a major league record. His last year in that streak, 1964, he stole a career-high 57 bases. He had an off year in '65, and Campy Campaneris took over as the leading base stealer. In '66 the Orioles asked Aparicio to break in a new partner at second base, Davey Johnson. Responding to the challenge, Aparicio had arguably his best season, getting a career-high 182 hits and scoring 97 runs. He finished ninth in the MVP voting, his only top-ten finish other than 1959.

The Orioles wanted to get Mark Belanger in the lineup, so Aparicio was traded back to Chicago, then to Boston. In 1969 and 1970 Aparicio posted the best offensive numbers of his career, hitting .300 for the only time (.313) in 1970, when he was 36 years old. In 1971, with the Red Sox, he went through a terrible slump, hitless in forty-four at bats; President

Nixon sent him a letter when he finally snapped the streak, commending his stoicism in the face of adversity, and thanking him for all the great moments he had provided over the course of his career.

At the end of the 1972 season Boston visited Detroit for the last three games of the schedule, nursing a half-game lead over the Tigers. In the third inning of the first game, Aparicio raced around third homeward bound, stumbled, and tried to retreat, only to find third base occupied by a teammate. The inning was killed, Boston went on to lose the game, and eventually the division title.

Playing regularly until the end of his career, Aparicio hit .271 in 1973, but was given his release during spring training, 1974. The Sox had decided to go with Rick Burleson. Luis had won nine Gold Gloves and was the all-time leader among shortstops in games played, assists, and double plays. He had never played an inning in the majors at any position other than shortstop. He was elected to the Hall of Fame in 1984.

—M.K. and B.J.

Bob Apodaca, relief pitcher with the Mets in the mid-seventies.

Apodaca, of Mexican-Portuguese descent, grew up in Los Angeles, where he attended Cerritos Junior College and later California State, majoring in political science. He was not drafted by any team, but got a chance to pitch in the Mets' system in 1971, and very quickly pitched his way to the majors.

Primarily a sinker/slider pitcher, Apodaca was part of the Mets' bullpen from 1974 through 1977, posting a 1.48 ERA and thirteen saves in 1975. His career was ended by elbow surgery at age 27. At this writing (September '90) Apodaca is the pitching coach for the Jackson Mets in the Texas League.

Luis Aponte, relief pitcher for the Boston Red Sox in the early eighties.

Aponte signed with the Red Sox twice. After spending four years in A ball, Aponte quit the Red Sox in 1977 to return to his native Venezuela. He re-signed in 1980 and this time moved through the system quickly. At Pawtucket in 1981 Aponte pitched four hitless innings, striking out nine men, in the legendary thirty-three inning game begun on April 18. According to teammate Mike Smithson, when he drove Aponte home the next morning his wife wouldn't let him in the house; she thought he'd been out drinking. He ended up sleeping in the Pawtucket clubhouse.

Aponte threw across his body with his left leg going *backward* as he delivered the pitch, an awkward, crossfire delivery. He pitched well for the Red Sox in 1982, mostly in a mop-up role, and started the 1983 season pitching well, earning the chants of "Looie, Looie!" previously bestowed on El Tiante. He faded as the season wore on, was traded to Cleveland and released after the 1984 season.

Ed (Whitey) Appleton, a kid from Arlington, Texas, who pitched with Brooklyn in 1914–15, and roomed with Casey Stengel. Forty years later, Harold Rosenthal was talking to Casey about a deep furrow extending from the corner of his mouth, and Casey told him about Whitey Appleton.

"One day when we had the day off and we went out to Coney Island which was very fancy in them days and where I had met a nice family which had a couple of nice young daughters. They give a party and invited me and told me I could bring a friend so I brought Appleton. It was okay except they had a punch bowl that had something kinda strong in it and my friend got into it and after a while he started to make some remarks to the girls so I figured I'd better get him home."

The story continues in a Stengelesque stroll for some time (see *The 10 Best Years of Baseball*), but the upshot of it is that Appleton and Stengel wind up in a dragdown, knockout fight until Appleton puts his fingers in Stengel's mouth and rips a hole in the side of his jaw, giving him a scar that never healed. Appleton died in Arlington in 1932, just short of his fortieth birthday. The scar in question can be seen in any photograph of Casey Stengel.

Pete Appleton (originally **Pete Jablonowski),** a pitcher for six major league teams from 1927 to 1945.

Jablonowski graduated from the University of Michigan in 1927, and made an impressive major league debut with Cincinnati that same year, pitching thirty innings with a 1.82 ERA. He dropped out of the majors in 1928, but won eighteen games with Columbus (American Association) in 1929, earning his way back to the majors with Cleveland in 1930. He pitched OK but unimpressively with Cleveland and Boston, and was released to Newark in 1932, where he went 11-1. He got a look with the Yankees, but didn't stick.

Jablonowski was married on November 9, 1933, and shortly after that changed his name to Appleton, which I gather is an English translation of Jablonowski. His story was that he changed his name to change his luck, but my theory has always been that his wife was behind it. His wife's maiden name was Aldora Leszczynski; I always figured that after all those years of being Aldora Leszczynski, she just couldn't handle being Aldora Jablonowski. In any case his luck did change, and he went 23-9 with Montreal in 1936 and was, according to his manager, Frank Shaughnessy, the best pitcher in the league. "Somewhere the guy has learned to pitch," he told Shirley Povich, after Appleton was sold to the Senators. "He's got an overhand curve that's as good as Tommy Bridges' and I'm not kidding. I don't see how he can miss in the American League."

He didn't, posting a 14-9 mark in 1936 with the league's fifth best ERA. His career sputtered along for nine years after that, although he was never again particularly effective. Apparently he liked to drop down sidearm. Shaughnessy, the manager who set his career aright with Montreal in 1935, had some advice for Clark Griffith on that subject. "Listen, Griff. If old Pete tries to give 'em that side-arm stuff, why, shoot him. He can't pitch that way, but he thinks he can. Fine him the first time he tries it, and he'll behave." After retiring as a player Appleton became a scout, serving with the Senators and later the Minnesota Twins from 1954 until his death in 1974.

(M.K./B.J.)

Luke Appling, Hall of Fame shortstop with the White Sox of the thirties and forties, and probably the greatest player the White Sox have ever had.

Lucius Benjamin Appling, Jr., was born in

Luke Appling
Susan McCarthy

High Point, North Carolina on April 2, 1909. The Applings, including seven children, moved around in the next few years, settling in Atlanta when Luke was two years old. Like his father, Luke was a natural left-hander, but a ruler-wielding elementary school teacher "cured" him of this affliction. He continued to bat and throw left-handed until the age of fourteen, when he switched his glove to the left hand so he could play the infield.

TRACERS

(Jimmy Dykes is talking about the young Luke Appling):

"One day we were playing in St. Louis. We were in the last half of the ninth inning with the score tied, two out and the bases drunk. The next hitter slapped one to Luke and he booted it. The man on third scored and the game was over. On the way to the clubhouse, Luke's head was down and he said to me, 'Why do they always have to hit the ball to me in a spot like that?' I grabbed him by the arm.

" 'Don't let me ever hear you say a thing like that again!' I said. 'You won't be a ballplayer until you want them to hit the ball to you in a spot like that.'

"He never forgot it. I think that was when he started to be a real ballplayer."

Jimmy Dykes
Quoted by Frankie Graham
"Indestructible Shortstop"
Collier's, July 9, 1949

Luke Appling also told this story, from his standpoint but almost word for word the same, as recently as two years ago.

In the memory of old ballplayers the bases are usually loaded and it is almost always the ninth inning, but it required only a minute to ascertain that this event, as it is reported here, did not occur. The event had to have happened in 1933, since that was Dykes' first year with the White Sox, and also the year that Appling became a star. Both Dykes and Appling specify that it happened in St. Louis, which gives us a field of eleven games. The White Sox won eight of those games, which cuts us to three. Two of the losses were lopsided, which cuts us to one. The remaining game, the game of August 5, 1933, was (oddly enough) the game often cited as Appling's best day ever at the plate, when he had five hits including three doubles, but the White Sox lost 10-9 in twelve innings on a double by Ed Wells.

No doubt something *like* this did happen, since both Dykes and Appling cite it as the turning point of his career. The game in question may have been the game of July 29, 1933, which was Rogers Hornsby's first game as manager of the Browns. The game was played in Chicago. According to the UPI account of the game:

The White Sox led, 2 to 1, going into the eighth, when, with the aid of errors by Luke Appling and Al Simmons, two unearned runs gave the Browns victory.

Gray faltered in the ninth, but Hadley made Earl Webb ground out, issued an intentional pass to Simmons to fill the bases, then slipped a third strike past Appling.

Bump Hadley, a hard-throwing right-hander most famous for beaning Mickey Cochrane, was a peculiar nemesis of Appling, and was often mentioned in his stories about his early struggles.

Luke Appling was a great story teller, and the story that appears on page 347 was perhaps his favorite story. An almost identical version of the story appears in *The Sporting News* of April 3, 1965, except that Lazzeri calls him "you little so-and-so" rather than "you little twirp", causing us to wonder whether *The Sporting News* was too squeamish to print the word "twirp".

This double-header would have had to occur between 1931, when Appling came up, and 1937, when Lazzeri retired. It would probably have had to happen no sooner than 1933, when Appling began to hit to right field. The White Sox and Yankees played nineteen double headers from '33 to '38, plus some in '31 and '32 which we also checked.

In some versions of the story Appling places the double-header in the season that he hit .388, which was 1936. In addition, the story has two elements which would make it fairly easy to spot: seven hits in a double-header by Appling, and a broken finger for Lazzeri.

Appling hit extremely poorly (.223) in double-headers against the Yankees. We found no double-header which met either of the two essential conditions.

The genesis of the story may have been the first game of the double-header of August 26, 1935. The White Sox and the Yankees were in the middle of a string of four straight double-headers, on the 25th, 26th, 27th and 28th. Appling went three-for-seven in the double-header of August 25, and had four hits in the first game on August 26, by far his best game in a double-header against the Yankees. Lazzeri did not play the second game of that double-header, did not play (except for one at bat as a pinch hitter) in the rest of the series, and did not return to the lineup until September 8.

The *New York Times* on September 3, 1935, reported that Lazzeri "hurt his shoulder in Detroit and became ill in St. Louis", but since the Chicago series came *after* the trip to Detroit and St. Louis, and since Lazzeri *did* play in the first three games of the Chicago series, this is less than an adequate explanation. Lazzeri had a Medwick-type incident with Marv Owen in Detroit, after which he fell into a terrible slump.

Our best guess is that Lazzeri injured his shoulder in Detroit, and aggravated the injury by diving to stop Appling's fourth hit in the first game on August 26, his seventh hit in two days, and that Appling's story came from this event. Also, Appling had gone six-for-seven in a double-header against Philadelphia just a week earlier, and this also may have figured in his memory.

Luke attended Fulton High School, near the site of the present-day Atlanta-Fulton County Stadium, where he was a standout athlete. At Oglethorpe University in Atlanta he starred as both a fullback and a shortstop, playing football for Wally Butts. As a baseball player he attracted offers from the Cubs and Dodgers. A scout from the Atlanta Crackers, an independent team in the Southern Association, came to watch him the final game of the 1930 season, against Mercer College. Appling hit four home runs in the game, and the Crackers were anxious to have him. Johnny Dobbs, Atlanta manager, and Rell Spiller, co-owner, met with Appling, trying to persuade him to turn pro. The Crackers had the great advantage of being in Atlanta. Appling negotiated a deal—a great deal, as it turned out, but that's getting ahead of the story.

Appling reported to Atlanta on June 17, 1930. "Atlanta thought I was a third baseman instead of a shortstop," he told Shirley Povich in 1949. "I proved I wasn't, right away. The first man up laid down a bunt and beat it out before I could get out of my tracks. It cost us a couple of runs, but I won my argument, and they moved me back to shortstop." Appling attracted attention as a prospect almost immediately. On August 7, 1930, the *Sporting News* reported that "There is a boy named Luke Appling from Oglethorpe College playing shortstop for Atlanta who will be a big league star if a patient, far-seeing manager obtains him. [Appling] is fast, rangy and has a fine arm. Chip Robert and Rell Spiller already have had several offers for the boy, but they are holding him for what will be a record price for a Southern Association player. And they'll get it, for Applings are scarce in this season's orchard." Appling hit .326 for the Crackers with seventeen triples in 104 games, although he also led the league in errors at shortstop.

Atlanta sold him to the White Sox for $25,000, his minor league apprenticeship consisting of slightly more than three months. (Stories written much later say that a deal had been reached to sell Appling to the Cubs, but that the White Sox came through with an eleventh-hour offer. There are, however, no contemporary accounts of the aborted sale to the Cubs.)

Under Appling's contract with the Crackers he received a $1,000 bonus, $500 a month (for four months), plus if he was sold to another team he was to receive one-fourth of the sale price. Appling got $750 for the last month of the seaon with the White Sox, and asked the Crackers for one-fourth of the $25,000. Atlanta refused to pay, and Appling filed a grievance, which was taken before the National Board of Arbitration. Appling presented his case, which was the contract and an affidavit about the sale price; the Crackers asked for, and were granted, more time to produce additional evidence. There was, of course, no other evidence, and in late 1930 the board ruled in Appling's favor, ordering the Crackers to pay him $6,250. Appling had negotiated a contract, an A.P. story observed that fall, under which "the 21-year-old Appling made more money during his first season as a professional baseball player than many established players of the majors earned during their best years. So astute was Appling in his dealings that he cleaned up $10,000 from June 17 to the close of the major league season. He paid an income tax on that amount to prove it, too."

For a while, it appeared that that might be his biggest payday. In six games with the White Sox in 1930 Appling hit safely in each game, batting .308 but with four errors. A line drive fractured his finger, and manager Donie Bush sent him home to Atlanta. He had an awful rookie season in 1931, hitting just .232 and committing 42 errors in 76 games at shortstop. The fans hooted him and the newspapers bestowed him with the nickname "Kid Boots". Tris Speaker, broadcasting a game, spoke up in his defense, and offered the opinion that Appling would be in the league for many years. Although outwardly calm, Appling admitted later that he was putting terrible pressure on himself. "Those fans may be surprised to learn that in my freshman year at Oglethorpe I waited on tables," Appling said. "I never dropped a dish."

He played somewhat better in 1932, but it was still unclear whether he would be a major league shortstop, much less a Hall of Famer. "The first couple of years," remembered Ted Lyons, "it seemed as if he were the worst enemy I had on the field. In nearly every game I pitched, he would throw a couple of balls into the stands. Even his wife rode him about it. She said it was a shame that he always had to ruin my ball games."

One day in Detroit, with Lyons on the mound, Luke played a perfect game at short, and then saved the game with a great play in the ninth inning. Appling was so excited that he dragged Lyons to his hotel room, put through a long-distance call to Chicago and forced Lyons to tell Luke's wife what a great game he had played for him.

The White Sox that Appling joined were one of the worst teams in the major leagues. Following the Black Sox scandal the team slid gradually toward the bottom of the league, and by the early thirties had reached a nadir, losing regularly around a hundred games a year. Charles Comiskey died in October, 1931, and his descendants began a sincere and determined effort to improve the team. On September 28, 1932, the White Sox paid the Athletics $150,000 for third baseman Jimmie Dykes and outfielders Al Simmons and Mule Haas.

Simmons, at the time, was one of the biggest stars in baseball. Jimmie Dykes played third and, according to Luke, also made a ballplayer out of Luke Appling. Dykes was ten years older than Appling, but the two men formed a lifelong bond. Dykes went to Lou Fonseca, managing the Sox, and told him, as he recalled, "That boy is never going to be a ballplayer as long as he is pushed around. Half the time he doesn't know where he is going to play—or when. If he makes an error, he worries and his hitting falls off, then you put him on the bench and it nearly kills him. What you've got to do is let him stay in there. I can do a lot for him." This event, if it actually happened, must have happened in spring training, since Appling played nearly every game at shortstop in Dykes' first season.

In any event, whether because of the addition of Dykes (see Tracer) or his own maturity, Appling arrived as a star in 1933. Originally a straightaway hitter, he began to

TRACERS

"In one double-header against the Yankees I got seven hits, slicin' the ball between Lou Gehrig and Tony Lazzeri. Everytime I came to bat, Joe McCarthy kept movin' 'em closer and closer together. 'I'm shakin' hands with him now, I'm so close,' says Lazzeri when Ol' Joe he done move him over some more. Me, I'm alaughin' and alaughin'.

"In my last time at bat I tried to jam one between 'em again, jes' for the hell of it even though there ain't no room and it was wide open nearer second base. Lazzeri makes a dive for the ball, stops it, breaks a finger and throws me out. He looks at the broken finger. He looks at me.

" 'At least I threw you out, you little twirp,' he says."

—Arthur Daley column
New York Times
March 21, 1965

concentrate on hitting to the opposite field, right field, which he would do for the rest of his career. In 1933 he gathered 197 hits with a .322 average, 85 RBI and 90 runs scored. His defense at short improved, for which he also credited Jimmy Austin (see Austin). That fall there were rumors that Joe McCarthy wanted Appling and that he would soon be traded to the Yankees, the sure sign that he had arrived as a top-flight player. After that he was a consistent .300 hitter, a decent base stealer and regularly among the league leaders in walks. The White Sox, as a team, began to improve a little, finishing 67-83 in 1933 (their best record in five years).

Dykes became manager of the Sox early in the 1934 season. "I knew before he did that he was going to be manager," Appling said. "Lou Comiskey asked me if I thought Jimmy could handle it, and when I told him yes, he sent me to find Jim. When I found him I almost scared the life out of him. I told him the boss was really hopping and wanted to see him." In 1935 the White Sox moved up to 74-78, and then were over .500 in '36, '37, '39 and '40.

As a player Appling was most famous for two things: hypochondria and foul balls. Luke's ability to slap pitches into the stands was legendary. Any number of stories relate this uncanny skill; perhaps the best known describes the time Lou Comiskey fined Appling twenty-five dollars for some minor offense. An angry Appling proceeded to foul twenty-five bucks worth of balls into or near the owner's box. Other versions of this story have Appling avenging himself on the White Sox because they denied him free passes to the game, or because he asked for a dozen free baseballs to distribute at a father/son banquet and was turned down.

Apart from getting even with onery executives, the real purpose of the skill was to wear down the pitcher, forcing him to throw Appling's pitch from fatigue and frustration, and many other stories tell of Appling doing this to Ruffing, or Gomez, or Bridges, or Newhouser. Lee Allen would write in *The Sporting News* that the repeated stories about his ability to hit foul balls "are irrelevant to his skill and project a false image of him as a player." Allen's point was that the attention given to the foul balls had consumed Appling's image as a player, but in fact the skill was central to his accomplishments. Appling was a lifetime .310 hitter who walked a hundred times a year. Take the ability to spoil pitches away from him, and he'd have been a .260 with fifty walks a year—in other words,

he'd have been Don Gutteridge rather than Luke Appling.

He was long considered the best hit-and-run man and the finest two-strike hitter in the league. Because Appling hit the ball late, the hardest ball for him to handle was a fastball right over the heart of the plate.

In 1936 Appling hit .388, the highest average ever posted by a shortstop in modern history. Hitting third behind Mike Kreevich (.307) and Rip Radcliff (.335), Appling drove in 128 runs in 138 games, and finished second in the MVP voting, behind Lou Gehrig. He was the first shortstop to win the American League batting title. That was by far his best season. He said that he concentrated that year, from beginning to end, on hitting to right field (see Tracer).

Dykes didn't like him to bunt, preferring to hit and run. To Appling, who took great pride in his bunting, this was a sore point. "Cain't I drop me a bunt, Jim?" he asked Dykes one afternoon.

"Only if you ain't got the guts to hit away."

Another of his favorite stories involved laying down a game-winning bunt against Mike Higgins, playing him deep. "You only bunt once a year," Higgins told him, giving him the game ball in the runway after the game. "Whaddaya have to pick on me for?"

On March 27, 1938, Appling sustained the only serious injury of his career. In one of the last exhibition games of the spring he was decoyed into sliding at second base on a no-play, and broke his ankle, causing him to miss half the season. White Sox Vice President Harry Grabiner computed that Appling's absence had saved the White Sox $1400 in foul balls.

Appling hit .348 in 1940, leading the White Sox to a fifth-place finish, just eight games behind the pennant-winning Tigers. In twenty seasons Appling would never get any closer to a flag than that. The Yankees had an off-year in '40, and on Sept. 18 the White Sox, now led by a non-playing Dykes, were just four-and-a-half games behind the first-place Tigers. That day in Comiskey Park the Sox lost a heartbreaker to the Yankees, and quickly fell out of contention. In Appling's twenty seasons, the White Sox finished with a winning record just five times. David Nemec would later write that, "No other player in the game's history would play for so long for a team that was never once in contention."

In 1941 Appling had a chance to stop Joe DiMaggio's streak at 29 games. In the seventh inning of the thirtieth game, June 17, Di-

Maggio hit a routine ground ball to short. The ball took a bad hop and hit Appling in the shoulder, allowing DiMaggio to reach first. Dan Daniel ruled it a hit. DiMaggio later cost the Yankees the game with a defensive screw-up in center field, and then lost a game-winning homer in the ninth inning on a sensational play by Taffy Wright.

Appling played in the All-Star game in 1936, 1940, 1946 and 1947, and backed out of the game in 1941 because he was tired and needed the rest.

As a fielder Appling had tremendous range and was very quick on the double play, but was also charged with many errors. Frank Graham wrote that "Since Luke does try for every ball hit into his sector, he is bound to miss some and this has earned him a mark of which he isn't proud (most years leading the league in errors, shortstop), although there is no reason for him to be ashamed of it." In each of the seasons that Appling led the league in errors, he also led in assists. Luke blamed the condition of Comiskey Park for some of the errors. The park was built on the site of a dump, or at least Appling claimed that it was, and was never properly maintained by the White Sox. Appling claimed that one time before the White Sox went on a road trip he planted peas and radishes around the shortstop position. When they got home, the radishes were up and the peas were six inches tall. Another time, Appling remembered, "I kept clicking a spike on something. I scratched around and found the handle of one of those old blue-and-white coffee pots. I pulled it out and they had to hold up the game while they filled the hole with dirt."

After nine straight seasons over .300 Appling dropped to .262 in 1942, leading to the natural supposition that he was on the downhill slide at the age of 33. He rallied strongly in 1943. On August 13, 1943 he got his 2,000th career hit, placing him among the active leaders. With DiMaggio and Ted Williams in the service, Appling beat out Dick Wakefield and Ralph Hodgin to win his second American League batting title, at .328, and once again finished second in the MVP vote, this time behind Spud Chandler. He remains the only shortstop to have won the American League batting championship more than once. *The Sporting News* named him the outstanding major league shortstop for the third time, the others being 1936 and 1940.

Appling was ordered to report for his physical that November, was drafted into the

Army in December and reported to Camp Lee, Virginia on January 3, 1944. Richard Goldstein wrote in *Spartan Seasons* that Appling

> let it be known upon reporting for induction . . . that "ducking bullets can't be much worse than ducking some of those bad hops in the infield." He did the latter, the Army putting him to work as manager-shortstop of the Camp Lee, Virginia, quartermaster post team.

When he entered the Army Appling announced that "he probably would not return to the major leagues as an active player after the war. He said that he already had had trouble with his legs and felt they wouldn't stand up under a major league season by the time he got out of the army."

Appling was discharged from the service late in the '45 season, and reported to the White Sox in time to hit .362 in eighteen games. In 1946 he was back to work at the same old vegetable stand, hitting .309 and leading the league in assists, double plays, and errors.

In the spring of 1947 the White Sox traveling secretary, or "road secretary" as he was called then, offered to bet Appling a $10 hat that Luke couldn't hit eight homers in the year. Appling hit eight homers the first half the season, but his average was low, and he had to rally to finish at .306. "Come to think of it, I never did get that hat," he told Joe McGuff years later. "If I had gone for homers, I think I could have hit about twenty a year, and I'd have hit about .240."

June 8, 1947, was Luke Appling day at Comiskey Park, with ceremonies scheduled between the halves of a double-header. The first game was 1-0—in eighteen innings, tying the major league record for the longest 1-0 game. (Frank Papish, apparently beginning a brilliant career, pitched thirteen scoreless innings, giving him a string of 27 straight. As so often happened, Papish's career went into the tank from that moment.) After the first game anything would have been an anti-climax, but Appling was presented an automobile, a traditional gift for the day. Comedian Jack Benny had a joke automobile, an ancient Maxwell tricked out in red wheels and brass. When Appling's "car" was presented to him, it was Benny's famous Maxwell. The crowd roared. Appling got in and took Ted Lyons for a spin. The crowd whooped. You probably had to be there. Appling was then presented with a long line of gifts including fishing tackle, a diamond-studded watch, a check for $1,700 (a hundred dollars for each year he had been with the team) and his *real*

automobile, a 1947 sedan. The watch was inscribed on the back "to aches and pains on Appling Day", and was presented by Johnny Rigney, who told him "As the saying goes, you're what we like about the south."

Early in the 1948 season, Ted Lyons, now managing the White Sox, decided to move Appling to third base, putting Cass Michaels at shortstop. Appling and Lyons were old friends, but Appling objected to the move, and said that his arm wasn't strong enough to play third. On June 20, 1948, Appling was assigned to play third base in the first game of a double-header. He complained of a sore arm before the game. "For the life of me," he told the reporters, "I can't work it loose. Boys, my arm is so sore I don't honestly think I can even lob the ball to first base." Appling recorded ten assists that day in a nine-inning game, breaking an American League record which had stood for 47 years. (The record has since been broken.)

I have always wondered whether the Senators, knowing that Appling was out of position and hearing talk about his sore arm, didn't try to bunt on him all afternoon, producing the ten assists. No game story says that this is what happened, but then, reporters have been known to miss things like that. Appling also had three hits in the game, an 8-5 victory completed in just over two hours.

In any case, it was this event which crystalized the image of Appling which exists today, the image of "Old Aches and Pains". Between games of the double header Appling talked to reporters again. "Gosh," he said, smiling. "My right leg is aching like it never ached before—and I still have a full game to go." Although Appling had been around for sixteen years, and in fact had been playing this game with the reporters and his managers for several years, prior to that game the public had no clear image of him—indeed, that was what the writers most often wrote about him, on those infrequent occasions that they wrote about him. Joe Williams wrote in 1943 that the average baseball addict, if asked to identify Luke Appling, would say "Who?" Even in 1949, Frank Graham wrote that "If someone should ask you quickly, without giving you much time to think, what forty-year-old ballplayer has twice led the American League in batting and has a lifetime average of .312, the chances are that you wouldn't be able to say, unless you live in Chicago." Modern fanatics may find it hard to believe that their grandfathers actually knew so little about the game, but as my dad often said, "Baseball didn't used to be the main thing in life."

Before June, 1948, all that the average baseball fan knew about Luke Appling was that he was a .300 hitter, he fouled off a lot of pitches and hit to right all the time. Appling, wrote the writers, was "a ballplayer's ballplayer", a quiet, almost colorless player who went about his business seriously and efficiently. There was no human, three-dimensional image associated with the numbers he put up.

But after that date, Appling had an image: the happy hypochondriac, the cheerful complainer, the wornout old man who always had seven things wrong with him, but who when gametime came would get out there and get the job done. Virtually every story written about him from 1948 on drew upon and embellished this image. This story, which comes from a 1949 magazine (I can't figure out what magazine) distills the story to its essence:

> Luke Appling, baseball's gift to the medical profession, filled the Chicago White Sox dugout with groans. Today, complained Luke, he was sicker than ever, suffering from an upset stomach, inflammation of the ankles and a strange lump on his left hip.
>
> The other Sox were happy to hear it. "That's great!" they said. "Now go up there and get a hit."
>
> Limping to the plate, Appling squinted at Pitcher Bob Lemon of Cleveland. "My eyes are all shot," he told Tribe catcher Jim Hegan. "It's that double vision again."
>
> Hegan grinned. "Yeah, I heard you were feeling bad enough to play today, Luke."
>
> Lemon pitched and Appling drilled a curve ball into center field, scoring the White Sox run that pinned an upset defeat on Cleveland. Luke moved to first base, rubbing his side. He had just discovered a new "crick" that was causing considerable pain . . .
>
> Baseball's foremost hypochondriac, Lucius Benjamin Appling, keeps fans chuckling as he claims to be a hospital case, then socks the ball for a .300 average. The worse he feels, the better he plays. Manager Jack Onslow says that if Luke arrives at the park complaining of chills and high fever, he's almost sure to get three or four hits and sparkle in the field. Over the course of a season, the ailing Mr. Appling may suffer from indigestion, a stiff neck, fallen arches, a sore throat, dizzy spels, torn leg tendons, insomnia, signs of gout, astigmatism and a throbbing sensation in the kneecap.

Stories of this nature were written *ad infinitum* from 1948 through 1950, always recounting a few familiar incidents and adding another one of uncertain origin. Appling, who had not had a baseball nickname since he outgrew "Kid Boots" almost twenty years earlier, suddenly had twenty of them—The

Moaner, Droopy Luke, The Indestructible Invalid, The Groaner. Old Moanin' Low. Dykes had called him "Old Moanin' Low" for years, but I doubt that the nickname "Old Aches and Pains", with which he is now so closely identified, was ever printed until 1948, and it certainly was not printed before 1946.

It was also in this era that there arose confusion about Appling's actual age. When he signed with Atlanta in 1930 Appling gave his date of birth as April 2, 1911—unquestionably a "baseball age". Some sources always had his age right, however, so his date of birth was listed in some places as April 2, 1911, and in some as April 2, 1909. When he reported for the service in 1944, he confessed that the 1909 date was the correct one. "Can't lie to the Government," he told Shirley Povich. "They might not like it." After this happened, however, some people got confused about which date needed to be corrected, and thought that Appling had confessed to being two years older than he actually was. Some reference books after that listed him as having been born on April 2, 1907, and a few even list April 2, 1906. The original *Macmillan* listed the date of birth as 1907.

Given conflicting sources for his age, reporters got cute with it, and began speculating that Appling in 1949 might be as old as 45. Playing games with Appling's age, as they did with Satchel Paige and Minnie Minoso, they lost interest in when he was actually born, creating additional confusion on the issue. When he celebrated his 40th birthday in 1949, it was written that he was celebrating his 40th birthday "again", and that Appling denied that he had ever played side by side with Cap Anson. When the White Sox roster came out in 1950 it listed his date of birth as "April 2, A.D." A teammate, Billy Pierce, was born on April 2 many years later. In San Antonio in 1950 (spring training) the fans presented Appling with a huge birthday cake smothered in candles, while Pierce was presented a tiny cake with just a few candles. Appling, fighting for his professional life and feeling strongly that he could still play, took it with the best humor that he could manage.

Ted Lyons was let go after the 1948 season, and Appling returned to shortstop in 1949. "Last year he was switched to third in then Manager Ted Lyons' drive to 101 losses," wrote Ed Burns sarcastically. "Others wanted to see Luke continue at his favorite position, but Ted wanted it known he was boss, and that was that." At age forty (1949) he had one of his finest seasons, hitting .301 with 121 walks, only 24 strikeouts and a .439

on-base percentage. He still ran reasonably well, and his defensive starts at shortstop, although he had no doubt lost some range, are pretty decent. With his new image he was, for the first time, one of the game's brightest stars.

On August 5, 1949, Appling broke Rabbit Maranville's record for the most games played at shortstop, 2,153. The White Sox hyped the event. Maranville was on hand and made a brief speech congratulating Appling, as did United States Senator Clyde Hoey of North Carolina, the state in which Appling was born. Media from around the country was in attendance. The White Sox handed him a check for "a sizeable amount of money", believed to have been $2,153. Ed Burns wrote that "When Luke Appling finally [retires] he not only will own the major leagues' non-stop shortstop record, but will have set the mark at such a lofty figure that it will be virtually unassailable in the foreseeable future." Of course Luis Aparicio, a generation later, would break the record by almost 400 games.

And then suddenly the next spring, he was old and out of a job. A young shortstop showed up in spring training, Chico Carrasquel. Like most players, Appling had difficulty accepting the end, probably more so because it had arrived with so little warning. The White Sox manager, Jack Onslow, asked Appling to go to first base. Appling tried it for three days in spring training, but then balked. He began the season on the bench. When the first base job opened up again he tried it again, saying that it was driving him batty to sit and watch. He wasn't happy, and he didn't hit. The White Sox started badly and Onslow was fired, but Carrasquel was anchored at short, and Appling, although convinced that he had several good years left, couldn't get back in the lineup.

The popular sentiment in Chicago was to hire Appling as the Sox' new manager for 1951, an idea to which Luke was quite receptive. Paul Richards was hired instead, in part because of fears that Appling, if hired to manage, would put himself back in the lineup. Released by the White Sox, Appling looked around the majors for other offers to play or manage. Nothing came. He was offered the job as manager of the Memphis Chicks, a White Sox affiliate, and accepted that on November 1, 1950. He announced immediately that he would not be a playing manager.

In Appling's second year at Memphis, 1952, the Chicks won the Southern Association Playoff, and Appling was named by *The Sporting News* as the Minor League Manager

of the Year. In 1953 he guided Memphis to a first-place finish, although they were quickly eliminated in the playoff.

The great unanswered question of Appling's life is why he never got a real chance to manage in the major leagues. Appling was a very popular player, a smart player in the general mold of a manager. He wanted to manage, and he was outspoken about that. He paid the price. He went to the minors and proved that he could do it—yet the chance never came. He was regarded as an excellent teacher, so much so that he was able to remain employed as a minor league instructor until his death at age 81—in fact, just a year ago the Braves still thought he was doing a great job in their system, that the kids really responded to him. The eight managers in the Southern Association in 1953 included Appling, Gene Mauch, Mayo Smith, Danny Murtaugh and Cal Ermer. Among those men one would have thought that Appling would be the first to get a shot at a major league job, but for some reason he never did.

He may have been perceived as too nice to be a manager, and that may or may not have been an accurate perception. Appling had a distinctly combative side to his personality. An article about a game in late 1949 notes that Appling was thrown out of the game for arguing for the fourth time that year. He enjoyed managing. George Lapides, interviewing him in 1979 about the Memphis teams he had piloted almost thirty years earlier, was amazed to discover that Appling remembered the most minor role players on the team in stunning detail.

Appling was a great talker, always had something to say to the reporters. Like George Brett today, he talked to everybody on the field—the umpire, the catcher, the first baseman, the first base coach, the opposition's coach, everybody. He got worse as he aged, a beloved but indefatigable talker. He told a lot of stories about the good old days. Some people probably didn't take him seriously because of that.

In any case Appling moved up to Richmond (International League) in 1954, and managed there for two years with no success, after which he would not manage again until 1959, when he returned to Memphis. In 1960 Jimmie Dykes was managing the Tigers. Dykes hired Appling to be his batting coach, replacing Tommy Henrich.

In mid-summer, 1960, there occurred the famous "managers trade" between the Indians and the Tigers. Dykes, managing the Tigers, was traded to the Cleveland Indians in exchange for their manager, Joe Gordon. A few days later, the teams also traded coaches, Appling going to Cleveland in exchange for Jo Jo White. Dykes was fired after the '61 season. Luke signed to manage Indianapolis in the American Association in 1962, and guided that team, whose best players were Tommy McCraw and Al Weis, to a record of 89-58, the best record in the American Association. It was his finest managerial accomplishment; no one can look at that team and explain why they should walk away from the league.

Appling coached for Baltimore in 1963. Charlie Finley had purchased the Kansas City A's a few years earlier. Finley, who grew up in Chicago in the thirties, collected the heroes of his youth for his coaching staff. In November, 1963, Appling signed to coach with the A's, joining Dykes, Gabby Hartnett and Ed Lopat on the Kansas City bench. They didn't win many games, but they had a lot of fun. As a hitting coach, Appling's approach was to try to teach everybody the virtues of hitting to right field.

In January, 1964, Appling was elected to the Baseball Hall of Fame in a special runoff election after no one had received the necessary seventy-five percent on the first ballot:

Someone asked me after I missed on the first ballot how I would feel if elected on the second.
I told him I don't care if I made it on the second, third or 40th or have to crawl in on my hands and knees. It's a great honor. This makes up for never having played on a pennant winner or in a World Series.

Appling was still coaching in Kansas City in 1967 when A's manager Alvin Dark was fired in August (see Jack Aker, 1990 book). Luke was named interim manager for the rest of the season. It was an awful situation in which to try to manage. The A's, a bad team to begin with, were miles away from the pennant race by the time Appling arrived, and seething bitterness between the players and Finley had erupted into open hostility. According to Herbert Michelson's book Charlie O:

As one player who was a rookie then recalls things, Appling spent moments of those managerial weeks eating in the dugout. During one critical point in a meaningless game, Appling wasn't even in the dugout. "He'd gone upstairs for another sandwich," says this player.

The A's won only ten of forty games under Appling's direction, although two of those were a doubleheader sweep of the White Sox

in the last week of the season, which effectively destroyed Chicago's pennant hopes.

Appling served as a "superscout" for the A's for the next two years, 1968–69, also doing some instructional work with the minor leaguers. In October, 1969, the White Sox, fulfilling the same pre-natal yearnings which had led them to re-acquire Luis Aparicio two years earlier, decided to bring back Appling as a coach for the 1970 season. Appling is one of the few ever to express sadness over leaving Charles O. Finley's employ. "Charlie's been a good ole' boy to work with," he said. "We got along fine." He served as a coach under Don Gutteridge in 1970. Gutteridge had an awful time as manager, and once more there were rumors that Appling would get the White Sox' job. Appling was in his sixties by this time, however, and the White Sox—wisely, no doubt—went with a much younger man, Chuck Tanner.

Leaving the White Sox after 1971, Appling retired, sort of, to Atlanta with his wife Faye (they were married in 1932, and had two daughters and a son, Luke III). The Braves hired Appling as a part-time organizational batting coach, and found him to be so effective that his "part-time" role grew steadily. In 1978, when Jerry Royster broke through as a regular after several years of struggle, he gave Appling much of the credit:

"Appling," he said, "taught me how to go to right field, and that has been so important. He didn't just tell me; he showed me."
Among other things, Appling placed a target on the right side of the infield for Royster to try to hit during spring training. And he showed him how. Even at 70, Appling can still handle the bat.
Impressed, Royster listened and practiced, and many of his hits have gone to right.

Royster scored 103 runs in 1979.

No discussion of Luke Appling's career would be complete without mention of his most famous at-bat, in the Cracker Jack Old-Timers Baseball Classic in Washington, D.C., on July 19, 1982. Appling, the oldest player in the game, was due to lead off the contest for the American League. Warren Spahn was on the mound. "I had a game plan," said Spahn. "I was going to pitch around the young guys and work on the old guys. I could see guys like Al Kaline and Bobby Richardson hitting one out, but not an old man like Appling. I didn't figure he could even hit a ball that far." Spahn threw him a hummer without much tune to it, right over the plate, and Appling ripped it over the left field fence, 320 feet away. Luke circled the bases slowly, with

Spahn trailing him all the way, pummelling Appling with his glove in mock furor. "I wanted him to retaliate, to ham it up for the crowd," Spahn said. "But he was so happy, all he could say was 'Oh, thank you, Spahnie. Thank you, Spahnie.'

"That just proves," said Spahn, "that I can still throw hard. I know Luke couldn't hit the ball that far by himself." Millions saw Appling's homer replayed on highlights shows, and the Hall of Famer was arguably more famous at seventy-three than he had been at thirty.

Appling died on January 3, 1991, at Lakeside Community Hospital in Atlanta; he was hospitalized for an aneurysm, and died during surgery. The date of his death was the 47th anniversary of his induction into the Army in 1944. He spent sixty years in professional baseball, at the end teaching hitters too young to be his grandsons.

A reporter once asked Appling what his saddest day in baseball was. "I had one day every year," he said. "The last day of the season, when I knew I couldn't put that uniform on again tomorrow."

(B.J. and R.N. We would like to thank the Hall of Fame library, Tom Heitz and Bill Deane, for sending the Appling clipping file. Rob also talked to Mr. Appling on the phone in 1989, and we appreciate his co-operation.)

Angel Aragon, who played 33 games for the Yankees from 1914 through 1917.

In 1912 a gentleman/promoter named Dr. George Henriquez imported an entire team from Cuba. Henriquez intended to play his team against semi-pro teams in the New York area, but heard that a new minor league was being formed, the New York-New Jersey League. He secured the Long Branch franchise in the new league, and supplemented the team with an American or two in preparation for the 1913 season.

His team was so good that everybody else in the league finished under .500. Long Branch was 65-29; Poughkeepsie finished second in the six-team circuit, at 48-49. According to Ira Smith in Baseball's Famous Pitchers (see article on Dolf Luque) "opposition managers and players attributed some of that success to the fact that the Cubans were able to discuss plays and lay plans openly on the field while the game was in progress. Shouting all over the place in Spanish, they had little or no use for signals."

They could also play. Two members of the team went on to outstanding careers in the major leagues. Catcher Mike Gonzalez, purchased by the Braves, played in the major leagues for seventeen years. Dolf Luque, 22-5 for Long Branch that summer, was the outstanding pitcher in the National League ten years later, going 27-8 with a 1.93 ERA. The five-foot, five-inch Aragon, though less successful in the majors, was the team's leading hitter in 1913, with an average of .358. Henriquez also played for the team, playing first base and hitting .320.

After his playing career Aragon returned to Cuba, where worked as a bird dog/scout for the Giants until his death in 1952.

Fernando Arango, head baseball coach at Cleveland State.

Luis Arango, third baseman with the Cuban Stars and New York Cubans, 1925–1939.

Jorge Aranzamendi, a scout in the Cardinal system and coach for the Louisville team in 1989.

Mike Arbuckle, a scout for the Atlanta Braves.

Maurice Archdeacon, Chicago White Sox outfielder for a brief period in the twenties.

Archdeacon was very small (153 pounds) and very fast. While with Rochester in 1921 he circled the bases in 13.4 seconds, a record at the time. He stole 225 bases over a five-year period in the minors, and was nicknamed "Flash" and "Comet."

Archdeacon was a player out of his time, a player who had *some* impressive skills, but lacked others, and happened to lack those which were in fashion at the moment. With Rochester, the second-best team in the International League, he was one of the outstanding players in the league from 1921 to 1923, leading the league in runs scored each year with totals of 166, 151 and 162, and hitting as high as .357. Purchased by the White Sox late in the 1923 season, Archdeacon hit .402 in 87 at bats, earning him a starting job for the 1924 season.

It seems absurd to say that Archdeacon failed his major league trial, and yet it impossible to say that he didn't. In 127 major league games (384 at bats) he hit .333, and scored 84 runs. He didn't throw well and had no power, and at the time major league teams were looking for left fielders who could drive in runs. Archdeacon returned to the International

League, playing for Baltimore, Buffalo and Toronto.

(—R.N.)

Jim Archer, long-time minor league pitcher who spent the 1961 and '62 seasons with the Kansas City Athletics.

Archer had a trial with LaGrange in the Georgia-Florida League in 1951, and was hit very hard, posting a 7.24 ERA in nine starts. He was out of baseball for three years, returning to the Pidemont League in 1955. He was no prospect, but he began a string of six straight solid seasons, working his way methodically through the Oriole system. The Orioles traded him to the A's in a multiplayer trade.

Archer was already 28 years old when he pitched in his first big league game, and surprised nearly everyone when he became not only the best pitcher on the K.C. staff, but one of the better pitchers in the American League, pitching 205 innings as a rookie with a 3.20 ERA. *The Kansas City Times* said, "Archer relies principally on a good curve, his control and an effective change-up. [Frank] Lane describes him as a left-handed Cal McLish." Archer also threw a fine screwball.

Archer pulled a leg muscle in spring training, 1962, and, favoring the leg, developed tendinitis in his left (pitching) shoulder. He was ineffective in 1962, mostly in relief, and his major league career came to a quick end.

(—R.N.)

Jimmy Archer, catcher with the Cubs in the teens, owner of the finest throwing arm of his era, and one of the first catchers to go into a full squat.

Archer was born in Dublin, Ireland, in 1883; his family moved to Canada when Jimmy was a child. Archer played in the Toronto City League from 1901 to 1903. According to Charles Cleveland in *The Great Baseball Managers,* Archer "was originally a pitcher but one day he slipped on a wet floor and his arm was plunged into boiling water and afterward his elbow was stiff." Stiff elbow and all, he entered professional baseball with Fargo in the Northern League in 1903, where he played for the first team managed by Spencer Abbott (see Abbott, 1990 Book). Playing for Boone in the Iowa State league in 1904, Archer hit .299 and earned a look by the Pirates late in the year. He failed the trial, and spent several years with Atlanta in the Southern League, polishing his defensive skills. Again according to Charles Cleveland, "In one game for Atlanta he picked off seven

Memphis runners from first. In another game against Memphis the bases were loaded with no cuts. On four pitches, Archer retired the side by picking men off second, third and first."

His portfolio of apocryphal defensive feats completed (Natty Bumppo would be hard pressed to shoot down three runners on four pitches), Archer was acquired by the Tigers in 1907, played eighteen games with them and, in a desperate attempt to control the Cubs' running game, started the final game of the 1907 World Series. The Cubs stole 16 bases in the five-game series, dominating the series; they stole three against Archer.

Archer was let go by the Tigers, sold to Buffalo. It was written many years later that Archer was sent out by the Tigers because "the late Hughey Jennings opined no catcher could operate while squatting" (1935 *Who's Who in the Major Leagues*). He hit only .208 for Buffalo, but continued to build his reputation as a defensive wizard. In 1909 Cubs catcher Johnny Kling held out, all year. The Cubs acquired Archer to split the catching job with Pat Moran.

Kling returned in 1910, making Archer a second-string catcher and first baseman, backing up Kling and Frank Chance. Chicago won the pennant, for the fourth time in five years, with the 1911 *Reach Guide* reporting that "in a team of such even strength it is almost ungracious to single out individual factors in success, but candor compels the statement that the greatest credit was due to [Frank Chance and] the fine catching of Kling and Archer, and the latter's splendid substitute duty as first baseman during Chance's frequent layoffs." Archer hit a respectable .259 in 98 games.

The Philadelphia Athletics trounced the Cubs in that fall's World Series. Johnny Kling hit .077 in the World Series, and was criticized by the writers and by his own pitchers for calling too many fastballs with men on base to prevent the A's from stealing bases. After the first three games were lost, with Kling catching, Archer started the fourth game. He played well defensively, and scored the game-winning run after hitting a double in the bottom of the tenth inning. He started again in the fifth game, but didn't play well, allowing four stolen bases. According to the 1911 *Reach Guide,* Archer "fell down badly in the final game, losing his head completely in the crucial eighth inning, when he let Zimmerman's wild throw get completely away from him, a lapse that cost two runs." The game was out of hand when the play occurred and the error was charged to Zimmerman, so Archer was far from the goat of the series; he was merely caught in the spray of criticism which inevitably follows defeat.

Kling, suffering from a winter of second-guessing, started slowly in 1911, hitting .177 through 27 games. Kling was traded to the Braves, and Archer became the first-string catcher. He caught over a hundred games in each of the next three years, hitting as high as .283 and establishing himself as the best throwing catcher of his time, if not the best of all time. In *The Glory of Their Times* Al Bridwell said that "Jimmy Archer was still catching for the Cubs in 1913, when I was there. Best arm of any catcher I ever saw. He'd zip it down there to second like a flash. Perfect accuracy, and under a six-foot bar all the way." Chief Meyers, in the same book, said that "The best throwing arm of them all was Jimmy Archer of the Cubs. He didn't have an arm. He had a rifle. And perfect accuracy."

In *Casey: The Life and Legend of Charles Dillon Stengel*, by Joe Durso, Stengel repeated a conversation he had with Jimmy Archer shortly after Stengel broke in (p. 34):

Jimmy Archer was catching and the first time I went up to hit he said to me: 'So you're Stengel, eh?' "

" 'Yes,' I said, 'I'm Stengel.' "

"I see you broke in pretty good," Archer said.

"Yeah, pretty good," Stengel replied. "Four for four and stole a couple of bases."

"Well," said Archer, squatting behind the plate with an air of expectation, "when you get on there, let me see you run."

"Not today, Mr. Archer," Casey said politely. "I know you."

To complete the story, Casey got on late in the game and was ordered to run, and Archer threw him out "from here to there."

According to some sources, Archer was the first white catcher to go into a full squat. Robert Smith referred to him in *Baseball* as "Jim Archer, the Dublin Irishman whose flat-footed throwing technique (learned from a black catcher named Buddy Petway) was soon imitated by every catcher in organized baseball." In another book, however, Smith says that it was Bresnahan who copied Petway's style, and the league copied it from Bresnahan.

One of the things that this book is about is documenting changes in the game over time. If Jimmy Archer did, in fact, introduce the full, flat-footed squat for a catcher, this is a large footprint in the history of the game. We took a look at the question of when catch-ers first went into a full squat. In the thirties and forties reporters would sometimes state flatly that it was Archer, without even mentioning Petway; black players didn't exist. Now Petway is usually given the credit, but what exactly the source for this is I don't know.

We have a collection of Baseball *Guides* going back to the start of the century, and we studied the photos of the catchers. The first photos of a catcher squatting are of Roger Bresnahan and Red Dooin in the 1909 *Spalding Guide*. These pictures would have been taken in 1908, at which time Archer had failed two brief trials and was playing for Buffalo.

It was many years after this, at least ten years, before catchers began to squat as an ordinary thing. By 1912 photos of catchers squatting are relatively common, but photos of catchers "crouching" or standing almost upright are still the rule. An action photo of Archer taken in 1915 shows Archer crouch-ing, *not* in a full squat. By 1918 most photos show catchers crouching, but this is not universal even up to the time of Mickey Cochrane and Bill Dickey. Action shots of Bob O'Farrell in the 1926 World Series and Earl Smith in 1925 show them standing to receive pitches, although certainly all of the young catchers were squatting by that time. My general conclusions are that

1. Archer, because of his tremendous throwing arm, probably did help to popularize the squatting position, but it is unlikely that he was the first white catcher to do this, and

2. the practice of "crouching" or catching almost upright continued much later than I would have thought. Probably if you talked to old men today, men in their nineties, you might find that as small boys they stood upright to catch when they passed the position in workup.

Catchers may, for some time, have crouched to give a target but stood up when there was a man on base, fearing that they couldn't throw out of a crouch. Archer's specialty was the snap throw to the bases, without getting out of the crouch, and very probably he was the first catcher to do this. Enough on that. According to Harold Seymour's second volume, *The Golden Age*, "Jimmy Archer once attacked a man he thought was flirting with his wife in the stands." Seymour is recounting a series of player/fan confrontations; we do not know the specifics of this incident.

The dead ball era returned after 1913, and Archer's hitting fell off with the rest of the league. By 1917 his fingers were bent and brittle, and he left the game, returning briefly in 1918, when the War thinned the talent. In 1918 he went to spring training with the Pirates, but got released a few weeks into the season. Brooklyn came to town and needed a catcher; he filled in for a week, and then quit them. As he was packing his bags, Cincinnati came to town, looking for a catcher. As he remembered it later, he wound up making three trips to the Polo Grounds in two weeks, with three different ball clubs. "How many times are we going to see you this year?" McGraw asked.

Returning to Chicago, Archer was hired by Armour Meat as a hog buyer, and worked at that job for almost fifteen years. The 1935 *Who's Who in the Major Leagues* reported that "the arm that won him everlasting fame when he was throwing out hostile baserunners, while in a squatting position back of the plate, now is employed by Jimmy Archer . . . in the advancement of bowling in one of Chicago's leading pin emporiums."

Archer happened to have played for a series of fascinating managers, starting with Spencer Abbott. His major league managers were, in order, Fred Clarke, Hughie Jennings, Frank Chance, Johnny Evers, Hank O'Day, Roger Bresnahan, Joe Tinker, Fred Mitchell, Hugo Bezdek, Wilbert Robinson and Christy Mathewson, eight Hall of Famers altogether. For his 1950 book about managers Charles Cleveland interviewed Archer at length about the men he had played for, which incidentally makes that book one of the best sources of information about Archer. Archer was near seventy by then, and convinced as old players inevitably are that the modern players were neither as tough nor as smart as the men of his day, and didn't care as much about the game. He recalled Fred Clarke during spring training going from room to room on a Sunday morning, "jabbing the men with a stiletto, trying to get them to go to church."

Archer died in Milwaukee in 1958.

Fred Archer, briefly a pitcher for the Philadelphia Athletics in the thirties.

In 1936 Archer was a 24-year-old left-hander who had washed out of the Bi-State League in 1934 and was pitching semi-pro ball. Connie Mack retained him to pitch for the Athletics. He was ineffective.

George Archie, Most Valuable Player in the Pacific Coast League in 1940, and a regular for the Senators in 1941.

Archie, a first baseman, was a tremendously consistent and valuable player in the best minor leagues of the late thirties. He hit .299 in the Texas League in 1936. With Indianapolis in 1937 he hit .315 with eleven homers, seventeen stolen bases. With Toledo in 1938 (American Association) he hit .312 with 107 RBI and 28 stolen bases.

At that time he was the property of the Tigers, but his path to the majors was blocked not only by Hank Greenberg, but also by Rudy York. After two at bats with the Tigers in 1938 he was traded to the Seattle Rainiers as a part of the Fred Hutchison trade.

Fast for a first baseman and an excellent fielder, Archie became a star in Seattle, leading the Rainiers to the PCL championship in 1939 and 1940. In 1939 he hit .330 with 7 homers, 88 RBI and, according to Gary Waddingham in *The Seattle Rainiers (1938–1942)* "furnished quiet leadership to a rollicking, aggressive ballclub." In 1940 he won the Pacific Coast League MVP award over Lou Novikoff, who had much better batting stats. (Novikoff hit .363 with 44 doubles, 41 homers and 171 RBI; Archie hit his usual—.324 with 46 doubles, 8 homers and 95 RBI.)

Drafted by the Washington club, Archie was projected as the Senators' starting first baseman in 1941. He struggled early, but by the end of camp had solidified a spot on the roster. The "Washington Post" on April 13, 1941, wrote that "You'll have to see him on first base, because you can't hear him. He'd give the sphinx a battle in a long-distance silence contest. What is left of his hair is red."

While Archie didn't play badly, Mickey Vernon, who had failed a trial in 1939, returned with avengeance, and won the first base job. Archie moved to third base, and hit a respectable .277 in 114 games, but couldn't handle the glovework at third. He entered the Army that fall; in Austria late in the war he became part of a team put together by General Reinhart, which had several other major leaguers. He played four games with St. Louis after the war, but apparently retired after that. He still resides in Nashville, Tennessee, where he was born in 1914.

(—R.N.)

Jose Arcia, a utility player with the 1968 Cubs and the expansion San Diego Padres.

Arcia, a native Cuban, was drafted by the Cubs from the Cardinals' organization, and got his break in the spring of '68 when, with Glenn Beckert off for two weeks of Army duty, he was awarded the second base job for the opening days of the season. When Beckert came back Arcia became a utility man, often used as a defensive replacement or pinch-runner.

The Padres selected Arcia from the Cubs in the expansion draft, and he played a hundred games for the Padres in 1969 and '70.

(—R.N.)

Valerie Arcuri, Director of Publications and Advertising Sales for the Cleveland Indians.

Frank Arellanes, pitcher with the Red Sox from 1908 to 1910, winner of sixteen games in 1909. Arellanes died of Spanish influenza during the deadly epidemic of 1918; he was 36 years old.

Hank Arft, first baseman with the St. Louis Browns in the late forties and early fifties.

In the minors since 1940, Arft re-emerged as a prospect by hitting .366 in the Three-I League in 1947, then .290 with power for Toledo in 1947. Purchased by the Browns on July 27, 1948, Arft made his major league debut the next day before the hometown fans in St. Louis (he was born and raised in Manchester, Missouri, a small town just outside St. Louis.) He drove in three runs with a homer and a triple as the Browns shut out the Yankees, 4-0.

When Hank came to the plate the next day he was greeted by choruses of "Arft, Arft!" from the fans; at some point, he also acquired the nickname "Bow Wow". He never lived up to his initial promise, and was out of the majors by 1952.

(—R. N.)

George Argyros, owner of the Seattle Mariners from January 14, 1981 until August 22, 1989.

Argyros bought the Mariners for an amount then reported as $10.4 million, later reported as $13.1. Dick Williams in *No More Mr. Nice Guy* described Argyros as "a self-made southern California millionaire who became rich in real estate and airplanes."

Argyros stewardship of the Mariners was carpeted with uninterrupted losing seasons, and highlighted by periodic rumors that the Mariners would leave Seattle. In the manner of self-made millionaires, Argyros was arrogant, loud and arbitrary. When Chuck Cottier was fired in May, 1986, he said that "Argyros had embarrassed him on many occasions," and alleged that Argyros had called him on the phone almost every day (*TSN*, May 26, 1986).

Argyros spent much of his time on the telephone. In the spring of 1987 he announced that he intended to sell the Mariners and buy the San Diego Padres. This was followed by several months of semi-public negotiations, including a period of time in which it appeared that baseball might try to get him to sell the Mariners, and then refuse to approve his purchase of the Padres. On April 16, 1987, Argyros called Padres' manager Larry Bowa in Bowa's office to congratulate him on a win. N.L. President Bart Giamatti happened to be in Bowa's office when the phone call arrived, and Argyros was fined $10,000 by the commissioner for tampering, or something.

According to Williams, "because Argyros and Armstrong didn't understand baseball, they lived by the rule that the player is always right. Make the player happy, they figured, and he'll help you win. More important for them, apparently, he'll be your friend. And they made sure they only had players they would cherish as friends."

Argyros, wrote Williams, was an awful baseball man, but a great businessman. "George's tenure as a Seattle owner wasn't about winning or losing. It was about making money. He had no concept of a final score, just bottom line. And he made that line pay off when he loaded his pockets by finally selling the Mariners in 1989 for $75,000,000."

Eleodoro Arias, a scout for the Los Angeles Dodgers.

Rudy Arias, Cuban relief pitcher for the 1959 Chicago White Sox.

Arias spent six seasons in the minor leagues before catching on with the "Go-Go Sox". He was used strictly in non-critical situations and after 1959 never again pitched in the majors. The "Chicago Tribune" on Apr. 9, 1959 spoke of his "live fast ball," and "good control," but also noted his "lack of stamina."

(—M. K.)

Homero Ariosa, outfielder with the New York Cubans, 1947–1949.

Michiyo Arito, Manager of the Lotte Orions (1989).

Roone Arledge, innovative head of ABC Sports.

Arledge graduated from Columbia University and, after a stint in the Army, made it into sports by producing college football games. He worked his way up to vice-president, and by 1968 president, of ABC sports. According to Bert Randolph Sugar in *The Thrill of Victory*, it was Arledge more than anyone who subverted the prevailing attitude towards sports production articulated by baseball commissioner Ford Frick: "The view a fan gets [on TV] should not be any better than that of the fan in the worst seat in the ballpark." Sugar wrote that Arledge took the "simple forthright approach, heretical up to that point, that television was not in the ticket-selling business, but in the business of projecting a game with all its color."

Arledge rose to fame with his productions of "Wide World of Sports," "Monday Night Football," and the 1972 terrorist-haunted Munich Olympics. He helped Howard Cosell become the most famous sports broadcaster of his era. At the Emmy Awards in 1976, ABC and Arledge took with thirty-two of the possible thirty-four statuettes. In 1977 he received additional responsibilities when he was appointed president of ABC News.

In the mid-seventies, Arledge brought "Monday Night Baseball" to the screen, and initially angered Commissioner Bowie Kuhn by bringing in Cosell, a long-time baseball detractor, as one of the announcers. The Arledge approach to baseball was not universally admired, and director Chet Forte later admitted that "out of the ten or fifteen home runs hit at the beginning of our first year, we probably saw four of them go into the stands." Even Arledge conceded it was "not our finest hour."

"Monday Night Baseball" never became a big success, and as years passed the number of games broadcast was scaled back. Eventually Arledge successfully bid for a share of the post-season telecasts, alternating the playoffs and World Series with NBC. Cosell managed to mollify Kuhn, but continued to drive baseball fans out of their minds. Cosell finally quit network television and Arledge assembled the generally admired team of Al Michaels, Jim Palmer, and Tim McCarver, who served until ABC lost baseball to CBS at the end of the 1989 season.

(—M. K.)

Buzz Arlett, the Babe Ruth of the minor leagues.

Russell Loris Arlett was born in Oakland, California, in 1899. By 1918 the Arlett family had moved to Boyes Springs, California, where the Oakland Oaks conducted spring training. Without anyone's invitation, Arlett began to hang around the camp and work out with the players. He was a huge kid (6 foot 3, around 205 pounds) and an obvious athlete, and the Oaks added him to their roster as a pitcher.

I will assume that most of you know this, but I will say it all the same: that the minor leagues in 1918 were not what they are today. They were not, at that time, primarily a training ground for the major leagues. The teams were by and large locally owned, and run for the benefit of the local owners and the local fans. They were small-scale imitations of major league teams, not servants of major league needs as they are today. No rule in 1918 required a minor league team to sell a player to a higher league—indeed, had Babe Ruth come along in 1918, rather than in 1914, Jack Dunn would not have sold Ruth to the Red Sox; he would have kept him in the International League, just as he did Lefty Grove for several years. Dunn sold Ruth to the majors only because the war with the Federal League was causing financial hardship for him, and he needed the cash. Arlett came along in 1918, rather than 1914, and this is one of the largest differences between Babe Ruth and Buzz Arlett.

A spitball pitcher, Arlett pitched 153 innings in 1918 with a 2.70 ERA, but finished with a 4-9 record for a last-place team. For the following four seasons, 1919 through 1922, he was the Oaks' best pitcher, and one of the best pitchers in the minor leagues. According to an article by Gerald Tomlinson in the 17th *Baseball Research Journal*, he was an excellent fielding pitcher, described by a reporter as being "like a cat on his feet for a big man fielding bunts". An instructive comparison is that Arlett pitched in rotation all four of those years beside Remy Kremer.

In 1919, when Arlett was 22-17 with a 3.00 ERA, Kremer was 15-23 with a 3.83 ERA.

In 1920, when Arlett was 29-17 with a 2.89 ERA, Kremer was 13-22 with a 3.02 ERA.

In 1921, when Arlett was 19-18 with a 4.37 ERA, Kremer was 16-14 with a 3.61 ERA.

In 1922, when Arlett was 25-19 with a 2.77 ERA, Kremer was 20-18 with a 2.78 ERA.

In 1923 Arlett hurt his arm and moved to the outfield, allowing Kremer to move up to the number one spot in the Oaks' rotation. Kremer had a good year and moved on to the National League where, beginning in 1924, he posted records of 18-10, 17-8, 20-6, 19-8, 15-13, 18-10 and 20-12 in his first seven seasons. I am not saying that had they gone to the majors together Arlett would have remained the better pitcher, nor am I trying to transfer to Arlett credit equal to Kremer's impressive accomplishments as a major league pitcher. I am merely pointing this out: that Arlett and Remy Kremer pitched in rotation beside one another for four seasons, and Arlett was a better pitcher. Arlett was 95-71 over the four years; Kremer was 64-77.

In any case, Arlett suffered an arm injury in 1923, and moved to the outfield in time to hit .330 with 101 RBI. A switch hitter, he would become perhaps the greatest hitter in the vast history of minor league baseball. The Pacific Coast League played a long schedule in those days, so Arlett would play 185 to 200 games a year. He was a lifetime .341 hitter, one point less than Ruth's major league average, and would hit as high as .382 (1926). He would drive in 140 or more runs in a season eight times, with a high of 189 (1929). He would hit consistently more than 30 homers a year, with a high of 54 in 1932. He would hit more than fifty doubles a year, with a high of 70 in 1929. He would steal more than twenty bases in a season six times. His first year as a regular he hit 19 triples, following that up with 13 and 16. He was durable, consistent, ran well and had a powerful throwing arm.

Arlett remained with the Oakland Oaks from 1918 through 1930, despite persistent rumors that he would be sold to a major league team. Modern fans looking back at the astonishing numbers he compiled in the best minor leagues are always puzzled by his failure to "get a chance" in the majors, so perhaps I should address that directly. There were several factors involved.

- The Oakland owners did not want to sell him, and until the mid- to late-twenties did not have to sell him if they did not want to. (In fact, I'm not really sure *when* the Pacific Coast League teams agreed to the structural arrangements which required them to sell players to the majors after holding them for a couple of years. It wasn't before 1925.) The Oaks set a price for Arlett of $100,000—the same price Babe Ruth sold for in 1919—and, not surprisingly, no major league team would come up with the money.
- Although Arlett had other pitches, he relied heavily on a spitball. The spitball was banned in 1920, but established pitchers were protected by a "grandfather clause".

In the Pacific Coast League, Arlett was grandfathered, allowed to throw the spitball. Had he gone to the major leagues, he would not have been; he wasn't on the major league list. Thus, from 1920 to 1922, Arlett's prime as a pitcher, major league teams were reluctant to shell out the big money for a pitcher who couldn't bring one of his best pitches with him.

- After Arlett moved to the outfield, it took him a couple of years to gain the same status as an outfielder that he had had as a pitcher.
- Like Ruth, Arlett was enormously *popular* with his local fans, which made it both difficult and counter-productive for an organization to peddle him. Arlett was, incidentally, an extremely handsome man, with dark, curly hair and a dimpled chin.
- Like Ruth, Arlett put on weight in mid-career, reaching 230 to 245 pounds by 1930. He lost some speed, and major league teams became somewhat wary of him because of this.

In any case, Arlett remained with Oakland until 1930, compiling consistently impressive batting statistics, and—like Ruth—continuing to pitch a game or two now and then and winning almost all of them until an ill-advised attempt to return regularly to the mound in 1929. From 1928 through 1930 he was a teammate of Hall of Famer Ernie Lombardi, who incidentally is listed in some sources as exactly the same height and weight as Arlett—6-3, 230. In 1929, when Lombardi hit .366 with 24 homers and 109 RBI, Arlett hit .374 with 39 and 189. In 1930, when Lombardi hit .370 with 22 homers and 105 RBI, Arlett hit .361 with 31 and 143. In fact, many if not most of Arlett's teammates in those years were players who had major league careers either before or after their years in the PCL.

In early 1930 Arlett was about to be sold to Brooklyn; according to Tomlinson's article, quoting contemporary sources, "the checkbook was on the table, fountain pen dripping." Arlett, however, got into a pushing contest with an umpire, Chet Chadbourne, who hit him below the eye with his mask, opening a cut under his eye. Brooklyn backed off, purchasing outfielder Ike Boone from another PCL team, and Ernie Lombardi from the Oaks.

At the end of that season, however, Arlett's chance finally came. The assumptions of the present are embedded in our language; there is no reason to believe that Arlett *wanted* to play in the majors, and it is very *unlikely* that he regarded his acquisition by a major league team as a "chance" which had "finally come". He probably saw it as the *end* of something—his wonderful career in Oak-

land—rather than the *beginning* of a major league career. In any case, the Philadelphia Phillies purchased Arlett after the 1930 season.

Arlett opened 1931 hitting very well. Again according to Tomlinson, a reporter later recalled that Arlett "gave promise of earning top ranking as the most valuable 'rookie' of the year, but injuries and advancing years took their toll. By the middle of August, Arlett had lost his regular place in the Phillies' lineup and served only as a pinch hitter for the balance of the year." Again, the present is being projected onto the past; the concept of a "rookie" was not a common part of the baseball vernacular in 1931, and I doubt that anyone at the time thought of Arlett as a rookie, or gave any thought to who the most valuable rookie would be. The Phillies moved Chuck Klein to left field, putting Arlett in right. Arlett hit .324 through August 9, then had a very brief slump, after which he was benched and Doug Taitt went into left field, Klein back to right. From the usage patterns it looks as if Arlett was nursing an injury of some sort from mid-August to mid-September.

In any case, Arlett wound up the year hitting .313 with 18 homers, 72 RBI and a .538 slugging percentage, fifth best in the league. Since he never played in the majors again, those are his major league totals. Among the thousands of major league players who had only one season, Arlett had the *best* one season. His career batting average and slugging percentage are better than most Hall of Famers.

At this time major league and minor league teams often made trades. The Phillies traded Arlett to the Baltimore Orioles of the International League—Babe Ruth's old team, although Jack Dunn was dead by then. On May 5, 1932, Arlett hit a home run that cleared the fence, cleared the street, broke through a window and hit a 45-year-old woman playing bridge in the head. On June 1, 1932, Arlett hit four home runs in a game. On the Fourth of July, he did it again—four more homers in one game. By early July he had 44 home runs, but suffered a shoulder injury and wound up with 54, leading the International League. Arlett also led the league that year in RBI (144) and runs scored (141), hitting .339. He played a second year with the Orioles, again leading the International League in home runs (39) and runs scored (135); he hit .343 and drove in 146 runs. (The International League played seasons of normal length.)

In 1934, playing for Birmingham (South-

ern League) and then Minneapolis (American Association), Arlett hit 48 more homers and drove in 155 runs in 151 games. In the second week of spring training, 1935, according to the 1936 *Spalding Guide*, Arlett "suffered a torn ring finger of the left hand, and part of the member had to be amputated." Starting late and minus part of a finger, Arlett hit .360 with 101 RBI and 122 games.

Arlett retired in 1937, stopped by injuries and age. In the movie *Bull Durham*, Crash Davis breaks the career record for home runs by a minor league player, with a figure in the low 200s. The man who in fact holds that record is Buzz Arlett, with 432 minor league home runs (unless you count Hector Espino of the Mexican League, which some people do and some people don't. Espino hit 484.) All but seven of those 432 homers were hit in the best minor leagues, the leagues that would now be considered Triple-A. He hit 251 homers in the Pacific Coast League, a record.

Persons familiar with Arlett's story inevitably wonder how good a player he would have been had his career been in the majors, rather than in the minors. This is a biography, not an evaluation, but there can be no reasonable doubt that he was a very good player, and would have had an outstanding major league career. Since Arlett competed side by side with many major leaguers in three leagues over a period of almost twenty years, it is not difficult to evaluate how he compares to those players. That he did play one year in the majors makes it even easier. In my opinion Arlett would have hit, as a major league player, somewhere between .290 and .315 for his career, depending on which park and which part of his career. Obviously, he was not Babe Ruth, but he was probably as good a player as some of the marginal Hall of Fame outfielders, including Chuck Klein, Hack Wilson and Heinie Manush. He may have been as good as Goose Goslin, but probably was not.

But while he was not Babe Ruth, I am struck by how firm many of the parallels to Babe Ruth are. He was Babe Ruth, only

1. he was in the minors, rather than the majors,
2. he was on the West Coast, rather than the East, and
3. he came along four years later.

Arlett was born in California in 1899, four years after the birth of Babe Ruth. He entered baseball in 1918, four years after Ruth broke in with Baltimore. Like Ruth, he was initially a pitcher, and a tremendous one. Like Ruth, he had a "transition season" when he moved to the outfield. Ruth's transition year was 1919; Arlett's 1923. Like Ruth, he attained his greatest fame as an outfielder. Like Ruth, he was a friendly, outgoing man who liked to have a drink and was free with his money. Ruth's career home run record was broken in the first days of the 1974 season; Arlett's record, if you consider Espino a minor leaguer, was broken in the last days of the 1977 season.

Arlett returned to Minneapolis after his retirement, running a restaurant/tavern until his retirement. Again quoting Tomlinson's article:

> In the summer of 1946 . . . Buzz Arlett had a gala "day" in Oakland. He arrived from Minneapolis at Oakland's Sixteenth Street Station aboard the City of San Francisco. On August 11 he was given a breakfast at the Hotel Leamington. That afternoon the Oaks played the San Diego Padres in a doubleheader. The fans turned out 12,000 strong at the old Emeryville ballpark, presented him with a new Ford convertible between games, and capped it off with a standing ovation for the player the Oakland Tribune dubbed "the mightiest Oak of them all."

Arlett died in Minneapolis in 1964, almost forgotten by the public, like the prince of a once-great nation reduced by time to a province. The work of members of the Society for American Baseball Research has reconstructed his career and salvaged his image to some extent, but in writing this article I am struck by how *little* we actually know about him. The statistical record exists and some other little pieces of information, but the anecdotal record is as barren now as it was at the time of his death. The series of quotes and quirks, the testament and apocrypha which can be put together for anyone from Max Carey to Riggs Stephenson to Howard Ehmke, simply does not exist for Arlett, or rather remains buried on the microfilm and in the memories of men near death. I would hope that our work has just begun, and that ten years from now the record would be a great deal more complete.

Harold Arlin, announcer of the first baseball game broadcast on the radio, the game broadcast on KDKA (Pittsburgh) from Forbes Field on August 5, 1921. Arlin at the time was a twenty-six year old man who worked for Westinghouse by days and broadcast nights and on weekends. According to *Voices of the Game,* Arlin was also the first man to broadcast a tennis match, the first man to broadcast a football game and the first man to broadcast game scores over the radio.

Steve Arlin, a pitcher who led the National League in losses in 1971 and 1972.

In 1966 the Phillies signed Arlin out of Ohio State for a bonus of $108,000. Part of his deal with the Phillies was that he would be allowed to continue going to dental school in the off-season. The lack of spring training interfered with his minor league performance. He was 5-15 in the minors in 1967 and '68, after which the Phillies let him go to the Padres in the Expansion draft. He posted a nifty 6.10 ERA for Salt Lake City in 1970, so the Padres brought him to the majors.

In 1972, despite leading the league in losses, Arlin pitched a series of spectacular games, including two one-hitters and three two-hitters. One of the one-hitters wasn't official, because he was lifted for a pinch hitter in the eleventh inning, with the score tied 0-0. Against Philadelphia on July 18 Arlin pitched no-hit ball for eight and two-thirds innings, losing the no-hitter on a bloop single by Denny Doyle over the head of third baseman Dave Roberts, who was in guarding against the bunt. Manager Don Zimmer second-guessed himself about Roberts' positioning.

"I bleeped it up," Zimmer told Phil Collier (*TSN*). "I had Dave [Roberts] playing shallow on the first two strikes because I was afraid Doyle might bunt or hit a swinging bunt. When Arlin got two strikes on Doyle, Roberts wanted to back up to a normal position, but I made him stay in close. If we play him normal, Steve gets his no-hitter." Zimmer handed Arlin a razor. "Here," he said, pointing to his throat. "Just make it quick."

Arlin's control wasn't particularly good, and, as noted by John Thorn and John Holway in *The Pitcher,* neither was his luck:

> Not every victory is deserved, nor is every defeat. In 1972 Steve Arlin of the Padres put together a string of seventy-one innings in which he gave up only thirty-three hits. Yet he lost twenty-one games that year after losing nineteen the year before. No wonder he went into dentistry.

Tony Armas, outfielder with three American League teams in the 1970s and '80s.

Antonio Rafael Armas was born in Anzoatequi, Venezuela on July 2, 1953, one of fourteen children. He had ten brothers, one of whom (Marcos, a younger brother) played in the A's system. Tony was signed by the Pittsburgh Pirates in 1971, and spent six years in the Pirate system, playing four games for the major league team in 1976.

The Pirates had an outfield of Al Oliver, Dave Parker and Omar Moreno, and so included Armas with several other prospects in a nine-player trade with the Oakland A's. The A's lost virtually their entire team in the first wave of free agency, and were collecting prospects. One of the other prospects coming over in the trade, Mitchell Page, was *The Sporting News* Rookie of the Year, but the A's lost 98 games in 1977, 93 games in 1978 and 108 in 1979. Armas joined cheerfully in the struggles, playing about half the time and hitting below .250. He was frequently injured, struck out a lot and had a reputation for making mistakes.

On the other hand, Armas as a player had three huge positives: he had power, he had a great throwing arm, and he played hard. Billy Martin was hired to manage the A's in 1980. Martin recognized in Armas a player with untapped potential, and developed a program to get it out of him. Martin stayed with him, day in and day out, mistake in and mistake out. Hitting coach Felipe Alou convinced Armas to switch to a lighter bat, and moved him back off the plate and deeper in the batter's box. On July 5, 1980, *The Sporting News* suggested that the A's outfield might be the best in baseball, a suggestion that over the next two years would become gospel—Armas, Rickey Henderson, Dwayne Murphy. Billy Martin said that "if Henderson and Murphy aren't named to the All-Star team, there shouldn't be any All-Star team." Armas, although leading the team in homers and RBI, was a third leg.

Just after the All-Star break Armas hit four homers in four games against the Angels. In the next series, against the Tigers, he drove in four runs in a game with a homer and a triple. In another game of the same series he dropped a fly ball, but picked the ball off the ground and nailed the runner going for second. In the next series, against Cleveland, he hit two tape-measure homers in a single game. That period—the two weeks after the 1980 All-Star game—marked Armas' emergence as a star. Rumors began to circulate that he was using a corked bat, but he was never caught with one, and the rumors were probably based on nothing other than his rapid improvement. In a game against Kansas City on September 20, 1980, Armas hit two homers, two doubles, drove in five runs, was intentionally walked and stole third base. He wound up at .279 with 35 homers, 109 RBI, and 17 baserunner kills. The A's improved by

29 games, moving from last in the division to second place. Eight voters found room for Armas on their MVP ballots.

In 1981 the A's broke from the gate like a busload of starving teenagers descending on the Golden Arches. They started out 11-0 and were 18-3 by the end of April. Armas had the hottest bat, winning the American League Player of the Week Award twice in a row. In the 21 April games he hit .329 with seven doubles, seven homers and 23 RBI. On May 5, 1981, Armas was on the cover of *The Sporting News*.

By May 7 Armas had nine homers and 25 RBI. Two weeks later, playing every day, he still had nine homers and 25 RBI. A headline in *The Sporting News* of June 6: Plunging A's Seek Help. Billy Martin was involved in a series of wild confrontations with the umpires and the league. A fan called the switchboard, and threatened Martin's life. By early June the A's five-game lead had shrunk to a game and a half, and then just like that the schedule was halted by a two-month strike, and the A's were awarded a title (if you haven't got a whole pennant, a ha'pennant will do.) Armas tied for the league lead in homers (22), and was second in RBI (76). He played in the All-Star game, and finished fourth in the MVP voting, one ballot placing him first. *The Sporting News* selected him the American League Player of the Year.

On June 12, 1982, with Rick Langford on the mound, Armas had eleven putouts and twelve total chances in a game, both establishing major league records for a right fielder (the twelfth chance was an assist.) He also had a single and a triple and drove in two runs, including the game-winner. It was a memorable game in the midst of a forgettable year, for in 1982 the inevitable happened: Billy Martin's ball of string unravelled. Armas slipped to .233 and went back to the Disabled List, although he still hit 28 homers and drove in 89 runs. The A's lost 94 games. The A's started over. On December 6, 1982, Armas was traded to the Boston Red Sox in exchange for Carney Lansford.

The Red Sox put Armas in center field, and installed him as the cleanup hitter. Armas started the year hitting about .150, and asked Red Sox manager Ralph Houk to be taken out of the cleanup spot. "You're my cleanup hitter," Houk told him. "You'll be fine."

Some of the fans had other ideas, and began to boo. "I don't know why they boo," Armas told Joe Giuliotti, "but it's only a small group. The majority are good fans who are pulling for me." He finished at .218 but hit 36 homers and drove in over a hundred. He had fallen into the habit of trying to pull every pitch. In spring training, 1984, Armas worked with Walt Hriniak on hitting the ball straight-away. On April 28, 1984, Armas hit a 500-foot home run off of Tom Seaver, only the sixth ball ever hit into the center field bleachers at Comiskey Park. He wound up 1984 with his finest statistical season, hitting .268 and leading the league in homers (43) and RBI (123). He was named to the All-Star team, although he did not play, and finished seventh in the MVP voting.

Ralph Houk said that Armas was as tough a player as he had ever managed, a fairly remarkable statement when you consider the players that Houk managed. His successor, John McNamara, reiterated this and extolled Armas's less evident virtues, calling him the best baserunner on the team, and the best center fielder in the league. As he had been in Oakland, Armas in Boston was a part of what was recognized as the best outfield in baseball—Rice, Armas and Dwight Evans.

After 1984 he was never healthy and in the lineup for a full season. In 1986, when the Red Sox came within a hop of winning the World Series, Armas was limited to one at bat in the series because of a twisted ankle, giving Dave Henderson the chance to be a hero. After that season he was a free agent, and wandered into the collusion market with an injury rap. He didn't find a job until mid-season, 1987.

If this record seems a little devoid of personality, there is a reason for that. Armas is very quiet, and his knowledge of English appears to consist largely of ballplayers' cliches about looking for an opportunity to contribute and running out ground balls 100%. He was rarely interviewed, and has never been known to say anything quotable. His managers loved him, seeing him as an incarnation of the old-school virtues of playing hard and keeping your mouth shut. He played three years with the Angels as a fourth outfielder, and returned to his native Anzoatequi in Venezuela, where he resides today.

Ed Armbrister, who was involved in one of the greatest controversies in World Series history in 1975.

Armbrister, a native of the Bahamas, was a reserve outfielder for the Big Red Machine, used primarily as a pinch runner and defensive substitute.

In the third game of the 1975 World Series the score was tied in the tenth inning, a man on first and nobody out. Armbrister went up to pinch hit, with orders to bunt. The bunt bounced a few feet in front of the plate, and as catcher Carlton Fisk scrambled after it he collided with Armbrister in front of the plate. Fisk got to the ball late, made a hurried throw to second and threw it into center field, leaving runners at second and third, none out, bottom of the tenth inning. The Reds scored the run, won the game and won the series.

Fisk, heads up as always, appealed immediately to home plate umpire Larry Barnett, asking Barnett to call interference on Armbrister, which would declare Armbrister out and freeze the runner at first. Fisk was joined quickly by his manager, Darrell Johnson, and the umpires went into conference to determine whether the call should be made. Their decision: no interference. The play stands.

Controversy sparkled for months afterward about the call, and dispassionate observers disagree to this day, although the consensus is that Barnett blew the play. According to *Baseball by the Rules*, by Glen Waggoner, Kathleen Maloney, and Hugh Howard, "The argument raged . . . not only on the interpretation of the rule—but on *which* rule applied. Umpire Barnett did not refer specifically to any rule, either during or after the game. But he did talk about 'intent': if the runner had intentionally obstructed the fielder, said Barnett, then it would have been interference." Since Armbrister hadn't intended anything other than to go to first, Barnett figured there was no basis for an interference call.

There were, however, two rules which applied to the play, rule 7.08(b) and rule 7.09(1). At that time, neither rule said anything about intent. Rule 7.08(b) said that a *runner* was out if he "hinders a fielder attempting to make a play on a batted ball." There was disagreement, at the time, about whether Armbrister could be considered a "runner", but rule 7.09(1) said that a batter *or* a runner was out if he "fails to avoid a fielder who is attempting to field a batted ball."

Since the two rules say basically the same thing, you might ask, why do you need two rules? That's a good question. Rule 7.08 begins "Any runner is out when . . .", and includes this on a list with stuff like running out of the base line to avoid a tag, passing another runner and being struck by a hit ball in fair territory. Rule 7.09 says "It is interference by a batter or runner when . . .", and then attempts to imagine every way in which the batter or runner could interfere with the fielders, which actually is pretty entertaining.

Anyway, the umpires were of course defensive, and the league was so determined to prove they were right that the National League office, in the calm light of reason several weeks after the play, sent a letter to Leonard Koppett of *The Sporting News* citing a third rule which was obviously irrelevant to the play, but which had the advantage of citing intent. Koppett made fun of them, and the powers that be used their ultimate weapon: they changed the rule to prove they had been right all along. Rules 7.08 and 7.09 were both amended to specify intent, and a paragraph was inserted after rule 7.09 (1) to memorialize this play. The paragraph begins:

> When a catcher and batter-runner going to first base have contact when the catcher is fielding the ball, there is generally no violation and nothing should be called.

Charlie Armbruster, a catcher with the Red Sox in the first decade of this century.

Juan Armenteros, a pitcher with the Kansas City Monarchs in the early fifties.

Bill Armour, Ty Cobb's first major league manager and a pioneer of platooning.

Armour began his career as a player with Toledo in 1891, and managed several minor league clubs before signing to lead the Cleveland Blues of the American League in December, 1901. According to Franklin Lewis in *The Cleveland Indians,* "Armour had managed the Dayton team for several years and had been credited with the development of many stars, including Elmer Flick, Wiley Piatt, Earl Moore, and Gene Wright."

The Cleveland team had finished seventh in the American League's first major league season, 1901, winning only 55 games. The American League was an upstart league, signing players away from the established National League. The players were bound by a reserve clause, but the American League believed the clause to be unenforceable. In late April, 1902, the supreme court of the state of Pennsylvania upheld the reserve clause, making it impossible for the Philadelphia Athletics to retain three outstanding players that they had signed away from their crosstown rivals, the Phillies.

To avoid losing the players back to the National League, American League president Ban Johnson assigned their contracts to another team, without compensation to the A's, who were going to lose them anyway. Apparently Cleveland was selected because

a. Connie Mack owed the Cleveland owner a favor, and
b. The Blues were one of the weakest teams in the league.

Assigning three outstanding players to another team might have destroyed competitive balance; assigning them to Cleveland created it. The three players were Nap Lajoie, one of the greatest second basemen of all time, Elmer Flick, also a Hall of Famer, and Bill Bernhard, a big pitcher.

The Indians, guided by Armour, continued to collect quality players. They purchased Addie Joss, another Hall of Famer, from Toledo. They traded Candy LaChance for Piano Legs Hickman. Still, Armour was so desperate for pitching that he was forced to conduct an open tryout for semi-pro and amateur pitchers at League Park. He signed Otto Hess, who would have a ten-year career as a pitcher and outfielder. One day in August, according to Lewis, Armour was so hard pressed for a starter to oppose the Athletics and Rube Waddell that he took the advice of a ticket taker named Herman Schleman and pulled a novice pitcher named Charlie Smith out of the stands and put him on the mound. Smith beat Waddell, 5-4, and he, too, was on his way to a ten-year career.

The Indians moved up to fifth place. Napoleon Lajoie became so popular in Cleveland that the team became the "Naps". Lajoie and Armour became partners in the ownership of a cigar store, even though, by 1903, there was agitation in the press and among fans for Napoleon to take over Armour's job. The Naps moved up to third in 1903, and were the choice of many sportswriters to take the flag in 1904.

Armour, like countless other managers before and since, became a victim of the high expectations, including his own. The details of his resignation have become garbled by history, and if you'll pardon me I'm going to take a minute to try to straighten them out. Franklin Lewis' account is given below:

> The Naps continued to play .500 baseball until early September. The team had dropped to fifth place. Armour finally called on Somers.
> "I'm resigning, Charley," he told the vice-president on September 9. "This team doesn't want to be managed. Lajoie isn't aggressive although he's a great ball player. I'm through."
> Somers accepted the resignation. As team captain, Lajoie took over the field direction of

the team for the balance of the season and at the completion of the schedule he was given the permanent appointment as manager.

First question: if Armour resigned on September 9, why do all the Encyclopedias list him as continuing to manage all year? Apparently they just don't know what else to do with it, since Lajoie wasn't "officially" named manager until after the year. The 1905 *Reach Guide* confirms that Armour resigned with several weeks left in the season.

Lewis, however, gives the erroneous impression that the team was playing badly at the time. A generally excellent article about Nap Lajoie by Jim Murphy, published by the Society for American Baseball Research in 1988 as an edition of the *National Pastime,* also gives an inaccurate account of the season, apparently following Lewis' lead. In fact, despite constant injuries including the loss of shortstop Terry Turner for almost two months with an illness, and despite a terrible slump in June, the team was 66-53, thirteen games over .500, before September 9, and split a double-header on that day. Boston and New York were hot and had pulled away from the league, and the Naps had dropped to fifth place, but they were *not* in a slump. Armour, expecting more from his team, was disenchanted with the performance and quit—but his team was playing better ball at the time than they had ever played before.

In any case, in 1905 Armour became manager of the Detroit Tigers, seventh place finishers the previous year. He moved them up to third and, according to the 1906 *Spalding Guide,* "the biggest surprise of the year was the Detroit club." The most significant event of the season, though little noted at the time, was the late-season arrival of a brash rookie from Georgia named Ty Cobb. In his autobiography, Cobb wrote:

> After signing the contract, I met Bill Armour, the manager. He was a fashion plate, with an impressive walrus mustache, who never wore a uniform in the dugout. I thought he was one of the most elegant men I'd ever seen.

In a 1912 newspaper interview Cobb said that Armour "appeared to take a friendly interest in my progress and he helped me a lot." An off-season letter from Armour to Cobb is extant, which states in part that "you have a bright future in front of you if I am any judge of a ballplayer."

In 1906, the Tigers fell back into the second division. Armour made Cobb a regular, not without misgivings, but was unwilling, or unable, to deal with the turmoil that Cobb's presence was creating. Other players, including Sam Crawford, were sulking over salary squabbles. According to Charles C. Alexander, in his biography of Cobb, "Crawford was one of several on the team who thought they knew more about how to run things than Bill Armour did." The season concluded with Cobb brawling with teammate Ed Siever before the final game. Armour was discharged during the off-season.

What no one noticed in that dissension-racked 1906 season was that Armour had instituted one of the first platoon arrangements in the history of baseball. Two rookies, Charley "Boss" Schmidt and Fred Payne, and a veteran, Jack Warren, shared the catching, with the right-handed hitting Payne getting the call against southpaw hurlers, and the switch-hitting Schmidt or lefty-swinging Warner standing in against right-handers. Although teams had experimented briefly with platooning as much as twenty years earlier, this was, so far as I know, the first twentieth-century platoon arrangement, and also the first time a platoon combination was used for an entire season. The strategy was popularized eight years later, when George Stallings platooned at several positions, leading the Miracle Braves to the World Championship.

Armour never again managed in the majors. He scouted for the St. Louis Cardinals for a year, managed in Toledo and Kansas City, and was for a time part-owner of the Milwaukee team in the American Association. He was out of baseball and living in Minneapolis when he died of a stroke in 1922.

(—M. K. and B.J.)

Alfred (Buddy) Armour, outfielder with the St. Louis Stars and other teams in the Negro Leagues, 1936–1947.

George Armstrong, President and Chief of Operations for the Seattle Mariners under George Argyros (see Argyros).

Herbert E. Armstrong, longtime business manager of the Baltimore Orioles, retired in 1972. He was also president of the Oriole foundation, a civic support operation funded by the Orioles.

Louis Armstrong, jazz great, who in 1931 sponsored a New Orleans baseball team called "Armstrong's Secret Nine."

TRACERS

[Rube] Waddell could throw the ball harder than any other pitcher of his era; his ability to strike out batters was exceeded only by his passion for liquor and for relaxation in general. A man who knew him when he played for the St. Louis Browns, from 1908 to 1910, recalls that Waddell took a bottle of bourbon to bed with him on an overnight train ride from Cleveland back to St. Louis, finished before he got up, and pitched a shutout against the visiting Detroit Tigers that afternoon . . .

—John Lardner. "That Was Baseball: The Crime of Shufflin' Phil Douglas." *The New Yorker,* May 12, 1956, Page 136+.

A quick check of *Total Baseball* confirms that Waddell was with the Browns from 1908 to 1910. But he only made two starts in 1910, neither of which were shutouts, so we can narrow it down to 1908 or 1909.

The 1910 *Reach Guide* lists all the shutouts of 1909; Waddell threw five of them, including three in a row in late May. However, I checked all five in the *New York Times,* and each followed a home game (or, in one case, a home rainout). And none involved Cleveland one day and Detroit the next.

The 1909 Guide does *not* list the shutouts pitched in 1908, so was of no help, so I checked the 1908 Guide for a schedule of that season. Again, the story above has the Browns playing in Cleveland one day, then returning to St. Louis overnight to play the Tigers. According to the schedule in the guide, that was supposed to happen on September 12 and 13.

Waddell did start for the Browns on the 13th. He ran into trouble in the first inning. Matty McIntyre singled to lead off the game, and after two were out, Ty Cobb tripled him in. Waddell got Claude Rossman to end the inning, but the damage had been done. Rube wasn't to pitch a shutout that day. Following the first inning, however, Waddell threw scoreless ball for *ten consecutive innings.* What's more, in the bottom of the second he singled in the tying run. Syd Smith's single in the bottom of the eleventh finally won the game for St. Louis, 2-1.

So Waddell didn't pitch a shutout, but it *was* an impressive performance. Especially if he'd gotten totally soused the night before.

—Rob Neyer

Mike Armstrong, relief pitcher of the 1980s.

Armstrong, a first round draft pick in 1974, got his first shot at a major league job with San Diego in 1980, and surfaced as a major league pitcher with Kansas City in 1982. For two years he was Dan Quisenberry's setup man, and very effective in the role.

On July 18, 1983, in a game eventually won by the Blue Jays, George Brett ripped an apparent triple down the right field line at Exhibition Stadium, scoring U.L. Washington. According to *The Sporting News* Armstrong, "sitting in the visitors' bullpen, fielded the ball, assuming it was foul. Umpire Bill Kunkel, slightly dumbfounded by this turn of events, halted play and returned Brett to second base and Washington to third."

"I told George I would have thrown him out at third anyway," Armstrong cracked.

After the 1983 season Armstrong was traded to the Yankees for Steve Balboni. He signed a four-year contract with the Yankees, but developed elbow trouble in 1984, and Steinbrenner filed a grievance with the commissioner, claiming that Armstrong was injured at the time of the trade. When his plea was rejected Steinbrenner trashed Armstrong, sending him to Columbus for most of the four years. Armstrong earned the respect of his teammates and the media for handling a difficult situation with as much grace as possible. He left baseball in 1987.

Harry Arndt, second-line ballplayer for various teams in the 1900's.

From *The Detroit Evening News* for July 3, 1902:

> Another feature [of the game] was the debut of Harry Arndt, the Lajoie of the State League. In spite of a strained position at the bat, he hit the ball and on one occasion he raised it almost to the clubhouse when there were two on bases. He fielded perfectly and made one fine catch which included a head spin. Arndt looks very much as though he will do, and although he does not stand very gracefully at the bat, what difference does it make if he stands on his head so long as he clouts the sphere?

Arndt lasted only ten games with Detroit before being sold to Baltimore. After a stint in the American Association he left organized baseball to play in the outlaw Tri-State League, being coaxed back by the Cardinals in 1905. After two years and a few games with the Cardinals he was released, and returned to the Tri-State outlaws. He was active in professional baseball as a minor league player and manager for several years after that.

Arndt died of tuberculosis at the age of 43.
(—M. K.)

Orie Edgar (Old Folks) Arntzen, longtime minor league pitcher who had one season with the Philadelphia A's during World War II.

Arntzen was named Minor League Player of the Year in 1949, when he won 25 games and lost only two for Albany in the Eastern League. He was 40 years old when the honor came. Arntzen played organized baseball from 1931 through 1953.

Chris Arnold, a minor player with the San Francisco Giants in the seventies. Arnold, an intense man, was a utility player in the truest sense of the term; at one time or another he caught, played the outfield, and played every infield position. Although Arnold hit .343 for Phoenix in 1971 he could never get enough major league at bats to build his offensive skills, and ended his career with three seasons in Japan.

Dorothy Arnold, actress and first wife of Joe DiMaggio.

Joe Arnold, head baseball coach at Florida University.

Paul Arnold, outfielder with the Newark Dodgers (Negro Leagues), 1934–1935.

Rick Arnold, a scout for the Baltimore Orioles.

Tony Arnold, briefly a pitcher with the Baltimore Orioles in the mid-eighties. Arnold, whose best pitch was a sinker, was in the Dodger system as recently as 1989.

Morrie (Snooker) Arnovich, outfielder with the Phillies in the late thirties.

Arnovich grew up in Wisconsin, and attended Superior State Teacher's College before entering baseball. In 1934 he led the Northern League in batting, hitting .374 with excellent power. After two more strong minor

league seasons he earned a late-season shot with the Phillies in 1936, hitting .313. He became a regular the next year.

In 1939 Arnovich, who was Jewish, made the N.L. All-Star team after hitting .375 for the first half of the year, but saw no action. In *The Philadelphia Phillies,* Fred Lieb and Stan Baumgartner report that

> even though Gabby Hartnett, the National League manager, had four occasions to use a pinch-hitter, he always looked the other way from Morrie . . . Jewish fans in Philadelphia and New York never forgave Gabby and booed him as long as he remained in the National League.

Arnovich didn't run well and was probably heavier than the 168 pounds at which he is usually listed. He was traded to Cincinnati midway through a sub-par 1940 season, and then to the New York Giants in '41. Arnovich was called for a draft physical in 1941, but failed the physical due to bad teeth. Hearing suggestions that he was a draft dodger, Arnovich popped out his false teeth for the benefit of reporters.

As the war heated up the Army became less picky, and Arnovich spent three years in the service. He played one game for the Giants after the war, and died in Wisconsin at the age of 48.

(—R.N. and B.J.)

Brad Arnsberg, contemporary pitcher in the Texas Rangers system.

Jerry Arrigo, pitcher in the sixties.

In spring training, 1961, Arrigo impressed Twins manager Cookie Lavagetto with "a big-league arm, [and the] best curve and fastball in camp." He debuted on June 12, his twentieth birthday, but was knocked out of the game in the second inning.

He spent most of that season and the next two in the minors. With Dallas-Fort Worth in 1963, Arrigo was suspended for a good part of the season for refusing to fly in what he called "an airplane that didn't look safe to me."

Arrigo made the majors in '64, and had his best season in 1968 with Cincinnati, pitching 205 innings with a 12-10 record.

Fernando Arroyo, a pitcher with three American League teams from 1975 through 1982, plus one appearance in 1986.

Arroyo signed with the Tigers in 1970, and got a trial with the Tigers late in 1975. He pitched fairly well, and at the end of spring training in 1976 was so confident of making

the team that he hired someone to drive his car from Florida back to Detroit. Pushed aside by the phenomenal development of Mark Fidrych, he was devastated to be sent to Evansville. "I saw the opportunities they were giving some other people, like Lerrin LaGrow and Dave Lemancyzk," Arroyo told *The Sporting News,* "and I wondered what was going on. I began to wonder if maybe it was something personal." He made the team in 1977, and when Vern Ruhle was ineffective in May, Ralph Houk called Arroyo aside and told him he was in the rotation.

Arroyo started out brilliantly, winning five of his first eight decisions. He threw a sinking fastball that tailed in on a right-handed hitter, and had excellent control. He pitched very well through the end of July, posting a 3.25 ERA in 144 innings, but suffered a series of tough losses. He began to press, trying to be perfect. Beginning with a start in Minnesota on August 3, when he failed to retire a single hitter, he was belted around over the last two months, winding up 8-18 with a 4.18 ERA.

Arroyo started the 1978 season in the minors, where he would be for most of the next ten years. The Tigers traded him to Minnesota, and he pitched fairly well for the Twins in 1980 and 1981, He stayed with it for several years after that, even going to the Mexican League in 1984 and 1985 to keep his career alive, then back to Class A ball to earn an opportunity.

At one point in 1977 Arroyo was the senior man in the Tiger rotation, at the age of 25; the rotation was Fidrych, Rozema, Sykes and Arroyo. The story of Fidrych is well known, and the story of the other three men is exactly the same. After pitching brilliantly for a short period of time, all four battled for many years to revitalize their careers, and none was ever successful.

Luis Arroyo, relief ace of the 1961 Yankees.

A native of Puerto Rico, Arroyo broke into professional baseball in 1948 with Greenville, a class D ballclub in the Cardinal chain. Arroyo spent years in the minors; he could throw hard, at that time, but had little control. In the Carolina League in 1949 he won 21 games and struck out 228 men. In 1954, with Houston of the Texas League, he pitched a no-hitter against Dallas. He made the majors in 1955, still as a starting pitcher, and won eleven games for the 1955 Cardinals.

Traded to the Pirates early in 1956, Arroyo spent the next four years splitting time between Pittsburgh, Cincinnati, and those teams' top farm clubs. Thirty-two years old, he spent the 1959 season pitching mop-up relief for Havana in the International League, at one point becoming so discouraged that he quit baseball and went home for two weeks. By this time, however, he had come up with a screwball, and also earned the friendship of Ralph Houk, then a coach with the Yankees. Houk had managed Arroyo one year with San Juan in the Puerto Rican winter league. "He was a great help to me there, and not just pitching," recalled Houk in *Season of Glory*. "I had a coach named Luis Olmo, an old Dodger outfielder, and he'd [translate] what I'd say in meetings, and so on. One day Arroyo came to me and said, 'Skip, watch out. That guy might be trying to get your job.' "

Arroyo pitched brilliantly for Havana in '59, posting a 1.15 ERA in 41 games. Early in the 1960 season the franchise had to be moved to Jersey City, which turned out to be another break for Arroyo, since it made it easier for the Yankees to scout him. A Yankee scout, Bill Skiff, saw him pitch several times, and turned in a good report on him. Ryne Duren was on the disabled list, and the Yankees needed help in the bullpen. On the recommendations of Skiff and Houk, the Yankees acquired Arroyo. He pitched well for the rest of the season, earning seven saves with a 5-1 record and an ERA below three, and made a brief appearance in the Series. Casey Stengel, of course, had a comment: Imagine finding a guy as good as him lying around dead somewhere.

With the help of Johnny Sain, Arroyo's control of his screwball improved. Early in 1961 the Yankees had to file a list of eighteen players they could protect from the expansion draft. To the surprise of everyone they protected Arroyo, letting Bobby Shantz go instead.

In 1961 Arroyo was the best relief pitcher in baseball, and a major contributor to a dream season. He saved twenty-nine games, and set an American League record (since broken) for relief wins, with fifteen. Whitey Ford had his greatest season, and Arroyo received a great deal of the credit—probably a disproportionate share—for saving Ford. Ford was 16-2 by the time of the second All-Star game. "I'll have a great season," he told reporters, "if Luis Arroyo's arm holds out." After winning twenty games Ford was presented several gifts on the field, one of them a huge, man-sized roll of Life Savers. Arroyo, of course, was hidden in the roll. At the

award banquet accepting the Cy Young Award, Ford announced that for his nine-minute speech he would speak for seven minutes and let Arroyo finish the last two, which he did.

Ford grew tired of the gag, which he felt was depriving him of credit for what he had accomplished; probably he began to tire of it about the time that Bob Feller wrote a magazine article suggesting that rather than individual pitchers going into the Hall of Fame, perhaps Ford and Arroyo could go in as a team.

Arroyo was a short, heavy-set man who looked nothing at all like an athlete. When he reported to the Yankees in 1960 the security guard refused to let him in the clubhouse. In the books he is listed at 5'8½", 178 pounds, but in fact he weighed more than 200. He was very neat, a nice-looking man with graying hair who wore good suits and Panama hats and smoked big cigars; Ralph Houk said he looked and acted like a guy who might own a bank somewhere. Dan Topping called him The Bartender. Despite this he was a good hitter, a lifetime .227 hitter. He spoke fluent English, and managed his money well.

After the 1961 season the Yankees asked Arroyo not to play winter ball, to save his arm. Arroyo told Hamey that he had been pitching winter ball and summer ball all his life and never had a sore arm, but Hamey wouldn't listen. Ralph Houk stood up for him, arguing that Luis needed to pitch to stay in shape, but Hamey wouldn't listen; he paid Arroyo $8,000, his winter salary, to take the winter off. Arroyo laid around the house that winter, eating and drinking and getting fat and lazy. When he reported to spring training in 1962 his arm had no snap. The Yankees went to Detroit in mid-April; it was very cold. Arroyo pitched in a game, but woke up at three in the morning, his arm screaming in pain. He couldn't lift the arm. He battled it for a year and a half, but his career was over.

Arroyo remained active in baseball. He was a manager and general manager for two years in Mexico, then was hired to scout for the Yankees, which he still does. He has two sons, one a dentist and the other an architect, and lives to this day in Puerto Rico, on the farm where he was born.

Rudy Arroyo, who pitched nine games for the '71 Cardinals.

Sal Artiaga, Commissioner of the National Association (the minor leagues).

Karl Artman, a sportswriter in Selma, Alabama, who conceived of and founded the National Hot Stove League.

Harry Arundel, sometime starting pitcher for Pittsburgh in the American Association in 1882.

Tug Arundel, a nineteenth-century catcher with a lifetime .173 batting average, and the kind of defensive reputation that you need to hit .173. His major league career was brief, but he was cited as late as 1914 (*Reach Guide*) as one of the best defensive catchers of the 1800s.

Randy Asadoor, who played briefly for San Diego in 1986.

Bob (Asby) Asbjornson, a catcher of the 1920s and 30s.
According to Lee Allen's *The Cincinnati Reds* (page 213):

> There was a young catcher on the [1932] team named Bob Asbjornson, who came from Concord, Massachusetts. When the Reds visited Boston one afternoon, his fellow townsmen decided to give him a "day." Remembering the experience of Bill Wysong the year before, the Reds wondered what would be in store for Asbjornson.

> Wysong, a starting pitcher, had been hammered on his "day" in 1931, losing the game 18-zip.

> As it turned out, his "day" was even more fantastic than Wysong's. Bob did his part, hitting the only home run of his National League career that afternoon. But something had apparently gone wrong with the plans of the committee of people from Concord. Bob was called to home plate and given a substantial check, but after the game he noted that no one had bothered to sign it. Then a party was scheduled for a Boston hotel after the contest, and when Asbjornson went there, he found that none of the guests had showed up. So, if anything, he suffered more on the day he was to be honored than did Wysong, though he was not stung with an 18-to-0 defeat.

Total Baseball lists Asbjornson's name as "Casper" Asbjornson, and says that he changed his name to "Asby". He batted only 221 times in the major leagues.

Gord Ash, Assistant General Manager of the Toronto Blue Jays.
Ash, a native of Toronto, wanted to get into baseball so much that he quit a job as a

bank executive to work in a ticket booth with the fledgling Blue Jays. After a year he switched jobs, being assigned to oversee the maintenance of the field. In the early eighties he got the job of player personnel administrator, from which he graduated to being Pat Gillick's assistant. Now 39 years old, Ash plays a lead role in negotiating contracts for the Blue Jays, although club persident Paul Beeston does most of the talking when the contracts get into seven figures.

Ash's innovations have included a nutritional program under which the Blue Jays pay half the cost of the meals for their farm hands if the players will eat balanced meals at specified restaurants, and a program borrowed from the military to teach concentration skills. (This item based on an article in *Scorebook* magazine, the Blue Jays' superb program/magazine. I have also dealt briefly with Ash in contract negotiations.)

Ken Ash, a minor pitcher with the Reds in the late twenties, who owns the distinction of throwing perhaps the single most effective relief pitch in baseball history.

At Redland Field on July 27, 1930, the Reds were trailing 3-2 in the top of the sixth inning and the Cubs, with Dan Taylor on first, Hack Wilson on third and none out, were threatening to extend their lead. Reds Manager Dan Howley called the right-hander Ash from the bullpen to replace Larry Benton, although with Charlie Grimm at the plate this gave the Cubs the platoon advantage.

Ash's first pitch was high and outside, but Grimm swung, slapping a grounder to shortstop Hod Ford. Wilson headed home, but for some unknown reason stopped running about halfway. Ford threw the ball to third baseman Tony Cuccinello, who threw to catcher Clyde Sukeforth; Sukeforth ran down Wilson and tagged him near third. Meanwhile, Grimm had put his head down and was digging for second, having not specifically observed that Taylor was still occupying that base. He finally did look up, reversed his direction and headed back to first, but wasn't able to beat Sukeforth's throw to first baseman Joe Stripp, and there were two out.

Taylor made a break for third, and you can guess what happened. Stripp made a perfect throw to Cuccinello, and the Reds had a triple play, 6-5-2-3-5.

Ash was pinch-hit for leading off the bottom of the inning, and the Reds scored four runs to take the lead, which they held. So for

Ash, it was one pitch, one inning, and one victory, one of his six in the major leagues.
(—R.N.)

Richie Ashburn, center fielder for the Whiz Kids of 1950, a two-time National League batting champion, and now nearing the end of his third decade as a Philadelphia broadcaster.

Don Richard Ashburn was born in Tilden, Nebraska on March 19, 1927. The son of a blacksmith and small-town businessman, Richie showed unusual athletic ability from an early age, starring in basketball at the Tilden public school (there was only one, for all ages.) Playing in the local summer leagues from the age of eight, Ashburn was such an outstanding player as a kid that, according to a 1956 article in the *Saturday Evening Post*, it was "taken for granted by the folks in Tilden that Richie Ashburn would be a major-league ballplayer." His father, afraid that Richie would get hurt and ruin his baseball career, prohibited him from playing football until he weighed 150 pounds, and by the time he reached that level the school had dropped the football program because of World War II shortages.

When Richie was sixteen a Cleveland scout mailed him a contract, which was prohibited; Commissioner Landis summoned

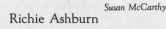

Susan McCarthy
Richie Ashburn

the wunderkind to Chicago to give evidence, and fined the Indians $500. (The reason it was illegal for the Indians to offer a contract to the sixteen-year-old Ashburn in 1943, but legal for the Reds to pitch the fifteen-year-old Joe Nuxhall in 1944 is that Nuxhall was a Cincinnati native, and so could play professionally without interrupting his education.)

After graduating from high school in 1944, Ashburn was signed to a contract by the legendary scout Cy Slapnicka, then working for the Cubs; he was to report to Nashville in the Southern League. The Ashburns, however, had negotiated a clause specifying that Richie was to receive a share of the purchase price if he was sold to a major league team. Such clauses were prohibited by 1944 (see Luke Appling), and the contract was declared invalid. Feeling a little snakebit, Ashburn enrolled at Norfolk Junior College, where he earned an Elementary Teacher's Certificate. The scouts continued to follow him, and Ashburn signed with the Philadelphia Phillies for a bonus of $3,500.

Ashburn began his professional career (finally) with the Utica Blue Sox in 1945, playing for Eddie Sawyer. As an amateur Ashburn had been a catcher, but after seventeen pro games behind the mask Sawyer moved him to the outfield to save his legs; his speed was one of his best assets. He hit .312 for Utica in 1945, spent a year in the Army, mostly in Alaska, came back to Utica in 1947 and hit .362; Ashburn, Sawyer, Stan Lopata and Granny Hamner led Utica to a rout of the Eastern League race. Invited to spring training with the Phillies in 1948, Ashburn had no real prospect of making the team. The Phillies' center field was Harry (the Hat) Walker, a very similar player to Ashburn—a left-handed singles hitter with speed. And Harry the Hat had hit .363 in the *National* League in '47.

Harry, however, hung his hat at home in spring training; he held out. Ashburn, noted since age eight for going full-bore from beginning to end, got a chance to show what he could do. Ted Williams, seeing him in an exhibition game, called him "Put-Put" because he ran as if he had twin motors in his pants. Walker had a minor injury coming out of spring training, and never got his job back. Beginning on May 9, 1948, Ashburn hit safely in 23 consecutive games, at that time a record for an NL rookie. For the season he hit .333, second in the league to Stan Musial, led the league in stolen bases and walked almost three times as often as he struck out; no rookie since then has hit for as high an average as a regular. His season ended in late August when he broke a finger sliding into second base, but *The Sporting News* still named him Rookie of the Year (the BBWAA chose Alvin Dark).

And the team began to improve. The Phillies for almost thirty years had been near the bottom of the National League; this is part of why Ashburn had signed with them. When William D. Cox was shown the door by Judge Landis and the Carpenter family bought the team, the Phils could offer a young player the best of both worlds—a short path to the major leagues, because the team was bad, but the prospect of being a part of a good team. When Eddie Sawyer was brought up to manage the team in late July, 1948, that dream began to materialize.

It must have been a wonderful thing to be a part of, this building of a team. In his first two years in the majors, Richie's parents came to Philadelphia and ran a family-style boarding house for several of the Phillies' young players. Curt Simmons lived there, and Robin Roberts; the house broke up when the boys started to marry and set up their own homes. In November, 1949, Richie married Herberta Cox, a Nebraska farm girl whom he had met at Norfolk Junior College; her first professional ball game was seeing Richie play in the 1948 All-Star game in St. Louis.

Ashburn didn't have a good season in 1949. "It was my own fault," he told a reporter. "I reported to spring training with a swelled head and a 'big-shot' attitude." The defenses adjusted to him, swinging around to left field since Ashburn rarely pulled the ball. I'm making it sound worse than it was; he had 188 hits in 1949, and the Phillies finished with 81 wins, their best record since 1917 (see Grover Cleveland Alexander, 1990 *Baseball Book*.)

Still, few people thought the Phillies' young players could do much better in 1950. In a poll of the BBWAA in the spring of 1950, 145 of 194 writers picked the Brooklyn Dodgers to defend their championship; the Phillies were picked fourth. With a core of young players signed at the end of the war—the "Whiz Kids"—and the help of an MVP season from a veteran reliever named Jim Konstanty, the Phillies battled for the top spot evenly with three other teams over the first half of the season; on July 17 the Dodgers were in fourth place, one game out of first. Almost everyone still expected the Dodgers to win it, but on July 25, Roberts and Bubba Church threw a double shutout at the Cubs, pushing the Phillies over the

Cardinals and into first place. They were never to relinquish the lead. Going 20-8 in August, they were seven games ahead on Labor Day, when they themselves were the victims of a double-header shutout from the Giants. Two days later, Don Newcombe almost performed a feat from the game's pre-history, shutting out the Phillies in the first game of a double header, then pitching seven innings of the second game before leaving for a pinch hitter; the Dodgers rallied to win that one, too.

Bailing out, the Phillies built their lead back to seven and a half by September 18, with the Dodgers nine games behind on the morning of the 19th. Incredibly, Brooklyn almost won. On September 29, the Phillies went to Brooklyn two games ahead with two games to be played. The Dodgers won the first one. Roberts opposed Newcombe October 1, 1950, in one of the greatest baseball games ever played. In the bottom of the ninth, with the score tied 1-1 and Cal Abrams, a fast man, on second base, Duke Snider ripped a single into center field. Ashburn, cheating in in anticipation of a pickoff play at second base, fielded the ball and gunned down the startled Abrams at the plate (see Cal Abrams, 1990 Book), the most crucial and most famous play of the season. The Phillies won the game in the tenth; the Whiz Kids had done it.

I have always suspected that had it not been for the unbelievable end to the 1951 National League race, the next year, this wonderful race, this classic game and this remarkable play might be even more famous than they are. Bobby Thomson, in a sense, blew Ashburn out of the water before the event had time to settle into myth. In any case, the Whiz Kids were annihilated in the 1950 World Series, and that was the end of the team. For some reason, although the core of the team stayed together for several years—Ashburn, Granny Hamner, Robin Roberts, Curt Simmons, Andy Seminick, Del Ennis, Willie Jones—they were never serious contenders again. In retrospect, the team had three critical failures:

1. They needed a power-hitting first baseman. Going up against the likes of Adcock, Hodges, Kluszewski and Musial, the Phillies would get about three homers a year out of their first basemen.
2. They needed a reliable number three starter, like Bob Buhl or Jim Hearn. They were unable to withstand things like the loss of Curt Simmons to the Army in '51 because they had only two consistent starting pitchers.

3. The farm system, after its spurt in the late forties, didn't even produce capable replacements or fill-ins. When the Phillies needed an infielder in the early fifties they'd come up with Putsy Caballero or Ted Kazanski.

Ashburn, far from the madding pennant race, was superb. He led the league in hits three times (1951, 1953, 1958), triples twice (1950, 1958), walks four times (1954, 1957, 1958, 1960), stolen bases once (1948), batting average twice (1955, 1958), and on-base percentage four times (1954, 1955, 1958, 1960). He is the only leadoff man to lead his league in batting average and walks in the same season, hitting .350 with 97 walks in 1958; other years he walked as many as 125 times. Although he wasn't with a running team and it wasn't a running era, he would steal some bases—29 in 35 tries in 1951, 16 in 20 tries in 1960. He scored more than ninety runs nine times between 1951 and 1960. His *defensive* statistics are by far the best of any outfielder ever to play major league ball. He led the league in putouts nine times, and had six of the top ten outfielder's putout totals of all time, a defensive equivalent of Nolan Ryan's strikeout totals. Though his arm was not strong it was accurate, and his quickness in center field frequently enabled him to cut off balls and surprise baserunners, so that he led the league three times in outfield assists. He led the league in at least one category every year from 1948 to 1958, and generally led in several. He was universally regarded as the best bunter of his time. *Look* magazine in 1954 did a photo essay on Ashburn's speed going down the line, setting up a series of clocks to show his progress down the line in fractions of a second; by the crude tools of the era, he was timed going home-to-first in 3.5 seconds. He was durable—in fact, from June 6, 1950 through the end of the 1954 season he played every game, the streak ending on opening day, 1955, when he was nursing a sore knee due to a pre-season collision with Del Ennis, and manager Mayo Smith didn't want to risk the knee on a muddy field. He had played in 731 games, just 91 games short of the National League record then held by Gus Suhr. Back in the lineup after a week, he played several hundred more games before needing another day off.

Staying close to home throughout his playing career, Richie worked winters as a basketball official to stay in shape, and invested in real estate in and around his hometown of Tilden. By 1959 the Phillies had reached rock bottom, and Ashburn, after an off season, was traded to the Cubs in exchange for three players. He gave the Cubs a good season in 1960, slipped badly in 1961 and became a member of the infamous 1962 Mets, the lovable losers of Casey Stengel's purgatory. "The 1962 Mets lost one hundred and twenty times," wrote George Vecsey, "and Ashburn went down kicking and screaming one hundred and twenty times."

"I don't know what's going on," said Richie, as the team lost daily and drew increasing crowds, "but I know I've never seen it before." Thirty-five years old, he hit .306, stole a dozen bases and, although missing by a few at bats of being officially qualified, again had the best on-base percentage in the National League. In the fifth inning of the first game of a September 3, 1962, Labor Day double header, Ashburn made a spectacular somersaulting catch on a line drive by Don Hoak. The next hitter, Bill Mazeroski, lifted a fly ball down the right field line. Ashburn crashed into the wall, falling on his face in the Mets' bullpen. The hit was ruled a ground rule double; Richie argued that the ball had been foul.

In any event, after the game a teammate began to suspect that something was wrong with Richie. Talking to him, they discovered that he remembered nothing about the crash, the argument—or the ballgame from that point on. He had played the last five innings of the game on pure reflexes.

He could still play, but he was offered a job as a Phillies' TV and radio commentator in 1963, and decided to take it. "I had to quit some time," he told Curt Smith in *Voices of the Game*, "and this gives me security. If it was any other job in any other city, I don't think I would have taken it. But Philadelphia has always been like a second home." I believe, although I'm not certain, that Ashburn is the last player to retire after a season in which he played regularly and hit over three hundred.

He had been one of the most popular men ever to play in Philadelphia—even the Philadelphia fans rarely booed him—and this popularity sustained him until he learned the job. "Those first few years," he says, "I thought at the time I was all right; looking back, I know I was awful." As he had as a player, he compensated for his weaknesses as a broadcaster by constant enthusiasm and hard work, never forgetting that he was one bad year away from carrying a lunch pail. A literate man with a sense of humor, Ashburn's broadcasting career has lasted almost twice as long as his playing career, and he remains to this day a part of the Philadelphia broadcast team.

Why do I like Richie Ashburn so much? I think because he combines the Pete Rose virtues and the Pete Rose style of play with the virtues of dignity, intelligence and style. He was, like Rose, a three-hundred-hitting singles hitter who ran out every ground ball of his career, a player who got out of his body every pound of ability that the Lord had put in there. But unlike Rose, Ashburn *didn't* extend his career past its natural limit to reach individual goals. (At the time he retired, Ashburn had only 188 fewer hits than Rose would have at the same age. Ashburn at retirement also had *more* hits than Rod Carew, Carl Yastrzemski, Willie Mays, Honus Wagner, Eddie Collins, Cap Anson or Lou Brock at the same age—seven of the sixteen 3,000-hit men. He was less than ten hits behind two others.) Unlike Rose, Ashburn *didn't* promote himself from morning to night; in fact, he has probably hurt his reputation as a player and a broadcaster by his self-deprecating remarks about not having a good throwing arm and never being able to steal bases because he couldn't read pitchers and not being a quick study as a broadcaster. His early retirement may have kept him out of the Hall of Fame—but then, Richie probably never thought of himself as a Hall of Fame type player, anyway. Unlike Rose, Ashburn is a reader, a family man, a man of restraint and taste. In the modern media world that may leave a man all but invisible—but if you have any faith in the bigger picture, there's got to be a place in your heart for Richie Ashburn.

(—B.J./M.K.)

Alan Ashby, Houston Astros catcher of the eighties.

Ashby was a third round draft choice of the Cleveland Indians in 1969, and after a minor league career extensively interrupted by injuries and military service came to the majors to stay in 1975. His rookie year he hit .165 and didn't play much the first half the season (79 at bats), but his playing time increased dramatically after John Ellis, who started the year as the number one catcher, threw a temper tantrum when Frank Robinson pinch hit for him. Ashby had a hot streak in August, pushing his average over .200. He was one of the best players in the Indians' camp in 1976, and opened the season as the starting catcher. He hit only .239 and the Indians re-acquired Ray Fosse, so they traded Ashby to Toronto, the first trade the Blue Jays ever made. Nominally a switch-hitter, Ashby had trouble hitting left-handers, and experimented with hitting left-handed all the way in both Cleveland and Toronto.

The Blue Jays had collected three young catchers (Ashby, Cerone and Ernie Whitt), and so passed Ashby on to Houston in 1979, where he began a long run as the Astros' almost-regular catcher. Over the years he suffered numerous broken fingers and toes trying to catch Joe Niekro's knuckleball, which he said took years off of his career. Originally a defensive catcher with a suspect bat, he evolved into a good-hitting catcher who couldn't throw.

Mark Bailey took over as the Astros' number one catcher in '84 and '85, but Ashby remained in Houston to back him up, and re-emerged as number one after Bailey bailed out. He hit .272 over the second half of the '86 season, and opened 1987 red-hot, solidifying his grip on the job. An injury to a calf muscle in June slowed him down, but at age 36 he posted career highs in home runs, batting average and RBI. For a while Hal Lanier installed Ashby as the cleanup hitter, dropping Glenn Davis to the sixth spot. In one game as a cleanup hitter Ashby had a single, double and home run in his first three at bats. A reporter asked him about the cycle. "Yes," he said. "I knew I had a shot at it if I'd had somebody else's legs."

Ashby's career went into a fatal tailspin in 1988 because of back problems and advancing age. In early 1989, with his average under .200 and Craig Biggio on the scene, Ashby was traded to the Pirates for outfielder Glenn Wilson. Being a ten and five man, Ashby had the right to reject the trade, which he did when the Pirates refused to almost double his guaranteed $550,000 salary. "I realize this may be a bad career move, but that's not what's most important to me. My family is my primary concern, but some people just don't understand that." The Astros released him, and Ashby retired.

(—M.K.)

Earl Ashby, Negro League catcher, 1945–1948.

Scott Asher, Administrative Assistant with the San Francisco Giants.

Emmett Ashford, the first black umpire in Organized Baseball, and the first in the major leagues.

Ashford was born in Los Angeles on November 23, 1914, making him two days older than Joe DiMaggio. His mother, a sharp, aggressive woman who worked as a secretary for the *California Eagle*, a black newspaper, was abandoned by his father when Emmett was one year old. According to *Porter's Biographical Dictionary* Ashford "attended Los Angeles public schools and served as the first black student body president and newspaper editor at Jefferson High School." (The article in Porter's is excellent, much better than usual. It was written by Larry Gerlach, who interviewed Ashford for *The Men in Blue.*)

Ashford was also a high school track star, as a hurdler and broad jumper. He earned a degree from Chapman College, where he played baseball and was an editor of the college newspaper. He also played on a semi-pro team called the Mystery Nine; they had a big question mark on their uniform, in the place of an insignia. He was the only black player on the team. He wasn't a very good player, and one day when the umpire didn't show up Ashford was dragooned into service behind the plate. The crowd loved him, and the collection that day was larger than usual. From then on, Ashford was the umpire.

Ashford got a job with the Post Office right after graduation (1936), and held that job for fifteen years except for a stint in the Navy during World War II. He continued to umpire—sandlot games, recreational league games, high school games, college and junior college. He was still in the Navy when he heard that the Dodgers had signed Jackie Robinson. The moment he heard the news, he knew what he wanted to do: he was going to be the first black umpire in the major leagues.

Ashford was always a go-getter, a man with unusual energy and enthusiasm. By this time he had already broken down countless tiny little barriers; it was just in his nature to do that. If he wanted to eat in a restaurant that didn't serve blacks, he'd just walk in and make friends with the manager. He made himself a spectacular umpire. On the recommendation of Rosey Gilhousen, a scout, he was offered a tryout by the Southwest International League on the Fourth of July, 1951.

The game was played in Mexicali, south of the border. There were three umpires for the game; the two white umpires refused to work with him. The league sent to El Centro, eleven miles away, for a substitute umpire, who turned out to be Doug Harvey's father; he was working semi-pro games in the area. Ashford impressed the league, and two weeks later was hired for the balance of the season. He became the first black umpire in Organized Baseball.

"Emmett's crazy!" That's what Ashford told Gerlach people said about him when he took the job. "The man's crazy to leave all that security to go out in the desert to umpire." By this time he was earning $4700 a year with the Post Office, a good salary in 1951; the S.I.L. paid him $350 a month, for two months.

By 1954 Ashford had worked his way up to the Pacific Coast League, where he would labor for twelve seasons. He was perhaps the most colorful umpire who ever lived, and the crowds on the coast grew to love him. He wore large cuff links and a huge smile. He called everything with a cheerful violence of exaggerated gestures. He raced around the field, wrote *The Sporting News* in 1966, with "the speed, grace and agility of a ballerina." He took over the game, again quoting *TSN*, "by the sheer power of his unbridled energy."

Bob Sudyk wrote a description of Emmett's style:

> Staying in a semi-squat, Emmett sweeps his right arm out to the side and up, and when it comes straight overhead, down it comes like a karate chop. That's phase one. Then he teasingly reaches up as if pulling a train whistle and gives two short jerks for phase two. Or there is an alternate phase two. While in that squat, he reaches out the side, grabs a handful of air and jerks it in as if yanking open a car door.
>
> When Emmett dusts the plate, he finishes by coming across sideways with the brush in a follow-through that leaves him on one foot.
>
> He runs around the field on tip-toes; sometimes he [will] do a little Charlie Chaplin shuffle.

All of this is true, and Sudyk adds one apocryphal detail: a story that Ashford, in the minors "often circled the bases with a base-runner and slid into the bag with him to make the call." Another story was that one time in the minor leagues his pants split open up the back before the game. A fan yelled at him "Hey, Emmett, your britches are split wide open."

"It's too late now," Emmett yelled back. "Play Ball." He umpired the whole game that way. He was so popular on the West Coast that he was assigned to extra games to hype the gate. People would actually pay to watch him umpire.

He was, of course, criticized for this approach, and not all of the criticism was displaced racism; umpires at this time were still expected to be invisible. Ashford had a saying, which appears in every story about him: Just because we dress this way doesn't mean we're presiding at a funeral.

Civil rights groups were pushing for a black umpire, and Ashford was the obvious choice. Jim Murray, the brilliant columnist of the *Los Angeles Times,* carried the banner to a national audience. American League President Joe Cronin, after watching Ashford from the press box, announced that he was "a little weak on balls and strikes." If Cronin could call balls and strikes from the press box better than Ashford could call them from home plate, wrote Murray, Ashford's problem couldn't be his color. It had to be glaucoma.

On September 10, 1965, the American League purchased Ashford's contract from the PCL. He had realized his ambition, set almost twenty years earlier, to become the first black umpire in the major leagues. "Broadway," he said. "I'm the wandering minstrel of baseball who has finally made it to Broadway."

The league noticed right away that he was different. When Birdie Tebbets called time in a spring training game to double-check Bill Rigney's lineup card, Ashford turned to the crowd, removed his cap and announced with mock solemnity, "Ladies and gentlemen (pause) Mr. Tebbetts was merely questioning the strategy (pause) of the opposing manager (pause) I thank you."

Ashford was assigned to the season opener. Vice-President Hubert Humphrey was at the game, so security was tight. When Ashford tried to enter the park a security guard told him that there were no negro umpires in the major leagues. "No," he said, "there aren't. But there will be if you'll let me in the park."

As the first black umpire he was, of course, subject to racial slurs and attempts at intimidation, and yet he had a way of taking charge of the game which kept everything under control. He'd been doing it for a long time by then, and anyway, next to him the loudest manager seemed dry and colorless. When the game was over they would call him a clown and a great many other things, but he was the teflon umpire, so to speak. There were no serious incidents.

Ashford worked the All-Star game in 1967, and the World Series in 1970. He retired as an umpire after the 1970 season; he was 56 by then, old for an ump. After his retirement he worked for Commissioner Kuhn as a public relations representative. He died of a heart attack at the age 65, March 1, 1980. He had violated all of the rules, for an umpire, yet if the rules say that an umpire cannot be a remarkable man, how can those rules be good ones?

Tucker Ashford, long-time minor league third baseman, who had several trials in the major leagues between 1976 and 1984.

Eliot Asinof, author of *Eight Men Out.*

As a young man Asinof played minor league baseball, a total of 56 games. He played fifteen games with Moultrie of the Georgia-Florida League in 1940, and 41 games with Wausau of the Northern League in 1941, hitting .296 each year. He was a left-handed hitting and throwing first baseman and outfielder, with no power.

In 1955 McGraw-Hill released Asinof's novel *Man on Spikes,* the story of career minor leaguer Mike Kutner; I haven't read it, but I'm told it is excellent. On July 17 of that same year, Asinof's television adaptation was shown on NBC as part of the Goodyear TV Playhouse series.

According to Jerome Holtzman's introduction to a reprint of *Eight Men Out,* the idea for a book about the Black Sox was suggested by Howard Cady, editor-in-chief at Putnam's, during a lunch probably in 1959 or 1960. Asinof leaped at the idea, but said that it would take him a year to research and write. It took him three, but the result is unarguably one of the best books in the literature of American sport. It provided the basis of John Sayles' 1988 movie with the same title, in which Asinof himself had a cameo role.

Asinof found the four surviving players who had been expelled in the fix, Chick Gandil, Swede Risberg, Eddie Cicotte and Happy Felsch. Gandil and Felsch talked to him; Cicotte and Risberg would not. He pieced together not a perfect account, but the best account of the fix that had ever been written, or ever can be.

In 1969 Asinof got a call from Lee Allen (see Allen, 1990 *Baseball Book*) telling him that Cicotte was dying, and, according to Holtzman "the word was out that he wanted to talk." Asinof flew to Detroit, but too late; Cicotte was comatose, and would die the next day.

Asinof is still alive and occasionally still writes an article, but he has done no interesting work in baseball since 1963.

Bob Aspromonte, original third baseman of the Houston Colt .45s.

Aspromonte was born and raised in Brooklyn, and signed with the hometown Dodgers in 1956. An older brother, Ken, was in the Red Sox chain, and was almost ready to surface with the major league team, and another brother, Charles, was in the Yankee system. The two who had major league careers look a great deal alike—dark, handsome men with wavy hair.

Aspromonte made his professional debut as an eighteen-year-old pinch hitter for the Dodgers on September 19 of that year, and struck out. He then began a four-year minor league career, mostly as a shortstop. Tommy Lasorda was a teammate at Montreal in 1959, and recalls that Manager Clay Bryant's "favorite whipping boy was Bob Aspromonte. He had Aspromonte so depressed he was considering quitting baseball. I wouldn't let him quit. I told him that we were all in it together, and if I was going to stick it out, he had to."

Aspromonte stuck it out, and was in the majors to stay by 1961. The Houston Colt .45s chose him in the expansion draft and made him their regular third baseman, a position he held for six years. He was an excellent fielder and, like everyone who played for Houston in those years, probably a far better hitter than his stats show. In 1962 he set a National League record by playing 57 consecutive errorless games at third, and in 1964 set the standard for fewest errors by a third baseman in 150 or more games (11) and highest fielding percentage (.973). (All of these records have since been broken.)

Aspromonte hit a career-high .294 in 1967, but things unravelled quickly on him in the dreadful summer of 1968. On April 15 Aspromonte played in the longest 1-0 game in history; the Astros beat the Mets 1-0 in 24 innings. Aspromonte went 0-for-9 in the game, which would probably be a major league record of some sort had not Tommy Agee and Ron Swoboda, hitting third and fourth for the Mets, gone 0-for-10.

Robert Kennedy was assassinated on June 5, 1968, and President Johnson declared June 9 a national day of mourning in memory of him. Spike Eckert, showing the dynamic leadership for which he was known, told each team to make its own decision about whether or not to play the games scheduled for that day. The Astros' players voted unanimously not to play the game, but General Manager Spec Richardson overruled them, and announced that he would fine any player who refused to play in the game. Aspromonte was one of two players who defied the ban, and refused to play out of respect for Kennedy. The other player was Rusty Staub.

It was probably just a coincidence, but Aspromonte and Staub were both gone from the team by the time the 1969 season opened. Aspromonte, still trying to get his average up after the disaster in April, lost his job almost immediately, being replaced at third base by Doug Rader. Staub played every game that year except the game of June 9, but after the season Staub was traded to Montreal, and Aspromonte to Atlanta.

Braves' manager Luman Harris decided to play him at many positions, and Aspromonte said, "It makes no difference to me, as long as I play." He did, despite struggling with injuries, and also got his only taste of post-season play, going hitless in three tries as a pinch hitter in the series against the New York Mets. Again struck by injuries in 1970, he played less, and was dealt to the Mets, who released him after the 1971 season.

Just after his release his brother Ken was hired to manage the Indians, and there were rumors that Bob would join the Indians as a player/coach, but Gabe Paul wouldn't approve it. A note in *The Sporting News* said that he had signed to go to Japan as a player/coach for the Hiroshimo Carp in 1972, but *Total Baseball* doesn't list him as having played in Japan, so we're not sure whether he did or not. By surviving until 1971, he had become not only the last Brooklyn Dodger to play in the majors, but also the last of the original Colt .45s.

(—M. K./B.J.)

Ken Aspromonte, manager of the Cleveland Indians from 1972 to 1974.

A middle infielder, Aspromonte played basketball at St. John's University before signing with the Red Sox system in 1950. After five years of minor league ball and two years of military service he was no particular prospect until he hit .334 for San Francisco in 1957, leading the Pacific Coast League. The Red Sox called him up and gave him a quick look late in '57, but traded him away when he started slowly in '58. (It is argumentative, but the Red Sox probably would have been better off to have put him at second base and left him alone.) Anyway, they traded him to Washington, and he became a journeyman major leaguer, playing for Boston, Washington, Cleveland, Los Angeles, Cleveland again, Milwaukee and the Cubs in a seven-year career. He went to Japan in 1964, and played three years with the Taiyo Whales.

In 1968 the Indians hired Aspromonte to manage their team in the Gulf Coast League, a short-season rookie league. His team did fairly well, and he remained in the system, managing Reno in '69 and Wichita, the Triple-A team, in '70 and '71. Wichita played around .500 ball, considered good for the Indians' system, and Aspromonte was credited with aiding the quick development of Chris Chambliss and Buddy Bell. When Alvin Dark was dismissed late in the '71 season, Aspromonte became the obvious candidate to replace him. Dave Bristol was offered the job, but rejected it; he was offered the job again, and rejected it again. On November 9, 1971, Aspromonte was hired to manage the Indians, at a reported salary of $27,000. Gabe Paul announced that "We hope this will be the first of many one-year contracts for Kenny."

Aspromonte gave the predictable Get-Tough speech that managers give when they take over bad ballclubs; the headline in *The Sporting News* was '**Country Club Kaput,' Aspro Warns Indians**. It must have been a ton of fun, managing the Indians. Early in the 1972 season Aspromonte made a platoon player out of Graig Nettles, for which Nettles ripped him. "I can hit lefties," Nettles told Russell Schneider, "but suddenly he doesn't believe it. I've hit them for two years. My records prove that. But he was down managing in the minors somewhere then."

"This is ruining my confidence," Nettles continued. "We got a good club, if they'd let the guys play the way they can." The Indians had lost 102 games in 1971, so the merit of this evaluation is open to question. Nettles and another player, Eddie Leon, asked to be traded; Gabe Paul announced that Nettles was a helluva player and the Indians had no intention of trading him. Nettles' platoon partner, Jerry Moses, couldn't play third and didn't hit, so Nettles got back in the lineup until season's end, when he was donated to the Yankees.

Shortly after the Indians hired Aspromonte, they traded Sam McDowell to San Francisco for Gaylord Perry. Aspromonte called Perry on the phone. "All I want," Perry told him, "is a chance to pitch every fourth day."

"With our club?" Aspromonte asked him. "How about every third day?" He wasn't kidding; Perry pitched 343 innings in 1972, although the season was shortened ten days by a strike, and won the Cy Young Award with a 1.92 ERA. The Indians won 72 games, a twelve-game improvement, and Aspromonte was rewarded with a new two-year contract.

The Indians restructured for 1973, trading veterans and building a younger team—Chambliss, George Hendrick, Charlie Spikes, Oscar Gamble, Johnny Ellis. They won 71 games and finished last again, but the team played well the last two months of the season, and Aspromonte remained optimistic about the future. He was retained for 1974, but his

three coaches (Warren Spahn, Joe Lutz and Rocky Colavito) were all fired.

With a core of young black players, the Indians wanted a black coach. After speculation about Tommy McCraw, Elston Howard and several other people, the Indians hired back local hero Larry Doby, then coaching for Montreal; bizarre as it now seems, Doby, Howard and Junior Gilliam were the only black coaches in the major leagues at the time. Wanting to hire his brother, Bob, Aspromonte got instead Clay Bryant, the old pitcher who had managed—and tormented—Bob at Montreal in 1959.

The Indians in 1974 had their best season in six years. They were at .500 in early September, and faded late to finish at 77-85, their best record since 1968. It wasn't enough to save Aspromonte's job—and oddly enough, it wasn't enough to get him another one. As bad as they are now, the Indians then were perhaps an even worse organization; in 1974 they hired only six full-time scouts, and would hire only three coaches to save on salaries. The farm system was small, frugal and disorganized. The bottom line on Aspromonte's career as a manager is the same as the bottom line on him as a player. He probably wasn't a great talent, but I'd like to know what he could have done with a *real* chance.

Brian Asselstine, outfielder with the Braves from 1976 to 1981.

Asselstine was a spare outfielder with the Braves in 1977, and won the starting center field job over Barry Bonnell and Rowland Office by playing well early in the 1978 season. At Fulton County Stadium on May 31, 1978, Mike Lum of the Reds hit a home run to center field. Asselstine leaped for the ball, caught his cleats in the wall and broke the bone just above his ankle. He was out for the year, and would never again run as well he once had.

Asselstine was all hustle, and he hit enough early in the 1980 season to force the young Dale Murphy into a platoon arrangement, a complicated five-men-for-four-positions situation. He began having recurring trouble with his knee and ankle, and his career ended after the 1981 season.

Paul Assenmacher, contemporary relief pitcher.

Weldon Aston, Financial Consultant with the Texas Rangers.

Joe Astroth, catcher with the Athletics in the fifties.

Astroth saw brief action with Philadelphia in 1945 and '46, but didn't stick with the club until 1949, when he became Mike Guerra's backup. On Sept. 23, 1950, Astroth tied an American League record with six RBI in one inning. That was a third of his season's total.

In 1951 Astroth became Bobby Shantz' personal catcher, and in 1952 Shantz was the Most Valuable Player in the American League, winning 24 games. Astroth caught 23 of the 24. In his autobiography, Shantz called Astroth "one of the main reasons for my success," adding that:

> [Astroth] knows the hitters like he knows his own name. I have complete confidence in his judgment behind the plate. Even sometimes when I think maybe he has signaled for the wrong pitch to a certain batter, I'll throw it anyway. Most of the time he turns out to be right.

Shantz, a small man, pitched 280 innings in 1952, and, suffering for most of the next two seasons from what writers of the time fondly called "flipper troubles", he saw little action. Astroth hit .296 in 1953, and continued as a half-time player through 1955.

(—R.N.)

Keith Atherton, contemporary relief pitcher.

Jim Atkins, Director of Sales for the Jacksonville Expos.

Tommy Atkins. The 1911 *Reach Guide* contains short profiles of all the members of the World Champion Philadelphia Athletics, and the entry on Atkins is worthy of verbatim reproduction:

> Frank M. Atkins came to the Athletics in 1910 via the Atlanta club. He is a southpaw pitcher and is chock full of nerve and spine. Tommy was born in Paucan, Neb., which ought to be fame enough for any ball player, but Tommy has been increasing his right along. When he reached the age of three his parents disregarded Horace Greeley's advice and moved East instead of West. They settled at Painesville, which is something over twenty miles outside of Cleveland. He pitched for the local high school there, and, being something of a rangy kid, made good. He gave the little hayseed high school such a reputation around the suburbs of Cleveland that he drew a professional engagement. He went to Akron, and then the left-hander merrily went the pace and was graduated to Bay City, Mich., famous as the home of King Cole, and thence to Augusta and Atlanta, where he was pitching when the Ath-

letic Club purchased him. He won his spurs by the manner in which he showed his nerve, and because Manager Mack is partial to the men who "have the stuff." Tommy has a fingernail fling which is a grand ball, and when modestly asked what he possesses, says "a fast one and a curve." Another year ought to see Frank M. Atkins with the frontrankers.

Atkins, 3-2 with a 2.68 ERA in 1910, never threw a pitch in the major leagues after that was written, and we do not know why.

Al Atkinson, who pitched two no-hitters in three seasons in the 1880s.

Atkinson was a busy man in his first major league season of 1884. He started with Philadelphia in the established American Association before jumping to the Union Association (in its only year of existence) and laboring for three teams there. Association owners took a dim view of this, and declared him ineligible for 1885. The Union Association folded, and Atkinson was out of a job.

At a meeting on October 17, 1885, Atkinson was reinstated and returned to Philadelphia for the 1886 campaign. He pitched no-hitters for Philadelphia in 1884 and 1886; in each of those seasons he pitched almost 400 innings. He was ineffective in 1887, and his major league career came to an end.

(—M. K.)

Billy Atkinson, relief pitcher with Montreal in the late seventies. Atkinson, a tiny right-hander, was born in Chatham, Ontario, across the street from the home of Ferguson Jenkins, who was eleven years his senior. He became the first native Canadian to work his way through the Expos' farm system, and pitched extremely well as a rookie in 1977. His career was ended by arm trouble just two years later.

John Atkinson, radio announcer for the San Jose Giants.

Abe Attell, a one-time featherweight boxing champion who became a pivotal figure in the 1919 World Series fix.

His boxing career having run its course, Attell by 1919 was a flunkie for Arnold Rothstein; he was the man who handled the money and carried the messages. Rothstein testified in court that it was Attell and Bill Burns who approached him about the possibility of arranging the fix.

Toby Atwell, the Greg Olson of 1952. A 28-year-old rookie catcher, Atwell hit over

.300 for the Cubs the first half of the season, and was named to the National League All-Star team. He had hit .233 with Montreal the year before, so you probably could have made a pretty good guess that he wasn't a legitimate .300 hitter. Atwell had come to the Cubs after six years in the Dodgers' system; the Cubs included him in the big trade for Ralph Kiner early in 1953, officially designating him as a journeyman. He stayed in the league until 1956.

Bill Atwood, a catcher with the Phillies from 1936 to 1940.

Atwood was a multi-sport star at Simmons University in Atlanta, and began his minor league career with a blast, hitting .385 in half a season for Augusta (1931). After five minor league seasons he started similarly well in the majors, hitting .302 for the Phillies in 1936 (71 games).

He completely stopped hitting after that, and eventually ran out of trials. The 1939 edition of *Who's Who in the Major Leagues* reported that "Last year, working little more than half the games, [Atwood] put weight on in proportion to the shrinkage in his batting average. Regular work and less avoirdupois may work wonders for him."

Jake Atz, one of the most successful managers of minor league history, who presided over the dynasty of the Fort Worth Panthers in the Texas League from 1914 through 1929.

Atz won born John Jacob Zimmerman in the nation's capitol in 1879, but had his name legally changed to Atz in 1900; he always said he made the change after he was last man in line to get paid, and the team he was playing for ran out of money before they got to Zimmerman. A minor league infielder of no great distinction, Atz did play parts of four seasons in the major leagues, and was the regular second baseman for the Chicago White Sox in 1909.

In 1914 Atz was hired as player-manager of the Ft. Worth Panthers. The Panthers, a sixth-place team in 1913, climbed to fifth in 1914, third in 1915, and second in 1917 and 1918. In 1919 the Panthers won the most games in the league and won the second half of the split schedule with a 56-30 record, but lost the playoff to Shreveport.

Remember that until 1925 a minor league team had a degree of independence (see Buzz Arlett). A team did not have to sell its best players to the majors or to a higher minor league if it did not choose to do so, and Fort

Worth did not choose to do so. With support from his owners, Atz added young players like Joe Pate, Paul Wachtel and Otto (Big Boy) Kraft. In 1920 they took over the league. Following more or less the same time frame as the great Baltimore team in the American Association, the Panthers (Atz's Cats, as they became known) posted consecutive records of 108-40, 107-51, 109-46, 96-56, 109-41 and 103-48, with the 109 wins in 1922 and 1924 still the standing mark in the Texas League. Pate and Wachtel were the star pitchers, Pate posting records of 15-4, 26-8, 30-9, 24-11, 23-15, 30-8 and 20-12 beginning in 1919, and Wachtel being only an inch behind. In 1924 Kraft, a first baseman, hit .349 with 55 homers and 196 RBI. A brawling, high-living outfit in step with their time, Atz said of his team that they could "drink any brewery dry at night and beat any baseball team the next day."

Although the Texas League played a split schedule, the Cats never had to face a playoff because they won both halves of the race every year. After the season the winner of the Texas League would play a "Dixie Series" against the winner of the Southern Association. The Cats won that with almost equal ease, although they did lose it once in the six years.

Minor league baseball in this era was split by a raging debate over whether teams in the higher classifications, beginning with the major leagues, should have an absolute right to purchase any player they wanted from a team at a lower level, as well as over other related issues regarding the balance of power between majors and minors. While players from some minor leagues could be drafted, other leagues (including the Texas League) were "draft exempt". Led by Jack Dunn in Baltimore, the owners of the successful minor league teams argued that without the exemption all of the best players would quickly wind up in the major leagues, and the minor league would be reduced to "farms", growing ballplayers for others to use. While history has shown the wisdom of his argument, the other side could point to a more present danger: that if minor league teams could keep their best players, some teams would grow too strong for the leagues in which they competed. With Atz's Cats dominating the Texas League and Baltimore towering over the American Association, this argument was eventually resolved in 1925 with a compromise permitting a minor league team to keep a player for two years, but then allowing him to be drafted.

This rule brought a quick end to the dynasty in Ft. Worth, as well as to Dunn's Orioles. Although at 34 he was past his prime, Pate, drafted by Philadelphia, went 9-0 with a 2.71 ERA in his first major league season in 1926. Fort Worth finished third.

In 1929 one of the Panthers' long-term owners died, and the other sold his stock in the team. Atz left the team. In the next few years he managed Dallas, Shreveport, Tulsa, and Galveston in the Texas League, as well as New Orleans in the Southern Association

and a partial-year return to Fort Worth, but he met with no success anywhere, and began to slip to the lower minors. In 1939 and 1940 he managed championship teams in Henderson in the East Texas League, but after an eighth-place finish in the Piedmont League in 1941 his managerial career drew to a close. Atz probably didn't know it at the time, but the Society for American Baseball Research later concluded that he had managed his teams to 1,972 minor league victories.

Four years later, Atz died in New Orleans, aged 65. In 1946 it was announced that the winner of the Texas League playoff was to be given the Jake Atz trophy.

(Information for this article is taken from *The Texas League,* by Bill O'Neal, as well as other sources. All existing Encyclopedias decline to confirm that Atz' original name was Zimmerman, which may mean that the story is apocryphal, but I like it anyway.)

NOTES UPON WATCHING A SMALL BOY WITH A MUSIC BOX

My little boy has just turned two, and he is trying to figure out a music box. It is a baseball music box, on which a small figure pivots with a tiny bat, swinging at a white cloth marble while the tinny sounds of "Take me out to the ball game" leak from below.

The music box has two operating mechanisms, an on/off switch which one pushes and pulls, but also a handle which must be wound to provide power. This is too much for a two-year-old boy to deal with at first. He pulls the switch and the music starts; he pushes it and the music stops—but then, when the tension winds down, he pulls the switch and nothing happens. Isaac is frustrated. "Broke," he says, handing me the worthless machine. "Ball payer broke."

He will, of course, soon figure out the concept of two switches. But I am struck by this: that ideas are harder things than machines, and many people will never master the two-switch concept as it applies to a logical inference. I find this to be an undeniable lesson of sports talk shows. A caller argues that a baseball manager makes no difference. Look at Whitey Herzog, he says; he was supposed to be such a genius a few years ago, but why can't he win now? The caller has not mastered the two-switch concept; the on/off switch must be turned on, but the energy must *also* be there.

If Ralph Kiner is in the Hall of Fame, demands a voter, shouldn't Roger Maris be there, too? The argument is perfectly satisfactory to him; one switch operates all machines. Indeed, the entire intellectual life of many sportswriters is a search for master switches. Baseball is 90% pitching, sportswriters argue, not because this makes any sense or because there is any evidence to support it, but because it reduces the terrifying complexity of the sport to a single switch. To win a pennant anymore you have to have a strong bullpen—never mind that a dozen teams have won titles in the last ten years with conspicuously weak bullpens. The key to winning on artificial turf is speed.

If only one could hold an idea in one's hand and play with the switches, I think, how quickly the arguments would advance. In the real world, arguments go around and around, advancing almost imperceptibly from generation to generation, and this is another way of explaining why I stopped writing the *Baseball Abstract*. After ten years, I realized the impossibility of advancing complex ideas in a world that only wanted to know where the switch was.

SUMMER OF '49
Or Was that '50
Wait a Minute, I'm almost sure that was '37
And I think maybe that was Vince DiMaggio

David Halberstam's best-seller of '89 begins with a look at the last game of the 1948 American League season, when the Cleveland Indians beat the Red Sox in a one-game playoff after the two teams had ended in a tie. It was assumed by the Red Sox media, fans, players and by Mel Parnell himself that Mel Parnell would start this game. Manager Joe McCarthy, however, "was wary of rookies," according to Halberstam, and so decided against starting Parnell. "Even more astonishing to Parnell was his choice: a veteran right-hander named Denny Galehouse, who had been used mostly in relief all season . . . The Indians won, 8-3, behind the brilliant pitching of young Gene Bearden. Bearden threw a particularly bewildering knuckle ball that seemed to dance in every direction. The playoff victory was Bearden's twentieth of the year, and it made him Rookie of the Year, just ahead of Parnell."

The decision to start Denny Galehouse in the last game of the 1948 season bombed, and has come to rank, with the sale of Babe Ruth and the failure to lift Bill Buckner, among the most famous blunders in Red Sox history. There are, however, a few problems with the story the way that Halberstam tells it, just a few:

1. Mel Parnell was *not* a rookie in 1948. Parnell had pitched 51 innings for the Red Sox in 1947. The standards used to determine whether a player is a rookie have changed many times since 1948, but Mel Parnell was not considered a rookie then, wouldn't be considered a rookie now, and wouldn't have been considered a rookie by any standards which have ever been applied between then and now. The man was not a rookie.

2. Gene Bearden *was* a rookie, but despite winning twenty games did *not* win the Rookie of the Year award.

3. Denny Galehouse was *not* used primarily in relief in 1948. Although he didn't pitch a lot that year, Galehouse started more often than he relieved, and seventy percent of his innings had come in a starting role.

Welcome to the world of 1949, where memory is truth and facts are whatever old ballplayers remember them to be. Pick out a story at random and check it out . . . on page 82 Halberstam says of Yogi Berra that "in 1947 it appeared that his future would be as a catcher. But then in the World Series Jackie Robinson humiliated him by stealing, it seemed, at will, and he did not seem to want to catch anymore." In fact, Jackie

Robinson stole only one base against Yogi in the 1947 World Series.

On page 226, Halberstam tells this story:

> The Yankee regulars were very much aware of Rizzuto's value. It was understood that since he was small and physically vulnerable, Rizzuto had to be protected. If any opposing player went into second hard at him, the Yankee players would immediately retaliate against the opposing infielders and the Yankee pitchers would throw at the offending player. Earlier that year, Pesky had taken Rizzuto out in a play at second. The next time DiMaggio was up he singled. DiMaggio turned at first, never hesitating, and raced for second, though it was obvious he had no chance. He laid a savage block on Doerr as revenge.

First of all, it has *always* been an unwritten rule in baseball that you need to defend your infielders—still is—so if the purpose is to establish that the other Yankees attached a special significance to Rizzuto's place in the lineup, this seems to me a peculiar way to make the case. That's neither here nor there, but the Yankees and Red Sox played only twenty-two games during the 1949 season, and all of those games are reported in great detail in the Boston and New York papers. If you were writing a book about the 1949 American League pennant race, wouldn't you think that one of the first things you would do would be to go to the library and gather up the accounts of those twenty-two games?

This event, as reported by Halberstam, never happened. The incident in question occurred in the game of June 28, which was the day DiMaggio returned from the disabled list. Pesky did take Rizzuto out on a double play, leaving the Scooter dazed for a minute and shaken up badly enough that the papers were still writing about it several days later.

But DiMaggio did *not* irrationally sacrifice a base hit to get even. What happened was, in the eighth inning DiMaggio was on first base when Yogi Berra grounded to second. DiMaggio crashed into *Vern Stephens*, not Doerr, while Stephens was in the middle of turning a double play. It was a hard slide and it no doubt conveyed a message, but it was just a natural part of the game, and not some Zulu warrior stunt to avenge the *paisano*.

None of these things really bother me. If David Halberstam doesn't know where to find a Macmillan *Encyclopedia* or how to use one, that doesn't disqualify him from writing baseball books. What bothers me are the ridiculous characterizations of men and events. What bothers me in the Parnell/Galehouse story is not that he didn't check to see whether Parnell was really a rookie or whether Bearden won the Rookie of the Year Award or whether Galehouse was used primarily in relief, but the statement that Joe McCarthy "was wary of rookies."

Saying that Joe McCarthy was wary of rookies is historical ignorance on the scale of saying that Whitey Herzog was wary of using the running game, or Lou Piniella was wary of going to his bullpen. No manager in the history of baseball was ever *less* wary of rookies than Joe McCarthy. McCarthy spent fifteen years as a minor league player, never getting a major league at bat. After that he managed in the minor leagues for several more years, earning a shot as manager of the Chicago Cubs by putting together dominant minor league teams at Louisville in the American Association. This was very unusual in the 1920s, when most major league managers were former star players. For much of his career McCarthy was the only major league manager who had not played in the majors.

In consequence of his years in the wilderness, McCarthy *knew* that there were good players stuck in the minor leagues, and he was not at all reluctant to use them. That was how he built his first great team in Chicago: by pulling players out of the minor leagues who had been stuck there after failing previous major league trials.

In New York and later in Boston, McCarthy would repeatedly take criticism for releasing a veteran player so that a rookie or a youngster could have the job—as, in fact, he had done with Parnell that very spring. Just one example: in 1936 Tony Lazzeri, a second baseman, drove in 109 runs. In 1937, although he missed a month with an injury and slumped to .244, Lazzeri still drove in 70 runs in 446 at bats. Lazzeri was only 33 that summer and almost everyone thought that he could still play, but McCarthy released him, and gave the second base job to a rookie, Joe Gordon, who did not have a major league at bat. The Yankee GM who hired McCarthy, Ed Barrow, wrote in his autobiography that McCarthy "not only could judge a new young ballplayer, but was extraordinary at being able to detect the first signs when a veteran or a star was beginning to go downgrade. Basically, he was a builder, and as soon as he saw those signs he would begin to think of the man to replace the fading star."

In fact, Halberstam tells a story (p. 31) of which this is the real point:

> Once in 1937 the Yankees split a doubleheader with one of the weaker teams in the league, losing a game they should not have lost. Afterward, McCarthy came prowling angrily through the locker room. A utility outfielder named Roy Johnson, relatively new to the team, saw McCarthy and complained just loud enough for him to hear that you could not win every game. McCarthy heard him. Later that day he called up his superiors. "Get me Henrich," he said. Tommy Henrich was brought up from the Yankee farm team in Newark, and Roy Johnson was waived out of the league.

As Halberstam presents it, the point of this story is that McCarthy was a despot, willing to get rid of anyone who said something he didn't like. But the *real* point, if he understood his own story, is that McCarthy had no fear of getting rid of veteran players and replacing them with untried rookies. That was, as much as anything, his defining characteristic as a manager, for whereas most managers believed that there was a shortage of players so you had to put up with things from the guys who had major league ability, McCarthy believed that there were lots of guys around who could play baseball, so if you didn't want to do things his way then the hell with you. There were a few players around who had special skills and you had to make a special effort to get along with them, like Ted Williams, but the rest of them had to get along with *you.*

Halberstam carries on his treatise on Joe McCarthy's dislike of rookies at considerable length. According to Halberstam, McCarthy "most emphatically did not like the new bonus-baby rule", which required that players who signed large bonus contracts go to the major leagues in their first full season. When Bobby Brown came to the Yankees in 1946 as one of the first bonus babies, McCarthy took him aside and told him 'Bobby, we don't have any rats on the Yankees.'

"He was even more resentful when he came to the Red Sox, which had a weaker farm system. In 1948 the Red Sox had an eighteen-year-old bonus baby named Chuck Stobbs . . . McCarthy made him feel as if he didn't exist. (Stobbs) stayed with the team for the entire 1948 season and pitched a total of nine innings."

Let's look at this:

a) *Of course* McCarthy hated the bonus baby rule. *Every* manager hated the bonus baby rule. The managers were *supposed* to hate the rule. That was why it was adopted—so that teams wouldn't sign young kids for large bonuses, because it would force the major league team to waste a roster space. What manager *wouldn't* hate being told that he had to carry one or two players that he would never have chosen on his own?

b) McCarthy hated the bonus baby rule, but *unlike the other managers* of the era, he *did* use the bonus babies. It is true that Chuck Stobbs sat on the bench all year in 1948—but this was not unusual for a bonus baby (see articles on Johnny Antonelli and Bobby Avila, Biographic Encyclopedia.) Bobby Brown, after being warned by McCarthy not to be a rat, played 69 games in his first year as a bonus baby, and 133 his second. Chuck Stobbs, after watching and learning as an 18-year-old in 1948, pitched 152 innings and won eleven games as a 19-year-old. No other manager in that era, with the exception of Eddie Sawyer of the Phillies, was equally willing to put these inexperienced, untried players out on the field.

c) The statement that the Red Sox had a weaker farm system in this era than the Yankees, which Halberstam makes repeatedly in various forms, is *extremely* questionable. First, the Yankees didn't even *have* a farm system when McCarthy signed to manage them in 1930, although they did have players stuck around with independent teams. Edward Barrow didn't believe in farm systems, and it wasn't until late 1931 that Colonel Ruppert, over Barrow's objections, bought the Newark team and began the Yankee farm system.

Second, between 1937 and 1952 the Red Sox farm system produced:

Ted Williams
Bobby Doerr
Johnny Pesky
Dom DiMaggio
Billy Goodman
Mel Parnell
Jimmy Piersall
Pee Wee Reese
Jim Tabor
Walt Dropo
Sammy White

Plus an extensive list of lesser talents like Hal Brown, Ike Delock, Bill Henry, Tex Hughson, Mickey McDermott, Charlie Maxwell, Sam Mele, Willard Nixon, John Peacock, Stan Spence, and Chuck Stobbs. I think I could live with it.

In fact, the Red Sox farm system in the years building up to the great races of the late forties was in one of the most productive cycles that any system has ever had. Halberstam ignores this, and instead hammers on the Red Sox for failing to sign Willie Mays.

Continuing his explanation of why Parnell should have started the final game of the 1948 season, Halberstam says that "Three of his victories had come against the Indians, a team loaded with right-handed power hitters—a sure sign that his ball was harder on right-handers."

In fact, the Cleveland Indians in 1948 had more left-handed hitting than almost any other American League team. Although their power was mostly right-handed, they missed by only ten of leading the American League in the number of at bats by left-handed hitters. Even if it were true that they were a right-handed hitting team, which it isn't, to regard the simple fact that Parnell had beaten them three times in five decisions as proof that his ball was harder on a right-hander than a left-hander would be really, really stupid.

I suppose I should resist the temptation to debate the choice of Galehouse over Parnell as the starter for the decisive game of the 1948 season. It is quite true that Joe McCarthy preferred to use a veteran pitcher in a crucial game. In 1929 McCarthy was managing the Cubs when Connie Mack pulled the famous stunt of starting Howard Ehmke, a seldom-used 35-year-old veteran, in the first game of the World Series. McCarthy had seen Ehmke shut down his team, one of the greatest offensive powerhouses ever built. In 1932 McCarthy had started Johnny Allen, a rookie, in the fourth game of the World Series. Allen was hammered.

After that, McCarthy preferred to use a veteran in a critical game. This is a perfectly reasonable policy. There were several other reasons to use Galehouse. Galehouse was rested; Parnell was not. Although Parnell was 15-8 on the season and Galehouse just 8-8, Galehouse actually had a better record against first-division teams than did Parnell. (5-3 as opposed to 4-5. Eleven of Parnell's 15 wins were against the second division.) Galehouse had far better control than Parnell at that time.

Playing a team with right-handed power in Fenway Park, McCarthy had awakened to find the wind blowing out to left field. That had tipped the scales, in his mind, to Galehouse. The decision didn't work out, but I hardly believe that that justifies treating McCarthy, one of the greatest managers of all time, with barely disguised contempt.

Halberstam's vision of Joe McCarthy appears to be, to a substantial degree, adopted from Mel Parnell, one of his chief sources for the book. McCarthy had his faults and prejudices, one of which was, according to Edward Barrow, that "He didn't like Southern ballplayers. He thought they were too hot tempered and defeated themselves." Parnell was from Louisiana.

All of us make errors in our books. All of us write things which turn out not to be true, and all of us are embarrassed when our readers point these out to us. People who haven't tried it sometimes think that if you're careful you shouldn't make mistakes in print, but being perfect in accuracy is as impossible as being perfect in other ways. Even magazines like *Sports Illustrated*, which spend a huge amount of time and money going through articles word by word, double-checking sources, still make a surprising number of errors, because sources turn out to have been mis-informed, and buried in every sentence are undiscovered assumptions, some of which will prove to be false.

Nor should it be suggested that Halberstam breaks any records for inaccuracy. Many baseball books are equally careless with the story. Another book dealing with the glory years of the Yankees is Dom Forker's *Sweet Seasons.* The interview with Art Ditmar in *Sweet Seasons* runs only seven pages, and contains at least sixty errors of fact. There are two differences. First, Forker is *quoting* what his subjects say; if a pitcher says "I was 14-7," the writer has to quote him as saying "I was 14-7," even if he knows damn well that his record was actually 12-10. You can *remove* the errors, and I would have, but you can't correct what is inside of quotation marks.

Second, Halberstam is not trying to be Dom Forker. I mean, he can if he wants to, but one presumes that David Halberstam holds himself to a different standard than Dom Forker, and that his reputation and success flow in some measure from upholding that standard.

I'm not trying to tell David Halberstam what his standards should be. I can't make up standards for anyone but myself. But hell, *I* hire a research assistant, and Halberstam's a lot bigger name than I am. Why on earth didn't he hire somebody who knows something about baseball to read this book carefully before it came out?

The intriguing question is, is Halberstam this careless with the facts when he writes about the things he usually writes about? There are two possibilities, one frightening and one irritating. It is frightening to think that Halberstam, one of the nation's most respected journalists, is this sloppy in writing about war and politics, yet has still been able to build a reputation simply because nobody has noticed.

What seems more likely is that Halberstam, writing about baseball, just didn't take the subject seriously. He just didn't figure that it *mattered* whether he got the facts right or not, as long as he was just writing about baseball.

And that, to me as a baseball fan, is just irritating as hell.

JEROME HOLTZMAN HAS A COW

In the spring of 1990 Macmillan published the eighth edition of the *Baseball Encyclopedia*. The book received generally good notices at first. Macmillan had made the pages larger, which enabled them to make the book thinner and more manageable, while at the same time containing more information.

When they were putting together the book, the editors of the new Macmillan undertook to rectify some errors in the old stats. Honus Wagner had previously been credited with 3,430 career hits, but Macmillan decided that the actual total was only 3,418. Larry Lajoie, credited with 3,251 hits, was pared back to 3,244.

Well, Jerome Holtzman just about shit in his pants.

In the June 10 issue of the *Chicago Tribune*, Holtzman wrote that the editors were "tampering with baseball's most sacred and trusted text". Wagner and Lajoie, said Holtzman, "have been the victims of a statistical grave robbery", which he compared to "a baseball Watergate."

Holtzman called Rick Wolff, Macmillan editor, and asked him to explain the changes in Wagner and Lajoie's hit totals. Wolff tried to explain the process of reviewing records, but couldn't specifically explain what had happened in these two cases. Wolff recommended he call Richard Topp, president of SABR. Topp couldn't explain it, either.

Holtzman concluded that the review process had been flawed, and recommended that in the future "all statistical adjustments be approved by the professionals at the Sporting News and Elias, not by a platoon of well-meaning but nonetheless amateur detectives."

Tom Barnidge of *The Sporting News* joined in. "There is no sport on this planet", wrote Barnidge, which "treats its records with greater reverance (sic) than baseball." In edition eight, wrote Barnidge, "Macmillan violated the trust bestowed upon it when it unilaterally changed existing accepted statistics."

Tracy Ringolsby signed on in *Baseball America*. "In altering the statistics," wrote Ringolsby, "Wolff and company have tampered with the very lifeblood of the game's historical perspective." He talked to Seymour Siwoff, head of the Elias Bureau, and gave Siwoff the last word on the subject.

"It's a disgrace," said Seymour Siwoff. "The best thing to do is let the statute of limitations exist and let written records stay. How dare Rick Wolff and the amateurs he deals with arbitrarily change the records of Hall of Fame players?"

Parenthetically, since when is there a "statute of limitations" on accuracy? Despite my quarrels with the Elias Bureau over the years, I always thought that they spoke *for* accuracy, rather than against it.

Well, this *is* an unexpected twist in the tempest. The Macmillan Company, which publishes the *Encyclopedia*, also publishes *The Baseball Analyst* for the Elias Bureau; Siwoff has cashed a number of checks from the company he now calls a disgrace, and for all I know intends to cash some more, so it is a bit of a surprise to see Siwoff snapping at the hand that feeds him.

Anyway, Ringolsby has some valuable insights into the process. "One theory," he explains, "is that Wolff, with the aid of members of the Society for American Baseball Research, examined old box scores. That's a risky business because of typographical errors and changes in official scoring." That's not what actually happened, as I'll explain in a minute, but it is a wonderful thing to see Tracy Ringolsby instructing Richard Topp on how to do baseball research. Perhaps, when he is through, he could give Larry Bird a few pointers on how to shoot free throws, or outline a conditioning regimen for Nolan Ryan.

Look, all you guys are fine baseball writers. Holtzman, Barnidge, Ringolsby—you're all among the best. But I challenge any one of you to come forward and try to tell us that you actually know doodly squat about how baseball record books are put together. Does any one of you have the stones to claim that you actually have some understanding of the process of researching a record book? Among the three of you, I'll bet I could write everything you know about the subject on one piece of paper, and have room left over for Rachel to cut out a couple of paper dolls and Cher to make a dress for next year's Academy Awards. You're *consumers* of baseball record books; you're not qualified to expound on how they're put together. Why can't you be honest enough to admit that?

I am not involved with SABR's efforts to review and correct old records, but I am acquainted with the people who do that. Some of those men, like Neil Munro and Pete Palmer, are friends of mine, while others, like Richard Topp, are on my list of people I would recommend to test experimental parachute designs.

But all of these men know vastly more about researching old baseball statistics than Tracy Ringolsby does. Do you honestly imagine, Tracy, that after twenty years of digging through old box scores, we haven't noticed that they tend to be a little unreliable? Do you think Richard Topp isn't aware that scoring decisions are sometimes changed?

Baseball record books do not sprout from the ground like mushrooms; they are put together from other sources. What Ringolsby doesn't understand, because he doesn't *really* know anything at all about the process of statistical research, is that *all* of these sources are unreliable. There are five basic sources from which the statistical portions of record books are compiled, which are:

a. box scores,
b. game summaries,
c. printed statistics in old guides and other contemporaneous publications,
d. copies of the worksheets which league statisticians used when initially compiling the stats, and
e. previous record books.

All of these sources are prone to errors, and none of them contains all of the information which we would like to have. Record books must draw on *all* of these sources to get the information that they want.

Since Ernest Lanigan compiled the first *Baseball Cyclopedia* seventy years ago, the process of reviewing records, extending and correcting them has been constantly at work. Thousands of people have participated in that process over the years, and the great bulk of the work has *always* been done by amateurs. There is a simple reason for this: economics. The process of reconstructing statistics from old records is enormously time-consuming, and the money to have it done by a professional staff simply doesn't exist.

When the first Macmillan *Encyclopedia* was published in 1969, there were thousands of "holes" in the data, especially the biographical data. There were players who were left out of the book entirely, and there were non-players—fake players—who were mistakenly included. There were cases where two players with the same or similar names had had their records combined into one. The birth and death dates for many, many players, hundreds of players, were unknown. Records for things such as which way the player batted or threw were missing for many players.

Who do you think it was that sorted all this out, and created the book which Holtzman now considers beyond refinement? Who do you think spent unimaginable numbers of hours at libraries and county courthouses, in cemeteries and small-town churches and most of all microfilm reading rooms, hoping to find a birth or death certificate or a headstone or a name on a list? Do you think it was "the professionals at the Sporting News and Elias" who paid for all this work, purchased at a rate of perhaps one line per hundred hours? Do you think the Commissioner's office did all this work? Do you think perhaps the Commissioner himself snuck down to the library on Saturdays and found most of this stuff? Or do you think maybe it was done by "a platoon of well-meaning but nonetheless amateur detectives."

These people—Topp, Bill Carle, Bob Hoie, Cappy Gagnon, Joe Overfield, hundreds of others—have given baseball something very valuable: a strong skeleton for its history. And the condescending, ignorant attitude of Holtzman and Ringolsby toward them, on the assumption that if an error has been made they must have been responsible for it because they're amateurs, is despicable.

Speaking for *The Sporting News*, Barnidge wrote that "Right or wrong, changing a Hall of Famer's stats would elicit outrage from a number of fans." Well, *The Sporting News* has changed the published stats of Hall of Famers hundreds of times in successive editions of *Daguerreotypes*. Did all of those changes elicit outrage?

Many of the changes to records that *The Sporting News* has made are much more significant than the revisions to Wagner and Lajoie. When I was a kid *Daguerreotypes* listed Cy Young with 510 career wins, rather than the 511 which is standard now. In the 1951 edition of *Daguerreotypes*, Walter Johnson is listed with 3,497 strikeouts, 415 wins and 113 shutouts. Now he is listed with 3,508 strikeouts, 416 wins and 110 shutouts. What happened to those figures?

What happened to those figures is that they were reconciled to the statistics in *Macmillan*—changes which were made necessary by the discoveries of those very same "amateurs" whose contribution is now being scorned. It was "amateur detectives" who discovered that Walter Johnson had been credited with shutouts in several games which he failed to complete, and had been credited with a shutout on one occasion when he pitched only four innings. Does the fact that the people who learned this didn't get paid for it invalidate the discovery? Do you want we should go back to printing the wrong figure?

Ringolsby warns us of the *danger* than an error could be made, doing research from box scores. But what we are dealing with, in the case of Wagner, is the *certainty* that an error has been made. The nature of baseball is that when a hitter gets a hit, a pitcher must also *give up* a hit. An earlier decision to allow Wagner's hit total to stay at 3,430 was causing the league totals not to balance. If the league totals do not balance, then it is *certain* that a mistake has been made.

Barnidge asked Rick Wolff whether any external committee, outside Macmillan, had approved the changes. Wolff told him that it was done internally. "This would seem to be a presumptuous decision," commented Barnidge.

I should say this, so there isn't any misunderstanding, that Wolff (and Macmillan) probably *did* make an error of process here. Nobody really knows exactly how many hits Honus Wagner had, but 3,418 is probably a better figure, on the basis of what we *do* know, than 3,430, so that's not the error. Corrections have been made and totals changed in every successive edition of the *Encyclopedia*, so continuing to do that cannot, on the surface of it, be faulted. But the difference is that there is a process of review now, and that process should have been given a chance to work. Bart Giamatti established or at least gave his kiss of approval to a committee intended to review significant changes in the official statistics. No one knows yet whether that committee can actually function, but Wolff should have run these changes by that committee before going into print.

But just a few years ago (1981) *The Sporting News* put out a new edition of *Daguerreotypes* in which, without the approval of anybody outside their own company, they changed the American League batting champion for 1910! Pete Palmer, another one of those "amateurs" who is now scorned, had found that the American League statistician in 1910 had double-counted a game for Ty Cobb, giving him two extra hits in a close race, and thus pushing back ahead of Lajoie in a race which had been hotly disputed for other reasons. *The Sporting News* saw the evidence, bought it, and changed the race.

They not only changed the 1910 batting championship, but they made a big point of it. They advertised this change, wrote articles about it in their weekly newspaper, and wrote editorials defending their right to change it. If Macmillan is "arrogant" now, what was *The Sporting News* then?

OK, they've changed their policy. The new edition of the *Daguerreotypes* restores the batting championship to Ty Cobb. Does that give them the right to dump on Rick Wolff, because Macmillan is doing the same thing that *The Sporting News* was doing just a couple of years ago?

Ringolsby interviewed Jerome Holtzman for his panegyric on the subject. "After that," Holtzman told him, meaning after he wrote the original article, "I found an even bigger travesty with Cap Anson." Holtzman is outraged that Anson dropped from 3,041 hits to an even 3,000, dropping him from thirteenth place on the all-time list to a tie for fifteenth with Roberto Clemente.

Well, pardon my pointing this out, fellas, but the figure 3,041 has only been around for a few years. At the time of Anson's death in 1922, the figure reported by the *Reach Guide* was 3,013 hits. The total arrived at by *The Sporting News* when they started publishing record books was three thousand, *eighty*-one, which incidentally is still the figure they use. The total appearing in the first edition of the *Macmillan Encyclopedia* was 2,995. The figure 3,041 made its first appearance sometime in the 1970s.

In fact, of the four major sources for player records, not one now uses the 3,041 figure which Holtzman would have us believe is revered. *Daguerreotypes* uses 3,081. *Total Baseball* uses 2,995. *The Sports Encyclopedia: Baseball* uses 3,022. *Macmillan* uses 3,000. So how did 3,041 get to be an accepted standard?

The figure 3,041 was arrived at by the very same people who now believe 3,000 is a more accurate count, and was an outcome of precisely the same process of review and correction which is now under attack. If the figure 3,041 had indeed become an officially sanctioned figure, then one can argue perhaps that it should not have been changed without the knowledge and ac-

quiescence of the review committee. This, however, creates a few problems.

Problem #1) If *The Sporting News* supports the process of official sanction for existing records, as Barnidge would have us believe that they do, then why do they continue to use their own records, which disagree with the "officially sanctioned" ones? If *TSN* would have us believe that there is one official total for each player and only one, then why don't they use that one? Why do they continue to list Cap Anson at 3,081 hits, when the "official" Macmillan lists him with 3,041, or 3,000, or whatever? There are hundreds of examples like this. *Daguerreotypes* lists Denny Lyons with 1,404 career hits, while Macmillan has him at 1,333. The figures are in dispute for nine of his thirteen major league seasons. The two sources also disagree on his date of death.

Problem #2) Do you know how the Macmillan Company maintains its status as the "Official" Encyclopedia?

They purchase it. That's right—Macmillan pays the Commissioner's Office an annual fee to be recognized as the official source.

Richard Levin of the Commissioner's Office told Ringolsby that "We take our statistics very seriously." Well, if you take your statistics so seriously, then is it really appropriate for you to sell your imprimatur?

Problem #3) Does this committee ever actually meet?

As best I can determine, this committee has never actually met. It appears to have no budget and no funds to, for example, fly all of the people who are on the committee to the same place. The committee seems to exist only in theory.

Problem #4) Does this committee have any standards? published or private, by which to direct the people who do the work in how to determine what the official stats should be? Do they place any priority on getting league stats which balance, or is that not important to them? If the statistician of the time clearly made a mistake, do you want to correct it? Do you want to correct it sometimes and not other times?

Problem #5) Who is on this committee?

Rick Wolff told Jerome Holtzman that the committee included "anybody we could find who had a sense of baseball history—researchers from the commissioner's office, from SABR, the Hall of Fame and ourselves."

Well, sorry to butt in here, but wouldn't that definition seem to include *me*? I appreciate that I have an extensive history of establishment-bashing, but if you want your little committee to be respected, you can't have a committee of good old go-along boys. You have to have the legitimate authorities in the field.

On the other hand, since this committee seems to exist only in theory, and nobody can supply a list of who is on it and who is not, maybe I *am* on it, but just didn't know about it. They just forgot to tell me.

Problem #6) Is the committee actually willing to approve revisions when errors are found?

If they aren't, then you can forget the whole thing, because there is no way in the world the committee can be respected if it intends merely to enshrine old errors. The concept of a "statute of limitations" on old errors is blatantly irresponsible, and the idea that such a thing could ever be accepted is preposterous. You cannot ask historical researchers to form a consensus around a statement which is known to be wrong; they simply will not fall in line.

Historians differ enormously in their thinking as to what extent it is possible to form a clearer image of the last century, with some arguing that historical revisionism is only beginning to develop, and others arguing that it has run amuck. But no historian in the world—none—would argue that there is a statute of limitations after which an error becomes a fact.

Baseball, incidentally, has a long history of this sort of thing. The Spalding Commission in 1907 was formed in theory to determine who invented baseball and where it came from. Under Spalding's influence, the Commission ignored the evidence and endorsed the myth that Abner Doubleday had invented the game. It was important to Spalding that the game be *American* in origin, and so that's what they had to conclude.

That was the official history—but did it hold? No—because a consensus of historians would not endorse a lie.

In some respects, the language of the debate is unavoidably slanted against accuracy. Holtzman says that twelve of Wagner's hits "have been taken away", which becomes the inevitable premise of the debate. But if Honus Wagner didn't *get* 3,430 hits, then how can those hits be "taken away" from him?

Holtzman says it's grave robbery. If you assume that the original total was correct, then of course it is wrong to remove them. But if the original total was wrong, then how can he be "robbed" of hits that he never got?

Holtzman says that hereafter, all "adjustments (should) be approved by the professionals at the Sporting News and Elias." Well, I think I speak for the entire world of baseball research when I say that we would be tickled pink if these two institutions would assume a place of leadership in the field. It would be wonderful if *The Sporting News* would stop being such prigs about access to their library. After that, maybe they could try to make *The Sporting News* microfilm available to researchers, rather than fighting tooth and nail to *keep it* from being available, as they have for the last quarter-century. Then maybe they could start reviewing baseball research, get involved with the Society for American Baseball Research, maybe publish a few of the better articles resulting from private research efforts. Finally, maybe they could even start to *support* research, pump just a little bit of money—$50,000, $60,000 a year—into the field. We'd be thrilled.

But what Holtzman is demanding is that Elias and *The Sporting News* be allowed to pass judgment on a process that *they refuse to have anything to do with*. Do you really think that's practical? Holtzman says that "Elias, by far, has the largest library of official box scores." Great. Did they ever consider letting anybody see them? Baseball researchers would be thrilled to work with Elias.

Macmillan *has* tried. This is a rival publisher I'm talking about here, but Macmillan *has* been involved in the world of baseball research. They *do* send people to the SABR convention. They *do* put a little money into the field. And that has made them, over a period of years, the legitimate leader.

OK, Rick Wolff, here's your slap on the wrist. If you've got a process, use the damn thing. If you don't have a process, stop pretending that you do.

More important than that, take a minute to *explain* what you have done. You've got 2,781 pages in the book; you can afford two paragraphs in an appendix somewhere to explain in plain English why Honus Wagner's hit total has been revised downward.

Why the change was made is the smallest issue in the argument, but I'd better clear that up before I quit here. As I understand it, when Macmillan published their first edition in 1969, they listed Wagner's hit total at 3,415. This was based on a thorough, if imperfect, review of his day by day performance.

Well, after a year or two the book came under the influence of Joe Reichler. Reichler used his position in the Commissioner's office to get himself listed as the editor of the Macmillan *Encyclopedia*. Actually, he didn't edit the thing at all, and really had very little to do with it. The only thing that Reichler *really* did was set a few policies.

One of those policies was that, while review and correction of the records of minor players would be permitted, a few records of a few players would be considered inviolable. Honus Wagner had always been listed with 3,430 hits, and by God, 3,430 hits was the right total for him. This caused the league totals for those seasons not to balance, but that's no problem; you can short-circuit the balancing routine. If tradition can take precedence over evidence, it can certainly take precedence over evidence *and* logic.

Well, with the grace of God, Reichler eventually dropped dead. Rick Wolff, dancing perhaps a little carelessly around the barnyard, simply decided to go with the best evidence. He changed Wagner's totals for his first three years, and don't ask me which is correct, because frankly I don't have any idea. Ask Jerome and Tom and Tracy; I'm sure they'll be able to fill you in on the details.

The "amateurs" attacked by Holtzman and Ringolsby actually had nothing to do with this change. The information which supported the change was a part of Macmillan's original data base, twenty-some years ago. Wolff simply made an "internal decision" to go with the evidence, rather than with tradition. He decided that Reichler's idiotic policy would die with Reichler.

Maybe he shouldn't have changed them, and probably he shouldn't have changed them without telling anybody, and certainly he shouldn't have changed them without *explaining* his decision.

But this is *not* a "sacred text", as Holtzman said. This is not a religion; it's a game.

Changing statistics is not robbing graves. It is not *like* robbing graves.

Macmillan has *not* violated any trust.

Nobody in his right mind treats baseball statistics "with reverance", or reverence, either.

Baseball statistics are not "sacred" or "honored" or "revered" or any of that crap. They are right, or they wrong.

Baseball statistics are like any other statements of fact. They are correct or they are incorrect. They are significant or they are insignificant. They are relevant to the discussion, or they are not relevant.

And *stop pretending that this stuff is central to your life.* Discovering that Honus Wagner has a different hit total than you remember him having is not a good reason to go mental on us. Frankly, whether Honus Wagner has 3,430 hits or 3,418 or 3,472 doesn't have a damn thing to do with your life or my life or anybody else's life. I mean, how much do you *really* care about Honus Wagner, Jerome? How often do you write articles about Honus Wagner? Once every two or three decades, maybe?

There is nothing at stake here except the accounting practices used in sorting out very minor discrepancies in the records of players who have been dead longer than the Cleveland Indians. You make a mountain out of molehill, and the moles will eat you alive.

Errata and Addendum

In the biography of **Grover Cleveland Alexander** last year, we wrote of Alexander's 1909 experiences as a member of the minor league team in Galesburg, Illinois:

According to later stories, Alexander was hit by a pitched ball during the season, knocked unconscious and had blurred vision for some time, apparently ending his career. (If you're in Illinois and can get to the microfilm for the summer of 1909, it would be a public service if you could document this event.)

Well, not one, but two kind souls spent time at the library doing the dirty work. Rick Partin and Scott Johnson each sent material on the incident and its aftermath, and the account below is drawn from their research.

Alexander was *not* hit by a pitched ball, but was seriously injured by a play in the field in late July, 1909. Alexander had been pitching and playing right field for the Galesburg Boosters, and was playing sensationally well, much better than revealed by his 15-8 record. On July 20, 1909, he struck out 11 men and drove in the only run of the game, beating Canton 1-0. On July 23, with two days rest, he pitched a no-hitter against Canton, striking out ten and walking one. On July 26, with two more days rest, he beat Macomb 1-0 in eighteen innings; in that game he pitched no-hit ball for the first nine innings, and wound up with an eight-hit, 18-inning shutout with 19 strikeouts.

The next day, July 27, Galesburg was playing Pekin (Illinois); Alexander was playing right field for Galesburg. Alexander hit a single in the eighth inning, and was on first when the Galesburg first baseman, Neer, hit a hard ground ball to second base. The second baseman flipped the ball to the shortstop covering second, and the relay throw to first base nailed Alex in the left temple.

According to the Galesburg *Daily Republican Register* (July 29, 1909), Alexander "was unconscious for ten or fifteen minutes. Alexander was removed from the field and taken down town where Manager Wagner and another player stayed up all night with him. At last accounts he was resting easily but somewhat dazed from the force of the blow and no real serious results are anticipated . . . He went down like a shot and will probably be out of the game for several days."

On July 31, the *Daily Republican-Register* had worse news.

ALEXANDER BAD OFF
Local Pitcher Still Suffering From
Blow Caused by Thrown Ball in
Wednesday's Game

Among the local people who have been in Pekin during the past week witnessing the Pekin-Galesburg games is Rus W. Sweeney. Mr. Sweeney states that Pitcher Alexander is quite bad off as the result of being hit with a ball thrown by Edwards in Wednesday's game in an effort to complete a double play. Alex has not been able to take hardly anything on his stomach since the trouble and is feeling quite poorly.

Alexander's head swelled up horribly, and he was bedridden for two weeks, unable to take food regularly. When he finally appeared in public on August 11, the *Register* noted that he "appears but a shadow of his former husky self, and he is still weak and unable to be about much . . . The big bump caused by the ball striking his face has almost disappeared."

The incident gave rise to several weeks of hard feelings and threatened violence between Galesburg and Pekin. The shortstop who threw the ball to first, Edwards, was also accused of spiking Neer and other Galesburg players, and Galesburg suffered four injuries in the series with Pekin. The Galesburg paper railed against Edwards, accusing him of deliberately trying to injure players, and Edwards was hanged in effigy in a Galesburg storefront. Emotions reached such a peak by August 10 that the manager of the Pekin team, a man named Horton, refused to play a game in Galesburg, fearing for the safety of his team. To the outrage of Galesburg, the league president supported Pekin:

BLAIN SIDES WITH PEKIN
President's Back Gets Weak
and He Lets Horton
Manage League.
Afraid of a Big Mob

President Blain of the league has again sided with Pekin, and we get the worst of it once more, as usual. Blain's feelings were so tender that when Manager Horton and Director Scholtz of the Pekin ball club got him on the telephone and told him that they were in imminent danger of great bodily harm if they stayed in Galesburg and played the game this morning, Blain said the game would have to be played at the regular league park, letting Skinny Horton abrogate entirely his agreement to play the games anywhere . . .

Why don't the league president get busy and suspend a player who according to half the people who saw the game spikes another player wilfully and makes a malicious peg of a ball and puts a Galesburg pitcher off of the working list—a man who is worth at least $1,500 to us in a deal with a major league team. The more fans here size up the situation, they feel that the team was lucky to get out of Pekin alive, let alone with four cripples. And when Pekin claims to the president that they are afraid to play on the college campus, Blain's kidneys give out and with a resulting weak back he gives in . . .

Alexander, though still suffering from blurred vision in his right eye and unable to pitch, was purchased by the Indianapolis club. On August 19 he left Galesburg for Indianapolis, where he had his eyes checked by a specialist, but never did pitch. Edwards, the hated shortstop, was released by Pekin on August 29.

In the entry on **Hank Aguirre** we reported that on May 26, 1962, "Al Kaline, off to a red-hot start, broke his collarbone on the last play of the game, crashing into the fence to make a game-saving catch." Dr. Barry H. Gross was a ten-year-old Tigers fan at the time and, remembering the play differently, decided to check. Sure enough, his memory was better than whatever our source was. As Barry tells us, *The New York Times* of May 27 printed a photo of Kaline's game-ending play showing Kaline *diving forward* (not crashing into the fence), captioned "BAD LUCK: Al Kaline, Tigers' right fielder, rolls over on his shoulder after making diving catch of liner by Elston Howard of the Yankees in the ninth at the Stadium." By the way, as Dr. Gross substantiates, Kaline *was* off to a red-hot start (13, 38, .336).

In **Bob Allison's** entry, we reported that he "has been stricken by 'a mysterious disease' ". Allison is suffering from a rare condition called olivopontocerebellar atrophy, a neurological disorder which falls under the general classification of ataxia. Basically, the nerve cells that coordinate Allison's motor activities, such as speech and balance, are dying. Though he has retained his mental faculties, his good looks and his powerful physique, Allison walks with a cane and his speech is slurred. The cause of ataxia is unknown, as is the cure.

We did a Tracer last year on whether Eddie Cicotte was promised a $10,000 bonus if he won thirty games in 1917 or 1919, and if so, was he unnaturally prevented from reaching the goal? *Eight Men Out* (both the book and the movie) offer this as a reason for Cicotte throwing the two Series games in 1919. Bob Hoie wrote us with some information that we missed.

As we wrote a year ago, in September of 1919 Cicotte, the Sox' top pitcher, was held out of the rotation for two weeks. In examining *The Chicago Tribune* for that month, the only explanation we found was that Cicotte had been suffering from poor control, and that he was being rested up in preparation for the World Series.

But as Hoie discovered, there were rumors circulating that Cicotte had had a sore arm. In the Oct. 1 *Tribune*, responding to the question "Is Cicotte's arm all right now?", Sox manager Kid Gleason was quoted: "Say, it always was allright and it's just the same now as it always was. Those stories about Cicotte having a sore arm were all wrong. He's ready [for the Series]."

Yet on the same day, *The New York Times* ran the following: "Cicotte told his friends yesterday that the lameness which impaired his pitching arm a few weeks ago had completely disappeared and he confided to them that he believed that it would stand the strain of the hard work which it will be called upon to perform in the series."

So you have Gleason saying that Cicotte didn't have a sore arm and Cicotte saying he did. As Hoie points out, this is *exactly the opposite* of what one would expect if Cicotte had been artificially held back from winning thirty games in order to cheat him out of a bonus.

Hoie also notes that in *The Hustler's Handbook*, Bill Veeck listed Cicotte's salaries for 1918: $5,000 plus a $2,000 signing bonus; and for 1920: $10,000. In neither year was there mention of an incentive bonus.

Comiskey *did* offer incentive bonuses. Lefty Williams' 1920 salary was $6,000, with bonuses of $500 for fifteen wins and $1,000 for twenty. But even if Cicotte was offered an unreported incentive bonus, Williams' contract indicates that a $10,000 bonus for winning thirty would have been way out of line in proportion to Cicotte's base salary.

Further, as Hoie points out—I don't know how we missed this—Cicotte prior to 1917 had been in the American League for ten years, and had never won more than eighteen games, that total having been reached several years earlier. Does it seem likely that a veteran pitcher who normally wins eleven to fifteen games a year would have a bonus in his contract for thirty wins?

No single piece of evidence introduced in the '90 book, or above, proves that Cicotte wasn't cheated out of a bonus for winning thirty games. But taken together, the evidence heavily suggests that there was no such bonus, or at the least that the amount of the bonus was greatly exaggerated.

In the article on Giants' pitcher **Red Ames,** Mike Kopf wrote that Heinie Groh "eventually won his battle with the bottle bat to star for the Reds." A typesetter, a copy editor or person or persons unknown changed the sentence to say that "Groh eventually won his battle with the bottle to star for the Reds", and we failed to notice the change until it was in print. Heinie Groh did not have a drinking problem, and we apologize to his descendants or to anyone else who was misled by the error.

In the '90 book we ran a Tracer on a story concerning Red Sox pitcher **Cy Morgan** and Ty Cobb. The way Cobb told it, Morgan regularly threw at his head. When Morgan threw a wild pitch with Cobb on second base, Tyrus saw his chance. He raced around third and straight at Morgan, who got the ball with plenty of time to make the play. Instead of tagging Cobb, Morgan turned tail and ran away. Unable to get hold of the appropriate Boston newspaper, our research was incomplete, but we determined that something like this probably did happen on June 4, 1909. Cobb did score on a wild pitch by Morgan, and Morgan, a pretty good pitcher, was traded the next day for the immortal Biff Schlitzer.

A reader named Ray Charbonneau went to the library and found the relevant *Boston Globes*. As it turns out, Cobb was exaggerating quite a space when he wrote that Morgan "turned and actually ran away from the plate." The June 5 *Boston Evening Globe* reported that Morgan missed Cobb while "trying to make an artistic tag at the plate after a throw from the back stop by [catcher] Donahue when all he had to do was to drop his hands and get [Cobb] as he came into the plate." In other words, daunted by Cobb's spikes, Morgan played too high and too nice.

After Morgan was traded, the *Daily Globe* said he "was unsteady at critical times in the game" and was "not showing the proper interest for a team fighting for everything in sight." These comments may very well have been referring in part to Morgan's perceived cowardice in the Cobb play, but Morgan went on to pitch excellent baseball for Philadelphia from 1909 to 1911.

THE SEVENTH SIGN

For several years, I have used a series of indicators to predict how a team's performance might change in the following year. This "Index of Leading Team Performance Indicators" is a compilation of several established facts, brought together in a way which predicts whether the team will improve or decline in the following season with about 80% accuracy.

There are six "leading indicators" which have been previously established. In writing about the White Sox in the 1990 *Baseball Book*, page 51, I wrote the following:

> I have six indicators—but if I had time to study the issue long enough, I could find more . . . If I had one guess of what the seventh indicator might be, it might be the performance of the team's AAA and AA players.

All six indicators for the White Sox last year indicated that they would probably be a better team in 1990, and the point I was making was that the seventh indicator, the strength of the AAA team, would also have been positive, had it been researched enough to know what it meant.

The White Sox, of course, had a terrific season, and this got me to thinking again about the seventh indicator.

I designed a matched set study to determine whether or not the performance of the AAA team is an indicator of the future performance of the major league team. First of all, I asked Greg Mount to mark off on a sheet of paper all the possible won-lost records from 100-62 to 62-100, these being the records of major league teams. Then, for each won-lost "niche", I asked him to find the *best* and *worst* won-lost records by a AAA affiliate between 1977 and 1988—actually, the two best and the two worst. For example, for the won-lost record 84-78, this is the data:

84-78	1988	Kansas City	(81-61)
	1979	Philadelphia	(72-63)
	1986	Cleveland	(58-82)
	1978	San Diego	(56-82)

All four major league teams had 84 wins—but the 1988 Royals and 1979 Phillies also had strong AAA affiliates, whereas the 1986 Indians and 1978 Padres had very poor AAA affiliates.

After rounding up the data, we then looked at the performance of the major league team in the following season:

84-78	1988	Kansas City	(81-61)	1989	Record: 92-70
	1979	Philadelphia	(72-63)	1980	Record: 91-71
	1986	Cleveland	(58-82)	1987	Record: 61-101
	1978	San Diego	(56-82)	1979	Record: 58-93

The conclusion is this: THE PERFORMANCE OF THE AAA TEAM *IS* AN INDICATOR OF THE NEXT-SEASON PERFORMANCE OF THE MAJOR LEAGUE TEAM. An indicator; not, of course, a dominant indicator, as might be suggested from the example above, but an indicator.

The teams which had good AAA affiliates did get better.

The teams which had poor AAA affiliates did get worse.

We had 67 "matched sets"—67 teams with good AAA affiliates, and 67 with poor AAA affiliates. The won-lost records of the two groups are, of course, virtually identical, this being the basis of the study. The aggregate winning percentage of the teams in each group in the "base season" was .501. Group A, however, had minor league affiliates with an aggregate record of 5322-4120, a .564 percentage. Group B had AAA affiliates with an aggregate record of 4118-5268, a .439 percentage.

In the following season, the teams in Group A (with strong affiliates) had an aggregate record of 5330-5130, a .510 winning percentage. In other words, these teams *improved* in the following season.

The teams in Group B (with poor affiliates) had an aggregate record of 5039-5395, a .483 percentage. These teams *declined* in the following seasons. Although the percentage difference was small, the aggregate difference between the two groups in the following season was 278 games.

Of the teams with good affiliates, 40 of the 67 played *better than .500 ball* in the following season. Of the teams with poor affiliates, only 28 played winning baseball the following season.

Next I looked at whether the team had improved or declined from its record in the base season. Oddly enough, the data is the same (although the teams are different); 40 of the 67 teams with strong affiliates improved in the following season. Only 28 of the 67 teams with weak affiliates improved in the following season.

One can make up all kind of reasons why the performance of the AAA team should or should not be an indicator of future major league performance. Before beginning this study, I asked Susie whether she thought that the won-lost performance of the AAA team should indicate the future performance of the major league team. She said that since the major league teams completely controlled the AAA teams, since they went down and picked up anybody who was playing well, she didn't see how the won-lost record could be very meaningful.

This argument, though, has a hole in it, which is this: what happens if the major league team reaches down for somebody, and there is nobody there?

I asked Rob Neyer the same question, and got the same answer for a different reason. Look at the people playing AAA ball, Rob answered. They're mostly old veterans who have had years as fringe players and several major league trials, all of which they have failed. What difference does it make who has more or better of these players?

But the problem with this argument can be seen by looking back at a year in the past—say, 1985. If you read the list of players playing in the league, you do indeed find the interminable list of one-time prospects on their way out (Tommy Dunbar, Alan Knicely, Gary Rajsich). But you also find that occasional player who is now a big star. Jose Canseco, Fred McGriff and Kevin Mitchell were in AAA ball in 1985, as well as many, many players who have since become major league regulars, like Larry Sheets, Milt Thompson and Jim DeShaies. The difference between good AAA teams and bad AAA teams may be the difference between having five major league prospects, and having one. And that difference could very well manifest itself in the major leagues in the next season.

It might also be, I suspect, that having a good AAA team is a true *indicator* of the quality of the organization. AAA teams being what they are, couldn't you argue that any organization which is paying attention ought to be able to put together a competitive AAA team? So if a team's AAA affiliate finishes 60-92, what does that tell you?

Greg Mount, on the other hand, argues that this study misses the real effect by being focused too tightly; the *real* effect, he argues, could be seen better by looking at both AA and AAA teams, and then by looking two or three years down the road. In principle, he may be correct, but the problem with such a study is making it manageable. How, *exactly,* do you design such a study?

Setting the arguments aside, it is now clear that the performance of the AAA affiliate *is* an indicator of whether the major league team is likely to improve in the following season. The series of six indicators now has seven.

THE 1991 SEASON

This book is due to the publisher within a few hours, and so I can no longer avoid the task of sitting down to figure out who is going to win what in 1991. Let's be honest about this: I know as much about who is going to win the divisions in 1991 as you do. If you know something about it, then I know less than you do.

It is a peculiar obligation afflicting a few professions—meteorologists, economists, baseball writers—to be asked not merely to understand the present, but to foresee the future. It is not merely that people want to know what you think, in a casual, off-hand way, but that many people seriously think that if you know what you are talking about you should be able to tell them who is going to win the race, and that therefore your ability to foretell the winners is a fair test of your expertise. Many people seriously believe that the fact that economists often disagree about where the economy is headed means that none of them really knows what they are talking about.

The reality, of course, is that:

a. a great deal of what happens is random. It is perfectly possible, in a baseball season, for one team to finish twenty games ahead of a *better* team by sheer luck.

b. a great deal of what is not random cannot possibly be foreseen. There is no way of knowing who will break a leg.

c. the game is so complicated, and there is *so much* to know about it, that none of us knows even one percent of what we would need to know to foretell the future, even absent luck and injuries.

Somewhere in baseball there is a fat player who has spent the winter lifting weights and drinking orange juice, and somewhere there is a good player who has spent the winter getting fat and lazy. Somewhere there is a two-pitch pitcher who has learned to throw a slider that will melt a hitter's knees. There is no way in the world that anyone can know all of these things, or can know what they will mean in September.

I give this disclaimer every year, but it doesn't relieve one of the itch to have opinions, or the responsibility to share with the reader what little I know about the future.

I use a series of seven indicators to help me predict a pennant race—quite simply, an Index of Leading Performance Indicators. What the indicators actually predict is whether a team will be *better* or *worse* this year than they were last year. The indicators are right on this limited point the great majority of the time, which is of less use in predicting a pennant race than you would think it would be. You can predict that the Oakland A's will win fewer games this year than they won last year, and you've got about a 99% chance of being right, but this is of absolutely no use in determining whether or not the A's will win the division, because in theory they could decline by twenty games and still win.

The seven indicators are seven scientifically established facts, five of which are:

1. Winning teams tend to decline; losing teams tend to improve. Everybody moves toward the center.
2. A team which declines in one year will tend to improve in the next year, and vice versa.
3. Young teams tend to get better; old teams tend to get worse.
4. Teams which play well late in the year do tend to have a positive carryover the next year. Teams which slump late in the year tend to also decline the next season.
5. Teams which have good AAA affiliates tend to improve. Teams which have poor AAA affiliates tend to decline.

The other two indicators, which I think in the future I'll combine into one for the purposes of explanation, are "luck indicators". Sometimes the won-lost record is an imperfect reflection of how well the team has played, and there are a couple of statistical tests to see whether or not this is true. These tests, if you combine them, form the sixth indicator.

In practice, each of these things has a "weight", which again has been empirically established. When the weights are combined into one, you get the Index of Leading Performance Indicators, which for 1991 are:

Kansas City	+ 19.7
Baltimore	+ 15.5
Atlanta	+ 15.0
Chicago (N)	+ 13.7
New York (A)	+ 12.2
San Diego	+ 9.8
Houston	+ 9.1
California	+ 8.8
Toronto	+ 8.2
St. Louis	+ 8.0
Cleveland	+ 4.4
Minnesota	+ 4.1
Milwaukee	+ 4.1
New York (N)	+ 1.1
Seattle	− .6
Montreal	− 2.1
Cincinnati	− 3.9
Philadelphia	− 8.1
San Francisco	− 8.1
Los Angeles	− 9.7
Texas	− 9.9
Boston	− 10.4
Pittsburgh	− 15.5
Oakland	− 20.3
Detroit	− 21.3
Chicago (A)	− 23.3

About eighty percent of the teams which have positive indicators will improve, and about 80% of those with negative indicators will decline.

Let us start with the American League East, since that is probably the easiest division to pick. Last year there were only two competitive teams, the Red Sox and the Blue Jays. One of those teams, the Blue Jays, figures to be better this year. The other doesn't figure to be as good.

The positive indicators for the Blue Jays are the ones you would expect:

1. They were probably a better team last year than their won-lost record reflected, and
2. They're still young.

Besides, I always pick the Blue Jays to win this division, so why should I stop now?

The Blue Jays, of course, have nuked their clubhouse, fumigated the latins and re-arranged the team photo. Whether they came out of this with a better team or a worse one is open to dispute. Devon White isn't the ballplayer that Junior Felix is, and, as Moss Klein pointed out, the Blue Jays have re-cooked their chemistry by bringing in two of the most selfish players in baseball. The uncompensated loss of George Bell can't be overlooked merely because the position was covered in the shuffle. Worse, the Blue Jays fixed their chemistry, or tried to, without addressing the fundamental problems on the team, which start with the starting pitching. It can be argued that the fundamental difference between the Red Sox and the Blue Jays is that the Red Sox have Roger Clemens, and the Blue Jays don't.

It remains to be seen whether the Blue Jays have a shortstop, in Manny Lee, or don't.

So naturally, I pick them to blow away the division.

The Blue Jays have talent; nobody doubts that. With Roberto Alomar, Kelly Gruber, Pat Borders, Joe Carter, John Olerud and several other guys who *might* have good years, they should score forty or fifty runs more than the league average. That means that Dave Stieb, Jimmie Key and David Wells will be able to win.

With Henke and Ward, the Blue Jays still have one of the best bullpens in the league. That means the other two starting pitchers, whoever they turn out to be, have a chance to fight the league to a standstill.

I've never been a Devon White fan, but I think he'll have a good year by his own standards. The defensive outfield—probably Carter, White and Whiten or Hill—should be the best in the league. Yes, Joe Carter is overrated, but when a talented player takes criticism, sometimes he'll surprise you. Sometimes a player like that will come out determined to prove the critics wrong. I'm not crazy about the team, but they're the best in the division. The key players, if they are to win, are Manny Lee, David Wells, Devon White and the four-five starting pitchers, whoever those are.

The Red Sox, despite their negative indicators, could certainly win the World Championship. I figure "team age" by looking at the age of the regulars, and the Red Sox score as an old team—worse, as an old team with a poor Triple-A affiliate. But the Red Sox can replace Dwight Evans, their oldest regular, with Mo Vaughn and come out, if not ahead on the deal, certainly not much behind.

Shortstop Tim Naehring could be not only the Rookie of the Year, but even potentially an MVP candidate, depending on his health and defense.

Ellis Burks is probably the best MVP candidate you could find.
Mike Greenwell is going to have a better year.
They still have Boggs.
Phil Plantier could be a big surprise.
Brunansky could bounce back.

You can probably say this about anybody, but if the pitching is good enough, the Red Sox will win. The pitching probably won't be good enough. Roger Clemens is the best pitcher in the world, but it's not a hundred percent certain that he's healthy. Tom Bolton was great last year, but nobody's sure if that's for real. Matt Young pitched well last year for Seattle, but Mike Boddicker for Matt Young isn't a trade that anybody would make if they didn't have to. Danny Darwin was brilliant last year for Houston, but Fenway Park ain't the Astrodome.

For years we have said that if the Blue Jays play as well as they are capable of playing, nobody else could beat them. Now that is no longer true. In 1991, if the Red Sox play as well as they are capable of playing, nobody else in this division can beat the Red Sox. But in the cold light of January logic, you can't pick a team with no proven closer and four question marks in the starting rotation to win their division. The key players: Naehring, Bolton, Young and Brunansky.

The Orioles will finish third. The Orioles were contenders in '89, and dropped off the pace last year but had two very positive indicators: they were the youngest team in baseball, and they had the best AAA team in the minors. Add that to:

1. Glenn Davis,
2. A full year of Ben MacDonald,
3. Leo Gomez, and
4. A full year of Randy Milligan (hurt last August), and you have a team that should win 85, 90 games.

On the other hand, the Orioles have some problems. The Orioles four best hitters are Davis, Milligan, Ripken and Gomez—four big, strong, right-handed sluggers. Four right-handed sluggers isn't my idea of a great offense. It's more like my idea of 170 double play balls. A great offense is more like four outstanding hitters, two right-handed and two left-handed, two sluggers, a leadoff hitter and .300 hitter with 35 doubles.

Chris Hoiles, who replaces Mickey Tettleton as the half-time catcher, could be outstanding. But guess what? He's another big, slow, right-handed slugger.

The Orioles have done nothing to improve the weakest-hitting outfield in the major leagues other than to sign Dwight Evans, another slow right-handed slugger. If they're all in the lineup that's six.

The Orioles are the best defensive team in the American League, if not in baseball, which gives their starting pitchers a head start. Even so, two Orioles who kept the team afloat last year, Billy Ripken and Dave Johnson, are extremely likely to disappoint in 1991. The starting pitcher who *could* have improved, Harnisch, went to Houston in the Glenn Davis trade.

The Orioles slumped late last year, primarily because of the injury to Milligan and a loss in effectiveness of Gregg Olson. They said Olson's arm was just tired, but what if it's something more serious?

In a good division, the Orioles would finish fourth. In this division, they'll finish third. The key players: MacDonald, Telford, Gomez and Brady Anderson.

Probably the question most asked about this division is "What ever happened to the Milwaukee Brewers?" The Brewers a few years ago were supposed to be brewing a dynasty, or a least a competitive team. What happened to them, in short, is:

1. They overrated their kids, and
2. Upper management diverted their attention to solving the problems of baseball as a whole, and lost interest in the ballclub.

It was Dalton and Selig, the Brewers' one-two punch, who came up with the owners' moronic plan to fix salaries by a series of performance-based statistical ratings. (I hate to be unkind, but can you imagine what people would say about *me* if Bill James had come up with this idea?) Intent on working to create a unified front among the owners, the Brewers allowed obvious problems of the ballclub to go untended. The ballclub turned into a collection of mediocre, slow white guys, enlivened by two really good players (Yount and Molitor).

The Brewers could be better this year because of Greg Vaughn, Julio Machado and Chris Bosio, but they won't contend.

The execution of George Steinbrenner may finally allow the Yankees to start back up. When a team starts back up it is anybody's guess how fast they will gather speed, and the Yankees have some good players. Mattingly will be back and Maas will be here all year, but the Yankees start the year with *no* proven starting pitchers. Intuitively it seems unlikely that they will find four of them before September.

The Cleveland Indians play .500 once every three or four years, and this could be the year for that, but that's about their upside potential. The Tigers were the oldest team in baseball last year and will probably be the worst this year, making the final standings:

Team	W-L
Toronto	91-71
Boston	86-76
Baltimore	84-78
Cleveland	78-84
Milwaukee	77-85
New York	75-87
Detroit	67-95

Other than the Blue Jays, the easiest team to pick for 1991 is the Los Angeles Dodgers. As with any team, there are some things you have to overlook. You have to overlook their leading indicators, to begin with (Minus 9.7). You have to close your eyes to the prospect of Juan Samuel playing second base.

The Dodgers, as an organization, like to stay competitive, and then gear up for a major charge at the pennant every few years. In the last ten years, every time they have geared up for a major effort, they've won—and obviously, this is one of their years. Signing Strawberry, they followed through by making a series of small moves designed to back up their options, like trading Vizcaino for Greg Smith, which backs them up at second base in case Samuel starts acting that way again.

The Dodgers have more than their share of old guys, and you never know who might suddenly blow out on them—Scioscia, or Murray, or Samuel, or Butler. Kal Daniels may not be ready to play on opening day. Javier, Harris and Sharperson, who all hit about .300 last year, probably will hit an aggregate .256 this year. The Dodgers have only three pitchers on their roster who pitched 100 innings in 1990 and had a winning record, and two of those are Bob Ojeda and Dennis Cook.

But the Dodgers also have some *positive* question marks. Can Orel Hershiser come back? Probably not—but suppose he does. Can Neidlinger pitch all year the way he did last August and September? Maybe not—but suppose he does.

The Dodgers have a great leadoff hitter, in Butler, and a super #2 hitter in Sharperson if they will use him there. Their 3-4-5 punch of Murray, Strawberry and Daniels is probably the best in baseball, although they won't have the best statistics because of Dodger Stadium. Backing them up are Scioscia, Samuel and Offerman. They're going to win this division.

The Giants' pitching should be better, with Burkett in the rotation from opening day, Bud Black added and a comeback likely from either Kelly Downs or Rick Reuschel. Trevor Wilson is a positive question mark, a player who could suddenly turn into one of the best in the league. A bullpen of Brantley and Righetti, at the worst, has got to be better than a bullpen of Brantley and Bedrosian.

The Giants have three kids that I just love—Steve Decker, who I think will be the Rookie of the Year, plus Mark Dewey and Mark Leonard. There's no place for Leonard to play, but then you ask: *why* isn't there any place for him to play? Because the two positions he could play are occupied by two of the best hitters in the league, Will Clark and Kevin Mitchell. Add Matt Williams, and the Giants' 3-4-5 punch may be a match for the Dodgers. Certainly, any of those six players (three Dodgers, three Giants) could hit cleanup for the Reds.

I don't think Willie McGee can carry Brett Butler's weighted donut, and I'd like the Giants better if I knew who was going to play shortstop for them. I hate the way Roger Craig handles his pitching staff. But if I could pick both the Dodgers and Giants to win this division, I would.

One thing I have noticed, as a sports fan, is that whenever you win something there is always somebody around who wants to take it away from you. There is always some reason why you were lucky, or the schedule worked in your favor, or the umpire blew a call, or something. What this overlooks is that *everybody* gets breaks, in the course of a season or a series, and the team that wins is the team that takes advantage of those breaks.

So I don't want anybody to think that I'm trying to take anything away from the Cincinnati Reds, because I'm not. I didn't think they were that good a team a year ago, and I don't think they're that good now. They got some breaks and—power to them—they took advantage of those breaks. The shortened spring training left the starting pitchers not quite ready to open the season, and that gave an advantage to the teams with the good bullpens. The Reds had the best bullpen, and by the time the season was a month old they were in control of the race.

Mariano Duncan isn't, as I see it, real likely to hit .306 again. Hal Morris will be there all year and will hit, let's say, .312—but is a full season of Morris at .312 worth more than a half-season of Morris at .340? I love Norm Charlton, and Jose Rijo could win the Cy Young Award—but Browning is a question mark, in my mind, and Danny Jackson is gone. Nobody knows what to make of Jack Armstrong.

The Reds have only three players that I regard as good players—Sabo, Larkin and Eric Davis. Maybe Doran makes four and maybe Morris will make five, but hell, you can say that about anybody. I think they're a third-place team.

San Diego is a wild card. Sometimes a team which is supposed to be good will get good when everybody gives up and stops picking them—I'm sure we've all seen that. With Whitson, Hurst and Benes the Padres have the solidest foundation for their starting rotation of any team in the N.L. West. With Harris, Lefferts and Larry Andersen nobody is carping about their bullpen.

The Padres have no power in the outfield—none. Fred McGriff is maybe the one hitter in baseball who most needs somebody coming up behind him, and he's got nobody. I'm not putting down Benito Santiago, but he's not a middle-of-the-order guy. As a catcher he can match up with anybody, but as a hitter he's being matched up against Matt Williams and Kal Daniels and Hal Morris, and that's a mismatch.

The Braves *will* be better this year, but they're not a contender, and of course everybody will be picking the Astros last, since they lost five relievers and traded Glenn Davis. They may not *finish* last, but I'm not going to argue, making the race:

Team	W-L
Los Angeles	90-72
San Francisco	89-73
Cincinnati	81-81
San Diego	80-82
Atlanta	74-88
Houston	68-94

The one sure thing about the American League West is that the Oakland A's will not be, in 1991, the dominant team that they have been for the last three years. The A's determined assemblage of over-the-hill veteran players to surround their stars has reached puzzling proportions. Vance Law, Eric Show, and Willie Wilson have been added to a cast of Willie Randolph, Harold Baines and Jamie Quirk. Several of the A's good and great players—Rickey Henderson, Eckersley, Welch, Honeycutt, Stewart, Dave Henderson—are well into their thirties. Carney Lansford is probably finished. The A's are a very, very old team—unnecessarily old, artificially aged by the additions of superfluous veterans.

The A's farm system is one of the weakest in baseball. Two players are probably ready to contribute, reliever Steve Chitren, as if the A's needed another reliever, and Scott Brosius, a shortstop from Double-A who may wind up at third base. Of course they have the young pitchers that they picked up with the extra draft picks.

I'm picking the A's to win this year, but I'm telling you: don't put any money on them. I'm picking them to win in this sense, that they are the *one* team with a better chance than any other

one team—but their chance of defending their title is 25% or 30%, not 65% or 70% as it was a year ago.

The A's are a close historical parallel to two other teams, the Yankees of 1926–1928 and the Orioles of 1969–1971. Neither the Yankees nor the Orioles was able to win the fourth time.

The A's will face improved competition from the two teams which were supposed to be there last year, but weren't, the Royals and the Angels. No team has seven positive indicators (or seven negative), but the Royals have the most positive indicators of any team. They're a relatively young team, and they have outstanding AA and AAA teams with several prospects who might help them in '91. They were a much, much better team last year than their won-lost record reflects.

This applies to both California and Kansas City: that there are probably more cases when free agent signings have helped the team the *second* year the player was there than cases where the player has helped the first year. Frank Funk, the pitching coach who contributed so much to 1990's debacle, has been fired and replaced by Pat Dobson, who worked with Mark Davis in San Diego.

The Royals still don't know who will play second base for them. Their first baseman is old and their catcher can't throw. Their four and five hitters get hurt every year. The fact that it's an odd-numbered year doesn't guarantee that Bret Saberhagen will be healthy, and Mark Gubicza hasn't started throwing off a mound yet. The organization remains peculiarly enamored of 33-year-old free agents. The key players: Saberhagen, Gubicza and Kevin Seitzer.

Of all the teams in baseball, the California Angels may have had the best off-season. The Angels traded Devon White, a "talent", for Junior Felix, a baseball player. For the first time in years, the Angels have a catcher (Parrish), a first baseman (Joyner), a second baseman (Sojo), a shortstop (Schofield) and a starting rotation. OK, so they still have four right fielders, no third baseman and no relief ace; at least they're moving in the right direction. Mark Langston will be back, if he can avoid the temptation to over-react to Dick Williams' hatchet job by trying to prove how tough he is or something. The Angels should contend.

The Rangers are the division's wild card; I can give you twenty reasons why they should be better, and twenty reasons they should be worse. I'll limit it to five each. They should be better because:

1. Bobby Witt could be the best pitcher in the league.
2. Ruben Sierra, if healthy, is as good a player as there is around.
3. Juan Gonzalez is the top candidate for the A.L. Rookie of the Year Award.

4. Jeff Russell could be back, and would make a tremendous difference if he is.
5. Pete Incaviglia is heading into his free agent year.

I also like this kid they got from the Dodgers, Poole. OK, that's six. They could be worse because:

1. Charlie Hough is gone.
2. Kevin Brown may not be able to contribute his 12 wins again.
3. They still don't have a shortstop or third baseman.
4. They still have Tom House.
5. Their catching sucks.

I'm picking the Rangers fourth—but really, I'd give them almost as good a chance to win the race as Oakland, who I picked first. If Oakland has a 25 to 30% chance, Texas is 20 to 25%. Any one of those four teams can win.

The White Sox, despite their stunning improvement of last year, and despite the addition of one of the best hitters in the league in Frank Thomas, really aren't a very good ballclub. Their second baseman ought to be replaced, their shortstop is overrated and their third baseman is all potential, no production. They've got two outfielders who could strike out 300 times and drive in 97 runs between them, Sosa and Snyder. Tim Raines is great, but he's not the player he was five years ago. They have one proven starting pitcher, Jack McDowell, and he's got a career record of 22-19. Even if things break right for them, meaning that Alex Fernandez wins sixteen games and Raines steals a hundred bases, the White Sox won't win the division.

The Seattle Mariners still have enough ability that sometimes you think you ought to win. For years, I've said that "this is the year the Mariners break through." With Erik Hanson and KG Jr. on hand, certainly that time has got to be closer now than it has been before.

The Mariners have *not* broken through, they have continued to lose, primarily because they have persisted in playing these godawful journeymen players like Henry Cotto, Jeff Leonard and Pete O'Brien, rather than giving their good young players, like Briley and Edgar Martinez, a fair shot.

Look, I'll still say that the Mariners *could* break through. The talent to play better than .500 ball is there. But:

1. The indicators don't tell me that they're going to be any better than they were.
2. A team doesn't normally improve suddenly under a manager who has been there for two or three years, and
3. Tino Martinez ain't that good.

I'm picking them sixth.

The Twins don't have a terrible ballclub, but the organization is run by a collection of dumb guys who probably won't be able to fix any problems that arise, making the finish:

Team	W-L
Oakland	89-73
Kansas City	87-75
California	87-75
Texas	86-76
Chicago	79-83
Seattle	74-88
Minnesota	74-88

Now as for this other division, it's the Mets. Yes, the loss of Strawberry will hurt them, but

a. people greatly over-estimate the value of any individual player, and
b. many times a team will rally around the loss of a key player, and play better without him.

The Mets and Pirates have the best pitching in the division, which puts them a leg up. The Pirates last year got tremendous years from their three best players—Bonds, Bonilla and Drabek. That won't happen again.

Leyland is a terrific manager, and let's say he's as good as LaRussa. But when the A's won for the first time, the Oakland management still acted to strengthen the team. The Pirates have let their talent thin out over the winter—Bream, Reynolds, Backman, Power, and a couple of other guys have left. Maybe none of those guys are great, but then, maybe you don't need any one particular pint of blood, either. They traded the minor leaguers all away last fall to make the push. I just don't see that they have enough resources left to solve a problem if they have one, and you know they will.

The Mets, on the other hand . . . well, they're still the Mets. They lost Strawberry, but they added Brooks *and* Coleman. They still don't have a shortstop or second baseman, and this still bugs the hell out of you, that they seem able to collect pitchers at will, but insist on supporting them with a gap-toothed defense. But their lineup one through six is the best in the division (Coleman, Magadan, Jefferies, Johnson, McReynolds and Brooks), so they'll still score runs. They're pitching is still good enough to win if they score runs. I still got to pick them.

The Expos, who a year ago were short of pitchers, now suddenly have pitchers coming out of the bleachers in waves. The core offense—Wallach, Galarraga, Calderon—remains mediocre. The Expos are a wild card, probably a contending team but probably not a winner. They're about where the Pirates were in 1988, meaning that I'll take them seriously a year from now.

The Cubs have added several free agents . . . Bell, Jackson, Smith. To win in Wrigley Field you almost have to lead the league in runs scored. To lead the league in runs scored, you have to be among the top two or three in on-base percentage, which just means that you have to have people on base to score runs, which would be common sense if it were not empirically demonstrable. The Cubs last year were tenth in the league in on-base percentage, and they've done absolutely nothing over the winter to change that. They'll finish third or fourth.

The Cardinals are starting over; it will be an interesting year to be a Cardinal fan, but certainly not a championship year. The Phillies have been building, which tends to obscure the fact that they still only have two good players, Dykstra and Von Hayes. This is the division as I see it:

Team	W-L
New York	91-71
Pittsburgh	86-76
Montreal	85-77
Chicago	84-78
St. Louis	73-89
Philadelphia	71-91

I promised several times in the comments to produce a list of the top candidates for the Rookie of the Year awards, so I'd better do that before I stop. These are my lists:

American League

1. Juan Gonzalez, Texas
2. Tim Naehring, Boston
3. Leo Gomez, Baltimore
4. Mark Whiten, Toronto
5. Scott Chiamparino, Texas
6. Hensley Meulens, New York
7. Pedro Munoz, Minnesota
8. Tino Martinez, Seattle
9. Scott Lewis, California
10. Mark Lee, Milwaukee

Some other guys that I can see winning the award if things go well for them include Steve Adkins (Yankee pitcher), Gerald Alexander (Texas pitcher), Kevin Belcher (Texas outfielder), Tito Bell (Baltimore shortstop—one of the things that needs to go well for him is that he needs to be traded); Joey Belle, Cleveland head case; Sean Berry, Kansas City third baseman; Joe Bitker, Texas relief pitcher; Kevin D. Brown, Milwaukee pitcher; Steve Chitren, Oakland relief pitcher; Milt Cuyler, Detroit outfielder; Jim Poole, Texas relief pitcher; Luis Sojo, California second baseman; Scott Brosius, Oakland infielder; and Chris Hoiles, Baltimore catcher. I will say without reservation that any one of those guys is capable of winning the Rookie of the Year award if he gets a chance early in the season and performs at the top of his range.

In the National League, the candidates are:

1. Steve Decker, San Francisco
2. Jose Offerman, Los Angeles
3. Ray Lankford, St. Louis
4. Wes Chamberlain, Philadelphia
5. Mickey Morandini, Philadelphia
6. Lance Dickson, Chicago
7. Bernard Gilkey, St. Louis
8. Julio Valera, Mets
9. Andres Santana, San Francisco
10. Chris Hammond, Cincinnati

Other guys who could win it with luck include Mark Dewey, Giants relief pitcher; Dave Hansen, Los Angeles third baseman; Mark Leonard, San Francisco outfielder; Kelly Mann, Atlanta catcher; Brian Meyer, Houston relief pitcher; Al Osuna, Houston relief pitcher; Greg Smith, Dodger infielder; and Jose Vizcaino, Chicago Cub infielder.

NOTE TO THE READERS

You will, if you read baseball publications, see my name associated with any number of other projects. I always want you to know as much as possible about whatever it is before you make a buy/don't buy decision, so I wanted to take a minute here to say a few words about what those other projects are.

There is, for one, *Bill James Fantasy Baseball,* which is a game vaguely like rotisserie baseball. I designed the game; STATS, Inc. markets and produces it. You draft players at the start of the year, and for everything they do you get points. If your player hits a single or a double or a triple or a homer, you get points. If a middle infielder turns a double play, you get a point. The design of the game is very simple, but we tried to include a broad enough range of accomplishments to make the values of the players realistic. Once a week STATS sends you a mailing on how your team is doing, or you can check everyday by modem, and also if you get on-line you can access a whole bunch of neat information from them. You can make trades, of course, or drop players and add players. If you're interested you can contact STATS at 7366 N. Lincoln, Lincolnwood, Illinois, 60646-1708, or call 1-800-63-STATS (1-800-637-8287).

Another thing that I do in collaboration with STATS is the *Handbook,* more formally entitled "Bill James Presents STATS™ 199X Major League Handbook." My name is on this book because it was my idea to do it, but the book has virtually no text; it's a reference book. The book has the complete batting records and pitching records, year by year, of all active major league players. It's like *Who's Who in Baseball* or *The Sporting News Register* except that the record is a lot more complete, containing things like caught stealing, grounded into double plays, sacrifice hits and flies, etc., and also in that it is available from STATS each year in November. The player register is 70% of the book, but then it also contains some other features, like 1990 fielding records. If, in this book, I say that Andy Van Slyke played 1,134.2 innings in center field, I am using the *Handbook,* which is the only source of that kind of information. The book has 1990 platoon data for pitchers and hitters, a few pages of "leaders lists" (Kevin McReynolds hit .800 last year with the bases loaded, the highest average of any major league player), extensive data for a few players (Doug Drabek threw 112 pitches at Philadelphia's Veteran's Stadium in 1990, as opposed to 1,711 pitches at Three Rivers) and projections for how every hitter will do in 1991. The projections have received a lot of press notice, almost all of it favorable, but I don't know myself how much value there is to doing that.

The people at STATS also produce a number of other books, which I will mention as a courtesy to them. *The Scouting Report,* which has been around for years, has replaced the intuitive ramblings of randomly chosen announcers with the fact-based analysis of John Dewan and Company. The Baseball *Scoreboard* is a wonderful collection of questions and lists which will tell you, for example, that Don Carman has the lowest career batting average of any pitcher in baseball, and that Craig Worthington in 1989 hit .692 (nine for thirteen) after the hitter ahead of him was intentionally walked.

I do a Sunday Night radio show, on seven to nine Eastern time (four to six on the West Coast). It's called *Baseball Sunday;* there are three of us in the booth, taking questions and talking baseball. Last year the three of us were Joe Garagiola, Hal Bodley (Baseball Editor of *USA Today*) and myself at the start of the year. Joe left in July, after he returned to the *Today Show,* and was replaced by Dan Quisenberry, who's also a lot of fun. If you'd like to know where you can pick up the show in your region, drop a card to *Baseball Sunday,* United Syndications, 108 West 11th St. Suite 1630, Kansas City, Missouri, 64105. Or you can try writing to me, but God knows whether I'll ever get around to responding.

I also wanted to add a quick note about this book, which is that it is still evolving, and may be a substantially different book next year than it is this year, so you might look through it at the store a minute before you buy it. I don't know if we'll have the *Biographic Encyclopedia* continued, for example, or whether we'll have any more of Jack Etkin's wonderful personality sketches. The stats section may be entirely different; it may even be missing. Don't assume that it's the same book before you buy, I'm saying. I'm going to continue the *Biographic Encyclopedia,* but whether I'll continue it *here,* or find some way to move it to a hardcover, that I don't know.

And then next year, summer of '92, we'll have another major book out, but that's a year away. Thank you so much for buying this one. Hope you enjoy it.